# Reflective Teaching in Secondary Education

# Reflective Teaching in Secondary Education

## A Handbook for Schools and Colleges

Andrew Pollard and Pat Triggs

CONTINUUM
London ♦ New York

**Continuum**

| | |
|---|---|
| The Tower Building | 370 Lexington Avenue |
| 11 York Road | New York |
| London SE1 7NX | NY 10017-6550 |

© Andrew Pollard 1997

First published 1997 by Cassell
Reprinted 2001 by Continuum

**British Library Cataloguing-in-Publication Data**
A catalogue record for this book is available from the British Library

ISBN 0–304–33535–5 (hardback)
       0–8264–5965–X (paperback)

*0826459565X*

Typeset by Kenneth Burnley, Irby, Wirral, Cheshire.
Printed and bound in Great Britain by Bookcraft (Bath) Ltd,
Midsomer Norton, Somerset.

# CONTENTS

# PREFACE

Welcome to the first edition of *Reflective Teaching in Secondary Education.*

The book is intended to provide flexible and comprehensive support for school-based and school-focused teacher education, in a form which is suitable for a wide range of circumstances. The book should thus be an excellent resource for students, teachers, mentors and tutors, and can be used in almost any form of professional development, teacher training and classroom research activity. Suggested *Practical Activities* and annotated *Notes for Further Reading* are designed to provide support for self-directed or group study with or without the support of tutors or teacher-mentors.

The book will contribute to the 'new agenda' for teacher education and professional development which the Teacher Training Agency has been developing in recent years. As the Chief Executive of the TTA has said:

> —Only through the efforts of teachers can the profession maintain and build its status. A profession with confidence in itself is a profession which takes responsibility for training and developing the next generation of teachers. It is also one which reflects on and improves its own performance. (Millett 1996)

At a time when the first-ever comprehensive national professional framework for teachers in the UK is being constructed, we are delighted that the importance of reflective professional practice and classroom enquiry is being reasserted.

This book was developed from a similar classroom handbook for primary schools, *Reflective Teaching in the Primary School.* The third edition of that book was published in early 1997, and with it came a totally integrated and very comprehensive collection of 134 edited readings (Pollard, *Readings for Reflective Teaching in the Primary School*). Where these readings remain relevant in the context of secondary education, they are cross-referenced in the present text and this is indicated by the use of a Reading icon. When the next edition of *Reflective Teaching in Secondary Education* comes out, it is intended that it will be supported by its own comprehensive and fully integrated book of readings.

*Reflective Teaching in Secondary Education* is meant to be used selectively, depending on judgements of what is needed for classroom problem-solving or for professional development. Put another way, it should be possible to take the activities and resources which the book offers and to use them to provide practical classroom support and targeted professional development for oneself and others. The framework and its contents provide continuous resources for teachers, students, mentors and tutors at all stages of professional development.

Our thanks to those who have contributed and offered comments, criticisms and suggestions regarding the production of this book, which has been developed with the support of a team of specialists in secondary education (see the Acknowledgements). Users of this new edition are invited to maintain a feedback loop to us, so that the book can be developed constructively in the future. Please write with ideas, experiences, criticisms and suggestions.

*Andrew Pollard and Pat Triggs, GraduateSchool of Education,*
*University of Bristol, Bristol, UK, 1st May 1997*

# ACKNOWLEDGEMENTS

The origins of this book lie in a book on reflective teaching for primary education which was initially co-authored by Andrew Pollard and Sarah Tann (now Sarah Villiers). We would like to acknowledge Sarah's early contribution with gratitude, though she should not be held responsible for any of the later developments.

*Reflective Teaching in Secondary Education* has been produced with the support of a team of consultants who advised us in the various stages in the production of the manuscript: strategic and detailed planning, writing, revising, taking stock and successive phases of editing. For their advice and support during what has been a three-year development period, we are very grateful to: Laurinda Brown, Jan Denton, John Homewood, Adrian Jackson, the late Robin Lawson, Rupert Lister, Pauline Marson, Roy Nevitt, Jean O'Reilly, Lynn Raphael Reed, John Simpson, John Spindler and Roger White.

Additionally, many initial revisions and drafts were produced by a team of 'contributing authors' who were commissioned to work on particular chapters. The required tasks varied in size and all the texts were developed further, sometimes very significantly, as the overall editing of the book proceeded. We are very grateful to all our contributors, without whom the book would have been extremely difficult to produce. We would particularly like to thank: John Quicke (University of Sheffield), Lynn Raphael Reed (University of the West of England), John Spindler (University of Northumbria), and John Furlong, Sally Power, Malcolm Reed, Paul Weeden and Jan Winter (University of Bristol).

The major contributors to this book are listed below. In a very simplified form, this indicates chapters which have been predominantly constructed by *revising* previous material, and those which have been predominantly *developed* for this book in particular.

Chapter 1    Revised by Andrew Pollard
Chapter 2    Revised by Sally Power
Chapter 3    Developed by John Furlong
Chapter 4    Revised by Andrew Pollard
Chapter 5    Developed by Pat Triggs
Chapter 6    Developed by Andrew Pollard and John Spindler
Chapter 7    Revised by Pat Triggs
Chapter 8    Developed by Lynn Raphael Reed and Malcolm Reed
Chapter 9    Revised by John Quicke
Chapter 10   Revised by Pat Triggs
Chapter 11   Revised by Pat Triggs
Chapter 12   Revised by Pat Triggs
Chapter 13   Revised by Pat Triggs
Chapter 14   Revised by Pat Triggs
Chapter 15   Developed by Andrew Pollard, Paul Weeden and Jan Winter
Chapter 16   Developed by Andrew Pollard and Pat Triggs
Chapter 17   Revised by Andrew Pollard

Following initial review and development, the book was thoroughly edited by Andrew Pollard and Pat Triggs to maximize coherence and to maintain structure and accessibility.

We would particularly like to thank Sarah Butler for her efficient support at many points in this process. Naomi Roth and her colleagues at Cassell have, as usual, been most helpful in bringing the project to its published conclusion.

We would like to thank the following authors and publishers for permission to reproduce previously published materials:

The Teacher Training Authority and OFSTED for the text in Figure 1.3, from the *Framework for the Assessment of Quality and Standards in Initial Teacher Training* (1996).

The National Council for Vocational Qualifications for Figure 6.6, The NVQ Framework.

Avon County Council for Figures 7.1 and 13.5.

Routledge and Patrick Easen for Figure 8.1, from *Making School-Centred INSET Work* (1985) (Croom Helm).

Boynton/Cook Heinemann and Douglas Barnes for Figure 13.1, from *From Communication to Curriculum* (1975) (Penguin).

Routledge and Alec Webster, Mike Beveridge and Malcolm Reed for Figure 13.2, from Webster, A., Beveridge, M. and Reed, M., *Managing the Literacy Curriculum* (1996).

Routledge for Figure 13.3, from Brown, G. A. and Edmondson, R. 'Asking questions', in Wragg, E. C. (ed.), *Teaching Skills* (1984) (Croom Helm).

Longman for Figure 13.6, from Alladina, S. and Edwards, V. (eds), *Multilingualism in the British Isles* (1991).

Routledge and Barry Fraser for the 'Classroom Environment Scale' in Practical Activity 14.2, from *Classroom Environment* (1986) (Croom Helm).

HMSO for Figure 15.3, from Gillborn, D. and Gipps, C., *Recent Research on the Achievement of Ethnic Minority Pupils* (1996) (Crown copyright).

The Geographical Association for Figure 15.6, from Leat, D. and Chandler, S., 'Using concept mapping in geography teaching', *Teaching Geography*, July 1996.

Cassell for Figure 16.2, from Hargreaves, D. and Hopkins, D., *The Empowered School* (1991).

DFEE for Figure 16.3, from OFSTED/DFEE, *Setting Targets to Raise Standards* (1996).

The International School Improvement and Effectiveness Centre, London University, Institute of Education, and Ken Spours for Figure 16.4 from, *Value Added and Raising Attainment* (BP Educational Series).

David Fulton and Jean Rudduck for Figure 16.6, from *School Improvement: What Can Pupils Tell Us?* (1996).

# INTRODUCTION

The main aim of this book is to support student teachers, school mentors and teachers who wish to reflect upon teaching in a systematic fashion. It is hoped that processes of enquiry, reflection and sharing could help to account for achievements, to analyse anxieties and to identify areas for future professional development.

The book is designed as a handbook which can be easily dipped into and from which ideas can be taken and developed. Selected issues, particular procedures and related *Practical Activities*, are set out so that analysis and practical suggestions are readily accessible. Each chapter also contains a section of *Notes for Further Reading*. This is an annotated list of particular books which are recommended to readers to extend study of certain issues and procedures. Many chapters also contain reading icons indicating cross-referencing to another book, *Readings for Reflective Teaching in the Primary School*. This is a very convenient source-book and many of its 134 edited readings are of relevance to all phases of education. A further and more specifically targeted sourcebook, *Readings for Reflective Teaching in Secondary Education*, is planned.

*Reflective Teaching in Secondary Education* is intended to be more than a practical guide to the self-evaluation of classroom practice and the work of students, mentors and teachers. The analysis and activities have been set within a theoretical framework which attempts to link classroom practice and educational theory with current educational, political and social debates. Thus, this book offers a broad context – the context of the 'extended professional' – within which to reflect upon teaching.

Of course, in the late 1990s, there are major national concerns with educational standards, school and LEA performance and target setting. In their 'New Labour' manifesto, these concerns are matched by particular prioritization of the needs of pupils in the inner cities. This emphasis on educational outcomes generates agendas to which all schools and teachers must respond. However, clarity in aspirations must be complemented by clear understanding of the teaching and learning *processes* through which improvements can be brought about. We see this as the core professional responsibility of teachers, to which reflective practices can make an important contribution.

All forms of action inevitably involve people in making judgements based on values and commitments and this is certainly true for teachers. We therefore wanted to maintain a framework which recognized the necessity of professional judgements by individual teachers and yet was also informed by a set of value-commitments that would command widespread support in moral and ethical terms.

We have considered many of the documents which have flowed from government agencies in recent years, reflecting wide-ranging concerns about the quality of educational provision. However, at a more fundamental level, we feel a particular need to emphasize the links between education, human rights and democracy. In this respect one can learn a great deal from looking at the Universal Declaration on Human Rights and the European Convention on Human Rights, which were both developed in the post-war years. There is also a specific educational Recommendation from the

Council of Europe's Committee of Ministers, entitled 'Teaching and Learning about Human Rights in School' (Council of Europe 1985), to which Great Britain is a signatory. It is worth citing some parts of this document here.

There is an important statement on the curriculum in relation to human rights:

*The understanding and experience of human rights is an important element of the preparation of all young people for life in a democratic and pluralistic society. It is a part of social and political education, and it involves intercultural and international understanding. (1.1)*

In terms of both knowledge to be acquired and the climate within schools in which such work should take place, it is stated:

*The study of human rights in schools should lead to an understanding of, and sympathy for the concepts of justice, equality, freedom, peace, dignity, rights and democracy. Such understanding should be both cognitive and based on experience and feelings. Schools should thus provide opportunities for pupils to experience affective involvement in human rights and to express their feelings through drama, art, music, creative writing and audio-visual media. (3.3)*

*Democracy is best learned in a democratic setting where participation is encouraged, where views can be expressed openly and discussed, where there is freedom of expression for pupils and teachers, and where there is fairness and justice. An appropriate climate is, therefore, an essential complement to effective learning about human rights. (4.1)*

For teacher education, the task is also spelt out clearly:

*The initial training of teachers should prepare them for their future contribution to teaching about human rights in their schools. For example, future teachers should:*
*(i) be encouraged to take an interest in national and world affairs*
*(ii) be taught to identify and combat all forms of discrimination in schools and society and be encouraged to confront and overcome their own prejudices. (5.1)*

These are challenging ideas, but ones which have to be faced if we are to provide the best possible quality of education for all the children in our society. The work of a professional educator thus involves a heavy degree of social responsibility. We hope that this book will help its readers to reflect on these concerns, as well as to improve their 'practice' more generally.

*Reflective Teaching in Secondary Education* has three parts.

Part 1 is entitled 'Becoming a Reflective Teacher'. Chapter 1 offers a theoretical rationale for the approach and Chapter 2 provides an analysis of the relationship between individuals, education and society. Chapter 3 is a guide to partnerships between schools and higher education institutions and to processes involved in mentoring from both student and mentor perspectives. The first part of the book then concludes with a review and examination of ways of investigating classrooms, Chapter 4.

Part 2, 'Being a Reflective Teacher', represents the classroom-focused, practical core of the book. Each chapter is devoted to a particular aspect of the teaching-learning process. Each has the same structure: a significant issue is discussed, practical activities for classroom investigation are presented, follow-up points are suggested and guidance for further reading is given.

The issues selected in Part 2 are ones which are basic to classroom life: Chapter 5 on examining the school context; Chapters 6 and 7 on curriculum structures at Key Stages 3 and 4 and at Post-16, and on curriculum planning; Chapter 8 on ourselves, our values, aims and commitments and those of the pupils; Chapter 9 considering how pupils learn; Chapter 10 on planning teaching sessions, followed by Chapter 11 on organizing the class and classroom. Chapter 12 is on classroom management and Chapter 13 on communication issues and skills. Chapter 14 addresses relationships, discipline and behaviour, and Part 2 concludes with a major treatment of assessment issues, Chapter 15.

Part 3, in Chapter 16, looks 'Beyond Classroom Reflection' to consider reflective teaching and innovation in schools as a whole. Finally, in Chapter 17, the place and responsibilities of reflective secondary teachers in society are also reconsidered.

A final point which may need some clarification concerns the terms by which we name young people as a group in school. They are sometimes referred to by teachers as 'children', although for most there comes a point around Year 10 or 11 when this becomes increasingly inappropriate and 'young people' may be substituted. Interestingly, 'young adults' is seldom heard. In the early years of secondary eduction some teachers use terms like 'kids' to get over the naming problem, although both 'children' and 'kids' have significant and possibly unhelpful connotations. The most commonly used term used by teachers is thus 'pupils', and this remains common even through Years 12 and 13 where the term 'students' may also sometimes be substituted. In further education colleges the term 'students' is almost always used. However, it is rare to hear a school staff referring to young people as 'students' throughout Years 7–13. For the purposes of discussion throughout this book, we have therefore chosen to use the terms 'pupils' and 'young people', since we felt these would be most readily and widely accepted by teachers across the sector. Our normal use of 'students' is in reference to student teachers, and 'children' normally refers to those below the age of 11.

# PART 1

# BECOMING A REFLECTIVE TEACHER

# CHAPTER 1

# Reflective teaching and competence

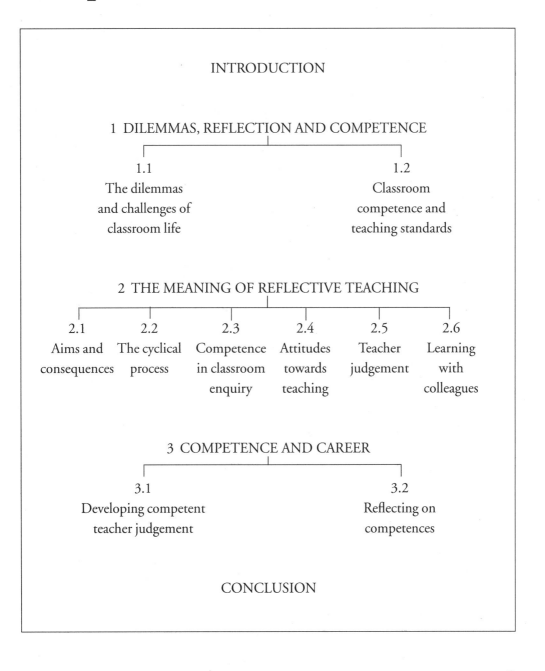

INTRODUCTION

1 DILEMMAS, REFLECTION AND COMPETENCE

1.1
The dilemmas
and challenges of
classroom life

1.2
Classroom
competence and
teaching standards

2 THE MEANING OF REFLECTIVE TEACHING

2.1
Aims and
consequences

2.2
The cyclical
process

2.3
Competence
in classroom
enquiry

2.4
Attitudes
towards
teaching

2.5
Teacher
judgement

2.6
Learning
with
colleagues

3 COMPETENCE AND CAREER

3.1
Developing competent
teacher judgement

3.2
Reflecting on
competences

CONCLUSION

## INTRODUCTION

This book is based on the belief that teaching is a complex and highly skilled activity which, above all, requires classroom teachers to exercise judgement in deciding how to act. We see reflective teaching as a process through which the capacity to make such professional judgements can be developed and maintained.

The book also relates directly to the practical 'competences' are increasingly required of teachers and which, in many respects, represent a constructive clarification of the particular skills, knowledge and understandings of the profession. However, when discussing competence, there is a tendency to concentrate on practical and technical matters with little reference to values, aims and consequences. Such consequences could be of a personal nature, for example, the effects of a classroom teacher's practice on a pupil's self-image. They could be of an academic nature, for example, concerning intellectual achievement, or they could be of a social nature, for example, relating to the cumulative effects of school experience on life chances.

The view taken in this book is that teaching concerns values, aims, attitudes and consequences as well as skills, knowledge and competence. Indeed, we shall argue that there is a constructive relationship between the *state* of classroom competence and the *processes* of reflection through which competence is developed and maintained.

This proposition simplifies a number of issues, but it remains at the core of the approach which we have taken in this book. We see successive levels of competence in teaching. Those which student-teachers may attain at the beginning, middle and end of their courses, those of the new teacher after their induction to full-time school life, and those of the experienced, expert teacher. Given the nature of teaching, professional development and learning should never stop. We believe that the process of reflection feeds a constructive spiral of professional development and competence. This should both be personally fulfilling for teachers, but also lead to a steady increase in the quality of the education which is offered to young people. This argument is represented diagrammatically in Figure 1.1.

This chapter has three main parts. The first introduces some of the dilemmas which teachers face and some of the issues surrounding competences. In the second part, six key characteristics of reflective teaching are identified and discussed. The final part focuses on developing successive levels of competence throughout a teaching career and also looks at some criticisms of competency approaches.

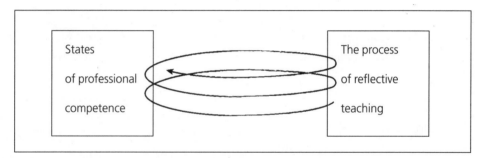

**Figure 1.1** *The spiral of professional development and competence*

# 1 DILEMMAS, REFLECTION AND COMPETENCE

## 1.1 The dilemmas and challenges of classroom life

The complicated nature of educational issues and the practical demands of classroom teaching ensure that a teacher's work is never finished. When practicalities, teaching competence, personal ideals and wider educational concerns are considered together, the job of rising to the challenges and reconciling the numerous requirements and possible conflicts often seems to be overwhelming. As one teacher explained to us:

> Teaching can be totally absorbing but there always seems to be more to do, more that you want to do, more that you have to do, than the time allows. It's a constant struggle to fit it all in and keep a family and social life. You always seem to be cutting time from somewhere.
>
> There have been so many changes in school. There are additional requirements to syllabuses and schemes of work so that as a subject teacher you always feel that you're taking on new things (some of which you want to take on, others you haven't always got your heart in). As well as the subject teaching there's all the other elements of teaching: there's your tutor group where there's a pretty constant stream of family and social issues to deal with as well as following up problems with learning and behaviour; there's the admin within school and the whole-school elements of teaching, trying to keep a career going and get some professional development and contact with other teachers in my subject outside school.
>
> The constant engagement with kids can be great but exhausting. They all need my attention; I want to help them all as learners but I can't always get the teaching right. When there are problems it's often because I haven't planned the lesson right, I've reacted in the wrong way, or I've just been boring. Some kids are difficult and although you do complain about their behaviour and fill out the right bits of paper you don't always feel that anything is being done. Sometimes you feel that because you complain you're seen not to be coping. I'm sure lots of teachers do keep things to themselves, within their rooms, because of this.
>
> I teach almost two hundred different pupils each week and keeping each class, each child working to their best is difficult. There always seems to be at least one class who don't get your best planning, and there's always an individual who, when they come to ask you about them, isn't getting all they need. As the year goes on I tend to find more of my attention going into the exam classes, and keeping up with this marking always seems to leave me with marking not done lower down the school. Nowadays there's checking by the Head of Department and the Senior Managers, so I feel guilty and vulnerable about that.
>
> It feels like a tightrope at times and you do fall off. I am happy to keep getting back on.

Such dilemmas are frequently expressed – by experienced teachers, and even more by student teachers.

One excellent analysis of the difficult dilemmas which teachers face has been pro-vided by Berlak and Berlak (1981, **Primary Reading 1.3**). The framework which they developed is a simple but very powerful one, the strength of which derives from the fact that, although they studied only three schools in detail, they took great care to relate their analysis of the dilemmas which arose in the 'micro' world of the classroom to the major factors, beliefs and influences in society as a whole. Such factors, it was argued, influence, structure and constrain the actions of teachers, children and their parents. However, they do not do so in ways which are consistent, because of existing complexities and contradictions – hence the dilemmas which have to be faced. The resolution of such dilemmas calls for teachers to use professional judgement to assess the most appropriate course of action in any particular situation.

But what are the major dilemmas which have to be faced? Figure 1.2 below, pre-sents our version of some of them.

This book is intended to provide a practical guide to ways of reflecting on such issues and it offers strategies and advice for developing the necessary classroom com-petences to resolve them.

| | |
|---|---|
| Treating each learner as a 'whole person' | Treating each learner primarily as a 'pupil' |
| Organizing the learners on an individual basis | Organizing the learners as a class |
| Giving learners a degree of control over their use of time, their activities and their work standards | Tightening control over learners' use of time, their activities and their work standards |
| Seeking to motivate learners through intrinsic involvement and enjoyment of activities | Offering reasons and rewards so that learners are extrinsically motivated to tackle tasks |
| Developing and negotiating the curriculum from an appreciation of learners' interests | Providing a subject curriculum which learners are deemed to need and which 'society' expects them to receive |
| Maintaining awareness of the relationships between subjects in the curriculum | Dealing systematically with each discrete subject of the curriculum |
| Aiming for quality in school-work | Aiming for quantity in school-work |
| Trying to build up co-operative and social skills | Developing self-reliance and self-confidence in individuals |
| Inducting learners into a common culture | Affirming the variety of cultures in a multi-ethnic society |
| Allocating teacher time, attention and resources equally among all learners | Paying attention to the special needs of particular pupils |
| Maintaining consistent rules and understand-ings about behaviour and school-work | Being flexible and responsive to particular situa-tions |
| Presenting oneself formally to pupils | Relaxing with pupils |
| Working with 'professional' application and care for learners | Working with consideration of one's personal needs |

**Figure 1.2** *Common dilemmas faced by teachers*

## 1.2   Classroom competence and teaching standards

There has been a great deal of discussion in recent years about the need to ensure that teachers are competent and meet appropriate standards in the skills, knowledge and understanding required for effective classroom management, pupil assessment, subject teaching and professional development. Indeed, competency criteria have been set by governments in many countries to provide a structure for teacher training. For instance, in England from 1996/97, the Teacher Training Agency established a new 'framework' for competences and inspection procedures. These are believed to 'focus on the practical outcomes of training and the factors which explain them' (OFSTED/TTA 1996) (see Figure 1.3).

*The students' (NQTs') subject knowledge for teaching in the secondary age-range* **is judged by the extent to which they demonstrate:**

a.   secure knowledge, concepts and skills in their specialist subject at a standard equivalent to degree level and sufficient grasp of their second or other teaching subject (where applicable) to enable them to teach it confidently and accurately in KS3 and, where appropriate, KS4 and post-16;

b.   as required for their subjects, a detailed knowledge and understanding of the National Curriculum Programmes of Study for KS3 and, where applicable, KS4, and familiarity with relevant KS4 and post-16 examination syllabuses and courses, including vocational courses;

c.   where relevant, an understanding of progression from the KS2 Programmes of Study;

d.   the ability to cope securely with subject-related questions which pupils raise.

*Students' (NQTs') planning, teaching and classroom management* **are judged by the extent to which they:**

a.   plan their teaching to achieve progression in pupils' learning, taking account, where applicable, of Programmes of Study or of vocational or Post-16 syllabuses;

b.   select learning objectives, content and teaching methods for lessons which are appropriate to what is being taught and the age, ability, attainment and prior learning of the pupils;

c.   make effective use of information on pupils' attainment and progress;

d.   are able to present content clearly and accurately, using appropriate specialist vocabulary, and communicate to pupils their enthusiasm for the subject;

e.   know how to make effective use of IT and other resources to improve standards of pupils' learning;

f.   achieve a good standard of discipline and classroom organization, and maintain a safe and purposeful environment for learning;

g.   teach whole classes well, monitoring and intervening as necessary to ensure sound learning; and ensure effective teaching of groups and individuals;

h.   ensure that pupils acquire and consolidate knowledge, skills and understanding of the subject;

i.   plan opportunities to promote pupils' spiritual, moral, social and cultural development;

j.   evaluate critically the effectiveness of their own teaching;

k.   stimulate pupils' intellectual curiosity and their enthusiasm for the subject.

*The students' (NQTs') assessment, recording and reporting of pupils' progress* **are judged by the extent to which they:**

a.   assess on a day-to-day basis how well learning objectives have been achieved and use this assessment to adjust their lesson planning and teaching methods;

b.   identify the learning needs of pupils, including able pupils and those with special educational needs;

c.   assess pupils' work regularly and provide oral and written feedback to help them make progress;

d.   record pupils' progress effectively;

e.   understand the standards required by the National Curriculum, GCSE and other Key Stage 4 courses and, where applicable, Post-16 courses, and can assess pupils against these with guidance from an experienced teacher;

f.   are familiar with the statutory assessment and reporting requirements and are able to prepare and present informative reports to parents.

**Figure 1.3** *Teaching competence of students and newly qualified teachers (from the Framework for the Assessment of Quality and Standards in Initial Teacher Training, OFSTED/TTA, 1996)*

Such competency criteria are very helpful in defining goals for students, tutors and teachers who are engaged in initial teacher education and, of course, others could be developed for the initial period of induction into full-time work or for in-service stages of professional development.

However, we need to be clear about the status of competency criteria. The example above describes the skills, knowledge and understanding which the TTA deemed to be appropriate for teachers in the particular context of England in 1996. By 1997 they were already being changed and represented as a set of 'standards'. Those required where a national curriculum and legally defined assessment procedures exist may well differ from those which are called for where such structures do not exist; those called for where class sizes are very high (as in many parts of the world) may vary from those needed when much smaller classes or groups are taught; those required in the 1990s are unlikely to remain constant into the next century.

We want to argue then, that officially endorsed competency criteria and standards are context-specific. They reflect the cultures, values and the priorities of decision-makers. In the case of teacher education, they describe a particular repertoire and level of skills, knowledge and understanding which has been deemed appropriate for the particular time and circumstances in which a new generation of teachers is to be trained.

This specificity brings both benefits and disadvantages, and we represent these in Figure 1.4, as elaborated from work by Whitty and Willmott (1991).

There has been considerable concern in some quarters about the use of competences in teacher education, and there have been some unfortunate and unsuccessful experiences in the United States. Nevertheless, we believe that the advantages of having a clear specification of goals for teacher education are very significant. They can provide a framework both for greater partnership between schools and higher education training institutions and for rational, career-long staff development.

However, we reassert our point that they represent states of teaching capacity to be attained. They do not define or prescribe the process by which these standards of competence are to be developed. For the latter, we would argue that the process of 'reflective teaching' is essential.

| Benefits of competency approaches | Disadvantages of competency approaches |
|---|---|
| May provide clear goals for students | May be hard to agree definitions of competence |
| May clarify the roles of schools and of colleges in the training process | May lead to a fragmented reductionism of the holistic capacity to teach |
| May give employers greater confidence in what beginning teachers can do | May be difficult to agree valid and reliable criteria for assessment |
| May give beginning teachers more confidence in themselves | May emphasize outcomes rather than learning processes in training |

**Figure 1.4** *Benefits and disadvantages of competency approaches*

## 2 │ THE MEANING OF REFLECTIVE TEACHING

The notion of reflective teaching, around which this book is based, stems from Dewey (1933, **Primary Reading 1.1**) who contrasted 'routine action' with 'reflective action'. According to Dewey routine action is guided by factors such as tradition, habit and authority and by institutional definitions and expectations. By implication it is relatively static and is thus unresponsive to changing priorities and circumstances. Reflective action, on the other hand, involves a willingness to engage in constant self-appraisal and development. Among other things, it implies flexibility, rigorous analysis and social awareness.

Dewey's notion of reflective action, when developed and applied to teaching, is very challenging. In this section, we review its implications by identifying and discussing what we have identified as six key characteristics. These are:

1. Reflective teaching implies an active concern with aims and consequences, as well as means and technical efficiency.
2. Reflective teaching is applied in a cyclical or spiralling process, in which teachers monitor, evaluate and revise their own practice continuously.
3. Reflective teaching requires competence in methods of classroom enquiry, to support the development of teaching competence.
4. Reflective teaching requires attitudes of open-mindedness, responsibility and wholeheartedness.
5. Reflective teaching is based on teacher judgement, which is informed partly by self-reflection and partly by insights from educational disciplines.
6. Reflective teaching, professional learning and personal fulfilment are enhanced through collaboration and dialogue with colleagues.

Each of these six characteristics will now be considered more fully.

## 2.1 Aims and consequences

*Reflective teaching implies an active concern with aims and consequences as well as means and practical competence.*

This issue relates first to the immediate aims and consequences of classroom practice for these are any teacher's prime responsibility. However, classroom work cannot be isolated from the influence of the wider society and a reflective teacher must therefore consider both spheres.

The recent history of educational policy-making in the UK will illustrate the way in which changes outside schools influence actions within them. Following the initiation of a 'Great Debate' by Prime Minister Callaghan (1976, **Primary Reading 7.7**) many of the 'taken-for-granteds' in education were progressively challenged during the 1980s. Successive Conservative governments introduced far-reaching and cumulative changes in all spheres of education. Many of these reforms were opposed by professional organizations (see for example, Haviland 1988, Arnot and Barton 1992) but with no noticeable effect on political decision-making. For instance, in the summer of 1992 three professionals who had been highly influential in the early development of the educational reforms, the former Chief Inspector of Schools, the architect of the assessment arrangements and the former director of the National Curriculum Council for England, each made public statements regarding their concern about the extent of political influence. Indeed, the allegation was again made that educational policy was being influenced by a closed system of beliefs – an 'ideology' – but this time under the control of a small number of right-wing politicians and pressure groups. Meanwhile, teachers and pupils in schools and classrooms worked to implement the new forms of curriculum, assessment, accountability, management and control which had been introduced – despite the fact that, in many respects, the profession at the time was largely opposed to the principles on which the reforms were based.

Such a stark example of the contestation of aims and values in education raises questions concerning the relationship between professionals, parents and policymakers. It is possible to start from the seemingly uncontroversial argument that, in a democratic society, decisions about the aims of education should be 'democratically' determined. It has been suggested (White 1978) that teachers should accept a role as active 'interpreters' of political policy. That most teachers accept this argument is shown by the way in which they implemented legislation even when they did not support it – though in the 1990s an unusual number of teachers did leave the profession.

However, such a stance is very different from the idea of the autonomous professional with which many teachers have traditionally identified. Yet it can be argued that the existence of unconstrained autonomy is only reasonable and practical if ends, aims and values are shared in some sort of social consensus. Obviously, in such circumstances, judgements about the technical effectiveness of various types of teaching would best be derived from the educator on the spot. However, as soon as questions about educational aims and social values are seriously raised then the position changes. In a democratic society, the debate appropriately extends to the political domain and this, of course, is what has happened recently.

This does not mean though, that teachers, even as interpreters of policy, should simply 'stand by' in the procedure. Indeed, there are two important roles which they can play. In the case of the first, an appropriate metaphor for the teacher's role is, as White suggested, that of 'activist'. This recognizes that teachers are individual members of society who, within normal political processes, have rights to pursue their values and beliefs as guided by their own individual moral and ethical concerns. They should thus be active in contributing to the formation of public policy. Second, whilst accepting a responsibility for translating politically determined aims into practice, teachers should speak out, as they have done, if they view particular aims and policies as being professionally impracticable, educationally unsound or morally questionable. In such circumstances the professional experience, knowledge and judgements of teachers should be brought to bear on policy-makers directly – whether or not the policy-makers wish for or act on the advice which is offered. Indeed, we would suggest that, within a modern democratic society, teachers should be entitled not only to a hearing, but also have some influence, on educational policy.

The reflective teacher should thus acknowledge the political process and be willing to contribute to it both as a citizen and as a professional.

## 2.2  A cyclical process

*Reflective teaching is applied in a cyclical or spiralling process in which teachers contin-
ually monitor, evaluate and revise their own practice.*

This characteristic refers to the process of reflective teaching and provides the
dynamic basis for teacher action. The conception of a classroom-based, reflexive
process stems from the teacher-based, action-research movement of which Lawrence
Stenhouse was a key figure. He argued (1975, **Primary Reading 3.1**) that teachers
should act as 'researchers' of their own practice and should develop the curriculum
through practical enquiry. Various alternative models have since become available
(Carr and Kemmis 1986, Elliott 1990, McNiff 1992), and, although there are some
significant differences in these models, they all preserve a central concern with self-
reflection.

Teachers are principally expected to plan, make provision and to act. Reflective
teachers also need to monitor, observe and collect data on their own and the pupils'
intentions, actions and feelings. This evidence then needs to be critically analysed and
evaluated so that it can be shared, judgements made and decisions taken. Finally, this
may lead the teacher to revise his or her classroom policies, plans and provision before
beginning the process again. It is a dynamic process which is intended to lead through
successive cycles, or through a spiralling process, towards higher-quality teaching.
This model is simple, comprehensive and certainly could be an extremely powerful
influence on practice. It is consistent with the notion of reflective teaching, as
described by Dewey, and, provides an essential clarification of the procedures for
reflective teaching. Figure 1.5 represents the key stages of the reflective process.

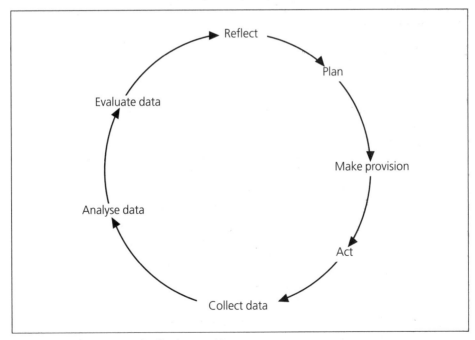

**Figure 1.5** *The process of reflective teaching*

## 2.3 Competence in classroom enquiry

*Reflective teaching requires competence in methods of classroom enquiry, to support the development of teaching competence.*

We will identify three types of competence, each of which contributes to the cyclical process of reflection (see Section 2.2).

### Empirical competence

This relates to the essential issue of knowing what is going on in a classroom or school. It is concerned with collecting data, describing situations, processes, causes and effects with care and accuracy. Two sorts of data are particularly relevant. Objective data, such as descriptions of what people actually do, are important, but so too are subjective data which describe how people feel and think – their perceptions. The collection of both types of data calls for considerable skill on the part of any classroom investigator, particularly when they may be enquiring into their own practice.

### Analytical competence

This form of competence is needed to address the issue of how to interpret descriptive data. Such 'facts' are not meaningful until they are placed in a framework which enables a reflective teacher to relate them one with the other and to begin to theorize about them.

### Evaluative competence

Evaluative competences are involved in making judgements about the educational consequences of the results of the practical enquiry. Evaluation, in the light of aims, values and the experience of others enables the descriptive and analytical results of an enquiry to be applied to future policy and practice.

Further practical discussion on competence in classroom enquiry is offered in Chapter 3 of this book and in Chapter 1 of *Primary Readings*. However, such competence is not sufficient in itself for a teacher who wishes to engage in reflective teaching. Certain attitudes are also necessary and need to be integrated and applied with enquiry skills.

## 2.4 Attitudes towards teaching

*Reflective teaching requires attitudes of open-mindedness, responsibility and whole-heartedness.*

### Open-mindedness

As Dewey put it, open-mindedness is an:

> active desire to listen to more sides than one, to give heed to facts from whatever source they come, to give full attention to alternative possibilities, to recognize the possibility of error even in the beliefs which are dearest to us. (Dewey 1933, p. 29)

Open-mindedness is an essential attribute for rigorous reflection because any sort of enquiry which is consciously based on partial evidence, only weakens itself. We thus use it in the sense of being willing to reflect upon ourselves and to challenge our assumptions, prejudices and ideologies as well as those of others. However, to be open-minded regarding evidence and its interpretation is not the same thing as declining to take up a value-position on important social and educational issues. This point brings us to the second attribute which Dewey saw as a prerequisite to reflective action – 'responsibility'.

### Responsibility

Intellectual responsibility, according to Dewey, means:

> to consider the consequences of a projected step; it means to be willing to adopt these consequences when they follow reasonably. . . . Intellectual responsibility secures integrity. (Dewey 1933, p. 30)

The position which is implied here is clearly related to the issue of aims which we discussed above. However, in Dewey's writing the issue is relatively clearly bounded and he seems to be referring to classroom teaching and to school practices only. Zeichner has taken this considerably further when, in considering teacher education, he points out that:

> Because of the intimate relationships between the school and the social, political and economic contexts in which it exists, any consideration of the consequences to which classroom action leads must inevitably take one beyond the boundaries of the classroom and even of the school itself and beyond the consideration of educational principles alone. . . . An exclusive focus on the level of the classroom and on educational principles alone does not enable the student teacher to contemplate the kinds of basic structural changes that may be necessary for his or her responsibility to be fully exercised. The attention of student teachers remains focused on the amelioration of surface symptoms in individuals and not on an analysis of the social conditions that stand behind, and at least partially explain, the existence of those symptoms. (Zeichner 1981/82, pp. 6–7)

Here, Zeichner is asserting the inevitable consequence of relating means and ends in education with systematic open-mindedness. Moral, ethical and political issues will be raised and must, he argues, be considered so that professional and personal judgements can be made about what is worthwhile. It clearly follows that a simple instrumental approach to teaching is not consistent with reflectiveness (see also Carr and Kemmis, **Primary Reading 3.2**).

### Wholeheartedness

'Wholeheartedness', the third of Dewey's necessary attitudes, refers essentially to the way in which such consideration takes place. Dewey's suggestion was that reflective teachers should be dedicated, single-minded, energetic and enthusiastic. As he put it:

> There is no greater enemy of effective thinking than divided interest. . . . A genuine enthusiasm is an attitude that operates as an intellectual force. When a person is absorbed, the subject carries him on. (Dewey 1933, p. 30)

Together, these three attitudes are vital ingredients of the 'professional' commitment which needs to be demonstrated by all those who aim to be reflective teachers.

## 2.5   Teacher judgement

*Reflective teaching is based on teacher judgement, informed partly by self-reflection and partly by insights from educational disciplines.*

Teacher knowledge has often been criticized. For instance, Bolster (1983) carried out an analysis of teachers as classroom decision-makers and concluded that teacher knowledge commonly has certain negative characteristics. In particular, he suggested that, since teacher knowledge is specific and pragmatic, it is resistant to change. Bolster argued that teacher knowledge is based on individual experiences and is believed to be of value if it 'works' in practical situations. However, since it 'works', there is little incentive to change, even in the light of evidence supporting alternative ideas or practices. On this analysis there is little need for teacher judgement, since teachers will stick to routinized practices.

However, Bolster's position does not seem to recognize adequately the very real strengths of the knowledge which teachers can develop. For an alternative view it is possible to draw on Donald Schon's work (1983, **Primary Reading** 1.2) on the characteristics of 'reflective practitioners'.

Schon contrasted 'scientific' professional work such as laboratory research, with 'caring' professional work such as education. He called the former 'high hard ground' and saw it as supported by quantitative and 'objective' evidence. On the other hand, the 'swampy lowlands' of the caring professions involve more interpersonal areas and qualitative issues. These complex 'lowlands', according to Schon, tend to become 'confusing messes' of intuitive action. He thus suggested that, although such 'messes' tend to be highly relevant in practical terms, they are not easily amenable to rigorous analysis because they draw on a type of knowledge-in-action – knowledge that is inherent in professional action. It is spontaneous, intuitive, tacit and intangible, but it 'works' in practice.

Schon also argued that it is possible to recognize 'reflection-in-action', in which adjustments to action are made through direct experience. As he put it:

> When someone reflects-in-action, he (*sic*) becomes a researcher in the practice context. He is not dependent on the categories of established theory and technique, but constructs a new theory of the unique case. His enquiry is not limited to a

deliberation about means which depends on a prior agreement about ends. He does not keep means and ends separate, but defines them interactively as he frames a problematic situation. He does not separate thinking from action. . . . His experimenting is a kind of action, implementation is built into his enquiry. (Schon 1983, p. 68)

Such ideas have received powerful empirical support in recent years, with the sophistication of teachers' classroom thinking and 'craft knowledge' being increasingly recognized and understood by researchers (e.g. Elbaz 1983, Calderhead 1987, 1988b, **Primary Reading 1.8**, Olson 1991, Brown and McIntyre 1992, Rowland 1993). It is clear that effective teachers make use of judgements all the time, as they adapt their teaching to the ever-changing learning challenges which their circumstances and pupils present to them.

However, there is a danger too in this affirmation of the sophistication of much teacher thinking, for a justifiable emphasis on the value and merits of teacher-generated classroom knowledge could devalue the enriching strengths of other forms of educational insight. Many of these derive from research or analysis undertaken by people outside classrooms. They may be based on comparative, historical or philosophical research, on empirical study with large samples of classrooms, teachers, pupils or schools, on innovative methodologies, or on developing theoretical analyses. Whatever its character, such educational research has the potential to complement, contextualize and enhance the detailed and practical understandings of teachers.

We thus strongly advocate attempts to maximize the potential for collaboration between teachers and researchers in relevant disciplines. For such collaboration to be successful it must be based on a frank appreciation of each other's strengths and weaknesses. While recognizing the danger of unjustified generalization, we identify these strengths and weaknesses below (see Figure 1.6).

|  | Strengths | Weaknesses |
|---|---|---|
| Researchers' knowledge | Often based on careful research with large samples and reliable methods | Often uses jargon unnecessarily and communicates poorly |
|  | Often provides a clear and incisive analysis when studied | Often seems obscure and difficult to relate to practical issues |
|  | Often offers novel ways of looking at situations and issues | Often fragments educational processes and experiences |
| Teachers' knowledge | Often practically relevant and directly useful | Often impressionistic |
|  | Often communicated effectively to practitioners | Often relies too much on situations which might be unique |
|  | Often concerned with the wholeness of classroom processes and experiences | When analysing, is sometimes unduly influenced by existing assumptions |

**Figure 1.6** *Comparison of researchers' and teachers' knowledge*

We arrive, then, at a position which calls for attempts to draw on the strengths of teachers and researchers and, by doing so, overcomes the weaknesses which exist in both positions. This is what we mean by the statement of the fifth characteristic of reflective teaching, that it should be based on 'informed teacher judgement'. The collaborative endeavour which is implied here underpins this whole book.

## 2.6 Learning with colleagues

*Reflective teaching, professional learning and personal fulfilment are enhanced through collaboration and dialogue with colleagues.* - All say this.

The value of engaging in reflective activity is almost always enhanced if it can be carried out in association with other colleagues, be they students, teachers or tutors. The circumstances in secondary schools and FE colleges, with high proportions of contact time with students, have constrained a great deal of such educational discussion in the past – though this is gradually changing as co-ordinated professional development assumes a greater priority. On teacher education courses reflection together in seminars, tutor-groups and workshops, at college or in school, should bring valuable opportunities to share and compare, support and advise in reciprocal ways.

Collaborative work capitalizes on the social nature of learning (Vygotsky 1978, **Primary Reading 6.4**). This is as significant for adults as it is for pupils (see Chapter 9) and it works through many of the same basic processes.

Collaboration produces discussion and action together. Aims are thus clarified, experiences are shared, language and concepts for analysing practice are refined, the personal insecurities of innovation are reduced, evaluation becomes reciprocal and commitments are affirmed. Moreover, openness, activity and discussion gradually weave the values and self of individuals into the culture and mission of the school or course. This can be both personally fulfilling and educationally effective (Kohl 1986).

In the 1990s, when the development of coherence and progression in school policies and practice has become of enormous importance, collaborative work is also a necessity. At one level, it is officially endorsed by the requirement to produce 'school development plans', a process which has been seen as 'empowering' (Hargreaves and Hopkins 1991, **Primary Reading 14.3**). However, whilst affirming the enormous value of whole-school staff teams working and learning together, we must almost acknowledge the complexity and fragility of the process.

Whatever their circumstances though, reflective teachers are likely to benefit from working, experimenting, talking and reflecting with others. Apart from the benefits for learning and professional development, it is usually both more interesting and more fun!

## 3 | COMPETENCE AND CAREER

## 3.1 Developing competent teacher judgement

In this section we look at career development and competence. This is important, if only because much present provision in this area is so haphazard. To explore some of these issues, we have simplified some work by Elliott (1991), who drew on Dreyfus (1981).

Dreyfus suggested that understanding and judgement in complex interpersonal situations is based on four basic capacities:

- Recognizing issues
- Discerning which issues are important
- Understanding the situation as a whole
- Making decisions.

Dreyfus and Elliott mapped five stages in the development of these capacities for situational understanding and judgement. We have simplified these to just three, those of the 'novice', the 'competent' and the 'expert' (see Figure 1.7).

These three stages can then be related to the four capacities for situational understanding and decision-making.

The value of the model is that it highlights key factors in the *development* of competence. This can be applied to teaching.

*Novice teachers* tend to need to proceed carefully, having only a limited understanding of the issues with which they are about to engage, and having to think hard about both the various features of their classroom situation and how best to act in it. Sometimes there is also a tendency for such teachers to seek security by conforming to the norms and culture of the school (Menter 1989).

*Competent teachers* have had more experience and know classroom situations better. They can thus interpret and respond to events with more confidence, even though they still have to work at their decision-making.

*Expert teachers* work at a higher level of competence, understanding the various dimensions of school and classroom contexts so well that many of their decisions

|  | Recognizing the issues | Discerning important issues | Understanding the whole situation | Making a decision |
|---|---|---|---|---|
| *Novice* | Out of context | No | Analytically | Rationally |
| *Competent* | In context | Yes | Analytically | Rationally |
| *Expert* | In context | Yes | Holistically | Intuitively |

**Figure 1.7** *Stages in the development of competence*

become almost intuitive. Where appropriate, they are also able to face the dilemmas of teaching with more self-confidence, to experiment with, and analyse, their own practice.

Of course, as with many developmental models, this model simplifies great complexity. For instance, for any one teacher it is very likely that levels of competence and self-confidence regarding different aspects of the teaching role will vary. More specific needs for professional development will need to be identified and met – a role which is increasingly being met by collegiate systems of appraisal (Hopkins and Bollington 1989, **Primary Reading 3.6**).

As we argued in the introduction to this chapter, reflective teaching is important as the process through which ascending levels of competence, in whatever sphere, can be developed. At a novice stage, reflection on one's practice can be unsettling and perhaps even painful at times. On the other hand it is part of the learning process and can also be affirming. At more competent stages there is a considerable danger that people may level out their aspirations for professional competence, and decide to coast along in routinized ways. Reflective practice will help to develop beyond this. As expert stages are reached, reflective teaching is likely to be an accepted part of the repertoire of teachers who are constantly asking questions of themselves and seeking to increase the quality of their provision.

Reflective teaching thus provides a means of constantly evaluating, developing and refining competences. It provides an essential underpinning for professional judgement, development and the provision of high quality education.

## 3.2    Reflecting on competences

Having suggested the value of defining competences and the role of reflective processes in developing them to meet appropriate standards, it is appropriate to consider some avenues of critique. Several are suggested by the disadvantages identified in Figure 1.4. However, we want to approach this using a comparative strategy and by thinking about generic competences drawn from the world of industry.

A great deal of work on competences has been carried out in businesses, particularly with regard to productivity and management. Among the early influential studies are those of McBer and Company in the 1970s, summarized in a book *Three Factors of Success in the World of Work* by Klemp (1977). Klemp's key suggestion is that it is possible to distinguish three basic generic types of competence which are needed in acting appropriately in complex situations involving problem-solving and decisions. These should thus apply to many types of occupation – including teaching. Klemp suggests that there are:

- *Cognitive abilities* – for instance, understanding, analysing and communicating information, reflecting on experience.
- *Interpersonal abilities* – for instance, empathizing with, relating to and supporting others.
- *Motivational abilities* – for instance, personal goal-setting, risk-taking and commitment to achieve; networking, goal-sharing and team work.

The development and maintenance of appropriate types of cognitive, interpersonal and motivational competence is obviously necessary for high quality teaching – but, as we have seen, teachers crucially need the professional judgement to select from their repertoire of teaching competences, as appropriate, to meet the needs of the pupils whom they teach.

Perhaps the major fear of those who oppose the use of competency statements and 'standards' in teacher education is that they will lead to itemization and fragmentation of what, when it is working well, is the holistic art of teaching. Teaching is only partly amenable to rational analysis, and, particularly in work with young people, the intangible contribution of rapport, intuition and imagination is often vital. This should not be seen as a weakness. Indeed, it is a necessary aspect of human interaction and part of what makes teaching fulfilling.

## CONCLUSION

We have considered ways in which states of classroom competence can be defined and the benefits of doing so. We have also discussed the way in which reflective teaching provides a *process* through which successive levels of competence can be developed and maintained. We have outlined six characteristics of reflective teaching.

Some readers may well be wondering if this isn't all just a bit much to ask. How is the time to be found? Isn't it all 'common sense' anyway? We would respond in two ways. First, we accept that engaging constantly in reflective activities of the sort described in this book would be impossible. The point however, is to use them, as appropriate, as *learning experiences*. Such experiences should lead to conclusions which can be applied in new and more routine circumstances. Second, we accept that there is what some may see as a good deal of 'common sense' in the logic of the process of reflective teaching, but we see this resonance as a strength. When reflective teaching is used as a means of professional development it is extended far beyond this underpinning. The whole activity is much more rigorous – carefully gathered evidence replaces subjective impressions, open-mindedness replaces prior expectations, insights from reading or constructive and structured critique from colleagues challenge what might previously have been taken for granted. 'Common sense' may well endorse the value of the basic, reflective idea but, ironically, one outcome of reflection is often to produce critique and movement beyond the limitations of commonsense thinking. That, in a sense, is the whole point, the reason why it is a necessary part of professional activity. The aim of reflective practice is thus to support a shift from routine actions rooted in commonsense thinking to reflective action stemming from professional thinking.

We believe that teachers can confidently expect to achieve an appropriate state of professional competence through adopting processes of reflective teaching – and the remainder of this book is designed to provide support in precisely that process.

## Notes for further reading

The dilemmas in educational decision-making, which suggest that reflection is a continually necessary element of teaching are analysed in:

Berlak, H. and Berlak, A. (1981)
*Dilemmas of Schooling,*
London: Methuen.                    📖 **Primary Reading 1. 3**

Rowland, S. (1993)
*The Enquiring Tutor: Explorations in Professional Learning,*
London: Falmer Press.

Two works by Dewey which have influenced our thinking are:

Dewey, J. (1916)
*Democracy and Education,*
New York: Free Press.                    📖 **Primary Reading 1. 1**

Dewey, J. (1933)
*How We Think: A Restatement of the Relation of Reflective Thinking to the Educative Process,*
Chicago: Henry Regnery.                    📖 **Primary Reading 1. 1**

The work of Zeichner on reflective teaching has been very influential in recent years. See a recent consolidation and a review of reform initiatives:

Zeichner, K. and Liston, D. P. (1996)
*Reflective Teaching: An Introduction,*
Mahwah, NJ , Lawrence Erlbaum Associates.

Zeichner, K., Melnick, S. and Gomez, M. L. (1996)
*Currents of Reform in Preservice Teacher Education,*
New York: Teachers College Press.

On the potential gains, embracing both practical competence and social emancipation, which are claimed to derive from self-evaluation and classroom enquiry see:

Stenhouse, L. (1982)
*Authority, Education and Emancipation,*
London: Heinemann.                    📖 **Primary Reading 3. 1**

Carr, W. and Kemmis, S. (1986)
*Becoming Critical,*
London: Falmer Press.                    📖 **Primary Reading 3. 2**

Elliott, J. (1991)
*Action Research for Educational Change,*
Buckingham: Open University Press.                    📖 **Primary Reading 1. 7**

Smyth, J. (1991)
*Teachers as Collaborative Learners,*
Buckingham: Open University Press.

Tripp, D. (1993)
*Critical Incidents in Teaching: Developing Professional Judgement,*
London: Routledge.

For a range of views on the nature of professional knowledge and its relationship to more theoretical analyses see:

McNamara, D. and Desforges, C. (1978)
'The social sciences, teacher education and the objectification of craft knowledge', *British Journal of Teacher Education,*
Vol. 4, No. 1, pp. 17-36

Schon, D. (1983)
*The Reflective Teacher,*
London: Temple Smith.                                    Primary Reading 1. 2

Van Manen, M. (1990)
*The Tact of Teaching: The Meaning of Pedagogical Thoughtfulness,*
London, Ontario: Althouse Press.

Tom, A. (1984)
*Teaching as a Moral Craft,*
New York: Longman.

Calderhead, J. (1988b)
*Teachers' Professional Learning,*
London: Falmer .                                    also Primary Reading 1. 8

Brown, S. and McIntyre, D. (1992)
*Making Sense of Teaching,*
Buckingham: Open University Press.

There are now many studies of teachers' practical reasoning. For instance, see:

Elbaz, F. (1983)
*Teacher Thinking: a Study of Practical Knowledge,*
London: Croom Helm.

Clandinin, D. J. (1986)
*Classroom Practice: Teacher Images In Action,*
London: Falmer Press.

Cooper, P. and McIntyre, D. (1996)
*Effective Teaching and Learning: Teachers' and Students' Perspectives,*
Buckingham: Open University Press.

The field of competences in teacher education is a rapidly developing one. For useful reviews of the issues, see:

Whitty, G. and Willmott, E. (1991)
'Competence-based teacher education: approaches and issues',
*Cambridge Journal of Education*, Vol. 21, No. 3, pp. 309—18

Hustler, D. and McIntyre, D. (1996)
*Developing Competent Teachers: Approaches to Professional Competence in Teacher Education,*
London: David Fulton.

For an analytical view of the relationship of competency and professionalism, see Chapter 8 of:

Elliott, J. (1991)
*Action Research for Educational Change,*
Buckingham: Open University Press.                    Primary Reading 1. 7

The holistic, intuitive and contextualized competence, which Elliott characterizes 'expert', is also often described as reflecting the 'art' of teaching. For an influential perspective on this, including the concept of 'connoisseurship', see:

Eisner, E. W. (1979)
*The Educational Imagination,*
New York: Macmillan.

The government quango responsible for teacher education in England is the Teacher Training Agency. See:

Teacher Training Agency (1996b)
*Corporate Plan, 1996: Promoting Excellence in Teaching,*
London: TTA.

Key documents for Scotland and for England and Wales which reflect their national contexts and specify competences for initial teacher education are:

Scottish Office Education Department (1992)
*Revised Guidelines for Teacher Training Courses,*
Scottish Office Education Department: Edinburgh.

OFSTED/TTA (1996)
*Framework for the Assessment of Quality and Standards in Initial Teacher Training, 1996/97,*
London: HMSO .

For a sustained attempt to identify competences of reflective teaching, see:

Hextall, I., Lawn, M., Menter, I., Sidgwick, S. and Walker, S. (1991),
'Imaginative projects: arguments for a new teacher education',
*Evaluation and Research in Education,*
Vol. 5, Nos. 1 and 2, pp. 79–95.

Recent approaches to teacher education and training are premised on large proportions of school-based work and on close partnership between higher education institutions and schools. This is now well studied. In the collections below, the first reviews the issues involved in school-HE partnerships and the second provides a case study of professional learning in a school-based scheme by both student teachers and established staff:

Booth, M., Furlong, J. and Wilkin, M. (1990)
*Partnership in Initial Teacher Training,*
London: Cassell.

Heilbronn, R. and Jones, C. (1996)
*The Quality of Our Learning: Beginning Teachers and Staff Development in an Urban Comprehensive,*
Stoke-on-Trent: Trentham Books.

Good reviews of changes in the status, autonomy, professional knowledge and training of teachers are:

Hoyle, E. and John, P. (1995)
*Professional Knowledge and Professional Practice,*
London: Cassell.

Wilkin, M. (1996)
*Initial Teacher Training: The Dialogue of Ideology and Culture,*
London: Falmer Press.

For international comparisons of changes in teacher education which track a tightening of state control in many countries, see:

Popkewitz, T. (ed.) (1993)
*Changing Patterns of Power: Social Regulation and Teacher Education Reform in Eight Countries,*
New York: State University of New York Press.

For a direct attack on Dewey and on educationalists in general (by the 1996 Chairman of the TTA's Research Committee) see:

O'Hear, A. (1991)
*Education and Democracy: Against the Educational Establishment,*
London: Claridge.

# CHAPTER 2

# Social contexts, teachers and pupils[*]

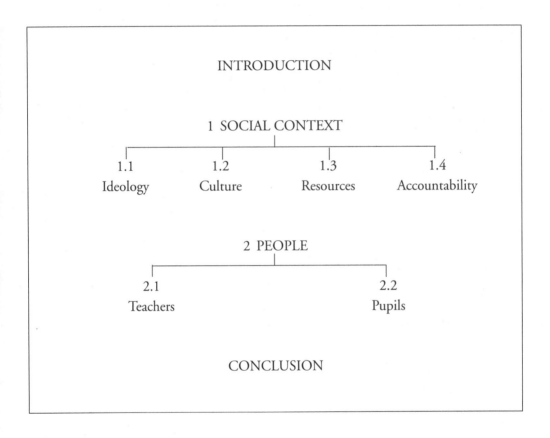

INTRODUCTION

1 SOCIAL CONTEXT

| 1.1 | 1.2 | 1.3 | 1.4 |
|-----|-----|-----|-----|
| Ideology | Culture | Resources | Accountability |

2 PEOPLE

| 2.1 | 2.2 |
|-----|-----|
| Teachers | Pupils |

CONCLUSION

[*] Revised by Sally Power

## INTRODUCTION

This chapter provides a brief review of some of the important contextual factors which affect teachers in secondary schools. The specific challenges of teaching and learning are considered in detail in Part 2 of the book.

Figure 2.1 represents the way in which the relationships between these factors have been conceptualized in this book.

We would argue that the influence of social context pervades everything that happens in schools and classrooms, and awareness of such issues is therefore an important contributing element of reflective teaching.

A second purpose of this chapter is to establish a theoretical model concerning the relationships of individuals and society. Indeed, the chapter is very deliberately in two parts. The first, 'social context', emphasizes the ideas, social structures and resources which *constrain or shape* action in various ways. The second part, 'people', is concerned with the various factors which, in some senses, *enable* action by individual teachers and children.

Of course, this argument can be applied to the education system of any country. However, for illustrative purposes, we have focused in this chapter on the United Kingdom. The Notes for Further Reading contain suggested sources concerning other countries.

We begin the chapter by discussing the social context and by introducing the theoretical framework.

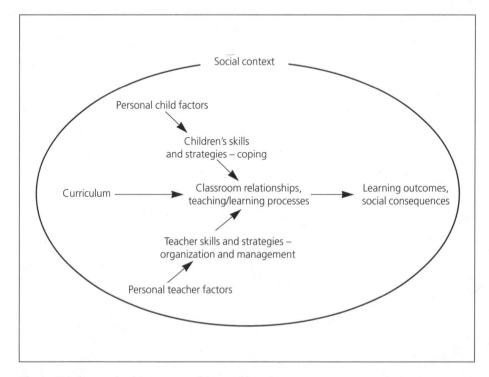

**Figure 2.1** *Factors in classroom teaching and learning*

# 1 | SOCIAL CONTEXT

A particular theoretical position underpins this chapter and, indeed, the book as a whole. At the core of this position is the concept of a dialectical relationship between society and individuals. This suggests the existence of a constant interplay of social forces and individual actions. On the one hand, the decisions and actions which people make and take in their lives are constrained by social structures and by the historical processes which brought about such structures. On the other hand, each individual has a unique sense of self, derived from his or her personal history or biography. Individuals have a degree of free will in acting and in developing understandings with others. Sets of these understandings, which endure over time, form the basis of cultures. Such understandings can also lead to challenges to established social structures and thus to future changes.

For example, there are differences between various social groups in terms of power, wealth, status and opportunities (Halsey 1986, Goldthorpe 1987, Reid 1989, *Social Trends 1996*). However, individuals, each with their own background and sense of self, will react to such factors in a variety of ways. Some in powerful positions might wish to close ranks and defend themselves by suggesting that their position is inherited by right or earned by merit. Some among those who are less fortunate may accept the social order or even aspire to success in its terms. Others may try to contest it for, of course, to be able to question existing social arrangements is a fundamental right in our democratic societies.

There is, thus, an ebb and flow in social change, a process of tension and struggle. At opposite poles are action and constraint, voluntarism and determinism, biography and history (Mills 1959, **Primary Reading 2.1**).

We believe that a reflective teacher has responsibilities within this process which should not be avoided. With this in mind, we will now discuss four aspects of the social context which we feel are particularly significant for practice in secondary schools: ideology, culture, resources and accountability. The influence of each can be traced at national, regional, local and school levels so that, although such issues sometimes seem distant, they affect children and teachers in classrooms in very real ways.

## 1.1 Ideology

A dictionary definition of ideology states that it means a 'way of thinking'. However, particular sets of ideas are often used, consciously or unconsciously, to promote and legitimize the interests of specific groups of people. Indeed, if a particular way of thinking about society is dominant at any point in time it is likely to be an important influence on education and on teachers' actions. It may produce a particular curriculum emphasis and even begin to frame the ways in which teachers relate with young people.

For instance, in the United States of America of the 1950s, the Cold War, anti-Communist feeling was so great that it not only led to the now discredited inquisitions of the McCarthy Committee but also to a range of nationalistic practices in schools, re-interpretations of history and pressures to compete, particularly after the 1957 launch of the Russian Sputnik satellite. Similarly, in the USSR and Eastern

Block countries, before the revolutionary changes which swept Eastern Europe in 1989, pupils were taught highly selective views of history, of the values and achievements of their societies. They too were encouraged to compete, particularly to sustain exceptional international achievements in areas such as science and sport. In both cases, despite widely differing circumstances, it can be seen that the ideologies of key political élites interacted with the 'commonsense thinking' of the wider population to create particular ideological climates (see the work of Gramsci (1978) for an analysis of such hegemonic phenomena). Although the influence of these ideological periods was enormous, they passed.

The ideologies which more specifically influence secondary education also come and go. There are, for instance, different trends in beliefs about what kinds of schools should be provided and who should go to them. After the Second World War, it was thought that the fairest way of organizing secondary education was to have different types of school – grammar schools, technical schools and secondary moderns. Pupils would be selected for each of these schools on the basis of how they performed in tests – commonly called the '11-plus'. However, it was not long before this 'tripartite' system came to be criticized for limiting rather than widening educational opportunities. This led many educationists to argue for the introduction of a system of common secondary schools, which would be 'comprehensive' in that there was to be no selection of students by ability.

In the post-war years, political pressure groups had relatively little influence on education policy. Indeed, civil servants and educationalists tended to moderate such political activity when it infrequently occurred. Of course, this was itself a reflection of the influence of policy-making professionals' own ideologies and 'assumptive worlds' (McPherson and Raab 1988). However, such policy-makers became unable to assert such influence in the late 1980s, and there followed a considerable struggle  for control between politicians, civil servants and professionals over education policy (Ball 1990, see also Bowe *et al.* 1992, **Primary Reading 2.4**).

More recently, the merits of the comprehensive school system, and the benefits of local education authorities through which it had been regulated, have increasingly been called into question. There have been repeated 'moral panics' (Cohen 1972), in which public concern was orchestrated by politicians and the media, over issues such as reading, spelling, 'failing schools', British history, Shakespeare, standards of A-levels and teaching methods. The comprehensive school has been blamed for educational mediocrity and poor discipline.

During the 1980s, such concerns were the focus of what have been termed 'New Right' pressure groups (e.g. Gamble 1986, Whitty 1989, Quicke 1988), which sought to influence the policies of successive Conservative governments. Amongst these pressure groups, often with interlocking memberships, were the Hillgate Group (e.g. 1987), the Adam Smith Institute (1984), the No Turning Back Group of MPs (1986), the Centre for Policy Studies (e.g. Cox and Marks 1982, Lawlor 1988), the National Council for Educational Standards (e.g. Marks and Pomian-Srzednicki 1985) and the Campaign for Real Education (e.g. Marks 1992). One important belief of the members of these groups was that educational standards needed to be raised and that the best way to do this was to provide more parental choice and school accountability, so that educational provision would be subject to market forces.

During the 1990s a whole range of policies were introduced which sought to reorganize education provision through the operation of market forces. Measures to enhance 'consumer' choice involved removing artificial limits on pupil enrolment, making private schools more accessible to the 'able' but 'poor' (the Assisted Places Scheme), establishing new kinds of schools (City Technology Colleges: CTCs), and enabling parents to take their school out of LEA control (the grant-maintained schools: GMS). Per capita funding arrangements and site-based management (Local Management of Schools) were also introduced to make schools more responsive to 'consumer' demand.

In addition, the National Curriculum became statutory, together with associated high profile assessment procedures. This not only provided a basis for comparisons between schools (discussed later in the chapter), but also addressed concerns that the content of school knowledge had been hijacked by 'trendy' educationists. Although there was some initial acknowledgement of cross-curricular elements, there is little doubt that the legislation endorsed a relatively traditional view of the school curriculum. It reinforced the dominance of subject-centred approaches, and elevated some subjects as being more important than others. It also appeared to emphasize a particular view of British history and culture (see, for instance, Whitty 1992).

In terms of examining the intended effects and likely consequences of recent changes, some historians have argued (for example, Simon 1985, 1992) that, by such means, attempts are made to make the education system more effective as a means of 'social control'. In other words, existing social and class structures are to be accepted and reproduced. Indeed, authors such as Althusser (1971) have seen education systems within capitalist societies as 'ideological state apparatuses' which are designed for precisely this purpose. On the other hand, sociologists such as Collins (1977),  Kogan (1978) and Archer (1979, **Primary Reading 15.1**) have argued that educational policies and provision are the product of competing interest groups and that control and power are more diffuse.

In any event, the national legislation of the late 1980s and the 1990s radically challenged what previously had been, in effect, a very decentralized system. The result was that educational priorities, structures, centres of control and accountability were all restructured. The values of a common system of schooling controlled by local authorities were replaced by those of a centrally regulated marketplace which celebrates parental choice and school diversity. The initial policies of the 'New Labour' government, elected in 1997, attempt to by-pass these issues. As David Blunkett put it: 'Standards, not structure, are now the prime concern' (Press Release, 30 May 1997).

The dominant patterns of thinking about secondary school practice have thus changed considerably in recent years. However, awareness of the concept of ideology makes it more likely that the values or interests that may lie behind new proposals will be considered by reflective teachers. It is also worth remembering that societies and dominant ideologies are never static. At some point in time, critique and experience lead to re-evaluation, counter-proposals, development and change. There will be no end to this story.

Nor should we forget that no one, including ourselves, is immune to the influences of ideologies. For instance, professional ideologies are likely to always remain strong among teachers – they represent commitments, ideals and interests. Reflective teachers should be open-minded enough to constructively critique their own beliefs, as well as those of others.

## 1.2  Culture

Cultures can be seen as sets of shared perspectives and as the products of people acting together. Cultures can develop from collective activity and from the creative responses of groups to situations. Furthermore, it must also be recognized that cultures endure over time and can thus represent sets of ideas, perspectives, values and practices into which individuals are likely to be socialized. For instance, when students come to school, they bring with them a range of ways of perceiving and responding to school life. Indeed, they may use these as a means of understanding school and coping with it. For example, Willis' classic study of a group of working-class boys shows how they draw on the workplace culture of their fathers to attain respect and status within the school (Willis 1977).

The community within the school serves to provide another cultural context. This is bound to influence and be influenced by the perspectives of parents, children and teachers. However, few communities can be characterized as single, united entities. Among the many divisions which may exist are those relating to ethnicity, language, religion, social class, sexuality and to political or personal values. The existence of such cultural diversity is particularly important in many inner-city schools, and reflective teachers are likely to explore the relationship between cultures in young people's homes, communities and school very carefully indeed. A great deal of research has shown problems arising when working-class cultures are regarded as being deficient by those in schools (for example, Keddie 1971, Ball 1981) and institutionalized forms of racism are likely to result if teachers fail to take appropriate account of the perspectives of ethnic groups (Mac an Ghaill 1988, Gillborn 1995). Stereotypical perceptions of teachers may also have gender or sexuality dimensions which impinge in a number of ways on the educational opportunities of both girls and boys (e.g. Davies 1984, Wolpe 1988, Mac an Ghaill 1995).

There are also likely to be significant cultures among the adults within each school. Within the secondary school, teachers' allegiances and identities tend to be strongly  influenced by the structure of the curriculum. Bernstein (1971, **Primary Reading 7.2**) used the term 'collection code' to describe the prevailing form of secondary school curriculum. Unlike the 'integrated code' which was once dominant within primary schools, the collection code divides school knowledge into sharply demarcated subjects. Teachers are specialists within these subjects, which become a powerful form of allegiance and identity. Within the staffroom, teachers of the same subjects can often be seen talking only with each other. These divisions are also underlain by a hierarchical ordering of school knowledge.

Within British education, there has also been a particularly pronounced tension between subjects which are deemed academic and those which are thought to be vocational (Reeder 1979, McCulloch 1989). Over the past 20 years there have been a series of initiatives designed to establish a more vocationally relevant curriculum, bringing with them a variety of acronyms – TVEI, CPVE, BTEC and NVQ. These culminated in the Dearing Review of Qualifications for 16–19 year olds (1996). However, despite such attempts to promote greater parity of esteem between academic and vocational courses, traditional school subjects still command the most prestige (Hodgson and Spours 1997). It is often held, even if implicitly, that the narrowly specialized A-level is the 'gold standard' of educational achievement.

A similar tension is evident between the pastoral and the academic dimensions of secondary education. In many schools, there is a formal system of pastoral care in which specialist pastoral staff have responsibility for student welfare and home-school liaison. They may also be in charge of the organization of tutorial work. Although the pastoral and academic dimensions are supposed to complement each other, there is often considerable tension between staff with a primarily pastoral role and subject specialists (Power 1996).

Such divisions within the curriculum are not only implicated in teachers' identities and allegiances, they are also a source of power. For instance, prestigious subjects, such as maths and science, are often able to command more resources, an area to which we now turn.

## 1.3 Resources

Adequate resources are essential in education, in particular people, buildings, equipment and materials. In both quality and quantity, these resources have an impact on what it is possible to do in schools and classrooms. A very consistent feeling from teachers in primary and secondary schools is that class size is a major factor in determining educational practice and there is much research which supports this  proposition (e.g. Glass *et al.* 1979, Pate-Bain *et al.* 1992, **Primary Reading 9.1**).

Many people are involved in the life of a successful secondary school and, for this reason, collaboration and team-work are needed, irrespective of status. Apart from the head and the teaching staff, there are many others, such as cleaners, dinner supervisors, cooks, secretaries, technicians, classroom ancillaries, and caretakers, who all have very important supportive parts to play. However, it is arguably the case that, from the educational point of view, the number, quality and range of expertise of classroom teachers are major factors in determining what is done and what it is possible to do in schools. Teachers themselves are the most important resource. School governors, who make staff appointments, have a particular responsibility to provide a teaching team with an appropriate balance of curricular expertise and teaching skill. This is far from easy, for schools are not funded on the basis of curriculum needs but on the basis of pupil numbers.

As already mentioned, since the 1988 Education Reform Act, all schools have had 'locally managed' budgets. Income is distributed annually from each LEA (on the basis of a locally determined formula) or direct from central government (with a 'common' funding formula). These formulae allocate a certain amount for each pupil on roll, plus certain other amounts in respect of social disadvantage, special educational needs or school size. Expenditure is the responsibility of the headteacher and governors. However, school managers often have relatively small sums to spend at their discretion, once fixed costs are taken out of the overall budget. In most schools, the salaries of teachers and other staff account for over 75 per cent of the budget, followed by costs of building maintenance and school running costs. Only a tiny percentage is left for direct educational expenditure.

All resources have to be paid for and, on a national basis, education is a significant expense. For instance, the annual education expenditure of public authorities in the 1990s has been around £30 billion, which is around 5 per cent of the UK Gross Domestic Product. About half of this is spent at local government level, and education is by far the largest item in council budgets (about 70 per cent in some cases, of which the most significant item is teachers' salaries). However, with up to 95 per cent of school spending delegated to the schools, the power of LEAs has been considerably reduced during the decade. Their statutory responsibilities are concerned mainly with allocating and monitoring budgets, promoting quality, co-ordinating some special services and intervening in schools where there are identified weaknesses.

Resourcing levels vary somewhat between local education authorities, for the levels of government support, the degree of priority given to education and the exact funding formula differs from one LEA to another. However, the most significant factor in all funding formulae is the 'age weighted pupil unit' (AWPU): that is, the sum of money which is allocated to the school for each pupil of each age (in England in 1996/7, the average 'standard spending assessment' per secondary school pupil was £2,728). The key factor in school budgets is thus the number of pupils on roll, and each school's position in the quasi-market for pupil enrolments in its area is thus crucial to its resource base. In most areas, some schools tend to flourish whilst others may face gradually declining resources (see Dale 1996, **Primary Reading 15.5**). Further resource differences emerge due to the fact that a considerable contribution to total school incomes can be made by parental fund-raising, appeals to 'old boys' and 'old girls', and through links with commercial companies which lead to donations or sponsorship. Such activities can produce very significant annual funds and these tend to increase social divisiveness because of wide differences in the distribution of wealth and incomes within local areas and between different regions of the country.

The grant-maintained schools policy initiated by Conservative governments also contributed to differences in the source and scale of funding for state schools. Grant-maintained schools received more money from the centrally controlled Funding Agency for Schools than their LEA counterparts and were able to bid for extra grants (Fitz *et al.* 1993). For instance the Department for Education and Employment made money available for specialist subject areas. The first initiative was the creation of City Technology Colleges (CTCs), new schools created from scratch, sponsored by business and funded centrally. Only fifteen of these colleges were built, far below the target of 300 set by Sir Cyril Taylor, chairman of the CTC Trust. However, the idea mutated first into the Technology Schools Initiative and then became, in 1993, an invitation to schools to be designated technology or language colleges. The specialist emphasis was extended beyond technology to include languages, IT, mathematics and science – all seen as promoting skills needed for the next century and to boost the British economy. The opportunity to have access to this funding was at first limited to grant-maintained and voluntary-aided schools and then opened up to all maintained secondary schools. At the beginning of 1996 there were 249 schools funded by the Technology School Initiative; 151 Technology Colleges and thirty Language Colleges.

Schools applying for specialist designation had to find at least £100,000 in sponsorship, produce a development plan showing how education will be improved and how the sponsors will be involved.

Overall then, the level of resourcing in particular classrooms is dependent on a combination of school-based decisions, numbers of pupils on roll, the legal status of the school, and the priority given to education by national and local governments. A good deal of political, as well as professional, judgement is involved at all points (Hewton 1986, Kingdom 1991, Byrne 1992).

While resources structure the material conditions in which teachers work, the actions which they might take are also likely to be influenced by the degree of autonomy which they feel they have. For this reason, we now focus on the issue of accountability.

## 1.4  Accountability

Teachers in the public education system are paid, through national and local taxation systems, to provide a professional service. However, the degree of accountability and external control to which they have been subject has varied historically and has been subject to considerable change in recent years.

In the first part of this century, the payment-by-results system of the late 1800s, although superseded, still left a legacy in the form of imposed performance requirements in reading, writing and arithmetic. Handbooks of Suggestions for good practice were published regularly, as guidelines, but were not enforceable. However, from the 1920s teachers began to develop greater professional autonomy and in this they benefited from the acquiescence of successive governments (Lawn and Ozga 1986). In particular, the independence of headteachers within their schools, and of class teachers within their classrooms, emerged to become established principles. After the Second World War, as professional confidence grew, this independence extended into the curriculum: so much so that, in 1960, it was described by Lord Eccles, Minister for Education, as a 'secret garden' into which central government was not expected to intrude. Such confidence was probably at a high point in the early 1970s.

Since then, the changing ideological, economic and political climate has resulted in teachers coming under increasing pressure: first to increase their 'accountability'; and second, to demonstrate their competence. These developments were presented as a necessary reduction in the influence of the 'producers' (seen as teacher unions, administrators and theorists) and as enabling educational provision to be shaped by the 'consumers' (seen as parents and industry, though with little direct reference to children and young people themselves) (Lawton 1995). In England, following the Education Reform Act, 1988, the government set up two organizations to implement this transformation – the National Curriculum Council (NCC) and the School Examination and Assessment Council (SEAC). They were replaced in 1993 by a single body – the School Curriculum and Assessment Authority (SCAA). Following the Dearing Report on 16–19 provision (1996), a new national priority of linking 'academic' and 'vocational' education and training became apparent. As a result, in October 1997, SCAA was merged with the National Council for Vocational Qualifications (NCVQ), and the Qualifications and Curriculum Authority (QCA) was established.

Some of the products of these trends can now be seen. For instance, regarding accountability, the role of governing bodies has been radically redefined giving them increased rights and responsibilities. In a maintained secondary school with 600 or more pupils there must be four or five parent governors, two teacher governors, five people appointed by the LEA, five or six governors co-opted according to choice. The numbers of governors drawn from parents, industry and the community have been increased, The headteacher can choose whether he or she will be a governor. (The composition for grant-maintained and voluntary-aided schools differs slightly.) Governing bodies are legally responsible for many aspects of their schools, including the budget, buildings, staffing and curriculum. According to DFEE guidance, governors are not expected to take detailed decisions about the day-to-day running of the school: this is the role of the headteacher. Nevertheless the guidance says that governors should be involved in setting the policy framework covering all the main aspects of school life as it is they who must answer to parents and the LEA for the running of the school. Governors have a responsibility to monitor the effectiveness of school management and to ensure that the school provides value for money. As a result many are concerned about the maintenance of 'standards', especially against national 'norms and targets' and with the articulation of plans for school development and improvement. This is a challenging role for non-educationists (Beckett, Bell and Rhodes 1991).

The governors must present an annual report to parents, and parents have their 'rights' enshrined by the government in a 'Parents' Charter' (DES 1992). Information from both standardized and teacher assessment of pupils must now be published to parents, together with written, annual reports. These results, and school attendance figures, can, it is claimed, be used to judge the effectiveness of schools.

As a further development of accountability, in 1992 Her Majesty's Inspectorate, a widely respected and independent body which had advised on both particular schools and the system for over 150 years, was scaled down and many of its functions passed to the Office for Standards in Education (OFSTED). This contracts teams of inspectors (including non-educationalist 'lay inspectors') to make a public report on every individual school in a regular cycle.

On the issue of teacher appraisal, following negotiations within the profession (National Steering Group 1989) and a significant increase in both LEA appraisal schemes and methods of school-based, self-evaluation, a national appraisal system was imposed in England and Wales. However, a 1996 HMI report suggested that implementation and impact on teaching and learning had 'not been substantial' (OFSTED 1996b). However, pressure for linkage of appraisal to salary levels also remained strong.

In an historical review of such developments, Grace has suggested:

We are now in a period where the social and political context of state-provided schooling in Britain is reminiscent in a number of ways of the climate of reaction in the 1860s. There is a growing emphasis upon tighter accountability; a required core curriculum and a concentration upon basics. The role and strength of the inspectorate is being reappraised and changes can be expected in the ideology and practice of inspection at all levels. Both teacher training and the work of teachers in schools are to be subject to more surveillance and to the application of more specific criteria for the assessment and evaluation of competence. (Grace 1985, p. 13)

Accountability is thus an important aspect of social context because it highlights both legal requirements and areas of independent and consultative decision-making. Nor should we forget that underlying all the specific measures which we have reviewed, is the conception of market competition 'forcing up standards'. Thus the greatest influence on accountability is supposedly the 'market'. Whether market strategies achieve their intended results or not, there is no doubt that accountability measures have enormous implications for each teacher's work experience. This is likely to remain an area of much flux and considerable contest, particularly between the government and teacher unions.

In a sense, accountability is an issue which crystallizes many of the considerations which are raised more generally by a focus on the social context of schooling. What relationship does education have to society? Should it be a relatively autonomous system or should it be under tight forms of control? The history of our education system provides many fascinating instances of attempts to resolve such questions (Silver 1980) and there are plenty of related current issues which a reflective teacher might consider. In particular, though, and following the dialectical model of social change which we discussed above, the issues of accountability, autonomy and control pose questions of a personal nature for teachers. How should each individual act (see Mills  1949, **Primary Reading 2.1**)?

## 2 │ PEOPLE

Within the dialectical model, which conceptualizes the constant interaction of social structures and individuals, personal factors are the counterpart of social context. For instance, classroom life can be seen as being created by teachers and children as they respond to the situations in which they find themselves. Thus, as well as understanding something of the factors affecting the social context of schooling, we also need to consider how teachers and children respond. We begin by focusing on teachers.

## 2.1 Teachers

Teachers are people who happen to hold a particular position in schools. We make no apologies for wishing to begin by asserting this simple fact, for it has enormous implications. Each person is unique, with particular cultural and material experiences making up his or her 'biography' (Sikes, Measor and Woods 1985). This provides the seed-bed for their sense of 'self' and influences their personality and perspectives (Mead 1934). The development of each person continues throughout life, but early formative experiences remain important. Indeed, because personal qualities, such as having the capacity to empathize and having the confidence to project and assert oneself, are so important in teaching, much of what particular teachers will be able to achieve in their classrooms will be influenced by them. Of even greater importance is the capacity to know oneself. We all have strengths and weaknesses and most teachers would agree that classroom life can be probing in this respect. Reflective teaching is, therefore, a great deal to do with facing such features of ourselves in a constructive and balanced manner and in a way which incorporates a continuous capacity to change and develop.

Teachers, as people, have opinions, perspectives, attitudes, values and beliefs. This particularly human attribute of being able to review the relationship of 'what is' and 'what ought to be' is one which teachers often manifest when considering their aims and examining their educational values and philosophies. While there has always been a good deal of idealism in the thinking of teachers at the start of their career, there has also always been a concern with tactical realism. Indeed, a very important factor which influences teachers' perceptions in the classroom is that the teacher has to 'cope', personally as well as professionally, with the classroom situation. Standing in front of a class of adolescent learners can be a nerve-wracking experience. For this reason, we would suggest that a fundamental element of classroom coping, or survival, is very deeply personal, for it involves teachers, with a particular image of their self, acting in the very challenging situation which classrooms represent. In this, it is important to remember that what it is possible to do in classrooms is constrained by the basic facts of large numbers of students, limited resources, compulsory attendance, a legally defined National Curriculum and other external expectations which exist about what should and should not take place (Hargreaves 1978, Pollard 1982, Woods 1990a).

In such circumstances, as we suggested in Chapter 1, teachers face acute dilemmas between their personal and professional concerns and the practical possibilities (Rowland 1993, Berlak and Berlak 1981, **Primary Reading 1.3**). They are forced to juggle with their priorities as they manage the stress which is often involved (Dunham 1992, Cole and Walker 1989) and as they come to terms with the classroom situation.

The final set of personal factors about teachers to which attention will be drawn relates to their position as employees. The first aspect of this is that teachers are workers and have legitimate legal, contractual and economic interests to maintain, protect and develop (Lawn and Ozga 1981, Lawn and Grace 1987). The notion of 'directed time', in reference to the 1,265 hours per year for which teachers are contracted, means that headteachers will specify activities, in addition to teaching contact, which teachers are contracted to undertake. These most commonly include attendance at meetings of different kinds, parents' evenings, administration, planning. The extra-curricular activities of various kinds – running teams, clubs, choirs, orchestras, drama productions – which many teachers did voluntarily may now be included in directed time. However, much of this is still voluntary. Some balance has to be struck between educational expectations and what it is reasonable to ask of people who happen to earn their living from teaching. It should never be forgotten that teachers also have their own personal lives outside the classroom. Many teachers have family responsibilities, as well as other interests which may be important to their own personal development (Acker 1989, Thomas 1995, Bell 1995).

## 2.2 Pupils

As with the personal factors associated with teachers, the most important point to make about the pupils is that they are thinking, rational individuals (James and Prout 1990, Cooper and McIntyre 1996, Rudduck, Chaplain and Wallace 1996). Each one of the many millions of school pupils in the UK has a unique 'biography'. The way in which they feel about themselves, and present themselves in school, will be influenced by their understandings of previous cultural, social and material experience (Bruner 1986).

Perhaps the most important fact for teachers to consider is the huge range of attributes and experiences which children may bring to school. Factors such as sex, social class, ethnicity, language development, learning styles, health and types of parental support, are so numerous and so complex in their effects that, although broad but important generalizations about patterns of advantage and disadvantage can be made (Rutter and Madge 1976, Halsey, Heath and Ridge 1980), it is foolish to generalize in specific terms about their ultimate consequences.

On a more individual level, children at the start of their secondary education have also experienced nearly seven years of schooling, and will bring with them a relatively well-developed sense of their educational identity. The interaction of social and classroom processes in the primary school may have already led them to see themselves as school failures or successes (Sharp and Green 1975, Hartley 1985, Pollard 1985, Pollard with Filer 1996). As pupils progress through the secondary school, with its complex systems of setting, banding, options and 'pathways', these self-perceptions will be further reinforced or modified. At the point of leaving and entering the worlds of college, work or unemployment, their life trajectories are likely to be well established.

Coming between pupils' origins and their educational destinations is the whole issue of how young people actually respond to their circumstances and, indeed, of how teachers provide for them. Like teachers, pupils have to learn to cope and survive in classroom situations in which they may well feel insecure. Of course, pupil culture and the support of a peer group are considerable resources in this. However, such cultural responses by pupils can also pose dilemmas in class when they try to satisfy personal interests by attempting to please both their peers and their teacher. Creative strategies are called for and these may cover a range from conformity through negotiation to rejection. Once again then, we wish to highlight the importance of the subjectivity of the perspectives which teachers and pupils develop as they interact.

Above all, though, we must never forget that young people are placed in the role of 'pupils' for only part of each day. It is no wonder that families, friends, relationships, TV, film, music, fashion, sport, etc., are important to them. A reflective teacher, therefore, must aim to work with parents and carers and with an understanding of the culture of young people.

## CONCLUSION

Our intention in this chapter has been to discuss the relationship between society as a whole and the people who are centrally involved in secondary education. This is because we believe that school practices and classroom actions are influenced by the social circumstances within which they occur. We have also argued that individuals can have effects on future social changes, though the degree of influence ebbs and flows at different phases of history. A theoretical framework of this sort is important for reflective teachers. The provision of high quality education is enhanced when social awareness is developed and when individual responsibilities for professional actions are taken seriously.

This fundamental belief in the commitment, quality and role of teachers underpins the book. At a time when central control over education has been tightened and when teacher morale is often low, the analysis is, essentially, optimistic. High quality education is not possible without the committed professionalism of teachers and, at some point, the extent of unilateral government interventions will recede, to be replaced, we must hope, by recognition of professional expertise and a new partnership.

Issues identified in this chapter are considered in greater detail in Section 2 of this book. You will find more on school context and organization in Chapter 5, on curriculum structures and planning in Chapters 6 and 7, on pupil identity in Chapter 8, on teacher and pupil coping strategies in Chapter 12, and on accountability in Chapter 16.

## Notes for further reading

These suggestions concentrate on the theoretical framework which has been introduced, rather than on the topics through which it has been illustrated. The latter are all covered in more detail elsewhere in the book, and can be accessed via the index.

On the theoretical framework which has been introduced, with its juxtaposition of social context and individuals, two classic books may be helpful. Chapter 1 of Mills and Chapters 4 and 5 of Berger are particularly relevant.

Berger, P. L. (1963)
*Invitation to Sociology: a Humanistic Perspective,*
New York: Doubleday.

Mills, C. W. (1959)
*The Sociological Imagination,*
Oxford: Oxford University Press.                    Primary Reading 2. 1

For more recent, but equally stimulating, texts, try:

Giddens, A. (1993)
*Sociology,*
Cambridge: Polity Press.                            Primary Reading 2. 3

Bauman, Z. (1990)
*Thinking Sociologically,*
Oxford: Blackwell.

For a readable analyses of modern British society, which illustrates aspects of this framework, see:

Halsey, A. H. (1986)
*Change in British Society,*
Oxford: Oxford University Press.

For a more international challenge, try:

Miliband, R. (1991)
*Divided Societies,*
Oxford: Oxford University Press.

Three very different illustrations of the uses of the basic framework are provided by:

Connell, R. W., Ashden, D. J., Kessler, S. and Dowsett, G. W. (1982)
*Making the Difference: Schools, Families and Social Divisions,*
Sydney: Allen & Unwin.

Humphries, S. (1982)
*Hooligans or Rebels?,*
Oxford: Blackwell.

Grace, G. (1978)
*Teachers, Ideology and Control,*
London: Routledge and Kegan Paul.

Case studies of secondary schools which attempt to trace links between individual actions, school processes and the wider social context are:

Corrigan, P. (1979)
*Schooling the Smash Street Kids,*
London: Routledge.

Willis, P. (1977)
*Learning to Labour: How Working Class Kids Get Working Class Jobs,*
London: Saxon House.

Burgess, R. G. (1983)
*Experiencing comprehensive education: a study of Bishop McGregor School,*
London: Methuen.

General reviews which locate education and secondary school practices within social, historical and political contexts are:

For the United Kingdom:

Connor, M. (1990)
*Secondary Education,*
London: Cassell.

Chitty, C. and Benn, C. (1995)
*Thirty Years On: Is Comprehensive Education Alive and Well, or Struggling to Survive?,*
London: David Fulton.

Hargreaves, D. H. (1982)
*The Challenge for the Comprehensive School: Culture, Curriculum and Community,*
London: Routledge and Kegan Paul.

and for Europe as a whole:

Husen, T., Tuijnman, A. and Halls, W. (1992)
*Schooling in Modern European Society*
London: Pergamon.

For Australia:

Henry, M., Taylor, S. Knight, J. and Lingard, R. (1990)
*Understanding Schooling,*
London: Routledge.

For the USA:

Spring, J. (1991)
*American Education: an Introduction to Social and Political Aspects,*
New York: Longman.

Chubb, J. and Moe, T. (1990)
*Politics, Markets and America's Schools,*
Brookings Institution.

Recent UK legislation on education has proceeded at an unprecendented rate and tracing requirements has thus become very complex. As a result, two consolidation acts have been passed and now provide the 'official' point of legal reference. From the 1944 Act onwards, these acts incorporate legislation which is still in force and repeal what is not. They are:

The Education Act 1996
The School Inspections Act 1996

A concise, but inspection-orientated, reference source to the legislative framework is:

OFSTED (1996c)
*School Inspection: A Guide to the Law,*
London: OFSTED.

Keeping abreast of new developments and policies is a considerable challenge. However, there are a number of useful newspapers and magazines for the UK:

*Times Educational Supplement* (weekly)
*Education* (weekly)

Many subject specialisms have their own professional associations (see page 174) and magazines (e.g. *Teaching History, Teaching Geography, Teaching Mathematics and Its Applications*), and there are also journals such as *Pastoral Care in Education.*

Legal requirements have also been changing rapidly and access to reliable, accurate and regularly updated sources of information can be invaluable. The National Association for Headteachers and the National Union of Teachers supply such services for their members in the form of ring-binders of information. An independent resource for all teachers, with a quarterly update routine and dealing with all legislation, management, staffing, special educational needs and day-to-day issues which occur in schools, is:

*The Head's Legal Guide,*
London: Croner Publications.

How should teachers act? An accessible Canadian book which urges teachers to have faith in themselves, collaborate and act in the face of centralized control is:

Fullan, M. and Hargreaves, A. (1992)
*What's Worth Fighting for in Your School?*
Milton Keynes: Open University Press.

# CHAPTER 3

# Partnership, mentoring and student development

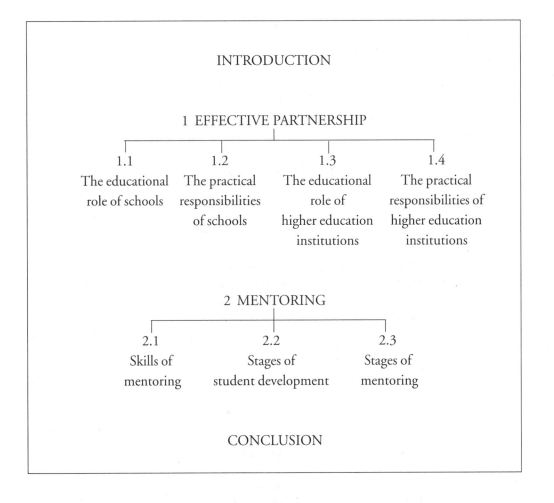

INTRODUCTION

1 EFFECTIVE PARTNERSHIP

1.1
The educational role of schools

1.2
The practical responsibilities of schools

1.3
The educational role of higher education institutions

1.4
The practical responsibilities of higher education institutions

2 MENTORING

2.1
Skills of mentoring

2.2
Stages of student development

2.3
Stages of mentoring

CONCLUSION

# INTRODUCTION

This chapter has been primarily written to support mentors in fulfilling their vital role in school-based teacher training. It clarifies the respective roles of schools and higher education institutions and of mentors and tutors. It describes mentor skills, characteristic stages through which student teachers develop, and ways in which mentors can support these developments as they occur. Students will no doubt find it interesting too! Indeed, understanding how others may be trying to support one's learning is a helpful step in making best use of such assistance, and in moving beyond it towards independence.

The role of practising teachers in initial teacher training has gone through a number of transformations over the last 100 years. At the end of the the nineteenth century, training was primarily seen as a practical affair and, through the pupil-teacher system, responsibility for that practical training was largely in the hands of teachers themselves (Gardner 1993, 1996). However, during most of the twentieth century there was a progressive exclusion of teachers from the training process. This exclusion reached its height in the 1970s with the development of a highly academic approach to professional preparation (Furlong and Maynard 1995). By that stage, training had become something that happened almost entirely within higher education institutions. Students studied academic courses which were sharply divorced from the world of schools. Schools were merely places where students were sent to 'practice' what they had learned in college, and officially at least, practising teachers were only assigned a very minor role in the training process – that of allowing students access to their classrooms and providing informal supervision and support.

Much has now changed. Since the early 1980s, governments have taken an increasingly direct interest in the training of teachers in England and Wales (Barton *et al.* 1994, **Primary Reading 2.5**). A series of circulars have progressively prescribed the structure and content of training, culminating in the publication of a 'framework' for the inspection of teacher training courses (OFSTED/TTA 1996, see Figure 1.3) and a commitment to specifying a National Curriculum for teacher training. A number of 'alternative' routes into the profession have also been established. Such initiatives have served, both by example and by decree, to re-establish the involvement of teachers in the preparation of the next generation of teachers.

Of these developments, the most significant of the early 1990s was Circular 9/92 which introduced three radical new features to all secondary training programmes in England and Wales. First, it insisted that the content of teacher education programmes be conceived of as a series of 'competences' on which students, lecturers and teachers would focus 'throughout the period of the training' (see also Chapter 1, Sections 1.2, 3.1 and 3.2, **Primary Readings 1.7** and **1.8**). Second, the amount of time students had to spend in school was substantially increased. For instance, in the case of the secondary PGCE, it was raised to twenty-four weeks out of the thirty-six-week course. Finally, and most radically of all, it insisted that responsibility for training students was something that was to be shared between institutions of higher education and partner schools. Moreover, in recognition of that shared responsibility, schools were in the future to be paid by higher education institutions for their part in the training process. As the circular put it:

The Government expects that partner schools and higher education institutions will exercise a joint responsibility for the planning and management of courses and the selection, training and assessment of students. The balance of responsibilities will vary. Schools will have a leading responsibility for training students to teach their specialist subjects, to assess pupils and to manage classes; and for supervising students and assessing their competence in these respects. Higher education institutions will be responsible for ensuring that courses meet the requirements for academic validation, presenting courses for accreditation, awarding qualifications to successful students and arranging student placements in more than one school. (DFE 1992: para 14)

Thus, as a result of Circular 9/92, practising teachers were once again being given a major role, working in partnership with higher education, in training the next generation of teachers. The 1996 Framework for the Assessment of Quality and Standards in Initial Teacher Training cemented this role and in 1997 development of a national curriculum for teacher training took it further still. However, it is important to recognize that the reason for adopting such an approach to professional preparation was not merely because government regulations insisted upon it. Even before government intervention, the role for schools was being increased in the vast majority of teacher training programmes. Government intervention increased the pace of change, but it did not fundamentally alter its direction.

## 1 | EFFECTIVE PARTNERSHIP

### 1.1 The educational role of schools

As early as the mid-1960s, Sussex University had established a school-based programme involving close partnerships with schools (Lacey 1977) and during the 1970s and 1980s a number of other courses began to be developed on similar lines (Furlong *et al.* 1988). However, it was probably the Oxford secondary PGCE course, developed in the late 1980s, that did most to convince the profession of the value of a partnership approach to training (Benton 1990).

Central to the Oxford scheme was a recognition that learning to teach involves the mastery of many different forms of professional knowledge: speculative theory; the findings of empirical research; and the craft knowledge of experienced teachers. However, none of these different forms of professional knowledge was presented as having prescriptive implications for practice. Rather, students were taught that all knowledge should be tested. Thus knowledge from university sources was to be tested against practicality criteria in the schools; and knowledge from school sources was to be tested against more academic criteria. The inevitable logic of this approach is that effective training involves a partnership between higher education and schools.

McIntyre (1991), one of the architects of the scheme, argues that the conditions of university lecturers' work:

enable and oblige them, much more than is generally possible for practising teachers, to know about alternative teaching approaches being used elsewhere, to study relevant research and theoretical literature and to explicate and critically examine the principles which should or could inform the practice of teaching. (1991, p. 114)

However, it is only practising school teachers, he suggests, who can directly introduce students to the practice of teaching and:

to the use of the contextualized knowledge of individual pupils, of established relationships with classes, of resources and their availability and of schools' customs and procedures, which is such a crucial element of professional teaching. (1991, p. 141)

As a result, students on the Oxford scheme spend much of their time in school working in pairs under the supervision of experienced teachers who act as mentors.

What the Oxford scheme highlights is that the partnership model of professional preparation does not simply involve a 'better' or 'longer' form of the traditional 'teaching practice' for students. School-based training involves a fundamental reconceptualization of the training process, both by those in higher education as well as by those in school. The role of schools is of vital importance, for student knowledge and skill can only be developed *in context* with their direct support.

Whilst training institutions are now obliged to plan, deliver and manage their training programmes in collaboration with schools, and teachers must be actively involved throughout, the role of schools has also been fundamentally changed. Individual schools are now likely to take on a significant number of students, perhaps as many as six or eight, and for a substantial part of the school year. As a result, arrangements for students' school experience can no longer be approached in an *ad hoc* way. Formal inter-institutional partnership arrangements have to be established and there are important implications for the school as a whole as well as individual teachers who act as mentors.

Given such innovations, schools and teaching staff can play a vital role in the development of practical, *professional* teacher education.

## 1.2 The practical responsibilities of schools

What are the implications for schools of joining a training partnership? Here, we focus on the costs and benefits of participation, and on the specific responsibilities of senior, co-ordinating mentors and teacher mentors.

### Costs and benefits

Taking partnership seriously makes demands on schools in many different ways. It is therefore vitally important that the school's senior school management team are fully aware of the responsibilities and costs of the scheme in which they are to participate, and are committed to it. The most significant resource demand of a partnership scheme is staff time for mentoring. Mentors need to be assigned at least one hour per week of 'protected time' in which to work in private with their students. If, in addition, the scheme involves the provision of 'school-based seminars' led by mentors or other teachers, then these too have to be accounted for. In-service time will also need to be assigned to the scheme in order to ensure that teachers are fully aware of what is involved and have the opportunity to develop appropriate skills. Students will make other demands on the school too: materials, photocopying, telephone, secretarial time. These too need to be clearly assessed and managed.

There are, however, important benefits of participation in initial teacher education. In one sense students could be seen simply as an additional staff resource, but their presence can also benefit experienced teachers. Indeed, taking responsibility for the systematic training of a new member of the profession is a very powerful form of staff development for those acting as mentors. Mentors establish close working relationships with those in higher education as well as mentors in other schools. They also develop their ability to articulate and justify their own professional practice. As a result, commentators such as Beardon *et al.* (1993) have argued that taking part in initial teacher education is the single most significant initiative that a school can take in supporting the professional development of its staff.

### Mentoring roles for teachers

Experience has shown that if a scheme is to be managed effectively in a school, someone at senior management level needs to be appointed to undertake responsibility for it. This senior, co-ordinating mentor will need to become familiar with the legal framework of the national training system and have a clear working knowledge of the particular teacher education programme and the role of their school within it. Effective working relationships with their higher education partners will also have to be established.

Within school the co-ordinating mentor will need to ensure that the scheme has a high profile; this is essential in that it potentially has implications for the whole school community. Governors and parents need to be kept fully informed and all staff, whether or not they are directly involved in the student programme, need to become familiar with the nature of the programme and feel committed to it.

But perhaps the most significant task for the senior mentor is the selection of other mentors. Indeed, the quality of the mentoring scheme necessarily stands or falls on the capabilities of the teachers appointed to take on this role. In selecting mentors, a number of factors need to be taken into account. For example, because modelling is a key teaching strategy in mentoring, mentors must themselves be effective classroom teachers. They also need good communication skills, and the ability to articulate the principles underlying their practice and to deal sensitively with adult learners at both professional and personal levels. Being a mentor also demands that the teacher has some status within the school; newly qualified teachers are therefore unlikely to be appropriate.

Checklist 3.1 (page 44) might be used by the senior management team in reviewing the partnership scheme within their school.

## 1.3 The educational role of higher education institutions

What is the contribution of those in higher education to initial teacher training?

At one level there is a very simple response here, in terms of the validation of courses at appropriate academic levels and the guarantee of quality. More profoundly however, the unique contribution of higher education to the professional development of teachers lies in higher education's commitment to challenge students with new ideas, expose them to research findings, and engage students in critical 'conversations' about both their own educational practices and those of others (Furlong 1996). As such challenges and conversations evolve though a course, students are encouraged to extend their knowledge; to develop their own views; to take an open and critical stance in the evaluation of practice; to experiment in the development of their own teaching; and to begin to develop their professional judgement.

Of course, teachers in schools may well foster an open-minded commitment to the critical scrutiny of practice. However, the school is certainly not a seminar – far from it. Indeed, as we suggested in Chapter 1, Section 2.5, it is the imperative of action in immediate contexts on which the judgement of practising teachers is grounded. The teacher is responsible for teaching this curriculum, to these pupils

---

## Checklist 3.1

*Aim:* To review issues involved in school participation in a partnership scheme for initial teacher education.

- Is an educationally sound and practically viable partnership scheme agreed with a higher education institution?

- Have other teachers, parents, governors been made aware of the training scheme?

- Has a senior, co-ordinating teacher been appointed?

- Are there clear criteria for the identification of appropriate teachers to be involved in the scheme? For instance, are the designated mentors appropriately qualified, experienced and committed to the training model?

- Is there appropriate in-service support for the different groups of staff involved – mentors, other teachers, assistant staff?

- Have effective procedures for appropriate liaison with tutors from the higher education institution been established?

- Are there regular planned meetings between mentors and students? Do mentors have adequate 'protected time' for this?

- Are there planned opportunities for students' involvement in the life of the school beyond their department, such as attendance at staff meetings, parents' meetings and participation in extra-curricular activities?

- Do students have access to adequate resources for teaching and training purposes?

- Have internal or external evaluation procedures identified any weaknesses in the school which might adversely affect teacher training?

- Have appropriate internal quality control procedures for the training scheme been established?

---

now, and, if teachers stopped to reflect on every action, then they simply could not teach effectively. Higher education can therefore claim to have a distinctive contribution to make to professional development by supporting a particularly analytic form of reflection.

But does this really matter? Why do student teachers need to know about new research, to be challenged by debates about curriculum, assessment, pedagogy, learning, etc., and to be engaged in 'conversations' about practice? This takes us back to the conception of 'reflective teaching' which we introduced in Chapter 1. There we drew attention to the complexity of teaching, to the multiple dilemmas which teachers face (Rowland 1993, Berlak and Berlak 1981, **Primary Reading 1.3**) and to the need for teachers to use professional judgement in resolving them.

Student teachers need to develop what Elliott (1990) calls 'intelligent skill knowledge'. (See also **Primary Readings** 1.4, Wragg 1993, and 1.7, Elliott 1991). Such knowledge is essentially practical, but it nevertheless involves an implicit appreciation of the complexities on which it is based. Higher education tutors can help students in appreciating these. Indeed, given their breadth of practical experience and their own engagement in research and study of education, tutors have access to a powerful range of questions that can help students confront the complexities underlying practice (see Figure 1.6 for a representation of the strengths and weaknesses of teachers' and researchers' knowledge). Most importantly for the development of an autonomous profession, it is through the challenge of such questioning, through being forced to look at their assumptions, articulate them and expose them to critical scrutiny, that students learn to bring their practice more effectively under their own control.

Higher education institutions and tutors can therefore play a vital role in the development of practical, professional teacher education.

## 1.4 The practical responsibilities of higher education institutions

Higher education institutions have a range of major responsibilities in most partnership models.

First, they are normally responsible for initiating work on the partnership model and, working with teacher colleagues, for appropriate integration, coherence and progression of courses. These must then be both validated by the higher education institution and accredited by the Teacher Training Agency. The higher education institution must also take responsibility for negotiating an appropriate level of remuneration to each school for their work with students.

A second major responsibility of a higher education provider is the basic one of providing a high quality and enriching course, through which student teachers are appropriately challenged. Tutors can broaden students' practical knowledge and skills, through activities such as discussions of research, the use of libraries and professional resource centres, by arranging visits and visiting speakers. However, given the national requirements of initial training courses, the amount of time for such activities is sometimes somewhat restricted with a wide range of activities often being packed into a short space of time.

Student teachers also often benefit from reviewing the practicalities of teaching away from the complexities of the classroom itself. In a college or university, the challenges of immediate performance are removed. Other important aspects of teaching also need sustained study. For example, students need to consider the National Curriculum in detail, they need to work on the preparation of lesson plans and to examine different strategies for assessing pupils' work. All of this work is highly practical in nature, but the higher education environment is sometimes the most appropriate place in which to engage with it.

Higher education tutors must also take on the very important responsibility of modelling forms of 'good practice'. Recent research has demonstrated that higher education tutors regard their own pedagogy as one of their key strategies in professional preparation (Furlong *et al.* 1994a). Through it, tutors model a wide variety of teaching strategies for their students. Many tutors also deploy the strategy of putting a group of students back into the role of learners themselves. Through this process, complex issues about teaching, learning and the nature of knowledge can be raised in an extremely effective manner.

Higher education institutions have a particular responsibility for ensuring that the assessment of students' practical competences is conducted constructively and fairly. Procedures within the partnership scheme will set out the complementary roles of mentors, tutors (and sometimes, students) in assessment. External examiners, appointed by the higher education institution, are used to monitor overall standards, resolve uncertainties and to confirm both failures and particular successes.

A final responsibility for those in higher education concerns quality control. School-based work must be monitored to ensure that schools are able effectively to perform their role. It must be remembered here that schools do not have the statutory responsibilities for initial teacher education which those in higher education work within. It is therefore the responsibility of those in higher education to make sure that students are appropriately placed and well supported by appropriately skilled mentors. Checklist 3.2, overleaf, summarizes these points.

The OFSTED/TTA Framework for the inspection of teacher training (1996) clarifies the criteria which all training routes have to satisfy. These cover all aspects of a programme, whether college or school-based, including:

- Teaching competences of students and of newly qualified teachers
- Quality of training and assessment of students
- Selection and quality of the student intake
- Quality of staffing and learning resources
- Management and quality assurance.

## 2 | THE PROCESS OF MENTORING

As we have seen, one of the most significant changes that has come about with the development of partnership schemes is a reconceptualization of the role of teachers in supporting students' school-based learning. At the heart of the partnership is the mentor, who will be a subject specialist with formal responsibility for the students within their department.

Mentoring is an active process, and in this respect is fundamentally different from traditional forms of student 'supervision'. Of course, it is itself a form of teaching and like any teaching, those undertaking it need to have a repertoire of different 'teaching'

## Checklist 3.2

*Aim:* To review the roles and responsibilities of higher education institutions in partnership schemes for initial teacher education.

- Has an educationally sound, practical and financially viable partnership scheme been offered to schools?

- Have appropriate LEAs, schools and governors been made aware of the training scheme?

- Has a clear administrative infra-structure been set up by the higher education institution?

- Are tutors appropriately qualified, experienced and committed to the training model?

- Has a high quality course been constructed, presenting student teachers with new knowledge, concepts and experiences, challenging their attitudes and enabling them to develop their skills?

- Do students have access to adequate resources for teaching and training purposes?

- Is there appropriate in-service support for the different groups of school and higher education institution staff involved – mentors, other teachers, tutors themselves?

- Have effective procedures for appropriate liaison between tutors and schools been established?

- Are there regular planned meetings between tutors, mentors and students? Do tutors have adequate time for these?

- Has provision been made for regular review and evaluation of the higher education contribution to the training programme, and of its fit with school provision?

- Are procedures for assessing the competence of student teachers clear and appropriate?

- Are the higher education institution systems for monitoring the quality of mentoring and school provision appropriately rigorous but professionally sensitive?

or mentoring strategies at their disposal. Mentors also need to have a clear understanding of the learning processes student teachers go through and an understanding of how they can work in a complementary way with higher education tutors in supporting students at different stages of their development.

It is worth considering the fundamental processes which mentoring involves, and this can be done by reference back to Chapter 1, Section 3, on 'competence and career'. There we distinguished between three stages of professional development – those of the 'novice', the 'competent' and the 'expert'. If mentor selection procedures have been carried out effectively, then school-based teacher training should bring experts and novices together. But how will they relate and communicate from their very different positions? This issue is squarely faced in the sections that follow.

We begin by looking at the 'skills' of mentoring – the range of strategies that mentors have at their disposal in supporting students learning to teach. However, it is central to our argument that the way in which mentors work with student teachers should vary and develop, depending on the particular learning needs and stage of development of the student. After discussing the skills of mentoring, we therefore go on to consider what is known about how students do indeed develop in the process of learning to teach. In the final section of the chapter we consider how mentors can respond to students' changing learning needs. The primary focus of that section is therefore on the role of mentors in supporting school-based learning. However, where appropriate, we will also refer to tutors' responsibilities.

## 2.1   Skills of mentoring

We identify four clusters of mentoring skill: preparation and induction, helping students observe, observing students and giving feedback, and collaborative teaching.

### Preparation and induction

Being responsible for mentoring a new entrant to the profession needs careful planning and preparation. It also calls for considerable skill in both preparing the ground with colleagues in the school, and providing appropriate clarity, sensitivity and encouragement to ensure that student teachers begin their period of school experience in positive ways.

Even before the student arrives it is necessary to prepare for them. For example, it is essential that colleagues, and most particularly those who will have regular contact with the student, fully understand what is involved. The mentor also needs to develop an overview of the complete course that the student is taking and to ensure that he or she can provide regular meetings to support the student's learning.

Once they arrive, student teachers need to be inducted into both the school as a whole and into the department and classrooms in which they will be working.

Inducting the student into the school as a whole may be the responsibility of the mentor or a senior teacher. The programme should be well planned in advance so that students can be contacted and told when and where to report. Appropriate members of staff need to be available. During the 'whole school' induction students should:

- receive key school documentation
- meet key people within the school
- be shown around the school
- be made aware of the school's expectations of them
- be made aware of the school's organization and procedures.

In terms of induction into the department where they will be working, students need to:
- receive important departmental documentation
- meet members of the department
- be shown around the department and relevant classrooms
- be made aware of the departmental expectations of them
- be made aware of the department's organization and procedures
- learn about teaching resources
- understand classroom organization procedures
- understand assessment and reporting procedures.

### Helping students to observe

Observing experienced practitioners is one of the most important strategies for learning any complex activity. It is for this reason that it has always been an important part of student teachers' introduction to teaching. But learning from observation is not as straightforward as it may seem. Particularly in the early stages, students often find it difficult to disentangle the complexities of teaching – they find it difficult to 'see'. Observation, if it is to be an effective use of time, therefore needs to be carefully planned and followed up. And if it is well managed then observation is not only valuable in the early stages of learning to teach, but can also be valuable at later stages too. The following are some of the key principles to follow in helping students get the most out of observation:

- Establish a clear focus for the student. In the early stages of teaching this might, for example, involve looking at the beginning and ends of lessons; observing how and for what purposes teachers ask pupils different types of questions. At a later stage more complex processes might be observed such as how teachers adapt and develop their lesson plans in response of pupils' learning needs.
- Suggest ways in which students might collect evidence to support their observations.
- Advise students about the role they should adopt when observing – it is not always necessary to be a passive observer.
- Ask students to report back on their observations as soon as possible afterwards.

The Practical Activities throughout this book will provide many structured ideas for observational, and other, investigative activities.

### Observing students and giving feedback

Informal observation and feedback by mentors is vitally important if students are to get the most out of their time in school. However, mentors also need to establish a more formal observation and feedback routine. This should happen on a regular basis

– at least once a week – and needs to be planned just as carefully as any other 'teaching' activity.

The routine of observation and feedback involves three distinct processes: preliminary planning, undertaking observation and giving feedback. Simply responding to 'whatever emerges' is not enough.

Preliminary planning of a teaching session is essential for student teachers, and their mentor should help constructively in this. Some of the issues may seem relatively basic to a skilled teacher, but the complexity and multiplicity of demands in teaching are very challenging for relative novices. Good plans can give confidence and lead, in turn, to more flexible responses to pupil needs. The advice and activities in Part 2 of this book contains much advice on planning. In respect of planning for particular teaching sessions, see Chapter 10, Section 3.

Where a lesson is to be observed, as part of the preliminary planning, mentors need to establish a clear focus for the observation and ensure that the student knows what it is. The nature of this focus will obviously change as the student develops, but official government competences can provide a useful framework (see Figure 1.3 for an edited list of these). Later, the observation might be focused on a particular area of student need. In planning the observation, it is also necessary for the mentor to think carefully about their own role in the classroom and whether they will participate in the teaching or simply observe. Whatever role is adopted, it is essential that it is explained to the student in advance so that they can present themselves appropriately.

During the observation itself, it is an advantage to collect evidence so that some form of record of the lesson exists for later reference and discussion. A considerable number of ways of collecting evidence in classrooms is reviewed in Chapter 4, 'Investigating classrooms', and Table 4.1 provides an overview of methods which are discussed across the book as a whole. Good evidence will be a great help in providing effective feedback later.

Formal feedback from the observation needs to be given as soon as is practicable following the lesson. The aim of such feedback is to help the student develop a clearer understanding of his or her own teaching, in terms of both its strengths and its weaknesses. It is through this developing understanding that students are able to bring their teaching more directly under their own control, and providing students with appropriate feedback that achieves this aim is one of the most challenging skills of mentoring.

One of the challenges of providing feedback is getting an appropriate balance between pointing out problems and providing positive comments. If mentors are too critical they can undermine the student's confidence; alternatively, mentors can 'kill by kindness'. It is important to remember that, however confident students may appear, they often feel vulnerable. Mentors therefore need to plan their feedback with care and strike an appropriate balance. If the lesson seems really weak, mentors should prioritize a few points that have to be made and still try and find some things to praise. However, in the long term, avoiding serious problems will not help, and mentors should aim to create a relationship of trust and respect in which difficulties can be faced frankly and constructively. It is particularly valuable that students have opportunities to express their views on teaching sessions, and hearing their perception of their own strengths and weaknesses may be highly illuminative. Attempts should be made to develop and support student self-evaluation (for relevant ideas, see Chapter 9, Section

2.5; Chapter 15, Section 2.3, **Primary Reading 6.5**, Tharp and Gallimore 1988).

The style of feedback also needs to be considered. Mentors need to have at their disposal a repertoire of different strategies that can be used in different circumstances. Indeed, the models of teaching and learning which are discussed in Chapter 9 of this book, are very relevant here. At times mentors may need to be *didactic,* giving tightly focused advice on specific teaching strategies. At other times they will be *discursive,* drawing the student out, and helping them to identify and analyse specific aspects of their own teaching. This is a particularly valuable way of opening up discussion of weaker areas of teaching. Finally, a *partnership* approach may develop where the student takes a degree of control in identifying issues that need to be discussed. In this scenario the mentor provides evidence, facilitates the discussion, offers advice and poses key questions in support of the student's line of enquiry. This strategy is particularly valuable at the later stages of student development where the aim is to encourage students to take greater responsibility for their own professional development and help them confront some of the complexities of the teacher's role. In reality, any one feedback session might well involve a combination of these different styles.

### Collaborative teaching

One of the main challenges of developing more effective school-based teacher education programmes is to find ways of giving students access to the wealth of practical knowledge that experienced teachers possess. Despite, or perhaps because of the complexity of teaching, teachers often find it difficult to articulate clearly what it is they are doing and why they are doing it. One of the great strengths of collaborative teaching, where student and mentor plan and teach together, is that the student becomes an 'insider' within the teaching process. Through the collaborative process the student teacher can start to gain insight into the mentor's practical knowledge.

However, it is important to recognize that there are many different ways of teaching collaboratively. They range from a situation where the student teaches one small aspect of a lesson, perhaps explaining a key concept or managing the introduction, to full and equal joint teaching. Whatever role is assigned to the student, an essential feature of collaborative teaching is that student and teacher plan together. If they are to gain insight into what the teacher is trying to achieve then it is essential that the student is part of the planning process and is fully involved in the classroom activities. For collaboration to work as an effective learning experience, students must have opportunities directly to experience and engage with the complexities of the teacher's contexualized thinking.

## 2.2  Stages of student development

Effective mentoring involves the use of skills, such as those reviewed above, in appropriate responses to the changing learning needs of students. But what do we know about the way in which student teachers develop?

An examination of research literature on the process of learning to teach confirms the commonsense observation that trainees typically go through a number of distinct stages of development, each with its own focal concerns. Maynard and Furlong (1993) argued that these concerns can usefully be grouped under the following headings: early idealism; survival; recognizing difficulties; hitting the plateau; and moving on.

## Early idealism

Before they have begun their training, students are often highly idealistic about teaching. For many, this involves wanting to identify closely with the pupils and their needs and interests. This identification with the pupils is hardly surprising, since, for the vast majority of students in training, their only experience of the teaching process has been as pupils themselves. Once student teachers enter the classroom, such idealism can fade very quickly.

## Survival

The first days and weeks in the classroom are extremely challenging for students both professionally and personally. One of the common complaints that students make in these early days is that they find it difficult to 'see'. They find it very hard to disentangle the complexities of teaching and to understand the processes involved. Either they assume that it is straightforward – something that anyone can do – or they are overwhelmed by its complexity. In the early stages of school experience, time is often given for trainees to observe classroom practice. However, as Calderhead (1988a) and Doyle (1977, **Primary Reading 10.1**) confirm, this is often wasted time because they cannot interpret the noise and movement around them and they do not understand the significance of the teacher's actions. In a nutshell, they simply do not know what it is they are supposed to be looking for. It is no wonder that at this stage students go in search of 'quick fixes' and 'hints and tips' (Eisenhart *et al.* 1991). Learning how to observe an experienced teacher and understand the different skills that he or she is using is thus an achievement in itself. It is something that students need to be taught how to do, and to which this book should contribute.

Another important feature of their early classroom experiences is that students frequently become obsessed with their own survival; 'fitting in' and establishing themselves as a 'teacher' often become major issues for them. Rather than wanting to identify closely with the pupils, they become dominated by their concern to 'manage' them. However, if achieving classroom management and control becomes the overriding concern, then teaching and learning activities begin to be judged almost entirely in terms of whether they contribute to achieving that end. Maynard and Furlong suggest that students are often personally very stressed by this early period of learning to teach. In particular, many find it hard to come to terms with themselves as authority figures. They have to get used to a new persona, 'me-as-teacher' (see Chapter 8, Section 1) and for some, it is not a character they particularly like. As a consequence it is not uncommon for students to go through a period of resenting the pupils for forcing them to be more authoritarian than they really want to be.

## Recognizing difficulties

Fortunately the confusion and challenges brought about by the first taste of teaching do not, in most cases, last more than a week or so. Slowly, the 'survival' stage gives way to a period where students can at least start to disentangle some of the complexities involved in teaching. They begin to identify some of the difficulties they face in learning to teach. However, this recognition brings its own pressures and they can be overwhelmed by the complexity of it all. As a result, despite assurances from teachers and tutors and attempts to help them view this as 'learning experience', the dominant concern for most students at this early stage is, 'Will I pass?' In this circumstance, a common reaction is for students to try to replicate or mimic other teachers' behaviour. They develop 'procedural' competence by focusing on teaching strategies and classroom organization, 'acting' like a teacher without necessarily understanding the underlying purpose or implications of those actions.

### Hitting the plateau

Eventually, most students do manage to at least 'act' like a teacher; they learn how to control the class and engage the pupils in some purposeful activity. However, Maynard and Furlong suggest that once students have achieved this level of competence, they may stop developing – they can 'hit a plateau'. They have found one way of teaching that 'works' and offers security, and they are going to stick to it! The challenge is then for the mentor, working in collaboration with the higher education tutor, to move the student on from 'acting like a teacher' towards 'thinking like a teacher'. We would suggest that the difference between these two states is that experienced teachers devote most of their attention to thinking about their pupils' learning rather than focusing on their own 'performance'. In other words, they are competent and confident enough to be able to 'de-centre' from themselves to the pupils. If students are to improve the quality of their teaching, we would argue that it is essential that they too gradually learn to de-centre. Evidence would suggest that without external support and some progressive development of practical teaching skills, students often find this transition difficult.

### Moving on

There is one further stage of learning to teach and that involves the further development of the student as a 'reflective practitioner' – a concept which was explored in Chapter 1 and to which this book contributes. Of course, whilst a programme of initial teacher training can lay foundations for the development of reflective practice, to teach in this way is an appropriate ambition at any stage of a professional career in schools. Nevertheless it is clear that as student teachers gain in confidence, they are capable of taking more responsibility for their own professional development, for broadening their repertoire of teaching strategies, deepening their understanding of the complexities of teaching and learning, and for considering the social, moral and political dimensions of educational practice. Mentors and higher education tutors, working collaboratively, are well placed to help students analyse and reflect on their own teaching.

## 2.3 Stages of mentoring

Mentoring needs to be developmental so that students can be supported through these different stages of learning to teach. However, it is important to emphasize that, in arguing for a developmental approach, we are not suggesting that mentors should simply give students whatever support they ask for. If students are to develop fully, then there will be times when mentors will need to be assertive in their interventions, providing students what it is judged that they 'need', even when this may not be what they immediately 'want'. However, we would support the idea that in essence, mentoring is no different from any other form of teaching; it is necessary to start from where the learners are and take typical patterns of development into account.

Following Furlong *et al.* (1994b), we outline a number of different stages of mentoring. In each stage we can identify different learning priorities for the student and a different 'role' for the mentor in supporting those learning needs. We also suggest a number of key mentoring strategies, although we do not intend these stages to be followed slavishly. The development of any one student will be much more complex than a simple stage model implies; they will develop at their own rate and will need to revisit issues because they have forgotten them or wish to relearn them in a different context or at a deeper level. We therefore intend these stages of mentoring to be considered flexibly and with sensitivity. In fact it is probably more appropriate to think of each stage as cumulative rather than discrete. As students develop, mentors will need to employ more and more strategies from the repertoire that we set out.

A summary of a developmental model of mentoring adapted from Furlong *et al.* (1994b) is set out in Figure 3.1.

| | Beginning teaching | Supervised teaching | From teaching to learning | Reflective teaching |
|---|---|---|---|---|
| Stage of development | Survival | Recognizing difficulties | Hitting the plateau | Moving on |
| Focus of student learning | Rules, rituals, routines and establishing authority | Teaching competences | Understanding pupil learning and developing effective teaching | Taking control and developing professionalism |
| Role of mentor and tutor | Providing models of effective practice | As trainers, providing focused advice and instruction | As critical friends, providing constructive critique for development | As co-enquirers, joining together in aspects of professional development |
| Key mentoring strategies | Student observation focused on class routines and teacher techniques | Focused observation by student, combined with structured observation of the student and feedback | Focused observation by and structured observation of the student. Re-examination of lesson planning | Partnership in teaching and supervision |

**Figure 3.1** *A developmental model of mentoring*

*Beginning teaching*

As we indicated earlier, when students first begin the process of learning to teach, they have two particular learning needs. They need to learn how to 'see' – to disentangle and identify some of the complexities of the teaching process. In particular, they are most concerned to discover how teachers achieve effective control within the classroom.

In developing an understanding of how to achieve classroom control, students face two particular difficulties. The first is that teachers often find it extremely difficult to explain how it is they achieve discipline and order. To an experienced teacher, classroom management is such a 'natural' process that it is difficult to discuss it in isolation from other aspects of teaching. The second difficulty is that by the time that the student arrives in school, usually part-way through the year, teachers have already established relationships with their pupils. Much of the 'work' that goes into achieving order takes place at the beginning of the school year and thereafter is simply understood by teacher and pupils alike (see Chapter 14, Section 2). By the time students arrive, many of the teacher's management strategies may be almost 'invisible'.

Because much of what the student most wants to learn may be tacit, and invisible to the untutored eye, we would suggest the focus for students in the earliest stages of learning to teach must necessarily be on the rules, routines and rituals of the classroom. By observing and copying these 'ready made' strategies, students can more quickly come to participate in the classroom and begin to 'act' like a teacher.

At this stage, students can best be helped to make sense of the classroom and understand its rules, rituals and routines by observing and teaching collaboratively alongside their mentor. By setting up focused observations and collaborative teaching, the mentor acts as a model for the student; interpreting events, guiding their observation, drawing their attention to what they are doing and why, and to the significance of what is happening in the classroom. Collaborative teaching also allows the student to begin to engage in substantive 'teaching', while the teacher, rather than the student, remains responsible for classroom management and control.

*Supervised teaching*

Once student teachers have gained some insight into the rules, routines and rituals of the classroom and, through carefully supported collaborative work, have themselves had some experience of teaching, then they will be ready for a more systematic and structured approach to training. As we indicated above, during this second phase of their teaching experience, students are likely to be mostly concerned with developing their own 'performance' as teachers. Their aim will be to achieve greater and grater control over the teaching and learning process. We suggest that this development can be supported best if the mentor, and when appropriate the visiting higher education tutor, explicitly develop a formal 'training' role, focusing directly on the 'competences' of teaching.

In reality, teaching cannot be fully characterized as a series of discrete competences because the whole is always more than the sum of the parts (see Chapter 1, Section 1.2, 3.1 and 3.2). Thus, to extract one particular element from a complex process like teaching, is necessarily artificial. Nevertheless, to simplify the complexity for training purposes, there are considerable benefits in mentors focusing on specific teaching competences in a systematic and structured way.

As part of their systematic training, students will continue to need to observe and investigate classroom practices, though now their focus might benefit by being even more tightly geared to issues which have been identified for further development. The Practical Activitites in this book should provide many ideas for worthwhile activities. In addition, we would suggest that mentors and tutors provide similarly focused observation and feedback on specific teaching competences.

In terms of the content of training, the broad focus is provided by 'official' competences which may be set by government (see Chapter 1, Figure 1.3). However, particular courses and individual mentors may well wish to add to the list provided. As was suggested earlier, the degree of specificity of guidance the mentor and tutor need to give the student will vary depending on the stage of the student's development and their success in managing the particular competence successfully. The more difficulty a student has, the more helpful it is for the mentor and tutor to give specific guidance.

### From teaching to learning

Once students have gained sufficient confidence in classroom management and control in order to 'act' like a teacher, then they are able to turn their attention away from their own performance, and look more deeply at the content of their lessons in terms of what their pupils are actually learning. Furlong *et al.* (1994b) called this process 'de-centring'.

Developing the ability to de-centre, to reassess one's teaching in terms of pupils' learning rather than one's own performance, is a vitally important part of becoming an effective teacher. However, experience shows that students often fail to move on in this way unless they are given some direct help. They may be satisfied with having established a particular formula for teaching which keeps the children quiet and occupied, but then fail to look critically at what learning is taking place.

Students who find difficulty in moving on to consider pupils' learning often embody two basic misconceptions.

First, they may hold views that are not supportive of the need for further development to focus on pupil learning itself. For example, they may believe:

- that teaching is simply about the transmission of knowledge and the accumulation of factual information
- that children are blank slates
- that school learning is 'discrete' and separate from learning going on elsewhere in pupils lives
- that giving correct answers denotes understanding.

Until these sorts of beliefs have been challenged and student teachers have begun to recognize the complexities involved in teaching and learning (see Chapters 9, 10, 13 and 15), they will not be open to developing a more appropriate approach to planning for pupils' learning over time.

A second difficulty may be that the student actually has insufficient confidence in classroom management and control (the ideas in Chapter 14 will help with this). An appreciation of how pupils learn also demands a willingness to experiment with different strategies of classroom organization (see Chapter 11). In particular, it demands that pupils take an active role in their learning and, when appropriate, to participate in investigation and inquiry. For some student teachers, especially those who have only a tentative hold on classroom control, this may appear very threatening. How much easier to keep pupils sitting in their places and have their attention focused on you!

Student teachers have to come to realize that effective classroom control is attained primarily through working with young pupils though well-matched activities that:

- take account of pupils' needs and interests
- take account of how pupils learn
- are supportive of pupils' developing understanding of the subject area

The development of a fuller understanding of effective teaching is often a slow and difficult process for students. Their understanding of how pupils learn, and what their role as a teacher should be, may initially be naïve and simplistic.

If students are to move on to develop a more realistic understanding of the processes involved in effective teaching, they need to be encouraged to look critically at the teaching procedures they have established and to evaluate their effectiveness. The Practical Activities in this book will help in this, but students will certainly need the consistent support and advice of both the mentor and the higher education tutor. Careful collaboration between the two is essential at this point and the task for the mentor and the tutor is particularly challenging at this stage of the student's development. Furlong *et al.* (1994b) characterize the role as providing 'critical friendship' through which the student is challenged to re-examine his/her teaching, while at the same time is offered practical support, encouragement and personal affirmation.

### Reflective teaching

As we indicated above, there is one further stage of student development that needs to be considered, and that is student development as reflective practitioners. We would suggest that the focus for student learning in this final stage of development should include:

- broadening the student's repertoire of teaching strategies
- encouraging the student to take more responsibility for his/her own professional development
- deepening their understanding of the complexities involved in teaching and learning including the social, moral and political dimensions

As the student begins to acquire greater skill and knowledge and develop a more appropriate and realistic understanding of the nature of teaching, so the mentor and the tutor should begin to modify their role yet again. While there will still be times when they need to act as 'model', 'trainer' or 'critical friend', they should also develop the role of 'co-enquirer'. As a co-enquirer, they will develop a more open and equal relationship with their student, spending more time working as equal professionals. Such a relationship has the advantage of encouraging the student to take greater responsibility for their own learning and allows student, mentor and tutor to address some of the complexities of teaching in a spirit of more open enquiry.

However, its most valuable role is in providing a framework for mentor and student to discuss planning and teaching at a more fundamental level than before. No longer should mentors present themselves as an authority, knowing the 'right' answers. Rather, through discussion of their planning and teaching, mentors should attempt to 'open up' their work. This can be achieved by, for example:

- focusing on the *complexity* of thinking underlying professional decisions
- exposing the moral, practical and other *dilemmas* underlying professional decisions
- evaluating the social and educational *consequences* of particular professional decisions
- discussing the social, institutional and political contexts in which professional decisions have to be made.

It is by participating in such open, professional discussions in relation to their own practice that students can be encouraged to confront the complexities of teaching more deeply.

## CONCLUSION

In this chapter we have reviewed the rationale for school-based teacher training and considered the important roles of schools and higher education institutions and of mentors and tutors. We have drawn attention to important mentoring skills, reviewed characteristic ways in which the competence and self-confidence of novice student teachers develops, and considered the ways in which mentors should support them as they progress.

Part 2 of this book provides an enormous bank of resources. There are comprehensive reviews of important issues, Practical Activities to try, and Notes for Further Reading, all of which can be selectively used to meet particular needs and support professional development.

As the chapter makes clear, becoming a 'reflective teacher' is almost bound to be challenging, but it is made considerably easier with appropriate support from mentors and tutors working in partnership.

### Notes for further reading

Recent approaches to teacher education and training are premised on large proportions of school-based initial teacher education and on close partnerships between higher education institutions and schools. For recent publications exploring the issues involved in partnership in initial teacher education see:

Benton, P. (1990)
*The Oxford Internship Scheme: Integration and Partnership in Initial Teacher Education,*
London: Calouste Gulbenkian Foundation.

Furlong, J. and Smith, R. (eds) (1996)
*The Role of Higher Education in Initial Teacher Training,*
London: Kogan Page.

McIntyre, D. and Hagger, H. (eds) (1996)
*Mentors in Schools: Developing the Profession of Teaching,*
London: David Fulton.

OFSTED (1995b)
*Partnership: Schools and Higher Education in Partnership in Initial Teacher Training,*
London: HMSO.

TTA (1996a)
*Effective Training Through Partnership,*
London: TTA.

Williams, A. (ed.) (1994)
*Perspectives on Partnership: Secondary Initial Teacher Training,*
London: The Falmer Press.

Whiting, C., Whitty, G., Furlong, J., Miles, S. and Barton, L. (1996)
*Partnership in Initial Teacher Education: A Topography,*
London: Health and Education Research Unit, Institute of Education, University of London.

The government organization which is responsible for teacher education is the Teacher Training Agency. For full information on its policies and activities, see the latest corporate plan, such as:

Teacher Training Agency (1996b)
*Corporate Plan 1996: Promoting Excellence in Teaching,*
London: TTA.

The role of experienced teachers in mentoring students in schools is of enormous importance in modern teacher education programmes and a substantial amount has been written on their role. See for example:

Furlong, J. and Maynard, T. (1995)
*Mentoring Student Teachers: The Growth of Professional Knowledge,*
London: Routledge.

Kerry, T. and Shelton Mayes, A. (eds) (1995)
*Issues in Mentoring,*
London: Routledge.

McIntyre, D. Hagger, H. and Wilkin, M. (1993) (eds)
*Mentoring: Perspectives on School-Based Teacher Education,*
London: Kogan Page.

Tomlinson, P. (1995)
*Understanding Mentoring: Reflective Strategies for School-based Teacher Preparation,*
Buckingham: Open University Press.

More practical advice on mentoring is provided in:

Furlong, J., Wilkin, M., Maynard, T. and Miles, S. (1994b)
*The Active Mentoring Programme,*
Cambridge: George Pearson Publishing.

Hagger, H., Burn, K. and McIntyre, D. (1993)
*The School Mentor Handbook,*
London: Kogan Page.

Stephens, P. (1996)
*Essential Mentoring Skills: A practical Handbook for School-based Teacher Educators,*
Cheltenham: Stanley Thorn Publishers.

Wilkin, M., Furlong, J., Miles, S. and Maynard, T. (1996)
*The Secondary Subject Mentor Handbook,*
London: Kogan Page.

For other useful books on teacher training see:

Shaw, R. (1995)
*Teacher Training in Secondary Schools,*
London: Kogan Page.

Hustler, D. and McIntyre, D. (1996)
*Developing Competent Teachers: Approaches to Professional Competence in Teacher Education,*
London: David Fulton.

Tolley, H., Biddulph, M., Fisher, T. (1996)
*Beginning Teaching Workbooks 1–6,*
Cambridge: Chris Kington Publishing.

On supporting new teachers in the first few years of work, see:

Tickle, L. (1994)
*The Induction of New Teachers: Reflective Professional Practices,*
London: Cassell.

# CHAPTER 4

# Investigating classrooms and schools

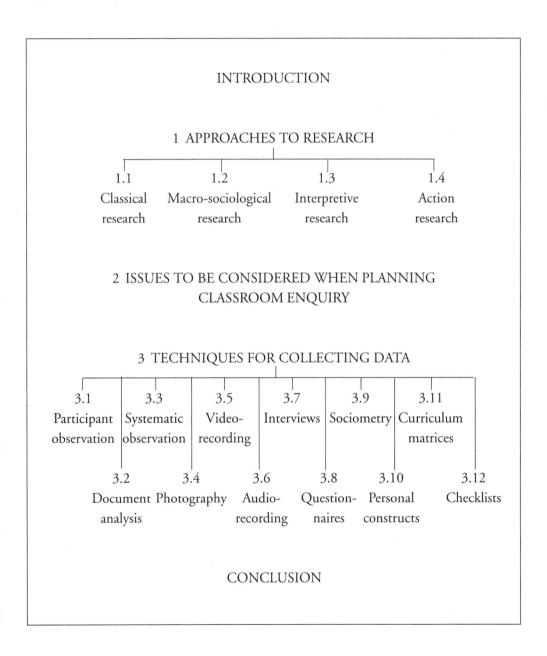

INTRODUCTION

1 APPROACHES TO RESEARCH

| 1.1 | 1.2 | 1.3 | 1.4 |
|---|---|---|---|
| Classical research | Macro-sociological research | Interpretive research | Action research |

2 ISSUES TO BE CONSIDERED WHEN PLANNING
CLASSROOM ENQUIRY

3 TECHNIQUES FOR COLLECTING DATA

| 3.1 | 3.3 | 3.5 | 3.7 | 3.9 | 3.11 |
|---|---|---|---|---|---|
| Participant observation | Systematic observation | Video-recording | Interviews | Sociometry | Curriculum matrices |

| 3.2 | 3.4 | 3.6 | 3.8 | 3.10 | 3.12 |
|---|---|---|---|---|---|
| Document analysis | Photography | Audio-recording | Question-naires | Personal constructs | Checklists |

CONCLUSION

# INTRODUCTION

The relationship between 'researchers' and teachers has often been an uneasy one. Teachers have identified a number of reasons for this state of affairs. First, teachers claim that researchers do not seem to focus on the kinds of concerns which teachers actually have. Second, researchers appear to be rather distant: they come to do research about teachers and their classrooms, but without clearly explaining the purpose or the methods. Third, the results are often presented through complicated statistical procedures or are embedded in technical language. Many teachers and some distinguished researchers have disclaimed such research as 'less than useful' (Hargreaves 1996, Freeman 1986). Although the Teacher Training Agency (TTA) seems to be rather ambivalent about existing work from universities (TTA 1996), it is very keen on the development of teachers as researchers of their own practices.

Constructive developments are thus seen to include researchers working alongside teachers in more collaborative ways, or teachers becoming their own researchers into classroom practice. In the latter case, this means that teachers need to develop the necessary techniques to research their own classrooms and have to be able to interpret and evaluate their findings appropriately.

Such developments raise important issues, the first of which relates to the nature of research itself. Research is traditionally characterized as being 'objective' – reliable, valid, generalizable and credible (Shipman 1981). If research were done by involved insiders, such as teachers in their own classrooms, would such research still be able to meet these criteria? If not, would this matter? In particular, could such research, which would be likely to be small-scale, provide a basis for theoretical explanations and generalizations? Again, if not, would it matter?

Such questions and doubts have been raised for many years about the feasibility of teachers becoming 'teachers-as-researchers'. However, more and more teachers have begun to gather evidence of their classroom practices routinely. Indeed, teachers are frequently aware of the discrepancies between their 'espoused theory' and their actual practice, and between their own descriptions of the practice and the descriptions made by others of the same practice (Elbaz 1983). Most of us realize how difficult it can be to 'see' what we are doing while we are in the middle of doing it. However, because it is difficult, it does not mean that it is not possible or that it is not worthwhile to try!

The model of a reflective teacher, as outlined in Chapter 1, suggests that critical reflection and systematic investigation of our own practice should become an integral part of our daily classroom lives. Such self-examination should lead to an improvement in our teaching judgements and help us to have a more professional control over our own development and that of others. Self-appraisal and professional awareness should provide the basis for a professional autonomy and educational quality.

If this is to happen, then an appreciation of the major issues involved in research and knowledge of some of the main enquiry techniques available are essential. This chapter has been written as an introduction to such matters. Readers are strongly advised to follow up issues and techniques in which they may be particularly interested via the Notes for Further Reading section.

The chapter begins by examining two issues: the nature of traditional forms of research and the status of the main alternative forms. There is then a section on what are essentially 'research design' issues for classroom enquiry. Finally the chapter reviews a range of possible research techniques which teachers could use in their own classrooms.

## 1 | APPROACHES TO RESEARCH

 Four main research approaches to education can be identified (see also **Primary Reading 3.5**, Bassey 1990). The first is the 'classical' scientific model which has traditionally laid great emphasis on quantitative data – for instance, by classifying and measuring behaviour. This approach is sometimes called 'positivistic'. A second approach is offered by some sociologists and focuses on structural features of society – for example, social inequalities, which are frequently measured and quantified. Such features are also examined in relationship to their historical, economic, cultural and political contexts. This may be referred to as a 'macro-sociological' approach. Forms of comparative education could be associated with this. The third approach is 'interpretive' research, which emphasizes the qualitative aspects of each situation being researched – for instance, by analysing people's perceptions. It is sometimes referred to as being 'phenomenological'. The final approach is one which has been developed in recent years by curriculum specialists working alongside teachers. This 'action research' is concerned with self-evaluation and the direct improvement of classroom practice.

## 1.1 Classical research

The classical model is based on the research style which has served the physical sciences for many years. Its characteristic stages are:

- to recognize and define a problem
- to develop an hypothesis
- to design a controlled research procedure to test the hypothesis
- to accumulate observations
- to analyse the data
- to interpret the data and form generalizable explanations.

The hallmarks of this classical model are, therefore, that the investigation has an hypothesis, which is testable and replicable, which provides an explanation and is generalizable. When such research is referred to as 'scientific', it is usually to highlight two features which are believed by some to be crucial: that it is 'systematic' in the way the research is carried out and that it is 'objective' in the interpretation of the data collected and in the conclusions drawn. How far such research is 'scientific' in practice and whether this is still a suitable model for some areas of the physical sciences (for example, astrophysics or microbiology as just two examples) is in dispute in the scientific community itself (Harré 1972, Capra 1982, Anderson *et al.* 1986).

When this model is transferred to the social sciences, certain inadequacies are evident. For instance, it is very much more difficult to test an hypothesis in a classroom situation with the same rigour as one might expect in a laboratory experiment.

It is more difficult because we cannot isolate the variables being examined and we cannot control all the myriad factors which might influence the test. In addition, we are dealing with human beings for whom we must have proper ethical concern about the way in which they, as with all living things, are treated. Further, because of the complexity of the classroom and because of the ethics of any such research, any 'experiment' can never be replicated exactly. Researchers have had to rely on sophisticated statistical methods to try to measure the impact of variables. Notwithstanding this, the difficulties weaken the claim that such research can provide generalizable explanations. For all these reasons, the argument runs, such study cannot properly be called scientific research.

Nevertheless, there has been a long tradition in education research of following the classical model as exactly as is humanly possible. For example, much of the laboratory-based psychological testing and measurement research has been of this nature (for example, Cattell and Kline 1977). Similarly, the extensive work on teacher effectiveness in classrooms in the USA during the 1960s and 1970s (for example, Flanders 1970) used systematic observation techniques.

## 1.2 Macro-sociological research

The second, 'macro-sociological', approach has many features which distinguish it from the 'classical' model. In the first place, it is far more wide-ranging, for it is based on the assumption that specific situations, practices and perspectives can only be understood in relationship to their historical, economic, cultural and political contexts. Comparative and historical studies provide one form of this (e.g. Altbach and Kelly 1986, Green 1990). In its sociological form it rejects narrow forms of positivistic empiricism which tend to prevent such wide-ranging factors being considered, and uses various forms of theorizing to try to make sense of social structures, their processes and development. Among a number of forms of theorizing, the most important influences on educational analysis have been structural functionalism (for example, Parsons 1951, 1959), structural Marxism (for example, Bowles and Gintis 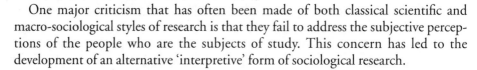 1976, **Primary Reading 13.1**), Weberianism (for example Collins 1977; Archer 1979 **Primary Reading 15.1**) and cultural Marxism (for example, Apple 1982). The latter offers ways of examining the tensions and dialectical forces of change or development within education and society. In recent years variants of such forms of analysis have been powerfully applied to educational policy-making (for example, see Whitty 1985, Ball 1990, Dale 1989, **Primary Readings** 2.4 Bowe *et al.* 1990, 2.5 Barton *et al.* 1994, 15.5 Dale 1996 and 15.6 Ball 1994).

One major criticism that has often been made of both classical scientific and macro-sociological styles of research is that they fail to address the subjective perceptions of the people who are the subjects of study. This concern has led to the development of an alternative 'interpretive' form of sociological research.

## 1.3 'Interpretive' research

The origins of this 'interpretive' approach can be traced to anthropology and the concern to understand, describe and analyse the cultures of particular societies and groups. Among the ethnographic methods which were developed are participant observation and interviewing. These techniques (which we will discuss in more detail later) are explicitly 'qualitative', rather than 'quantitative', and are concerned with opinions and perceptions rather than only observable facts or behaviour. Interpretive researchers tend to aim, in the first place, simply to describe the perspectives, actions and relationships of the people whom they are studying. Typically, they study a limited number of cases in depth and try to achieve a view of the whole situation in a way which is seen to be valid by the participants. This process often requires the personal involvement of the researcher and is rarely a neat, linear progression of research stages. The approach is pragmatic and flexible, as the researcher seeks data and understanding (Burgess 1984, Hammersley and Atkinson 1983, Woods 1986). The outcome of such research is usually a detailed case study within which concepts, relationships and issues are identified and analysed. Glaser and Strauss (1967) provided the classic statement of the challenge of such work when they argued that interpretive sociologists should start from the grounded base of people's perspectives and, through the simultaneous collection, classification and analysis of data, should develop systematic and theoretically refined perspectives of the social institutions and relationships which they study. Some examples of such work available concerning secondary education are Ball 1980, Aggleton 1987, Mac an Ghaill 1995, Woods 1979, Wolpe 1988).

Interpretive research has strengths and weaknesses, as with the classical model. Indeed, in many respects, they can be seen as complementary. For instance, a phenomenological researcher's 'generation' of theory may be balanced by a positivistic researcher's 'testing' of theory; qualitative data on perspectives may be balanced by quantitative data on behaviour; and a focus on detailed whole cases may be balanced by generalization from sampling across cases.

Whatever their differences and the degree of their complementarity, these alternative approaches to social science each share one important feature: they have all tended to distance themselves from actual practice. In the mid-1980s a direct concern with practical action emerged (Finch 1986, Shipman 1985, Woods and Pollard 1988), and it was argued that to understand thoroughly is a precondition of acting effectively, and there is clearly some merit in this point. However, a quite different approach has also been developed, which seeks to improve and understand practice through the direct action and involvement of practitioners.

## 1.4 Action research

'Action research' was originated by Lewin (1946). His model for change was based on action and research. It involved researchers, with teachers or other practitioners, in a cyclical process of planning, action, observation and reflection before beginning the whole process all over again.

 Further development of this model was instigated by Stenhouse (1975) **Primary Reading 3.1** and elaborated by Elliott and Adelman (1973) in their work with the Ford Teaching Project, based at the Centre for Applied Research in Education at the University of East Anglia. It was this generation of researchers who coined the term 'teacher-as-researcher' to refer to the participants in the movement they helped to create. This encouraged teachers to assume the role of researcher in their own classrooms as part of their professional, reflective stance.

The approach is sometimes criticized for encouraging a focus on practical class-room ideas while wider, structural factors are accepted as unproblematic (e.g. Barton and Lawn 1980/81, Whitty 1985). However, Carr and Kemmis (1986) **Primary Reading 3.2** argue that such work provides a means of 'becoming critical'. They sug-gest that action-research involves:

- the improvement of practice
- the improvement of the understanding of the practice by the practitioners
- the improvement of the situation in which practice takes place. (1986, p. 165)

Overall, they, like Stenhouse (1983), see the potential of action-research as being 'emancipatory': releasing practitioners from 'the often unseen constraints of assump-tions, habits, precedents, coercion and ideology' (Carr and Kemmis 1986, p. 192).

There are now some excellent published examples of teachers' action research (Nixon 1981, Hustler *et al.* 1986, Webb 1991) (see also **Primary Reading 3.4** Winter 1989).

In this section we have identified four major forms of research: the classical or pos-itivistic, the macro-sociological, the interpretive or qualitative and, lastly, action-research. The position which we have adopted in this book borrows a great deal from action-research in terms of the processes of enquiry which we suggest. In addition, its sense of purpose draws on macro-sociological awareness. With regard to specific substantive topics, we aim to utilize the findings and methods of both posi-tivistic and interpretive approaches to research as well. However, regardless of whichever approaches to research or enquiry are adopted, there are certain basic ques-tions which have to be addressed and these form the subject of the next section.

## 2 ISSUES TO BE CONSIDERED WHEN PLANNING CLASSROOM ENQUIRY

Before any research can begin there are general decisions to be taken concerning the overall design of the study. The most significant of these design issues will be dis-cussed below.

1. *Which facet of classroom life should be investigated and why?* Identifying the issue for investigation is sometimes a problem in itself. We do not always have a particular topic in mind, but merely want to explore first and see what emerges. Dillon (1983) offers a threefold categorization of the kinds of problems that might be explored: existing problems which we can already recognize; emergent problems which we discover in our initial investigations; and potential problems which we anticipate might develop if we took a particular course of action. The issue chosen for investigation may emerge from any of these three types of problem.

2. *What data to collect and how?* This decision is very important, for it must be remembered that no data can ever wholly represent the events or phenomena which are studied. Therefore, data should be selected which are valid indicators of what it is we want to study. Judgements about which data to collect are thus cru-

cial, so that we do not distort the 'picture'. It is important to remember that what we choose to collect and how we will collect it affect what we find and, therefore, our understanding of the situation. Thus, however objectively we try to collect data, the choice of methods inevitably results in some distortion. One way of limiting this problem is to use several methods so that data on a single issue is collected in several ways. This is known as 'methodological triangulation'. However, our choice must, to a certain extent, be determined by what is feasible, given the time we can set aside to collect data and the time we can spend analysing it.

3. *How can we analyse, interpret and apply the findings?* The basic strategy is to look for patterns, for places where regularities and irregularities occur. In order to do this, the data have to be sorted using various sets of criteria. All patterns of frequencies, sequences and distributions of activity are likely to be of interest. In addition, it is also important to look for spaces and omissions – where something does not occur which might have been expected. Where examples of co-occurrence exist, they can be misinterpreted as implying a cause–effect relationship. Such judgements should be viewed with caution until further data reinforce the pattern.

The important question of interpreting findings leads us into the issue of the relationships between research and the theoretical explanations to which it can lead. We would argue that theorizing is an important and integral part of reflective teaching. This is because it represents an attempt to make sense of data and experience. It is also an opportunity to develop creative insights and an occasion to consider any discrepancies between 'what is' and 'what ought to be'. In a sense, we are all theorists in our everyday lives in the ways in which we develop hunches and use our intuition. This might be a starting-point, but, as reflective teachers, we would need to go further. In particular, we would want to generate theory relatively systematically and consciously. One way of doing this is to engage in a continuous process of data collection, classification and analysis of our own practice. The 'theory' which emerges is likely to be professionally relevant and may also offer insights with regard to other cases. This kind of theory resembles what Glaser and Strauss (1967) refer to as 'grounded' in that it is developed from and grounded in our own experiences.

Such theorizing is particularly important for conceptualizing teaching and learning processes and for developing a language with which they can be discussed and refined. Indeed it has been argued that the lack of such an appropriate conceptual vocabulary is a serious constraint on professional development (Hargreaves 1978).

Grounded theory, developed from the study of individual cases, is valuable. However, such particular 'micro' studies can only offer a partial analysis of social and educational structures, processes and practices. This is where macro-sociological models can help by offering explanations which may challenge 'commonsense' assumptions and place particular events in a wider context (for example, Apple 1982, Archer 1979, Bourdieu and Passeron 1977, Carnoy and Levin 1985, Halsey 1986, Whitty 1985, Simon 1985, 1992). Such studies may well raise more issues than they resolve, but they are likely to make an important contribution to the sense of commitment and social responsibility which we have identified as being characteristic of reflective teaching. A particularly useful insight from Mills (1959), **Primary Reading 2.1** is his observation of the way in which people often worry about 'private troubles'

without seeing how they manifest 'public issues'. There is nothing then to prevent reflective teachers from developing their own theories and conceptualizations of the relationships between education, the individual and society.

For the most part though, reflective teachers are likely to be concerned more directly with specific aspects of their practice. This calls for the use of a range of techniques for gathering data, which we will now review.

## 3   TECHNIQUES FOR COLLECTING DATA

For many teachers, busy teaching, it is difficult to collect the information we need to make the necessary day-to-day decisions and judgements, much less the information needed for anything more systematic and research-like. Our usual impressionistic data are collected sporadically and are often incomplete. They are selective and are probably based on what we have found in the past to be useful (one of the reasons it is so difficult to break out of old habits). They also tend to be subjective, because we have so few chances of discussion to help us to see things from any other viewpoints. If we could manage it, the most helpful forms of data might be:

- descriptive (rather than judgemental)
- dispassionate (not based on supposition or prejudice)
- discerning (so that they are forward-looking)
- diagnostic (so that they lead us into better action).

That data should be as valid and reliable as we can make them must be accepted, but technicalities should not blind us to some relatively simple underlying processes in research. Essentially, these boil down to looking, listening and asking, though, of course, with an unusual degree of care in selection and use.

In Figure 4.1 we use this simple distinction between 'looking, listening and asking' to produce an overview and typology of the data-gathering techniques which are introduced at various places in the book. We also distinguish between those which occur routinely in classroom life and those which must be undertaken specially. Whilst, for the most part, the former are more convenient to use, the latter often produce more structured data which may be easier to analyse.

There are many uses for such techniques and they can be applied to the issues considered in all the chapters of this book. However, an important case of this concerns methods which are particularly appropriate for gathering evidence for the assessment of pupils' learning. Such methods are *italicized* in Figure 4.1. Where **bold italic** is used, the methods are discussed in the communication chapter, Chapter 13. Where *plain italic* is used, the methods are discussed in the assessment chapter, Chapter 15. The other, more generally applicable forms of data gathering, are introduced below. References for further consideration of data-gathering issues are provided in the Notes for Further Reading section at the end of this chapter.

| | Looking | Listening | Asking |
|---|---|---|---|
| ROUTINELY OCCURRING | Participant observation (C4, 3.1, C15, 4.1) Document analysis (C4, 3.2) *Marking pupils' work* (C15, 4.5) | ***Active listening*** (C13, 2.4) | ***Questioning*** (C13, 2.2) *Setting tasks* (C15, 4.4) *Subject based tests* (C15, 4.9) |
| | | ***Discussing*** (C13, 2.3) *Oral assessment* (C15, 4.3) *Conferencing* (C15, 4.7) | |
| | *Assessing practical competence* (C15, 4.8) | | |
| SPECIALLY UNDERTAKEN | Systematic observation (C4, 3.3) Photography (C4, 3.4) | Audio recording (C4, 3.6) | Interviewing (C4, 3.7 and C15, 4.7) *Concept mapping* (C15, 4.6) Questionnaires (C4, 3.8) Sociometry (C4, 3.9) Personal constructs (C4, 3.10) Curriculum matrices (C4, 3.11) Checklists (C4, 3.12) *Examining* (C15, 4.10) *Cognitive testing* (C15, 4.9) |
| | Video recording (C4, 3.5) | | |

**Figure 4.1** *A typology of data-gathering methods and their location in this book*

## 3.1 Participant observation

Participant observation refers to a way of actively, carefully and self-consciously describing and recording what people do whilst one is, oneself, part of the action. Personal involvement is not necessarily seen as a weakness if the benefits of direct experience are complemented by care in avoiding hasty judgements. The emphasis, in the first place, should be on description. Recording is usually done in the form of field-notes which contain detailed descriptions of events, incidents or issues. Such field-notes may record individual or group activity. They may record conversations together with features of the situations in which conversations or events took place. The participant observer will also often try to discuss the situation observed to elicit the participants' interpretations of events. Thus the observer's, teacher's and the student's views will be sought, and a process of triangulation may be employed.

Although this may be a time-consuming procedure, such records can contain a wealth of information and can be applied very flexibly. Over a period of recording, it is normally possible to discern recurring themes which may lead to a greater understanding of the complex whole of a classroom environment. This technique, because it is relatively open-ended, can be particularly comprehensive and responsive to the unique features of the situation.

However, field-notes can generate an enormous quantity of wide-ranging data from which it may be difficult to draw conclusions. On studying such notes, the teacher may identify specific insights which it might prove fruitful to follow up in greater detail. The follow-up could then be in terms of a further set of more focused observations designed to test out an emerging idea. Alternatively, the teacher may decide to use another technique to provide a further source of insights.

## 3.2  Document analysis

It can be revealing to examine official documents. For instance, this is a very important aspect of policy analysis and of historical and comparative work. In such approaches, official documents will be 'interrogated' with questions to generate an analysis. Do there appear to be any hidden aims, as well as those which are explicit? What are the underlying assumptions which are embedded in the document? Which groups are likely to gain from the document? Which groups are likely to lose? Does the document reflect the influence of any particular interest group, or a combination of concerns? How has it been created? Who was consulted? Who was not? How is this reflected in its final form?

The Conservative government of the United Kingdom helpfully provided a steady flow of education documents on which this form of analysis can be used (e.g. DES 1987, DES 1992, DFEE 1996a,b, OFSTED 1995a). Those of other political parties may be just as interesting. For instance, compare the tone of successive Labour Party statements (1994, 1995) reflecting 'old' and 'new' Labour (see **Primary Reading 7.11**). Glossy designer production features, should, of course, be questioned in the same way as the content.

At a school level, examination of documents might include the brochure for parents containing introductory information. Similarly, curriculum policy documents (for example, maths, English or science policies should provide some insights to collective staff thinking – their aims, values, commitment). The contents of such documents are likely to indicate the assumptions held by their author about how young people learn, what they should learn, why, and how it should be taught. Similarly useful and indicative documents are annual school development plans.

Working papers, which might have been produced for staff meetings, may also throw light on the issues discussed during the formation of school policies and development plans. Similarly, minutes of governors' and parents' meetings, documents from community organizations, communications from the school to the community (for example, notice-boards/letters/bulletins) can also be of value to the reflective teacher.

However, it is worth remembering that even school documents tend to be relatively 'official' products and may thus gloss over internal debates which took place in the process of their creation. It is important, therefore, to read 'between the lines' and to be aware of what is not considered as well as the issues that are included. For instance, written planning devices, such as school policy documents, attempt to describe what is expected in terms of the intended curriculum. They do not, of course, reflect what is actually conveyed through the 'hidden' curriculum. Distinguishing between these two aspects is a very important task for a reflective teacher (see Chapters 5, 7 and 13).

## 3.3  Systematic observation

This is a way of observing behaviour in classrooms by using a schedule, or list of categories, of probable behaviour. The categories are chosen by the observer who has decided which ones are important to the issue in hand. Each category is then 'checked off' each time the behaviour is observed or by time sampling. The technique assumes that the teacher has already carried out sufficient preliminary, exploratory investigations to be able to decide which behaviours are relevant. Nevertheless, having devised the schedule, it can be a very quick and easy-to-administer technique for collecting information.

Information collected in this way can easily be quantified, and the frequencies and distribution patterns of the listed behaviours can be calculated. It could be used to note how teachers distribute their time among different young people; which pupils seek attention; which ones avoid it; or which ones 'get forgotten'. Another common use is to measure the possible differences in the ways teachers interact with boys and with girls.

To reduce the possibility of misrepresenting the behaviour which is seen, it is often considered advisable to use categories which can be clearly identified and involve little interpretation by the teacher (that is, low-inference categories rather than those which involve high levels of inference). An example of a low-inference category would be 'pupil talks to neighbour' rather than 'pupil helps neighbour'. Further, to make it easier to code quickly in a busy classroom situation, it is advisable to use categories which do not overlap – exclusive rather than inclusive categories. Exclusive categories would be 'teacher asks open question', 'teacher expands pupil's response', rather than 'teacher discusses'.

Such information can indicate frequencies and patterns in what happens but it cannot explain why. The technique is designed to be selective, but might distort the picture. It relies on the appropriateness of the predetermined categories on the schedule.

## 3.4  Photography

Recording what happens inside a classroom, by any of the next three techniques, provides a very valuable source of information, for they 'fix' events which are so fleeting. This is particularly valuable because no one can have ears and eyes everywhere and even the most alert of teachers misses a great deal of what goes on.

Photography is a relatively unobtrusive form of visual recording, especially if fast film (with a high ASA/ISO rating) is used so that flash is not needed. Photography, of course, only captures frames of action rather than the sequence of action itself, though stop-frame techniques can overcome this to some extent (Adelman and Walker 1975). A particular advantage is the ease of use of photographs once they are developed. They can provide an excellent basis for discussion with others.

## 3.5  Video-recording

Video-recording is particularly helpful in providing contextual information in class-rooms and in capturing non-verbal behaviour as well as some speech. Sampling selections must be made, and, before filming, it is important to think through exactly what is required. The presence of cameras is likely to affect some pupils and may dis-tort the normality of the classroom, but, if done periodically, the novelty usually soon wears off. Modern video-cameras, with automatic focusing and low-light adjustment facilities, make videoing a relatively easy task.

This is a convenient and very powerful form of data. The quality of the sound-track is usually the weakest point.

## 3.6  Audio-recording

Audio-recording of a class discussion is a common and simple procedure. However, tape recorders often only pick up a few of the students, or perhaps only the teacher's voice. Nevertheless, the procedure can provide excellent information about the amount, type and distribution of teacher talk – a very worthwhile, though often salu-tary experience. It could also be useful for oral assessment (see Chapter 15, Section 4.3).

Recording small groups or pairs is technically easier if background noise can be controlled and can similarly provide valuable insights into the language strategies used and into social dynamics. Of course, the presence of a recorder may affect some students – either to put on a performance or to clam up. Time could be allowed for familiarization and discussion of the purposes of the activity.

A radio-microphone or portable recorder could also be worn by an individual teacher or pupil for a period of time. The main advantage of this is that the quality of the recording is frequently excellent.

It must be remembered that it takes time to play back tapes: at least three times the length of the recording is often needed to study effectively and to distinguish who said what. Still more time will be needed for transcription.

Photography, video- and audio-recording capture and record what is said or done. They can therefore be used to produce high quality descriptive data, leaving us to analyse and infer our own explanations. We could also discuss them with the partici-pants and thus gain insights into their interpretations of the same events or we could discuss them with other colleagues. Each of these uses is likely to make a powerful contribution to reflection.

## 3.7  Interviews

Interviews are structured or semi-structured discussions which can be used to find out what people think or do, and why. The interviewer can explore and negotiate under-standings because of the possibility of immediate feedback and follow-up. However, because of the person-to-person situation, some people may feel threatened – by the interviewer or, if it is a group interview, by other participants. The success of this tech-nique of data collection rests heavily on the relationship established and on the way in which the event is conducted. Interviews can be used with varying degrees of formality and structure. The term 'interview' is usually reserved for the more formal, more structured one-to-one situations. As the event becomes more informal and less structured, it may be more appropriately seen in terms of a 'conference' or discussion (see also Chapter 15, Section 4.7 on conferencing and action planning).

## 3.8 Questionnaires

This form of data collection uses questions and statements to stimulate responses to set items. Questionnaires are usually given to the respondents to fill in (which, therefore, demands a certain level of reading and writing skill). The technique can be used for collecting factual information as well as opinions. Hence, it may provide data about what people do or think, and also why.

The format of a questionnaire can be closed (e.g. asking for specific data or yes/no responses) or open (e.g. asking for general and discursive responses). Open forms of response encourage relatively free answers which have the advantage of enabling the respondent to express their thoughts and priorities in their own way. However, it also makes greater demands on the respondents' writing abilities and poses the problem of how to categorize a wide range of replies which such an item may well evoke.

The wording and design of questionnaires is important, so that the respondents do not misunderstand, or are led to respond in any particular way. For example, some words are emotive and can exaggerate responses. Sometimes people react differently to a positive statement compared to a negative statement. Questionnaires can be filled in independently of the teacher and thus not interrupt the flow of teaching time. On the other hand, they could be completed through discussion with individual students.

Questionnaires can be useful in a variety of ways, such as to provide information to include on school records. They can be used to try to discover how respondents feel about aspects of classroom life: for example, for feedback on a particular lesson or topic of work. Questionnaires can also be used for evaluative purposes at the end of a unit of work. They encourage students to reflect on their recent learning experiences and to comment on them by answering specific questions to focus their response. The answers may be required as written sentences, by ticking boxes, or by ringing a word/number on a rating scale (e.g. hard/quite hard/just right/easy, or, from 'exciting' 5-4-3-2-1 'boring').

## 3.9 Sociometry

Sociometric techniques have been developed to help students and teachers gain insights into friendship patterns (Evans 1962). The basic procedure is to ask young people, in confidence, to name three pupils from their class with whom they would like to work or socialize. This can also, with care, be extended to ask pupils to identify anyone with whom they would not like to work or socialize. The friendship groupings which emerge from an analysis of these choices as a whole can then be represented in diagrammatic form, known as a sociogram. Such representations provide a visual display of social relationships: mutual pairs and groups (where choices are reciprocated), clusters of friends (though not all with reciprocated choices); isolates and even rejectees.

However, this technique does not tell the whole story. In particular, it provides a static picture of friendships, and given the dynamic nature of the social relationships of some students, this needs to be borne in mind. Nevertheless, the data are structured and descriptive and can provide a starting point for analysing further aspects of relationships between students.

## 3.10 Personal constructs

This is a structured method of indirectly finding out about the way people think and feel about each other. Personal constructs are evident in our thinking when, for example, we appraise or comment on pupils. Using a technique called 'triadic elicitation' (finding distinguishing criteria within a group of three) it is possible to reveal the constructs we are using. You can do this yourself or work with a colleague whom you ask to guide you through the process.

For instance, if you wanted to investigate the constructs you have about your pupils you would make name cards for each pupil in the class, then, successively, draw three names. For each group of three, you should identify which two are most alike, and then explain in what way the two are similar and how they differ from the third. In this way it is possible to elicit relatively instinctive reactions and the actual 'bi-polar constructs', or criteria, which we use. Such a procedure is usually more effective than asking, in the abstract, what constructs we think we might use to distinguish students. Having obtained such a list, it is then possible to classify the constructs – for example, those which are intellectual, affective, physical or social.

The patterns which may emerge could indicate underlying assumptions that the teacher has about what school is for and how he or she perceives pupils. However, construct elicitation only provides information which the respondents choose to give. It may provide information about what respondents say they feel, but, in itself is unlikely to indicate why they feel it or to describe what they actually do.

This method can be used to investigate our view of other aspects of the work – for example our view of different roles and responsibilities amongst school staff, different parts of the curriculum. Just create a new set of cards, with different labels, to use for your triadic elicitation.

## 3.11 Curriculum matrices

Different forms of matrix can be used for both planning and review purposes. Given the complexity of modern curriculum planning, the two-dimensional character of matrices gives them enormous utility, particularly where coherence, progression and interrelation of provision is necessary.

For instance, a matrix could be used be used for subject and classroom planning purposes, for locating units for study and organizing resources. Matrixes could also be used to review balance, breadth, coherence and progression amongst the components of the curriculum – for example, in terms of concepts, knowledge, skills and attitudes.

Matrices are often enormously useful to represent relationships and to aid planning and review. However, it is vital that the two axes are appropriately conceptualized. Additionally, one must always bear in mind that educational provision cannot often, in reality, be reduced to two simple dimensions.

## 3.12 Checklists

Checklists provide a simple and practical form of record which has been tried and tested by generations of teachers. Indeed, checklists have been developed in sophisticated ways to support a variety of teaching concerns such as records of pupils' basic skills, stages in curriculum planning or procedures in assessment.

Indeed, checklists are both simple to implement and practical to use. Targets, competencies or other attainments can be clearly listed and ticks, crosses or other symbol systems can be used to record students' achievements against these criteria. However, judgements should be checked with evidence before a checklist is completed. Sometimes checklists are completed relatively impressionistically, which may not always produce an accurate record.

The process of devising a checklist can also be helpful in clarifying aims, so that they can be itemized and shared with others.

## CONCLUSION

This chapter has provided a brief introduction to some of the theoretical issues and practical techniques of undertaking classroom research as reflective teachers. We would advise readers to follow up other more detailed references, such as those given below. However, 'doing research' is not just about collecting data. The next stage is to be able to interpret the data and to design further investigations to refine our understandings. We need to be able to relate our findings to those of others and to consider our results in the context of the current debates about educational issues. Finally, as reflective teachers and collaborating professionals, we need to be able to turn our data into action and articulate to others what we are doing, and why.

Part 2 of this book is designed to help to put this reflection into practice.

### Notes for further reading

These notes are more extensive than those provided for some other chapters. It is important that suggestions on methodology are followed up to provide detailed information on techniques prior to their use. See also Chapter 3 of Primary Readings.

Gathering information about the existing state of knowledge on educational issues is obviously important. Databases, abstracts, journals and research indices are available, often on CD Rom, or through the internet.

British Education Index (BEI)
University of Leeds

Register of Educational Research in the United Kingdom
National Foundation for Educational Research

Educational Resources Information Centre (ERIC)
United States Department of Education

One easy way of accessing hundreds of sources of educational information on the World Wide Web is through the BUBL Information Service. The WWW address is:

http://www. bubl. bath. ac. uk/BUBL/education. html/

See, for instance:

Department for Education and Employment:

> http://www. open. gov. uk/dfee/

Guide to Education and Training in Scotland:

> http://www. ed. ac. uk/~riu/GETS/

Rapid, the database of the Economic and Social Research Council:

> http://edina. ed. ac. uk/rapid/

Ask-ERIC, a site which makes it possible to question some US researchers and access this very important database:

> http://ericir. syr. edu/Eric/

Selections from the *Times Educational Supplement* are now available on-line:

> http://www. tes. co. uk/

Many university education departments use the World Wide Web to provide excellent introductions of what they have to offer, such as research training or particular research foci. For an example, you can see training opportunities and new developments on learning, culture and organizations at Bristol University's School of Education site, see:

> http://www. brist. ac. uk/Depts/Education/

If you want to find out more about educational research, the major UK association is the British Educational Research Association (BERA):

> http://www. sbu. ac. uk/~bera/

The Collaborative Action Research Network (CARN) has a particular emphasis on classroom-based research and professional development activity. It has strong international links:

> http://www. uea. ac. uk. care. carn/

For more complete advice on these rapidly evolving sources of information consult your librarian.

For **statistical data on education** in the UK see the latest edition of the sources below. The first is exceptionally well presented and comprehensive for all countries in the UK.

Steedman, J. and MacKinnon, D. (1991)
*The Education Factfile,*
London: Hodder and Stoughton.

Government Statistical Service
*Statistical Bulletin,* (published monthly)
*Education Statistics for the United Kingdom,* (published annually)
London: DFEE.

For **general overviews and discussion of the most common research methods** used in the study of education, see:

Cohen, L. and Manion, L. (1990)
*Research Methods in Education (Third Edition),*
London: Croom Helm.

Hitchcock, G. and Hughes, D. (1995)
*Research and the Teacher: A Qualitative Introduction to School-Based Research,*
London: Routledge.

To focus thinking on important **research issues** see:

Hammersley, M. (1986)
*Controversies in Classroom Research,*
Milton Keynes: Open University Press.

Shipman, M. (ed.) (1985)
*Educational Research: Principles, Policies and Practice,*
London: Falmer Press.

Walford, G. (1991)
*Doing Educational Research,*
London: Routledge.

**The classical 'scientific' research tradition** is discussed in:

Popper, K. R. (1968)
*The Logic of Scientific Discovery,*
London: Hutchinson.

For useful guides to the application of this approach in education see:

Borg, W. R. (1981)
*Applying Educational Research: A Practical Guide for Teachers,*
New York: Longman.

Cohen, L. (1976)
*Educational Research in Classrooms and Schools: A Manual of Materials and Methods,*
London: Harper & Row.

An excellent and extensive series of pamphlets on particular methods is provided by:

*Rediguides,*
Nottingham University School of Education.

Systematic observation is particularly well covered by:

Croll, P. (1986)
*Systematic Classroom Observation,*
London: Falmer Press.

**Statistical analysis** would be helped by books such as:

Cohen, L. and Holliday, M. (1979)
*Statistics for Education,*
London: Harper & Row.

Anderson, A. J. B. (1989)
*A First Course in Statistics,*
London: Routledge.

The methods which are appropriate to **macro-sociological approaches** are, in one way, properly seen as being those involved in conceptualizing the links between individuals, classroom practices and wider social structures. The classic book is:

Mills, C. W. (1959)
*The Sociological Imagination,*
New York: Oxford University Press.                     ▢ **Primary Reading 2. 1**

For more recent examples of sociological, historical and comparative work respectively, see:

Whitty, G. (1985)
*Sociology and School Knowledge,*
London: Methuen.

Green, A. (1990)
*Education and State Formation,*
London: Macmillan.

Combs, P. H. (1985)
*The World Crisis in Education: The View from the Eighties,*
Oxford: Oxford University Press.

A rather different approach to macro-sociology issues is through the collection of **survey** data. A book for guidance in this method is:

Fink, A. and Kosecoff, J. (1986)
*How to Conduct Surveys: A Step by Step Guide,*
London: Sage.

An excellent example of work using a survey approach are:

Halsey, A. H., Heath, A. F. and Ridge, J. M. (1980)
*Origins and Destinations,*
Oxford: Oxford University Press.

**Interpretive research** has a long history. A general collection of papers, in which the major methodological issues are discussed, is:

Burgess, R. G. (ed.) (1982)
*Field Research: A Sourcebook and Field Manual,*
London: Allen & Unwin.

Further discussions of these issues can be found in:

Burgess, R. G. (1984)
*In the Field: An Introduction to Field Research,*
London: Allen and Unwin.

Hammersley, M. and Atkinson, P. (1984)
*Ethnography: Principles in Practice,*
London: Tavistock.

For a feminst approach to ethnography, see:

Ely, M. (1990)
*Doing Qualitative Research: Circles within Circles,*
London: Falmer Press.

**Analysis** can be a particular problem, but see the first few chapters of:

Strauss, A. and Corbin, J. (1990)
*Basics of Qualitative Research,*
New York: SAGE.

For a book on **qualitative methods** which was specially written for teachers who want to engage in their own studies:

Woods, P. (1986)
*Inside Schools,*
London: Routledge & Kegan Paul.

For the study of language, see:

Edwards, A. D. and Westgate, D. P. G. (1987)
*Investigating Classroom Talk,*
London: Falmer Press.

The **action research approach** is introduced in **Primary Readings** 3. 1, 3. 2, 3. 3 and 3. 4. There are also many good books, each of which provides advice on the use of a variety of methods:

Hopkins, D. (1986)
*A Teacher's Guide to Classroom Research,*
Milton Keynes: Open University Press.

Altrichter, H., Posch, P. and Somekh, B. (1993)
*Teachers Investigate their Work: An Introduction to the Methods of Action Research,*
London: Routledge.

Walker, R. (1986)
*Doing Research: A Handbook for Teachers,*
London: Routledge.

Kemmis, S. and McTaggert, R (1981)
*The Action Research Planner,*
Victoria: Deakin University.

For guidance on **the principles and design of an action research study** for classroom or school use:

Elliott, J. (1991)
*Action Research for Educational Change,*
Milton Keynes: Open University Press.

McNiff, J. (1988)
*Action Research: Principles and Practice,*
London: Routledge.

Winter, R. (1989)
*Learning From Experience: Principles and Practice in Action-Research,*
London: Falmer.

Illustrations of **action-research studies** are becoming more easily available. See for instance:

Hustler, D., Cassidy, T. and Cuff, T. (eds) (1986)
*Action Research in Schools and Classrooms,*
London: Allen & Unwin.

Nixon, J. (ed.) (1981)
*A Teachers' Guide to Action Research,*
London: Grant McIntyre.

Vulliamy, G. and Webb. R. (1992)
*Teacher Research and Special Educational Needs,*
London: David Fulton.

# BEING A REFLECTIVE TEACHER

# CHAPTER 5

# How is the school organized?

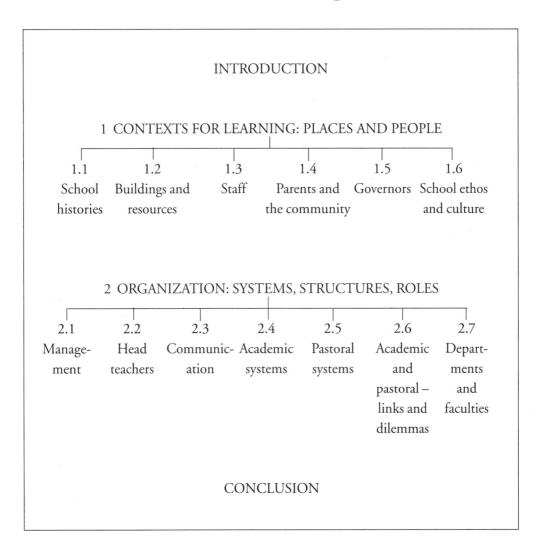

INTRODUCTION

1 CONTEXTS FOR LEARNING: PLACES AND PEOPLE

| 1.1 | 1.2 | 1.3 | 1.4 | 1.5 | 1.6 |
|---|---|---|---|---|---|
| School histories | Buildings and resources | Staff | Parents and the community | Governors | School ethos and culture |

2 ORGANIZATION: SYSTEMS, STRUCTURES, ROLES

| 2.1 | 2.2 | 2.3 | 2.4 | 2.5 | 2.6 | 2.7 |
|---|---|---|---|---|---|---|
| Manage-ment | Head teachers | Communic-ation | Academic systems | Pastoral systems | Academic and pastoral – links and dilemmas | Depart-ments and faculties |

CONCLUSION

## INTRODUCTION

Teachers are employed to teach: to make sure that pupils learn, make progress, achieve. Every day teachers make decisions about how to teach; but what happens in lessons is affected by the wider context outside the classroom. In this chapter we focus on that context, on the whole school and its community.

As we saw in Chapter 2, the ERA (1988) produced an enormous increase in the significance of schools as free-standing and self-managed organizations. From the professional perspective, the significance of schools as organizations is very strong. Twenty years of evidence indicates that variation in the internal policies and practices of schools does influence educational effectiveness, and more recently there has been a move to look carefully at processes for bringing about and measuring school improvement (Gray and Wilcox 1995, Sammons and Nuttall 1992). These enquiries tell us that positive educational developments are almost impossible to sustain without leadership, teamwork and coherent planning at an institutional level (Hargreaves and Hopkins 1991). Roger and Richardson (1985) characterize a 'self-evaluating school' as follows:

> It is the school which is aware of the pressures of accountability being experienced in education yet is concerned to maintain and advance its professionalism, not least in the area of autonomy of decision-making. It is a school which sees itself as having many relationships with its employers, its community and particularly its clients. These relationships . . . are susceptible to improvement. It is a school in which the staff see themselves as part of a collaborative venture aimed at the purposeful education of children. . . . It is a school which also recognizes that it may lack experience and expertise in particular areas and is therefore prepared to be open to advice and information from outside agencies. It is a school which is prepared to devote precious time and energy to reflective activities. . . . Above all, it is the school which has a genuine desire to find out about itself. (1985, pp. 20–21)

This view is consistent with the position which we are advocating in the present book but we have to recognize that not all schools fit the model which Roger and Richardson suggest. In fact, in many cases the schools in which reflective teachers find themselves may be far more static, 'routinized' and locked into 'taken-for-granted' conventions. We deal with issues of effectiveness and school improvement in more detail in Chapter 16. This chapter with its associated practical activities is intended to:

- clarify the context in which secondary schools now find themselves
- assist reflective teachers to gather and analyse information about the various strands which together interact and make up the complex organization of the secondary school.

## 1    CONTEXTS FOR LEARNING: PLACES AND PEOPLE

We begin by looking briefly at the historical development of secondary education in this country. This is followed by a closer look at the school, the people in it and the community it serves. The intention is to 'place' your school in this historical, geographical and social context and to consider what impact this has on how the school operates, sees itself and presents itself.

## 1.1   School histories

Picking out a thread from Chapter 2 we will start with the tripartite system, introduced as a result of the Education Act 1944, and some of the assumptions on which it was based. The creation of grammar, technical and secondary modern schools indicated that 'ability' was seen as the most important variable in determining the kind of education that was most suited to any pupil and it was thought that ability could be reliably and validly tested at age 11. There was also the assumption that full-time education beyond the statutory school-leaving age was likely to be appropriate only for the small number with more academic dispositions. In effect, as Lowe (1989) argues, the differences between the curricula of the three kinds of schools were not as different as might have been expected. So strong was the status of the grammar schools that relatively few technical high schools were established. Secondary modern schools had low status and the vocational and pupil-centred curricula they tried to develop were not accepted as having widespread value. (At the end of the century we are still grappling with these issues as you will see in Chapter 6.)

During the 1960s the reliability and validity of selection at 11-plus, and the idea that some notion of general ability determined potential achievement in all curriculum areas, was increasingly disputed. It was argued that pupils had a range of aptitudes and might achieve a great deal in some subjects while making only modest progress in others; also that aptitude changed over time and selection at 11 did not allow for those whose potential became apparent later. Worse, that potential might never be recognized. Identifying the majority of the population as 'failures' at 11 resulted in low self-esteem and lack of interest in school; the 11-plus contributed to under-achievement; its predictions became self-fulfilling prophecies. Underlying all this was a concern about the impact of selection on the life chances of those, mostly working-class, pupils who attended secondary modern schools and about the resulting waste of talent. These concerns led gradually to the introduction of comprehensive schools.

The first comprehensives in the 1960s were purpose built and established alongside existing secondary modern and grammar and technical high schools. In 1966 comprehensive education became national policy and through the 1970s secondary provision in LEAs was reorganized so that most or all of their schools became comprehensive. However, the independent sector continued to exert an influence on state provision in the UK, especially in England. This effect was intensified in 1975 when a Labour government removed the category of 'direct grant' under which many independent day schools had (while retaining selection) come into the LEA state sector. Faced with the prospect of having to become comprehensive, the majority returned to the private sector. With their reputations for long-established 'traditions' and academic excellence, independent schools competed for the most able (and affluent) pupils.

By 1980, 80 per cent of the pupils in state secondary education were in comprehensive schools. These years of change, however, delivered a very mixed picture of provision across the different parts of the UK. Academic selection was never abandoned in Northern Ireland; in contrast, Scottish secondary education is fully comprehensive; Wales had no secondary schools which operate selection by ability and no grammar schools. In some English LEAs, isolated grammar schools (mainly in urban areas and with middle-class catchment areas) managed to resist reorganization and the ideal of universal access to socially mixed, democratically accountable schools, giving equal value to all learners and all forms of learning proved difficult to achieve.

During the late 1980s a new belief in the power of market forces to 'raise standards' developed (Chubb and Moe 1990) and 1993 legislation to provide 'choice and diversity', positioned parents as 'consumers' of education and provided for specialist, centrally funded City Technology Colleges (see also Chapter 2, Section 1.3). The Assisted Places Scheme, which provided support to parents paying fees to independent schools, was also expanded before being ended by the new Labour government which took office in 1997. In England at the start of 1997, there were still 160 grammar schools and Conservative party policy was for 'a grammar school in every town'.

Contrasts in provision between urban and rural, inner city and shire counties became increasingly marked in the 1990s, with middle-class parents in particular exercising market choice. For example, the following figures suggest the impact of the market on 11-year-olds in London. Of some 20,000 children, 10 per cent went to twenty-six academically selective fee-paying schools, 15 per cent went to twenty-three schools which took only the occasional pupil from the top 25 per cent of the ability range. Only 35 per cent went to schools which could be described as having a broadly balanced intake (Newsam, 1996).

Margaret Maden *(TES,* 10 May 1996) characterized schools at the extremes of secondary provision:

> At one end . . . is the boys' 'comprehensive' which enrols pupils at 11, few of whom have a reading age near their chronological age, many of whom have been unable to gain admittance to the schools nearest to their home and most of whom are black. . . . It is highly probable that throughout the school year there are further enrolments – of the recently-arrived homeless, of immigrants and of those excluded from other schools. At 16, more than 20 per cent of the pupils have achieved no GCSE grades at all, compared to a national average of 8 per cent. At the other end . . . is the mixed comprehensive which has opted out of its LEA and made use of its grant-maintained status so it can select up to 50 per cent of its intake at 11. On the basis of a series of tests (in verbal reasoning, non-verbal reasoning and maths) which are skewed towards identifying the top 10 per cent of the age cohort (not simply the top 25 per cent) the school is already 'super-selective'. The other half of the intake is drawn from the school's mainly middle-class catchment area, with priority given to siblings of present pupils and to the children of staff. It is frequently oversubscribed – 1,200 applications for 250 places.

In 1996 a Conservative government White Paper proposed the gradual introduction of greater selection through to the end of the century. New grammar schools were to be established; existing schools could create selective streams. Grant-maintained schools could select up to 50 per cent of their intake; specialist schools up to 30 per cent. All schools would be required by law to vote annually on whether to introduce more selection, although changing admissions criteria would be subject to the consent of the LEA. This enthusiasm for selection reflected opinions of some social commentators outside education who argued that 'grammar schools and grammar school streams in comprehensives need to be revived in order to attract members of the middle class back to the state system' (Hutton 1995). However, other evidence suggests less dissatisfaction with comprehensive education. *Half Way There* (Benn and Simon 1970) is an account of the early years of comprehensive schools. Between 1993 and 1994 Caroline Benn and Clyde Chitty returned to the subject and surveyed 1,560 schools and colleges (35 per cent of all secondary institutions) collecting evidence on a variety of topics. Among their findings is that comprehensive schools in the 1990s were more socially mixed than those of the 1960s. In 1968 none of the schools in the study had a mainly middle-class intake; less than half could be described as socially mixed. In 1994 two-thirds were socially mixed and 6 per cent mainly middle class. The authors suggest that, contrary to the frequently voiced view, there was widespread support for comprehensive education among the majority of parents, teachers and communities . In addition, the majority of schools exhibited little enthusiasm for selection; relatively few chose to take advantage of the 'permissions to select' successively offered by government from 1979. Tellingly, the research revealed the detrimental effect on the majority of that minority of schools which chose to select. Where a school practised selection other schools in the vicinity experienced bad effects: distortion in their social and attainment intakes, falling numbers, worse staying-on rates and depressed examination results. Comprehensive education, the research argues, is not compatible with the existence of an open market (Benn and Chitty 1996). The Labour Party has pledged to end the assisted places scheme but is wary of policies to strengthen comprehensive education where these can be construed as a reduction of parental choice. However, the social mix of pupils attending a school is important because where there is a significant body of more motivated and demanding pupils (and parents) teachers tend to have higher expectations, peer culture is often influenced positively and pupil performance improves. Choices by individuals thus certainly impact on the opportunites and experiences of others.

The intake of a school depends on both the demand for admission and on the school's admissions criteria. Most LEA schools have criteria that ensure that most pupils live close to the school – within its catchment area. Grant-maintained schools can agree their own criteria with the Secretary of State for Education. Denominational church schools can also apply criteria of their own. Unless a school is designated 'selective' on some basis (general academic ability, musical talent, technological promise) it should not have 'selective' criteria or entrance tests. However, where a school is over-subscribed decisions have to be made on some basis. In 1993 a government circular advised against using interviews with parents and pupils as a basis for controlling admissions, but the practice is not illegal and many popular schools interview all applicants. Admissions criteria are frequently so vague as to be capable of interpretation as required. For instance, 'the aims, attitudes, values and expectations of the parents and the boy are in harmony with those of the school', or 'the governing body may, in exceptional circumstances, refuse admission to any applicant if, in its view, to admit that pupil would be to prejudice the fulfilment of the school's aims. . . .' Parents applying to such schools report feeling that they are subject to selection as much as their child. Schools are accused of favouring middle-class children or those with parents who have particular skills, contacts or prestige. Children who have a history of deviance or disruption, who might present a drain on resources or adversely affect the school's performance statistics are, it is claimed, not welcomed.

See Dale 1996, **Primary Reading 15.5** for an analysis of how these various factors create a 'multiplier effect' to differentiate schools within our communities.

This brief history indicates how much our schools are a product of philosophical, ideological, political, social beliefs about what education is for. As a teacher (perhaps as a parent, certainly as a voter and tax-payer) you will work out where you stand in all this, what your values are. More immediately, Practical Activity 5.1 asks you to focus on the school you are in. As well as tracing its history you will want to consider other factors: is it single-sex or co-educational? What age range does it serve? 11–16? 11–18? LEAs' ideas about how secondary education should be organized have been varied and changing. Some authorities favoured Middle schools (with the middle years variously defined). In some authorities there has been a move to sixth form colleges and to a greater role for colleges of further education; competition between these and 11–18 schools has sometimes been intense.

## Practical activity 5.1

*Aim:* To compile information about the school with particular emphasis on its history and development to the present.

*Method:* Use as many sources of information as are appropriate to build up a history of the school. For instance check the school library; ask for up-to-date documents such as the school prospectus.

Ask about the admissions criteria. How are these operated?

*Follow-up:* Think about the relationship between the history you have discovered and what you see of the school today. Has the school experienced much change? How conscious is the school of its past? Does the past have any noticeable impact on the present?

What is the social mix in the school? What is the relationship between your school and others in the area? Find out how staff and pupils feel about the school. What do parents think of it?

## 1.2 Buildings and resources

The environment for learning which a school creates has a noticeable impact on attitudes, behaviour and achievement. In this section you will find a number of Practical Activities which will help you to explore this area and focus your thinking about it.

## The use of buildings and grounds

Decisions about how to teach are frequently affected by the size, shape and location, even availability of teaching areas. Few schools will tell you that everything is ideal. Most heads, deputies, heads of departments or faculties can produce ideas and plans for how they would like things changed in order to teach more effectively. Many schools built in the last thirty years were designed with scant input from educators. Trends in education-related design – separate classrooms, open plan classrooms, linked suites of rooms, separate buildings on a campus – have come and gone. Some schools are in older buildings, some have split sites. Frequently the physical limitations of a building force schools or individual teachers to compromise how they would like to teach.

As important is the way in which the design of the school affects how people move around in it; where pupils can gather together socially, where staff can meet. The Practical Activity which follows will help you to consider these and other aspects of the school you are in.

## Practical activity 5.2

*Aim:* To consider the school as an environment for teaching and learning

*Method:* Get hold of (or make) a plan of the school building and grounds. Look carefully at the way the school is using the space for different purposes. (You might like to colour code the map – devise your own key).

1. Teaching areas
Where does teaching happen? Are there specialist areas for different activities, subjects or groups of subjects? How do these areas relate to each other? Look at the size and shape of teaching spaces. What kind of teaching and learning do they seem to have been designed for? How is the school using the space? How are classrooms furnished? How is the furniture arranged for teaching? How are resources made available to pupils? How are the outside areas used?

2. Non-teaching areas
Mark on the plan all the areas not directly used for teaching. What are these areas used for? Where are they located in relation to teaching areas? Are there any areas which are double-purpose – used sometimes for teaching? Where are the social areas? How have you categorized the library?

3. Circulation areas
How do people move around the space? How much movement is there? When do people move? Are there any trouble spots?

*Follow-up:* Ask staff in your subject area how their teaching is affected by the physical environment. Have they made any adaptations? What changes would they make if they were given the chance?

Find out, if you can, whether the school has a building plan. What are the priorities for development?

Over a period observe how pupils and staff use and react to the space. Reflect on how the space is enabling or impeding learning.

How does the way the building is used reflect the school's approach to teaching and learning?

### The appearance and atmosphere of the buildings and grounds

An early research study in school effectiveness (Rutter et al 1979) found 'a significant association between good pupil behaviour and good maintenance of decorations and care of the building generally'.

Maintenance of the building features in every school budget and often the funding available is not sufficient to do all a school might wish. Nevertheless most schools consciously pay attention to the environment and some give it a specific focus. For instance, the *Schools Make a Difference* project (Myers 1996) involved all the secondary schools in Hammersmith and Fulham, London. One group of schools in the project decided to concentrate their research on improving the learning environment. Pupils, staff and parents made proposals for how money allocated should be spent. As a result of this consultation the schools were involved in a range of activities: creating flexible learning centres, improving display areas for pupils' work, refurbishing entrance areas, corridors and pupil toilets, creating pupil study and common room facilities, carpeting corridors, staircases and classrooms, providing benches and litterbins for the playground and lockers for pupils. The improvements were completed as quickly as possible so that pupils could see that their ideas were being implemented. The aim was to affect pupil morale and self-esteem, both of which can contribute to achievement.

### Practical activity 5.3

*Aim:* To consider the impression created by the school's environment and the attitude of staff and pupils to the environment.

*Method:* Try to experience the school as a stranger. What impression does the entrance make? Walk around the school and the grounds; look into the teaching areas, the social areas, the toilets. What does it look like? What does it smell like? How do pupils and staff treat the environment? What kinds of behaviour are encouraged or discouraged?

Find out whether the school is or has been involved in any project to improve the environment. Why did they choose to do this?

Ask some pupils what they think of their surroundings. How does the environment affect them – if at all? What would they improve if they could?

*Follow-up:* Consider what you have discovered. Does it seem to support the findings of the Rutter *et al.* research quoted above? What would you improve first if you could?

### Resources

As we saw in Chapter 2, Section 1.3, resource provision varies markedly between schools. This happens for a number of reasons: schools are funded differently; they have different priorities for the funds available ; they have access to differential funding – for example, government initiatives, sponsorship, parental fund-raising.

Differential funding clearly has a huge impact on the balance of staff expertise, class size and the quantity and quality of learning resources available for pupils and teachers. Government initiatives encouraging schools to compete for additional funding have been criticized as unfair – giving money to the few (often those schools already doing well) rather than to all schools which need it. In connection with the Technology School Initiative, for instance, Professor Alan Smithers, director of the centre for education and employment research at Brunel University, drew attention to schools where technology was being taught in sub-standard facilities. 'Technology is part of the core curriculum of Key Stage 4, yet many schools are grossly underprovided in terms of accommodation, teachers, technological support and materials' (*TES*, 7 June 1996).

Spending on books and learning resources is also very varied. A 1996 survey by Book Trust suggested that secondary schools were spending less than half of what is needed to ensure an adequate supply for learners. A recommended figure for 'good' provision was £67 per pupil, for 'adequate' provision, £56. The report records schools' awareness of the gap between what they feel they should be spending and what they can afford. It suggests that, with LMS, governors may have to cut book spending to build up contingency funds.

## Practical activity 5.4

*Aim:* To review the overall resourcing of learning in the school.

*Method:* Find out where computers are situated in the school. What are they used for? Who can have access to them?

Look at the provision of facilities and equipment in the specialist areas featured in the DFEE initiative – technology, science, languages, mathematics.

Look at the provision in other areas, e.g. PE, art, music, English, history.

You may want to focus on provision in your own subject area but try to get some comparison with other curriculum areas.

Look at the books and resources in your subject area. Visit the library and if possible talk to the person in charge about how it is funded.

*Follow-up:* Are some areas better equipped than others? Try to discover how this has happened. Is there a school plan for development? How does provision in your school compare with other schools in the area?

Does your school receive sponsorship of any kind? Do parents contribute to funds for resources?

What is your view of the DFEE Specialist Schools Initiative?

## 1.3 Staff

Members of staff have a designated role in the hierarchy and organization of a school (we will be looking at this in more detail in Section 2 of this chapter). However, the informal networks within a staff group are very significant and influence schools in different ways. How long a teacher has been in a school, out-of-school relationships, access to the head, who gets on with whom – all have their effect. A teacher acting as co-ordinator in a school improvement project reported that the real reason the project was succeeding was that its aims had been endorsed by a group of teachers who lunched at the local pub every Friday. They were not senior staff but they were opinion-formers and no innovation would be accepted without their say-so (Hopkins and Ainscow 1994). Paechter (1995), who investigated co-operation between teachers in different subject areas for GCSE, says 'When we go into a school and the teachers ask which subjects it will work for, the first question to ask is "Who do you drink coffee with in the staff room?" It works best where there is a good relationship between the teachers.' This cross-subject project revealed how much teachers can be locked into their own subject groups.

> Teachers learn the power balance of their own departments – but encounter problems working with other subject teams; as well as factors associated with the specific academic discipline and how it is taught. Teachers did not have access to each other's implicit subcultural understandings of progression and differentiation. (Paechter 1995)

A staff-room culture can exert considerable influence on the school and on individual teachers. It is possible to identify 'pressures' to do certain things and 'constraints' not to do certain things. If a teacher or student teacher is accepted into a staff (or departmental) group then a considerable source of support and advice is provided. However, there may be pressure to conform in such things as dress, speech, opinions and practice. Constraints may take the form of a withdrawal of support and a questioning of membership if conformity is not observed. Sometimes then a coherent culture can be oppressive and can even stifle innovation rather than underpin constructive teamwork.

As we saw in Chapter 2, the notion of 'directed time' for which teachers are contracted has raised issues related to the relative priority given to, for instance, meetings, staff development and extra-curricular activities. In some schools there has been a reduction in extra-curricular activities available for pupils. However, many staff ('directed' or not) still maintain a great variety of extra-curricular provision and attest to the value this has for their relationship with their pupils.

It is important to remember that the staff of a secondary school is made up of more than just teachers; equally significant are the technical support staff in laboratories, workshops, library, resources and reprographics; the administrators and secretaries; the school nurse, school meals supervisory assistants ('dinner ladies'), the caretakers, cleaners, ground staff; etc. And there will be a number of people from outside agencies, for instance educational welfare officers, educational psychologists, advisers, who work regularly in the school. There are good reasons for doing everything one can to understand the roles, work experience and perspectives of other people who work for or are associated with the school.

## Practical activity 5.5

*Aim:* To increase familiarity with composition of the school staff and to consider informal networks within the staff.

*Method:* If possible obtain a list of staff. Note the balance between teaching and non-teaching staff. Get to know the non-teaching staff that you have most contact with and become familiar with their roles and routines. Find out about people from outside agencies who work with the school. What is their role?

Discover which of the staff are involved with extra-curricular activities. What is the range of activities offered? Where and when do these occur? Is extra-curricular work part of the teaching contract or is it undertaken as a voluntary activity?

Do colleagues go into each other's lessons to observe, collaborate on the improvement of teaching and learning? Is there any form of collaborative/team teaching?

Observe the informal network of contact among the staff. Can you identify opinion-formers? Who exerts influence? What are the networks among teachers in your subject area? Where are the cross-subject alliances?

*Follow-up:* Consider how all this affects the school as an organization.

## Practical activity 5.6

*Aim:* To monitor the support, pressure and constraint which results from your relationships with other staff.

*Method:* One appropriate way to collect data on this is by keeping a private diary over a period of time. Use this to focus the issue of your relationships when making entries. After a period, reflection on the diary, your account and memories of various incidents should make it possible to review the support, pressures and constraints which you perceive.

*Follow-up:* Bearing in mind one's aims and value position, it may or may not be a good thing, to be drawn into an existing staff culture. Carrying out this exercise may make you more conscious of staff relationships and may provide a basis for actively contributing to future understandings, developments and innovation.

## 1.4 Parents and the community

Before the legislation of the late 1980s, educational administration was based on a so-called 'partnership model' in which government, local education authorities and schools worked together, at different levels of organization, to provide appropriate education within each community. As we saw in Chapter 2, Part 1, this model was challenged in the 1980s and 1990s for being dominated by professionals and for failing to produce sufficiently high standards of education. An alternative conception of schools responding directly to their client consumers was suggested and it is this 'market model' which has begun to dominate.

The market model is based on the belief that, if schools are made autonomous and exposed to market forces, then competition between schools will produce steadily increasing standards of education (Chubb and Moe 1990, DES 1992, DFE 1996b).

Legislation of the late 1980s and early 1990s and the associated 'Parents' Charter' of 1991 gave parents significant rights. These include the rights:

- to have access to standard information about aggregated results of school performance (including the standardized tests)
- to select the school which their children attend (subject to certain limits)
- to receive written reports on the performance of their children
- to receive an annual report from the school governors.

Such rights provide parents with certain kinds of information and with clear opportunities to exercise choice. The law positions parents as consumers of education and, in so doing, defines parents, for the present, as the group to which teachers and schools should primarily be held to account.

Research (McClelland *et al.* 1995) shows that when choosing a secondary school parents pay attention to test and examination results published in a school's prospectus. Over 70 per cent of parents in this study said they found the information valuable in making a decision. However, these parents were less interested in league tables. Many did not even look at them, and of those that did only 2 per cent said it would make them consider a different school. Many schools now put a considerable amount of effort into 'marketing' themselves through the prospectus, promoting coverage of their activities in the local media, and through community involvement.

## Practical activity 5.7

*Aim:* To consider the 'image' a school projects to its potential clients.

*Method:* Read the school's prospectus. Look at the school entrance area – note any display of trophies, newspaper cuttings, pupils' work. Make a list of all the public performances – concerts, plays etc. in the last year. Find out about the performance of the school sports teams. Note any other achievements particularly celebrated by the school.

List the points the school seems to be emphasizing as its strengths. Are these curricular? Extra-curricular? Pastoral? What sort of pupil/parent does it seem to want to appeal to?

*Follow-up:* Consider the make-up of the school's intake. What is the social mix? Do most of the pupils live in the area or do they travel some distance to attend? What is the proportion of pupils receiving free meals? How many have statements of special educational need? How do staff describe the attitude of parents to the school?

Is the nature of the school's intake consistent? Or has it been changing in recent years? Can you or the school account for this?

Of course, schools have a variety of contacts, formal and informal, with the parents of pupils. Direct parental involvement in school is often hard to develop at secondary level (not least because it is frequently discouraged and subverted by pupils). However, there is evidence that parents do want access to clear and constructive reports on their children's progress and achievements. For this reason perhaps the apparently objective assessment of tests is particularly valued. Communicating with parents, on this and other topics, is an important feature of school life. School governors are required by law to produce an annual report – content headings are strictly prescribed. Some schools even submit their reports for a national award. A recent winner was decribed as 'really stylish, but also conveyed a tremendous commitment to and pride in the school, and a real understanding by governors of its rich curriculum offerings, of where it was going, the standards it was aiming at, and the problems'. Schools use many different ways of involving and informing parents: termly letters or newsletters; advisory groups; parent-governors' committees. Particular efforts may be made in connection with aspects of the Personal and Social Education curriculum, the development of policies on behaviour or homework and the curriculum options available for pupils. More traditionally there are open evenings, a formal opportunity for parents to talk to teachers about progress and achievement. Of these, teachers usually say they rarely see the parents they really need to. However, many of these, whose children may be giving cause for concern, will have individual contact with the school (see also Chapter 15, Section 5.2).

Some schools actively seek parental views as part of their monitoring and evaluation, sending out questionnaires on aspects of school life, conducting surveys to get parent (and pupil) perspectives. In secondary schools it is notoriously difficult to ensure that communications sent home with pupils actually reach the intended destination. Schools adopt innovative strategies to overcome this, based on their intimate knowledge of their community. One Scottish school achieved a 100 per cent return of questionnaires by numbering each and offering a bottle of whisky to the 'lucky number'.

Parents may organize themselves into a PTA or 'Friends of the School' group. They may arrange social activities and engage in fund-raising. In this country (as opposed to, for instance, the USA), such groups rarely seek to influence any of the educational aspects of the school.

## Practical activity 5.8

*Aim:* To investigate ways in which a school communicates with parents.

*Method:* Look at a copy of the governor's annual report. Collect examples of any written communication with parents. Have parents been invited to take part in surveys, questionnaires or had their opinions sought in any way? What evidence in the school is there of parental involvement?

*Follow-up:* What picture of parental involvement emerges from this? What attitude does the school take to parents?

The community of a school can be defined as its staff, pupils and parents. But there is also the relationship of a school with its immediate physical surroundings. Where pupils travel long distances to school there may not be such a strong sense of 'neighbourhood'. Sometimes the relationship between a school and its immediate neighbours can be strained and in need of management. In some schools pupils make a positive contribution to the neighbourhood by, for example, visiting or shopping for the elderly, clearing wasteground.

In recent years schools have been encouraged to seek links with 'the business community' to gain sponsorship, to arrange work experience for pupils or staff, to appoint governors with management skills. Many also make links with local churches, community groups, voluntary organizations. Schools seeking income from lettings will make the building and grounds available to local groups. In some places schools are more specifically defined as 'community schools' where the premises are used more extensively out of (and sometimes during) school hours for educational activity.

## 1.5 Governors

As we saw in Chapter 2, a considerable part of schools' accountability to parents and the community is exercised through governing bodies. It is interesting to consider the composition of a school's governing body, what expertise the members bring, how they are appointed/co-opted, what role the head plays. Sub-committees and *ad hoc* working parties are frequently created to focus specific areas and issues. Teachers may meet with or compile reports for governors when things are being discussed that touch on their area of reponsibility or interest. In some instances a teacher or teachers may initiate discussion by making a suggestion or applying for support for a particular development. The Practical Activity that follows suggests one way in which you might become more familar with the workings of the governing body of your school.

### Practical activity 5.9

*Aim:* To consider the role of a governing body.

*Method:* Ask if you can study minutes of the governing body meetings of your school. Note and classify the range of issues covered – staffing, curriculum, finance etc. To what extent would you regard the issues covered as 'professional' matters and to what extent were the decisions taken enhanced by the deliberations of the governing body?

*Follow-up:* Attend a governing body meeting as an observer.

Did it provide a constructive forum for school management and professional accountability?

In the context of their accountability perhaps the most significant part of governors' responsibility under LMS is control of the school budget. Figure 5.1 below sets out the budget of a secondary school in the 1995/6 financial year.

**INCOME**

**Formula allocation income**

| | |
|---|---|
| Age weighted pupil units | 2247530 |
| Special needs allowance | 56000 |
| Floor area allowance | 23000 |
| **Total formula allocation** | **2326530** |

**Miscellaneous income**

| | |
|---|---|
| Donations | 18000 |
| Lettings | 20000 |
| Services | 14000 |
| **Total miscellaneous** | **52000** |

| | |
|---|---|
| **TOTAL INCOME** | **2378530** |

**OVERALL BUDGET BALANCE**

**Income and expenditure**

| | |
|---|---|
| Total income | 2378530 |
| Total expenditure | -2417766 |
| **Deficit** | **-39236** |

**Method of funding deficit**

| | |
|---|---|
| From reserves | 26594 |
| From enrolments | |
| 7 pupils @ £1808 | 12642 |
| Total deficit funding | **39236** |

| | |
|---|---|
| **FINAL PROJECTED BALANCE** | **0** |

**EXPENDITURE**

**Staffing expenditure**

| | |
|---|---|
| Permanent teachers | -1664332 |
| Supply teachers | -47727 |
| Foreign language assistants | -9280 |
| Visiting lecturers' fees | -1600 |
| Insurance for teacher sickness | -10000 |
| General assistants | -40723 |
| Librarians | -19783 |
| Technicians | -43190 |
| School meals supervisory staff | -6736 |
| Caretakers and cleaners | -34072 |
| Administrative staff | -109503 |
| Recruitment expenses | -3000 |
| **Total staffing** | **-1989946** |

**Premises expenditure**

| | |
|---|---|
| Building repair and maintenance | -28000 |
| Health, safety and servicing | -6100 |
| Cleaning contract | -53000 |
| Building improvements | -8000 |
| Grounds maintenance contract | -24000 |
| Electricity | -22000 |
| Gas | -32500 |
| Water rates | -4000 |
| Sewerage | -6500 |
| Refuse collection | -1500 |
| **Total premises** | **-185600** |

**Direct educational expenditure**

| | |
|---|---|
| Equipment | -47978 |
| Reprographics | -16000 |
| Books | -11744 |
| Stationery and materials | -4408 |
| Examination fees | -30000 |
| Educational visits | -3600 |
| **Total direct educational** | **-113730** |

**Miscellaneous expenditure**

| | |
|---|---|
| Furniture and fittings | -8000 |
| Adult meals | -4200 |
| Postage | -3750 |
| Telephones | -7500 |
| Governors' clerk | -900 |
| Vehicle maintenance | -2080 |
| Staff travel | -640 |
| School brochure and publicity | -4000 |
| Insurance | -12000 |
| **Total miscellaneous** | **43070** |

**Contingencies**

| | |
|---|---|
| Staff salary settlements | -59500 |
| General | -25920 |
| **Total contingencies** | **-85420** |

| | |
|---|---|
| **TOTAL EXPENDITURE** | **-2417766** |

**Figure 5.1** *Projected budget for a secondary school, 1995–96 financial year*

There are three salient points to make:

1. 94 per cent of the income comes in relation to the 1,045 pupils on roll. This is an average of £2,150 per pupil, though the actual amount per pupil is age weighted – an 'Age Weighted Pupil Unit' (AWPU).
2. 85 per cent of the expenditure goes to pay for salaries and other staffing costs including related contingency funds (on eighty-two teachers – sixty-seven in terms of full-time equivalence – and forty part-time non-teaching staff, including school meal supervisory assistants).
3. After taking out staffing, premises and miscellaneous costs, there is only £114,000 (5 per cent) left for the annual direct educational expenditure on the 1,045 pupils.

It is essential to link the budget with the school development plan (Chapter 16). Costing, projecting ahead and examining different alternatives enables governors to make more informed decisions. However, governors often feel that, because the room for manoeuvre is so limited, they are prevented from getting to grips with more central issues of class size, teacher workload, organization and resourcing the curriculum.

 Following extensive research on how governing bodies work, Deem, Brehony and Heath (1995) ask whether school governors should be seen as 'empowered citizens' or as 'state volunteers' (see also **Primary Reading 14.7**). Their concern is that, despite the apparently wide-ranging responsibilities of governors, the actual scope for decision-making is severely constrained. National requirements pervade many areas of a school's provision and resource constraints often restrict opportunities for innovation. Thus governors come to act more as passive agents, enacting and seeming to

## Practical activity 5.10

*Aim:* To consider the impact of school budget constraints.

*Method:* Consider the budget in Figure 5.1 with a colleague. If you were part of a school governing body, what implications might it have for your policies on:

- pupil enrolment?
- staff appointments?
- staff development?
- curriculum development?
- buildings maintenance?
- publication of assessment results?
- class size?
- provision for pupils with special educational needs?
- liaison with parents?
- education equipment and materials?
- car boot sales?

*Follow-up:* Enquire about the budget of a school that you know well. Have budgetary constraints and opportunities affected teaching processes? Has budgetary awareness increased the accountability of the school to parents? Have the roles of central and local governments been considered?

legitimate the requirements of central government, rather than being active, empowered, local decision-makers for their schools.

The relationship between schools, in particular headteachers and governors, is a delicate one and often requires skilled negotiation. Whether governing bodies are relatively inactive and 'rubber-stamp' a headteacher's decisions, drawn into unproductive clashes with their schools or engaged in a productive and mutually supportive enterprise depends very much on the attitudes and skills of individuals involved.

It is legitimate to expect professionals to be accountable. However, it is necessary to create educationally constructive structures and processes through which such accountability can be expressed. How the systems of the 1990s will develop in the new millennium remains to be seen.

## 1.6   School ethos and culture

We conclude this section by discussing the social character of schools. This is an important initial consideration because of the way in which perspectives, behaviour and action in schools are very often influenced by established conventions, expectations and norms. Such norms often remain tacit and may easily be taken for granted by people who know a school well. Other people, as relative 'strangers' are likely to be more explicitly aware of them.

'School ethos' or 'school culture' are well-established concepts but they are not always easy to describe.

Practical Activity 5.11 suggests one way in which this might be done.

### Practical activity 5.11

*Aim:* To describe a school ethos.

*Method:* Rate the school on the mapping device below derived from Rogers and Richardson 1985. Ask some colleagues to do the same and discuss the results.

| | | | | | | |
|---|---|---|---|---|---|---|
| inactive | 1 | 2 | 3 | 4 | 5 | busy |
| happy | 1 | 2 | 3 | 4 | 5 | miserable |
| purposeful | 1 | 2 | 3 | 4 | 5 | aimless |
| relaxed | 1 | 2 | 3 | 4 | 5 | tense |
| enthusiastic | 1 | 2 | 3 | 4 | 5 | apathetic |
| noisy | 1 | 2 | 3 | 4 | 5 | quiet |
| messy | 1 | 2 | 3 | 4 | 5 | tidy |
| chaotic | 1 | 2 | 3 | 4 | 5 | organized |
| welcoming | 1 | 2 | 3 | 4 | 5 | formidable |
| open | 1 | 2 | 3 | 4 | 5 | closed |
| disciplined | 1 | 2 | 3 | 4 | 5 | unruly |
| confident | 1 | 2 | 3 | 4 | 5 | insecure |

*Follow-up:* Use of the mapping device and conversations with colleagues should provide a good idea of the subjective feel of the school ethos. An excellent extension would be to ask children or non-teaching staff to carry out the exercise too. They are likely to have different perspectives. All sorts of issues for school practice and provision might follow if particular patterns emerge from the exercise.

Work on schools as 'learning organizations' has proliferated in recent years (e.g. Fullan 1993). Nias *et al.* (1989) analysed primary school cultures as the subjective perceptions, understandings, conventions, habits and routines which are held collectively by school staff. Such school cultures can be seen as having been negotiated over time between all those who are, or have been, involved in the school. Such analyses suggest a high degree of consensus, and this expectation has been challenged by research which highlights conflict and micro-political struggle (Hoyle 1986, Ball 1987). Within large organizations like secondary schools, despite attempts to achieve coherence through 'school development planning' it is likely that differences in staff perspectives and some degree of conflict will exist. Indeed, distinct sub-cultures may exist in particular departments which may be more or less congruent with the dominant school ethos.

On this argument a school is seen as an institution which, despite the efforts of its management team, is likely to remain 'loosely coupled' (Hoyle 1986). Staff bring their perspectives, opinions, skills and enthusiasms. These are used, over time and in interaction with others, to construct understandings about the 'way the school is'.

Clearly, a headteacher has a particular degree of power to initiate and influence the development of a school culture (see Section 2.2 in this chapter). The Practical Activity below suggests two particular ways of developing an understanding of a headteacher's point of view.

## Practical activity 5.12

*Aim:* To understand a headteacher's perspectives and aims for her/his school.

*Method:* The first method is simply to ask. Try to arrange a time for an interview. You may want to prepare questions, perhaps structured around statements of aims which may be contained in a school prospectus. What you are aiming for is an account of the head's perspective and goals. Second, we would suggest that the headteacher's account is triangulated with some data of actual behaviour. An excellent source of data here are assemblies. Assemblies have symbolic and ritual functions as well as being used for practical managerial purposes. Because large numbers of pupils are involved, the control and discipline conventions in the school are likely to be evident and the normative structure of the school and expectations of the headteacher are likely to be made explicit. Look out too for other expressions of ethos – some headteachers, for instance, make a practice of walking around the school at dinner time, talking to pupils, or perhaps making a point about litter.

*Follow-up:* This exercise will produce a clearer understanding of the way the key leadership figure in the school conceptualizes goals and attempts to enact them. For reflective teachers the application of such understanding derives from the way in which it can inform decisions about future action.

It is important to understand the views and actions of headteachers but, as we have seen, it is certainly not the case that they are the only influence on a school culture.

Many other individuals and groups within a school also have power to influence events and contribute to the formation of expectations, but influence will depend on their degree of status, power, charisma and authority. It is likely that governors, deputy heads, heads of department or faculties will all have some influence. Other people, such as junior teachers, non-teaching staff and students on school experience programmes, may feel and be much more marginal.

In summary, the emergence of understandings about the 'way the school is' should be seen as a result of a contested negotiation between a number of different and competing influences and interests. It follows that a school culture may change and develop over time, in the ebb and flow of micro-political activity.

Documents produced by the school – statements of aims or mission statements, policies on different areas, for example equal opportunities, behaviour, can be seen as expressions of school ethos and values. Statements of aims and policies have been accused of being worthy statements which mean little to staff and pupils and have only a passing connection with what happens in schools. But at best they give a sense of purpose to the school and provide a framework for improving the quality of learning and standards of achievement (see Section 2.1 and Chapter 7 for more on processes which produce policies.)

## Practical activity 5.13

*Aim:* To consider how a school expresses its ethos.

*Method:* Look carefully at the school's aims statement and policies. Observe how (and if) these aims and policies are reflected in the day-to-day life of the school. Look at staff and pupil behaviour.

*Follow-up:* You might want to talk to some pupils about how they would describe their school. It could be useful to look in more detail at a specific area (behaviour, equal opportunities) to see how aspirations match with what happens.

The concept of school culture thus leads to an analysis of the micropolitics of schools as a constantly developing and adapting set of negotiated practices and expectations (Ball 1987). Underpinning this, it is suggested, is a close identification by individual staff with collective beliefs. Thus the 'self' of teachers (see Chapter 8) may be reflected in and affirmed through the development of the school culture.

There is a connection here with the educational quality of the school, for there is some evidence that teamwork and purposive coherence are effective (Mortimore *et al.* 1988, MacGilchrist *et al.* 1996). We will look more closely at this in Chapter 16.

If you want to enquire further into this area, the following Practical Activity provides a framework.

## Practical activity 5.14

*Aim:* To describe and analyse a school culture.

*Method:* This is a long-term activity which draws on ethnographic methods. It will take several weeks to do. We suggest that all possible opportunities are taken to listen, observe and understand the perspectives, assumptions and taken-for-granted understandings of the various people who are involved in the school. Make notes so that these are not forgotten. Review these notes and look for patterns in the understandings. Consider if the patterns relate to particular groups of people and use this awareness to orientate your future observations. Make comparisons between the views of different people and/or groups. This should help to refine your understanding. Try to produce a summary analysis. You might distinguish:

1. The main individuals and/or groups and their perspectives.
2. The shared understandings which exist about policy and practice in the school.
3. The degree of agreement with these understandings which exists from individual to individual or group to group.

*Follow-up:* Through this activity you should produce a clearer understanding of the school culture, of the groups in the school and of the degree of agreement between them. Such understanding is a very useful starting point for taking a new initiative which is strategically well judged or simply for 'fitting in' to a school.

## 2 ORGANIZATION: SYSTEMS, STRUCTURES, ROLES

In recent years there has been an increasing application of management and organizational theory to the way that schools operate and are led. Much of this theory is drawn from research done in commercial or industrial contexts and there is much discussion of how appropriate some of these ideas are to schools. Nevertheless there is a growing body of evidence that offers insights into the way schools are organized and managed. In this section we consider some of the systems, structures and roles which are found in secondary schools.

## 2.1 Management

The business of a school is teaching and learning, and this involves a huge variety of activities: producing a timetable, organizing resources, assemblies, liaising with parents, visits and events, checking attendance, school meals, playground duties, cover for absent staff, pupils with headaches, pupils in fights, homework, appraisal and staff development, careers advice, curriculum development, admissions, links with primary schools, producing magazines and newsletters, marking, behaviour problems, writing reports, mentoring student teachers, etc. There is clearly a need for ways of coping efficiently with the myriad things involved in the day-to-day operation of the school. Of greater significance perhaps is the need for schools to engage in review and longer-term planning for change and development (we look at this in more detail in Chapter 16).

The basis of school organization is the assignment of jobs and roles to staff, with varying degrees of responsibility acknowledged by the allocation of 'points' on the salary scales – though some teachers have responsibilities with no additional pay reward. Such an approach sounds essentially hierarchical with the headteacher (highest pay, most responsibility) at the top and the main professional grade teachers at the bottom and there is much emphasis on 'leadership' as a necessary quality of headteachers. However, the ways in which schools define and operate their organizational systems create an ethos and culture which may be more or less hierarchical. Over the last twenty years ideas of collegiate approaches to management have been developed in schools. These are intended to produce a culture of involvement where every member of staff knows what is going on and is involved in decision-making.

We will start by looking at the structures most frequently found in secondary schools.

In a line management system groups of teachers take on management responsibilities related to different functions of the school. These groups interact in different ways. All members of staff are linked into the structure in that everyone has at least one 'line manager' to whom they 'report' and are accountable for the discharge of particular roles and responsibilities. These lines run up and down and across the system. Accountability can involve passing and receiving information, reporting on activity, decision-making, innovating, using initiative. How well this works depends on how clearly roles are defined (in job specifications for instance) and how effectively the 'lines' work.

Most secondary schools have a Senior Management Team (SMT) and Middle Management Team which meet very frequently. The SMT usually includes the headteacher, deputy heads, senior teachers. These may have major areas of responsibilty attached to their title – staffing, curriculum, finance, pastoral.

The Middle Management Team usually includes staff with subject responsibility (heads of departments or faculties) and with key responsibilities for issues such as Key Stage co-ordination, assessment, examinations, year groups. There may be more than one middle management group; for instance subject leaders and heads of year may both meet as discrete groups. In addition there will be other 'middle managers' with individual responsibilities for things like careers, public relations, learning support/special needs, sixth form, who meet less frequently with other managers in variously constituted groups. In addition to the established management structures there may be working groups which meet for specific purposes over a defined period of time as different school priorities come into focus.

Most staff will probably have more than one management responsibility. A timetable of meetings provides a framework within which the formal groups/committees meet.

The head of mathematics in an 11–16 school with 900 pupils, gives a flavour of his various roles:

I run a team of five full-timers, plus four part-timers in five purpose-built class-rooms; I'll meet with them formally and informally about what we are doing. I'm responsible to the senior management team for what happens in mathematics. I have termly meetings with the head – she's my line manager – where we discuss the mathematics department. I'm also a member of the middle management team – that's heads of all major departments, some teachers in charge of minor depart-ments, two of the four year heads and two senior teachers from the SMT. We meet once a month to discuss wider polices and issues – anything from pupils wearing earrings to development plans for the next five years – and use it for information distribution. The head has also instituted special policy-making meetings – people attend who have an interest or contribution to make. Things go to this meeting from middle management and vice-versa. Another of my responsibilities is to analyse examination results and I have meetings for that. I'm a member of the assessment working group, and the IT working group. I also meet with heads of department in neighbouring schools three times a year – that's my curriculum support group. I also have a tutor group so I may meet with my year group head. Then there are whole-staff meetings. Sometimes I find myself going to too many meetings.

## Practical activity 5.15

*Aim:* To investigate the organizational and management systems of your school

*Method:* Collect as much information as you can about the school's management systems. Your mentor or subject department head should be helpful here. You may find what you need in a staff handbook or other existing documentation in the school. Note the overall structure and the specific roles staff are given. Look particularly for job descriptions which should set out the purpose, duties and responsibilities of any role and make clear the lines of management. Find out about the membership, remit and functions of different groups and committees (including governors). How often do they meet? Who chairs them? Where are discussions and decisions recorded? Who has access to the information?

Ask your subject head about the different roles s/he has in the school.

*Follow-up:* Ask staff how they feel about the structures and systems they work with. What are the strengths and weaknesses as they see it? Where does the power and influence in the school lie? Do pupils have a place in the system in the form of a School Council or other forum?

## 2.2 Headteachers

Fullan and Hargreaves (1992, p. 69, see also **Primary Reading 14.1**) suggest that headship is best discharged with the 'kind of leadership which makes activity mean-ingful for others', rather than being 'the charismatic innovative high-flyer that moves whole school cultures forward'. For change to be effectively managed those involved must feel 'empowered', have 'a sense of ownership' – words and phrases which occur again and again in the literature. But Fullan and Hargreaves make it clear that empowerment comes with individuals taking control rather than being controlled. The 'total schools' they advocate are created not by elaborate and inflexible systems but by frameworks which allow the development of a 'culture of collaboration' where individuals can learn from each other and the social and professional environment in which they exist.

Fullan and Hargreaves identify two kinds of existing cultures among teachers which work against collaboration. In the 'culture of individualism' teachers are not used to sharing ideas, resources; they work largely in isolation with perhaps the occasional foray into joint planning. In 'Balkanized cultures' teachers work in 'self-contained sub-groups' – like subject departments – that are relatively insulated. Both cultures 'fragment relationships . . . and stifle the moral support necessary for risk-taking and experimentation.' 'Reculturing' seeks to reverse these situations. It means creating contexts in which people can work together and build relationships. In this process they pool ideas, experience and resources; they approach problems looking for solutions, not to apportion blame; they see conflict as a necessary part of developement and come to appreciate the contribution that dissident, sceptical and critical voices can make. Individual learning becomes shared learning and is continuous. The role of the head, then, in making a school a 'learning organization' is to create structures which help people to connect and systems which increase opportunities for learning across the organization.(For further discussion of this, see Chapter 16, Section 2.1.)

At one 11–16 school a fairly traditional structure is operated with a light hand but with clear targets and great flexibility, providing openings for initiative and collaboration. Three teachers give their perspectives on organization:

*Deputy Head:* 'One of the things I think is exciting about the way we work in this school is that we make a point of not compartmentalizing our approach; middle management really cuts across the whole school. Our ideas and strategies for development come in a number of ways – from up, from down and from across. There is a lot of listening, a lot of thinking, a lot of sharing ideas at SMT, at department level, at tutor and pastoral level and then bringing these together. Sometimes we bring in outside help. Of course, the final decision has to be the Head's. That's the bottom line in any school.'

*Head of department:* 'I genuinely think, having been in an environment before where there was no discussion, that staff do feel more involved here. Meetings are open, the agendas are always published. At meetings we are all participants – I don't think there are any meetings here where people are observers. There is ownership – when things have been agreed you have actually participated in the discussion, even though you might not totally agree with the final decision. The problem with collaboration and consultation is it can be quite exhausting and exhaustive and slow.'

*Teacher in charge of PSE:* 'The Head's style of management is to throw access to innovate open to anybody. So one doesn't have to worry about belonging to any particular line or group. If you have got an idea you can go and discuss it, and if it's good then you will do it or it will be done.'

In Garibaldi School in Mansfield structural changes have been part of turning a school around. In seven years the school went from near the bottom of the county league tables to the top third, vandalism practically disappeared, pupil numbers rose, the sixth form expanded, truancy was almost completely eradicated. It was featured as an example of good management on television by John Harvey Jones and hailed as 'a model school' by David Blunkett. Accounts of how this was achieved focus attention on systems and the head's removal of the conventional management pyramid of deputies, heads of faculties, departments and years. According to the headteacher (*TES*, 23 June 1995) 'It took three months for an idea to go down through the hierarchy and then three months for it to come back again – in the meantime someone had changed their mind. The plans for Records of Achievement did three laps of the circuit – and this was in a school which needed massive, instant change.' The number of deputies and heads of year was reduced and heads of faculty were abolished; formal meetings were scrapped and the focus placed on 'the motivation and development of all staff as our greatest asset'. Senior staff were given new roles. Faculty heads were made leaders of review and working groups which looked at different areas of the curriculum and of school life. The management pyramid was replaced by a 'bobbing corks' model giving individuals freedom to emerge and make progress. That some might get stuck or fail was accepted. As the Head said, 'I want a risk-taking culture in which inertia is the only crime.'

Teachers at Garibaldi speak of the head's 'positive' approach, the ease of access to him, his encouragement of individual interest and talent, 'his willingness to let you have a go and make mistakes'. Observers point out the raising of morale and expectations among the pupils – and to the head's success in raising money from industry, charitable trusts, the EC and sponsorship to support teachers' ideas and aspirations.

These examples, and others in the literature, show schools which, though hierarchical by nature, have managed to create a culture where team work is the foundation of the way teachers work and there are high expectations of professionalism in day-to-day activity. Argument, debate, criticism are accommodated alongside celebration of success, and heads can lead from the front while promoting change from the bottom up.

## 2.3 Communications

One key factor in successful organizational systems is effective communication. Communication in secondary schools is varied and sometimes difficult to analyse. The formal systems – pigeon holes, noticeboards, bulletins, daily briefings, staff meetings – are all subject to human error. Things 'go astray' or are ignored. One person's priority is another's candidate for the wastepaper bin. Schools are awash with paper; teachers traditionally hate paperwork. The informal systems which are often influential are sometimes difficult to 'see'. Where do staff gather at break and dinner time? Is the staff room a focus or are social groups dispersed around the school? For the reflective teacher, wanting to know what makes an organization 'work', a close look at communications can be interesting and revealing.

> ### *Practical activity 5.16*
>
> *Aim:* To investigate formal and informal communication systems in the school.
>
> *Method:* Spend some time researching the school's communication systems. Trace the formal systems by which information is passed: paper circulation, noticeboards, daily briefings, meetings etc. Try to identify the informal systems – private communication, word of mouth.
>
> *Follow-up:* Where is it effective? Does it break down? Is misinformation a problem?
>
> Who are the key figures in that they act as 'gatekeepers' either impeding or supporting information flow?

## 2.4  Academic systems

### *Managing the curriculum*

A significant feature of this aspect of organization lies in the terminology schools use to identify subjects in the curriculum. Some identify subject departments, each a separate curriculum subject. In this system some subjects may be combined, for example home economics or textiles may become part of technology. Other schools organize subjects into faculties, groupings of subjects. In this system a faculty head manages and administers the whole area, and individual subjects within the faculty have 'subject leaders'. This may have implications for the status which different subjects enjoy. Faculty titles suggest an approach which is cross-curricular or inter-disciplinary but since the introduction of the National Curriculum (expressed as subjects) timetables tend to be organized using single subject headings. There are variations between schools in the way they define a faculty. These variations may reflect a school philosophy, be a pragmatic response to existing factors, or the result of a combination of both. Examples of ways schools have created faculties include: aesthetics and technology (art, home economics, design and technology, IT); expressive and communicative arts (drama, English language and literature, music); humanities (geography, history, religious studies); social and individual development (careers, health education, parenting, PSE, PE, social sciences). Teachers involved with catering for special learning needs may be designated as a separate department for learning support.

At whole-school level, academic planning will be concerned with curriculum and with associated issues such as equal opportunities, provision for special needs. Faculty heads, heads of department, subject leaders are key contributors here, especially to curriculum planning and the discussions that surround the creation of the timetable – the visible expression of a school's approach to delivering the curriculum.

## Timetable

As so often in school life, in creating the timetable idealism must be constrained by practicality – the rooms, laboratories, workshops available, staff availability and time available. Nevertheless a timetable reveals priorities, most evident in the amount of time allocated to different subjects.

Timetables are usually organized with a one-week or two-week cycle. There are differences between schools as to number and length of lessons and length of day. National guidance is that secondary schools should teach for between 23.5 and 25 hours each week. Subjects have different preferences for time allocation which arise from the way the subject is taught. For example Mathematics teachers usually favour regular contact; art and PE prefer longer blocks of time. For subjects in which pupils are to be 'set' by 'ability' the timetable may need to be 'blocked', that is all pupils in a year group do a subject at the same time. In Key Stage 4 the timetable has to accommodate statutory requirements and a variety of options offered to pupils; in some cases pupils may even be learning off-site for part of the time. (See Chapter 7 for more detail on this.)

## Organizing learners

The way a school groups pupils has an impact on the timetable and on the pupils. 'Mixed ability' groups, 'streaming' a whole year group by attainment, 'setting' by attainment within subjects are all possible approaches to organization. The mid-1990s saw an attack on 'mixed ability' teaching which, it was claimed, was the prevailing orthodoxy and largely responsible for pupils' underachievement. The argument was pursued vigorously in political circles and in the popular and educational press. Associated with this was the debate about selection at 11 (see Chapter 2 and Section 1.1 of this chapter). Most secondary schools had always, and continue to, set by attainment in some subjects and increasingly in later years. For example, in Year 7 pupils may be taught mainly in their tutor groups. In Year 8 they may be in sets for mathematics, science and modern languages. In Years 10 and 11 the academic organization may be determined by the 'pathways' pupils have selected. There are possibilities for considerable variation of this pattern and you will find more or less use of organization by attainment in different schools.

In the USA and Canada where pupils are frequently 'tracked' by ability there is pressure to discontinue this because of its undesirable social and educational consequences (Wheelock 1992). Able pupils in top streams progressed faster but lower-ability pupils, mainly from lower socio-economic groups and ethnic minorities, got less well-qualified teachers who had lower expectations and gave them less challenging work. Pupils also felt stigmatized and had low morale. The suggestion has often been made that to return to selection and structured grouping is not likely to be beneficial.

*Practical activity 5.17*

*Aim:* To consider the academic organization of the school and the expression of this in the timetable.

*Method:* Go back to the data on organizational structure you collected in Practical Activity 5.16. Make a plan and trace the parts which relate to 'academic' activity. Look at the way the academic curriculum is organized by the timetable for different year groups.

How are subjects grouped, organized and managed? Are there any evident differences in status between subjects? How much streaming or setting is there? How does the allocation of time meet the needs of different subjects and different approaches to teaching and learning? How does the grouping of pupils vary from year to year? What constraints have been operating on the design of the timetable? What principles seem to underpin it?

*Follow-up:* Check the conclusions you have drawn from your analysis with staff. Find out their views of mixed ability teaching, setting and streaming. If possible obtain the views of teachers from different subject areas. Is there any evidence that teachers' views are associated with their subject?

## 2.5   Pastoral systems

The pastoral system in a school is designed to keep track of pupils throughout their school careers, focusing attention on their progress and attainment as learners and on their development as people. This is achieved usually through a system of class tutors who, where possible, stay with the group as it moves through the school. For each year, there is a year head who manages and supports that group of tutors. Sometimes pupils are grouped in 'houses' which act as the basis for cross-year activities, sporting and other competitions.

Secondary schools are frequently too large for every pupil to be individually known by every teacher so the class tutor plays an important role. Year 7 tutors may be be involved with pupils in the summer term in which they leave primary school; they will certainly be involved in the pupils' induction into their new school and with the creation of a positive group identity.

Most teachers have a tutor group and will act as the first point of contact for all issues, meeting parents, dealing with day-to-day problems, keeping track of attendance (often an early indicator that something is wrong), establishing and maintaining a relationship with the group and individual pupils. Tutors are often the start of the chain of activity a school has devised for dealing with problems of attendance and behaviour should they arise.

As well as daily routine and trouble-shooting there are various record-keeping and assessment features to this role (see also Chapter 15, Part 5). Tutors often take on the annual task of writing profiles based on information collated from all subject areas and in collecting information of a pupil's activities that would contribute to a Record of Achievement which is completed in Year 11. They may also take responsibility for writing references where pupils leave at age 16. Pupil records held by schools should be clear, factual, up-to-date, reliable and readily available. The tutor plays a major role in ensuring this is the case. Now that pupil records are accessible by parents on demand, it is vital that this function is carried out professionally and impartially. School records can play an important role in cases involving child protection issues, so they must be as reliable as possible.

Often the form teacher will have a teaching role with his/her tutor group. In some schools Year 7 tutors will be timetabled to teach English or humanities to enable them to get to know their pupils. In almost all schools the timetable will show a period of tutor time once a week or fortnight. What happens in this time can be left up to the tutor; more usually there is a programme developed by the year team within a whole-school framework and with input from the teacher who co-ordinates Personal and Social Education (PSE). An active tutorial programme may be followed where the class engages in specific activities related to aspects of PSE.

The National Curriculum, with its fairly rigid division of the curriculum into academic subjects, has made the tutor's role of helping pupils make sense of the whole school experience even more important. Assessment linked to this part of a form tutor's role may be very informal but will certainly involve the teacher in gaining knowledge of quite a different type from that which they will gain in their role as a subject teacher. Many schools arrange programmes of activities, often residential, in which tutors take part with their groups. Other extra-curricular activities, such as sport or drama, add to this contact and are often very highly valued by teachers for the insight they help them obtain into their pupils' characters and interests.

Personal and Social Education is a 'subject' within which schools may fulfil the legal requirement to include sex education and education about substance abuse in the curriculum. PSE programmes may be taught by form tutors or by a team of volunteers. Teachers involved with PSE will be supported by a teacher in a co-ordinating role, possibly the year or house head or possibly by a head of social education. Schools' organizations vary considerably in this area. There is constant debate about how far the role of teachers extends – where does teaching end and social work begin? (Galloway 1990). There is no doubt that teachers can become very important people in young people's lives and can play a major supporting part through some of the difficulties they face in adolescence. They can offer a useful 'friendly ear' and informal counselling for pupils who feel comfortable talking to them. What is important is that the 'rules' of professionalism are not breached and that teachers are constantly mindful of the position of trust and power they are in. Schools will all have guidelines for support of this kind and teachers must follow them rigorously. It will not necessarily be the tutor to whom a pupil will turn if they are in difficulty, but the tutor will still be the person who brings together the whole picture of the pupils and will therefore need to be kept informed by others involved of any relevant matters.

## 2.6 Academic and pastoral – links and dilemmas

How far the academic and pastoral systems in a school interact or overlap has been a subject of considerable discussion. Most teachers have a role in both areas and frequently face dilemmas in allocating priorities (particularly of time) between them. In some schools the two areas seem to have acquired differential status, evident in the allocation of resources, the attitudes of management and consequently of teachers. At best the two areas work together in the best interests of pupils as learners

In the past a school's pastoral systems have often been characterized, as one teacher reports, as 'butt kicking and picking up the pieces when things go wrong'. More recently there has been a more clearly articulated understanding of the inter-relationship of academic and pastoral in ensuring that pupils achieve their full potential. A deputy head puts this point of view:

> Quite often pastoral priorities are triggered or driven by academic monitoring. If pupils are not feeling safe and secure their academic achievement is affected – we can see where they are failing. Obviously day-to-day crises and discipline are part of the tutor's job but pastoral work is just as much about monitoring and looking ahead as it is for the academic side. They have the same aims and objectives. Heads of year work with tutors at monitoring the overall picture for pupils in the same way that teachers and heads of department monitor progress in the curriculum. The knowledge of pupils that tutors build up is invaluable in ensuring they achieve as much as possible.

For instance, in 1993 teachers at King James's School, Knaresborough decided to investigate some disappointing fluctuations in examination results, the relative success of girls compared with boys and the underachievement of the most able pupils. A wide-ranging enquiry produced some interesting findings, most particularly the crucial importance to academic performance of the work of the pastoral tutor. Among other things the investigation revealed patterns of achievement associated with tutor groups. To develop the crucial advisory role for tutors there was a move to ensure more consistent use of specific strategies. Headteacher John Forster described (*TES*, 10 May 1996) how tutors consciously set out to be 'more active in monitoring homework, showing an interest in particular pieces of work, offering judicious praise, giving advice on note-taking and revision, emphasizing the importance of presentation'. In addition at the start of each day they were asked to establish a 'work ethos, by requiring a degree of appropriate formality, insisting on times when there must be full attention and silence, and in other words setting the tone for the working day'.

How teachers prioritize the various demands of their subject teaching and their pastoral role is a long-term issue. Questions of status, reward, most importantly of pressure of time are relevant here. Teachers can be torn between the various demands of the roles. When problems arise the knowledge which the tutor or year head has of the pupils involved may be needed quickly and a class may have to be left to 'get on' or will have 'cover'. The dilemma is neatly illustrated by one year head:

> It's difficult to make teaching a priority when one of my youngsters is caught mooning in the window. I tell the class to get sorted out and I'll be back in five minutes. They don't create a problem but it makes you feel uncomfortable that the lesson hasn't started as you planned; you sometimes lose the direction of it and it can ruin it. Wielding the big stick – off to the head to deal with it – would be quicker. But there is great satisfaction in the way we work, through relationships and negotiation. And it works.

A head of department, equally, may need to talk to a teacher before classes start or deal with an urgent problem. At such a time looking after a tutor group may appear an unnecessary intrusion to be got through as fast as possible.

The pastoral role is one of the most satisfying for teachers in that it provides them with contact with young people growing up and discovering themselves as adults. It is also one which it is easy to neglect when other pressures call on our time. It is important therefore to remember how important is the continuity which it can provide for pupils in a large institution.

## Practical activity 5.19

*Aim:* To investigate links and dilemmas in the pastoral and academic systems of the school.

*Method:* Talk with staff about how the academic and pastoral systems work. How far are they seen as complementary? How do they contribute to monitoring and maintaining pupils' progress? What dilemmas do staff encounter when carrying out their various roles?

*Follow-up:* Investigate pupils' perspectives on the pastoral system. Perhaps you could select some constrasting groups of pupils to talk with: high/low attaining, boys/girls, older/younger?

## 2.7 Departments and faculties

Each academic subject has its own way of organizing knowledge and as a result its own ways of passing on that knowledge to learners. Inevitably some of this rubs off on the way different subjects in schools are organized and managed. In this section, however, we will concentrate on some of the features that seem common to departments that 'work'.

A study of departments which added significantly more to pupils' achievement than might have been expected from their intake (Harris, Jamieson and Russ 1995) provides a very useful starting point. This study was carried out in six schools and included English, mathematics, science and geography/humanities departments. In all of these the following factors were evident.

### Shared vision

All teachers in the team were enthusiastic about their subject and had a clear and shared view of its nature; they also shared an enthusiasm and concern for pupils' learning. They were in 'talking departments' where there was a constant exchange of professional information, formally and informally. Heads of department were active in creating this context .There were frequent departmental meetings, often more than were scheduled in the school diary, all with clear purposes. A departmental handbook, revised each year, with job descriptions, guidelines on assessment and record-keeping, statements of rationale for the team's approach to teaching, provides an example of ways in which departments demonstrated their cohesion.

### Leadership

Responsibility for different areas of their work was shared in an atmosphere of mutual trust. Heads of department were 'leading professionals' and their practice was seen as a model to follow; but there was no prescription about teaching styles or stategies; possible innovations were carefully scrutinized and discussed and adopted only when there was a match with the department's view of 'good practice'.

### Schemes of work

All the departments had detailed and agreed schemes of work which had been produced either by the whole department or by individuals working to their strengths and within a shared vision. The schemes were very detailed with clear guidance, easily accessible and regarded as important documents. A key element was finding content and ways of teaching that matched the capacities and interests of the pupils. This approach was evident also in the time and care taken to select the 'right' examination syllabus for GCSE.

### Resources

None of the departments in the study were particularly well resourced but they had deployed what they had very effectively. The criterion for allocation or acqusitions was the enhancement of teaching and learning for all pupils. This was also followed in the allocation of human resources.

### Homework

Departments had consistent and consistently applied homework policies. There was a clear routine for setting and marking homework; it was returned quickly and good work was celebrated and displayed. Teachers actively sought home–school links and often used the potential of homework tasks to involve parents.

### Induction into the subject

Teachers, from Year 7, set out to induct pupils into the subject, to establish what was different or special about it. Particular attention was given to establishing the discourse of the subject, its language and ways of working.

### Record-keeping

Ways of monitoring pupil progress were firmly in place throughout the department. Each of the departments could produce, almost instantly, a detailed profile of a pupil's progress with detailed assessments of strengths and weaknesses. These were often systematically shared with the pupils, and pupil self-evaluation was encouraged. These procedures enabled teachers to identify at an early stage pupils who were under-achieving and apply strategies to offset this.

### Review

Departments also kept their own progress under review. Aspects of the work were subject to systematic review; members of staff felt free to raise issues concerning them. The approach to review was co-operative and collegial.

### Teaching and learning

All subjects had in common aspects of classroom routines, planning and structuring learning, feedback to pupils. While styles of teaching varied there was a consistently pupil-centred ethos.

In all the schools in the study heads and senior management were beginning to stress the scrutinizing of examination results in a formative way. The heads of department accepted that they were being held accountable but felt that this process was justifiable and necessary for further improvement (see Chapter 16 for more on these issues).

The researchers involved in the Harris, Jamieson and Russ study concentrated on the similarities between departments rather than the differences. As they point out, there are dangers in seeing their findings as a recipe for success. They identify some fundamental aspects of organization, teaching and learning that all departments have to address. Of these departments some achieved success by binding teachers tightly into shared culture and values, others by greater emphasis on structure and organization. In all these successful schools, the selected strategy seemed appropriate for the individuals involved and for their pupils.

### Practical activity 5.20

*Aim:* To consider the organization and management of your subject department.

*Method:* Use the headings from the Harris *et al.* study (above) to create a picture of the workings of your subject group. If you can, talk to your departmental head or subject leader about how they see their role, what challenges or problems they face.

*Follow-up:* How does your subject group fit into the overall organization of the school? What do you see as the significant features of the way your subject is organized and managed?

## CONCLUSION

In this chapter we have looked at how schools are affected by their history and location. We have also considered schools as complex organizations with many different functions and inter-relating systems.

How all these aspects combine to create an 'effective school' has been touched on here and is developed more fully in Chapter 16.

At this point we turn our attention to one of the questions which schools organize themselves to address: what should we teach? The next two chapters consider curriculum structures and the processes and issues associated with curriculum planning.

### Notes for further reading

For an overview of the histories of different types of school in the UK and excellent analyses of recent developments, see:

Lowe, R. (1989)
*Changing Secondary Schools,*
London: Falmer Press.

Kerckhoff, A. *et al.* (1996)
*Going Comprehensive in England and Wales,*
Woburn Press.

Gray, J., McPherson A. F. and Raffe, D. (1982)
*The Reconstructions of Secondary Education: Theory, Myth and Practice Since the War,*
London: Routledge.

Carr, W. and Hartnett, A. (1996)
*Education and the Struggle for Democracy,*
Buckingham: Open University Press.

Pole, C. J. and Chawla-Duggan, R. (1996)
*Reshaping Education in the 1990s: Perspectives on Secondary Education,*
London: Falmer Press.

Interesting recent studies of particular types of secondary schools are:

Benn, C. and Chitty, C. (1995)
*Thirty Years On: Is Comprehensive Education Alive and Well, or Struggling to Survive?,*
London: David Fulton.

Tomlinson, J. (1992)
*Small, Rural and Effective: A Study of Secondary Schools,*
Stoke-on-Trent: Trentham Books.

Halpin, D., Fitz, J. and Power, S. (1993)
*The Early Impact and Long-term Implications of the Grant-Maintained Schools Policy,*
Stoke-on-Trent: Trentham Books.

Walford, G. (ed.) (1984)
*British Public Schools: Policy and Practice,*
London: Falmer Press.

The management of resources in schools is a vital factor in their quality as work and learning environments. For an empirically based review of how secondary schools tackle this, see:

Thomas, H. and Martin, J. (1996)
*Managing Resources for School Improvement,*
London: Routledge.

An introduction to secondary school practices, written specifically to guide novice teachers, is:

Dean, J. (1996)
*Beginning Teaching in the Secondary School,*
Buckingham: Open University Press.

There has been a great deal of emphasis in recent years on the development of 'collaborative, whole-school staff cultures' and this is reflected in the first book below. However, the second reveals a more challenging picture of endemic differentiation in UK schools.

Lieberman, A. (1990)
*Schools as Collaborative Cultures: Creating the Future Now,*
London: Falmer Press.

Abraham, J. (1995)
*Divide and School: Gender and Class Dynamics in Comprehensive Education,*
London: Falmer Press.

For accounts of teachers fulfilling their personal and professional commitments in widely different school settings, see:

Hansen, D. T. (1995)
*The Call to Teach,*
New York: Teachers College Press.

Ball, S. and Goodson, I. (eds) (1985)
*Teachers' Lives and Careers,*
London: Falmer Press.

Little, J. W. and McLaughlin, M. W. (1993)
*Teachers' Work: Individuals, Colleagues and Contexts,*
New York: Teachers College Press.

A comprehensive overview of a wide range of contextual factors which affect teachers' work experience in the modern UK situation is:

Preedy, M., Glatter, R. and Levacic, R. (eds) (1997)
*Educational Management: Strategy, Quality and Resources,*
Buckingham: Open University Press.

For books on the impact on the Education Reform Act and parental choice on secondary schools, see:

Bowe, R. and Ball, S. with Gold, A. (1992)
*Reforming Education and Changing Schools,*
London: Routledge.

Glatter, R., Woods, P. and Bagley, C. (1996)
*Choice and Diversity in Schooling: Perspectives and Prospects,*
London: Routledge.

The best recent study of school governors is:

Deem, R., Brehony, K. and Heath, S. (1995)
*Active Citizenship and the Governing of Schools,*
Buckingham: Open University Press.

A classic book on the culture of secondary schools and issues in their development, now updated, is:

Sarason, S. B. (1996)
*Revisiting 'The Culture of the School and the Problem of Change',*
New York: Teachers College Press.

Other milestone publications on the school culture, climate and organization, are:

Rutter, M., Maugham, B., Mortimore, P. and Ouston, J. (1979)
*Fifteen Thousand Hours,*
London: Open Books

Hargreaves, D. (1982)
*The Challenge for the Comprehensive School,*
London: Routledge.

Fullan, M. (1991)
*The New Meaning of Educational Change,*
London: Cassell.

A simple introduction to the internal working of secondary schools is:

Smith, R. (1995)
*Successful School Management,*
London: Cassell.

For more detailed studies of senior leadership, management processes and micro-political activiety, see:

Evetts, J. (1995)
*Becoming a Secondary Headteacher,*
London: Cassell.

Wallace, M. and Hall, V. (1994)
*Inside the Senior Management Team: Teamwork in Secondary School Management,*
London: Paul Chapman.

Blase, J. and Anderson, G. (1995)
*The Micropolitics of Educational Leadership,*
London: Cassell.

Ball, S. J. (1987)
*The Micropolitics of the School,*
London: Routledge.

Hoyle, E. (1986)
*The Politics of School Management,*
London: Hodder and Stoughton.

Mortimore, P. and Mortimore, J. (eds) (1991)
*The Secondary Head: Roles, Responsibilities and Reflections,*
London: Paul Chapman.

On departmental organization, consider the issues raised by:

Gold, A. (1996)
*Managing a Department,*
London: Heinemann.

Siskin, L. S. and Little, J. W. (1995)
*The Subjects in Question: Departmental Organization and the High School,*
New York: Teachers College Press.

On taking reponsibility for a 'tutor-group', see:

Marland, M. (1989)
*The Tutor and the Tutor Group: Developing Your Role as a Tutor,*
London: Longman.

Waterhouse, P. (1990)
*Tutoring,*
Stafford: Network Educational Press.

For a good overview of issues in pastoral and socal education, see:

Best, R., Lang, P., Lodge, C. and Watkins, C. (eds) (1995)
*Pastoral Care and PSE: Entitlement and Provision,*
London: Cassell.

Lowe, P. (1988)
*Responding to Adolescent Needs: A Pastoral Care Approach,*
London: Cassell.

The best recent empirical study of the tensions between pastoral and academic systems is:

Power, S. (1996)
*The Pastoral and the Academic: Conflict and Contradiction in the Curriculum,*
London: Cassell.

For a comprehensive survey of secondary school teachers' work in the 1990s, see:

Campbell, R. J. and Neill, S. R. St. J. (1994)
*Secondary Teachers at Work,*
London: Routledge.

For pupil perspectives on secondary school settings, read:

Ruddock, J., Chaplain, R and Wallace, G. (1995)
*School Improvement: What Can Pupils Tell Us?,*
London: David Fulton.

# CHAPTER 6

# What are the main curriculum structures?

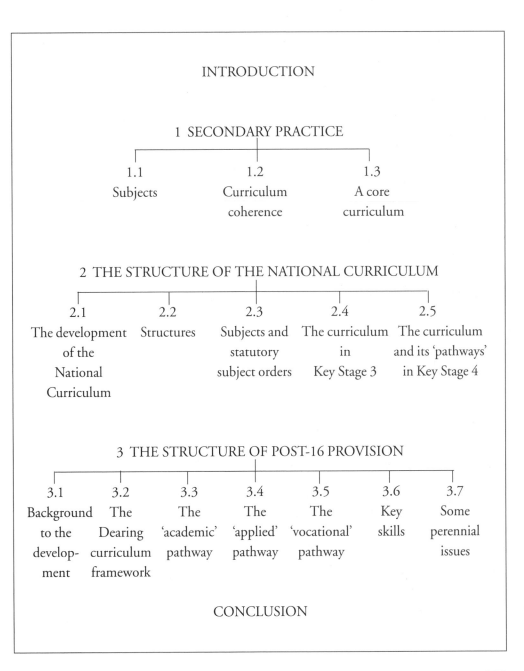

INTRODUCTION

1 SECONDARY PRACTICE

| 1.1 | 1.2 | 1.3 |
|---|---|---|
| Subjects | Curriculum coherence | A core curriculum |

2 THE STRUCTURE OF THE NATIONAL CURRICULUM

| 2.1 | 2.2 | 2.3 | 2.4 | 2.5 |
|---|---|---|---|---|
| The development of the National Curriculum | Structures | Subjects and statutory subject orders | The curriculum in Key Stage 3 | The curriculum and its 'pathways' in Key Stage 4 |

3 THE STRUCTURE OF POST-16 PROVISION

| 3.1 | 3.2 | 3.3 | 3.4 | 3.5 | 3.6 | 3.7 |
|---|---|---|---|---|---|---|
| Background to the development | The Dearing curriculum framework | The 'academic' pathway | The 'applied' pathway | The 'vocational' pathway | Key skills | Some perennial issues |

CONCLUSION

## INTRODUCTION

We begin this chapter by identifying four important conceptions of 'curriculum'.

### The official curriculum

The official curriculum can be defined as 'a planned course of study', i.e. an explicitly stated programme of learning, perhaps incorporating a national curriculum which has been endorsed by government. Such a course of study is likely to have three elements. First, there will be an intended curriculum content which will have been consciously planned. However, it may not always actually be taught nor is it likely to include learning which may take place outside school. Second, the official curriculum will usually structure sequence and progression, thus framing the content and course of activities. Third, the planned course of study will be designed with the intention of challenging young people appropriately and matching their learning needs.

The development of national curricula and of coherent whole-school planning are undoubtedly the most significant developments in curriculum provision in recent decades. Parallel developments have taken place in many parts of the world and, whilst there are obvious differences in each country, there are also many similarities in the ways in which aims are identified and structures created. However, for this chapter, we have focused mainly on developments within the UK, though suggestions for following up the initiatives of other countries are offered in the Notes on Further Reading.

In 1988, for the first time in the UK's history, parliament set out aims for educational provision in state-maintained schools. The Education Reform Act states that the curriculum must:

- be balanced and broadly based
- promote the spiritual, moral, cultural, mental and physical development of pupils
- prepare pupils for the opportunities, responsibilities and experiences of adult life.

A structure, content and assessment system for the official curriculum was developed so that teachers and student teachers are now required to accommodate their classroom planning within the statutory curriculum and assessment framework.

Of course, the intention of all official curricula is that the structure will ensure that the learning experience of young people is coherent and that they will benefit from curricular progression as they move through the education system. However, high quality curriculum provision for the classroom will always be enriched by the particular imagination, knowledge and enthusiasms of individual teachers. In Chapters 7 and 10, we identify how this unique contribution can be made, and the issues and constraints schools face in making official curricula available to pupils.

### The hidden curriculum

The hidden curriculum consists of all that is learnt during school activities which is not a designated part of the official curriculum. It is what is 'picked up' about such things as the role of the teacher and the role of the learner, about the status and relationships of each, about attitudes towards learning and to school. For instance, pupils may develop ideas about gender roles, or about about differences 'because' of ethnicity or social class. Thus the hidden curriculum is implicit and is embedded within taken-for-granted school procedures and curriculum materials. It may be unrecognized and is often unexamined, but it can have a profound effect on the self-image of pupils, upon their images of school and on their attitudes to other social groups.

### The observed curriculum

This is the curriculum that can be seen to be taking place in the classroom. It may, of course, be different from the intended official curriculum. If so, it may be useful for teachers to identify and evaluate such differences. It must be remembered however, that what can be seen in terms of subject content or activities, is not the same thing as how the young people feel about it, or what they learn through it.

### The curriculum-as-experienced

This way of conceptualizing the curriculum identifies the parts of the curriculum, both official and hidden, which actually connect meaningfully with young people. Arguably, it is only this aspect of curriculum which actually has an educational impact upon them. The rest is often forgotten.

In this chapter we focus mainly on the official curriculum, attending to the hidden, observed and experienced curriculum in many other ways throughout the book. The chapter is in three main parts. In Section 1, we take stock of developments in curricular practices in secondary schools and consider three main issues: the use of subjects as the basis of the secondary school curriculum, the challenge of achieving differentiation so that the curriculum is suited to the needs of learners, and the extent to which a core curriculum is necessary or desirable. In Section 2 we review the way the National Curriculum was introduced into England and Wales and begin to explore curriculum provision for the age groups: 11–14 (Key Stage 3), 14–16 (Key Stage 4). In particular, we discuss some of the ways that the issues identified in Section 1 of the chapter are reflected in the curriculum at these different stages. Section 3 reviews important developments in the structure of the Post-16 curriculum. Approaches to planning and implementing the curriculum at whole-school and faculty/department levels and the work of the individual subject teacher in planning classroom teaching and assessment are the subjects of Chapters 7, 10 and 14.

## 1 · SECONDARY PRACTICE

Separate subjects have traditionally provided the basis of the curriculum in secondary schools. As we have seen in previous chapters, they are significant in shaping the professional identity of secondary school teachers and in influencing their roles in schools' organizational structures. We start this part of the chapter by exploring why subjects are so fundamental in secondary schools, and begin from philosophical and historical perspectives.

## 1.1 Subjects

A subject-based curriculum is one which maintains high subject boundaries and thus sustains distinctions between subjects. The resulting curriculum, therefore, is a collection of separate subjects. Indeed, it has been called a 'collection curriculum' (Bernstein 1971, **Primary Reading 7.2**).

A philosophical rationale for a subject-based curriculum is that each element is based on logical structures of knowledge. Indeed, Hirst (1967) has suggested a classification of knowledge into seven 'forms':

- Mathematical
- Empirical (physical and social sciences)
- Aesthetic (the expressive arts)
- Mental (values and intentions)
- Philosophical
- Moral
- Religious.

However, Hirst distinguished between ' forms' of knowledge and 'fields' of knowledge:

> Although the domain of human knowledge can be regarded as composed of a number of logically distinct forms of knowledge, we do in fact for many purposes, deliberately and self-consciously organize knowledge into a large variety of fields which often form units employed in teaching. (Hirst 1967, p. 44)

Thus whilst some school subjects might be seen as 'forms' of knowledge, having logical structures and distinct concepts, others may be regarded as 'fields' of knowledge, characterized by their subject matter and drawing upon more than one form. Hirst cites geography as an example of a field of knowledge, whereas mathematics he suggested was a form of knowledge. This argument suggests that a school subject may be justified either because it is a fundamental and logical form of knowledge, or because it involves study of a particularly significant field of human activity (see also **Primary Reading 7.3** Barrow 1988).

An alternative perspective suggests that the classification of knowledge is socially and historically determined, rather than based on logical structures. Perhaps this was most powerfully argued in a collection of papers published in the early 1970s, *Knowledge and Control* (Young 1971). From this perspective, what counts as knowledge is contested and the dominant view arises from the competing definitions that are offered by various groups in a society. It follows that the way knowledge is classified and valued will reflect the distribution of power within a society.

> It may be useful to view curricular changes as involving changing definitions of knowledge. . . . Furthermore, as we assume that patterns of social relationships are associated with any curriculum, these changes will be resisted in so far as they are perceived to undermine the value, relative power and privileges of the dominant group involved. (Young 1971, p. 34)

This argument would suggest that the curricula of secondary schools do not reflect a logical division of knowledge, but arise from a struggle between alternative ways of conceptualizing knowledge and alternative beliefs about what it is worthwhile for young people to know. From this perspective, to understand the subject-based curriculum that is common in secondary schools, it is necessary to look at the historical development of secondary curricula.

In its early stages, the education system evolved to enable the elite of society to reproduce itself. Accumulated knowledge and skills were to be passed on to a new generation. It was only at a much later stage, with advanced industrialization and urbanization, that the need for the further education of the wider workforce was required. Thus we had provision for a national system of elementary education in the Education Act of 1870, and for secondary education in 1904.

Robert Morant, an influential civil servant, drafted the 1904 Regulations for Secondary Schools. However, he did not believe in secondary education for all and he based the regulations on the curricula of the established and independent 'public schools', thus reflecting the dominant view of knowledge at the time. The following subjects were required to be taught: English language, English literature, a language other than English, geography, history, mathematics, science, drawing, provision for manual work and physical exercise, and, in girls schools only, housewifery. From 1917 onwards, with the introduction of the School Certificate, examination boards began to exert increasing influence on secondary school curricula, which further reinforced the emphasis on subjects. The list of subjects in the 1935 regulations was thus virtually unchanged.

Secondary schools were initially intended for a small minority, the sons of the middle classes, and this expanded first to include middle-class girls and then all social groups. Nevertheless, in the 1930s only a minority of young people were in secondary schools. The situation was transformed by the 1944 Education Act, which provided for universal secondary education up to the age of 15, with the school-leaving age raised to 16 only as recently as 1972. The public and grammar schools, originally intended for middle-class boys, were generally regarded as providing the best available kind of schooling and became the model for the other kinds of school which were to follow, thus reinforcing the influence of relatively traditional views of subject knowledge.

However, it was recognized at an early stage of the development of state secondary education that the academic curricula of the public schools might not be appropriate for all young people. The Hadow report (Board of Education 1926) suggested that the majority of young people were likely to benefit from more practical curricula. It distinguished 'practical' from 'vocational' curricula, arguing that the former were concerned with intellectual training whilst the latter were focused on specific skills and understanding required for particular occupations. Though the report suggested that the majority of young people required different provision from that offered in public schools, it argued that practical curricula should not be regarded as inferior, and called for parity of esteem. As we saw in Chapter 5, neither the post-1944 tripartite system nor the comprehensive system realized this aspiration and traditional academic curricula, based around separate subjects, has continued to enjoy a higher status than the alternatives.

In Section 3 of this chapter we will explore the way this issue is re-emerging in the context of vocational and academic qualifications for Post-16 education.

At this point we suggest you undertake Practical Activity 6.1 to gain some perspective on how your own subject has been defined and constructed in the National Curriculum.

### Practical activity 6.1

*Aim:* To consider social influences on the construction of curriculum subjects.

*Method:* Study your own specialist subject and its development in recent years. If possible, focus down further, say to how your subject is taught in a particular Key Stage.

- Collect available national and school documentation specifying content and forms of assessment over the period.
- Talk to experienced teachers who taught the subject during the period and ask about the major influences which they recall.
- Search in sources such as the *Times Educational Supplement* for evidence of any major debates which influenced your subject's development (in many education libraries as hardcopy, microfiche or CD Rom).

Try to integrate and take stock of this material. What were the major developments? Were they associated with particular social or political pressures, 'moral panics' on standards, events, or with evolving professional opinions and experience?

*Follow-up:* The history of the development of curriculum subjects is a fascinating topic (see the Notes for Further Reading). Above all, it helps in putting new pressures and events into some sort of perspective. What are the current debates concerning your specialist subject? Can you detect social and political interests lying behind those debates?

## 1.2  Curriculum coherence

Though the dominant and traditional way of understanding secondary schools' curricula has been based on subjects, some have tried to encourage a perspective in which attention is focused on the relationships between subjects and the achievement of curriculum coherence. In the mid-1970s, for example, HMI started to encourage teachers to look beyond their subjects to the learning opportunities they provided for young people, and they expressed reservations about curricula expressed as lists of subjects:

> It is not proposed that schools should plan and construct a common curriculum in terms of subject labels only. Rather it is necessary to look through the subject or discipline to the areas of experience and knowledge to which it may provide access, and to the skills and attitudes which it may assist to develop. (DES 1977, p. 6)

HMI initially proposed eight 'areas of experience' but the list was later amended and expanded to nine areas: the aesthetic and creative; the human and social; the linguistic and literary; the mathematical; the moral; the physical; the scientific; the spiritual; the technological (DES 1985b, p. 16). The idea that all teachers shared responsibility for developing pupils as language users (talkers, listeners, readers and writers) was highlighted by the Bullock report (DES 1975, see Chapter 13).

> We must convince the teacher of history or science, for example, that he (*sic*) has to understand the process by which pupils take possession of the historical or scientific information that is offered them; and that such an understanding involves his paying particular attention to the part language plays in learning. (DES 1975, p. 188)

In the early 1990s, the concern for curriculum coherence was manifested in the introduction into the National Curriculum of cross-curricular issues, dimensions, skills and themes (NCC 1990).

> *Dimensions:* with particular reference to equal opportunities for both sexes, and to multi-cultural education.
>
> *Skills:* which are transferable and can be taught by teachers across the whole curriculum: communication, numeracy, study, problem-solving, personal and social, information technology.
>
> *Themes:* which were regarded as providing an integrative focus on pre-eminent issues: for England, these were economic and industrial understanding, careers education and guidance, health education, education for citizenship, environmental education.

Provision of careers education and guidance, and health education pre-existed in some form in most secondary schools. These were developed and in the case of health education frequently gained increased focus and status in the form of programmes in personal and social education (PSE). For the other topics, hopes and expectations that schools would weave these into their subject planning proved extremely difficult to sustain (Whitty, Aggleton and Rowe 1994). In the review of national qualifications (Dearing 1996) there was relatively little reference to cross-curricular themes, though 'key skills' were stressed (see Section 3.6). SCAA continued to produce guidance to schools, apparently in response to government priorities in areas of public interest and concern. For instance, in 1996 the foreword to the booklet, *Teaching Environmental Matters through the National Curriculum*, indicated:

> In view of the interest in environmental issues, we . . . were glad to respond to a request from the Secretary of State for Education and Employment to provide guidance to schools. . . . It is for schools to decide to what extent they wish to develop work in this area beyond their statutory obligation. (SCAA 1996e, foreword)

Enthusiasm for economic and industrial understanding waned in the late 1990s and concern for the 'moral climate' nationally brought 'citizenship' back into the discourse. An indication of the increased attention to the 'moral' in the ERA statement of the purpose of education ('to promote the spiritual, moral, cultural, mental and physical development of pupils at the school and of society') is provided by the publication in quick succession of two SCAA discussion papers. No. 3, *Spiritual and*

*Moral Development* (September 1995d) gives guidance to schools 'to demonstrate that these dimensions apply not only to Religious Education and collective worship but to every area of the curriculum and to all aspects of school life'; No. 6, *Education for Adult Life: the Spiritual and Moral Development of Young People* (July 1996b) reports on a conference convened by SCAA as a result of concern about 'a lack of focus on pupils' spiritual and moral development and its consequences.' Among many other suggestions was the proposal that, from the non-statutory curriculum, 'PSE, economic and political awareness and citizenship education' could provide routes into teaching in this area.'

Across the curriculum, it is often difficult for secondary teachers to know how the work they are doing fits in with that of colleagues teaching other subjects and this makes it difficult for them to build on and develop each other's work. How to ensure curriculum coherence, so that young people are able to synthesize the learning opportunities offered to them in the various subjects, is thus one of the main challenges that face secondary schools and teachers. Chapter 7 considers this further.

A core curriculum, which reduces diversity, has been seen as yet another way in which curriculum coherence might be enhanced and it is to this that we now turn.

## 1.3 A core curriculum

A 'core curriculum' has been defined as:

> Learnings judged to be basic and essential for all students: basic in that they provide both a foundation on which subsequent learning may be built and also the conceptual and methodological tools to continue their own learning. They are essential through their intention to equip students for a satisfying and effective participation in social and cultural life. (Skilbeck 1994, p. 98)

There is a sense in which, before the Education Reform Act, 1988, each school defined its own core curriculum which was common and required for all its pupils. However, since the Education Reform Act, 1988, the core curriculum has been determined by central government and each school in the maintained sector is required, by statute, to meet its requirements.

The Skilbeck quotation not only defines a core curriculum; it also provides a justification rooted in a view of what education is for. Arguments for a core curriculum generally proceed from ideas about the purposes of education. One strong case is based upon the principle of entitlement: whatever the kind of school young people attend, their background, ability or individual circumstances, they should have a right to experience and be taught certain key skills and forms of knowledge. This argument can be linked to the philosophical idea, which we discussed above in Section 1.1, that knowledge logically falls into a number of forms, each of which has its own purpose and value. This suggests the need for breadth and balance in the curriculum so that young people are able to develop a rounded understanding of human experience. Being unfamiliar with any of the forms of knowledge, according to this argument, would limit the students' understanding.

Another argument for a core curriculum is based on the view that schooling should prepare young people to participate as members of society, a view which was important in the initial development of comprehensive schools. Some argued that the tripartite system of grammar, technical and secondary modern schools, set up following the 1944 Education Act, had been socially divisive and that a common curriculum would help to eradicate social division and class distinctions. Others stress the role of schooling in strengthening a common culture. For instance, Lawton viewed the curriculum as a 'selection from the culture' (Lawton 1983) and suggested that there is a need for a core which includes some teaching related to each of the dimensions of social life. Connected to these arguments is the suggestion that young people need to be prepared to participate in a democracy. This requires them to be introduced to values which underpin democracy and to be able to understand, and make judgements about, social and moral issues. According to this view, a core curriculum is needed not only to induct young people into the traditions of their society but also to encourage them to be critical citizens, able to contribute and develop the society of which they are part.

A third argument for a core curriculum is derived from a concern for standards. During the 1970s and 1980s the diversity and curricular innovations evident in comprehensive schools and the growth of child-centred and integrated curricula in the primary sector were held responsible for a decline in standards, particularly in 'the basics'. These arguments were taken up by the press and received much public attention. A compulsory core curriculum has thus been seen by some as a means of re-establishing traditional values and ensuring the achievement of high standards, particularly of literacy and numeracy. Related to this argument is a concern about curriculum coherence, with a lack of continuity between primary and secondary schools and discontinuity in students' learning in secondary schools threatening progression. A core curriculum thus becomes a means of defining the standards that might be expected, enabling more careful monitoring of performance and securing progression in students' studies.

Finally, we must emphasize the importance of the needs of the economy in relation to arguments for a core curriculum, with industrialists and politicians having felt that  schools' curricula were not well matched to the needs of commerce and industry (see Callaghan 1976, **Primary Reading** 7.7). To some extent this concern is related to worries over standards, with some employers complaining that many young people lack the basic skills required for the workforce. However, there has also been a view that the study of academic subjects was not, in itself, a sufficient preparation for the world of work, and a concern that the extent of student choice in secondary schools has resulted in too few students studying science and technological subjects to the level required by the labour market. There was thus a need, it was suggested, for a more vocational orientation to the curriculum in order to secure a sufficiently highly skilled workforce to facilitate economic growth and enable the nation to compete effectively in the world economy. A core curriculum was seen as a way of ensuring that schools addressed the needs of industry and the nation as well as the needs of their individual students. Aspects of all of these arguments found expression in the National Curriculum and concerns for the relationship between schooling and the economy powerfully informed Sir Ron Dearing's review of the Post-16 curriculum. Following this through, in July 1995, the government departments dealing with education and employment were merged to become the Department for Education and

Employment (DFEE), and in October 1997 the two bodies dealing with school education (SCAA) and vocational training (NCVQ) were integrated into the Qualifications and Curriculum Authority (QCA).

We now turn to consider National Curriculum structures more closely.

## 2    THE STRUCTURE OF THE NATIONAL CURRICULUM

### 2.1   The development of the National Curriculum

It is possible to argue that the National Curriculum emerged from debates during the post-war period about the content and organization of the secondary school curriculum. Those debates were bound up with questions about: the nature of knowledge, the aims and purposes of schooling, and the ways in which secondary schools should be organized. This debate resulted in extensive, and sometimes rapid, curriculum change.

The specific origins of the policy initiatives which led to the National Curriculum are often traced back to the speech given by Prime Minister, James Callaghan, at Ruskin College in 1976 (**Primary Reading 7.7**). He referred to unease about informal methods of teaching, the case for the curriculum to cover 'basic knowledge', the importance of high standards to be maintained and to the need for improved relations between industry and education. The speech was followed by a 'Great Debate' in which these concerns were widely discussed and support began to grow for more central control of the curriculum. Initially, Secretaries of State in the new Conservative government, elected in 1979, showed little interest in a National Curriculum. However, after the appointment of Kenneth Baker in 1986, and following lobbying of Margaret Thatcher by right-wing pressure groups, the idea was energetically and quickly pursued. A consultation document was published in July 1987 and the Education Reform Act was passed in 1988. This introduced a clear structure for the education system in England and Wales and was intended to raise standards, broaden pupils' studies, and meet the needs of industry. It was meant to provide a clear specification of what children should be taught and what they might be expected to achieve at various stages through their schooling, backed up with testing of pupils to monitor achievement.

In 1989, a 'Task Group' for each subject was set up. Each group worked separately and a timetable was established for the introduction of the regulations relating to each subject. As a consequence, the requirements of some subjects became mandatory before final decisions on others had been made, and the planning lacked coherence. It also soon became clear that the curriculum was extremely overloaded with content and was too complex to manage. As difficulties accumulated, the need for the requirements to be 'slimmed down' was recognized. The problem at Key Stage 4 was particularly acute, as it became clear that it would be difficult to maintain the standards of GCSE at the same time as teaching all of the foundation subjects and whilst also allowing some degree of choice and specialization for students.

Sir Ron Dearing was appointed to slim down and simplify the National Curriculum. After receiving evidence from a large number of organizations and consulting teachers, he produced a report which included recommendations for significant, if not fundamental, change (Dearing 1993). For Key Stages 1, 2 and 3, he proposed that: 20 per cent of the time available for teaching should be left for use at the discretion of the school, the number of attainment targets should be reduced, but the requirement for all ten foundation subjects to be taught at Key Stage 3 should be retained. At Key Stage 4, he proposed that mandatory requirements should be limited to English, mathematics and single science, physical education and short courses in a modern foreign language and technology. He also emphasized the importance of careers education at Key Stage 4 and suggested that vocational courses should feature more prominently. He suggested that a General National Vocational (GNVQ) option should be developed in the medium term and that there should be discussions about how GCSE courses could count towards GNVQ accreditation. Very little emphasis was placed on cross-curricular elements, but attention was drawn to the need to enhance the profile of information technology as a distinctive part of technology. There were also proposals to reduce the complexity of assessment and to reduce the workload it placed on teachers, and these are discussed in more detail in Chapter 15. The proposals were accepted by the government and implemented from the 1995/6 school year.

## *Practical activity 6.2*

*Aim:* To review the *present* development of the National Curriculum.

*Method:* As we have seen, things change very rapidly in education and it is necessary to try to keep in touch. However, the system is now very complex and, for this reason, our first suggestion is that you need to set some specific objectives, such as:

- to get a broad overview of National Curriculum developments
- to study changes in relation to a specialist subject.

We suggest two main strategies:

- talking and discussing with appropriate colleagues
- studying key sources from a library, such as:

  - Newsletters and official documentation from the Qualifications and Curriculum Authority or from the DFEE

  - the *Education Journal* (for a commentary from teacher associations and LEAs);

  - the *Times Educational Supplement* (the main source of professional news and comment).

- studying latest developments through the DFEE or QCA internet home page:

  - http://www.open.gov.uk//dfee

*Follow-up:* Think about the future and, having tried the Practical Activity, consider how you can continue to keep up to date. It will make you much more effective professionally and in the development of your career.

## 2.2 Structures

There are many important features of the National Curriculum and of the modern education system of England and Wales, some of which we describe below. In doing so, we have drawn, in particular, on a SCAA/ACAC/TTA document, *A Guide to the National Curriculum* (SCAA 1996c). We have tried to use 'official' language. The following sections are thus a descriptive account of national structures and curriculum as they exist in the 1996/7 school year.

*Key Stages* denote periods of compulsory schooling which relate to the age of pupils and which, in terms of curriculum and assessment, are administered and provided for in somewhat similar ways. Key Stage 3 relates to the first three years of secondary education(11–14), and Key Stage 4 to the two-year preparation for GCSE and vocational examinations (14–16).

*Assessment points* come at the end of each Key Stage. In the case of secondary schooling, this is at the end point of the year in which pupils reach the ages of 14 (when SATs are completed) and 16 (when assessment is by GCSE) (see Chapter 15)

*Pupil year* is a way of describing the year-group of pupils.

Figure 6.1 clarifies the relationship between Key Stage, pupil year and pupil age. It also shows the way in which assessment takes place at the end of each key stage. We show the development from the primary years and across those of secondary education because one of the most valuable aspects of the National Curriculum is the expectation of continuity in the learning experiences provided between schools at transfer points.

| Age of pupils | Pupil year | Key Stage | School | Assessment |
|---|---|---|---|---|
| 5 or under | Reception (R) | Key Stage 1 | Infant school | |
| 6 | Year 1 (Y1) | | | |
| 7 | Year 2 (Y2) | | | At age 7 |
| 8 | Year 3 (Y3) | Key Stage 2 | Junior school | |
| 9 | Year 4 (Y4) | | | |
| 10 | Year 5 (Y5) | | | |
| 11 | Year 6 (Y6) | | | At age 11 |
| 12 | Year 7 (Y7) | Key Stage 3 | Secondary school | |
| 13 | Year 8 (Y8) | | | |
| 14 | Year 9 (Y9) | | | At age 14 |
| 15 | Year 10 (Y10) | Key Stage 4 | Secondary school | |
| 16 | Year 11 (Y11) | | | At age 16 |

**Figure 6.1** *Age of pupil, school year and Key Stage*

## 2.3 Subjects and statutory subject orders

In England, the Education Reform Act, 1988, established ten subjects as the basis of the National Curriculum for secondary education, and also required that pupils should receive appropriate religious education. In Wales, Welsh provides an additional subject.

The *foundation subjects* of the National Curriculum are thought to cover the range of knowledge, skills and understanding commonly accepted as necessary for a broad and balanced curriculum for individual pupils.Of these 'foundation subjects', some are officially identified as 'core foundation subjects' with the remainder as 'other foundation subjects'. However, in practice, they are commonly known simply as 'core' and 'foundation subjects'. There are slight variations in the National Curriculum subjects for Key Stages 3 and 4, as shown in Figures 6.2 and 6.4.

'Subject orders' are statutory and consist of 'common requirements', 'programmes of study' and 'attainment targets'. There is non-statutory guidance to support schools, and some variations of parts of the National Curriculum are possible to meet pupil needs.

- *Common requirements* apply to each of the 'subject orders'. They cover issues such as access to the curriculum for all pupils, the use of spoken and written language (including grammatically correct sentences and correct spelling and punctuation), provision of opportunities to use information technology and, in Wales, opportunities to apply knowledge and understanding to Wales.

- *Programmes of study* set out essential knowledge, skills and processes which need to be covered in each subject by pupils in each stage of schooling. These are minimum statutory entitlements. Programmes of study are intended to be used by schools in constructing schemes of work.

- *Attainment targets* are defined from within programmes of study to represent the knowledge, skills and understanding which pupils are expected to master as they progress through school. Attainment targets are used in assessment procedures. As we shall see in Chapter 15, Section 1.1, pupil attainment for each attainment target is described by 'levels of attainment', using either 'level descriptions' or 'end of Key Stage descriptions'.

- *Non-statutory guidance* comes in a variety of publications from the Qualifications and Curriculum Authority, and was formerly produced by SCAA, NCC and SEAC. It is intended to offer helpful advice on the implementation of the National Curriculum and assessment procedures.

- *Modifications, disapplications and exceptions* are terms used for various arrangements for lifting part or all of the National Curriculum requirements to meet the particular circumstances of pupils or schools. These procedures might, for instance, be applied tochildren with special educational needs, working within the SEN Code of Practice (DFE 1994).

We now move on to consider curriculum provision for each phase of secondary education.

## 2.4 The curriculum in Key Stage 3

This section is matched by Chapter 15, Section 1.1, which considers assessment at Key Stage 3.

The first Dearing Report (Dearing 1993) emphasized the need for breadth at Key Stage 3, the opportunity for pupils to deepen their understanding of the subjects they had studied in primary schools, and the need to provide a basis for informed choices at Key Stage 4. However, the report also recognized the importance of students being well motivated and the ways in which, at this age, they were becoming more independent and clearer about their own interests.

The subjects required at Key Stage 3 are identical to those that must be taught in the primary school, with the addition that study of a modern foreign language becomes compulsory once students enter secondary school. An overview of this is provided in Figure 6.2.

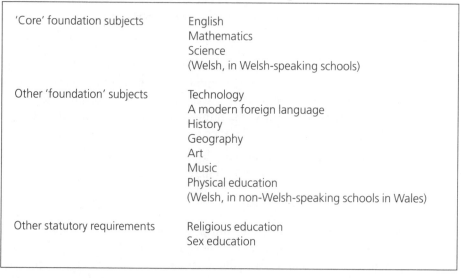

| 'Core' foundation subjects | English |
| | Mathematics |
| | Science |
| | (Welsh, in Welsh-speaking schools) |
| | |
| Other 'foundation' subjects | Technology |
| | A modern foreign language |
| | History |
| | Geography |
| | Art |
| | Music |
| | Physical education |
| | (Welsh, in non-Welsh-speaking schools in Wales) |
| | |
| Other statutory requirements | Religious education |
| | Sex education |

**Figure 6.2** *Statutory National Curriculum requirements for Key Stage 3 in England and Wales*

Figure 6.3 lists the Attainment Targets which are associated with each subject for Key Stage 3 in England and Wales.

Key Stage 3 of the National Curriculum therefore seeks to balance the need for broad entitlement with some flexibility. As we indicated above, the balance that has been struck involves about 80 per cent of the time available for teaching being devoted to mandatory requirements, with the remaining 20 per cent or so to be at the discretion of the school. It might be thought that curriculum planning at Key Stage 3 needs only to concern itself with the 20 per cent of time which is at the discretion of the school but, as we shall see in Chapter 7, there are many detailed organizational decisions which need to be made to implement the National Curriculum in individual schools.

At the end of Key Stage 3, pupils move on to the required elements of Key Stage 4, but must also make 'option choices' for those elements which are discretionary.

| Subject | Attainment targets in England | Attainment targets in Wales |
|---|---|---|
| English | Speaking and listening<br>Reading<br>Writing | Speaking and listening<br>Reading<br>Writing |
| Welsh | Not applicable | Oral (speaking, listening & viewing)<br>Reading<br>Writing |
| Maths | Using and applying mathematics<br>Number<br>Algebra<br>Shape, space and measures<br>Handling data | Using and applying mathematics<br>Number<br>Algebra<br>Shape, space and measures<br>Handling data |
| Science | Experimental and investigative<br>    science<br>Life processes and living things<br>Materials and their properties<br>Physical processes | Experimental and investigative<br>    science<br>Life processes and living things<br>Materials and their properties<br>Physical processes |
| Design and technology | Designing<br>Making | Designing<br>Making |
| Information Technology | Information technology capability | Information technology capability |
| Modern foreign language | Listening and responding<br>Speaking<br>Reading and responding<br>Writing | Listening and responding<br>Speaking<br>Reading and responding<br>Writing |
| History | History | History |
| Geography | Geography | Geography |
| Art | Investigating and making<br>Knowledge and understanding | Understanding<br>Making<br>Investigating |
| Music | Performing and composing<br>Listening and appraising | Performing<br>Composing<br>Appraising |
| Physical education | Physical education | Physical education |

**Figure 6.3** *Attainment Targets within each National Curriculum subject for Key Stage 3 in England and Wales*

133

## 2.5 The curriculum and its 'pathways' in Key Stage 4

This section is matched by Chapter 15, Section 1.2 on assessment in Key Stage 4.

Following the first Dearing Report (1993), the range of subjects required at Key Stage 4 became much narrower than that at Key Stage 3 (compare Figure 6.2 with Figure 6.4 below). This occurred because experience in the early 1990s showed a considerable risk of overloading both the timetable and the learning capacities of many pupils as each subject became more detailed.

| | |
|---|---|
| Core foundation subjects | English<br>Mathematics<br>Science<br>(Welsh, in Welsh-speaking schools) |
| Other foundation subjects | Physical education<br>Technology*<br>A modern foreign language<br>(Welsh, in non-Welsh-speaking schools in Wales) |
| Other statutory requirements | Religious education<br>Sex education<br>Careers education<br>Information technology |

*Technology is not compulsory in Wales

**Figure 6.4** *Statutory National Curriculum subject requirements for Key Stage 4 in England and Wales*

For Key Stage 4, these statutory requirements are expected to take up about 60 per cent of curriculum time, leaving 40 per cent for teaching which is locally determined. This reflects the thinking of Sir Ron Dearing whose report argued that:

> We need a framework at Key Stage 4 that encourages schools to provide a curriculum which:
> * continues to develop knowledge and skills in key subject areas
> * motivates all students and ensures high expectations
> * develops a range of talents and raises standards
> * provides recognition and progress at age 16
> * keeps open a range of education and training options and promotes progression through to education and training Post-16.
>
> (Dearing 1993, p. 44)

Reducing National Curriculum requirements for Key Stage 4 meant that schools were thus able to begin to respond to the particular aptitudes and inclinations of students. For instance, the notion of 'full', 'short' or 'combined' courses developed as a way of providing a range of curricular options, such as history, geography, art and music, and new subject options such as classical studies or a second foreign language were introduced.

However, of perhaps even greater significance was the fact that the new dispensation also made possible the gradual development of a range of 'pathways' into Post-16 education and training. Indeed, Dearing developed this concept considerably in his second report (1996) which focused on 16–19 education (see Section 3.2). There he explicitly suggested identifying three pathways, the 'academic', the 'applied' and the 'vocational' – and the influence of these is now rolling back into Key Stage 4.

The three pathways, with their major qualifications and underlying purposes are:

- *Academic (GCSE and A-level).* Where the primary purpose is the development of knowledge, understanding and skills associated with a subject.
- *Applied (various levels of GNVQ).* Where the primary purpose is to develop and apply knowledge, understanding and skills relevant to broad areas of employment.
- *Vocational (various levels of NVQ).* Where the primary purpose is to develop and recognize mastery of a particular trade or profession at the relevant level.

Four 'National Levels' were envisaged: 'advanced', 'intermediate', 'foundation' and 'entry'. The three lower levels could be achieved in Key Stage 4 and the overall framework provides a structure for mixing and transfer between pathways with the equivalence of work in each pathway being denoted by a system of 'National Awards' for each level. Reference to Figure 6.5, which sets out the overall framework of pathways, levels and qualifications from age 14–19, may be helpful in clarifying these distinctions and also in the following discussion of the pathways at Key Stage 4.

## The Key Stage 4 'academic' pathway

The academic pathway is the dominant route through Key Stage 4 and is structured by the General Certificate of Secondary Education (GCSE), taken by over 80 per cent of pupils each year. This qualification was established in 1986 following the merger of GCE O-level and CSE. The new examination aimed to be more broadly based than O-level and involved more practical work, school-based assessment and coursework. Since the development of the National Curriculum, the syllabi have been co-ordinated, so there is more commonality and limitations regarding the proportion of the award that can be determined by coursework. Students are entered for separate subjects and their performance is graded on a scale of A–G, with the A grade being starred (A\*) for those candidates whose achievement is assessed as exceptional. New 'short courses' at GCSE were introduced in 1995. Whilst the GCSE was originally designed for all pupils, there has been concern about their suitability for pupils with learning difficulties. 'Subject certificates' and unit-based subject schemes are sometimes used to meet these needs. However, public perception of the value of the lower grades of GCSE is variable, with many employers still looking for the equivalent of a pass at O-level (Grades A–C).

## The Key Stage 4 'applied' pathway

A significant recent development at Key Stage 4 is a gradual increase in the number of schools offering General National Vocational Qualifications, Part One (mainly at foundation level). GNVQs were originally developed for use Post-16 as a middle pathway between academic and NVQ provision (see Section 3.5 and Figure 6.5).

In 1996/7 Part One GNVQ courses were piloted in business, health and social care, manufacturing, art and design, leisure and tourism and information technology. Such courses are set to become increasingly significant at Key Stage 4 because of the route they offer to more established Post-16 pathways. Work can count towards a full GNVQ but is accredited only if the course is completed in Post-16 education.

### The Key Stage 4 'vocational' pathway

The call for a vocational pathway at Key Stage 4 arose from the concern to motivate and encourage achievement in those who have little interest in the sort of syllabuses normally provided by GCSE. More direct, vocational responses came in a variety of forms and from different sources. The main influences here are filtering down from Post-16 vocational initiatives, particularly the development of National Vocational Qualifications (NVQs). In the mid-1990s the various providers of these qualifications were in competition which produced considerable complexity (see below). A process of merger, collaboration, co-operation, brought about by a combination of market forces and government initiative, is gradually leading to rationalization, with the formation of the Qualifications and Curriculum Authority (QCA) being of enormous importance. In your school or college you may find some of the following, or their successor courses. These may be taken as 'link courses' between workplace training experiences and other educational provision.

- *'Initial Awards':* offered by The Royal Society of Arts Examination Board (RSA) and intended as 'stepping stones' into vocational studies. Available in: agricultural studies, care, computer graphics, environmental studies, food technology, media studies, travel and tourism, office studies, sports and recreation, and textiles.
- The *'Technological Baccalaureate':* offered by the City and Guilds of London Institute (CGLI). This provides a way of covering the core subjects and some foundation subjects at Key Stage 4. Students gain credit in units which fit with the National Curriculum. Since it is a course for 14–18 year olds, it offers opportunities for progression beyond 16.
- *National Vocational Qualifications, Level 1 (NVQ).* NVQs were first established as workplace-based training at 16-plus and awarding bodies accredit units related to specific occupations, with Level 2 being more advanced. See Figure 6.5 for equivalence with GCSE and progression to A-level equivalence at Level 3. We should note that NVQs are specifically intended for life-long learning, and may be taken at any point in a working career.

The development of academic, applied and vocational pathways at Key Stage 4 is likely to continue. As we saw in Section 1.3, the formation of the Department of Education and Employment (1995) and of the Qualifications and Curriculum Authority (1997) were powerful indicators of the trend towards the progressive integration of education and training. There are proposals that some pupils at Key Stage 4 should divide their time between school or college and training in workplaces. In this way young people less interested in what schools have to offer, would be able to undertake school-based study of National Curriculum requirements, whilst also being engaged in unpaid workplace training. Announcing the plan, the Secretary of State for Education and Employment was quoted as follows:

I think there is a case for having closer integration and more workplace-based education for certain groups of young people if, thereby, we can avoid demotivation and do something useful for employers at the same time. I think we can afford to be quite radical in the sorts of programmes we offer from age 14 onwards. (Shephard 1995, The *THES*, 14 April)

As we have indicated above and will focus on in Section 3, a major revision of the Post-16 curriculum and qualification framework took place in 1996. This has consequences for age 16 as a transitional point. Already there is discussion on how the 14–19 curriculum can be developed to retain in education the large numbers of disaffected pupils who drop out – a particular concern of Sir Ron Dearing. For example, from September 1996 pupils may be awarded a new national qualification in literacy, numeracy and IT. The aim is to motivate pupils who are not ready for full GCSEs at 16. The qualification (which must gain a national 'kitemark' approval) is seen as a basis for progress to GCSE and NVQ, a first step towards a new 'entry level' award. This, together with the Foundation Level GNVQ courses mentioned earlier, indicates the widening of options in Key Stage 4. Schools are likely to be involved in further development of the vocational Key Stage 4 curriculum in partnership with industrial companies and other organizations.

A key issue for the future is the relative status that will be given to the vocational and academic pathways. There is a danger that vocational courses will be seen as inferior to academic study which even the introduction of 'National Awards' to assert equivalence may be unable to prevent. There is some resonance here with the issues surrounding the tripartite system, set up by the 1944 Education Act, that we discussed in the first part of the chapter, and we will return to this question in Section 3.8, following our introduction of the Post-16 curriculum.

### Practical activity 6.3

*Aim:* To review the structure and range of Key Stage 4 curriculum provision in a school.

*Method:* In the school you are working in, talk to teachers and collect appropriate curricular documentation from planning documents and option guides for pupils, etc. Then classify the available courses in terms of the 'pathways' to which they relate:

- Academic pathway: required by the National Curriculum
- Academic pathway: discretionary
- Applied pathway
- Vocational pathway.

Consider the amount of time being devoted to each course and the range of pupil experiences which necessary constraints on school organization may impose.

*Follow-up:* Explore any patterns regarding which pupils are studying each type of course. For instance, is there any influence of social class, gender, ethnicity, disability, ability, etc?

## 3 | THE STRUCTURE OF POST-16 PROVISION

### 3.1 Background to Post-16 developments

The proportion of young people aged 16–19 in full-time education and training is steadily rising but remains low in comparison with other comparable countries. For instance, in 1990, 35 per cent of those aged 16–19 were participating in the UK compared with 70–80 per cent in countries such as Belgium, Canada, Denmark, Japan, the Netherlands, Sweden and the USA (DES 1991a). Given the growing importance to the economic well-being of the nation attached to education and training, it is not surprising that the government set ambitious new targets for participation and achievement of the age group. National Targets for Education and Training for the year 2000 include:

- 75 per cent of young people achieving NVQ level 2 competence in communication, numeracy and technology by the age of 19, with 35 per cent achieving level 3 competence by 21 years of age.
- 60 per cent of young people achieving two A-levels, an Advanced GNVQ or NVQ level 3 by the age of 21;
- 85 per cent achieving five GCSEs at grade C and above, or an Intermediate GNVQ or NVQ level 2 by the age of 19.

However, in 1996, national performance caused doubt that these targets would be met. For instance, the second target was achieved by 40 per cent of 21-year-olds and the third set of goals by only 63 per cent of 19-year-olds.

Greater participation has already meant that the range of young people continuing in education beyond the statutory school-leaving age has broadened and there has been a need to revise the curriculum in response to the greater diversity. Post-16 education has become available in a wide variety of organizations including schools, colleges of further education, sixth-form and tertiary colleges and in the workplace. Some schools do not provide courses Post-16 and their students must transfer to another organization to continue their education. Nevertheless it is important that all secondary school teachers are familiar with the kinds of courses on offer Post-16. As we shall see, the need for different providers involved with education Post-14 to work within a common framework, and possibly in partnership with each other, is becoming even more significant following a second review by Sir Ron Dearing, this time of the Post-16 framework of qualifications (Dearing 1996).

### 3.2 Dearing's Post-16 curriculum framework

This section is matched by Chapter 15, Section 1.3 on assessment in Post-16 education.

*The Review of Qualifications for 16–19 Year Olds* (Dearing 1996) was primarily commissioned because of a concern to improve standards of training and education for young people as they approached the workforce and higher education, but it was also important because of the enormous confusion in certification which then existed. Sir Ron was asked to produce a simpler and more coherent system. As he explained to the House of Commons Education Committee:

> People want something in which there is coherence, which they can understand, and the great problem at the moment is that there are upwards of 14,000 qualifications – and they keep changing. People find this incomprehensible, especially people in work such as employers and trade unions. If I may say so, I should think about half of employers still call the GCSE O-levels; A-levels is the one currency which everybody has got hold of, because it has been there for forty years. The NVQ is getting known; the GNVQ is known by name, but, amongst employers, it is very new, it has only been in the marketplace a short time and they are looking for something they can readily understand in which there is stability.
>
> I am interested in simplicity, especially things that can be done quickly rather than take a decade.
>
> I think it would be possible, if people were so minded, to say, 'We have got these three main pathways: academic, applied and vocational. In what way can we set them within a framework so that there is ready understanding amongst those who are not daily involved in this business?'
>
> Then I think it is a very, very simple thing to say, 'We have these qualifications, let us recognize four levels, perhaps suggesting to the awarding bodies that all their awards should be badged in these four levels, so an employer can look at the certificate and see right away.' And then we can have notes at the back of the qualification, which tell him, or her, all those things that are regarded by us, the community, as being at that level.
>
> Then one talks about coherence. For example, if someone begins on one pathway it may be possible to move over to another in a neighbouring subject without having to start at the bottom again. And so you start looking at structures of qualifications. And, happily, the GNVQ was developed at twelve units plus the three core skills; the A-level, when it is modularized, is most frequently six units. The A-level is regarded, for national target purposes, as half a GNVQ at the Advanced level. So the units intrinsically are the same size, and we have a good basis for proceeding.
>
> So I think there is scope, Sir, for developing something quickly that employers can quickly understand, and in doing so we can establish the national esteem which must be enjoyed by all achievement, whether it is within the vocational, applied, or general pathway.
>
> (Edited from a statement by Sir Ron Dearing to the
> House of Commons Education Committee, 17 January 1996)

There are three clear 'pathways', each with slightly different 'underlying purposes', and there are four 'national levels' and 'National Awards'. This yields a clear framework, as Figure 6.5 summarizes. This framework indicates equivalences, and thus provides scope for mixing elements of different pathways and for transfer between them.

| National Award | Academic pathway | Applied pathway | Vocational pathway |
|---|---|---|---|
| Advanced level | A-level and AS-level | GNVQ Advanced level | NVQ Level 3 |
| Intermediate level | GCSE Grades A*–C | GNVQ Intermediate level | NVQ Level 2 |
| Foundation level | GCSE Grades D-G | GNVQ Foundation level | NVQ Level 1 |
| Entry level | Key skills Communication; application of number; information technology Grades A/B/C | | |

**Figure 6.5** *The Dearing framework of pathways, levels and qualifications*

'National Entry provision', as the DFEE paper building on the Dearing Report put it (DFEE 1996), is intended to provide 'a bridge to learning' particularly for those young people who may not be ready to undertake NVQ Level 1, those with special education and training needs and those unclear about their career direction. The focus is on 'Key Skills' and the provision is structured by a formal agreement with a training provider, local Training Enterprise Council (TEC) or Careers Service.

## 3.3   The Post-16 'academic' pathway

In the UK, GCE A-level has been almost universally regarded as a 'gold standard' and it has traditionally provided the main gate-keeping function for entry into higher education. Following the clear preference of the Conservative government of the time, the 1996 Dearing Report took this as a given and sought to gain parity of esteem for alternative forms of study. To set the Dearing approach in context, it is useful to look at some of the recent history concerning debates about the Post-16 curriculum. A-levels, which were originally designed to select the 20 per cent of university entrants, have often been criticized for the narrow range of study that results from them. In an attempt to broaden the A-level curriculum, Advanced Supplementary (AS) levels were introduced. These are two-year courses which make the same kind of demands as A-level but have only half the content. In 1988, the Higginson Committee went further and argued that Post-16 provision should provide an experience which was broad and valuable in its own right, rather than being over-confined by preparation for higher education (DES 1988a). It proposed that students' A-level studies should consist of five subjects (rather than the traditional three A-levels) with syllabuses having reduced content. The proposals did not find favour with the government. However, they were shortly followed by suggestions from the School Examinations and Assessment Council (SEAC 1990) that AS-levels should become basic units from which students would build their academic studies. It was argued that, since the basic study unit would be one-sixth of the whole of the student's programme, this would facilitate broader studies. These proposals were also rejected by the Conservative government at the time which reaffirmed its commitment to A-levels as they had always existed.

Within Dearing's 16–19 report (1996) there was also encouragement for more breadth in Post-16 study, and the redefining of AS-level as 'Advanced Subsidiary' (rather than 'Advanced Supplementary')is significant. In this format, AS-level becomes a worthwhile exit point after one year of A-level study but is also a first half 'foundation' to which pupils may add a second year extension (to be known as 'A2'), thus achieving a full A-level. To be introduced in September 1998, this restructuring could lead to a broader curriculum in the first year of study and delay specialization.

Concerns have been expressed about inconsistencies between the demands of different subject syllabuses. A particular focus has been those A-level courses which are modular in design, with assessment points throughout the course. Some commentators have claimed that this has increased both participation and achievement, (Crombie White *et al.* 1995), and have argued that modular systems are more flexible and allow students to vary the length of time in which they complete their studies. The possibility of re-taking individual modules is seen as a way of supporting learning. Critics however, have been concerned that modular A-levels may result in reduced standards, and they point to the difficulties of monitoring many individual modules. Ironically the success of students in achieving higher grades in modular A-levels than they might have been expected to secure after a conventional course, has been cited as evidence of the lower standards of modular A-levels (Burstall 1995). From 1998, modular A-levels will have co-ordinated examinations twice a year, and re-takes will be permitted only once per module. Above all the A-level 'gold standard' in the academic pathway is to be maintained with rigour.

Whilst A-level is the predominant academic course available at Post-16, the International Baccalaureate has provided one alternative. Students study six subjects. All take maths, a science, social studies, two languages and a course in world literature in translation, though a fine arts subject can be taken as an alternative to one of these. Intended originally for international and multi-national schools, a small number of (mainly independent) schools in the UK have been attracted by the broader range of subjects that it offers and the 'international currency' of the award. However, in 1997 the incoming Labour government were attracted by the capacity of the Baccalaureate to combine breadth with depth. It is possible that it could be used as a model for further revision of A-level course structures.

## 3.4 The Post-16 'applied' pathway

Introduced specifically to meet the needs of the many young people for whom A-level was considered inappropriate, GNVQs are presented as an alternative route into higher education and employment, different from but of equal status with A-level. Indeed, Dearing initially recommended that GNVQs should be re-named 'applied A-levels' to signal his desire to position these courses alongside the more traditional 'academic' subjects.

GNVQs focus on the application of knowledge, skills and understanding in broad vocational areas, such as business, health and social care, engineering and art and design. An important feature of the GNVQ model is its clear specification of outcomes and its encouragement of independent, active and applied approaches to learning.

Advanced GNVQ is equivalent to two A-levels and is normally offered as a two-year full-time programme. A strong feature of GNVQ is its unitized or modular structure. Students take four mandatory units at Intermediate Level (which are the same irrespective of the awarding body) and two optional units (which vary from one awarding body to another). At Advanced Level students take eight mandatory units and four optional units. There are also three mandatory 'key skill' units on 'communication', 'application of number', and 'information technology' (see Section 3.6). Other units, such as 'improving own learning and performance' and 'problem-solving', may also be accredited.

However, although there were almost 200,000 GNVQ registrations in 1994/5, take-up by pupils, parents and schools has been perceived as relatively slow. There are several possible reasons for this. First, there is the question of the social status of the qualification. For instance, in the summer of 1995 the *Times Educational Supplement* reported a lack of confidence in GNVQs as a preparation for study in higher education amongst some university lecturers. A Director of Admissions was quoted as saying, 'the "good" do A-levels: the rest do GNVQs'. Second, there is the issue of the effectiveness of GNVQs as a preparation for work. BTEC, in its 1995 annual report, observed that the proportion of students with GNVQs who failed to secure employment was unacceptably high. Whilst it acknowledged that this might be due in part to lack of awareness of GNVQs by employers, it also suggested that the vocational elements needed to be enhanced and made more job-specific. A third problem, that of the overload of a complex assessment system, caused huge manageability problems in schools and colleges and was recognized by the Capey Report (1995).

Overall, whilst GNVQs were intended to provide an alternative to A-level, in their first few years there was certainly some doubt about the extent to which they provide appropriate preparation for both employment and higher education (Wolf 1997). However, they remain of national significance as a very important attempt to link the academic and the vocational and to enhance the relevance of education.

Dearing's 1996 proposals addressed these major concerns. Knowledge and understanding within the 'applied pathway' was made more explicit and the system of 'national awards' reaffirmed the parity of esteem of 'vocational' subjects in relation to traditional 'academic' study. Shorter courses (six units plus the three key skills units) made it possible to follow a single Advanced Level GNVQ (Applied A-level). There was also encouragement for the development of AS (Advanced Subsidiary) units within the 'applied pathway' to parallel those in the 'academic pathway'. Endorsing the Capey Report (1995), Dearing recommended that the assessment regime should be made simpler, more rigorous and cost-effective. A new system, including much greater use of external tests, is to be introduced from 1998 (see also Chapter 15, Section 4.8).

## 3.5 The Post-16 'vocational' pathway

This pathway has its origins in the variety of, mainly workplace-based, training courses which once had little status and were not part of a coherent framework of qualifications. The 1986 establishment of the National Council for Vocational Qualifications was designed to counteract this. Following the 1996 Dearing Report, NCVQ become part of the Qualifications and Curriculum Authority and began to work within the national framework of qualifications which Dearing had created (see Figure 6.5).

The system of National Vocational Qualifications (NVQs) provides a structure for organizing and recognizing vocational training throughout working lives. Most NVQs are therefore taken by adults as part of a 'lifelong learning' commitment. NVQs tend to be vocationally specific and are therefore often designed by employer organizations acting as 'lead bodies'. They frequently cover a wide range of standards and competences, are not constrained by any particular time period, use a flexible, unit-based system to combine elements, and enable credit to be transferred between workplaces. These versatile features make them valuable in industry, but they can be difficult to integrate into the structures of schools. NVQs were 'relaunched' in 1997, with a new separation of responsibility for setting standards and the design of qualifications.

Figure 6.6, below, shows the NVQ framework with the key distinction between eleven 'areas of competence' and five 'levels of competence'.

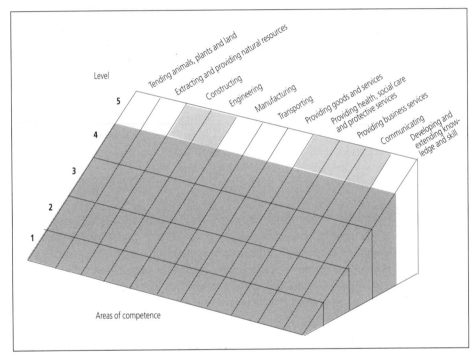

**Figure 6.6** *The NVQ framework at March 1997 (NCVQ)*

The five competency 'levels' normally represent gradations of the following (NCVQ 1995):

- breadth and range of competence
- complexity and difficulty of competence
- requirements for special skills
- ability to undertake specialized activities
- ability to transfer competences across a broad range of contexts
- ability to innovate and cope with non-routine activities
- ability to organize and plan work
- ability to supervise others.

NVQs have become the building blocks of 'National Traineeships' and 'Modern Apprenticeships'.

*National Traineeships* were launched following the 1996 Dearing Report as a response to national training needs and the plight of over 70,000 young people on the 'Youth Training Scheme' which existed at the time. This was commonly regarded as a low-status alternative to unemployment, or even as a way of massaging the national statistics of those out of work. The new National Traineeships are designed by Industry Training Organizations (ITOs) and local Training and Education Councils (TECs) and will be delivered as NVQ courses in association with FE colleges. Key skills are particularly important (see Section 3.6, below), as is the development of Entry level courses to pick up those who may have previously dropped out of the system.

*Modern Apprenticeships* began in 1995 to support able young people seeking Level 3 NVQs. Again, they were developed by ITOs working with TECs and FE colleges, and by 1996 they covered over fifty sectors of industry and commerce, ranging from accountancy to wool textiles. A distinctive feature of the scheme is that most Modern Apprentices are paid for their work during training. Dearing anticipated that around 60,000 young people per year could eventually take advantage of Modern Apprenticeships.

The National Record of Achievement may be particularly significant for the learners on the 'vocational pathway'. It acts as a way of recording 'lifetime learning', encouraging more coherent development of qualifications and improving completion rates (see Chapter 15, Section 5.3 for more details).

## 3.6 Key skills

There is a strong emphasis on 'key skills' at the Entry Level of each of the three pathways and across all the various routes to national qualifications. This reflects long-standing concerns over transferable skills in literacy and numeracy as young people enter the workforce, and a new awareness of the significance of computers and technology in all walks of life. The mandatory key skills are thus:

- communication
- application of number
- use of information technology.

However, three non-mandatory key skills have also been identified:

- working with others
- improving own learning and performance
- problem-solving.

The importance attached to such skills has grown in recent years. In 1990, the NCC identified a similar list of core skills for all 16–19-year-olds: communication, numeracy, problem-solving, information technology, personal skills and competence at a modern foreign language. However, it was felt that performance in these skills could be most appropriately recorded in a Record of Achievement rather than through 'academic' examinations. Now however, the Qualifications and Curriculum Authority is committed to working on the incorporation of key skills across vocational, applied and academic pathways and within all forms of assessment. In addition, schools and colleges may enrol pupils in specific skill development courses. These skills are seen as being highly appropriate for developing as independent learners, for teamwork, lifelong learning and employment. A new Key Skill qualification will apply across academic, applied and vocational pathways.

## 3.7  Some perennial issues

The Dearing Review of 16–19 qualifications was commissioned, as we have seen, in the context of considerable criticism of the UK education and training system, with extensive calls for fundamental reform. The changes which have followed are certainly radical – but will they succeed? Some perennial issues remain. What should be the relationship between academic and vocational study? How can flexibility and coherence be provided? Is it possible to maintain 'parity of esteem'?

Finegold *et al.* (1990) saw the origin of the exclusivity and narrowness of the UK education system in its separation of vocational and academic tracks. They suggested that the divided system was based on the questionable assumption that the economy required the separation of mental and manual labour; was dominated by selection despite the need to improve participation and achievement for all; and was inflexible in the way it inhibited movement between the tracks. Their proposal was for a 'British Baccalaureate' which would have involved a single national qualifications authority and a single diploma to replace A- and AS-levels and vocational awards. This call for a unified system was articulated more recently by Dunford (1995), President of the Secondary Heads Association. The latter suggested:

> We are told by government ministers that, Post-16, the dual carriageway has become a three-lane highway with A-level, GNVQ and NVQ in parallel. This analogy misrepresents the present situation since there is no opportunity for students, unlike motorists, to change from one lane to another, except by returning to the start. (Dunford 1995, p. 51)

If this argument turns out to be well founded, then opportunities and potential could both be constrained.

This was an immediate concern of the new Labour government which took office in 1997. The basic commitment to the Dearing structure was affirmed, but there was more emphasis on the need for flexibility. Announcing a delay in the implementation of Dearing's Post-16 proposals to allow time for further consultation, Baroness Blackstone explained:

> We need a qualifications framework which: raises levels of participation, retention and achievement; promotes flexibility and choice, and encourages life-long learning; secures high and consistent standards; and offers clear progression routes into higher education, employment and further training. (Press Release, 11 June 1997)

From a more optimistic perspective, Young (1993) has linked the argument for a unified curriculum with an analysis of new relations between education and the economy. He suggested that the proposals for a unified Post-16 system are necessary responses to changes in industry, and the need for increased flexibility and initiative associated with new technologies, flatter management structures and an emphasis on teamwork. As he put it:

> In curriculum terms there are two key issues: flexibility (the opportunity to make choices and combine different kinds of learning in new ways) and coherence (the sense of clarity that students need in order to be clear about where a particular course of study will lead). (Young 1993, p. 214)

A unified system would, he argued, provide this opportunity for flexibility and coherence.

Flexibility is a strong argument of proponents of modular systems, who are particularly attracted by the possibility of Credit Accumulation and Transfer (CATs). The opportunity to combine study of particular units in one pathway with those in others, it is argued, could provide excellent opportunities for choice, enabling students to develop study programmes which meet particular needs and aspirations. Indeed, new AS (Advanced Subsidiary) courses in the academic and applied pathways may enable Post-16 pupils to delay their choices. However, how far the new structures will help to bridge the vocational/academic divide, reduce segregation and division of students and promote parity of esteem between academic, applied and vocational pathways remains to be seen (Hodgson and Spours 1997).

Although new vocational developments were developed by Conservative governments throughout the 1990s, they also sought to preserve the distinctive contribution of A-level, and this was seen by many as a significant obstacle to progress towards a common framework. In addition, some on the political right (e.g. Pilkington 1991) continued to argue for differentiation and segregation of the academic elite. The case for preserving A-levels seems to rest on the assumption that different curricula are needed for those with different kinds of mind, while the arguments for a unified and comprehensive system at Post-16 are based on curricula which respond to a diversity of aptitude, interest and learning styles whilst attempting to avoid the low self-esteem and alienation which may result from selection. There is a tension here.

As we have seen, Sir Ron Dearing's 1996 recommendations work through a national framework of awards at all levels from 'Entry' to 'Advanced', and which seeks to encourage open access and equality of status between pathways. His proposals were welcomed by the Secretary of State, the Labour Party, the Confederation of British Industry and by a range of professional associations including Secondary Heads Association, National Association of Headteachers, Association of Principals of Sixth Form Colleges and other teacher associations. However, the preservation of A-levels and the maintenance of three clearly differentiated pathways, with 'different but parallel' courses and each with its distinctive mix of assessment procedures may be very hard to sustain. Will public perceptions enable parity of esteem to become a reality? In the first place, the role of universities and their admission policies is likely to be crucial. British culture, and the complexity of its underpinning social-class system, make this whole enterprise very worthwhile – but parity of esteem will not be easy to achieve whether the new Labour government intervenes or not.

*Practical activity 6.4*

*Aim:* To reflect on the relationships between academic and vocational courses.

*Method:* Talk to higher- and lower-attaining pupils in Key Stage 3, Key Stage 4 and Post-16 about the curricular choices that are available to them. Keep notes on the views of each group. How do they perceive their options? Do they perceive parity of esteem? What do they see as the relative merits of the qualifications?

*Follow-up:* You could extend this activity by talking to teachers, parents or employers about the same issues.

## CONCLUSION

In this chapter we have described the structure of the National Curriculum and Post-16 provision of England and Wales, as we approach the millennium. We have also introduced the major issues which have to be faced in relation to the curriculum of secondary schools.

It is clear that what constitutes an appropriate curriculum is problematic. Whatever form curricular structures may take and however curriculum content may be prescribed, these are, in themselves, social products. They reflect a balance of power, influence and concern at the particular socio-historical period in which they were set out.

We believe that it is the professional responsibility of teachers to both recognize such structures and also to go beyond them. Rather than merely 'delivering' a given curriculum, reflective teachers have an important role in evaluating the effectiveness of national provision, and of using their specific knowledge and judgement to shape the learning opportunities available to young people. In Chapter 7, we look at some of the ways in which schools do this through curriculum development and curriculum planning activities. Chapters 10 and 15 also consider the role of individual teachers in planning and developing curricula in their own subjects.

In Chapter 1 we emphasized the need for reflective teachers to be involved in debate and discussion of professional issues. The curriculum must be of central importance to reflective teachers and we should value understanding of the political, cultural and historical contexts in which curricula are constructed and of the values that underpin them. Such historical perspective helps us to contribute, both within our schools and beyond them, to the future of what is taught and learned in the name of secondary education.

## *Notes for further reading*

The seminal paper on classification and framing of knowledge is:

Bernstein, B. (1971)
'On the classification and framing of educational knowledge,' in Young, M. *Knowledge and Control: New Directions in the Sociology of Education,*
London, Collier-Macmillan.                                 📖   **Primary Reading 7.2**

Hirst, P. (1967)
'The logical and physiological aspects of teaching a subject,' in Peters, R. (ed.) *The Concept of Education,*
London, Routledge and Kegan Paul                📖   **see also Primary Reading 7.3**

For a general overview of the history of the secondary school curriculum:

Goodson, I. (1984)
*Social Histories of the Secondary Curriculum: Subjects for Study*
Lewes: Falmer Press

Price, M. (1986)
*Development of the Secondary Curriculum*
London: Croom Hellm

For some more specific insights into previous policy thinking on the secondary school curriculum, see:

Board of Education (1926)
*The Education of the Adolescent,* (Hadow Report),
London: Board of Education.

Callaghan, J. (1976) 'Towards a national debate',
*Education,* Volume 148, No. 1, pp. 332–3.                   📖   **Primary Reading 7.7**

DES (1977)
*Curriculum 11-16,*
London, HMSO.

DES (1985)
*Better Schools,*
London: HMSO.                                              📖   **Primary Reading 7.8**

The Labour Party (1994)
*The Curriculum for a Learning Society,*
London: The Labour Party.                                  📖   **Primary Reading 7.11**

An overview of policy changes since 1979 is provided in:

Docking, J. (1996)
*National School Policy: Major Issues in Education Policy for Schools in the UK,*
London: David Fulton.

The National Curriculum and its assessment system were initially produced from 1989 and then revised from 1995. The key document in this revision is:

Dearing, R. (1993)
*The National Curriculum and its Assessment: Final Report,*
London, SCAA.                                              📖   **Primary Reading 7.12**

Useful guides to the post-Dearing National Curriculum are:

SCAA (1996c)
*A Guide to the National Curriculum,*
London, SCAA.

Pring, R. (1996)
*The New Curriculum*, (2nd edition)
London: Cassell.

On cross-curricular themes, see collection of four books edited by Verma and Pumfrey. The first is:

Verma, G. K. and Pumfrey, P. (eds) (1993)
*Cross-curricular Themes in Secondary Schools*,
London: Falmer Press.

There is a process of continuous review, with the possibility of significant further developments expected around 2000. For instance, one topic on which media interest has focused is reflected in the following discussion document:

SCAA (1996b)
'Education for Adult Life: the Spiritual and Moral Development of Young People', *Discussion Paper No 6*,
London: SCAA.

There are many constructive critiques of the National Curriculum structures which are described in this chapter. Of those below, Ball analyses the political forces which produced the 'reform'; Carr and Hartnett consider its contribution (or otherwise) to democracy; Learner *et al.* raise the question of how selections of curriculum content reflect particular values; Elliott argues that the whole conception of system-wide specification and measurement of performance is outmoded and fails to meet the challenge of rapid social and technological change; Richardson reflects on the past and hopes to find new ways forward.

Ball, S. (1994)
*Education Reform: A Critical and Post-structural Approach*,
Buckingham: Open University Press.

Carr, W. and Hartnett, A. (1996)
*Education and the Struggle for Democracy*,
Buckingham: Open University Press.

Learner, R., Nagai, A. K. and Rothman, S. (1995)
*Molding the Good Citizen: the Politics of High School History Texts*,
Westport, CT: Greenwood.

Elliott, J. (1996)
*Changing Curriculum*,
Buckingham: Open University Press.

Richardson, R. (1996)
*Fortunes and Fables: Education for Hope in Troubled Times*,
Stoke-on-Trent: Trentham Books.

Regarding Post-16 education key documents, reflecting a growing consensus, are the second Dearing Report and the Conservative government's 1996 White Paper which built on both Dearing and the Labour Party's plans for education and training:

Dearing, R. (1996)
*Review of Qualifications for 16–19 Year Olds: Full Report*,
London, SCAA.

DFEE (1996b)
*Learning to Compete: Education and Training for 14–19 Year-olds*,
London: DFEE.

Guides to new forms of Post-16 education are:

Higham, J., Sharp, P. and Yeomans, D. (1996)
*The Emerging 16–19 Curriculum: Policy and Provision,*
London: David Fulton.

Gibson, J. (1996)
*All You Need to Know about GNVQs,*
London: Kogan Page.

NCVQ (1995)
*NVQ Criteria and Guidance,*
London: NCVQ.

However, for one of the most cogent critiques of competence and vocationalism in education see:

Hyland, T. (1994)
*Competence, Education and NVQs,*
London: Cassell.

For an excellent review of the enduring issues tackled by Dearing and an assessment, see:

Hodgson, A. and Spours, K. (eds) 1997
*Dearing and Beyond: 14–19 Qualifications, Frameworks and Systems,*
London: Kogan Page.

A major problem regarding the relationship of education and British society is undoubtedly the impact of social class. This has been studied extensively over many years and we may well see a new manifestation of old processes of reproduction as the academic, applied and vocational pathways become established. For insights into this issue, see:

Bourdieu, P. and Passeron, J-C. (1977)
*Reproduction in Education and Culture,*
Beverley Hills: Sage.

Willis, P. (1977)
*Learning to Labour: Why Working Class Kids Get Working Class Jobs,*
London: Saxon House.

Walford, G. (ed.) (1984)
*British Public Schools: Policy and Practice,*
London: Falmer Press.

Salter, G. and Tapper, T. (1985)
*Power and Policy in Education: The Case of Independent Schooling,*
London: Falmer Press.

Benn, C. and Chitty, C. (1995)
*Thirty Years On: Is Comprehensive Education Alive and Well, or Struggling to Survive?,*
London: David Fulton.

# CHAPTER 7

# How do we plan the curriculum?

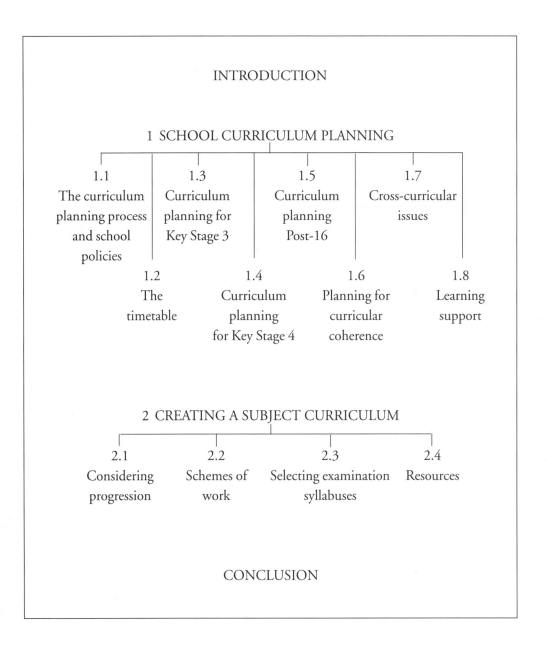

INTRODUCTION

1 SCHOOL CURRICULUM PLANNING

1.1 The curriculum planning process and school policies

1.2 The timetable

1.3 Curriculum planning for Key Stage 3

1.4 Curriculum planning for Key Stage 4

1.5 Curriculum planning Post-16

1.6 Planning for curricular coherence

1.7 Cross-curricular issues

1.8 Learning support

2 CREATING A SUBJECT CURRICULUM

2.1 Considering progression

2.2 Schemes of work

2.3 Selecting examination syllabuses

2.4 Resources

CONCLUSION

## INTRODUCTION

Underlying all curriculum planning are fundamental concerns about coherence, diversity, choice and entitlement. Schools, working within their particular contexts, have the opportunity to shape curriculum plans which reflect the needs and aspirations of pupils and their parents. However, these plans have to be developed within the constraints of the budget. Inevitably as schools go through the process of deciding how to meet statutory requirements and what to offer beyond that they will, of necessity, have in mind the constraints and possibilities arising from available time, space, learning resources, staff availability and expertise. Priorities have to be established and compromises are probably inescapable. It is within this overall plan that faculties and departments will develop their subject teaching.

In this chapter we look at the processes involved in curriculum planning at whole-school, faculty and departmental levels. We begin by considering one model of the curriculum planning process and discussing how the creation of whole-school policies can contribute to decision-making.

## 1    SCHOOL CURRICULUM PLANNING

### 1.1    The planning process and school policies

Curriculum planning, of whatever sort, is likely to reflect the overall philosophy of the school. Good practice is to tie this in with the process of school development planning (see Chapter 16) and with consultations with school governors, who have legal responsibility for the school curriculum.

Avon LEA (1992) produced a model to represent these processes (Figure 7.1).

*Policy statements* for individual subjects and whole-school issues such as equal opportunities, library use, information technology, are intended to act as a simple statement of purpose and a framework for action and decision-making. They are not usually long but should be endorsed by school governors and will reflect the overall school philosophy. Very often policy statements amount to single A4 sheets with simple, standard headings such as:

- Rationale
- Purposes
- Guidelines.

Policy statements provide for an input from governors without involving them in implementation detail.

Moving from policies to the practicalities of planning at whole school level will involve consultation with subject leaders or departmental heads, each of whom will have preferences and priorities based on how they see their subject developing in the school.

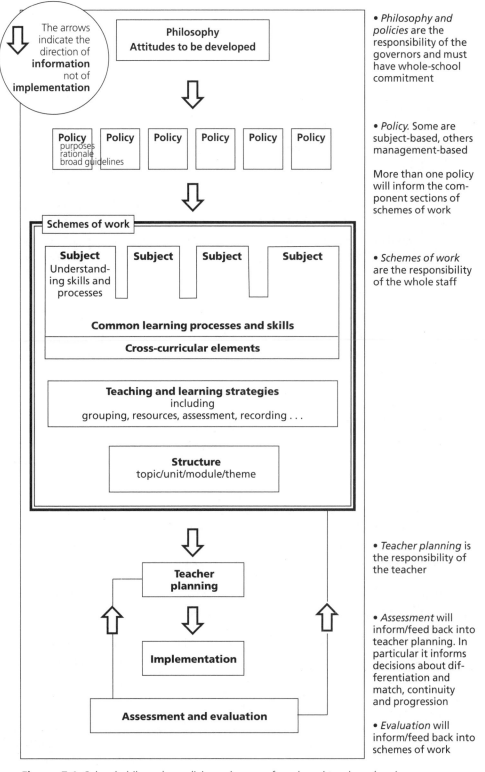

**Figure 7.1** *School philosophy, policies, schemes of work and teacher planning*

## Practical activity 7.1

*Aim:* To investigate the approach to whole-school curriculum planning in your school.

*Method:* Insights on this are likely to come from two main sources – documents and discussion. Begin by studying available policy statements (especially for your subject) and any other whole-school curriculum planning documentation. Ask your department or faculty head if she or he could talk to you about how they have been able to contribute to planning at whole-school level and whether decisions made at whole-school level have affected subject planning.

If possible try to talk also to teachers involved in planning curriculum at whole-school level – there may be a deputy head curriculum, a co-ordinator for assessment, etc. Ask about any challenges faced by the school in fulfilling the legal requirements for the curriculum and how the school has exercised discretion in complementary provision.

Write a concise summary of the position.

*Follow-up:* Consider what the implications of the approach to whole-school planning are for you and your subject. How does the process in your school compare with the model in Figure 7.1?

## 1.2 The timetable

As we saw in Chapter 5, 2.4, the configuration of the timetable is a fundamental planning decision. Indeed, once constructed, a timetable enables or prohibits aspects of planning.

The first step then, is to define the basic framework. What should be the pattern of the teaching week? How long is a lesson? Where do the breaks come? How long are the breaks? When does school start and finish?

You will find many variations on the 'traditional' 9 a.m. to 4 p.m. with breaks morning and afternoon and an hour for the midday meal. Some schools choose to operate a 'continental day' with an 8.30 start, a break for 15 minutes in the morning, thirty minutes at midday and finishing at 2.30. This, it is suggested, provides a lot of time for extra-curricular and after-school activity. It also cuts down on potentially troublesome 'playground time'. Making decisions about start and finish times may involve considerations of pupils' travelling time, the operation of school buses, before- and after-school activity etc. Length and positioning of breaks will involve thinking about providing food, the rhythm of the day, pupil and staff stamina.

The most significant question to be answered is: How long is a lesson? This unit of time becomes the basic building block of the curriculum structure. Should all lessons be the same length? Should they be short (as preferred by teachers of some subjects)? Able to be offered as double periods (as required by other subjects)? Are there advantages in having lessons of different length? What units of time should be allocated to registration, other administration, tutorial sessions, assemblies? Involved in this very significant decision are questions of how to maximize time for pupil learning: How long can pupils concentrate? How long is needed for different tasks and activities, e.g. changing for PE, practical work? How much time is lost on moving around, starting and finishing lessons? You might like to consider, for example, the factors that would be taken into account in choosing between a week of twenty-five lessons of sixty minutes or one of thirty lessons of fifty minutes or one of forty lessons of forty minutes.

Associated with this goes the decision about whether to have a timetable that repeats every week (five days) or runs over two weeks (ten days). With a two-week timetable subjects can be allocated an odd number of lessons per fortnight, rather than an even number per week.

Decisions about school organization, e.g. banding, streaming, setting, will be reflected in the timetable and may also enable or constrain it. In addition, schools may timetable before school/dinner time/after-school activities of various kinds – curricular and extra-curricular.

In subsequent sections we will be looking at how schools plan to fulfil the requirements of the National Curriculum and meet the entitlement, needs and preferences of pupils and their parents. At this stage we suggest you undertake Practical Activity 7.2.

## Practical activity 7.2

*Aim:* To consider the timetable of a school in which you are working and the factors that contributed to its construction.

*Method:* Examine the school timetable with different points in mind.

Look at: start and finish times; length and positioning of breaks; length of lesson; timetabling of administration, assemblies.

How are organizational features such as banding, streaming, setting or option choices reflected in the timetable?

Consider the allocation of time to your subject. Count the number of lessons (total time) per week for each Year Group/Key Stage. Is this the same for all pupils in a Year Group? How is this time allocation spread across the week and throughout the day?

Discuss with other teachers in your subject group how their preferences and priorities for teaching are met by this timetable. What are the strong points for them? Where are the weaknesses? What would they want changed? Are your subject's priorities in competition with other subjects? How is competition resolved?

Consider the nature of any before-school, dinner time or after-school activities.

Find out whether the school has changed or adapted the configuration of the timetable in recent years. Why was this done?

*Follow-up:* Compare your findings with those of a student or colleague from another subject area. Consider whether/ to what extent timetabling is affected by available space, staffing, other resources.

## 1.3 Curriculum planning for Key Stage 3

The first concern of planners is to make provision for the statutory requirements of the National Curriculum. The Dearing Report (1993) based its proposals around a view about the number of hours per year that might be given to each subject. At Key Stage 3, English, maths and science might have ninety hours per year each, modern foreign languages sixty-three hours per year, with forty-five hours per year for each of the remaining foundation subjects (including information technology) and forty-five hours per year for religious education. However, the report stressed that these figures were 'not to be seen as guidance to schools' (Dearing 1993, p. 35). In other words, though there needed to be some idea of the relative amount of time to be devoted to each subject and to avoid curriculum overload, schools would still need to make decisions about how to allocate time to different subjects and activities. Time has also to be allocated to sex education, health education, careers education and guidance, the moral and spiritual dimension of the curriculum, the common cultural heritage. There is a notional 20 per cent of time available for additional subjects or for treating some topics, themes, subjects in greater depth. Views about this are widely varied. To take one example: for Dr Nicholas Tate, chief executive of SCAA 'The flexibility is real' (*TES,* 2 December 1994) and should enable schools to direct their attention to planning for pupils' moral education and to 'developing pupils' sense of identity and their involvement in this country's common culture'. He also urges the case for classics to be offered now that time has been freed up in Key Stages 3 and 4. 'For the past thousand years and more the study of Greek and Roman civilization and their languages has been at the core of education. To toss this aside in one generation may not be wholly wise.'

In summary, whilst schools' curriculum planning for Key Stage 3 is constrained in many ways, there is still the requirement (set out in the Education Reform Act, 1988) to provide a curriculum which meets criteria for breadth and balance and coherence. This can be interpreted in its widest sense, with reference to 'spiritual, moral, cultural, mental and physical development' and preparing pupils for 'the opportunities, responsibilities and experiences of adult life'. In other words, breadth and balance cannot be simply reduced to a concern about the provision of specified subject matter; it requires us to address a more holistic question about educational provision to which pupils are entitled. This involves considering not only what is included in the curriculum but also how it is constructed and presented. These decisions may be based on principled beliefs about learning, but they may also be tempered by practical necessities.

If you consider the curriculum offered by a school at Key Stage 3, how broad and balanced does it seem as a learning experience? It is perhaps understandable if subject teachers develop 'tunnel vision' and have only a vague idea about the range and variety of learning that pupils are experiencing across the curriculum. Practical Activity 7.3 will help you to investigate this in relation to the idea of pupil entitlement.

In addition to this, schools must find time in Year 9 to give pupils advice and guidance about the curriculum they will select for Key Stage 4. In the next section we consider curriculum planning for Key Stage 4, the provision of options and the challenge of giving pupils (and their parents) their preferred choices.

*Practical activity 7.3*

*Aim:* To consider the breadth and balance of planned curriculum experiences.

*Method:* Select one Year Group in Key Stage 3. Use the timetable and, if possible, subject schemes of work to gain some sense of what pupils in this group will experience as the planned curriculum. Identify where the statutory elements of the National Curriculum appear. What use has been made of the notional 20 per cent 'free' time?

Seen as a whole and in conjunction with other, whole-school activities, how does this planned curriculum relate to pupils' spiritual, moral, cultural, mental and physical development? To what extent does classroom and school provision prepare pupils for the opportunities, responsibilities and experiences of adult life? What cross-curricular/transferable skills are being developed? Are there any planned links between different subjects/attempts at integration of learning?

How far is the curriculum differentiated for different pupils, e.g. starting a second foreign language, providing for special needs, learning a musical instrument?

*Follow-up:* What have you discovered about the planned curriculum? How useful is thinking about pupils' learning experiences as a whole? What implications may there be there for future curricular or cross-curricular planning? Can you discover how much of the planning is the result of principled educational beliefs and whether any of it is constrained by necessity/seen as a reluctant compromise?

What do you see as the priorities which have informed the planning?

## 1.4 Curriculum planning for Key Stage 4

All of the issues highlighted in relation to Key Stage 3 apply at Key Stage 4; in fact they come into sharper focus and can present schools with difficult dilemmas in making curricular provision. In theory schools have greater flexibility at Key Stage 4. The National Curriculum requirements are limited to six subjects plus RE and IT. Of the six only three (English, mathematics and a science) have to be 'full' courses; PE, a modern foreign language and technology can be offered as 'short' courses – but these can themselves bring logistical problems for the timetable. 'Thin' short courses (e.g. one hour a week for two years) can be difficult for teachers and learners to sustain. 'Fat' short courses (e.g. two hours a week for one year) require a follow-on course in the second year to fill the timetable gap. There is still a need to ensure appropriate coverage of sex education, health education, drugs, careers education and guidance, the moral and spiritual dimension of the curriculum, the common cultural heritage. This mandatory curriculum, it is suggested, will occupy 60 per cent of available time, leaving 40 per cent for schools to deploy as they wish. However the vision of a wider choice of options, access to vocational courses, more learning support, a generally enriched curriculum, often fades in the harsh light of budgetary and time constraints. In their different ways schools manage the gap between their aspirations for their pupils and the reality of what can be achieved. Here we set out some of the factors which arise in curriculum planning at this stage.

At Key Stage 4 a timetable may be in 'blocks' offering pupils restricted choice. Alternatively pupils may be offered a 'guided choice' from everything that is on offer. Beyond the National Curriculum minimum, 'core subjects' can now appear in more than one guise: English literature, drama, theatre studies, media studies, 'double' science. Different perceptions of the relative status of subjects at GCSE or of GNVQ equivalents may appear within the school and from parents. The way in which 'options' are offered is frequently affected by a school's resources and raises issues of entitlement. The illustrations in Figure 7.2 show how one school has approached the challenge. The compulsory courses are firmly at the heart of provision and option choice is related to the total number of GCSE courses a pupil is likely to follow. Options are clustered under Arts and Humanities with one other choice available for pupils aiming for ten GCSEs.

| For those aiming for up to ten GCSEs | For those aiming for up to 9 GCSEs | For those for whom a full GCSE course is too much |
|---|---|---|
| *Compulsory main courses* | *Compulsory main courses* | *Compulsory main courses* |
| English and English literature | English and English literature | English and English literature |
| Mathematics | Mathematics | Mathematics |
| Double Modular science | Double modular science | Double modular science |
| Modern foreign language | Modern foreign language | Design technology |
| Design technology | Design technology | Physical education |
| Physical education | Physical education | Careers |
| Careers | Careers | |
| | | |
| PLUS | PLUS | PLUS |
| | | |
| *Option courses* | *Option courses* | *Additional course* |
| *Arts choice* | *Arts choice* | Accreditation for life and living skills (RSA) |
| Art | Art | |
| Drama | Drama | |
| Media studies | Media studies | |
| Music | Music | |
| | | |
| *Humanities choice* | *Humanities choice* | |
| History | History | |
| Geography | Geography | |
| RE | RE | |
| | | |
| *Additional choice* | PLUS | |
| Art | Computer literacy and Information technology (RSA) | |
| Drama | | |
| Second foreign language | | |
| Geography | | |
| PE | | |
| Social science | | |

**Figure 7.2** *Option choices and blocking constraints: an illustration*

Choices may be limited or considerably more open and free. However, greater flexibility and choice may call into question the aim of breadth and balance. For instance, a school offering five option courses to add to the statutory core may find a pupil choosing four full GCSE courses (another science, design and technology, another foreign language, economics) and two GNVQ short courses in IT and business studies. Is this desirable? The core as defined, combined with free choice of options can squeeze out the humanities and the creative and expressive arts. Is this acceptable? Is it a good idea for academic and vocational pathways to cross? Should choices be constrained? Schools inevitably have to have a view of what kind of curriculum best fits their pupils' needs. What is most important? Breadth and balance? Motivation? Preparation for A-level? There is also the DFEE's concern that more pupils should take up mathematics and science Post-16, and the impact of pupil choices on school targets and published 'league tables'.

At whole-school level, three other related factors will affect the decisions of curriculum planners: available teacher expertise, resources, the cost of courses. Considering this last factor involves calculating financial outlay for things like travel, field work as well as materials and examination entry fees (e.g., in 1996, a 'short' course cost £10 per pupil entry, a 'full' GCSE cost £12). Launching GNVQ courses can require considerable investment in resources and staff training. The way of working ideally needs 'base' rooms with computers and phones. NVQ courses often involve day release and off-site travel. Available resources and existing staff expertise are clearly relevant. Teacher expertise is also an issue when mandatory courses in technology and a modern language have to be offered. Are there enough specialists? Who can be trained to cover this? With changes in curriculum content how will staff keep up to date? Staff involved in GNVQ courses will need time for training in new forms of working and assessment, new management skills. All this costs, and inevitably schools will have to establish priorities. In this situation small schools are at a disadvantage and may have to offer reduced choice.

The example within Figure 7.3 shows how one school has begun to build a post-Dearing curriculum for Key Stage 4. This 11–16 school has 800 pupils and is situated in an economically depressed area of a city. A quarter of the pupils have special needs. The aim of the curriculum re-think was to 'raise pupils' self esteem and remotivate their learning'. Figure 7.3 shows the choices offered to Year 10 pupils in the first year of development, 1996/7.

The school was able to meet 96 per cent of pupils' first choices. Parental involvement increased as did pupil motivation. In 1997/8 there will be two Year Groups following this Key Stage 4 curriculum and a greater timetabling challenge. Meanwhile the school looks to introduce GNVQ Part 1 courses (see Chapter 6, Section 2.5) to 'strengthen the programme without loss of flexibility' and to improve guidance to pupils.

Time-table: The school moved to a weekly timetable of twenty-five sixty-minute lessons.

Core time: Thirteen periods:
English, maths, science (x3)
Technology (x2)
Physical education, PSE (x1)

Option time: Twelve periods: one of which must be French

Full GCSE (three periods):
art, child development, drama, economics, expressive arts, information systems, IT with business studies, media studies, music, geography, history, French

Short courses (one or two periods)
GCSE art, French; RSA art, electronic music, French, health and social care, IT, orienteering, travel and tourism

'Support' (up to eleven periods)
Pupils needing extra help can book time with special needs teachers on a programme agreed with subject teachers.

**Figure 7.3** *Key Stage 4 curriculum with options: an illustration*

## Practical activity 7.4

*Aim:* To consider the curriculum at Key Stage 4 offered to pupils in your school.

*Method:* Obtain access to copies of material provided for pupils and their parents before Key Stage 4. Carefully study the documents with these questions in mind.

- How is the minimum National Curriculum delivered?

- Has the school elected to make use of short courses?

- What options are offered?

- How, if at all, are choices constrained?

- What qualifications (e.g. GCSE, GNVQ) are courses leading to?

Talk with relevant teachers about the choices pupils have made and the range of subjects and areas of study they are following. How differentiated is the curriculum for different pupils? On what grounds are pupils differentiated? How far have pupil and parent choices been met?

*Follow-up:* Talk with pupils in Key Stage 4 about the courses they are following. How did they make their choices? What are their feelings about workload?

## 1.5    Curriculum planning for Post-16

Year 11 pupils intending to continue in full-time education frequently have a choice about where they will study. Their present school may have Post-16 provision or a 'sixth form', or their LEA may have established a Sixth Form College or Post-16 courses may be available at local further education colleges. From an institution's point of view, the number of pupils who elect to stay on or come into a school or college for this phase determines the level of funding provided. Schools and colleges thus offer a Post-16 curriculum in the hope that pupils will want to study with them in sufficient numbers for them to be able to deliver their plans and promises. The aim is to remain viable which means calculating a minimum teaching group size for a course to run – usually six or eight students.

Post-16 providers are in competition for students – glossy brochures, open evenings, statistics of previous student attainment are all much in evidence as the drive to recruit Year 11 pupils gets under way. The importance of good careers advice and guidance at this stage is clear. The whole process is 'client led' and it is a question of whether would-be providers can offer courses of the kind and in the combinations that students want. Schools and colleges with well-established and consequently well-funded Post-16 curricula have an advantage. They may have chosen to specialize in some areas, building up teaching expertise or well-equipped facilities (computer suites, laboratories, video studio and editing, learning resource centres etc.) so important for subjects like science, communications, photography, art, music, theatre studies, sports studies etc. There are also decisions to be made about which A-level and/or GNVQ courses to offer. Can subjects such as sociology, psychology, health and social care be taught by existing staff? Is training needed? Can new appointments be made? Can modules be offered in different orders so that Years 12 and 13 can be taught together?

The Post-16 stage may also involve providing for students who want to re-take or add GCSE subjects or GNVQ at Intermediate level. They may be following courses below 'Advanced' level but they will want and expect to be treated differently from younger pupils.

For 11–18 schools the Post-16 stage raises a number of issues: How should students be timetabled? Should they be located in a separate building? Should uniform and other rules be suspended? What kinds of learning and pastoral support do they need? What is the role of the sixth form in the school? Schools with small numbers of Post-16 students but who want to maintain or increase their numbers may make a feature of their commitment to the pupils who have been with them for five years, focusing on the personal support students will get in small groups.

If your school is 11–16, find out what options are available for Post-16 education and training. What factors are most important for Year 11 pupils when they are making choices about whether to go on and where to study?

## 1.6    Planning for curricular coherence

As we saw in Chapter 6, Section 1.2, coherence refers to the extent to which the various parts of a planned curriculum actually relate meaningfully together. The opposite would be fragmentation. Clearly this is an important issue if we conceive of learning as a process of 'making sense' (Bruner and Haste 1987), for that process calls for understanding at overall levels as well as in more detail. Indeed, Gestalt psychologists such as Kohler and Lewin established the enormous significance which developing an overarching understanding and frame of reference has on learning. In planning we may look for coherence across subjects and within subjects.

One way in which schools address curriculum planning is through the organization of the school itself (see Chapter 5). This may involve departments or faculties embracing a number of individual subjects. Of course, the creation of these larger departments sometimes simply produces administrative and managerial structures, and curriculum planning continues to be based around individual subjects. However, in some schools, larger departments have provided opportunities for teachers to share perspectives and to plan their work with more knowledge of their students' experience in colleagues' lessons. This planning can produce more subject integration, particularly for work with younger pupils. For example, in schools with Humanities Departments, an integrated approach to teaching history and geography is not unusual. Sometimes such integrated courses have developed to embrace subjects like English and religious education. However, integrated approaches to humanities and science can have lower status than more traditional and specialized subjects. In addition, the subject-based National Curriculum has militated against integration and schools have found it difficult to maintain integrated courses after the age of 14, when students start to follow syllabuses leading to public examinations.

Coherence is only partially amenable to planning, for it derives its force from the sense, or otherwise, which the children make of the curriculum which is provided. Thus, whilst consideration of the issue at the planning stage is obviously important, we have chosen to focus Practical Activity 7.5 on the actual experience of the curriculum by pupils. People tend to enjoy and value learning more when they understand it as a whole. Rather than experience anxiety, overload or bewilderment, they feel more in control and are more willing to think independently and take risks. Whilst feelings of incoherence can lead to feelings of frustration and strategies such as withdrawal, coherence leads to satisfaction and engagement. In this respect, it is likely to be associated with the extent of subject confidence and expertise of teachers. Where teacher knowledge and competence is weak, the provision of coherent learning experiences will almost certainly be more difficult.

The data from this activity will bring us far greater awareness of the 'curriculum-as-experienced' than any amount of careful planning can do.

## 1.7 Cross-curricular issues

There are a number of cross-curricular issues which provide a focus for whole-school reflection and provision. Decisions have to be made about statutory aspects of the curriculum which may be provided by a combination of separate courses and cross-curricular planning. For instance, specific courses in personal and social education (PSE) usually include aspects of learning about sex, health, drugs abuse, and careers. A central question for most schools concerns who will teach the programme. There may be a specialist PSE team (with a leader) made up of teachers who have volunteered and/or been selected for the work. This team will often receive special training in this area. Alternatively PSE may be the responsibility of form tutors under the guidance of the Year Head. In another model, schools may suspend the timetable for one day at prescribed intervals for a PSE focus. Careers education (involving the careers service) will come to the fore as pupils reach decision points, e.g. selecting options for Key Stage 4, considering Post-16 education and training, applying for jobs. Work experience may form part of cross-curricular provision. Education about sex, health, drugs abuse and careers will also feature in subject teaching, and whole-school planning ensures that these contributions are combined to produce a complete 'map' of the provision.

Similarly a school may want to map how the 'moral, cultural and spiritual' dimensions are being addressed in different subjects, in addition to what is included in RE and through the required collective worship. Subject leaders may be asked to indicate where in their schemes of work these cross-curricular themes are being addressed. The same strategy could be applied to equal opportunities, environmental education, citizenship.

A whole-school perspective can also take us directly back to the debate about the value of focusing a curriculum on transferable skills and attitudes – a 'process oriented' curriculum (see Chapter 6, Section 1.2). In terms of national curricula, such cross-curricular potential is often narrowed. Many schools, however, are looking across the curriculum at the planned development of 'skills'. An obvious concern of the Dearing reviews was that all pupils develop key skills in communication, numeracy and IT. The interpersonal skills associated with working with others and collaborating in groups have also been identified as needing attention. In addition we might choose to plan and monitor pupils' development of skills we want them to have for learning. To undertake this involves identifying these skills quite specifically and mapping onto the different subject curricula where and how these will be developed.

This may involve general principles consistently and persistently followed or the identification of opportunities for specific focus and activity (for instance, see Chapter 13 for more detail on the development of literacy).

Co-operation between different subject teachers over work for GCSE can also bring positive gains, as research by Paechter (1995) indicates. The project which ran over two cycles of GCSE involved twenty-nine schools in eleven LEAs with more detailed work in four schools. The focus was on teachers identifying overlap in different subject syllabuses and using this in planning coursework assignments that enable pupils to work in greater depth. For instance assessment requirements in English and art were met in coursework that involved designing and illustrating children's books; a river study for geography combined statistical work for mathematics. Evidence in the study indicates that the approach can work for arts, science, technological and vocational subjects equally. It can also deliver academic and vocational subjects for the same pupil without any sacrifice of depth.

> ## Practical activity 7.6
>
> *Aim:* To enquire into cross-curricular planning in your subject.
>
> *Method:* Ask your subject leader about any ways in which the subject has been involved in cross-curricular planning. Consider whether dimensions and themes such as 'moral, cultural and spiritual development', 'equal opportunities', 'environmental education' etc. feature in your subject curriculum. Does this occur in isolation or as a result of consultation with other subjects? Find out whether there is a whole-school strategy for the development of any or all of the key skills.
>
> *Follow-up:* Try to discover the way in which other subjects approach the idea of cross-curricular planning. If this is a feature of your school, think about what makes it work. If it is not very evident, can you suggest why?

## 1.8 Learning support

The 1981 Education Act focused on the needs of pupils with physical and mental disabilities and with learning difficulties. A wide-ranging definition of special educational need was introduced, which could potentially incorporate one-fifth of the whole school population. However, commensurate resources have not been made available and an increasing focus on the integration of as many children as possible in mainstream schooling has highlighted the issue of equality of access to a common educational experience for all pupils. The identification of special needs, in particular, the securing of statements of special educational need which attract funding or other forms of support, is an important aspect of whole-school planning. Following the 1994 Code of Practice (DFE) there is an obligation to provide an appropriate curriculum for those pupils who are on a school's special education needs register, specifically to ensure that identified needs are met. As significant is the expectation that pupils' access to the full curriculum should not be compromised by arrangements to support their learning difficulties. For schools, this expectation raises issues associated with withdrawal of pupils for special support and of the disapplication or modification of the National Curriculum for some pupils.

These issues are relevant to planning a curriculum for many pupils who, though they do not have statements of special need, have difficulties in learning and are in need of support. How, for instance, does a school offer equality of access to the curriculum and opportunity to learn to pupils whose attainment at the end of Key Stage 2 has been assessed at Level 1 or Level 2? How can curriculum planning best support pupils for whom English is a second language? At the other end of the attainment spectrum, what planning supports the entitlement of pupils who in Year 7 arrive with attainment assessed at Level 6?

The role of learning support and the way time and staff expertise are deployed is, therefore, a crucial aspect of whole-school and subject planning. Here we will confine our discussion to a limited number of issues which schools currently face, and which present challenges to all teachers involved in planning and managing the learning.

### Withdrawal

This strategy, for many, is associated with the idea of 'remedial' classes. Pupils are 'withdrawn' from 'normal' classes to be given special help to enable them to rejoin their peers. Decisions must be made about the extent and frequency of the withdrawal and how to cope with the teaching which has been 'missed'. An associated strategy is to withdraw a whole group of pupils identified as having learning difficulties and plan a curriculum matched to their needs. Issues here concern the composition of such classes, their duration, movement in and out of them.

### Classroom support

In this strategy specialist teachers have time in classes to support pupils with identified need. Pupils with statements of educational need have specified entitlement to support. For pupils without statements, schools are faced with the deployment of scarce resources. Is it better for a learning support teacher to work with a group that has been withdrawn or to work with another teacher in a mainstream class? How is classroom support to be allocated?

### Modification of the curriculum

There is a statutory obligation on schools to teach the National Curriculum programmes of study for each Key Stage. As appropriate, materials may be selected from earlier or later stages, suitably adapted for the age of the pupils, to enable them to progress. This form of differentiation presents challenges to planners.

Low attainment, particularly in literacy, makes it particularly difficult for secondary pupils to access the full curriculum. Subject specialist teachers are not usually equipped with the skills to support literacy learning. Some schools are considering the idea of temporarily suspending the full curriculum for some pupils in Year 7 to concentrate on 'the basics'. These pupils would then be better equipped for accelerated progress through Key Stage 3.

We suggest that you explore some of these issues by considering the situation in your school.

> ## *Practical activity 7.7*
>
> *Aim:* To consider the school's planning for learning support
>
> *Method:* Find out how learning support is defined and organized in your school.
>
> If possible look at the school's Code of Practice special needs register to discover the range of pupils with statements of need. How are these needs met?
>
> Discuss with other teachers in your subject what aspects of whole-school planning affect how they can support the learning needs of pupils. How is learning support deployed?
>
> What support is provided for: very low attaining pupils; pupils with low attainment in literacy; pupils whose first language is not English?
>
> Consider and evaluate the range of support strategies you have discovered. Do they ensure entitlement and equality of opportunity? How do they help you, as a teacher, to meet the challenges of learners who are in need of particular support?
>
> *Follow-up:* You might like to try to discover, by talking to them, the perceptions pupils have of the kinds of learning support the school plans. Try to discuss this with pupils who receive learning support and those who do not.

## 2 CREATING A SUBJECT CURRICULUM

Implementation of the National Curriculum requires the exercise of professional judgement in various ways. There is scope within the National Curriculum for making *choices* and for *interpretation* and *selection* from within the prescribed content and about the order in which various aspects are covered. In whatever forum a subject scheme of work is produced, it will reflect teacher judgement in the selection of content, activities, teaching strategies and resources and in the balance and sequencing of activities over time. Content may be prescribed by a national curriculum or examination syllabuses; but teachers will use their professional judgement to make crucial decisions about the ways in which this is broken down and ordered for learning. Effective planning of this kind has regard for the nature and structure of the subject matter and uses principles appropriate to this for devising learning sequences based on its internal logic and organization (Bruner 1966, Gagne 1965).

In Chapter 10 we look in more detail at how individual teachers plan their teaching. Here we are concerned with planning at departmental or faculty level

### 2.1 Continuity and progression

The concept of 'progression' highlights the intended, cumulative outcomes which a planned curriculum is expected to produce: the expectation is that pupils should make progress in their learning, should build on and integrate their knowledge so that they deepen their understanding and skills. The underpinning rationale of the National Curriculum is of progression from stage to stage. At this stage it would be useful to look at the model of progression contained in the National Curriculum for your subject.

### Practical activity 7.8

*Aim:* To investigate the model of progression in the National Curriculum for your subject

*Method:* Obtain the National Curriculum documents for your subject for all Key Stages.

Consider the nature of progression that emerges as you read. Look in particular at the transition from Key Stage 2 to Key Stage 3.

*Follow-up:* Find out as much as you can about liaison between the feeder primary schools and your school. How much information is available about what happened in Key Stage 2? What use, if any, is made of that information? If you can, get the pupils' perception about whether they are 'doing things again' or moving forward.

The sequencing of tasks within the curriculum raises several issues depending, as we discuss in Chapter 8, on our view of knowledge and of how children learn. At a classroom level (see Chapter 10) it is possible to be more specific and more flexibly responsive to the evolving understanding of the children we teach. Schemes developed by subject teams will consider progression between and across Key Stages.

So far we have focused on the overall issues of structure and content in the curriculum. More detailed analysis is sometimes valuable to identify the various learning elements contained within a scheme. This is particularly useful in planning for progression and considering how to monitor a sequence of teaching-learning experiences.

First it is necessary to decide how we wish to analyse learning experiences. One common way of doing this is to distinguish between knowledge, concepts, skills and attitudes all of which may be considered as 'elements of learning' across the whole curriculum:

- *Knowledge:* Selections of that which is worth knowing and of interest.
- *Concepts:* The 'big ideas' which inform a subject or generalizations which enable pupils to classify, organize and predict – to understand patterns, relationships and meanings, e.g. continuity/change, cause/consequence, interdependence/adaptation, sequence/duration, nature/purpose, authenticity, power, energy.
- *Skills:* The capacity or competence to perform a task, e.g. personal/social (turn-taking, sharing), physical/practical (fine/gross motor skills), intellectual (observing, identifying, sorting /classifying, hypothesizing, reasoning, testing, imagining, and evaluating), communication (oracy, literacy, numeracy, graphicacy) etc.
- *Attitudes:* The overt expression of values and personal qualities, e.g. curiosity, perseverance, initiative, open-mindedness, trust, honesty, responsibility, respect, confidence, etc.

The items listed above provide a very useful analytic framework but they are not without problems. In particular, the concept of a 'skill' has some ambiguities of meaning. First, it can be used in the sense of analysis of the component skills of a task. Skill analysis can thus provide a way of diagnosing difficulties and can assist in planning new learning provision. In such instances, the word 'skill' is associated with the mechanistic break-down of activities into the basic components which are believed to contribute to mastery. On the other hand, the concept of 'skills' is also used to denote key elements in learning to learn, attributes which are heralded as being flexible and transferable rather than specific and mechanistic. In this context it is argued that skills are especially useful in a time of rapid change when particular knowledge may rapidly become obsolete. This sense of the term is used to encourage a consideration of what is considered as key elements in learning to learn, indeed, in meta-cognition (see Chapter 9, Section 2.5).

The attempt to define 'attitudes' and to distinguish them from 'skills' has raised further conceptual issues. This is particularly evident when considering social skills and attitudes. For example, what is the relationship between social behaviour and attitudes? Does it require skill to be able to behave in a chosen way?

There is also an important relationship between attitudes and intellectual skills, for learners are likely to have feelings and attitudes towards what they are trying to learn. A reflective teacher may therefore want to ask to what extent positive attitudes can foster intellectual development and to consider the role which motivation might play in learning (see Chapter 9, Section 2.4; Chapter 10, Section 2.1 and **Primary Readings** such as **6.7**, **10.2** and **10.3**).

Despite these complexities, the analytic power of the distinction between skills, attitudes, knowledge and concepts is very useful in gauging what it is that we are actually asking learners to do when we present them with new challenges (see Practical Activity 7.9).

The purpose of analysing curriculum content in this way is threefold. In the first place, it allows us to examine aspects of planned progression in a subject. Second, it encourages us to think more precisely about what we are trying to do. Third, it provides a detailed framework which we can use to monitor pupils' learning.

## 2.2 Schemes of work

A scheme of work translates a syllabus or programme of study into a statement of how this prescribed content is to be taught and learned.

At Key Stage 3 schemes of work incorporate the programmes of study of the National Curriculum. In the same way, in Key Stage 4 and Post-16, programmes of study and syllabuses specified for award-bearing courses must be expressed as schemes of work.

In drawing up schemes of work subject teams may well refer to non-statutory guidelines or other resources. In any event, new curriculum plans and schemes of work are usually modified in the light of experience. In general, schemes of work should guide teachers in developing their individual planning and ensure that continuity and progression through the school is provided. Schemes of work may be expressed as a series of units or modules of work to be taught over a period of time, e.g. four weeks, half a term. Subject teams may decide to design short 'fat' units in

*Aim:* To consider knowledge, concepts, skills and attitudes in planned schemes of work/units/modules/lesson sequences.

*Method:* Select a particular part of a programme of study in your subject area. Working on your own or preferably with a colleague, identify and list the knowledge, concepts, skills and attitudes which are targeted for development.

| TOPICS | Knowledge | Concepts | Skills | Attitudes |
|--------|-----------|----------|--------|-----------|
|        |           |          |        |           |
|        |           |          |        |           |
|        |           |          |        |           |
|        |           |          |        |           |

*Follow-up:* How easy was it to identify elements in the four categories? What relationship between knowledge, concepts, skills and attitudes did you arrive at?

Your subject team may have already written a scheme of work for this area. Consider it in the light of the analysis you have just done.

which all teaching time over a concentrated period is spent on one theme; alternatively they may design a long 'thin' unit using one lesson a week over a longer period. These units or modules will include specific aims and objectives; they may indicate outcomes and planned assessment; some may be expressed only in outline; others may be more detailed and specific.

Subject teams may also vary in how they sequence progression. Some plan for Year 7, then for Years 8 and 9, then for Years 9, 10 and 11. Year 9 is planned as a prelude to Key Stage 4 as well as the culmination of Key Stage 3 – in part because, for external examination purposes, there are only five terms available.

In general schemes of work address four basic issues:

### 1. What do we teach?

The outline knowledge, concepts, skills and attitudes to be developed, and any cross-curricular elements. Attainment Targets in the National Curriculum may be specifically identified, also key skills (including IT) and other cross-curricular content. Links with other subjects may also be identified. Issues of progression are relevant here particularly where, as in many subjects, progression is spiral rather than linear. A scheme of work will be aware of and show how 'big ideas' are being dealt with, e.g. if they are being introduced, revisited for consolidation, revisited for development, increased sophistication. Possibilities and methods for differentiation will also be considered.

### 2. How do we teach?

To cover how the curriculum and learning processes are to be organized: units or modules of work; suggestions for appropriate content, learning activities and processes; forms of pupil grouping to provide differentiation; resources needed; time allocations and opportunities for assessment.

### 3. When do we teach?

To address the issues of curriculum continuity and progression throughout appropriate Key Stages, i.e. what has gone before; what will follow. Relevant here are judgements about the order in which content is addressed. Is it always necessary to do X before Y or are there opportunities for flexibility?

### 4. How do we know that children are learning?

Methods and plans for assessing and monitoring progress and attainment. Specific outcomes may be identified.

Programmes of study for Key Stage 3 are very full and coverage is an issue for teachers when planning schemes of work. Especially for teachers of the core subjects of the National Curriculum, there is the possibility of a 'test-driven curriculum'. In English, for instance, the end of Key Stage 3 tests which focus on reading comprehension, Shakespeare, spelling, punctuation and grammar could well influence curriculum balance, especially where a school is particularly concerned about league tables as a measure of success.

## 2.3   Selecting examination syllabuses

At Key Stage 4, as we have seen, subject teams have to select appropriate accredited courses to fulfil the requirements of the National Curriculum and to offer pupils other learning options.

Subject groups will have views about, for instance, which examination board syllabus they favour for Key Stage 4 and Post-16. Examination boards are now in a 'market' for candidates. Many are offering quantities of 'support materials' for teachers – something which concerns SCAA in that teachers may be teaching the material provided rather than the subject as a whole.

The best way to get to grips with this area is to familiarize yourself with the approach your colleagues have taken since 1996 to developing the curriculum for this stage. Practical Activity 7.10 suggests how you might approach this.

> ## Practical activity 7.10
>
> *Aim:* To review the various syllabuses selected or developed by your subject team for Key Stage 4
>
> *Method:* Talk to your head of department or faculty about the factors which influenced the selection of the courses currently in use. Were these connected with: finance, assessment of pupils' needs, assessment of pupils' ability, availability of resources, familiarity with examination board, staff expertise? What range of courses are offered: GCSE, GNVQ, RSA, NVQ, short/combined etc?
>
> Study the literature associated with different courses. Familiarize yourself with the content and assessment.
>
> *Follow-up:* Find out how happy the subject team is with the courses currently in operation. Would they change anything if they could?

## 2.4   Resources

Resources, in the form of books, equipment, apparatus, artefacts and media, are all factors to be considered when developing schemes of work. Different resources have particular implications for the curriculum-as-experienced and for the skills, attitudes, knowledge and concepts which are likely to be developed through them. Resources should thus be seen to support a curriculum rather than as a means by which it is selected.

The advances in and increasing availability of desk-top publishing has led to many schools producing their own materials, often of a very high quality and specially matched to pupils' learning needs. Commercial publishers, too, especially since the advent of the National Curriculum, have seized the opportunity to produce very specifically targeted textbooks and other materials.

The artefacts, visits, programmes, books, CD Roms or other resources which are selected may also indicate to pupils that certain things are legitimate objects of learning whereas others are not. For many years, attention has been drawn to the books used in school with regard to the implicit values that they contain, particularly with reference to gender, class and ethnic stereotyping. The difficulties in finding appropriate resources are diminishing as publishers address such issues though problems still occur and, of course, schools still possess (and may use) unacceptable material. We suggest you undertake Practical Activity 7.11 as a way of considering the resources in your subject.

In connection with resources we should also mention briefly the allocation of human resources: Which teachers teach which classes. Which classes should have 'second subject' teachers? Where do you place the 'star performers' (or, if you prefer, the 'expert teachers')? What are the priorities? Raising the attainment of pupils on the C/D border at GCSE? Laying a solid foundation in Year 8 and 9?

### Practical activity 7.11

*Aim:* To become familiar with and evaluate resources for use in your subject.

*Method:* Identify the resources held by your subject which are associated with schemes of work at Key Stage 3 and examination syllabuses at Key Stage 4. Consider: a) their intrinsic quality (including their present physical state) and appeal, and b) their usefulness in supporting the intended learning.

Would you want to select, amend, adapt these materials in any way? How might you usefully supplement them with other available or purpose-made resources?

Investigate any centrally held resources which you could draw on or direct pupils to.

*Follow-up:* Develop your personal collection (or database of sources and locations) of resources to support your teaching.

## CONCLUSION

In summary then, the major task at whole-school or departmental level is to select, implement and justify the curriculum that is actually provided. Planning is, of course, crucial so that the decisions that are taken in the face of dilemmas and constraints are the most appropriate and effective. There is also a requirement for processes that enable review during the process of implementation. The most important thing for a reflective teacher is to be aware of the issues, to accept the difficulties and to work progressively and constructively to develop competence at curriculum planning, as suggested by the cyclical model in Chapter 1.

### Notes for further reading

The importance of a purposeful curriculum is well established as a contribution to effective schooling. For an early classic on the importance of coherent school practices, see Rutter *et al.* and also the suggested reading for Chapter 16. Marsh *et al.* is an example of a considerable body of work on school-based curriculum development. Core messages about whole-school curriculum planning are now incorporated within school inspection requirements.

Rutter, M., Maughan, B., Mortimore, P. and Ouston, J. (1979)
*Fifteen Thousand Hours: Secondary Schools and their Effects on Children,*
London: Open Books.

Marsh, C., Day, C. Hannay, L. and McCutcheon, G. (1990)
*Reconceptualizing School-based Curriculum Development,*
London: Falmer Press.

OFSTED (1995c)
*Guidance on the Inspection of Secondary Schools,*
London: HMSO.

For a useful resource on all aspects of curriculum planning and management:

Marsh, C. J. (1991)
*Key Concepts for Understanding Curriculum,*
London: Falmer Press.

The management of the curriculum in the context of other issues is very complex. For some insights into this, see:

Everard, B. and Morris, G. (1996)
*Effective School Management,*
London: Paul Chapman.

Gold, A. (1996)
*Managing a Department,*
London: Heinemann.

HMI, Scottish Education Department (1990)
Management of Education Resources 4
*Curriculum, Staffing and timetabling: a commentary on aspects of secondary school management,*
London: HMSO.

On issues surrounding option choices see:

Stables, A. (1995)
*Subjects of Choice: The Process and Management of Pupil and Student Choice,*
London: Cassell.

Glover, L. (1995)
*GNVQ into Practice,*
London: Cassell.

For a more analytic approach, see:

Goodson, I. R. (1994)
*Studying Curriculum: Cases and Methods,*
Buckingham: Open University Press.

On cross-curricular issues, see:
Murray, R. with Paechter, C. and Black, P. (1994)
*Managing Learning and Assessment Across the Curriculum,*
London: HMSO.

Paechter, C. (1995)
*Crossing Subject Boundaries: the micropolitics of curriculum innovation,*
London: HMSO.

Haydon, G. (1996)
*Teaching about values – a practical approach,*
London: Cassell.

Irving, A. (1996)
*Study and Information Skills Across the Curriculum,*
London: Heinemann.

Lowe, P. (1988)
*Responding to Adolescent Needs: A Pastoral Care Approach,*
London: Cassell.

On the experience of pupils with special educational needs, see:

Wade, B. and Moore, M. (1992)
*Experiencing Special Education: What Young People with Special Educational Needs Can Tell Us,*
Buckingham: Open University Press.

Beveridge, S. (1993)
*Special Education Needs in Schools,*
London: Routledge.

HMI (1992)
*Educating very able children in mainstream schools: a review,*
DES London: HMSO.

Selecting resources for lessons:

Powell, R. (1990)
*Resources for Flexible Learning,*
Stafford: Network Educational Press.

For information on the many excellent subject associations, write or ring their national offices:

The Association for Science Education, College Lane, Hatfield, Hertfordshire, AL10 9AA. Tel: 01707 267411.

National Society for Education in Art and Design, The Gatehouse, Corsham Court, Corsham, Wiltshire, SN13 0BZ. Tel: 01249 714825.

The Design and Technology Association, 16 Wellesbourne House, Walton Road, Wellesbourne, Warwickshire, CV35 9JB. Tel: 01789 47007.

Schools Music Association, 71 Margaret Road, Barnet, Hertfordshire, EN4 9NT. Tel: 0181 440 6919.

The Physical Education Association, Suite 15, 10 Churchill Square, Kings Hill, West Malling, Kent, ME19 4DU. Tel: 01732 875888.

National Association for Special Educational Needs, NASEN House, 4/5 Amber Business Village, Amber Close, Amington, Tamworth, Staffs, B77 4RP. Tel: 01827 311500.

The Association of Teachers of Mathematics, 7 Shaftesbury Street, Derby, DE23 8YB. Tel: 01332 346599.

The Mathematical Association, 259 London Road, Leicester, LE2 3BE. Tel: 0116 2703877.

Professional Council for Religious Education, Royal Buildings, Victoria Street, Derby, DE1 1GW Tel: 01332 296655.

The Geographical Association, 343 Fulwood Road, Sheffield, S10 3BP. Tel: 0114 267 0666.

The Historical Association, 59a Kennington Park Road, London, SE11 4JH. Tel: 0171 735 3901.

National Association for the Teaching of English, 50 Broadfield Road, Broadfield Business Centre, Sheffield, S8 0XJ. Tel: 0114 255 5419.

Association for Language Learning, 150 Railway Terrace, Rugby, CV21 3HN. Tel: 01788 546443.

# CHAPTER 8

# Who are we, as teachers and pupils?

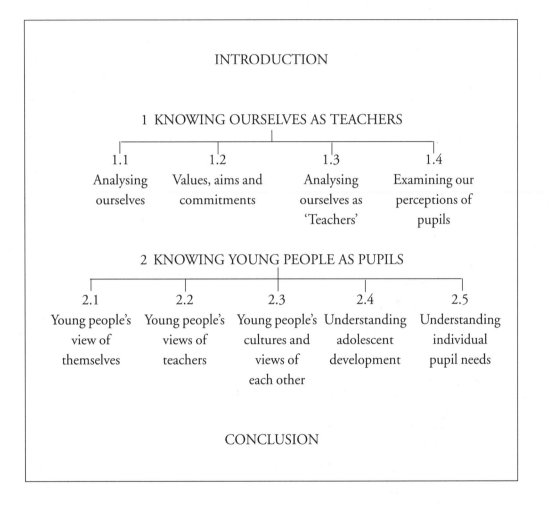

INTRODUCTION

1 KNOWING OURSELVES AS TEACHERS

| 1.1 | 1.2 | 1.3 | 1.4 |
|---|---|---|---|
| Analysing ourselves | Values, aims and commitments | Analysing ourselves as 'Teachers' | Examining our perceptions of pupils |

2 KNOWING YOUNG PEOPLE AS PUPILS

| 2.1 | 2.2 | 2.3 | 2.4 | 2.5 |
|---|---|---|---|---|
| Young people's view of themselves | Young people's views of teachers | Young people's cultures and views of each other | Understanding adolescent development | Understanding individual pupil needs |

CONCLUSION

## INTRODUCTION

In the first section of this chapter we focus on ourselves as teachers and pay particular attention to three central issues: the qualities of ourselves as unique individuals; our strengths and weaknesses in taking on the role of teacher; and the values and commitments which we hold. The second section focuses on understanding young people as pupils.

## 1 KNOWING OURSELVES AS TEACHERS

In considering ourselves as teachers, the first step is to consider the person we are. We could do this in terms of social, cultural and educational background, experience and qualifications, position, interests and personality. Such factors make up our 'personal biography' and together they can be seen as contributing to the development, within each of us, of a unique sense of 'self': a conception of the person we are. Social psychologists argue that this sense of self is particularly important because of the way in which it influences our perspectives, strategies and actions (Secord and Backman 1964, Rosenberg 1965). This is as true for teachers and young people in classrooms as it is for anyone else (Hargreaves 1972, Nias 1989, Claxton 1989, Kohl 1986, Salmon 1995). Each individual is thus seen as having a 'self-image' which is based on a personal understanding of the characteristics which he or she possesses and on an awareness of how others see his or her 'self' (Hall and Hall 1988). Individuals may also have a sense of an 'ideal-self', that is, of the characteristics which they may wish to develop and of the type of person which they might want to become. An individual's self-esteem is, essentially, an indicator of the difference between their self-image and their ideal-self.

The concept of ideal-self introduces the question of values, aims and commitments which individuals hold and to which they aspire. This is important because individuals in society, including teachers and pupils, actively interpret their situation in terms of their values, aims and commitments. Furthermore, teachers' values have considerable social significance because of the responsibilities of their professional position. Thus reflective teachers need to consider their own values carefully and be aware of the implications of them.

This brings us to a second set of factors which are to do with the 'roles' which are occupied by a teacher – or by a pupil too. Whilst teachers and pupils do not simply act out particular ascribed roles, it is certainly the case that expectations have developed about the sort of things that each should do. These expectations come from many sources: for example, headteachers, parents, governors, school inspectors, government and the media. Unfortunately expectations are frequently inconsistent. Thus teachers and pupils have to interpret these pressures and make their own judgements about the most appropriate actions.

Finally, more recent work in the field of educational studies has brought a new and more dynamic perspective to bear on the process of looking at teacher and pupil identity. This work suggests that we all inhabit multiple 'subject positions', and that our identities are fluid and fragmented, and are negotiated in social, political and cultural contexts through our interactions and relationships with others. Such a 'postmodern' perspective leads us to challenge simplistic, inflexible and externally imposed notions of teacher or pupil identity, for example, by asking what it means to be 'male' or 'black' (Wexler *et al.* 1992, Marshall 1994, Blair *et al.* 1995, Griffiths 1995).

Few teachers, however committed, can hope to fulfil all their aims if the context in which they work is not supportive. For instance, some parents may have one set of educational priorities: staff may take up another value position. The established practices of the school may not support the particular styles of teaching which a teacher would wish to adopt. Staff may disagree with some aspects of government policy; the resources needed may not be available. For reasons such as these, teachers must continually adapt: they must know themselves and the situations in which they work, and they must be able to make astute strategic judgements as they seek to achieve personal and professional fulfilment and to resolve the dilemmas posed by idealism and pragmatism.

Such reflection is a personal process and is very effective when undertaken with a self-aware integrity. However, such professional self-development is now complemented, as a national requirement for England and Wales, by teacher appraisal systems in each local education authority. 'Appraisal' is a formal procedure through which reflection on personal goals and teaching roles is managed by LEAs and headteachers. In England and Wales, following extensive discussion across the teaching profession (ACAS 1986), appraisal is deliberately not linked to pay so that there was no hindrance to openness. Such procedures should be professionally constructive and often require teachers to identify goals on which they may be appraised and to review their personal development and professional capacities in terms of their job descriptions. Such job descriptions should, of course, fit within the framework of the school's overall structure and development plans (see Chapter 5), and should help teachers and schools to identify priorities for further professional development (see Section 1.3).

Appraisal procedures thus provide a more formal contribution towards the process of knowing oneself as a person, establishing a clear set of values, aims and commitments, and understanding the context in which we work (Simons and Elliott 1989, Trethowan 1991 see **Primary Reading 3.6**). These are three essential elements in any reflective consideration of teaching and they are examined in more detail below.

## 1.1 Analysing ourselves

Studies such as those of Huberman (1993), Goodson (1992), Thomas (1995) and Nias (1989) have shown that most people enter the profession with a strong sense of personal identity and of personal values. For instance, Nias reported that this sense of self was so strong that many teachers saw themselves as 'persons-in-teaching' rather than as 'teachers' as such. Clearly, if this is so, then the openness and willingness to change and develop, which is implied by the notion of reflective teaching, is dependent on the qualities and degree of confidence of each teacher's sense of self and the relationship of 'self' to 'role'. One issue of particular interest is that of achieving personal fulfilment from teaching. This seems to be most likely when there is a congruence between each teacher's personal sense of self and the ways in which they are expected to present their self in school – their public display.

This work raises a number of important points, particularly the need to develop self-knowledge. Easen (1985) has provided a useful framework for developing such understanding. He suggests that we can distinguish between a set of characteristics which we see as being part of ourselves (as representing our self-image) in contrast to a set of attributes which other people attribute to us on the basis of observation and interaction with us. There is also an unknown area of potential for self-development. Using a model of this sort, one can distinguish between the following:

- our public display: aspects of ourselves which we project and others also see presented
- our blind spots: aspects of ourselves which others see but we do not recognize
- our dreamer spots: aspects of ourselves which we know are there, or would like to be there, but of which others are unaware
- our untapped reservoir: our unknown potential, of which we are also unaware.

These aspects are indicated in Figure 8.1.

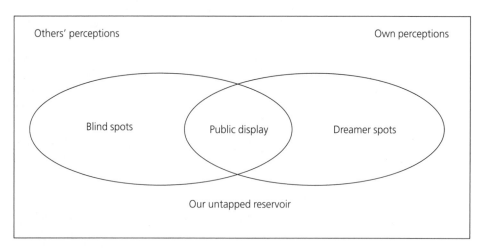

**Figure 8.1** *Seen and unseen aspects of 'self' (Easen 1985)*

Gaining self-knowledge is not something which one can simply 'do' and complete in a single activity. It is something which develops over time, as a conscious process which goes on throughout life. As reflective teachers we will be aware of how much our biographies affect what we think and do. It is helpful and interesting to recall experiences at home and at school which you feel were significant – exchanging memories with a colleague is a good way to do this. However, in Practical Activity 8.1 our main purpose is to draw attention to a different aspect of self-awareness.

It is necessary to consider the fact that developing such self-awareness can involve a process of self-discovery which may, at times, be threatening and painful. The work of Carl Rogers (1961, 1969, 1980) is useful here. Rogers writes as a psychotherapist who has developed what he calls a 'person-centred' approach to his work. His central argument is that 'individuals have within themselves vast resources for self-understanding and for altering their self-concepts, basic attitudes and self-directed behaviour' (1980, p. 115).

**Practical activity 8.1**

*Aim:* To analyse dimensions of our 'selves'.

*Method:* Think of specific and memorable incidents in which you were centrally involved.

Try to identify the most prominent characteristics of your 'self' which they reveal.

It may be helpful to situate your reflection (e.g. as a 'parent', as a 'child', as a 'pupil', as a 'student', as a 'teacher').

Try to identify:

1. Dreamer spots . . .           1
   (parts you would like to develop)    2
                                        3

2. Blind spots . . .               1
   (parts you do not often face up to)   2
                                        3

3. Public display . . .           1
   (parts you publicly present)       2
                                        3

4. Untapped reservoir . . .      1
   (parts you think might be there)    2
                                        3

It would probably be beneficial to do this exercise with a friend. It could help you to deepen your understandings, share and explain your perceptions, whilst providing mutual support.

*Follow-up:* Clearly, the challenge of being a reflective teacher is intimately bound up with reflection on such personal issues. It is about replacing blind spots with insights, about developing dreams and ideals into realities, about tapping potential and facilitating learning.

In addition to the focus on inner self-development, Rogers also suggests that personal development is facilitated by genuine acceptance by others. This has great relevance for professional and personal development in teaching. In particular, it points to the importance of working collaboratively with colleagues and developing open, trusting relationships. Such relationships should not only provide an alternative source of insights into our own practice but should also provide the support to face and deal with whatever issues may be raised. Recent work in the field of school effectiveness identifies the importance of schools developing cultures in which teachers are supported in taking risks, changing their practices and growing in effectiveness, creating 'learning communities' in which teachers are also learners (Barth 1990, Preedy 1993, Hopkins *et al.* 1994, Nixon *et al.* 1996).

## 1.2   Values, aims and commitments

In beginning to consider our personal sense of values and how, when and where they arise, it is important to establish a basic point: our perspectives and viewpoints influence what we do both inside and outside the classroom. The values we hold are frequently evident in our behaviours, and thus, in our teaching.

Identifying values and aims is difficult, and so, too, is trying to identify what to look for in the learning environments we create and inhabit, which could tell us whether we are putting our aims into practice. The reflective teacher needs both to identify values, aims and commitments and to consider indicators of their actual implementation. Only then will we be able to judge whether what we do really matches what we say we believe.

One important step is to see that our own individual beliefs do materialize in this area, but reflect our social position, previous experience and historical location. This is one reason why beliefs can be so difficult to change, since there can be significant material and cultural foundations to them, or edifices built upon them. Indeed, beliefs can often appear to be representations of 'objective truths', or 'natural facts', rather than socially constructed perspectives. One useful way forward can be to group such beliefs and to link them to educational ideologies (see Chapter 2, Section 1.1). These value positions and ideological perspectives can be labelled in many different ways – itself a challenging activity for a reflective teacher. We have identified six positions below which we feel are, or have been, particularly important.

- *Social democracy.* This is characterized by an egalitarian value-position and a focus on the potential of education as an instrument of gradual social change. This was a prevalent ideology in the post-war years and, for a period, seemed to have a degree of all-party support in the UK.
- *Liberal romanticism.* An example of this is the highly individualistic, 'child-centred' view of education focusing on the unique development of each child, a view which values diversity and individual difference. This is the ideology which was endorsed by the Plowden Report (CACE 1967), and which underpinned the Free School Movement.
- *Traditional educational conservatism.* A perspective that emphasizes, the transmission of established social values, knowledge and culture through a subject-oriented approach and which also has a particular emphasis on upholding 'standards'. This was the explicit ideology of the Black Papers (e.g. Cox and Dyson 1969) and was an important element of the thinking of the 1970s and 1980s (Boyson 1975, Hillgate 1987, Scruton 1986) which led to the Education Reform Act (1988), the National Curriculum, and particular forms of assessment and testing.
- *Economic pragmatism.* An instrumental approach focusing on the individual's acquisition of useful skills. The term 'vocationalism' is sometimes used where the emphasis shifts, perhaps at times of high unemployment, to directing individuals to acquire skills economically useful to society. In England and Wales this approach is evident in recent debates concerning the reformation of the Post-16 curriculum, the development of GNVQs, and experience in the 1980s of TVEI and TVEE (Crombie White *et al.* 1995).
- *Social radicalism.* An approach which is based on a commitment to develop educa-

tion as a means of combating inequalities in society and promoting social justice. Proponents support positive action regarding such issues as sexism, racism, homophobia, social class, disability, rights and the distribution of power and wealth (Arnot and Weiler 1993, Gillborn 1995, Griffiths and Davies 1995). Some 1980s policies of the Inner London Education Authority reflected this approach before it was disbanded, and the commitments, if not the actions, are reflected in UK laws (e.g. Race Relations Act 1976, Sex Discrimination Act 1975, Disability Discrimination Act 1996) and international conventions (e.g. European Convention on Human Rights, United Nations Convention on the Rights of the Child).

- *Neo-liberal conservatism.* A set of beliefs, going back to Adam Smith, about the efficiency of free market forces in allocating resources and raising standards in the provision of goods and services (No Turning Back Group of MPs 1986, Sexton 1987, 1988, Chubb and Moe 1990). As O'Keeffe (1988) put it:

> If you do not like the groceries at one supermarket, try another. The system which has utterly out-performed all others in history in the production of a wide range of goods and services needs trying out in education too.

In the 1980s, this ideology was applied in education in combination with that of traditional educational conservatism, to produce a radical set of 'New Right' ideas which see educational provision as a market and parents as consumers. Among the many implications of this conception are to reduce the importance of local educational planning (e.g. through LEAs in the UK) and to increase the importance of information for consumers on pupil and school performance. These ideas were very influential in the 1990s restructuring of education in countries such as New Zealand, Australia and the United States of America, as well as in the UK (Bridges and McLaughlin 1994, Gewirtz, Ball and Bowe 1995).

Such educational ideologies are often not expressed or experienced in their 'pure' form. In addition, throughout the 1980s and into the 1990s (under the auspices of a Conservative government), there were significant tensions and conflicts around which 'voices' and whose 'perspectives' would dominate in determining national educational policy; for example, between traditionalist interests in authoritative traditions and curriculum content, and a more modernizing tendency interested in curriculum process and flexible life skills (Jones 1989, Flude and Hammer 1990, Moore and Ozga 1991). In the late 1990s it was possible to identify an interesting coalescence between the Conservative political agenda for education and that of New Labour, with convergence over their articulation of concerns about 'standards' (Barber 1996).

The multiplicity of voices attempting to influence national educational policy has the potential to make it harder for teachers and school communities to clarify their own value positions. However, reflective teachers should aim to develop their own clearly defined personal perspective as a guide to everyday action and practical policies. The lack of explicitly conceived values and aims often results in an inconsistent commitment to implement any relevant policy.

The series of Practical Activities which follows should help you to explore different aspects of your aims and values.

## Practical activity 8.2

*Aim:* To identify general aims which you hold for the pupils' learning.

*Method:* List your 'top three' aims, and number them in order of importance.

*Follow-up:* How do your aims relate to your 'value-position'? How do your aims compare with your colleagues? What are the implications of any similarity or difference?

To investigate our value positions in greater depth the work of Eisner and Vallance (1974) is helpful. They distinguish three main dimensions upon which varied value positions are held. They suggest these are best represented as continua.

individual  society

(i.e. whether education should be geared to meet individuals' needs and demands, rather than to educational provision being planned to meet the needs of society).

values  skills

(i.e. whether education should focus on developing individuals' sense of values in a moral and ethical context, or on developing their skills and competencies.

adaptive ◄————————► reconstructive

(i.e. whether education should prepare individuals to fit into the present society, or should equip them to change and develop it).

By identifying these three dimensions, it may be possible to clarify where each of us stands regarding our value positions. For example, a student teacher might place herself at the 'individual' extreme of the first dimension, tend towards the 'skills' extreme of the second dimension and feel most comfortable with the 'adaptive' extreme of the third dimension. Such a person would, therefore, be committed to an educational system which aimed at developing individuals with the skills and competencies to fit into the given present society. She would feel less ethical concern for the needs of society as a whole or desire to consider the possibilities and processes of change.

## Practical activity 8.3

*Aim:* To identify individual value-positions.

*Method:* Try to place yourself along each of the three continua discussed above and clarify where your 'position' is.

*Follow-up:* Having tried to do this, you may find other dimensions need to be added as well – or taken away. This exercise can be extended so that a whole group could identify their 'positions'. Then it is possible to clarify areas of conflict and reassess policy issues in the light of such discussions. Consider the implications each 'position' may have for teaching styles.

Of course, as reflective teachers, we will also need to consider to what extent our classroom behaviour is consistent with our expressed beliefs. Practical Activity 8.4 will help to do this.

## Practical activity 8.4

*Aim:* To interrogate our actions as teachers in relation to our professed values.

*Method:* Make a chart as below. Complete the first two sections as honestly as possible and then move on to try to answer the questions posed in sections 3 and 4.

|  | When organizing learning groups | When teaching a class | When assessing pupils' work |
| --- | --- | --- | --- |
| 1. Most usually I . . . |  |  |  |
| 2. Sometimes I . . . |  |  |  |
| *Look at your answers and then address these questions with reference to assessment, organization of groups, teaching style* |  |  |  |
| 3. What values are my predominant behaviours projecting? |  |  |  |
| 4. How congruent is this with my core beliefs and values? |  |  |  |

*Follow-up:* In discussion with a colleague who has also completed the chart, ask yourself: a) How do you feel about the situation recorded here? b) If there is a lack of congruence, why is this? c) Is there anything you can do to change or improve the situation? d) What conditions do you need to effect this change?

It may be useful at this point to stop and reflect upon underlying value positions and the ideological perspectives underpinning your own practices, as an individual teacher, department/faculty, or school. A starting point might be to interrogate policy texts; for example, you could choose to focus on a document produced by central government (e.g. the Statutory Orders of the National Curriculum), or a document published by inspectors and advisers (e.g. from HMI, OFSTED, or QCA), or educational associations (e.g. the Geographical Association), or LEAs, or examples of school policies. Practical Activity 8.5 provides a sample text for this exercise.

## Practical activity 8.5

*Aim:* To identify value commitments and ideologies through consideration of educational policy statements.

*Method:* We suggest that a variety of policy statements (including school policy statements) are discussed with colleagues with a view to identifying both underlying value positions and practical implications. We provide an example from parts of a 1996 speech by Tony Blair on his 'new vision for comprehensive schools'.

'New Labour is committed to meritocracy. We believe that people should be able to rise by their talents, not by their birth or the advantages of privilege. We understand that people are not born into equal circumstances, so one role of state education is to open up opportunities for all. That means we need to provide high standards of basics for all, but also recognize the different abilities of different children, and tailor education to meet their needs and develop their potential.

'It is essential for this country to have both a good education for all and an education system that stretches our best brains. It is not a choice between the two. We need both if we are to thrive as a nation in the next century. Equality must not become the enemy of quality. True equality means giving everyone the education that helps them achieve all that they can. That implies special help for those who need it, a challenging education for the average pupil and the full extension of the capabilities of the intellectually gifted. In other words, an equally good education – whether you are brilliant, average or slow learner – is not learning in the same classes for everyone but the experience best suited to you as an individual with your own particular needs. That is why I argue for a flexible system of grouping pupils within comprehensive schools to ensure that everyone can get the education best suited to their needs . . .

'The Conservatives are delving deeper and deeper into the failed policies of the past. Take for example the Prime Minister's idea of a grammar school in every town. . . . It would be yet another policy designed to benefit a tiny minority at the expense of everyone else. It would also be a dangerous distraction from the central issue of raising standards for all children. . . .

'Mixed ability teaching is for some people as much of an ideology as the principle of comprehensive admission itself. It works in some cases – when done by the best teachers with proper support and a well-motivated and cohesive group of children. But mixed ability teaching makes heroic assumptions about resources, teachers and social context. While an overly rigid system of streaming can lead to the same problems as the 11-plus, not to take account of the obvious common sense that different children move at different speeds and have different abilities, is to give idealism a bad name. The modernization of the comprehensive principle requires that all pupils are encouraged to progress as far and as fast as they are able. Grouping children according to their ability can be an important way of making that happen.'

(Source: Speech at Didcot Girls School, 7 June 1996, reprinted in Blair 1996, pp. 173–6.)

*Follow-up:* Discussion of policy statements or documents should bring questions about educational aims and commitments into the open, and thus expose them to debate.

For instance, regarding Tony Blair's arguments above, consider the issues of: ideology (Chapter 2, Section 1.1), choice, diversity and education markets (Chapter 16, Introduction), 'intelligence' (Chapter 9, Section 2.1), curriculum pathways (Chapter 6, Sections 2.5 and Part 3), school organization and internal differentiation (Chapter 5, Section 2.4, Chapter 7, Sections 1.4 and 1.8, Chapter 10, Section 2.2.).

## 1.3   Analysing ourselves as 'teachers'

One way of representing and beginning to reveal our own ideological complexity to ourselves, is to select a broad area of our work (e.g. teaching style, or attitude to discipline), and 'objectify' it according to different ideological persuasions. In attempting to place our beliefs within contrasting categories, we reveal something of the complexity of our belief systems, particularly when we find that we don't always conform consistently or neatly to the 'standard', or 'conventional' approach we might expect (or claim) to fit into. Figure 8.2 below, uses the 'progressive' and 'traditional' dichotomy as a contrastive framework for representing some of teachers' beliefs about their practices. Ask yourself as you read through the statements to what extent a teacher is ever driven by all of the beliefs of one side.

| Progressive | Traditional |
|---|---|
| 1. Teacher as guide to educational experiences (e.g. pupils participate in curriculum planning) | 1. Teacher as distributor of knowledge (e.g. pupils have no say in curriculum planning) |
| 2. Active pupil role (e.g. learning predominantly by discovery techniques) | 2. Passive pupil role (e.g. accent on memory and practice and rote) |
| 3. Intrinsic motivation (e.g. enjoyment and fulfilment emphasized, interests followed) | 3. Extrinsic motivation (e.g. rewards and punishment used: points and penalties) |
| 4. Integrated subject matter and flexible timetable | 4. Separate subject matter and rigid timetable |
| 5. Concerned with personal/social/academic potential: accent on co-operative groupwork, and creative expression | 5. Concerned with academic standards: accent on competition and correct expression |
| 6. Continuous informal forms of monitoring | 6. Periodic formal testing and assessments |
| 7. Teaching not confined to classroom base | 7. Teaching confined to classroom base |

**Figure 8.2** *Characteristics of pedagogy*

Thinking about beliefs in this way can be revealing. We can use it to analyse public policy on education as well as our personal perspectives as teachers. However, such characterizations of ideology are over-simplified and generalized – a consequence of attempting to capture categories of meaning in the form of a table.

In practice, teachers' views and values about teaching and learning:

1. depend upon the setting within which we work
2. are more complex than simple models can capture
3. change over time.

Knowing ourselves as 'teachers' involves investigating our beliefs and conceptualizations of the practices which support and enable young people as 'learners'. What we need are more complex maps and more sensitive descriptions. Many of the Practical Activities in this and other chapters in Part 2 of this book should help you to develop such maps and descriptions.

In addition to investigating our values and conceptualizations of teaching, we also need to be able to identify our capability to fulfil our expectations of ourselves, and other people's expectations of us as teachers. Do we have the necessary personal and social attributes, as well as pedagogic skills and competences? How are we to acquire them, sustain them and develop them over time? Increasingly, being an effective teacher requires the ability to operate successfully in classrooms with pupils as a 'subject' teacher and as a 'pastoral' teacher. Furthermore, we need to build positive working relationships with other colleagues, and with other interested parties to whom we are accountable – notably: parents, governors, and inspectors of the school. Learning how to manage the multiple demands and expectations placed upon us has an important consequence for our ability to maintain our energy and sustain our willingness to change.

Of course, meeting the challenges of teaching is not a once-and-for-all process and professional development should continue throughout a teaching career.

Whatever the actual career pattern, the process of professional development should be broadly similar – that of the continuous identification, development and refinement of skills, knowledge and competencies (Calderhead 1988). Reflective teachers should aim to develop a coherent and progressive professional development programme which meets both their short-term needs and their career aspirations (Fullan and Hargreaves 1992, Smyth 1995).

Perhaps the most important aspect of analysing self involves considering whether what it is 'to be a teacher' is compatible with how we see ourselves 'as a person'. For some, there may be a conflict between these two images. For example, certain aspects of 'being a teacher' have been described as being willing to take a leadership role, to be 'in authority'. This may result in a conflict between personal values and aims and other people's expectations of a teacher's role.

A final aspect, which at many different times in our teaching lives we need to consider, is the question of what part 'being a teacher' is going to play in our lives. We have to decide how we are going to balance the demands of the job with our own personal needs, with regard for example, to our own family, social life and interests (Acker 1989, Evetts 1990). In addition, schools might be encouraged to develop and defend human-centred qualities where teachers feel 'looked after' as rounded indi-

## Practical activity 8.6

*Aim:* To identify the demands that teaching makes of us as individuals.

*Method:* Divide the page into two vertical columns.

In the left-hand column make a list of the aims you have for yourself as a teacher, as you did in Practical Activity 8.2.

In the right-hand column, make a list of the personal qualities, skills, knowledge or competencies which are needed to implement each aim.

Perhaps reference back to the discussion of competencies in Chapter 1 would be helpful.

| Aims | Personal qualities, skills, knowledge or competencies |
|------|-------------------------------------------------------|
|      |                                                       |

*Follow-up:* Review the qualities, skills, knowledge and competencies which are required. Consider which ones would be easy for you and which ones might be more difficult. Try to identify steps that could be taken to help to meet your particular challenges. It would be interesting to carry out or discuss this activity in a group with friends or peers.

viduals, with lives and commitments outside as well as inside school. In the UK the late 1980s and early 1990s were times of great stress for teachers (Cole and Walker 1989, Dunham 1992, Gold and Roth 1994) and it is doubtful if such an imbalance in personal/professional matters can be sustained in the long term.

## 1.4 Examining our perceptions of 'pupils'

Just as it was important to understand how we perceive ourselves as 'teachers', so, too, it is important to understand how we perceive 'pupils'.

All of us are likely to have preconceptions and prejudices about what young people should be like as pupils. For instance, it has been found that teachers are affected by the gender, ethnicity, or social class of the pupils and even by their names (Meighan 1981, Kyriacou 1986, Salmon 1995). Such preconceptions can result in treating pupils in different ways. If pupils then respond differently, the original preconceptions are reinforced. Such labelling, or stereotyping, can lead to a phenomenon known as a 'self-fulfilling' prophecy and could result in considerable social injustices (Brophy and Good 1974, Nash 1976, Mortimore *et al.* 1988), particularly if they emerge in official assessment (Burns 1982, Filer 1993).

This is a complex area for teachers, since our own identities and location by gender, ethnicity, social class etc. can make it difficult for us to change our perceptions of the pupils we work with or our interactions with them. Much work has been done in examining the nature of interactions within schools as institutions and between teachers and pupils, and the ways in which racism, sexism, class bias are implicated and sustained through the schooling process (Ball 1984, Davies 1984, Mirza 1992, Mac an Ghaill 1988, 1995, Epstein 1993).

As reflective teachers, focusing on the importance of supporting and enhancing the achievement of all pupils in our care, we need to step back from our initial or routine reactions to pupils, and interrogate our conscious or unconscious processes of labelling. For instance:

1. How does school organization reproduce and sustain differentiation and labelling of pupils (Hargreaves 1967, Lacey 1970, Ball 1981), and what are the implications of this for teachers and pupils?
2. How do we personally acknowledge, categorize and label the pupils we work with?
3. How can we think about and work with pupils, moving beyond the labels?

In Chapter 5 we considered aspects of school organization. Practical Activity 8.7 suggests a way to consider some possible consequences for pupils of decisions made about organization.

### Practical activity 8.7

*Aim:* To identify some elements of school organization that differentiate and label pupils.

*Method:* Write down a list of all the ways in which the school groups pupils for different purposes. If you have worked on them, you may find it useful to look at the academic and pastoral systems you identified in Practical Activities 5.17 and 5.18.

Consider, for each in turn, the pupils assigned to these groups. Is there any pattern of differential distribution of pupils by gender, ethnicity and social class? If so, what explanations do you have for this distribution? List the explanations under three headings and note which explanations you tend to favour:

1. Reasons residing within the pupil
2. Reasons residing within the pupil's family
3. Reasons residing within school processes.

*Follow-up:* What are the different implications of locating explanations under (1) and (2) rather than (3)?

Just as the school describes and defines pupils through its organizational structures, as teachers we also use shorthand defining categories as we try to deal with and respond to large numbers of pupils. The following Practical Activities suggest ways of making our generalizations visible for reflection.

### Practical activity 8.8

*Aim:* To find out our response to pupils we teach.

*Method:* Write down the names of the pupils in one class you teach (without referring to the register or any lists). Note which order you have listed them in and which names you found hard to remember.

*Follow-up:* What does the order tell you about which pupils are more memorable than others, and for what reasons? How does this reflect those you get on best with, those with problems, those who present you with problems, pupils who are withdrawn, those you would like to forget . . . ? Are there any differences between those of different gender, ethnicity, ability or social class?

The next activity suggests that we take this initial analysis a step further by using the idea of personal constructs. You may want to look at Chapter 4, Section 3.10, where this technique is described.

## Practical activity 8.9

*Aim:* To understand our perceptions of 'pupils'.

*Method:* Use a list of the pupils in one of your classes to generate the 'personal constructs' which you employ. To do this, look at groups of three names and write down the word that shows how two pupils are most alike. Then write down another word which shows how the third is most different.

*Follow-up:* When you have done this with each triad, review the characteristics that you have identified as the ends of a series of bi-polar constructs.

What does this suggest to you about the characteristics by which you distinguish pupils? What additional qualities do the young people have which these constructs do not seem to reflect and which perhaps you do not use?

Consider the constructs and note any patterns which might exist: for example whether some constructs are used more with boys than girls, with pupils from different class or ethnic backgrounds. There may also be a variety of constructs which relate to such things as academic ability, physical attributes or behaviour towards teachers or other pupils.

Most of us encounter pupils who present us with a challenge and we don't always like the reaction they provoke in us. Practical Activity 8.10 asks us to think about these pupils.

## Practical activity 8.10

*Aim:* To think through and beyond our hostile reactions to pupils who present us with challenging behaviour.

*Method:* Think of three different pupils you work with whom you find difficult or feel hostile towards. Write a brief pen portrait of each.

For each pupil, ask yourself the following questions and record your thoughts. It might be helpful to do this with a colleague who also works with the pupil concerned. Which labels are easily attached to each pupil? What might the implications of these labels be for each pupil and her or his teachers? What needs might each pupil have (cognitive, emotional, physical, social etc.) which need to be understood in supporting them through school? What might you need to understand better about each pupil in order to engage with her/him? What might you need to understand better about yourself to engage with her/him?

*Follow-up:* How do you feel about each pupil now that you have done this activity?

What might you want to now do to take this further forward? Chapter 14 may be relevant here.

## 2 | KNOWING YOUNG PEOPLE AS PUPILS

Developing an understanding of young people as pupils requires that a reflective teacher should empathize with what it is like to be a 'pupil' at school as well as develop personal knowledge of and rapport with individual pupils.

This can be challenging to do since a secondary school teacher will have contact with several different classes in a week across subject and pastoral responsibilities. It is also true that the 11–18 years encompass a huge range of developments in young people, and the understandings one might draw upon to inform a relationship with an 11-year-old pupil will, to some extent, be different from those required to build a positive relationship with an 18-year-old. What has been noted however across the secondary age range is that pupils characterize 'good teachers' as combining teacher 'authority' (understanding of the subject and good classroom management skills) with the ability to develop mutual respect and rapport between teacher and pupil (Kyriacou 1986).

## 2.1 Young people's views of themselves in school

What pupils think of themselves is important and will influence their approach to learning. Some may be highly anxious and continually undervalue themselves. Others may seem over confident. Some may be very well aware of their own strengths and weaknesses whilst others may seem to have relatively naïve views of themselves. Pupils may be gregarious, or loners, or they may be lonely. In a recent longitudinal study of the primary years, Pollard and Filer (forthcoming) traced the home, playground and classroom experiences of a small group of children through their primary school careers. They argued that such experiences contribute to a sense of identity and thence to confidence and achievement in learning.

This study emphasizes the complexity of pupils' lives, that there are no simple and causal explanations for how and why pupils respond to schooling as they do, but that interactions in a variety of social contexts are significant in the development of pupil identities and learning stances. The same is true for pupils in the secondary years. There are problems however in this phase: for pupils who see a succession of different teachers; and for teachers who deal with large numbers of learners.

Perhaps it is in the pastoral role, as form tutors or PSE tutors, that teachers most explicitly engage with this, or in curricular activities which allow pupils to reveal and reflect upon something of their individual identities (e.g. in drama or English) or in extra-curricular activities. A wide range of pastoral materials exists to enable teachers and pupils to explore elements of identity (Button 1981, 1982, Bliss and Tetley 1993, Mitchell and Stocks 1993, Best *et al.* 1995). Particular activities are often age-related, as illustrated below. However, there is also a school of thought which suggests such investigation into pupil identities could be intrusive and operate as a form of 'policing' (Hargreaves 1989).

Here we suggest just two possible activities that allow pupils to reveal something of themselves.

## *Practical activity 8.11*

*Aim:* To allow pupils in a new class on transfer to secondary school to reveal and share something of their individual identities.

*Method:* Each pupil draws a shield shape with a central hub and four quadrants. In each of the five spaces they draw something or someone of importance in their lives. The teacher can model this and reveal something of themselves by doing one to begin with.

*Follow-up:* Pupils in a tutor group could design questions and interview each other, take photos of each other and produce a biography page to display in the tutor base.

Like adults, pupils can also benefit from opportunities to reflect in more detail on their sense of themselves. This next activity is a variation on activity 8.1 suggested for use by teachers.

## *Practical activity 8.12*

*Aim:* To explore one of the features of adolescent experience: the multiple and sometimes contradictory expectations that different people have of them.

*Method:* This can be explored through 'picture maps' of different senses of themselves. Pupils can draw or write in boxes set out on a page.

| How my parent(s) see me | How other members of my family see me | How my teachers see me |
|---|---|---|

| MY OWN SENSE OF MYSELF |
|---|

| How my friends see me | How the media sees me | How my classmates see me |
|---|---|---|

*Follow-up:* The activity, as well as giving you insights into your pupils, may provide opportunities for discussion of how they could handle differing expectations of different people, and how it feels to feel uncertain of who we are.

A central strategy in the development of positive self-concepts among the pupils in school lies in encouraging individuals to identify qualities within themselves which they can value. It is important to provide opportunities where a wide range of qualities can be appreciated. In classrooms where competitive achievement is greatly emphasized, some pupils may quickly come to regard themselves unfavourably, or else learn to resent and oppose the values of the teacher. It is, however, possible to create a climate where many different qualities are valued and where pupils are encouraged to challenge themselves to improve their own individual performance. In this way the dignity of the individual child can be protected and individual effort and engagement rewarded (see Chapter 14).

One of the ways of establishing such a climate is to encourage pupils to evaluate their own work and to set their own personal goals. This is a practice now well established in many schools through the culture of Records of Achievement (Pole 1993) and formative forms of assessment (Gipps 1994). However, it is important that the procedures are meaningful for the pupils and worthy of their respect. Tokenistic self-evaluation form-filling, or rewards without currency amongst an adolescent audience, can be counter-productive.

## Practical activity 8.13

*Aim:* To encourage pupils to evaluate themselves and to review their work.

*Method:* This can be done informally, e.g., when a piece of work is brought for marking the pupil can be asked for his or her opinion on it. More formally, perhaps at the completion of a project, pupils could fill in a comment form to indicate what they had liked best/least about it, what they had found easy/difficult about it, what they had learnt from it (content and skills), what they think they need to practise more, have more help in understanding or try harder at etc. Another strategy is to ask them to keep a journal in which they can review their achievements on a regular basis.

In designing such strategies it can be very productive to discuss with pupils which criteria they would want to use to evaluate their work by, or if you are working to externally set criteria, to discuss fully how to interpret the criteria, fulfil them, and evaluate work against them. It is important to recognize in this that pupils, to some extent, are 'experts' in their own learning needs, and that we can empower them to know that they can know what it is they need to ask or to do in order to improve.

*Follow-up:* Such procedures will reveal specific difficulties which pupils experience and help the teacher to match future tasks appropriately. However, it is necessary to consider what difficulties some pupils might experience in undertaking self-evaluation. How could the teacher help them to articulate their own needs? In addition, such activity can make pupils feel exposed or individually vulnerable. What sort of strategies with a class might a teacher adopt to tackle this?

## 2.2   Young people's views of teachers

If we are trying to negotiate a positive working relationship with young people, it is important to know how each of the individuals involved in the relationship view one another. It is, therefore, important to know how pupils perceive their teachers.

A considerable amount of evidence has been collected in this area (Blishen 1969, Makins 1969, Meighan 1978, Kyriacou 1986, Keys and Fernandes 1993, Rudduck *et al.* 1995). Much of the evidence suggests that pupils like teachers who 'make them learn'. They expect teachers to teach, by which they seem to mean to take initiatives, to be in control and to provide interesting activities. On the other hand, they also like teachers who are prepared to be flexible, to respond to the different interests of the individuals in the class and to provide some scope for pupil choice. Pupils dislike teachers who have favourites or who are unpredictable in their moods. Most pupils like a teacher who can sometimes 'have a laugh'. Overall, it seems that pupils like teachers who are firm, flexible, fair and fun, and who help them be successful as learners.

You could check these findings with some of the pupils you teach.

### *Practical activity 8.14*

*Aim:* To find out young people's criteria for a 'good teacher'.

*Method:* Hold a discussion (with the whole class, or in small groups which can then report back to the whole class) on what makes a 'good teacher'. Perhaps the discussion could be couched in terms of suggestions for a student on how to become a good teacher. Discussions with pupils on such a topic must obviously be handled very carefully and only with the agreement of any teachers who are involved.

*Follow-up:* Such information can be interesting in two ways:

1. It reveals something of the young people's expectations of what it is to be a 'good teacher'.

2. It can contribute to reflection on our own effectiveness as teachers and in implementing our values, aims and commitments. It could also lead to a reconsideration of those values, aims and commitments.

In the world of the adolescent in school, part of becoming self-confident as a young adult is about being given increasing responsibility and autonomy as a learner. Important in this is some degree of power-sharing between pupils and teachers over lesson content and learning objectives (Hughes 1994). This may involve risk-taking for a teacher, and open up contested spaces in the classroom. Having a clear sense of 'self' as a teacher and a commitment to respect pupils in the process of learning is fundamental (Raphael Reed 1995a).

In addition, recent research shows that many pupils experience tension and pressure in reconciling the demands of work with the demands of personal and social development, and that schools and teachers have an important role to play in acknowledging these strains and helping young people to cope with these demands (Rudduck *et al.* 1995).

Involving pupils in the evaluation of your teaching is a significant act of power-sharing.

## *Practical activity 8.15*

*Aim:* To provide an opportunity for young people to analyse and comment on the teaching they experience.

*Method:* At the end of a sequence of work, a unit or module, you could invite pupils to comment on the experience. To help them to focus their thinking and to give you useful information to act on, you might like to design a *pro forma*. You could use some of the following prompts or invent your own which relate to what you would like to find out..

- What have you enjoyed most about doing this topic?
- Can you say why?
- What have you enjoyed least?
- Can you say why?
- What has been most useful to you in this topic?
- What was the easiest thing to learn? What was the most difficult thing to learn?
- The thing that we did that most helped me to learn was . . .
- I would find it helpful if you would . . .

*Follow-up:* This kind of activity might also be incorporated as a whole-school or departmental strategy. At the end of each year, when pupils receive reports from teachers, they could be invited to write evaluative reports on their teachers, or on the work they have done that term. It would be possible to use frameworks similar to those suggested, or develop something specifically for the purpose.

Pupils will also have views on the running of the school as a whole.

## *Practical activity 8.16*

*Aim:* To find out pupils' views on their place in the running of the school, as part of a democratic community of learners.

*Method:* Hold a discussion on how schools might find out more about pupil views on a range of issues, and about how schools might benefit from involving pupils more as active partners in the running of the school.

*Follow-up:* If there is already a School Council in some form, this may be a discussion of how to make that a more effective instrument. If there is no such tradition, what are the implications for the school of the views expressed?

## 2.3   Young people's cultures and their views of each other

So far the focus has been on the teacher, the pupil and their mutual perceptions. However, it is most important to remember that, although the teacher is a central figure, classrooms are a meeting place for many pupils – indeed, Jackson (1968) referred to 'the crowd' as being a salient feature of classroom life. How young people learn to cope with being one of a crowd and how they relate to each other is of consequence. This can affect how well they settle in the class socially, and, in turn, may affect their learning. There is, thus, a social dimension to classroom life.

The next Practical Activity explores pupils' friendship patterns using sociometry. You may find it useful to look at Chapter 4, Section 3.9 which deals with this technique.

### Practical activity 8.16

*Aim:* To try to identify the class friendship patterns.

*Method:* It is possible to construct a sociogram to indicate friendships.

1. Ask each pupil, confidentially, to write down the names of the three people in their class whom they would most like as friends, or with whom they would most like to work when doing a classroom activity.
2. As a variation or extension, each pupil could also be asked for the names of those whom they would least like as friends or to work with.
3. Having collected the data, friendship groupings can then be picked out and plotted. It is often easier to start with the reciprocal choices, where these are also positive (i.e. two or more pupils name each other as people with whom they would like to play, or work).
4. Where the choices are positively reciprocated, write down the names, linked with a double-headed arrow (i.e. ◄──────► ).
5. Where the choice is not reciprocated link the names with a single-headed arrow (i.e. ──────► ).
6. Where a negative choice is reciprocated, i.e. there is mutual dislike, link the names with a dotted, double-headed arrow (i.e. ◄┄┄┄┄► ).
7. Where a negative choice is one-way link the names with a dotted single-headed arrow (i.e. ┄┄┄┄► ).

From the diagram thus created (which will probably take more than one attempt) it should now be possible to isolate various features, such as:

- Clusters (i.e. three or more pupils who show mutual, positive relationships – a clique).
- Pairs (i.e. two pupils who show mutual choices).
- Isolates (i.e. those whom no one positively chooses but towards whom no one displays negative feelings).
- Rejectees (i.e. those who are negatively identified and actively disliked).

*Follow-up:* A number of questions need to be considered:

1. Are there any isolates or rejectees? If this results in any negative behaviour on the part of any pupils, what can a teacher do to help all the pupils in their social development, so that they learn to handle differences in positive ways and try to find ways by which they can accept each other? At the same time, it is important to remember that some pupils may choose to be outsiders for a time: they may be very cautious in establishing relationships and may, at first, prefer to be loners.
2. Have groups emerged which are based on ethnicity, social class, ability or gender? To what extent are these a reflection of criteria used in the school?
3. Have the friendship patterns discovered got any implications for classroom management policies (e.g. seating and collaborative groupwork activities)? Is understanding a particular individual, or group, enhanced by greater knowledge of their place in the pupil's social structure?

In addition, adults are keenly aware of the ways in which some young people mark their need to belong to a particular group (inside or outside school). This often causes anxiety or distrust amongst adults, uncertain as to how to interpret and respond to these cultural signals. This is reinforced by the fact that social scientists have often concentrated on aspects of adolescent peer culture which seem to indicate opposition, antagonism or confusion about relationships with the adult world. One has to ask how far this is adults projecting their own anxieties onto youth culture (Delamont 1990). Interestingly, for a long time there were few studies of how young people themselves saw their lives, and where young people's perspectives were explored, there was a tendency for this to be focused on the bizarre, outrageous or oppositional, rather than the ordinary, unremarkable or conventional. In addition, early writing on adolescent culture tended to focus on the experience of white working-class boys (Mungham and Pearson 1976, Hall and Jefferson 1975, Willis 1977).

Increasingly, the actual experience of a wide range of young people has been documented, across the lines of ethnicity, social class, gender and SENs, often allowing considerable space for young people themselves to tell their own stories in their own words (Aggleton 1987, McRobbie 1991, Mac an Ghaill 1988, 1995, Mirza 1992, Lloyd-Smith and Davies 1995). This is an important shift, since it demands that we as educators enquire as to, and listen to, the lived experience from the perspective of the young people themselves. Whilst not denying the importance of ethnicity, social class etc. to people's life experiences, this approach does challenge some of the ways in which adult constructions of 'diversity' can end up as stereotyping young people into groups and types (Pheonix and Tizard 1995).

A significant feature of school experience for many pupils is peer group provision and peer group conformity. There is evidence that this exists for girls as well as boys (Fuller 1980, Delamont 1983, Hey 1996). One important aspect of peer group relations is to do with status.

As young people try to establish their individual identities among their peers each will be valued in particular ways. Sometimes this value will be based on prowess in a

### Practical activity 8.18

*Aim:* To gain a greater understanding of how the world looks to young people we work with.

*Method:* Identify a group of young people, possibly a group or number of individuals you feel you do not easily understand. Interview them individually, or in a group, tape recording their responses if they agree. Formulate a set of questions you feel (a) would give them a chance to express clearly what matters to them – what counts, and (b) would give you a chance to enquire about aspects of their identities/attitudes/behaviours which you find puzzling, and need to understand better. Consider issues of ethics and confidentiality before you begin.

*Follow-up:* What issues are raised which you find illuminating for you as a teacher? What influences of the 'group' on individual responses are you aware of?

number of domains: for example at sport, or at exploiting their emergent sexuality, or by the wearing of designer label clothes, or by the music they listen to. In addition, the identity which young people develop through their school-work and their relationship with parents, siblings and teachers may influence the way they are perceived by their peers. Where this is the case, there are clear implications for us as teachers. This process of differentiation of pupils, in terms of their status with both teachers and with other pupils, affects their own self-image. The process starts during the early years at school and has been found to increase during school lives (Breakwell 1986, Pollard with Filer 1996). It may lead to a polarization of pro-school and anti-school cultures (Lacey 1970, Abraham 1995) and it has been cited as of particular significance in the underachievement of boys, when to be good at school is considered 'uncool' (Raphael Reed 1996). Hence, the status and self-image of a young person have significant consequences for their development during the school years – and these can last into their adult lives.

One particularly issue which could be watched for, in relation to pupils' relationships with each other, is that of bullying (Elliott 1992, Tattum and Lane 1989, Robinson *et al.* 1995 ). This is an unacceptable aspect of young people's culture and often reflects both its tendency to emphasize conformity and its concern with status, as well as, frequently, the relative insecurity of the perpetrators. Thus pupils who are different in some way – new to school, overweight, or possibly have an unusual accent or simply a different culture – are picked on physically and verbally and are excluded by other pupils as their unacceptability for cultural membership is asserted or as a pecking order is maintained. In one of its worst forms this can degenerate into overt racism (Troyna and Hatcher 1992) or sexual harassment (Lees 1987).

Adult intervention must be firm but sensitive to the realities of the social situation. All people need to have friends and feel accepted by others. The teacher's task is therefore to stop the bullying whilst facilitating the entry of the 'victim' into an appropriate niche within the school culture. It can be important to have a whole-school policy in relation to bullying (Maines and Robinson 1994). Issues of racism and sexism need to be addressed explicitly, and in this teachers and pupils can be supported by the creation of shared whole-school equal opportunities policies (Raphael Reed 1994). (See also Chapter 14, Section 4.2.)

## 2.4 Understanding adolescent development

There are many different theories and perspectives on what the years from 11 to 18 mean in our society. To some extent, we must start by acknowledging that childhood and adolescence are social constructions, i.e. during different periods of history and different parts of the world, young people are considered 'adult' at widely varying ages (Boas 1966, Steedman *et al.* 1985, James and Prout 1990). Influential perspectives in our own context at the current time tend to reside in physiological, psychological and sociological paradigms, with all identifying adolescence as a period of transition, where significant changes are experienced.

The physiological changes associated with puberty are many, and happen at different rates and at different stages for different people (McCoy and Wibbelsman 1989, Coleman 1992). These changes can lead to a loss of self-confidence and self-esteem, e.g., when a boy of 15 has not yet reached the growth spurt stage, has no facial hair or broken voice, and still looks like a boy whilst his peers look like young men. The scale and rate of physical changes can sometimes lead to physical exhaustion, or clumsiness and poor co-ordination. Changes in hormonal activity are sometimes used to explain adolescent outbursts of emotional energy, or moodiness and depression. It is debatable to what extent these mood swings are physiological alone, rather than psychological states related to uncertainties about changing identities and roles.

Other psychological features of adolescence relate to changes in cognitive state, particularly young people's ability to be increasingly sophisticated in their manipulation of abstract concepts and complex thought (Inhelder and Piaget 1958), and their ability to de-centre and evaluate moral and ethical dilemmas with sensitivity and reflexivity (Kohlberg and Lickona 1986).

Psychoanalytic analyses raise the issue of identity crisis for adolescents, with a loss of sense of 'self' as the relationship with significant others and the 'ego' begin to shift. Certainly, adolescence is a time when young people struggle to reshape their relationships with their parents and adults in general, and at the level of the unconscious, there is transference of 'attachment', particularly separating from a parent and finding new 'love objects'.

Finally, sociological interpretations of adolescence tend to focus on the transitional and sometimes contradictory roles that young people sometimes adopt or are expected to adopt. Within this there may often be a tension between autonomy and reliance, mediated through different forms of power. Although we might wish to see schools as 'self-actualizing' institutions, some sociological analyses propose that schools are agencies of social control, where young people are socialized into dominant or subservient roles (Willis 1977, Wolpe 1988). Resistance to, or compliance with this may then be a feature of adolescent identity.

One increasingly noted contradiction is the focus of schools in the secondary years on preparing young people for the world of work, when high levels of youth unemployment mean a job may be increasingly hard to find. The transition to adulthood may thereby be broken, producing disillusionment and marginality amongst groups of young adults (Griffin 1985, Wilkinson 1995).

## 2.5  Understanding individual pupil needs

Just as we looked at personal and personality factors in the teacher, so a similar kind of 'biographical' knowledge about each pupil is valuable in understanding them as individual people and as learners. Many schools collect basic information about each pupil's medical history and educational progress, but such records, although sometimes helpful, rarely convey an impression of the 'whole person'. As a move in this direction, profiles, portfolios or 'records of achievement' may be kept in some schools. These forms of record tend to focus on each individual's progress, together with examples of their work at different ages. However, they are often enhanced by information about hobbies and interests, abilities and tastes, and materials which reflect each pupil's social attitudes, behaviour, out-of-school achievements and family context. Each pupil also helps in decisions about what to include.

Such records may provide an excellent starting point for understanding each individual learner, in terms of their material, social and cultural circumstances as well as their development in school. They thus provide one sort of context for understanding young people in school. However, such records cannot replace the awareness which will come from personal contacts with pupils both inside and outside school.

### Practical activity 8.19

*Aim:* To deepen understanding of the biography of a pupil.

*Method:* Take an interest in a pupil's general behaviour inside and outside the classroom. Consider how they interact with other pupils and how they tackle learning tasks.

Present open-ended opportunities where a pupil can write, draw, talk or otherwise communicate about herself or himself. Discussions about friends, experiences, family or about favourite activities can be revealing. Make notes.

If possible, discuss the pupil with parents and other teachers.

Discuss the pupil's own perception of their individual needs with them.

Summarize what you have learned.

*Follow-up:* Consider what implications your new understanding has for shaping the educational provision that is appropriate for the young person concerned.

It is often argued that the 'needs' of the learner should be seen as the starting point for teaching and learning policies. However, the notion of appropriate needs is a very problematic one, since it begs questions about prior aims, and judgements about what is worthwhile (Barrow 1984). Nevertheless, it may be valuable for us as reflective teachers to articulate what we see as the basic 'needs' of every learner which we commit ourselves to trying to meet.

The work of Maslow is interesting here, since he linked the drive to have needs met with motivation in learning (Maslow 1970). Maslow proposed a hierarchy of basic needs, with a necessary human requirement that the lower-level order of needs must be met as a pre-requisite to people's abilities to fulfil their higher-level needs:

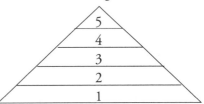

5. Self-actualization eeds
4. Esteem needs
3. Belongingness and love needs
2. Safety needs
1. Physiological needs.

The lowest level (1) encompasses the need for food, shelter, oxygen, water etc. The second level (2) encompasses the need for security and freedom from anxiety. The third level (3) includes the need to feel that one belongs and to be loved and be able to love in return. The fourth level (4) addresses the need for prestige and status, to be successful and to feel good about oneself. The final level (5) might be seen as the ultimate goal of education – the need people have to fulfil their full potential. Teachers and pupils are no different in their needs to have each of these elements addressed and fulfilled. An effective classroom and an effective school is one where both teachers and pupils feel safe, feel that they belong and are loved or respected, and where the experience of being in school enables all to move in the direction of self-actualization.

## CONCLUSION

The process of engaging in activities such as those suggested in this chapter should help us as teachers to place our aims in a realistic personal perspective. If the many unconscious influences on our teaching can be made explicit, it is easier to identify where we are being most successful and where perhaps our aims and our practice don't match as well as they might. It is also possible, by trying to make the implicit explicit, to be more aware of how we get to know young people and of the evidence upon which we base our understanding. Furthermore, by becoming more aware of the pupils' perceptions of us as teachers, of their culture and of their perspectives on themselves and each other, we are more likely to be able to take account of their needs when planning and making provision for classroom experience.

### Notes for further reading

An accessible and insightful introduction to the importance of considering the 'self' of teachers and children remains:

Hargreaves, D. H. (1972)
*Interpersonal Relationships and Education,*
London: Routledge & Kegan Paul.

For classic studies of teachers' work and lives, see:

Lortie, D. (1975)
*Schoolteacher: A Sociological Study,*
Chicago: University of Chicago Press.

Huberman, M. (1993)
*The Lives of Teachers,*
New York: Teachers College Press.

Ball, S. and Goodson, I. (1985)
*Teachers' Lives and Careers,*
London: Falmer Press.

In the book below, Easen provides many suggestions for coming to understand our 'selves' more clearly:

Easen, P. (1985)
*Making School-Centred INSET Work,*
London: Croom Helm.

Work on self-concept and self-esteem includes:

Robinson, G. and Maines, B. (1988)
*You can . . . you know you can!,*
Avon, Lame Duck Publishing.

Mecca, A. M., Smelser, N. J. and Vasconcellos, J. (1989)
*The Social Importance of Self-esteem,*
Berkeley: University of California Press.

A considerable amount of work on teacher biography has been conducted in recent years. This illustrates links between the personal and professional spheres of activity and demonstrates effects on careers. Further readings here are:

Connell, R.W. (1985)
*Teachers' Work,*
London: Allen & Unwin.

Sikes, P. J., Measor, L. and Woods, P. (1985)
*Teachers' Careers,*
London: Falmer.

Goodson, I. F. and Walker, R. (eds) (1991)
*Biography, Identity and Schooling,*
London: Falmer Press.

Goodson, I. F. (1992)
*Studying Teachers' Lives,*
London: Routledge.

An important book on teacher cultures and the challenges of modern societies is:

Hargreaves, A. (1994)
*Changing Teachers, Changing Times: Teachers' Work and Culture in the Postmoderm Age,*
New York: Teachers College Press.

On questions of aims, values and commitments, there are a number of distinctive philosophical analyses. Contrast for example:

Peters, R. S. (1966)
*Ethics and Education,*
London: Allen & Unwin.

O'Hear, A. (1981)
*An Introduction to the Philosophy of Education,*
London: Routledge.

Barrow, R. and Woods, R. (1988)
*An Introduction to Philosophy of Education,*
London: Routledge.

Bottery, M. (1990)
*The Morality of the School,*
London: Cassell.

For analyses which demonstrate the importance of considering aims and value positions within their social context, see:

Grace, G. (1978)
*Teachers, Ideology and Control,*
London: Routledge & Kegan Paul.

Hawthorne, R. K. (1992)
*Curriculum in the Making: Teacher Choice and the Classroom Experience,*
New York: Teachers College Press.

Hansen, D. T. (1995)
*The Call to Teach,*
New York: Teachers College Press.

Biklen, S. K. (1995)
*School Work: Gender and the Cultural Construction of Teaching,*
New York: Teachers College Press.

Two books which, together, will provide an interesting comparative perspective on teachers and teaching are:

Neave, G. (1992)
*The Teaching Nation: Prospects for Teachers in the European Community,*
Oxford: Pergamon.

Newman, J. W. (1990)
*America's Teachers,*
New York: Longman.

Teaching is, of course, work, and teachers are employees with both contractual duties and rights which need to be protected.

Hewett, P. (1993)
*About Time: The Revolution in Work and Family Life,*
London: River Oram Press.

For historically informed analysis of the ways in which teachers organize collectively to protect their interests and influence policy in the UK, see:

Ozga, J. (1988)
*Schoolwork: Approaches to the Labour Process of Teaching,*
Milton Keynes, Open University Press.

Barber, M. (1991)
*Education and the Teacher Unions,*
London: Cassell.

Many professionals feel that teacher associations in the UK would be greatly strengthened if a General Teaching Council could be formed. For an elaboration of this aspiration, see:

Sayer, J. (1992)
*The Future Governance of Education*,
London: Cassell.

On adolescent development, see:

Rosenberg, M. (1965)
*Society and the Adolescent Self-image*,
Princeton, N. J.: Princeton University Press.

Kroger, J. (1996)
*Identity in Adolescence*,
London: Routledge.

Hendry, L. (1993)
*Young People's Leisure and Lifestyles*,
London: Routledge.

Bates, I. and Riseborough, G. (eds) (1993)
*Youth and Inequality*,
Buckingham: Open University Press.

For the perspectives of pupils, read the findings of an important study:

Rudduck, J., Chaplain, R. and Wallace, G. (1995)
*School Improvement: What Can Pupils Tell Us?*,
London: David Fulton.

On issues to do with ethnicity and schooling, see:

Commission for Racial Equality (1987)
*Learning in Terror: A Survey of Racial Harassment in Schools*,
London: CRE.

Duncan, C. (1989)
*Pastoral Care: An Antiracist/Multicultural Perspective*,
Oxford: Blackwell.

Donald, J. and Rattansi, A. (eds) (1992)
*'Race', Culture and Difference*,
London: Sage.

Klein, G. (1993)
*Education Towards Race Equality*,
London: Cassell.

Gillborn, D. (1995)
*Racism and Antiracism in Real Schools*,
Buckingham: Open University Press.

In relation to concerns around gender and sexuality see:

Hey, V. (1996)
*The Company She Keeps: an Ethnography of Girls' Friendships*,
Buckingham: Open University Press.

Thorne, B. (1993)
*Gender Play: Girls and Boys in School,*
Buckingham: Open University Press.

Mac an Ghaill, M. (1995)
*The Making of Men: Masculinities, Sexualities and Schooling,*
Buckingham: Open University Press.

McLaughlin, C., Lodge, C. and Watkins, C. (eds) (1991)
*Gender and Pastoral Care: Personal-Social Aspects of the Whole School,*
Oxford: Blackwell,

Measor, L. and Sikes, P. J. (1992)
*Gender and Schools,*
London: Cassell.

Myers, K. (ed.) (1992)
*Genderwatch! After the Education Reform Act,*
Cambridge: Cambridge University Press.

Salisbury, J. and Jackson, D. (1996)
*Challenging Macho Values: Practical Ways of Working with Adolescent Boys,*
London: Falmer Press.

NUT (1991)
*Lesbians and Gays in School: an Issue for Every Teacher,*
London: NUT.

On issues relating to disability and special educational needs see:

Rieser, R. and Mason, M. (eds) (1990)
*Disability Equality in the Classroom: A Human Rights Issue,*
London: ILEA Publications.

Clough, P. and Barton, L. (1995)
*Making Difficulties: Research and the construction of SENs,*
London: Paul Chapman Publishing.

On social class see:

Jackson, B and Marsden, D. (1962)
*Education and the Working Class,*
London: Ark.

Hargreaves, D. H. (1967)
*Social Relations in a Secondary School,*
London: Routledge and Kegan Paul.

Lacey, C. (1970)
*Hightown Grammar,*
London: Routledge and Kegan Paul.

Corrigan, P. (1979)
*Schooling the Smash Street Kids,*
London: Macmillan.

Willis, P. (1977)
*Learning to Labour: How Working Class Kids Get Working Class Jobs,*
London: Saxon House.

Aggleton, P. (1987)
*Rebels Without a Cause?*,
London: Falmer Press.

Brantlinger, E. A. (1993)
*The Politics of Social Class in Secondary School: Views of Affluent and Impoverished Youth,*
New York: Teachers College Press.

# CHAPTER 9

# What do we know about learning?

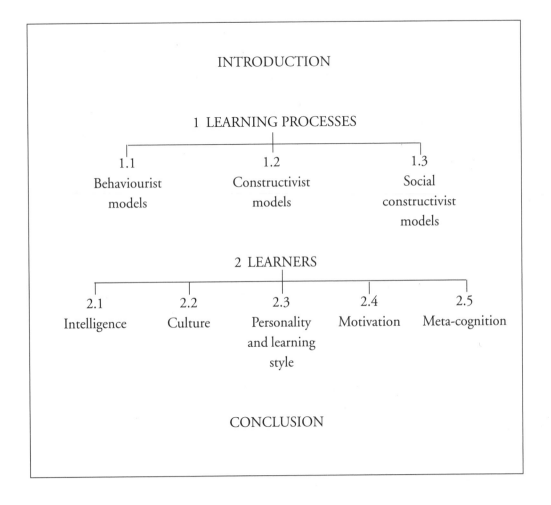

INTRODUCTION

1 LEARNING PROCESSES

| 1.1 | 1.2 | 1.3 |
| --- | --- | --- |
| Behaviourist models | Constructivist models | Social constructivist models |

2 LEARNERS

| 2.1 | 2.2 | 2.3 | 2.4 | 2.5 |
| --- | --- | --- | --- | --- |
| Intelligence | Culture | Personality and learning style | Motivation | Meta-cognition |

CONCLUSION

## INTRODUCTION

Learning can be considered as the process by which skills, attitudes, knowledge and concepts are acquired, understood, applied and extended. Children also learn about their feelings towards themselves, towards each other and towards learning itself. Learning is thus partly a cognitive process, and partly social and affective. Successful learning may result in confidence, pleasure and in a sense of achievement. However, failure may result in low self-esteem, apathy, avoidance or aggression.

Of course, all teaching is about developing, deepening and extending pupil thinking. There must be both engagement with the learner's understanding and support for its extension, hence the importance of diagnostic assessment and of teacher's subject knowledge. Pupil learning should thus not be confused, as it so often is, with mere completion of tasks. Indeed, in the routinized work of many classrooms, children may complete a task 'correctly' but have learnt nothing new. They may also learn things which the teacher did not intend. Such unintended learning could be productive – an appropriate match to their current needs. On the other hand, they might also learn things which could cause them problems later, e.g. incorrect spellings or letter-formation skills, inefficient subtraction procedures or inaccurate information. There is no doubt then, that effective learning is greatly enhanced by appropriate teaching. Learning cannot be left to chance.

In this chapter we introduce a framework for considering and investigating some of the ways in which learning occurs in secondary schools. We begin by setting the scene in a practical way, by taking stock of existing practices using three simple analytic models of classroom learning processes. The second part of the chapter moves the focus on to children directly and we consider the influence on the learning of individuals of factors such as 'intelligence', culture, learning stance, personality and cognitive style. The issues raised in this chapter are taken up again in Chapters 7 and 10, in the practical context of planning a curriculum which matches cognitive and motivational aspects of school tasks to pupils' learning needs.

A specific word about the role of language in learning is appropriate here for there is probably no more significant factor. Indeed, that is the reason why a whole chapter of this book is devoted to it (Chapter 13). In this chapter the use of language within teaching and learning situations is a recurring theme; it will be seen to have a pivotal role in social constructivist approaches.

## 1    LEARNING PROCESSES

Learning is a highly complex aspect of human capacity and one which, even now, is not fully understood. Philosophers and psychologists have worked to analyse and research it for centuries and this will undoubtedly continue. The result is that there are many alternative theories which attempt to describe the learning process. Most rest on an element of valuable insight, but, it follows, each has both strengths and weaknesses. Over the years, many theories have influenced teaching methods and, having been tested by the realities of classroom practice, have left their mark as part of the pedagogic repertoire of teachers. The key professional judgement concerns the 'fitness for purpose' of different methods. Which teaching strategy is most appropriate for our aims?

We have simplified this complex field by identifying just three theories of learning which have been of particular influence in education.

## 1.1 Behaviourist models

This theory suggests that living creatures, animal or human, learn by building up associations or 'bonds' between their experience, their thinking and their behaviour. Thus as long ago as 1911, Thorndike expressed both the 'law of effect':

> The greater the satisfaction or discomfort, the greater the strengthening or weakening of the bond.

and the 'law of exercise':

> The probability of a response occurring in a given situation increases with the number of times that response has occurred in that situation in the past.

Thorndike was confident and claimed that these 'laws' emerged clearly from 'every series of experiments on animal learning and in the entire history of the management of human affairs' (Thorndike 1911, p. 244).

A variety of versions of behaviourism were developed and provided the dominant perspective on learning until the 1960s. Perhaps the most significant of these later psychologists was Skinner (e.g. 1968) who, through his work with animals, developed a sophisticated theory of the role in learning of stimulus, response and consequence.

The influence of behaviourist theory in education has been immense for, in the early part of the century, it provided the foundations of work on a 'science of teaching' based on whole-class, didactic approaches through which knowledge and skills were to be taught. The 'law of effect' was reflected in elaborate systems and rituals for the reward and punishment of pupil responses. The 'law of exercise' was reflected in an emphasis on practice and drill.

Behaviourist learning theory casts the learner in a relatively passive role, leaving the selection, pacing and evaluation of learning activity to the teacher. Subject expertise can thus be transmitted in a coherent, ordered and logical way, and control of the class tends to be tight – because the children are often required to listen. There is a problem though in whether such teaching actually connects with the learner's existing understanding.

Teaching which has been influenced by behaviourism can be seen in all secondary schools. The importance of reinforcing children's work and effort is well established and, of course, there is still much use made of negative sanctions – strategies which reflect the 'law of effect'. The use of practice tasks is also widespread, particularly for teaching aspects of the core curriculum such as numerical computation, spelling and writing, and this type of work reflects the influence of the 'law of exercise'. The use of teacher-controlled explanation and of question and answer routines are important parts of any teacher's pedagogic repertoire. They will be found, for instance, in school assemblies, when new topics are being introduced and when taking stock of achievements. The idea of building progressive steps in learning (e.g. Gagne 1965, **Primary Reading 6.2**) is, of course, directly reflected in the organization of the National Curriculum of the UK and other countries into 'levels'.

Figure 9.1, below, represents the roles of pupils and adult in behaviourist influenced teaching and learning processes.

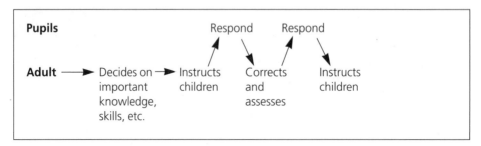

**Figure 9.1** *A behaviourist model of roles in the teaching-learning process*

Some particular points could be noted. First, there is a high degree of adult control in the process; deciding on the subject-matter, providing instruction, pacing the lesson, correcting and assessing pupil responses. In principle, this makes it relatively easy for teacher expositions and explanations to be logical, coherent, linear and progressive as subject-matter or skills are introduced to the pupils. This is likely to be of great benefit to those learners for whom such teaching is appropriate. Second, this approach lends itself to the teaching of large groups or whole classes, in which circumstances large numbers of pupils can benefit from teacher expertise.

However, there are also some difficulties in teaching in this way. The most important is the question of connecting with the existing understanding of pupils. In this respect, the strength of subject exposition can also be a weakness if a learner does not recognize subject divisions as being relevant to daily experiences. Such a mismatch can reduce motivation and achievement as the learner cannot use the knowledge which is offered to build a meaningful understanding. In such circumstances, learning tends to be superficial and fragmented. This problem may be made acute when large groups are taught because it is very hard for a teacher to 'pitch' the lesson appropriately for all learners. If this proves to be a problem, pupil motivation can be adversely affected.

The influence of behaviourism has been greatest on what are commonly termed 'traditional' teaching methods, and particularly those associated with whole-class, subject-based teaching. It is a relatively simple model and it is unfortunate that the value which it does have, when used appropriately, tends to be generalized by non-educationalists. Perhaps this is because of its association with tight discipline and strong subject teaching. However, as we have seen, these can also be weaknesses. The responsibility of teachers is to interact with pupils so that they actually learn, not simply to expose them to subject matter and drill.

Use of teaching methods based on behaviourism must, therefore, be fit for their purpose.

## 1.2  Constructivist models

This theory suggests that people learn through an interaction between thought and experience, and through the sequential development of more complex cognitive structures. The most influential constructivist theorist was Piaget (e.g. 1926, 1950) whose ultimate goal was to create a 'genetic epistemology' – an understanding of the origin of knowledge derived from research into the interaction between people and their environment.

In Piaget's account, when learners encounter a new experience they both 'accommodate' their existing thinking to it and 'assimilate' aspects of the experience. In so doing they move beyond one state of mental 'equilibration' and restructure their thoughts to create another. Gradually then, learners come to construct more detailed, complex and accurate understandings of the phenomena they experience.

Piaget proposed that there are characteristic stages in the successive development of these mental structures, stages which are distinctive because of the type of cognitive 'operation' with which children process their experience. These stages are:

- the sensori-motor stage (approximately birth–2 years)
- the pre-operational stage (approximately 2–7 years)
- the concrete operations stage (approximately 7–12 years)
- the formal operations stage (approximately 12 years onwards).

In each of the first three stages the role of the child's direct experience is deemed to be crucial. It is only in the formal operations stage that abstract thinking is believed possible. In the sensori-motor and pre-operational stages children are thought to be relatively individualistic and unable to work with others for long. Children are believed to behave rather like 'active scientists', enquiring, exploring and discovering as their curiosity and interests lead them to successive experiences. Practical experimentation has a crucial role in this process (Piaget 1951).

The influence of constructivist theory in primary education was considerable following the report of the Plowden Committee (Central Advisory Council for Education 1967) in which it was suggested that:

> Piaget's explanation appears to fit the observed facts of children's learning more satisfactorily than any other. It is in accord with what is generally regarded as the most effective primary school practice, as it has been worked out empirically. (CACE 1967, para 522)

In the secondary school, child-centred approaches based on interpretations of Piaget and other cognitive psychologists have never become a dominant influence, and there has never been the same commitment to these approaches as there has with younger pupils. However, cognitive psychology and constructionism played a significant part in the curriculum reform movements of the 1960s and 1970s, particularly in relation to the development of integrated curricula and 'active learning' methods. Both the Schools Council Integrated Studies Project at Keele University (see Jenkins 1973) and Humanities Curriculum Project (see MacDonald 1973) were opposed to the behaviourally-oriented objectives model of curriculum development and evaluation, and emphasized the importance of allowing pupils to explore issues for themselves and arrive at their own conclusions. Thus curricula were considered in terms of the principles and procedures which enabled pupils to construct their own meanings rather than in terms of the achievement of detailed, pre-specified objectives.

Perhaps, the most significant influence of constructivism in the secondary school has been in the 'pastoral curriculum' or what is more often described as personal and social education. Although not a legally required subject in the National Curriculum (see Galloway and Edwards 1992), many secondary schools have a slot for PSE in the timetable. The content varies from school to school , although many schools use it as a way of including material relating to cross-curricular themes (NCC 1990), e.g. health education, citizenship, careers guidance, etc. What most approaches have in common is a commitment to methods which encourage pupils to become morally informed, self-regulated learners. Teachers often employ tutorial methods based on a developmental model of moral development, such as that of Kohlberg whose model parallels Piaget's model of cognitive development (Kohlberg and Lickona 1986). Kohlberg proposed three levels (two stages within each level) corresponding to the cognitive stages after the sensori-motor stage:

- Level One: 'Preconventional' (2–7)
  - Stage One: Obedience/conformity due solely to fear of punishment
  - Stage Two: Morality based on fair trades.
- Level Two: 'Conventional' (2–12)
  - Stage Three: Judgement based on desire to please others
  - Stage Four: Judgement based on respect for authority.
- Level Three: 'Postconventional' (approximately 12 years onwards)
  - Stage Five: Rules can be changed if general agreement
  - Stage Six: Respect for human dignity: abstract principles.

There have been a number of criticisms of Kohlberg's and Piaget's work. For instance, Kleinig (1982) sees Kohlberg's scheme as a depersonalized, over-intellectual view of moral reasoning which does not explain why people in particular contexts should choose to engage in moral reasoning in the first instance. One consequence of this has been the way it fails to identify the moral sensitivity of which young children are capable, even when they are not mature enough to express themselves verbally. Similar points have been made about Piaget's stages of cognitive development. Psychologists such as Donaldson (1978) and Tizard and Hughes (1984) have demonstrated that children's intellectual abilities are far greater than those reported by Piaget. Such findings emerge when children are observed in situations which are meaningful to them. In such circumstances they have also shown considerably more social competence at young ages than Piaget's theory allows. From a different perspective, sociologists such as Walkerdine (1983, 1988) have argued that Piaget's stages became part of child-centred ideology and a means through which teachers classify, compare and thus control children. Critics have also suggested that this form of constructivism over-emphasizes the individual too much and ignores the social context in which learning takes place. In so doing, the potential of teachers, other adults and other children to support each child's learning is underestimated.

Constructivist learning theory, as adapted by educationalists, casts the learner in a very active and independent role, leaving much of the selection, pacing and evaluation of the activity to the learner to negotiate. There is considerable emphasis on pupil interests and some compromise on the specifics of curriculum coverage. In its place, there tends to be more emphasis on learning concepts and skills through work on pupil-chosen topics.

Teaching which has been influenced by constructivism can be seen in some secondary schools. It is reflected in the provision of a rich, varied and stimulating environment, in individualized work and creative arts. Above all though, the influence of constructivism is reflected in the ways in which teachers relate with children. Perhaps this is an unintended legacy, but the spirit of constructivism, with its close identification with the challenges which the learner faces, has influenced secondary school teachers' conception of the 'quality' of the teacher-pupil relationships.

Figure 9.2 represents the roles of learner and adult in constructivist influenced teaching and learning processes.

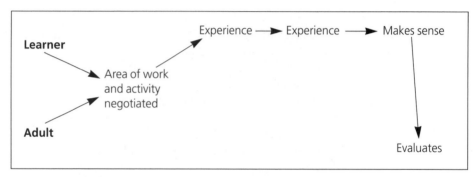

**Figure 9.2** *A constructivist model of roles in the teaching-learning process*

Some particular points could be noted, in particular, the negotiation of pupil activity and the emphasis placed on direct experience in learning. In principle these have the enormous strength of creating high levels of pupil motivation and engagement. In the right circumstances, creativity and other forms of pupil achievement can reach exceptional levels of excellence. However, coverage of a particular curriculum is hard to monitor and the diversity of individual pupil interests tends to produce relatively complex forms of classroom organization as a range of activities are provided. Research shows that teachers then tend to be drawn into managing this complex environment rather than teaching itself.

As with behaviourist approaches, professional judgements about 'fitness for purpose' will guide decisions about the use of teaching methods based on constructivism. Practical Activity 9.2 will help you to consider constructivist influences on teaching in your school.

## 1.3 Social constructivist models

This is another constructivist theory but, this time, one which emphasizes the importance for learning of the social context and of interaction with others.

The most influential writer on this approach has been Vygotsky (1962, 1978) whose publications in Russian actually date from the 1930s. The increasing availability of Vygotsky's work in English coincided with reappraisals of the strengths and weaknesses of Piagetian theory. Psychologists such as Bruner (1986), Wood (1988) and Wertsch (1985) have been able to demonstrate the considerable relevance of Vygotsky's work to modern education and this has coincided both with complementary empirical work by other child psychologists and with curriculum development initiatives by primary school teachers. Social constructivist theory is, it seems, beginning to provide a new model of effective practice.

We will focus on just two of the insights originating from Vygotsky.

The first concerns what Vygotsky calls the 'zone of proximal development' (the ZPD). This is:

> The distance between the actual developmental level (of the learner) as determined through problem-solving and the level of potential development as determined through problem-solving under adult guidance or in collaboration with more capable peers. (Vygotsky 1978, p. 86)

## Practical activity 9.2

*Aim:* To consider the influence and strengths of constructivist psychology when applied to pupils' learning and secondary school practice.

*Method:* Map for a single pupil for one day his/her experiences of teaching methods influenced by constructivism. If this is difficult to arrange, you could record the teaching methods a pupil encounters over a series of lessons in your subject.

Note each learning situation, each teaching method and then consider the reasons for its choice.

| Learning situation | Teaching methods used | Reason for choice of teaching methods |
|---|---|---|
|  |  |  |

*Follow-up:* Consider the extent, strengths and weaknesses of the constructivist influence on teaching in your school. Are the teaching methods used 'fit for their purpose'?

The ZPD concerns each learner's potential to 'make sense'. In other words: given a pupil's present state of understanding, what developments can occur if the learner is given appropriate assistance by more capable others? If support is appropriate and meaningful, then, it is argued, the understanding of learners can be extended far beyond that which they could reach alone.

Such assistance in learning can come in many ways. It may take the form of an explanation by or discussion with a knowledgeable teacher; it may reflect debate among a group of learners as they strive to solve a problem or complete a task; it might come from discussion with a parent, another 'expert', or from watching a particular television programme. In each case, the intervention functions to extend and to 'scaffold' the learner's understanding across their ZPD for that particular issue. An appropriate analogy is that of building a house. Scaffolding is needed to support the process as the house is gradually constructed from its foundations – but when it has been assembled and all the parts have been secured the scaffolding can be removed. The building – the learner's understanding – will then stand independently.

The second key insight originating in Vygotsky's work concerns the role of the culture and the social context of the learner in influencing their understanding. This influence starts in informal ways from birth. Thus infants and young children interact with their parents and family and, through experiencing the language and forms of behaviour of their culture, also assimilate particular cognitive skills, strategies, knowledge and understanding (Richards and Light 1986, Dunn 1988). Cognition, language and forms of thought, thus depend on the culture and social history of the learner as well as on any particular instruction which may be offered at any point in time. This influence of culture on learning continues throughout life (Rogoff and Lave 1984); indeed, it is what makes learning meaningful. Ideas, language and concepts derived from interaction with others thus structure, challenge, enhance or constrain thinking. Whatever role they play, they cannot be excluded from our consideration. Thus, learning is social as well as individual. We therefore have to look at the context in which learning takes place in schools as well as at the nature of specific learning tasks.

The influence of social constructivist theory in education has been considerable since the early 1980s. Perhaps this is because the approach seems to recognize both the needs of learners to construct their own, meaningful understandings and the strength of teaching itself. Indeed, a key to the approach lies in specifying constructive relationships between these factors. As Tharp and Gallimore (1988) put it, learning, particularly in schools, can be seen as 'assisted performance'.

Teaching which is influenced by social constructivism can be seen in many secondary schools, although it is rarely the dominant teaching and learning model. It is particularly associated with various processes of group work. Thus, for instance investigational work in science, maths or technology often involves small groups of pupils in collaborative problem-solving. Sometimes the discussion between pupils augments their experience and they 'scaffold' each other's thinking; sometimes the thinking of the group is challenged by the teacher. In all cases the emphasis is on starting with the pupils' 'spontaneous' concepts, which are often unverbalized and have been built up over the years in day-to-day interaction with people and objects in the world. Even in subjects like science and maths where such concepts may be considered erroneous from a teacher's point of view, pupils are encouraged to express their ideas and explore them with others. The role of the teacher is to help pupils see connections between their 'spontaneous' concepts and the formal concepts of the discipline (e.g. specific gravity, ratio). In their overview of this process in relation to science teaching Bentley and Watts (1992) refer to the way in which 'spontaneous' concepts (those developed from everyday experience) create structures for the 'evolution of a concept's more primitive elementary aspects, which give it body and vitality'. Formal, scientific concepts 'supply structures for the upward development of the child's spontaneous concepts towards consciousness and use'. In maths social constructivism has led to a similar focus on pupils' initial mathematical beliefs and strategies for making connections with these (see Ernest 1991).

In English, Vygotsky's work has underpinned many developments which have emphasized the importance of the role of language and speech in the development of thought (see Barnes 1975). The recognition of the centrality of language in learning has implications for teaching and learning in all subject disciplines, leading to the call for schools to have policies for 'language across the curriculum' (see Bullock Report, 1975, discussed more fully in Chapter 13). Social constructivist approaches in English have also focused on language both as a means for taking part in communities, including the community of the classroom, and as a means of actively 'making meaning' within those communities. In recent years this has led to an awareness of the ways in which common understandings can be fostered and communication between teachers and pupils and between pupils and pupils improved. Likewise, the reasons for 'failures' in teaching and learning can be pinpointed by analyzing them as breakdowns in communication. Many problems stem from pupils not fully understanding or being fully committed to the 'ground rules' of educational discourse (see Edwards and Mercer 1987). For example, as Sheeran and Barnes (1991) point out the rules for thinking about the world in the context of school subject disciplines require pupils to indulge in hypothetical thinking, giving rise to 'What if?' realms where ideas can be tried out. Yet many pupils operate in accordance with the ground rules of their pragmatic, everyday knowledge about the world; and want activities which have obvious practical relevance to their lives. If pupils do not recognize these differences in rules, then they are unlikely to play the academic game well. Many people feel that these misunderstandings and failures to appreciate ground rules are linked with pupils' social and cultural back grounds. For instance:

> Our own experience as teachers leads us to think that children from middle-class, especially professional, homes find it easier to accept success in schooling as an end in itself or at least a route to qualifications. Working-class parents know that for some young people schooling is a way to advancement, but may have been led by past experience to exclude themselves and their children from this. Perhaps as a result pupils from working-class homes are quicker to demand that what they learn in school has a visible relevance and usefulness in their present and future lives. This would be likely to make them less willing to take the 'What if?' mode seriously . . . (Sheeran and Barnes 1991, p. 16)

Figure 9.3, below, elaborated from Rowland (1987), represents the roles of pupils and adult in social constructivist teaching and learning processes.

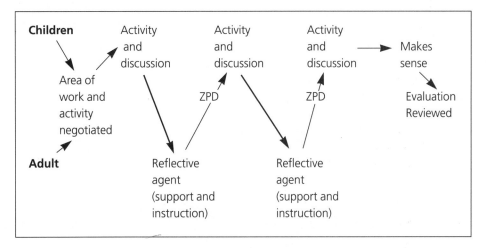

**Figure 9.3** *A social constructivist model of roles in the teaching-learning process*

Figure 9.3 shows some key social constructivist processes in classrooms analytically. Negotiation, focused perhaps on a National Curriculum topic, is followed by activity and discussion by children. However, the teacher then makes a constructive intervention – a role which Rowland named as that of the 'reflective agent'. This draws attention to the fact that any intervention must be appropriate. It must connect with the understandings and purposes of the learners so that their thinking is extended. If this is to happen, teachers need to draw on both their subject knowledge and their understanding of learners. They must make an accurate, and reflective, judgement themselves about the most appropriate form of input and, in this, various techniques of formative assessment (see Chapter 15) are likely to be helpful. If such judgements are astute then the input could take the learners' thinking forward, across the ZPD and beyond the level of understanding which they would have reached alone. Clearly there could be successive cycles of this process.

The influence of social constructivist ideas is implicit in much of the documentation of the National Curriculum in the UK and, for the last decade has progressively underpinned the work of curriculum associations and teacher-based curriculum innovation in all subjects. The role of language and of discussion is paramount in learning in each area. However, whilst social constructivism might, in a sense, seem

### Practical activity 9.3

*Aim:* To consider the influence and strengths of social constructivist psychology when applied to pupils' learning and secondary school practice.

*Method:* Review the learning situations and teaching methods, influenced by social constructivism, which a class you teach has experienced in several lessons.

Note each learning situation, each teaching method and then consider the reasons for its choice.

| Learning situation | Teaching methods used | Reason for choice of teaching methods |
|---|---|---|
|  |  |  |

*Follow-up:* Consider the extent, strengths and weaknesses of the social constructivist influence on teaching in your school. Are the teaching methods used 'fit for their purpose'?

to embody the most valuable educational implications of both behaviourism and constructivism, it provides little relief from the pressures of class size or from the wide range of curricular objectives to which secondary school teachers are increasingly subject. These challenges remain. The result is that secondary school teachers will continue to have to make judgements and compromises as they face the tension between how they may like to teach, and how they feel it is possible to teach in their particular circumstances. The practical implications of social constructivism are undoubtedly great, for it is an approach which will test the subject knowledge, judgement and organizational capacity of most teachers. Nevertheless, it is an approach with enormous strengths and should undoubtedly be in the repertoire of a reflective teacher.

Again, it is a question of fitness for purpose and circumstances.

## Summary

Figure 9.4, over, provides a very simple summary of some of the key points in the previous discussions.

So far in this chapter we have considered three key theoretical influences on learning and teaching in secondary schools. We now move on, in Part 2, to consider some issues which are likely to produce differences between individual pupils as they approach learning in school.

## 2 | LEARNERS

### 2.1 'Intelligence'

Teachers meet the specific needs of learners by knowing them well. It is thus right and proper that concepts to describe the attributes of pupils should exist. However, such concepts should be accurate, discriminating and capable of impartial application. Notions of 'intelligence' are common, but they quickly lead towards dangerous stereotyping and generalization.

The validity of the concept of intelligence has been in dispute among psychologists for many years. As one expert in the field recently commented:

Intelligence provides a rich source of confusions, augmented by the fact that psychologists fail to agree about even the most basic issues, such as how the term should be defined and whether or not it can be regarded as providing an explanation as well as a description of human variability. (Howe 1991, p. 382)

When it comes to attempting to measure intelligence the field is even more difficult, which is perhaps not surprising since no one is precisely sure what it is!

However, the concept is very powerful since it has passed into our culture to denote a generalized form of ability. It is part of our language and it influences our ways of thinking about pupils. For instance, parents often talk about their children in terms

|  | **Behaviourism in classrooms** | **Constructivism in classrooms** | **Social constructivism in classrooms** |
|---|---|---|---|
| Image of learner | Passive | Active | Active |
|  | Individual | Individual | Social |
| Images of teaching and learning | Teacher transmits knowledge and skills | Teacher gives pupil opportunity to construct knowledge and skills gradually through experience | Knowledge and skills are constructed gradually through experience, interaction and adult support |
|  | Learning depends on teaching | learning can be independent of teaching | Learning comes through the interdependence of teacher and learner |
| Characteristic pupil activities | Class listening to an adult | Individuals making, experimenting, or otherwise doing something | Discussing an issue with an adult or other pupil(s) |
|  | Class working on an exercise |  | Problem-solving with a group |
| Some characteristics | Draws directly on existing subject knowledge in a logical, linear manner | Uses direct experience and allows pupils to explore in their own way at their own pace | By structuring challenges can clarify thinking and produce meaningful understanding |
|  | When matched to existing understanding, can be a fast and effective way to learn | Can build confidence and practical understanding which clarifies thinking and produces insight | Encourages collaboration and language development |
| Some issues | May not connect with existing understanding and may thus lead to superficiality | Has major reource and organizational implications | Has major resource and organizational implications |
|  | Difficult to motivate all pupils in class | Management of the class and resources often dominates actual teaching | Requires a very high level of adult judgement, knowledge and skill |
|  | Difficult to adapt structure of subject matter to varied pupil needs | Assumes high level of motivation and autonomy from learners | Assumes high level of social and linguistic maturity from learners |

**Figure 9.4** *Some features of behaviourist, constructivist and social constructivist models of learning applied to secondary schools*

of 'brightness' or 'cleverness', and teachers routinely describe pupils and classroom groupings in terms of 'ability'. The concept of intelligence is important too because it is often used in the rhetoric of politicians and the media when they communicate with the public. It is thus routinely assumed that there is both a generalized trait of intelligence and that it is possible to measure it objectively.

Of course, such beliefs underpinned the UK use in the 1950s and 1960s of intelligence tests, at 11-plus, to select children for secondary education. Belief in the context-free, objectivity of such testing was severely undercut by studies at the time such as those by Simon (1953) and Squibb (1973). More recent research in areas where 11-plus is still used, such as in Northern Ireland, continues to show the lack of objectivity of the measurement. For instance, Egan and Bunting (1991) recorded gains of 30 to 40+ points, out of a total possible 100 points, for a coached group of 11-year-olds compared with an uncoached group. The results showed clearly that children can be taught to do intelligence tests and that it is not possible to identify or measure some context-free generalized ability with any confidence. Such tests are therefore likely to systematically disadvantage those who receive less coaching or experience a less advantageous cultural background.

The debate about the nature and origins of intelligence also continues. Psychologists such as Kline (1991) argue, on the basis of complex statistical factor-analysis, that general ability remains a valid concept to describe inherited attributes. On the other hand, Howe (1990) used experimental and biographical evidence from different cultures to argue that there are many types of ability and that generalized measures, such as IQ scores, are misleading. According to Howe, the origins of exceptional abilities lie in an interaction of intellectual, motivational and temperamental factors produced within a social and cultural context, and this may, itself, enhance or inhibit achievement. As Howe puts it:

> Faced with a new task, the chances of a person being successful depend on a myriad of contributing influences. These include the person's existing knowledge in relation to the particular task, existing cognitive skills, interest, motivation, attentiveness, self-confidence and sense of purpose, to mention only a few. (Howe 1990, p. 221)

The idea that there are many forms of intelligent behaviour, and that these are influenced by the social context in which people act, is thus now largely accepted by most psychologists. Some form of interaction between the influence of heredity and of environment is therefore agreed but it is doubtful if the nuances of the nature/nurture debate will ever finally be settled. In one sense, this hardly matters, because whilst the genetic potential of children is set, teachers and parents can take on the specific, and uncontested, role of acting to enhance the quality of environmental factors.

One important aspect of this role lies in encouraging pupils to make maximum use of their cognitive skills, to encourage them to think about their reasoning and to draw on their skills, strategies and conceptual understanding in the most appropriate ways for the task in hand. This issue of metacognition will be considered in detail in Section 2.5 of this chapter. But at this point it is worth noting that teachers' assumptions about the nature of intelligence will have a direct impact on these processes. Dweck and Bempechat (1983) have distinguished between teachers who define intelligence as a quality or a trait that a pupil possesses (an 'entity' perspective), and those who define it as an ever-growing quality that is increased through the pupil's actions (an 'incremental' perspective). The latter are more likely to facilitate the development of pupils' metacognitive strategies.

For reflective teachers then, it is worth remembering some simple points about intelligence:

- the use of generalized terms such as intelligence, ability, etc. is imprecise, insecure and unreliable – but is often put to rhetorical use
- a teacher can dramatically influence the variable, environmental quality of pupil experience – by providing support which will enhance, broaden and develop each pupil's inherited potential
- there are many kinds of ability and one challenge for teachers is to enhance their pupils' lives by identifying, developing and celebrating the diverse attributes of each learner.

## Practical activity 9.4

*Aim:* To monitor the use and abuse of concepts of 'intelligence'.

*Method:* A simple method is proposed based on noticing, recording and studying any use of language which denotes generalized ability.

This could be done in a school, in discussion with governors, teachers, parents, non-teaching staff or pupils, from printed articles in newspapers and the educational press, from school or government documents, from the speeches of politicians. It will require active listening – becoming attuned to things which are said which are relevant – and the period of awareness may need to extend over a week or so.

Whatever sources are chosen, the statements and the context in which these occur should be recorded in notes as accurately as possible.

When you have a collection of statements, study them.

Think about them in their context. For instance: What particular expectations about future attainment are implied? Do they recognize the richness and diversity of pupils' abilities?

*Follow-up:* Try to monitor your own use of language. Be explicitly aware of the words and concepts which you use. Distinguish between abilities and attainments. Try to satisfy the criteria of accuracy, discrimination and impartiality in your thinking about pupils' capacities and potential.

## 2.2  Culture

The cultures which pupils experience are significant for their learning. Of course, it has always been thought that home background, peer relationships, the cultures of different schools and, increasingly, the media, do influence how pupils learn, but the development of social constructivist psychology has led to a much greater understanding of the processes which are at work.

Three major cultural influences on learning can be identified:

- *Learning framework.* Learning is a process of 'making sense' and whatever is taken as being meaningful ('makes sense') will be strongly influenced by the culture, knowledge, values and ideas of social groups which the learner has previously experienced. Such cultures provide an initial framework of understanding. Thus, each pupil's construction (learning) will tend to elaborate and extend the knowledge which is embedded in their experienced culture.
- *Medium of language.* Language is the medium of thinking and learning and is created, transmitted and sustained through interaction with other people within the cultures of different social settings. These settings influence the range of 'languages' we use – the register, styles, dialects etc. Flexibility and appropriateness can enhance communication and thus learning.
- *Learning stance.* The learning stance adopted by each pupil is crucial to educational outcomes. Will a pupil be open or closed to experience and support, will they be confident or fearful, willing to take risks or defensive? For secondary schools the issue of the learning stance pupils have developed in the primary school (the first formal institution which most children experience in a sustained way) is particularly significant.

Four major sources of cultural influence on children can be identified.

- *The family:* Family background has been recognized as being of crucial significance in educational achievement for many years. This occurs not just in material ways, depending on the wealth and income of families, nor simply because of ownership or otherwise of overt forms of 'cultural capital' (Bourdieu and Passeron 1977), which is often associated with high status groups in society. The most significant issues for school learning, concern what the culture of the family provides in terms of a framework of existing understanding, a language for development and a disposition to adopt a positive stance regarding learning.

  Of course, families are themselves part of communities and the rich cultural diversity of modern societies ensures that most schools will provide for pupils from a variety of cultural backgrounds.

  Schools also have to take on board problems arising from other socio-cultural factors, like the lack of equality that exists between cultures and the existence of prejudice and discrimination. All these features of the wider society are reflected in the learning process and make an impact on pupils' orientation towards school. Teachers are themselves not immune from these influences, which often show up in their assumptions about the learning capacities of disadvantaged and minority groups (see Chapter 8 for more on this). As Bartolome (1994) points out, it is all too easy for teachers to fail to recognize 'the pedagogical implications of asymmetrical power relations among cultural groups' (p. 177) and to adopt a deficit orientation towards differences arising from cultural factors.

- *Peers at school:* As we saw in Chapter 8, peer group culture is important to pupils as a way of both enjoying and adapting to school life. As pupils get older, the culture of boys and girls tends to become more distinctive as the young people explore and come to terms with their sexuality (Hey 1996, Mac an Ghaill 1995, Wolpe 1988). Pupil culture also articulates with both academic achievement within school and social factors outside such as social class and ethnicity (Sewell 1996, Eckert 1989). Such differentiation is particularly important to pupil motivation and to the learning stance which is routinely adopted. Some peer cultures favour school attainment and are likely to reinforce teacher efforts to engender a positive approach to learning. Other peer cultures derive meaning from alternative values and pupils who are influenced by such cultures may approach school with minimal or even oppositional expectations. Such pupils will still be constructing understanding, but it may not be the type of understanding for which teachers would have aimed.

- *The school:* As we saw in Chapter 5, schools each have their own unique culture. Such cultures are created by those who work in the school and those who are associated with it.

  A school culture must be seen as a learning context which is at least as important as the bricks and mortar, books and equipment which make up the material environment of a school. Again, we have to ask how this culture influences the framework for understanding which is offered to the pupils, the language in which teaching and learning is transacted and the stance which learners adopt. For instance, are pupils encouraged to take risks in their learning? What learning stance is engendered through the symbolic rituals and events of the school, the assemblies and demonstrations of 'good work'? What criteria about standards of school work are communicated? What are the underlying assumptions about learning and knowledge within the school – and how do these impact on the pupils?

  It is also important to recognize that the school culture will not necessarily have the same meaning for all those who work and study in the institution. For instance, some teachers may find the cultural milieu constraining and inhibitive of the kind of teaching approach they favour, whereas other teachers may find it enabling and supportive. A further factor is the existence of subcultures within the school. Although looked at from the 'outside', so to speak, schools have their own distinctive culture; on closer inspection (as we suggested in Chapter 5) this can be seen to be made up of a number of separate cultural groupings amongst staff and pupils, each of which has a different relationship to the official dominant culture. This heterogeneity is often reflected in classroom practice (giving rise to different 'ethoses' in different classrooms) and in the way teachers identify with their subject subcultures.

- *The media and new technologies:* The influence of the media on young people is sometimes a controversial topic (Morley 1992) but it is known that, whilst book reading often seems in relative decline, television viewing is increasing, as is the apparent influence of advertising. With contradictory research findings abounding, it is impossible to say how this affects young people's thinking overall.

However, many teachers and parents believe that the influence is noticeable with individuals.

There is little doubt however that television, film and access to new communication technologies such as the Internet can 'broaden the mind' by presenting experiences and tapping emotions – even if this is only done indirectly. Young people may identify with particular 'imagined communities' (Anderson 1983), perhaps from soap operas, or adopt particular forms of consumption or behaviour associated with popular music or events (Willis 1990). The key question is how new cultural experiences are interpreted, and what sense is made of them.

Clearly, the nature of these influences on each learner will dramatically affect the way in which he or she approaches learning at school. Practical Activity 9.5 focuses on this issue.

### Practical activity 9.5

*Aim:* To map the influence of culture on the learning of a pupil.

*Method:* Draw up a table, as below, on a large sheet of paper.

| Four sources of cultural influence | Three influences on learning | | |
| --- | --- | --- | --- |
| | Framework of understanding | Language | Learning stance |
| Family | | | |
| Peers | | | |
| School | | | |
| Media and communication technologies | | | |

Think of one pupil whom you know well. Consider the way cultures influence the framework of the pupil's understanding, the language they use and the learning stance he/she adopts. Complete each cell of the table, far as you can, to map what you know about the cultural influences on that pupil.

If you have time it would be valuable to talk to the pupil and others – peers and teachers – to improve the quality of your data.

*Follow-up:* Repeat this exercise with different pupils, or compare the results of similar activities by colleagues. What insights are produced by comparisons of pupils of different sex, ethnicity, religion, social class, attainment?

Moving to another level of analysis, we also need to consider the different ways in which individual pupils tackle actual learning tasks. We do this by focusing on the psychological implications of personality on learning style and on meta-cognition.

## 2.3 Personality and learning approaches

Psychologists' understanding of personality has, according to Hampson (1988), derived from three contributory strands of analysis.

The first is the *lay perspective* – the understandings which are implicit in common-sense thinking of most of us about other people. This is evident in literature and in everyday action. It is a means by which people are able to anticipate the actions of others – ideas about the character and likely actions of others are used for both the prediction and explanation of behaviour.

Such understandings have influenced the second strand of analysis – that of *trait theorists* – although their work also reflects a concerted attempt to identify personality dimensions and to objectively measure the resulting patterns of action.

For instance, among the most frequently identified dimensions of personality are:

- *Impulsivity/reflexivity:* (Kagan *et al.* 1964) from impulsives who rush at a task without stopping to think first; to reflexives who like to chew it over, sometimes endlessly.
- *Extroversion/introversion:* (Eysenck and Cookson 1969) from extroverts who are outgoing and gregarious; to introverts who are more 'private' and may prefer to keep themselves to themselves.

As the work of trait theorists has become dated, a third strand of personality analysis has become prominent, and Hampson calls this the *self perspective*. This approach sees the development of personality in close association with that of self-image. Crucially, it draws attention to the capacity of humans to reflect on themselves and to take account of the views of others. The social context in which individuals develop, their culture, interaction and experiences with others is thus seen as being very important in influencing views of self and consequent patterns of action.

Of course, this approach has considerable resonance with social constructivist ideas and with our earlier discussion of culture. As Hampson puts it:

> The most important consequence . . . is that personality is no longer viewed as residing exclusively within the individual. Instead, personality is viewed as the product of a process involving the conversion of the individual actor's behaviour into socially significant acts by the observer and the self-observer. In this sense, personality should not be located within persons, but between or among persons. (Hampson 1988, p. 205)

The self perspective has generated many insights into how pupils approach learning tasks. Studies in this area have provided a useful vocabulary to describe some common ways in which activities and challenges are typically approached. Various aspects have been identified. For instance:

- *Task v. ego involvement.* In task involvement the focus is on the task rather than the self; learning is seen as an end in itself and dependent on effort rather than ability.

    In ego involvement the learner is more self-conscious and more concerned about the way they will be perceived by others (e.g. 'bright' or 'stupid'). They are more likely to perceive learning as dependent on ability rather than effort (Nicholls, 1983).

- *Internal v. external control.* The term 'learned helplessness' has been applied to pupils who never engage in learning tasks on their own initiative but always wait for guidance from an adult or peer. For such learners the 'locus of control' of their learning is outside themselves. The internal control leading to autonomy and independent learning is under-developed (Lawrence, 1987).

- *Forthcoming/unforthcoming.* Forthcoming pupils have a positive self-image, are self-assured in learning situations and enjoy challenges. Unforthcoming pupils have a poor image of themselves as learners and as a result lack confidence, particularly when tackling new learning tasks (Stott, 1976).

In a sense, the three theories of personality which we have reviewed differ in their view of the source of personality but reveal considerable overlaps in their descriptions of the personality characteristics. Insights on learning approaches can thus be helpful, but such approaches should be seen as being amenable to change and development through social and educational processes.

### Practical activity 9.6

*Aim:* To analyse individual pupils' approaches to learning.

*Method:*

1. Observe individual pupils when working in a range of situations – different types of tasks, different time demands, different social contexts. Note their behaviour carefully. Later, review your notes in the light of the dimensions of personality and learning approach listed above.

2. Try to monitor yourself in a similar range of situations, and thereby identify aspects of your own approaches to learning.

*Follow-up:* Use this information to review the match between task and learner, and to consider the relationship between your teaching and pupils' learning approaches. From these insights, consider the range of teaching strategies which are available to you.

## Practical activity 9.7

*Aim:* To analyse our responses to different learning approaches.

*Method:* Tape-record, take diary notes, or ask a colleague to observe your teaching during selected sessions. Monitor the way you help pupils.

Review the range of help that you offer. Try to distinguish reasons for the variety and assess whether the action taken did enhance the pupils' learning. Then use the information to analyse your response to others. For example:

1. Do you seem to prefer some pupil learning approaches to others, or to respond differently?

2. Do you expect different kinds of learning behaviour from boys and girls? Do you reward them differently?

3. Do you provide different kinds of tasks and opportunities for each of these approaches to develop, or do you tend to prepare tasks which suit your own favoured approach?

*Follow-up:* What are the implications of the answers to such questions?

## 2.4 Motivation

So far in this chapter we have considered the relationship between learning styles and the task. Whilst this is clearly important it is also essential to consider motivational aspects of learning, for an activity in which learners fail to see any purpose or meaning is unlikely to be very productive – however well-intended and carefully planned.

Motivation is highly subjective and is likely to be related to pupils' perceptions of themselves, teachers and schooling in general (see Chapter 8). It can also be affected by very specific, immediate moods and situations which arise in classrooms.

Learners' positive motivation towards learning is important not only for maximizing learning outcomes but because of the disruptive effects which pupils who are poorly motivated can produce. A reflective teacher thus needs to consider the meaning and worthwhileness which an activity is likely to have for learners, as well as its potential for developing learning.

A very common perception of children regarding schools is that they are 'boring'. For this reason, engendering enthusiasm can require a certain amount of imagination, skill and shedding of inhibition on the part of teachers. However, being able to motivate learners is basic to the smooth running of a classroom and to effective learning. Yet, few teachers can be certain of how pupils will respond to a particular activity. Developing a motivational match thus requires sensitivity to the learners, flexibility, spontaneity and imagination.

Motivation can stem from a wide range of factors, from positive interest to negative fear. The most commonly identified types of motivation are:

- *intrinsic* – based on a learner's personal interest
- *collective* – where pleasure derives from sharing work with friends, the class, school or family
- *extrinsic* – manipulation through the use of rewards and such devices as stars and house points
- *coerced compliance* – where learners carry out tasks in order to avoid punishments.

A teacher can influence the kinds of motivation learners may develop and the attitudes they show towards learning by the ways in which activities are set up and encouraged and by the nature of the activities themselves. For instance, co-operative group work for reflective learning can be encouraged by arrangements which enable all pupils not merely just to 'act' together but to express themselves as individuals, to explore their ideas and to discuss different viewpoints (Johnson and Johnson 1982, Phillips, 1985).

## Practical activity 9.8

*Aim:* To review the motivational qualities of a series of classroom activities.

*Method:* Consider a teaching/learning session and list the requirements which were made of selected pupils. This might be done by asking a colleague to observe, or by interpreting a tape-recording. From the perspective of each of the selected pupils, make a judgement of the type of motivation which you feel influenced their actions. Record your judgements.

If possible, discuss the session with the pupils involved and record their accounts.

*Follow-up:* By comparing teacher judgements and pupils' accounts it should be possible to obtain many insights which could help in developing more appropriate approaches to motivating learners in the future.

Chapter 10, Section 2.1 looks further at this important subject in connection with planning to teach.

## 2.5 Meta-cognition

We have considered some major factors which are likely to produce patterns in pupils' approaches to school tasks. The interplay of such factors is, however, extremely complex and will never be entirely predictable. Furthermore, learners have the crucial capacity to reflect on their own thinking processes and to develop new strategies. This capacity for self-awareness regarding their own mental powers is called 'meta-cognition'.

Since meta-cognition involves self-knowledge and since the self is socially constructed, this form of knowledge involves several factors. In his classic article, Flavell (1979) provides a definition of meta-cognitive knowledge which includes psychological factors such as various learning strategies (e.g. self-monitoring, planning, self-evaluating) and the more sociological factors such as beliefs about others and their impact on the learning process. It is a short step from here to seeing meta-cognition in terms of a broader perspective, one which encompasses all social and psychological influences on learning in an institutional context. For instance, pupils' awareness of how they are labelled by teachers or how their self-image is affected by peer relations would count as meta-cognitive knowledge.

The concept of meta-cognition has come to the fore recently in secondary schools because of growing concerns about the problem of 'transfer of learning', whether this refers to transfer across knowledge domains in the context of the school or transfer of school subject knowledge to the practical contexts of everyday life outside school (Quicke, 1994). Can metacognitive knowledge *per se* assist transfer between one subject and another? If pupils, say, know how to approach problems and monitor their performance in maths, will this be transferable to geography? In the literature on critical thinking and thinking skills there has been much debate about this issue. Some argue that cognitive strategies cannot simply be transposed from one subject area to another because thinking can only take place within the frameworks of specific subject disciplines (McPeck, 1981). Others are of the opinion that there is some value (i.e. in terms of transfer effects) in helping pupils to reflect upon the 'generalizable skills' which they deploy in any learning task. Others think that the proponents of each position have a point and that teachers should make use of both approaches.

Many innovative teaching strategies have drawn on research studies which have been carried out in school and non-school settings. In their co-investigational approach Scardamalia and Bereiter (1983) suggest several activities designed to elicit pupils' existing meta-cognitive knowledge:

1. Teaching and encouraging learners to think aloud
2. Giving pupils something concrete to talk about
3. Asking pupils to give advice to others on how to approach tasks
4. Attending to non-verbal cues and discussing them with pupils
5. Enlisting learners' help in getting the teacher to understand.

Pupils may then be introduced to more advanced strategies, such as using planning cues to provide support for others and switching roles so that they can see processes from different viewpoints. These issues are taken up again in practical ways in Chapter 15, Section 2, where we discuss formative assessment and pupil self-assessment.

The PEEL (Project Enhancing Effective Learning) (see Baird and Mitchell 1986) is a good example of teacher-controlled action research in this area. In a multi-disciplinary study of low achievers in the secondary school the problem of content versus process was resolved by distinguishing between two discourses – one the formal discourse of the subject (in this instance science) and the other the discourse of learning or the metacognitive curriculum (Quicke and Winter 1994).

## Practical activity 9.9

*Aim:* To consider ways in which meta-cognitive discussion can be enhanced in the classroom.

*Method:* Focus on a class with which you have a good relationship and try some of the strategies suggested by Scarmadalia and Bereiter. For instance, discuss the idea of 'talking one's thinking whilst doing'. Perhaps this could be practised in pairs. Then, or on a later occasion, divide the pupils into small groups and provide each with a clear but challenging learning task. Visit each group and encourage the pupils to reflect on how they are approaching the task. Ask one or two to articulate what they have been thinking and to offer advice to others. Watch for, and point out, non-verbal behaviours which may indicate perceptions which are forming or have formed. Ask the pupils to explain to you what they have been doing. Finally, encourage the pupils to reflect on what learning took place in the group and how this was achieved.

*Follow-up:* Review the pupils' learning. Has your work on meta-cognition caused them to become more aware of the social dynamics in group work? To extend these ideas, consider Chapter 15, Sections 2.3 and 4.7. The first focuses on pupil self-assessment for learning, and the second addresses conferencing, action planning and process review – each based on the encouragement of meta-cognition about learning and progress.

## CONCLUSION

Learning is an immensely complex topic and this chapter has simply touched the surface of the issues which are involved. In one sense, perhaps the provisional nature of our understanding is no bad thing, because, if we knew it all, then one of the greatest sources of fascination and fulfilment in teaching would be diminished. The vocation of teaching will certainly always include this element of intellectual challenge as teachers seek to understand what learners understand, and to provide appropriate support.

In this chapter we have reviewed three influential approaches to learning and discussed some of the key issues which are involved: as we stated in the introduction to the chapter, language provides the crucial medium through which learning takes place and consideration of it has pervaded our discussions here. The issue is taken up again later as the explicit focus of Chapter 13.

We conclude with three key insights on learning derived from the work of Margaret Donaldson (Grieve and Hughes 1990):

- One needs to consider the learner as a whole person, including the social context from which he or she derives meaning and understanding.
- One needs to consider any learning situation from the learner's point of view.
- One needs to remember the overarching difficulty of formal education for learners as their thinking develops from being embedded in particular contexts to become capable of more abstraction.

Whatever the strength of their subject knowledge, teachers are likely to be more effective in supporting young people's learning if they bear such insights in mind.


## *Notes for further reading*

Fascinating insights into the thinking of young people is provided by:

De Bono, E. (1972)
*Children Solve Problems,*
London: Penguin Education.

For basic psychological introductions to alternative theories of teaching and learning see:

Child, D. (1986)
*Psychology and the Teacher,*
London: Cassell.

Fontana, D. (1988)
*Psychology for Teachers,*
London: Macmillan.

Galloway, D. and Edwards, A. (1992),
*Secondary School Teaching and Educational Psychology,*
London: Longman.

A well-designed reference book, with excellent coverage by leading psychologists is:

Coleman, A. M. (1994)
*Companion Encyclopedia of Psychology,*
London: Routledge.

A concise and accessible review of approaches to classroom learning is:

Entwistle, N. (1987)
*Understanding Classroom Learning,*
London: Hodder and Stoughton.

For some classic behaviourist work see:

Skinner, B. F. (1953)
*Science and Human Behaviour,*
New York: Macmillan.

Gagne, R. M. (1965)
*The Conditions of Learning,*
New York: Holt, Rinehart and Winston.

Some classic constructivist work is:

Piaget, J. (1950)
*The Psychology of Intelligence*,
London: Routledge and Kegan Paul.

Inhelder, B. and Piaget, J. (1958)
*The Growth of Logical Thinking from Childhood to Adolescence*,
London: Routledge.

A comprehensive introduction to Piaget's work is:

Ginsberg, H. and Opper, S. (1969)
*Piaget's Theory of Intellectual Development*,
New York: Prentice Hall.

For classic social constructivist work see:

Vygotsky, L. S. (1962)
*Thought and Language*,
Massachusetts: Massachusetts Institute of Technology.

Vygotsky, L. S. (1978)
*Mind in Society: The Development of Higher Psychological Processes*,
Cambridge, Massachusetts: Harvard University Press.

The best detailed reviews of Vygotsky's work are:

Wertsch, J. V. (1985)
*Vygotsky and the Social Formation of Mind*,
Cambridge, Massachusetts: Harvard University Press.

Daniels, H. (1996)
*An Introduction to Vygotsky*,
London: Routledge.

Jerome Bruner is always worth reading. See his beautifully crafted books with brilliant insights into the 'inspiration of Vygotsky':

Bruner, J. S. (1986)
*Actual Minds, Possible Worlds*,
Cambridge, Massachusetts: Harvard University Press.

Bruner, J. S. (1990)
*Acts of Meaning*,
Cambridge, Massachusetts: Harvard University Press.

The significance of the imagination in learning is becoming seriously underestimated in these days of detailed curriculum planning. For sources which assert its importance see:

Smith, F. (1990)
*To Think*,
New York: Teachers College Press.

Eisner, E. (1994)
*Cognition and Curriculum Reconsidered*,
New York: Teachers College Press.

Abbs, P. (ed.) (1987)
*Living Powers: The Arts in Education,*
Lewes: The Falmer Press.

On intelligence, Richardson provides a useful introduction:

Richardson, K. (1991)
*Understanding Intelligence,*
Milton Keynes: Open University Press.

For dramatically contrasting views of the nature, origins and study of intelligence see:

Howe, M. J. A. (1990)
*The Origins of Exceptional Abilities,*
London: Basil Blackwell.

Kline, P. (1991)
*Intelligence: the Psychometric View,*
London: Routledge.

For the argument that there are in fact 'multiple intelligences', see:

Gardner, H. (1985)
*Frames of Mind: The Theory of Multiple Intelligences,*
London: Paladin Books.

Two interesting longitudinal studies of 'gifted children' provide case-study material with which to consider the nature/nurture intelligence debates. They are:

Freeman, J. (1991)
*Gifted Children Growing Up,*
London: Cassell.

Gross, M. (1992)
*Exceptionally Gifted Children,*
London: Routledge.

For a review of the history and state of work on dyslexia, see:

Miles, T. and Miles, E. (1990)
*Dyslexia: A Hundred Years On,*
Buckingham: Open University Press.

For a good introduction to personality, see:

Hampson, S. E. (1988)
*The Construction of Personality: An Introduction,*
London: Routledge.

An interesting book which tries to synthesize much previous work on personality into an overarching theoretical framework is:

Kegan, R. (1982)
*The Evolving Self: Problem and Process in Human Development,*
London: Harvard University Press.

Important sources on adolescent development and identities are:

Rosenberg, M. (1965)
*Society and the Adolescent Self-image,*
Princeton, N. J.: Princeton University Press.

Breakwell, G. (1986)
*Coping with Threatened Identities,*
London: Methuen.

Kroger, J. (1996)
*Identity in Adolescence,*
London: Routledge.

Hendry, L. (1993)
*Young People's Leisure and Lifestyles,*
London: Routledge.

The following books contain interesting articles relating to individual differences in learning approaches, particularly Section 2 in Entwistle (1985):

Entwistle, N. (ed.) (1985)
*New Directions in Educational Psychology: Learning and Teaching,*
London: Falmer.

Entwistle, N. (1987)
*Understanding Classroom Learning,*
London: Hodder and Stoughton.

On motivation there is a wide range of both psychological and sociologically inspired work. For instance, see:

Spaulding, C. L. (1992)
*Motivation in the Classroom,*
New York: Mc Graw Hill.

Furlong, V. J. (1985)
*The Deviant Pupil,*
Milton Keynes: Open University Press.

On memory, see:

Badderley, A. (1990)
*Human Memory: Theory and Practice,*
London: Allyn and Bacon.

Amongst a range of different recent work on meta-cognition:

Robinson, E. (1983)
'Meta-cognitive development', in Meadows, S. (ed.) *Developing Thinking,*
London: Methuen.

Nisbet, J. and Shucksmith, J. (1986)
*Learning Strategies,*
London: Routledge.

Quicke, J. (1994)
'Metacognition, Pupil Empowerment and the School context',
*School Psychology International,* 15(3), 247–60.

The two books below are more concerned with the philosophy and practice of thinking critically:

Siegel, H. (1990)
*Educating Reason: Rationality Critical Thinking and Education,*
London: Routledge.

Smith, F. (1990)
*To Think,*
New York: Teachers' College Press.

# How are we preparing and planning our lessons?

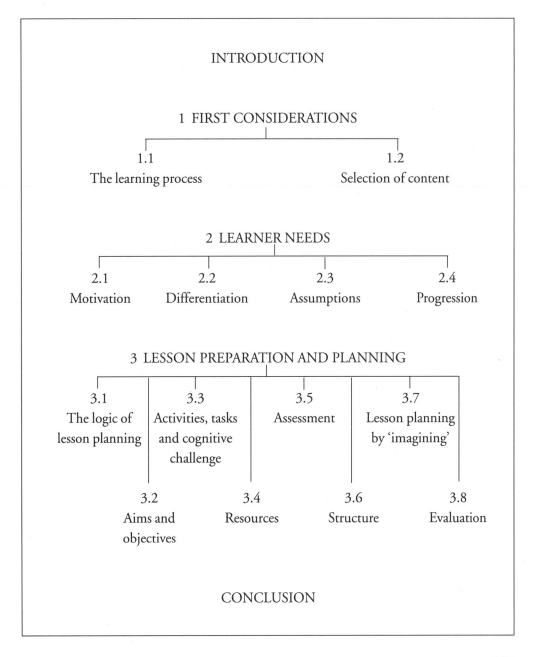

INTRODUCTION

1 FIRST CONSIDERATIONS

1.1
The learning process

1.2
Selection of content

2 LEARNER NEEDS

2.1
Motivation

2.2
Differentiation

2.3
Assumptions

2.4
Progression

3 LESSON PREPARATION AND PLANNING

3.1
The logic of
lesson planning

3.3
Activities, tasks
and cognitive
challenge

3.5
Assessment

3.7
Lesson planning
by 'imagining'

3.2
Aims and
objectives

3.4
Resources

3.6
Structure

3.8
Evaluation

CONCLUSION

## INTRODUCTION

The decisions you make as you prepare and plan your lessons will depend in part on your image of yourself as a teacher. What kind of teacher do you want to be? What teaching styles are you drawn to? In Chapter 9, 'What do we know about learning?', we set out various theories about how pupils learn, and discussed some of the factors which have an impact on how and whether learning happens. The teaching approaches derived from these theories come with a variety of labels: traditional, progressive, didactic, learner-centred, chalk and talk, experiential, practical, individualized, resource-based, skills-based, and so on. In practice (whatever the media and other sources may suggest to the contrary), teachers rarely sign up exclusively with any one approach; but the selections you make will be based firmly in your sense of who you are, what you know and what you believe. It is important to recognize this for a number of reasons. Our experiences as pupils inevitably affect our ideas about teaching; it is not unusual to find student teachers, especially in moments of crisis, replicating the teaching style they received (even when they have been critical of it). It is a good idea to talk about different experiences of school with other students and with your tutor or mentor. Another influence on how you teach is the setting, in particular the school's view of the teaching task (Calderhead 1987). It may be necessary to compromise or negotiate, another reason to be clear and articulate about the basis for the choices you make.

The preparation and planning of lessons fall into what Jackson (1968) defined as the *pre-active* phase of teaching. This is where you do all the thinking that lays firm foundations for your encounters with your pupils (the *interactive* phase). Feeling secure in your preparation leaves you relatively free to react to the unexpected, to adapt your routines and to respond more flexibly, dynamically and sensitively to pupils. This chapter is designed to help you focus on the factors you need to consider as you get ready to teach. It will be helpful to cross-refer as necessary to the other chapters in this central section of the book for more detailed consideration of organization, management, communication, and assessment.

## 1 FIRST CONSIDERATIONS

Put at its simplest, planning to teach a lesson is a two-step process: deciding what to teach, followed by deciding how to teach it. However, like most things associated with teaching, things are less neat and simple than this characterization suggests. In the first part of this chapter we look more closely at the learning process and at an important aspect of the selection of content.

## 1.1 The learning process

In preparing and planning to teach, you will be making decisions based on your thinking about learning. Abstract ideas about 'active learning', 'deep processing', meta-cognition, interaction, learning to learn, ownership, motivation, have to be translated into what will happen between you and a specific group of pupils at a particular time and in a particular place. In this section we want to focus on the individual experience of learning and to consider which (if any) aspects of the learning process can be generalized to the group.

We start by asking you to think about your own experiences as a learner.

### *Practical activity 10.1*

*Aim:* To reflect on your own learning experiences and to consider what made the learning easy or difficult.

*Method:* Sit down with a sheet of paper divided as shown:

| Things that made learning easier | Things that made learning more difficult |
| --- | --- |
| | |

Start by recalling a recent experience where you had to learn new knowledge or a new skill. List all the things about that experience that fit the headings.

Go on to recall learning experiences from your secondary school days. Make a note of what you were trying to learn; factors which make learning easier or more difficult for you may vary from subject to subject.

Compare your list with a colleague or fellow student. Are there many differences? Make a list of the positive and negative factors you agree on.

(As an alternative this could be done in a group with members discussing in pairs, and listing positive and negative factors on a flip chart for whole-group discussion.)

*Follow-up:* Consider aspects of school life which may make it difficult to arrange the optimum conditions for learning as set out in your list.

As an alternative (or additional) way to consider learning you might like to undertake Practical Activity 10.2

## Practical activity 10.2

*Aim:* To consider a list of ways in which people learn and discuss them in relation to your own experience.

*Method:* Consider the following list of statements about how we learn:

- individually
- socially, by interacting with others
- by being told
- by finding out
- by asking questions
- by answering questions
- collaboratively
- competitively
- by taking risks
- by being protected from failure
- under pressure
- in our own time
- holistically
- in separate compartments
- by doing/looking/reading/writing/talking/drawing/imagining
- by learning how to learn
- by being told what to do
- by evaluating our own success
- by being assessed by others.

Use the list to think about and/or discuss with others different aspects of learning. Relate these statements to your own experiences of learning and being taught.

Some of the points are contradictory. Does this mean that one is always positive and the other negative? How is your thinking about this affected by what is being learned, the age and experience of the learner?

How did you develop your personal stance to learning? Is it constant? How did you learn to learn? What positive and negative learning habits do you think you have?

*Follow-up:* Which of these factors will you try to incorporate in your own teaching?

An interesting and thought-provoking description of individual learning is provided by Michael Polanyi (1958). Factors involved in this description include:

- discovering that there is something that we want or need to know, understand or be able to do
- being immersed in the problem
- being puzzled
- active engagement, especially in obtaining information and testing hunches
- repeated experience of the learning situation
- the presence of an expert who sets up the situation, acts as a model, can answer questions
- moments of insight when things 'click'
- getting pleasure from such moments
- feeling doubtful that we will ever really understand/be able to do it
- having faith that we eventually will understand/be able to do it.

(List adapted from Sotto 1994, p. 54)

### Practical activity 10.3

*Aim:* To consider the description of individual learning derived from Polanyi.

*Method:* Alone or with a colleague consider the list of factors (above) of the characteristics of individual learning. Does the list ring true for you when you think of your own learning? Which parts do you recognize most strongly? Is there anything you would want to add?

What are the implications of this list for how you approach planning for your pupils to learn?

*Follow-up:* Apart from planning, what other implications are there for teachers in this description?

Two themes – the importance of 'activity' and of interaction – constantly recur in discussions of learning. In any event, the incorporation of activity and direct experience, in proportions and ways which are appropriate to the age of the learners, is an essential part of any curriculum provision. Whether or not pupils are aware of the role of activity in learning, in interviews they consistently report a preference for 'doing something interesting'.

Practical Activity 10.4 suggests a way of looking at a unit or sequence of work developed by your subject team.

## Practical activity 10.4

*Aim:* To consider the extent of activity and direct experience provided for pupils.

*Method:* Consider a unit or sequence of work in your subject. Annotate it to show where pupils are likely to be most active and obtain direct experience of the intended learning.

Discuss with another teacher who has worked on this unit the kinds of activity experienced by the pupils.

If possible talk to pupils to get their perspective on learning. How do they think they learn best? Is activity important to them?

*Follow-up:* Reflect on what you have found out and have it in mind when you move to other sections of this chapter, especially 3.3, and when you prepare to teach.

Planning for pupils to be active learners is often associated with phrases like 'problem-solving', 'discovery learning', 'resource-based learning', 'collaborative group work'. All of these do require pupils to be active. They also place demands on pupils' learning process skills (see Chapter 13) and on teachers' skills in organizing and managing learning. The approach was attacked in the mid-1990s by Her Majesty's Chief Inspector who questioned the effectiveness of 'progressive methods', discovery learning where children are never told anything and groupwork with teachers as facilitators (Woodhead 1995). In main the criticism was directed at primary teachers but the claim was that secondary teachers were equally guilty of 'unquestioning and ultimately irrational commitments' which undervalued the teaching of knowledge. This was followed by a widespread recommendation of whole-class teaching: at least half of all teaching should be in this form, more in mathematics (Woodhead 1996). We suggest that the polarization of didactic (transmission, telling) teaching and 'active learning' is not helpful. The challenge, as we see it, is to ensure that pupils' minds are engaged, that they are active as thinkers whatever the learning situation. Active engagement in learning can also be achieved by building interaction into whole-class didactic teaching; by devising short, straightforward tasks, carefully structured into a learning sequence that may be essentially 'teacher-centred' and include teacher telling. The significant factor is the nature of the task and the extent to which it requires pupils to be 'active' as learners. Consider how pupils might be more active as thinkers in traditionally didactic situations such as listening to the teacher, copying notes from the blackboard, reading.

You will find more about selecting activities and tasks in Section 3.3 of this chapter. For a further discussion of 'transmission' see Chapter 13, Section 1.1

## 1.2 Selection of content

Secondary teachers are appointed to teach a subject; they have a subject expertise. Subject curricula are expressed in terms of the knowledge, concepts and skills associated with that particular discipline. In lessons teachers teach and pupils learn that subject content. It might, therefore, be reasonably assumed that the more teachers know about a subject the more their pupils will achieve. However, studies of teaching have not found a straightforward correlation between what teachers know and what pupils learn (Dunkin and Biddle 1974). On reflection you may find echoes of this in your personal experience. Can you recall an occasion when an 'expert' tried to explain something to you with little success? To be a successful teacher of a subject requires two sorts of knowing – knowing the subject and knowing how best to present it so that it can be learned. The link between the two, however, is not straightforwardly linear. Deciding what we want pupils to learn is only the first step. Selecting the content for lessons in which we hope they will acquire this knowledge and understanding sends us back to the subject to examine our personal understanding of what we intend to teach.

Cognitive psychology is helpful here in identifying what Gardner (1985, **Primary Reading 6.6**) defines as 'mental representation' – the way in which knowledge develops through our ability to represent experience internally. Teaching another person what you know involves finding ways of *representing* subject matter to assist their learning (Dewey 1902, Byrne 1983) and being aware of the representations they develop as they work to understand the subject content. Very interesting American

research into the ways novice teachers prepare to teach subject matter (Shulman 1986, see also **Primary Reading 7.13**) refers to the ways in which teachers move from the representations of their personal understanding to those designed to initiate and develop pupil understanding as 'transformations'. These transformations take many forms: metaphors, analogies, illustrations, demonstrations, examples, narratives, associations, activities. In generating transformations teachers use:

- *content knowledge* – the concepts, structure and organization of the subject
- *knowledge from other content areas* – particularly where connections are seen
- *teaching knowledge* – general pedagogic principles and techniques
- *knowledge of learners* – their experience, current understanding, interests
- *curricular knowledge* – specific programmes, syllabuses, materials and resources.

Shulman (1986) calls this special understanding of content for the purposes of teaching *pedagogical content knowledge* and defines it as a form of subject content knowledge that:

> embodies the aspects of content most germane to its teachability. Within the category . . . I include, for the most regularly taught topics in one's subject area, the most useful forms of representation of those ideas, the most powerful analogies, illustrations, examples, explanations and demonstrations – in a word the ways of representing and formulating the subject that make it comprehensible to others . . . [It] also includes an understanding of what makes the learning of specific topics easy or difficult: the conceptions and preconceptions that students of different ages and backgrounds bring with them to the learning. (p. 9)

With experience, teachers develop a 'representational repertoire' for the subject they teach which may itself enrich and extend their own subject understanding – it's a truism that a good way to understand something is to try to teach it. This repertoire is part of the result of 'thinking like a teacher' about a subject. In one lesson a teacher may use a number of different strategies of this kind. The successes and failures of our *transformations* in making learning meaningful for our pupils, individually and as a group, add to our knowledge – of the subject and of how it may be learned, in particular of subject-specific difficulties which pupils experience.

In another study, this time of experienced teachers, Hashweh (1985) found that those with thorough subject knowledge were more likely to adapt and modify text books and other published materials where they found the organization of content and the representations of concepts unsatisfactory. They were also more likely to identify where learners might misunderstand, to recognize dawning insights and to see where connections, within the subject and with other subject areas, might be usefully pointed out. Teachers with what Hashweh refers to as 'surface knowledge of the subject' used representations that were often inappropriate and sometimes misleading; they also did not make within-subject connections.

In preparing to teach you may have as your starting-point modules or units of work which have been developed or selected by your subject team (see Chapter 7). Whether they have been written in-house, bought as a published programme, or a bit of both, these will probably be part of a larger scheme of work which sets out the subject curriculum over a longer time-scale. You may find that the units or modules you are going to teach are very detailed, with materials and other resources and teaching approaches clearly specified. In other cases there may be no more than a broad indication of the subject matter to be covered. Whatever the situation, you will be faced with the challenge of finding ways to transform the content for your pupils. Practical Activity 10.5 is designed to help you think about this.

## Practical activity 10.5

*Aim:* To consider the idea of *transformations* when preparing to teach.

*Method:* For a particular lesson or series of lessons focus specifically on what you know about the content and what you want your pupils to learn about the content. If teaching materials are prescribed, review them in the light of your understanding of the subject matter.

How do you represent your personal understanding of this content? How might you make it meaningful for your pupils? Consider some ways in which you might *transform* the content. How might you introduce ideas/concepts/principles? How can you best move pupils from what is known or familiar to new knowledge? Are there any analogies, metaphors, etc., which seem appropriate? What makes you think they will work? Are there parts of the learning where pupils may misunderstand or be misled? How might you avoid this? What language will you use? How will you approach any subject-specialist language?

If possible discuss your ideas for *transformations* with another teacher or student teacher.

*Follow-up:* Teach the lesson and try out your *transformations*. How did they work? Is there anything from the lesson that you will to add to your representational repertoire?

## 2 | LEARNER NEEDS

A consistent feature of our consideration of the learning process and of the selection of content has been, of course, the learners. Learning can only happen within the learner. As teachers frustratingly discover, having taught something is no guarantee that it has been learned. Worse perhaps is the knowledge that what teachers do can impede learning as much as support it. The ever-present challenge is to gain insights into our pupils as learners. You may want to refer or return to Part 2 of Chapter 8 at this point. In the second part of this chapter we develop further some of the factors identified in Part 2 of Chapter 9 which are particularly relevant to preparation and planning for learning.

## 2.1 Motivation

When motivation falls, with it goes concentration, commitment, quality and in some cases, control. No wonder then that it features so prominently in the concerns of novice teachers. And not only of novices. There is widespread concern in the profession and in society generally about 'disappeared, disaffected and disappointed pupils' (Barber 1996) and in particular about the high proportion of boys in this category. A secondary school in Suffolk offered this characterization of 'the stereotypical boy ... unable to concentrate or to organize himself, presenting work lacking in quality and quantity, broadly uninterested and unmotivated'. Such views are connected to per-ceived opportunities, but Dweck (e.g. 1986, **Primary Reading 6.7**) has also shown how motivation may be connected to pupils' views of their own intelligence as fixed or malleable. Clearly this has huge implications for positive engagement with learning and can, unfortunately, lead to dependency or alienation. So what is to be done? Irrespective of the age of the learners, factors that seem to produce greater effort and commitment include:

- the quality of the learning challenges presented – an appropriate level of challenge, and not too many undemanding tasks
- the opportunity to succeed and to sense progress
- clear feedback on performance, with reinforcement of good work through reward and/or recognition
- a supportive attitude and positive relationship with the teacher.

It seems that most pupils do want to work, learn and succeed. Why then are some so unco-operative, even to the extent of voting with their feet and truanting? We may find some answers by looking more closely at the factors noted above and at some associated concepts.

### Relevance

When pupils complain that an activity is 'pointless', is 'boring' or that they 'don't see what it is for', then the curriculum is failing to satisfy the criterion of relevance. Relevance in the educational context can be construed in different ways. Pupils often dismiss as 'boring' activities which are too challenging, where they fail or fear they will fail. In this instance the selection or presentation of the activity is not relevant to their learning needs. On another tack, is the general idea of making connections between pupils' learning and their lives and interests. In the selection of content, for instance, there is often a concern to take account of learners as adolescents, acknowledging teenage culture and preoccupations. This can work for a generalized view of adolescence, but has its dangers. 'Youth culture' is noticeably fragmented and fast-moving and materials and specific references planned on the basis of second-hand sources (or even, with young teachers, a personal perspective) can misfire or be quickly outdated. A genuine 'relevance' of this kind would be based on an in-depth and very specific understanding of the pupils being taught – and would be used judiciously as pupils do not always react positively to lessons which make regular and routine incursions into their private frames of reference. If badly done or overdone this becomes a kind of spurious relevance and counter-productive.

Where the life-experience of pupils is more significant is in making judgements of relevance in connection with learning. In the previous section we considered the idea of *transformations*. Selecting metaphors, examples, analogies etc. which connect with learners because they lie within their experience is fundamental. It is perhaps particularly important where it is difficult to make a direct connection between pupils' lives and what the curriculum requires them to learn.

To look at another conception of relevance, public discourse about schools and curriculum currently associates education with preparation for work and meeting the requirements of the job market. In interviews pupils in primary and secondary schools, when asked about what school is for, invariably mention getting a job, passing exams, getting qualifications. As we noted in Chapter 8, Section 2.4, this creates a poignant paradox for pupils who can see no prospect of being employed. If this is the purpose of school, how can it be relevant? The suggestion has been made that, when asked about purposes, pupils fall back on the idea of employability not only because they are pragmatic, or because this view is socially pervasive, or held by their parents, but also for want of anything better to say (Cullingford 1991). Teachers might usefully discuss with pupils alternative views of what school is for. More specifically there is evidence that pupils respond more positively when they are clear about *why* they are doing something in terms of its relevance to their learning. Motivation can be increased when teachers make explicit the reasoning which underpins their selection of activities.

### Enthusiasm

Teachers often rate highly their own enthusiasm for their subject as a factor in motivating learners. Reflecting on our own experience of enthusiasts may suggest the need to qualify this view with 'it depends how it is expressed'. Enthusiasm can lead us to talk too much, to 'oversell' the product. Those on the receiving end are as likely to feel alienated, oppressed, or antagonistic as they are to be inspired. Alternatively they may be quite happy to sit back and let the enthusiast do all the work. In school, motivation more often arises from enthusiasm which expresses itself indirectly, in a positive, purposeful approach and a genuine, obvious commitment to wanting pupils to learn, keeping them on-task and moving forward. One of the rewards of learning from an enthusiast who quietly opens a door for us is to share the particular enjoyment of that subject.

## Structuring learning

Two practical aspects of planning are particularly related to motivation.

Varying the teaching/learning methods over the period of a lesson will help in retaining attention and interest (Kounin 1970, Primary Reading 10.6). It is important to consider pupils' attention span in different activities and at different stages of the lesson. Variety needs to be balanced with time. It is demotivating to feel there is not enough time to learn properly, even when you are working hard, or not to complete a task or achieve a satisfying outcome through lack of time. Pressure from the teacher to achieve 'coverage' and completed 'product' can be counter-productive. One suggestion for keeping up the pace of learning while still maintaining a sense of purpose is to give more responsibility to the learners, negotiating targets with them and providing support by consistent monitoring.

## Extrinsic/intrinsic

In Chapter 9, Section 2.4 we talked about motivational 'match' and different forms of motivation. Motivation resides in the learner. Where it is lacking, teachers can only try to create situations where it reappears or increases. Ideally pupils will be intrinsically motivated by the pleasures of learning and wherever possible we try to make that happen. Realistically we realize the place of extrinsic motivation, and even, if regrettably, of the need for coercion and compliance. Rewards (if not intrinsic) can come in various forms; many (especially younger) pupils respond positively to Merit Marks, Effort Marks, and a host of other forms of reward (including chocolate bars and other treats). These can operate within a particular class or be part of a whole-school approach with public recognition in assemblies or other contexts. Perhaps the most significant form of recognition for learners is the feedback from teachers, especially the much-looked-for praise. This may occur formally in marks and comments on work, in planned oral review, or informally in 'off-the-cuff' comments. It may be public or private. Creating a culture where achievement is acceptable will be significant, especially in the face of peer pressure not to work hard or do well.

Competition can be a factor in rewards. The arguments for and against competition are well rehearsed. Most pupils have a clear idea of their 'abilities' and can place themselves in the 'pecking order' of achievement. A sense of personal progression (perhaps in relation to some self-chosen others) is motivating. Attitudes to rewards and competition can be different from school to school and, more consistently, it will vary with older and younger secondary pupils. For older pupils the relationship with the teacher, rather than public recognition, is likely to be more significant.

It is useful here to make the connection between motivation and personality and learning approaches (Chapter 9, Section 2.3). A pupil who is 'ego-centred' and 'unforthcoming', that is lacking in confidence, risk-averse, and self-defined as 'stupid' (Holt 1982, **Primary Reading 10.3**) will not react well to a highly competitive environment. In such a case non-competitive extrinsic rewards may have a part to play in developing confidence so that intrinsic motivation is increased. Equally, if motivation is to be intrinsic it is necessary to move pupils beyond 'learned helplessness' to taking more responsibility for their own learning.

As teachers we can try to create the best conditions for learning: a responsive and supportive climate where learning is intrinsically rewarding and progress is recognized and reinforced.

To end where we began in this section, the most productive approach to 'motivation' is to listen to learners. Practical Activity 10.6 suggests a way of doing this. If you haven't already tried it you might also find Practical Activity 9.8 useful at this point.

### Practical activity 10.6

*Aim:* To investigate the perceived motivation and relevance of a classroom programme of work.

*Method:* The simple method here is to ask the pupils about a specific piece of learning.

This can be done by asking them to write – as a minimum filling in a short *pro forma* provided by you, more ambitiously by asking them to keep a learning diary or journal. Alternatively you could interview individuals or small groups.

Try to discover: whether they know why they are doing this work; how they think/feel about working on this topic; how they feel about the way they are working – what about it makes learning easy/difficult; how do they feel about the feedback they are getting on their learning. (Your *pro forma* could be designed as a questionnaire using these ideas to inform the framework.)

Analyse the responses to see how meaningful they found the topic, how aware they were of why they were doing the work, how they valued the learning opportunities and processes, their level of motivation.

*Follow-up:* Review what you have learned about the pupils' views. Does this relate to their interest and application and to the standard of the work which they are producing or have produced? How good was your 'motivational match'?

What are the implications for your future planning for relevance and motivation?

## 2.2 Differentiation

The concept of differentiation highlights the nature of the demands which a curriculum or an activity makes of the learner. Awareness of differentiation should help teachers to match tasks and pupils as appropriately as possible, in the expectation that greater progress will be achieved.

Differentiation can be seen at a general or specific level. At a general level it relates to the appropriateness of provision for learners with particular needs. For instance, the needs of young children are significantly different from those of older pupils. Delivering a full National Curriculum in some circumstances is extremely difficult for learners with some categories of special educational need (Jones and Charlton 1992) and it may be necessary to 'disapply' parts to the curriculum where they are inappropriate. The concept of special educational need has focused attention both on those pupils most in need of learning support, and those 'most able' or 'gifted' who need opportunities to extend their learning.

At a more specific level, differentiation relates to the appropriateness, or otherwise, of particular tasks and activities planned for lessons and lesson sequences. At this point, while holding on firmly to the concept of 'match' as important in the progression of learning, we have to consider the practicalities of enacting a differentiated curriculum in class. We know that learning is uniquely and individually constructed in the mind of each learner. Does that mean differentiated activities for each pupil? In some subjects where teachers have adopted a particular approach, it does. SMILE Mathematics, for instance, is an individualized resource-based approach to learning. Each pupil works progressively through tasks on cards with periodic assessment by the teacher. Individualized learning on similar lines also occurs in other subjects: sometimes programmes are textbook-based, sometimes they are built around resource-packs commercially published or created by teachers. One criticism of schemes like SMILE is that the opportunities for pupils to work together co-operatively (which social constructivism suggests is essential for learning) are limited. In some individualized approaches, though, co-operative and collaborative activities are built in. Where tasks and activities and resources already exist, the task for the teacher is to plan the pupil's progress through the materials, monitoring and recording progress.

How does differentiation apply to whole-class teaching? Where pupils have been streamed or set, a degree of differentiation has been enacted by school organization, though this is still only broad brush. In mixed ability classes the teacher has to decide how to respond to individual needs. Teacher-centred whole-class activity has been advocated by, among others, HM Chief Inspector. Working in this way a teacher cannot closely differentiate for needs; of necessity there must be some general approximation in the 'level'. In whole-class interaction decisions about how far to follow the responses of some children have to be made in the light of the need to maintain the interest and attention of the whole group. With experience and practice teachers can adjust the level of questioning to individual pupils. A range of associated strategies: inviting pupils to build on each other's contribution, ask questions of each other, clarify their thinking, be more explicit and articulate in their responses, aids learning for everyone in the group. In the same way stopping to develop a shared summary (orally or in writing) is helpful to all learners. The issue remains of 'levelling up' or 'levelling down'. Research evidence suggests that in general teachers pitch for the middle. In Sweden, Dahllof and Lundgren (1970) identified the notion of a 'steering group', pupils below average in attainment used by teachers as an informal reference group. In whole-class instruction if the steering group seemed to be understanding, teachers would move on; if the pupils in the group seemed to be having trouble or under-performing the teacher slowed the pace for all.

When whole-class teaching is combined with group work and individual activity, differentiation can be by task or outcome. Either the activity itself or the outcome required of individual pupils as a result of the same activity can be more or less demanding depending on the teacher's assessment of potential attainment.

There is some evidence (Doyle and Carter 1984, Doyle *et al.* 1985) that complex, higher order tasks and activities are relatively rare in classrooms. Routinized activities or those where pupils are very familiar with the processes involved are preferred. The reason for this, it is suggested, is teachers' desire to maintain on-task activity flow, ensure a high level of product and sustain order. Challenging tasks present risks for learners (and for teachers). Where pupils hesitate, teachers often respond by reducing the risk and the level of challenge which may lead to underachievement. Work in many classes is not differentiated to any extent, particularly where the class is streamed or set.

In contrast, planning for lower attaining pupils with special educational needs may be more evident. Statemented pupils may have the support of a teacher in class; others will be known to the learning support team. In either case these pupils will probably have carefully planned differentiated programmes. Differentiation for those who are not designated with special needs is more likely to be determined by management priorities than by learning needs.

### Practical activity 10.7

*Aim:* To consider strategies for achieving differentiation with whole-class teaching of mixed ability classes.

*Method:* Select a topic you are going to teach and consider how you might plan your teaching and the pupils' learning to achieve appropriate differentiation. Think about the strategies you might use. What use will you make of differentiation by task and by outcome? For whole-class exposition select and practise strategies that will help you to differentiate in the interactive phases. How will you plan to support different learners' needs with resources, planned intervention, one-to-one or small group teaching?

Put your plans into action and consider how successful your strategies were in supporting learning.

*Follow-up:* Decide which strategies you want or need to develop by practice. Discuss your experience with a mentor or colleague. Plan some action research to develop your understanding and skills.

If we plan to progress learning by differentiating the learning experiences of pupils it is necessary first to be aware of where they are. The next section, 2.3, considers this aspect of planning. Section 3.3 considers in more detail the selection of activities and tasks and looks at how to provide cognitive challenge.

## 2.3 Assumptions

One of the major challenges in progressing learning is to allow for the prior knowledge, understanding, skills, interests and experiences of pupils. Whenever we plan to teach we must make a number of assumptions about what pupils know, understand and can do. The effectiveness of the lesson depends to a large extent on the accuracy of our estimates.

At this point you may want to refer back to Chapter 7, Section 2.2 to clarify your thinking about knowledge, concepts, skills and attitudes.

The assumptions to be made are of different kinds. It is useful to ask:

- What do they already know about the subject matter?
- What grasp do they have of the concepts underlying the planned learning?
- What practical skills do they have?
- What learning skills do they have?
- What social skills do they have?
- What experiences have they had that might be drawn on for the intended learning?
- What is their current attitude to the subject?

This information is most likely to be gathered over time from experience of working with a class. In your planning you will, of necessity, be making generalized assumptions about the whole class or groups within it. You may find it more practical to look at the tasks and activities you are considering in the light of your assumptions, rather than to work from assumptions to activities. It is always possible to adjust your thinking or to make provision for the required learning in your plans. Resources and activities call for particular skills from pupils if they are to be used successfully to develop learning. For example, pupils need to learn how to listen actively to explanations, to look carefully at objects, to extract information from books, television and other sources, to set up experiments, to use the library, to discuss in groups, to use computers for different purposes etc. so that they can 'make knowledge their own' and develop strategies for learning. We discuss the development of these cross-curricular process skills in Chapter 13.

The analytic power of the distinction between skills, attitudes, knowledge and concepts is very useful in gauging what it is that we are actually asking learners to do when we present them with new challenges. Practical Activity 10.8 (overleaf) should help you to check the assumptions you are making about prior learning in the lessons you are planning.

## 2.4 Progression

A major aim for teachers is to encourage and support the learning of individual pupils. Given a whole class and the complexity of the learning process it is unrealistic to expect to be able to keep individual progress constantly under review. Periodic assessments, marking of written work, checking that tasks and activities have been undertaken, all form part of a record of progress. In reviewing lessons teachers are more likely to have a sense of the way the class or groups within it are progressing then to recall any specific progress made by individuals. Nevertheless it can be valuable from time to time to plan to monitor individuals' learning through a unit of work. Observation of the insights, problems, mistakes, misunderstandings, misconceptions of individual pupils can inform understanding of the way the whole class is learning. Although learning is individual, learners go through many similar processes in developing understanding. Knowing more about this can help to plan progression for larger groups.

## Practical activity 10.8

*Aim:* To consider the prior knowledge, concepts, skills and attitudes assumed in a proposed lesson sequence and to identify learning that will need to be introduced or reinforced.

*Method:* Use the grid provided to help you identify the prior knowledge, concepts, skills and attitudes you assume your pupils will have as they approach the lessons you are planning. Fill in the proposed content and activities session-by-session, so that you can identify what is required of the learners.

| Content/activity | Prior knowledge assumed | Prior concepts assumed | Skills assumed | Attitudes assumed |
|---|---|---|---|---|
| Session 1 | | | | |
| Session 2 | | | | |
| Session 3 | | | | |
| Session 4, etc. | | | | |

*Follow-up:* How will you set about checking your assumptions and finding out what they know etc? Can you do this before you teach or will you have to build in a way of checking at the beginning of the sequence? Will you need to differentiate learning for individuals or groups?

If you find during the lesson that you may have overestimated what your pupils know, understand or are able to do, can still you use the proposed activities to teach what is required? How will you need to adjust your plans?

## Practical activity 10.9

*Aim:* To monitor the learning of individual pupils.

*Method:* Make an audio recording of a lesson. Put a small recorder in your pocket and clip a remote microphone to your collar. This will pick up your interactions when working with individual pupils or groups who are beside you. During the lesson try to be aware of the cues or signals from pupils that indicate they are learning something or having problems. Try to remember learning-related episodes; if possible make brief notes as soon as possible after your observation.

Listen to the tape. Identify questions or comments that indicate when pupils have learned or understood, and when they have failed to 'make sense' or have misunderstood.

Can you see any pattern in the responses? Are the mistakes, misunderstandings similar to any you have seen before? Can you suggest any origin for the misunderstandings, e.g. deficiencies for that learner in your explanations; misapplication of 'common sense'; confusion by other learners; careless observation/reasoning etc? Can you suggest what helped some learners to succeed, e.g. your explanation; a well-matched activity; your questioning; talk with other learners etc?

*Follow-up:* What implications can you see in your findings for when you next teach this topic or this class?

This activity has involved you in formative assessment of pupils' learning – an essential part of planning for progression. You will find more on this important topic in Chapter 15.

## 3 | LESSON PREPARATION AND PLANNING

### 3.1 The logic of lesson planning

The whole of this chapter (in conjunction with other chapters in Part 2 of this book) is about preparing to teach and becoming a reflective teacher. The many factors involved may seem daunting and research constantly throws up new insights. Nevertheless, teaching and learning remains a fascinating mystery which resists tidy categorization. In this section we suggest you get a sense of one way of planning a whole lesson. Subsequent sections look in more detail at different parts of planning and propose alternative approaches.

One approach to planning a learning session is to consider a number of questions:

#### Context
1. What are the present capabilities and knowledge of the children?
2. Where and when will the lesson take place? How (if at all) will this affect it?

#### Objectives
3. What are the specific objectives, in terms of learning elements: (skills, attitudes, concepts and knowledge) and learning domains (intellectual, social, moral, physical-motor and aesthetic)?

### Action

4. What learning opportunities will be provided for the selected objectives to be developed?
5. What organizational strategies will be required in terms of people, time, space and resources?
6. How will the session start, develop and end?
7. What will the teacher be doing at each of these stages and what range of things will the children be doing?

### Assessment of learning

8. How will the progress of the pupils be monitored, assessed and recorded?
9. How will such information be analysed and used?

### Evaluation of teaching

10. How will the quality of the session be evaluated?
11. How will such information be analysed and used?

### Practical activity 10.10

*Aim:* To manage a learning session, through consideration of context, objectives, action, assessment of learning and evaluation of teaching.

*Method:*

1. Prepare responses to the questions listed in connection with the three sections below. In this way you should be able to produce an outline sketch of what will happen during the session.

   CONTEXT . . . .

   OBJECTIVES . . . .

   ACTION . . . .

2. Teach the session. Keep some notes or some examples of pupils' work to refer to later.

3. Now use your evidence and your judgement to assess the pupils' learning and to evaluate the quality of your teaching. Refer back to the objectives you set.

   ASSESSMENT OF LEARNING . . . .

   EVALUATION OF TEACHING . . . .

*Follow-up:* How effective was your planning? Did you need to/want to depart from your plan? Was it easy to judge what your pupils were learning? How would you evaluate your own planning?

## 3.2 Aims and objectives

The previous activity involved you in using one approach to lesson planning using a sequence of logical steps. In this section we look more closely at what is traditionally assumed to be Step One – specifying aims and objectives.

*Learning objectives* are statements of what you want pupils to learn. For example, in schemes of work for a Year or Key Stage and in units of work that extend over several weeks, long-term learning objectives will already be decided. Within this broader context the short-term learning objectives for a lesson sequence or single lesson should be more precise and focused. With clear learning objectives, it is argued, you are able to make appropriate decisions about how you will plan to teach and for pupils to learn. The selection of *learning activities* – what you will do, what pupils will do – should relate directly to your objectives. Well-defined objectives will also help you to make decisions about *learning outcomes* – what you expect pupils to be able to do which will give evidence of their learning. If challenged, you should be able to justify what is happening in your lesson in terms of your objectives; you will assess pupil learning and evaluate your teaching with reference to your objectives.

It can be useful to give some thought to how you express learning objectives. One frequently-used formulation uses the opening phrase: *By the end of this lesson pupils will be able to . . .* which should push you to be precise. The things pupils 'will be able to do' should be observable so it is useful to select active verbs such as *list, describe, compare, identify, explain, solve, apply, discuss, evaluate, demonstrate the ability to, demonstrate an understanding of. . . .* Alternatively objectives can be expressed more developmentally – bearing in mind that you are aiming at moving learners forward. The opening *By the end of the lesson pupils will* can be followed by, for example: *be aware of, have had practice in, been introduced to, have considered, developed the ability to, gained increased insight into, improved performance in, have considered, have an understanding of, begun to analyse, identified.*

A lesson usually has more than one objective. They can be cross-curricular as well as for your subject. As well as general objectives for the class you may want or need to define objectives for particular groups or individuals. Objectives can also relate to your intentions in connection with pupils' attitudes and behaviour; or to your own performance, e.g. *to investigate the effects of making objectives explicit for pupils; to try out a new way of explaining; to consider question and answer sections of the lesson.*

The whole process as described is beguilingly logical. And indeed it can be valuable, especially for beginning teachers, to think clearly about objectives in this way. However, as Calderhead (1984) makes clear, the realities of planning by experienced teachers are more intuitive than the structured approach outlined above. Studies of teacher planning suggest that it is not a neat linear process and that the definition of aims and objectives is not a first step. In a study of the long-term planning of secondary teachers of English, science and geography, Taylor (1970) found that contextual factors such as available materials, resources and pupils' interests were considered before aims and purposes. In this and other research (Zahorik 1975) teachers appear to be concerned with decisions about subject content and learning activities well before learning objectives *per se*. In connection with this, the 'integrated ends-means' model (Eisner 1967) which views objectives as being implicit in activities may be applicable.

These are early studies in the area and it is likely that the introduction of the National Curriculum and OFSTED inspections has formalized the ways in which teachers' planning is made explicit. However, it remains likely that experienced teachers have an implicit sense of objectives for teaching and learning which they do not usually articulate on paper but which informs their actions and decisions. A 1993 study of twelve secondary and four primary teachers – all identified by pupils as 'good' – found that the teachers assessed the success of their teaching in terms of whether or not pupils were working appropriately (i.e. in a 'normally desirable state' for each stage of a particular type of lesson). Rarely was success claimed because formal learning objectives had been attained, though it was associated with various forms of 'progress': pupils' confidence, attitudes, understanding or skills; completion of artefacts, coverage of work (Brown and McIntyre 1993).

Overall, it seems clear that the demanding complexity of classroom practice is overlaid on the precision of formal 'learning objectives'. However, as experience is gathered, a teacher who has thought clearly about objectives is likely to be better equipped to analyse and respond to that complexity.

## 3.3  Activities, tasks and cognitive challenge

The choices you make of learning activities and tasks arise from your beliefs about learning, your assessment of your pupils, your appraisal of the setting, the time available, the approach you decide to take, your confidence in your own management skills. A mark of good teaching is the ability to transform what has to be learned into manageable tasks or problems, matched in size and complexity to learners so that they are stimulated, able to cope and hence learn (Nisbet and Shucksmith 1986, Entwistle 1985). This is not as easy to do as it is to say and reflective teachers will be alert and sensitive to the responses learners make to activities and tasks as they encounter them.

The 'learning pyramid' (see Figure 10.1) indicates the average retention rates arising from different forms of teaching/learning. It seems to support the points made elsewhere in this book about the value of activity in learning. This is not to suggest that there is no place for straightforward transmission via the teacher or other sources. However, you might like to consider how the retention rates for the top four categories might be increased by strategies to make them more active or interactive by creative use of the chalkboard, overhead transparency projection with overlays and windows, question and answer, frameworks to support listening and looking, or 'buzz groups' (see Chapter 13 for more on this).

Central to the idea of cognitive challenge is the proposition that there are different ways (or levels) of thinking. Bloom's Taxonomy of Educational Objectives (1956) identified six different kinds of thought processes: knowledge; comprehension; application; analysis; synthesis; evaluation. The taxonomy implies a hierarchy and much of the work derived from Bloom is concerned with developing 'higher order' thinking in pupils through activity or teacher questioning. Alternatively Bloom's classifications (or variations on them) have been used to analyse the range and variety of activity provided in classrooms.

Interesting work analysing activities and tasks on the basis of the level and variety of challenge to thinking/concept development has been undertaken in primary and secondary schools. We want to refer here to two studies.

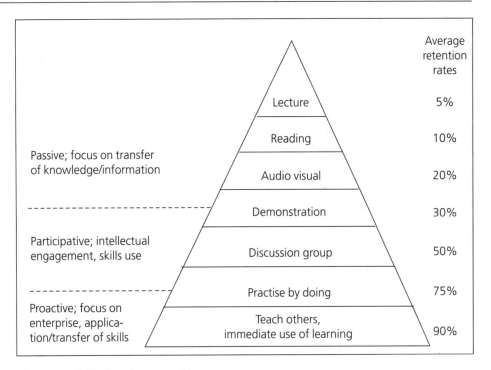

**Figure 10.1** *The learning pyramid*

In a study conducted in infant schools (Bennett *et al.* 1984), the researchers distinguished between five types of task demands:

- *Incremental:* which introduces new ideas, concepts, procedures and skills which are acquired during a task.
- *Restructuring:* which requires children to invent or discover for themselves, so that existing skills, knowledge and concepts are advanced.
- *Enrichment:* though which, by using familiar ideas, concepts, procedures, knowledge and skills on new problems, learning is applied.
- *Practice:* which reinforces ideas, concepts, procedures, knowledge and skills which are assumed to be already known.
- *Revision:* which reactivates known skills, concepts, knowledge, etc., which may not have been used for some time.

The study found that 60 per cent of tasks set in language and maths were intended as short-term practice, 25 per cent were 'incremental', 6 per cent were enrichment, 6 per cent were intended as long-term revision and only 1 per cent were intended as 'restructuring'.

The very high figure of tasks set for practice needs to be considered carefully. What were these children learning, cognitively or affectively? Practice tasks may be useful in confirming knowledge or skills, but one would have to consider at what point such tasks might cease to increase confidence and cause frustration. Interestingly, the percentage of practice tasks was even higher when examined in terms of how the tasks were perceived and performed by the children. This was particularly so for high-attaining children, who were often set tasks intended as incremental or enrichment, but which, in fact, involved yet more practice. Three reasons were suggested for this: that the children were already familiar with the knowledge or skills demanded by the tasks, that tasks were not well planned to meet the teacher's aims, and that tasks were not clearly explained with the result that children misunderstood them.

The secondary study (Kerry 1984) was undertaken in five comprehensive schools and focused on first-year mixed ability classes (Year 7). As indicated in Figure 10.2, tasks were designated 'low-level' or 'high-level' tasks for cognitive demand.

| Low-level tasks | High-level tasks |
| --- | --- |
| Disciplinary – writing rules etc. as a punishment | Imaginative tasks – includes writing poems, stories |
| Adminstrative – moving furniture, clearing up, collecting equipment | Collecting evidence, problem-solving, deducing, reasoning, such as devising questions to be answered and finding answers |
| Copying, drawing, colouring in | |
| Copying from the board | Application tasks – using knowledge gained in a new situation |
| Reading aloud around the class, singing together, repeating phrases from a tape recorder | Analysis tasks – find out why, differentiate facts from hypotheses, find patterns, clarify relationships |
| Silent reading; listening; watching – passive audience | Synthesis tasks – reorganizing ideas in a new statement, developing plans to test ideas, discovering relationships, proposing changes or improvements |
| Memorizing – learning dates/vocabulary | |
| Revising/revision test | Evaluation tasks – appraise, assess, criticize against justified criteria |
| Making simple observations of results of a demonstrated experiment/ Replicating a demonstration | |
| Simple cloze comprehension or note-taking – data supplied in textbook, worksheet or by teacher | |
| Reinforcing practice of a skill already learned | |
| Looking up simple factual information (Applying or using this information or a more complex information-finding task was placed in a higher category) | |

**Figure 10.2** *The cognitive demand of common secondary school tasks*

The study found that on average there were 4.3 tasks per eighty-minute double lesson. Tasks were categorized as set by teachers rather than by pupils' response; but pupils' written responses were collected to see if ambiguous tasks were interpreted as categorized. Analysis of tasks set produced the following results:

- 85 per cent of tasks were low-level and 15 per cent high-level.
- Of the low-level tasks, the three most frequent were:
  - Reinforcing/Practising
  - Copying (16 per cent)
  - Drawing and Colouring (14 per cent)
- Of the high-level tasks the most frequent were:
  - Imaginative (4 per cent)
  - Collecting evidence, problem solving, etc. (3 per cent)
  - Application (3 per cent)
  - Evaluation (3 per cent)

In these mixed ability classes, tasks were aimed at classes not pupils; less than a handful (0.3 per cent) were set specifically to provide differentiated work for the most or least able pupils.

Of the subjects, integrated studies, English and science featured most high-level tasks; RE and geography least high-level tasks.

The findings are strikingly similar to those from the infant school study. In considering the description and categorization of tasks from each study, reflective teachers might argue that tasks of various types are probably necessary if learning is to develop positively and surely. As we have seen, increases in learning do not necessarily occur in a smooth, ever-upward fashion. If learning occurs from somewhat unpredictable developments of insight and understanding then occasional plateaus may also be experienced and needed. A reflective teacher needs to monitor the match of task to pupil closely to try to ensure the best balance between boredom with too easy tasks, frustration with tasks that are too hard, comfort from consolidation tasks and excitement from a task that is challenging but not too daunting. Practical Activity 10.11 may be useful here.

The concern raised by both these studies is the comparative rarity with which pupils met with stimulating and demanding tasks, and the lack of differentiation. A positive move would be to analyse tasks you ask pupils to undertake in terms of the level of demand they make, their appropriateness and worthwhileness, and their potential for 'match' and differentiation.

## 3.4 Resources

Different resources have particular implications for the curriculum-as-experienced and for the skills, attitudes, knowledge and concepts which are likely to be developed through them.

However, all activities require resourcing in some way: text-books, worksheets, overhead projector transparencies, advance work on the board, etc. Time spent thinking about resources and how they will be used is well spent as part of your preparation to teach. Checklist 10.1 and Practical Activity 10.12 may help in this.

## Practical activity 10.11

*Aim:* To examine tasks in terms of their learning demands.

Method: Analyse the demands of tasks you have observed or those you plan to use by using the grid below:

|        | Incremental | Restructuring | Enrichment | Practice | Revision |
|--------|-------------|---------------|------------|----------|----------|
| Task 1 |             |               |            |          |          |
| Task 2 |             |               |            |          |          |
| Task 3 |             |               |            |          |          |
| Task 4 |             |               |            |          |          |
| Task 5 |             |               |            |          |          |
| Task 6 |             |               |            |          |          |

For activities you have used or observed, try talking to pupils to get their view of what they thought they were doing.

If you prefer, you could construct a grid using the categories from the Kerry study (see Figure 10.2).

*Follow-up:* From this evidence, what can you deduce about the balance of activities in the classroom? Can you identify the reasons for it? What can you do about it? What can you say about the range and variety of learning activities provided for pupils?

## Checklist 10.1

*Aim:* To consider resource requirements for a lesson.

Are the resources I plan to use:
• appropriate for the task?
• appropriate for the learners?
• of good quality?
• readable?
• in good condition?
• available at the time I want them?
• available in sufficient quantity?

If equipment is involved:
• is it available when I want it?
• do I know how it works?
• what happens if something goes wrong?

*Practical activity 10.12*

*Aim:* To consider the resource implications of a sequence of lessons.

*Method:* Review your outline plans for teaching a topic area in your subject. Make a list, such as the one below, of the resources which are required, and of any preparation or booking which is needed.

| Curriculum topics and activities to be covered | Resources available within school | Resources to be made and prepared | Resources to be borrowed or collected |
|---|---|---|---|
| | | | |

*Follow-up:* Use your list to check off the necessary jobs as you do them.

## 3.5 Assessment

We focus on assessment in Chapter 15. However, as you deal with lesson preparation and planning you will need to consider what role assessment may play.

In planning for learning at the level of the lesson, the idea of 'feedback and feed forward' is a useful one. Informal monitoring and formative assessment procedures will help you to consider what may, or may not, have been learned, understood or applied in one lesson that will 'feed forward' into the next. To gain this information, you can use your observations of what happens in a lesson as well as the evidence of any learning outcomes you have planned (see Chapter 15, Section 4 for a full range of ideas on gathering evidence for the assessment of learning). For instance, if the learning outcomes are written assignments you can gain useful information as you assess and mark pupils' work. In the press of teaching, especially as a beginner, it is hard to get more than a generalized impression of pupils' learning. As you feel more in control, it may be possible to make your observations of individual pupils or groups more focused and specific. Talking to pupils about their learning can also provide insights, especially where you have shared learning objectives and processes with them. One insight into pupil learning is suggested in Practical Activity 10.13

> ### *Practical activity 10.13*
>
> To investigate the understanding pupils have of lesson content and of their progress against learning objectives
>
> *Method:* We suggest that the technique of concept mapping is ideal for gathering data on this issue. Focus pupils' thoughts on the topic on which you have worked with your class or group and follow the advice on concept mapping in Chapter 15, Section 4.6. When the pupils have identified the content, pay particular attention to the connections which they draw, or fail to draw, between the parts. Discuss this with them to explore fully their understanding and to assess what they have learned.
>
> *Follow-up:* To what extent do you feel pupils are meeting your learning objectives for them? How will this assessment affect your next-step planning?

It is also worth considering how you might plan for pupil self-assessment (see Chapter 15, Section 2.3). This not only saves you time, it can also provide you with information and pupils with useful insights, especially where appropriate criteria have been discussed. An extension of self-assessment is to plan for pupils to negotiate assessments and criteria. These can be expressed in the form of an 'action plan' or learning contract between pupil and teacher (see Chapter 15, Section 4.7).

At the end of a topic or learning sequence you may want to plan for summative assessment. Conventionally this will be a written test or practical; but it is possible to devise other ways in which pupils can demonstrate their mastery of content, skill development and ability to apply or transfer their learning in new situations.

## 3.6  Structure

Thinking through how you are going to structure a lesson or lesson sequence is one of the most important aspects of your planning. It involves thinking about organizational issues, such as the grouping of pupils, use of time, space and resources (see Chapter 11) and class management issues, such as the pace, flow and sequencing of different phases of each lesson (see Chapter 12). All of these issues have to be considered with the specific learners in mind and in relation to the range of teaching strategies with which you feel comfortable or wish to deploy.

One useful way of thinking about this is to use the framework developed from the Technical and Vocational Education Initiative (TVEI) (Barnes *et al.* 1987). This identifies three styles of teaching: 'closed', 'framed' and 'negotiated', and these are broadly characterized as having the following features:

- *Closed:* Content controlled by the teacher; pupils accept teachers' routines; typical methods – teacher exposition, worksheets (closed), note-giving, copying, individual exercises, routine practical work; teacher evaluates.
- *Framed:* Content defined by the teacher, criteria for activities and tasks made explicit for pupils; pupils operate teacher's structural framework, join in teacher's thinking, make hypotheses, set up tests; typical methods – teacher exposition with

discussion eliciting pupil ideas; individual or group problem-solving; lists of tasks given, discussion of outcomes; teacher adjudicates.

- *Negotiated:* Content discussed, joint decisions; pupils involved in discussion of goals and methods, share responsibility for frame and criteria; typical methods – group and class discussion and decision-making, pupils plan and carry out work, make presentations, evaluate outcomes.

The TVEI project was set up to increase pupils' involvement in their own learning, to develop pupil initiative and autonomy through increased participation.

### Practical activity 10.14

*Aim:* To consider the strengths and weaknesses of closed, framed and negotiated teaching styles.

*Method:* We suggest you use a technique known as a SWOT analysis. This stands for Strengths, Weaknesses, Opportunities and Threats. You will need to look at the three styles and identify first what you see as the strengths and weaknesses of each. Then consider the styles with respect to the opportunities each offers you and the threats to you each might contain.

You might want to consider these from the point of view of the opportunities for teaching and learning, the organizational and management skills required by teacher.

| Style | Strengths | Weaknesses | Opportunities | Threats |
|---|---|---|---|---|
| Closed | | | | |
| Framed | | | | |
| Negotiated | | | | |

*Follow-up:* Use your analysis to help you think about style and structure in relation to fitness for purpose and contextual constraints of time, space, available resources etc.

There is evidence that teachers can influence pupils' learning behaviour by making structuring comments, what Gage and Berliner (1975) call *advance organizers*. This simply means telling them in advance what is going to happen, what is expected of them. To explain also why you are doing things, where it is leading, is also a productive strategy. During the course of the lesson 'verbal signposting' can maintain a sense of direction and summarizing at significant points and certainly at the end of lessons is helpful for learners who rarely do this for themselves.

*Practical activity 10.15*

*Aim:* To consider structuring of learning.

*Method:* For a topic you plan to teach think about how the learning might be sequenced. What steps or 'chunks' might you plan for? Identify possible tasks and activities; experiment with their scheduling, arrive at your first draft plan.

Think about the ways in which your selection should provide for progression and differentiation.

Think about time. How many lessons will you need? Have you got enough? How does the programme divide into lessons? Will you need to keep pupils together or is it possible to plan for fast and slow tracks?

Identify the elements of your proposed curriculum which are likely to be seen as highlights by the pupils. Do they come at appropriate places?

Examine the structure you are developing and identify where there will be teacher telling, where pupil activity? What does the balance look like? Where are the opportunities for interaction?

Revise your programme as necessary.

*Follow-up:* Keep structure under review as you plan. Make it a focus of your evaluation and adjust your planning accordingly.

Another aspect of structuring lessons is concerned with the stimulus and variety of tasks over time. Kounin (1970, **Primary Reading 10.6**) drew attention to this when arguing that teachers should avoid 'satiation' (i.e. letting the pupils get bored by monotonous activities) through an over-reliance on schemes, worksheets, or through the setting of repetitive individualized activities. Resources in the form of published or departmentally created schemes can offer a secure basis for implementing the curriculum in which progression has been systematically considered. However, over-reliance on such materials can have a narrowing effect on the curriculum and lead to boredom. Considerable amounts of pupil activity will inevitably be directed through print, accompanied by a requirement for written recording and a remorseless, hierarchical structure is often in-built. All these aspects impose a relatively depersonalized and technical control on children. Indeed, it has been argued that the preponderance of such routine activities in some schools may have consequences in terms of the reproduction of a docile workforce, rather than develop children whose  creativity and critical thinking have been stirred (Bowles and Gintis 1976, **Primary Reading 13.1**, Apple 1982).

*Practical activity 10.16*

*Aim:* To evaluate the stimulus and variety of tasks and activities.

*Method:* This evaluation could be carried out by an observer who focuses on a particular pupil for a day. All activities should be recorded in terms of their motivational appeal, explicit purpose and in terms of what the pupil was required to do (write, read, talk, draw, listen, watch, move, sing, etc.).

As alternatives, you could undertake the observation in your own subject over a longer period and compare findings with a colleague who has observed another subject area. Or you could involve pupils in recording what they do in lessons over a given period. They might do this by filling in a *pro forma* you have designed, or by keeping a log.

Some questions which might be asked could include:

a) Is there a planned highlight for any lessons?

b) How much writing are pupils required to do?

c) How much reading is required?

d) How much work is based on schemes or worksheets?

e) What is the balance between active and passive tasks?

f) What is the balance between collaborative and individual activity?

*Follow-up:* Consider the findings from this exercise and try to deduce the reasons for any patterns you identify. How do you evaluate the results? Discuss your thoughts with your mentor and other students. If you judge it appropriate, what could be done in your subject to increase the stimulus and variety of tasks?

## 3.7 Lesson planning by 'imagining'

Committing a lesson plan to paper is the last step in Jackson's (1968) 'pre-active' phase. Starting the lesson moves you into the 'interactive' stage where you are 'on your own' and, it seems, anything can happen. Only a small part of all the thinking you have done as part of your preparation will appear in your lesson plan, the tip of the iceberg. However, if you have done your preparation well, what is underneath will keep you afloat and on course in the uncharted waters of interaction, helping you to make good decisions in the press of activity. Remember too, the significance of the routines, norms and relationship you will establish with your classes and can then assume will underpin your classroom decisions (see also Chapters 11 and 12).

We need though, to be able to complement the logical form of planning (suggested in Section 3.1) with an approach which highlights the reality of the expected action of both teacher and pupils. In Practical Activity 10.17, we suggest a way of 'imagining' the lesson in your head; something which many experienced teachers do. If you can 'rehearse' the lesson in advance; 'run the film' in your imagination, it can help to anticipate possible problems and hitches. For instance: How long will it take them to do that? What if some of them haven't got pencils, textbooks? Is that long enough for them to get something worthwhile done? Should I give a deadline here? Can I get what I plan to say in the time allowed? What if I run over or they get interested and ask a lot of questions? What if they finish early? As you gather experience it will feed into your planning and your decision-making.

## *Practical activity 10.17*

*Aim:* To consider an approach to lesson planning.

*Method:* Use the *pro forma* outline given here as the basis for planning a lesson. Use your own judgement about how much detail to include but try to keep to one side of A4.

---

Class:                          Date:                          Time:

Subject:

Objectives:

Activities:

| Phase of lesson | What will I be doing? | What will they be doing? | Resource implications |
|---|---|---|---|
|  |  |  |  |

Particular things to remember (safety?)

---

*Follow-up:* Rehearse the lesson in your imagination. You might want to rehearse aloud what you will say at the beginning of the session, any 'advanced organizers' you will use, your first bit of 'telling', some questions. Trying out a 'script' (in front of a friend or a mirror or into a tape recorder) can be very effective.

## 3.8 Evaluation

The evaluation section of your planning is a reflection-on-action activity. This should inform future planning and general development as a teacher. At its simplest it is probably enough to ask a few questions:

- What went well?
- Can I say why it went well?
- What didn't go so well?
- Can I say why it didn't go so well?

An extension of this might ask:

- On what aspect of my teaching should I now focus for development?
- How might I work at this? (the index of this book will lead to ideas)

A general issue for evaluation concerns pupils' response to the learning activities and tasks. On this, the concept of 'match', between teaching and learners' needs, is again useful. A 'mis-match' could occur with regard to: the initial perceptions and intentions of the teacher and the pupil; the pupil's existing knowledge, concepts, skills and attitudes; the process by which the task is tackled; or the product, or final outcome, of the task. For example, at the first stage of a lesson a teacher could set a task for a particular purpose, but, if it were not explained adequately then pupils might misunderstand. Any task might be done 'wrongly', or it may be done 'blindly' without seeing its underlying purpose. At a second stage, the task may be found to be too hard for a pupil because it requires certain knowledge or skill which the learner does not have. At a third stage the suggested processes may be inappropriate. A task may thus be set with an instruction to use certain apparatus, or to present the outcome in a certain way, but this may actually confuse the pupil, or the style of presenting the outcome may assume some skill which the pupil has not yet acquired.

At a fourth and almost final stage, teachers often 'mark' the end-products of pupils' learning. However, a high percentage of 'errors' cannot necessarily be assumed to relate to 'bad' work or 'poor' learning. Indeed, the 'errors' can be very important clues regarding the learning that has taken place. In this respect they can be seen as 'miscues' which indicate where misunderstandings may have occurred. On the other hand, miscues can also be misinterpreted themselves. For instance, an absence of miscues could be taken to indicate a good cognitive match, but it could also hide the fact that the task was too easy and that little cognitive learning had taken place. This could have resulted in two contrasting affective outcomes: either that the pupils had gained in confidence in their abilities, or that they had become bored. Conversely, the existence of many miscues might be interpreted as a poor match where the task had been too hard and thereby frustrating. However, a large number of miscues could also indicate that the task had been too easy, uninteresting or unchallenging, and that the pupils either had not followed the instructions or had not wanted to be bothered with it.

As can be seen from the example above, the productive evaluation of learning processes requires observation, analysis and judgement. Nevertheless it is a powerful way through which a reflective teacher can gain a better understanding of the learning experiences of pupils.

## CONCLUSION

In this chapter we have considered various factors and processes that are part of preparation and planning to teach. We end with a reminder of research that questions the rationality of the planning process (Calderhead 1984, **Primary Reading 8.6**, Brown and McIntyre 1993). This suggests that the lesson planning of experienced teachers is a pragmatic, problem-solving process which draws significantly on professional 'craft knowledge'. When faced with a range of complex factors – pupils, resources, curriculum, timetable, expectations, personal experience, etc. – teachers have to solve the problem of how to structure the time and experience of pupils in the classroom. The tension between the ideal and the pragmatic must be faced, and the outcome reflects a professional judgement of how far it is possible to achieve educational goals, given particular circumstances.

This view of planning as problem-solving and an exercise in the art of the possible is one experienced teachers will recognize. Novice teachers too may well find that their planning gradually assumes these characteristics. However, it would be rash to rush into this mode. Both logical planning (Section 3.1) and the process of 'imagining' each phase of the lesson (Section 3.7) are forms of thoughtful preparation which provide a teacher with structure and security. The resulting confidence can then be used to be responsive to pupils as each lesson unfolds. Good planning underpins flexibility.

## Notes for further reading

For two important recent analyses of classroom teaching and learning, see:

Brown, S. and McIntyre, D. (1993)
*Making Sense of Teaching,*
Buckingham: Open University Press.

Cooper, P. and McIntyre, D. (1996)
*Effective Teaching and Learning: Teachers' and Students' Perspectives,*
Buckingham: Open University Press.

For a personal, idiosyncratic account which stimulates reflection and discussion try:

Sotto, E. (1994)
*When Teaching Becomes Learning,*
London: Cassell.

On the critical role of subject content knowledge for teaching, see:

Shulman, L. S. (1986)
'Those who understand: knowledge growth in teaching',
*Educational Researcher,* Vol. 15, No. 2, pp. 1–16          **Primary Reading 7.13**

Goodson, I. and Marsh, C. J. (1996)
*Studying School Subjects: A Guide,*
London: Falmer Press.

Interesting work on pupil motivation includes:

Dweck, C. S. (1986)
'Motivational processes affecting learning',
*American Psychologist,* October, pp. 1040–6          **Primary Reading 6.7**

Spaulding, C. L. (1992)
*Motivation in the Classroom,*
New York: McGraw Hill.

Hendry, L., Sanders, D. and Glendinning, A. (1996)
*New Perspectives on Disaffection,*
London: Cassell.

Nixon, J., Martin, J., McKeown, P. and Ranson, S. (1996)
*Encouraging Learning: Towards a Theory of the Learning School,*
Buckingham: Open University Press.

On differentiation see:

Hart, S. (1996) (ed.)
*Differentiation and the Secondary Curriculum,*
London: Routledge.

Dickinson, C. and Wright, J. (1993)
*Differentiation: A Practical Handbook of Classroom Strategies,*
Coventry: National Council for Educational Technology.

Stradling, R, Saunders, L. and Weston, P. (1991)
*Differentiation in Action: A Whole School Approach for Raising Standards,*
London: HMSO.

Peter, M. (ed.) (1992)
*Differentiation: Ways Forward,*
Stafford: National Association for Special Educational Needs.
(reprinted from a special issue of *British Journal of Special Education,* 1992, Vol. 19, No. 1)

The classic analysis of teaching and learning objectives remains interesting to consult:

Bloom, B. S. (ed.) (1956)
*Taxonomy of Educational Objectives: Handbook 1, Cognitive Domain,*
London: Longman.

Bloom, B. S., Krathwohl, D. and Masica, B. (eds) (1964)
*Taxonomy of Educational Objectives: Handbook 1, Affective Domain,*
London: Longman.

For accounts of how experienced teachers draw on professional craft knowledge to prepare and develop lesson plans, see Brown and McIntyre, above, and:

Connelly, F. M. and Clandinin, D. J. (1988)
*Teachers as Curriculum Planners,*
New York: Teachers College Press.

Calderhead, J. (1984)
*Teachers' Classroom Decision Making,*
London: Holt.

Calderhead, J. (ed.) (1987)
*Exploring Teachers' Thinking,*
London: Cassell.

For practical guidance and ideas on lesson planning, see:

John, P. D. (1993)
*Lesson Planning for Teachers,*
London: Cassell.

Pasch, M., Sparks-Langer, G., Gardner, T. G., Starko, A. J. and Moody, C. D. (1991)
*Teaching as Decision Making: Instructional Practices for the Successful Teacher,*
New York: Longman.

Primary Reading 8.6

Gibbs, G. and Habeshaw, T. (1989)
*253 Ideas for Your Teaching,*
Bristol: Technical and Educational Services Ltd.

# CHAPTER 11

# How are we organizing our classes and classrooms?

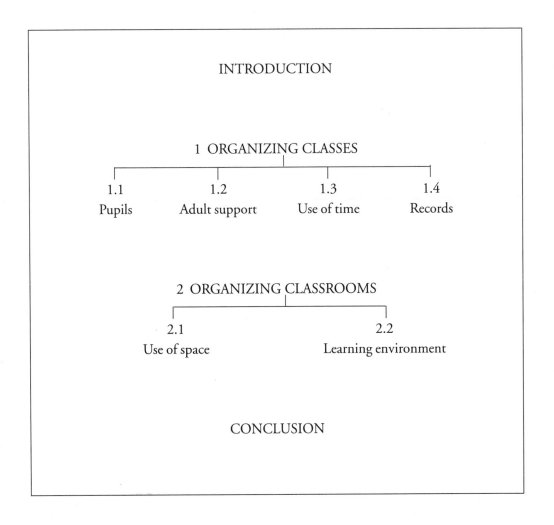

INTRODUCTION

1 ORGANIZING CLASSES

| 1.1 | 1.2 | 1.3 | 1.4 |
| Pupils | Adult support | Use of time | Records |

2 ORGANIZING CLASSROOMS

| 2.1 | 2.2 |
| Use of space | Learning environment |

CONCLUSION

## INTRODUCTION

Organization is vital in implementing our plans for learning.

By organization, we mean the way in which each class and classroom is structured in order to facilitate teaching and learning. For such teaching and learning to succeed, classroom organization must relate to values, aims and curriculum plans as a whole and also to practical circumstances.

Getting your organization right – appropriate to people, place and purpose – provides a common framework within which teachers and pupils can work. The strength of such a framework will derive from its internal consistency (the mutual reinforcement of its elements) and its legitimacy (the reciprocal acceptance of it by the teacher and the pupils).

However, organizational structure does not mean rigidity, for if the rules and routines of classwork are clear and agreed, good organization can free the teacher to teach and the learner to learn. The lack of ambiguity provides pupils with security and the possibility of ordered autonomy. The teacher should thus have more time to support learning and to teach rather than having to spend time on 'housekeeping' aspects of administration and routine class or task management (Campbell and Neill 1994).

In this chapter we identify and discuss six key factors related to the organization of classes and classrooms.

## 1     ORGANIZING CLASSES

People in a classroom need to work together in ways which are most appropriate for supporting the learning activities which have been planned. Obviously this involves pupils but, in some classes, it also involves adults such as ancillary staff and visiting specialists. However, we will begin by focusing on those who will always be present: the pupils.

## 1.1   Pupils

Perhaps the most important decision we make is how we choose to organize pupils for teaching purposes. Our choices must be made with regard to both pedagogical and practical considerations and always with the over-riding principle of fitness for purpose. Pedagogic considerations will include the general aims of the teacher as well as the particular objectives for a specific lesson or sequence of lessons (considered in more detail in Chapter 10). Practical factors affecting the decision might include the number of pupils, the size of the room and the availability of resources – these are discussed in more detail below. In planning a lesson we make decisions about *how* we think our pupils will best learn what we want to teach. Here we set out the three basic organizational choices available to us – classwork, group work and individual work – identify the main characteristics of each and discuss the idea of 'match' between organization, activity and learning.

## Classwork

This is the long-established form of organization for starting and ending a lesson, for giving out administrative instructions and introducing tasks and activities. It is also used for teaching specific concepts and knowledge, for demonstrating, and for extending and reviewing work. Whole-class activity is generally assumed to be teacher-centred but there is a continuum of teacher dominance even when the whole class is involved in the same activity. At one end of the scale is the situation where the teacher talks and the pupils listen, take notes or copy from the board. At the other however, the teacher may plan to give control of the activity to the pupils who may 'teach' by, for example, reporting what they have learned, demonstrating the result of activity, offering solutions for problem-solving, discussing alternative or conflicting ideas, asking questions. These activities can create a sense of class identity and shared endeavour. In the middle, we find the whole-class lessons and activities which to varying degrees can be defined as interactive, question and answer sessions, discussions, eliciting existing knowledge and understanding, constructing hypotheses, reviewing sequences: these are just a few possibilities. The teacher for the most part remains the focus of control, probably with the support of chalkboard, overhead projector, or other stimulus materials. These sessions can be highly interactive with a great deal of pupil participation – from time to time the teacher may 'hand over' to pupils who become actively involved.

Using whole-class organizational procedures may give the teacher a chance to instruct the class more directly and economically and to stimulate pupils' thinking by exploring ideas, asking more 'probing' questions, sharing common problems and encouraging pupils to join in trying to solve them. However, classwork can pose a severe strain on both the teacher and the listener. It is very difficult to match the instruction appropriately to each pupil's different needs, as we saw in Chapter 10, Section 2.2, when we discussed differentiation in the context of whole-class teaching. There is a tendency for teaching to be pitched at the 'middle', failing both to extend those capable of more and to meet the needs of lower attainers. Also engagement can be uneven, with some pupils 'opting out' even if they retain an apparent 'listening posture'. The ability of listeners to remain focused on one speaker is limited and affected both by the listeners' motivation and the speaker's skill. Involvement through activity or questioning can help but participation can be uneven. There is evidence of teachers addressing questions only to pupils in a V-shaped wedge in the centre of the room, or to particular groups or individuals (Wragg 1984). Some pupils are reluctant to face the risks involved in contributing to the whole class. We address some of these issues in more detail in Chapter 13.

## Individual work

Pupils spend a great deal of time working individually. They may be learning via tasks which require them to work alone, perhaps from textbooks, worksheets or other resources. They may be demonstrating the results of their learning in individual outcomes. Individual work is thought to be particularly useful for developing pupils' ability to work independently and autonomously. It is essential for most course work.

Working individually may be the dominant mode in lessons. For instance, mathematics is a subject in which pupils sometimes use individualized resource-based schemes and work at their own pace through the materials. Alternatively you may plan for pupils to work individually on specific tasks in or out of the classroom, including for homework. The amount of time spent working individually in any lesson may be a few minutes or an extended period.

The approach has its limitations. For example, a teacher who relies heavily on setting individual work in lessons may find that similar teaching points have to be explained on many separate occasions to different pupils. It is therefore particularly important to establish that pupils understand the aims and requirements of the set activity, before individual work begins. Individual work also often results in a lot of movement in the classroom, with either the teacher moving around the classroom seeing each pupil in turn, or pupils moving from their seats and queueing at the teacher's desk. This emphasis on working with each individual separately inevitably means that only a limited amount of time can be spent with any one pupil. In addition, It has been  shown that most of this time is spent in monitoring pupils' work, rather than in developing their understanding (Galton *et al.* 1980, **Primary Reading 9.2**).

When setting individual work, for example library research, which requires a degree of independence and is not based on specifically provided resources, it is important that the pupils have the necessary skills to undertake the task successfully (see Chapter 6, Section 3.6 for a discussion of key cross-curricular skills).

### Group work

This is often recommended for developing social and language skills and as a means by which pupils can support, challenge and extend their learning together, for instance, through problem- solving or work on a creative task. Group work can provide teachers with opportunities to observe pupils' learning more closely and, through questioning or providing information, to support them as they move forward to new knowledge, skills or understanding. The approach draws particularly on social constructivist psychology (see Chapter 9, Section 1.3 for the theoretical underpinning of this approach).

The form and function of groups may vary considerably from subject to subject and teacher to teacher, but three main types of groups can be identified:

- *Task groups.* The teacher decides on a group of pupils to work together on a particular task. The criteria for the composition of the group may vary (see below).
- *Teaching groups.* Groups may be used for teaching purposes, where the teacher specifically plans to instruct pupils who are at the same stage or doing the same task. This may be followed by the pupils working individually. Such a system can be an economical use of teacher instruction time and, possibly, of resources. The teaching may be directive or be based on a problem-solving activity where a task is designed to challenge pupils' learning in a particular way. In science for example, a teacher might plan an investigation to challenge commonsense ideas and introduce them to scientific concepts.
- *Collaborative groups.* This is a more developed form of group work, where there is a shared group aim, work is done together and the outcome is a combined product perhaps in the form of a model, play or problem solved. As a variant, the collaboration may lead to a number of different and differentiated outcomes from individuals or pairs. Although less teacher-centred than teaching groups, teachers may observe pupils and, as a result, plan to intervene to support learning.

A variant of this is 'reciprocal teaching' where pupils work in pairs, one taking the role of 'teacher partner', offering evaluation and feedback. It is particularly evident in subjects like PE, drama and languages which involve 'performance'. The teacher supports by intervening to develop the quality of the evaluation and feedback.

Although groups are very commonly found for task allocation and teaching purposes, collaborative group work is less common. Teachers have identified a number of problems which they associate with group work and, therefore, consider to be disadvantages. First, there is the issue of motivating the pupils and helping them to recognize that being in a group is for the purposes of learning together. Second, the monitoring of group work can pose problems. Third, the management of groups, in terms of such issues as who should be in the group, how many pupils and where they should work, may pose difficult dilemmas which have to be resolved.

Group work most frequently fails where pupils do not have the necessary skills to work together effectively. In recent years schools, prompted by initiatives like TVEI, have recognized the importance of these process skills. As we saw in Chapter 6, Section 3.6 their significance has been further endorsed by the Dearing Review's emphasis on 'key' or 'core' skills, including interpersonal skills. Many secondary schools build skill development in as a cross-curricular theme (for further detail on this see Chapter 7, Section 1.7).

In the same way that we use our professional judgement to achieve a balance between different general strategies for organizing pupils, we will look for an appropriate balance in the use of particular types of groups. Each has a different purpose and specific potential and, therefore, each has its own justifiable place in the classroom. As we plan however, we should have in mind the research finding that 'group work' is too often only individuals sitting or standing together and working individually. This may be something to look out for as you try out Practical Activity 11.1.

There is one more aspect of group work which we need to consider and that is how groups are composed. What size should groups be? Which pupils should work together?

### Teacher-selected groups, based on pupil attainment or 'ability'

In Chapter 5, Section 2.4 we discussed whole-school decisions about how pupils are organized in mixed ability classes, setting or by streaming. In organizing pupils for lessons then, we are dealing with classes which are already composed on some basis of selection. Within this context, when deciding how to group pupils, teachers are involved with many of the issues faced by the school – streams and sets are still to some extent 'mixed ability'.

Where the whole class is 'mixed ability' teachers face a number of challenges. Research on mixed ability classes in the first year of comprehensive schools (Kerry and Sands 1984) reports teachers having problems providing for fast and slow learners: work was finished quickly or not finished; boredom and frustration led to lack of motivation and sometimes disruptive behaviour. In general, this occurred with whole-class teaching where work was mainly undemanding or undifferentiated. However the research also noted the characteristics of teachers who taught effectively in mixed ability classes. They were flexible, using a variety of teaching modes in the

## Practical activity 11.1

*Aim:* To consider the balance of classwork, individual teaching and group work which a class experiences across a period of time.

*Method:* Arrange to observe one class over several lessons. Ideally you will follow the class for a day or half a day. Whatever the arrangement, try to ensure that you see a range of subjects.

Find a way of recording the 'shape' of each lesson in its use of classwork, individual work and group work. You might find it useful to note, approximately, the amount of time spent on each type of working.

As you observe, make notes on some things you find interesting. For instance, you may want to focus on: the balance of time the teacher spends between administration, management and teaching; how often an individual pupil is 'on task' during different types of activity; how effectively groups seem to be working.

Consider the data you have collected. What was the dominant way of working experienced by pupils in the class you observed over the time you were with them? How varied is the experience they get? Did the 'shape' of lessons vary? Can you suggest why this is? How did pupils respond to different ways of working? What was the teacher doing during different ways of working? What evidence have you seen of the strengths and drawbacks of classwork, individual work and group work which are identified in this chapter? How will this affect your own planning?

*Follow-up:* If possible discuss your findings with other people who have done this activity? Are your findings similar? If not why might this be? Is it to do with the pupils observed? The subjects you observed? The teachers you observed?

You might want to identify aspects of different ways of working to investigate in further observations and in your own teaching.

lesson, varying the pace and style, using a variety of resources (including audio-visual) and planning for a number of different pupil activities. Thus grouping within the class had a positive contribution to make to learning, especially where pupils were directly involved in the learning and decision-making. However, managing this successfully involved considerable preparation by the teacher (see Chapter 10, Section 3.3 for discussion of cognitive challenge) and some pressure on resources. In addition, effectiveness was also associated with a degree of informality between teachers and pupils, something which (as we indicate in Chapter 14) works only if it is based on well-established relationships and mutual understandings.

We are still left with decisions to make about whether in-class grouping (whatever the pupil mix) should be by attainment or mixed ability. Groups based on attainment levels are useful for setting up specific and well-matched tasks. They can be divisive if used as a permanent way of grouping. There is evidence that working in mixed ability groups is beneficial for lower attaining pupils (Kerry and Sands 1984, Howe 1995). Howe, however, suggests that there may be all-round gains. Her study of secondary pupils' learning concepts in physics noted that where pairs of pupils with differing conceptions worked together on computer-based tasks participants with high pre-test scores also showed gains in understanding. The restriction of groups to pairs may be significant in that working in groups makes considerable demands on pupils' management and social skills. Where attainment differs, there may be a tendency for fast learners to get impatient and take over and for the less able to be happy to let that happen.

### Teacher-selected groups, based on pupil interests

It can be productive from time to time for teachers to plan for pupils with shared interests to work together. As well as the motivational aspect, there may be gains where learners have shared understanding and experience. There are also advantages for the social cohesion of the class when pupils are of different attainment, sex, race, social class.

### Pupil-selected groups

These are popular with pupils and provide opportunities for social development. In addition pupils are frequently aware of those they work well with – not always those with whom they choose to socialize. However friendship choices can often result in a form of 'hidden streaming'. In addition, teachers need to be aware of any isolate and marginal children and alert to the possibility that friendship groups can set up divisive status hierarchies among the children, or reinforce stereotypes about gender, race or abilities.

Practical Activity 11.2 suggests a way of thinking about group type and size.

## Practical activity 11.2

*Aim:* To decide the most appropriate type and size of grouping for activities planned for your curriculum subject.

*Method:* First, list the major activities you might use in a sequence of lessons or to teach a unit of work. Then use the rest of the matrix to help you think about how you will organize your teaching. As you think about the type of grouping, justify your choice with reference to your teaching and learning aims, availability of resources, management, control etc.

| Activity | Individual work | Whole class work | Group work |
|---|---|---|---|
|  |  |  |  |
|  |  |  |  |
|  |  |  |  |
|  |  |  |  |

*Follow-up:* This sort of analysis should help in ensuring coherence between learning aims and organizational strategies. You could also use it to review and evaluate your previous practice.

## 1.2 Adult support

In studies of 'classroom management' it is suggested that the quality of classroom teaching is very greatly enhanced if all the adults in a classroom plan together so that they understand and carry out specific activities in a co-ordinated and coherent fashion (Balshaw 1991, Thomas 1992, Thomas 1989 **Primary Reading 9.7**). In secondary classrooms, subject teachers may need to work with learning support colleagues and technicians. From time to time governors or representatives from industry or the community may participate in classroom activities or an external specialist, such as an 'artist in residence', may work with the pupils as a one-off or over a specified period. All of these situations require careful organization. It is worth spending time clarifying purpose, role and responsibility with adult 'partners' and in making sure pupils understand the situation. Planning, review and feedback are also important.

### *Practical activity 11.3*

*Aim:* To prepare for having other adults working in the classroom.

*Method:* A *pro forma*, such as the one below, could help to structure a conversation with an adult who will be working with you in your classroom, though obviously it is a matter of professional judgement about how helpful it is to commit this to paper. Discussion alone should be enough with a fellow-professional such as a learning support teacher though you may want to make notes. With volunteers, occasional visitors, specialists to whom you pay fees, it can be very useful to write down what you have agreed and to provide basic information about the class and the school.

**Initial discussion**

Contribution offered:

Availability:

Any anticipated problems:

**Proposed activities**

Objectives for sessions:

Agreed role and contribution for partner:

Resources to be provided:

**Review and feedback**

*Follow-up:* Try to talk to learning support teachers, technicians, volunteers, to get their perspective on working with others in their lessons. What do they identify as factors that contribute to success? What are their main concerns? How can a partnership be made most productive for all involved, including the pupils?

## 1.3 Use of time

The way in which time is used in a classroom is very important indeed. About one-third of a secondary teacher's hours are spent on teaching the curriculum. The rest of the time in an average fifty-four-hour week is taken up by non-teaching contact with pupils, preparation, administration, professional development and other activities such as extra-curricular activities (Campbell and Neill 1994).

It follows that there is a need to maximize teaching time and try to ensure learning. A study of primary teachers (Campbell and Neill 1992), however, shows that almost 10 per cent of teaching time is lost as 'evaporated time' in the classroom management activities which are necessary to create teaching and learning opportunities. Pupils have to get books out, change, move locations, tidy up, etc. It is useful to pursue this notion of 'evaporated time' in secondary teaching and to look at the balance between time spent by pupils in organizing themselves or being organized and time spent engaged in learning.

Bennett (1979) has related pupil progress not only to the time which is actually made available for 'curriculum activity' but also to the pupil time spent in 'active learning'. Active learning is both a qualitative as well as quantitative category, and is linked to further factors such as motivation, stimulus and concentration. In order to maintain active, engaged learning, appropriate variety in activities is needed (see Chapter 10, Section 3.6). We thus have two aspects to consider in the use of time:

- the time available for curriculum activity
- the time actually spent in active, engaged learning.

The first of these, time available for curriculum activity, is explored in Practical Activity 11.4.

### Practical activity 11.4

*Aim:* To investigate 'evaporated time' in secondary school contexts.

*Method:* Distinguish between 'curriculum activity' when pupils are engaged in learning tasks as opposed to 'evaporated time' when pupils may be, for instance, waiting outside a room, coming into the room, getting books out, changing for PE, packing up. Observe a lesson, using a notebook and watch to record the use of the available time. Record from the time the lesson should begin and note all time that is not 'curriculum activity', taking your observation up to the start of the next lesson. What proportion of the available time was actually used for curriculum activity?

More ambitiously, you could take a longer period of time – a morning, afternoon or whole day – and track a class, pupil or teacher to calculate the ratio of 'evaporated' to 'curriculum' time. You might monitor yourself.

*Follow-up:* If possible compare your findings with those collected by others who have done a similar activity. Are any patterns emerging? It may be interesting to multiply your totals for the lesson or session to produce a figure for a week, term or year.

What is the reaction of other teachers to the idea of 'evaporated time'?

This analysis can be taken a stage further. Focusing on curriculum time it distinguishes between the time pupils are actively engaged with a task, the time they spend managing the task (fetching equipment/resources, sharpening pencils, waiting for the teacher etc.) and the time they are 'distracted' from the task.

## Practical activity 11.5

*Aim:* To monitor an individual pupil to estimate the use of curriculum time.

*Method:* Watch a chosen pupil during a lesson, perhaps using a time-sampling form of systematic observaton (see Chapter 4, Section 3.3). Judge the times at which:

1. The pupil is 'task engaged' (i.e. actively engaged on the given task).

2. The pupil is involved in 'task management' (i.e. doing other necessary activities related to the task – sharpening pencils, fetching equipment).

3. The pupil is 'off task' (i e. distracted, wasting time, messing about, day-dreaming).

Calculate the total amounts of learning time in each category:

| | | |
|---|---|---|
| Task engaged time | [ | ] |
| Task management time | [ | ] |
| Off-task time | [ | ] |

*Follow-up:* Are there any changes in class organization or management strategies which could help to maximize pupil use of curriculum?

Whilst the time spent on active learning can be assessed at any point it may also be seen as providing summative information: in a sense it is a product of the overall organization, relationships and teaching which are provided for the pupils. Practical Activity 11.6 may be helpful in considering these.

## Practical activity 11.6

*Aim:* To evaluate procedures for routine activities of the school day with a view to maximizing time for teaching and learning

*Method:* Use this list as a starting point for considering the routines that affect your lessons. Amend the list to match your situation. Consider possible improvements. Identify any aspects of organization you can deal with in advance of the lesson. Can you improve your own routines? Are you planning far enough ahead or practising crisis management? Can you actively involve pupils, giving them routine responsibility for specific aspects of lesson organization?

| Purpose of procedure | Procedure | Evaluation of procedure | Possible improvement |
|---|---|---|---|
| Pupils moving around the school | | | |
| Pupils entering the classroom | | | |
| Teacher checking attendance | | | |
| Teacher introducing/ assigning activities and tasks | | | |
| Pupils going to the toilet | | | |
| Pupils working somewhere other than the classroom during a lesson | | | |
| Teacher ensuring health and safety | | | |
| Pupils getting help from the teacher in class | | | |
| Pupils collecting/ using equipment/ resources | | | |
| Pupils getting work marked in class | | | |

| Pupils knowing which task to move on to | | | |
|---|---|---|---|
| Teacher setting homework | | | |
| Pupils giving in homework | | | |
| Teacher giving back homework | | | |
| Pupils tidying up/ cleaning the chalk board | | | |
| Pupils leaving the classroom for the next lesson | | | |

*Follow-up:* As a student teacher you will be discovering the existing procedures operated by the school or by individual teachers. It takes time to establish routines and it can be dangerous to attempt wholesale change in a short period. Nevertheless it is possible to sharpen your understanding and practice in this area. Think about discussing and reviewing procedures with pupils as part of establishing your operational ground rules.

## 1.4 Records

There are two basic types of record which teachers have to keep: those relating to class and school organization and those relating to the assessment of pupil progress. We deal with organizational records here and with assessment records in Chapter 15.

By organizational records we simply mean those records which are necessary to ensure the smooth running of the school and classroom. These range from attendance registers, which are extremely important to the administration of the school, to such things as records of group membership for various activities in lessons, timetables/booking arrangements for use of shared facilities such as classrooms or other spaces, video playback, computers, cameras, and records of resource maintenance or loan periods.

Records of classroom organization are essential for smooth lesson-to-lesson operation. The nature of these records – and whether the pupils or the teacher will be responsible for keeping them – depends on the extent of teacher or pupil control over the timing and selection of tasks and activities. A teacher may keep a simple list to show which pupils are doing or expected to do what activity and in which order. This information may be kept in a teacher's record book, be written on the blackboard before each lesson or kept by pupils individually in a progress record. At some point in a learning sequence pupils may negotiate an 'action plan' or draw up a 'contract' with the teacher indicating the work intended to be covered and targets to be attained. Whatever system is chosen, it is most important that a record system should be quick and easy for the teacher to refer to, and also for anyone else who may have to take over the class in an emergency.

Organizational procedures for homework are equally important. There may be a school-wide system involving, for instance, a homework diary kept by pupils and seen by parents. It is vital, as a part of establishing your expectations of pupils, to keep track of homework. Has it been done? Has it been given in on time?

## 2    ORGANIZING THE CLASSROOM

Relatively few secondary school teachers have their own classroom which they can organize to suit the way they want to teach. However, subject departments may have designated rooms or areas and some teachers may do the majority of their teaching in the same room or area; but in reality a classroom is normally shared by several teachers or, for some lessons, it may be necessary for one subject to be taught in another's specialist area. Thus a history teacher may end up teaching in a science laboratory or geography room. Spaces which are not clearly designated may be 'colonized' by a subject or, alternatively, may appear rather bleak and neglected. Where space is used by several teachers, compromises may have to be reached on how the space is used.

## 2.1   Space

The way a teaching space is organized has considerable impact on the kind of teaching that can happen, the attitude of learners and the quality of learning. Where these factors are unpropitious, a teacher has to work to overcome disadvantages. A first step is to review the space, and Practical Activity 11.7 offers a framework for this. For rooms where you will spend a lot of teaching time, and over which you have more control, it can be useful to produce a plan with which the existing constraints and the possibilities of the room and furniture can be explored. Reviewing space in this way is often a productive and enjoyable part of departmental discussion of teaching and learning strategies.

## 2.2   Learning environment

Research by ecological psychologists (e.g. Barker 1978, Bronfenbrenner 1979) has suggested the importance of the quality of the environment and the fact that it can influence behaviour. Secondary schools of late have given a great deal of attention to their internal and external environment. Much thought has been given to 'public spaces' used by everyone in the school, entrance areas have been redesigned, pupils' work is displayed. The link between the environment, school ethos and pupils' behaviour and attitude is generally accepted. In addition, the impact of the 'marketplace' and creating a good impression for visitors has made schools more conscious of this aspect of their presentation.

## Practical activity 11.7

*Aim:* To review space assigned to you for teaching.

*Method:* Stand in the room and, using this list as a starting point, consider carefully various aspects of the room as a space for teaching.

*Pupil seating:* What is available – tables, desks, chairs, benches, stools, floor etc? How is it arranged – rows across the room, in clusters, around the perimeter? How will pupils sit – singly, in pairs, in groups? How flexible is it? Can it be moved or re-arranged easily?

*Circulation:* How easy is it to move around the space? Where are the aisles? Are there areas which are inaccessible? Where is the natural place to stand as a teacher to command the whole class? Are there any blind spots – where pupils can 'hide'? Consider the sightlines – with the seating as it is, will all the pupils be able to look at you comfortably wherever you stand? Is there easy access to the teacher's desk?

*Learning resources:* How much of what you need is already in the room? How will the pupils have access to these resources? Can you anticipate any problems, e.g. with queues or bottlenecks? If you have to bring in resources where will you put them? How will you make them available?

*Teaching equipment:* What is permanently in the room – chalkboard/whiteboard, overhead projector, flip chart, audio/video playback, computers, specialist subject equipment? Can you make these work – e.g. where is the chalk and board cleaner? Where are the pens and cleaning cloth? Are you expected to bring these with you? Where does the electrical equipment switch on? Does anything need to be unlocked? Will anything that is kept in the room constrain your plans for teaching?

Is there any equipment you plan to use that will need to be brought into the room? What arrangements will you need to make for this? Where will you put it?

*Strengths and weaknesses:* Note any other positive or negative features of the space e.g. poor natural light; no blinds or curtains – gets hot in summer; is carpeted; poor sound-proofing – can hear next-door class and vice-versa. Make a list of the kinds of teaching strategies the space will positively support. Is there anything you might want to do that would be difficult in this space?

*Follow-up:* Talk to other teachers who use this space. How do they feel about how it is organized? If you make adjustments will this affect them? If you make changes will you have to restore the space to its usual arrangement at the end of the lesson? Imagine yourself teaching in this space. How can you maximize its possibilities and overcome the constraints?

It has often been asserted that classroom environments should be aesthetically pleasing, stimulate interest, reinforce learning and set high standards (e.g. Clegg and Billington 1994, **Primary Reading 9.5**). However, this is by no means easy to achieve in secondary schools. Some of the problems faced by secondary teachers in changing this image have been outlined above – of which, multiple use of rooms without a strong a sense of ownership or responsibility is probably the most significant. The creation of subject areas, with designated rooms etc., enables departments to do more to create some continuity within an appropriate learning environment. However, individual teachers still face the challenge of what to do about their particular teaching spaces.

Reflective teachers will aim to structure the environment to reinforce their overall educational purposes. This is the underlying rationale for the questions in Practical Activities 11.8 and 11.9.

### Practical activity 11.8

*Aim:* To examine the classroom environment.

*Method:* Use the framework below to consider a classroom as an environment for learning. Do so in relation to your own particular subject and aims.

1. *Design.* What are the main design features of the room? What is the dominant colour? What is the state of maintenance of the fabric and decor?

2. *Appearance.* What is the aesthetic feel of the room? What 'messages' are conveyed in terms of an environment for learning in your subject?

3. *Organization:* How is space in the room organized? Is it functionally efficient for your subject and for your more specific educational aims?

4. *Display:* What is currently displayed? What is or was its purpose – to stimulate, to inform? Is it serving that purpose? What state is it in? When was it put up? Has it been maintained? Does it contribute positively to the learning environment of your subject and your pupils?

5. *Display potential:* What are the possibilities for display on walls, on windows, on flat surfaces, off the ceiling? What are the possibilities for plants?

*Follow-up:* Discuss with other teachers who use it the possibilities for improving the room as a learning environment. What are their priorities? What claims on the space would each want to make? What would create problems for any of you? Are there any limitations set by the school on what might be done?

## Practical activity 11.9

*Aim:* To consider the potential of display in promoting learning.

*Method:* Think about some of the ways you might use display to enhance the learning environment. Could you use displays to stimulate and inform? Could they provide opportunities for pupils to interact with them, for example, by posing questions; inviting their participation in a problem-solving challenge; offering alternative viewpoints to consider; encouraging the pupils to look carefully, tracking progress through a sequence? What would be the effect of displaying pupils' work? Could displays support learning by revealing processes/work in progress which might be used for discussion, sharing problems, giving mutual support and advice? Could displays provide a model which pupils may apply to their own work? Could displays set standards for presentation?

How often would it be desirable to change displays? Could the pupils be involved in their creation and maintenance?

Having thought about the possibilities, and if you have been able to negotiate access to a suitable space, try out one or two of your ideas and evaluate the effect on pupil learning.

*Follow-up:* Talk to other teachers in your subject to get their views on displays. Look around the school and in other classrooms. Consider why some subjects make more use of displays than others.

## CONCLUSION

As reflective teachers we need to analyse the degree of coherence between the aims and values underlying our curriculum planning and the organizational strategies which are adopted when we try to implement those plans. There is thus no one best method – but we would suggest that there are two crucial criteria for judging all organizational approaches: appropriateness and coherence. You might like to pose two questions of yourself:

• Given my educational aims, is my form of organization appropriate for its purpose?
• Do all aspects of the classroom organization mesh coherently and consistently together?

In this chapter we have discussed six key aspects of class and classroom organization and the need for consistency between them. We have also emphasized the importance of coherence between classroom organization and educational aims and values. This can only be achieved through the exercise of professional judgement by reflective teachers who have the knowledge, skill and confidence to draw on a range of forms of classroom organization and thus maximize 'fitness for purpose'.

It is now time to turn to the issue of managing the implementation of those plans in action.

*Notes for further reading*

**Organizing for learning**

For an excellent review of research on classroom organization and management issues, see:

Doyle, W. (1986)
'Classroom organization and management', in Wittrock, M. C. (ed.) *Handbook of Research on Teaching (3rd edition)*,
New York: Macmillan.

Three very practical books on the organization of classes are listed below. Waterhouse is particularly effective on linking whole-class teaching with active learning, and on independent learning. Cruickshank *et al.* is an extremely comprehensive American text.

Waterhouse, P. (1990a)
*Classroom Management*,
Stafford: Network Educational Press.

Stern, J. (1995)
*Learning to Teach*,
London: David Fulton.

Cruickshank, D. R., Bainer, D. and Metcalf, K. (1995)
*The Act of Teaching*,
New York: McGraw-Hill

The question of 'ability' or 'mixed-ability' based grouping (remember these words actually normally refer only to attainment) is a complex one. For research and important inspection reviews, see:

Slavin, R. E. (1990)
'Achievement effects of ability grouping in secondary schools: a best evidence synthesis',
*Review of Educational Research*, Vol. 60, No. 3, pp. 471–500.

HMI (1978)
*Mixed Ability Work in Comprehensive Schools*,
London: HMSO.

Scottish Office Education and Industry Department (1995)
*Achievement for All: A Report on Selection Within Schools by HM Inspectors of Schools*,
Edinburgh: HMSO.

For a clear expression of the rationale for mixed-ability grouping and an excellent case-study of its implementation, see:

Kelly, A. V. (1978)
*Mixed-ability Grouping: Theory and Practice*,
London: Harper and Row.

Evans, J. (1985)
*Teaching in Transition: The Challenge of Mixed-ability Grouping*,
Buckingham: Open University Press.

On organizing group work, try:

Lloyd, C. and Beard, J. (1995)
*Managing Classroom Collaboration*,
London: Cassell.

Kutnick, P. and Rogers, C. (1995)
*Groups in Schools,*
London: Cassell.

Guidance on working with other adults in the classroom is offered in:

Thomas, G. (1992)
*Effective Classroom Teamwork: Support or Intrusion?,*
London: Routledge.

Mortimore, P. and Mortimore, J. with Thomas, H. (1994)
*Managing Associate Staff: Innovation in Primary and Secondary Schools,*
London: Paul Chapman.

An illustration of the ways in which precious school time is used up is provided by Delamont and Galton, whilst Campbell and Neill document teachers' work-time and Nelson offers advice on time management.

Delamont, S. and Galton, M. (1986)
*Inside the Secondary Classroom,*
London: Routledge.

Campbell, R. J. and Neill, S. R. St. J. (1994)
*Secondary Teachers at Work,*
London: Routledge.

Nelson, I. (1994)
*Time-management for Teachers,*
London: Kogan Page.

The good introduction to 'ecological psychology', which underpins the importance of providing a suitable learning environment is:

Barker, R. G. (1978)
*Habitats, Environments and Human Behaviour,*
San Francisco: Jossey Bass.

Practical advice on ways of setting out a classroom to link layout and educational purposes is provided in Waterhouse (1990), referenced above.

For a wide-ranging review of issues concerned with the learning environment, full of practical advice, see:

Hodgson, N. (1988)
*Classroom Display: Improving the Visual Environment in Schools,*
Diss: Tarquin.

# CHAPTER 12

# How are we managing our classes?

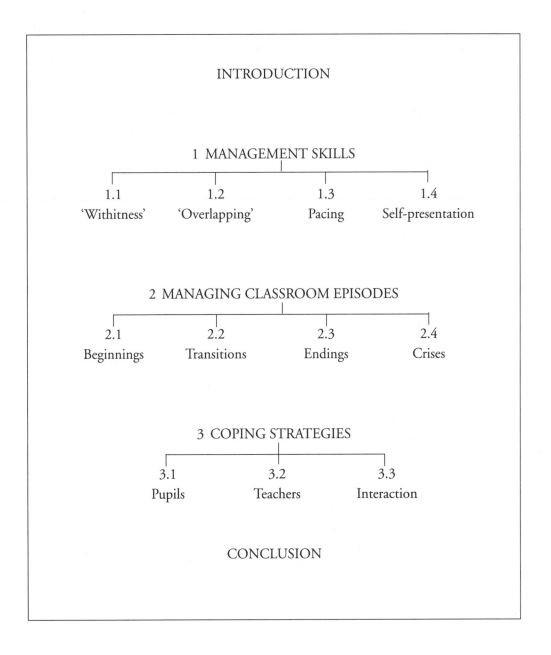

INTRODUCTION

1 MANAGEMENT SKILLS

| 1.1 | 1.2 | 1.3 | 1.4 |
|---|---|---|---|
| 'Withitness' | 'Overlapping' | Pacing | Self-presentation |

2 MANAGING CLASSROOM EPISODES

| 2.1 | 2.2 | 2.3 | 2.4 |
|---|---|---|---|
| Beginnings | Transitions | Endings | Crises |

3 COPING STRATEGIES

| 3.1 | 3.2 | 3.3 |
|---|---|---|
| Pupils | Teachers | Interaction |

CONCLUSION

# INTRODUCTION

Having considered the issues involved in organizing classes and classrooms, we now move into the 'action' part of the reflective teaching cycle. This chapter turns to a consideration of classroom management. This includes reflecting on how to manage and cope with learning situations.

In one sense the teacher is always dealing with a 'crowd' (Jackson 1968, **Primary Reading 5.5**). Control of that crowd must, therefore, be a priority. It is a well-documented finding that for many student teachers in particular, this concern initially displaces almost all other aims as they take on the challenge of coping with the class. This is a legitimate concern and an issue about which it is important to develop both skills and judgement. Without a calm and ordered atmosphere it is difficult to achieve learning objectives, however well conceived.

Thus, the focus of attention should arguably be directed at the prevention of managerial problems, so that crises are avoided, and to the maintenance of a positive climate for learning. This is by no means easy, since classrooms are such complex places, where events can unfold very quickly. Doyle's analysis of the 'multidimensionality, simultaneity and unpredictability' of this is excellent (1977, **Primary Reading 10.1**). Any number of factors – events outside the lesson, a group of difficult and disruptive pupils, ambiguous school systems, teacher fatigue, the weather – can affect what happens in a lesson. Success in coping with this complexity and with the particular challenges posed by different teaching groups is more likely to be achieved by reflective teachers who are willing to look squarely at their experiences, think carefully about teaching skills and look for ways to develop and improve.

However, it is all too easy for classroom management objectives to take precedence over learning requirements. It has often been argued that, despite high teacher control of classrooms, pupils are sometimes very unclear about the aims of learning tasks. The combination is a sense of ambiguity and risk, which then undermines the quality of pupils' engagement with learning. Holt (1982, **Primary Reading 10.3**) makes this idea more controversial by suggesting that pupils 'learn to be stupid' in schools. They do this when teacher requirements for conformity with managerial rules, structure and order over-ride the pupil need for understanding and engagement in high quality learning tasks. The vital message of such work is that classroom management is an absolutely necessary means to an end – but it is not the end itself.

This chapter has been structured in three sections. The first section focuses on some key management skills. The second considers some of the most regularly occurring classroom episodes which require management. Section 3 analyses some of the coping strategies which teachers and pupils may develop.

A consideration of classroom management would be incomplete without discussion of teacher-pupil relationships and the management of disruptive and challenging behaviour. This chapter concerns itself with basic management skills and begins to further develop the topic with the discussion of coping strategies in Section 3. To take your thinking further you should read this chapter in conjunction with Chapter 14, 'How are we managing relationships and behaviour?'

# 1    MANAGEMENT SKILLS

This section builds on the work on planning and preparing for a teaching session which was discussed in Chapters 9 and 10. Having considered how a lesson might be planned (Chapter 10), we now look at four important management skills which relate to the maintenance and development of such sessions in action: 'withitness', 'overlapping', 'pacing' and 'self-presentation'. Many of the issues in this and the following section on managing classroom episodes are also addressed in **Primary Readings 10.5 and 10.6**.

## 1.1  'Withitness'

This is a term coined by Kounin (1970, **Primary Reading 10.6**) to describe the capacity to be aware of the wide variety of things which are simultaneously going on in a classroom. This is a constant challenge for any teacher and can be a particular strain for a new teacher until this skill is acquired.

Teachers who are 'withit' are said to 'have eyes in the back of their head'. They are able to anticipate and to see where help is needed. They are able to nip trouble in the bud. They are skilful at scanning the class whilst helping individuals and they position themselves accordingly. They are alert; they can pre-empt disturbance; and they can act fast. They can sense the way a class is responding and can act to maintain a positive atmosphere.

## 1.2  'Overlapping'

This is another of Kounin's terms and describes the skill of being able to do more than one thing at the same time. This can be related to withitness if, for example, a problem emerges concerning occasions when giving sustained help to a particular pupil results in relatively neglecting the rest of the class. In addition, overlapping is also an important and separate skill in its own right. Most teachers work under such pressure that they have to think about and do more than one thing at a time. Decisions have to be made very rapidly. For instance, it has been calculated that over a thousand interpersonal exchanges a day typically take place between each teacher and the pupils in their care. For these reasons, reflecting, anticipating and making rapid judgements are very much a necessary part of any teacher's skills.

## 1.3  Pacing

Pacing a teaching-learning session is another important skill. In discussing lesson planning in Chapter 10 we discussed the importance of making appropriate judgements about the timing and phasing of the various activities and parts of a session. During the lesson, the management skill lies in maintaining an awareness of pace, of how the class is reacting, and taking suitable actions as necessary. At the simplest level, there is the practical judgement to be made at the end of a session about when to switch into a 'finishing up phase' – it is very easy to get involved in activities, forget about the clock and suddenly to find that it is time for the bell. More complex educational judgements are necessary in relation to learning activities and the various phases of a typical session. For instance, the activities have to be introduced: this is often an initial 'motivational phase' where the pupils' interest is stimulated. This motivation also has to be maintained. Sessions then often enter an 'incubation and development phase' in which pupils think about the activities, explore ideas and then tackle tasks. From time to time there may be a need for a 'restructuring phase' where learning objectives and procedures may need to be clarified further. Finally, there may be a 'review phase' for reinforcing good effort or for reflecting on overall progress.

Judgements about pacing – about when to make a new initiative – depend crucially on being sensitive to how pupils are responding to activities. If they are immersed and productively engaged then one might decide to extend a phase or run the activity into the next lesson. If pupils seem to be becoming bored, frustrated or listless then it is probably wise to retain the initiative, to restructure or review the activity. This may be an indication that the activity is too challenging so you might choose to restructure the task into smaller steps with more teacher direction; alternatively it may be that the activity is becoming unfocused and pupils are 'drifting' so you might choose to increase the pace by assigning a time-limited target or move on to something new. If pupils are becoming too 'high', excited and distracted, then it may be useful to review and maybe redirect them into an activity which calms them down by rechannelling their energies.

## 1.4  Self-presentation

The last of the four management skills which we have identified is self-presentation, for how to 'present' oneself to pupils is also a matter for skill and judgement. Teachers who are able to project themselves so that pupils expect them to be 'in charge' have a valuable ability. There is a very large element of self-confidence in this and student teachers, in particular, may sometimes find it difficult to enact the change from the student role to the teacher role. Perhaps this is not surprising, for a huge change in rights and responsibilities is involved. The first essential, then, is to believe in oneself as a teacher.

A second range of issues concerned with self-presentation is more skill-based. Here non-verbal cues are important. Self-presentation relates to such things as gesture, posture, movement, position in the room, facial expression, etc. These will be actively interpreted by pupils. The intended impression might be one of sureness, of confidence and competence. The reflective teacher will need to consider how non-verbal cues can help to convey such attributes.

A further very important skill is voice control. A teacher's use of voice can be highly sophisticated and effective in managing both learning and behaviour. Changing the pitch, volume, projection and the intensity of meaning can communicate different aspects about self. If a voice is to be used in this way then it will require some training and time to develop. Teachers, like singers and actors, can learn to use their diaphragm to project a 'chest voice', to breathe more deeply and speak more slowly so that their voice and their message is carried more effectively.

A fourth and more general area of skill which is involved in how teachers present and project themselves is that of 'acting' – as though on a stage. In this sense it is the ability to convey what we mean by 'being a teacher', so that expectations are clear and relationships can be negotiated.

Acting is also an enormous strength for teachers for one other particular reason. When one is acting, one is partially detached from the role. It is possible to observe oneself, to analyse, reflect and plan. Acting, in other words, is controlled behaviour which is partially distanced from self. In the situations of vulnerability which sometimes arise in classrooms this can be a great asset.

The skills which we have been reviewing above need to be put in a context. They are simply skills and have no substantive content or merit in their own right. A self-confident performer who lacks purpose and gets practical matters wrong (for example has ill-defined objectives, mixes up pupils' names, plans sessions badly, loses books, acts unfairly, etc.) will not be able to manage a class. A teacher has to be competent as well as skilled and must understand the ends of education as well as the means.

## Practical activity 12.1

*Aim:* To gather data about your management skills and judgement.

*Method:* Ask a colleague to observe one of your lessons and to make notes on the way in which you manage the class. They could watch out for examples of appropriate withitness, overlapping, pacing (or chances missed). Also of interest would be observations of how you present yourself (how confident and teacher-like you appear, where you stand in the room, non-verbal gestures and expressions, how you use your voice). Discuss the session together afterwards.

*Follow-up:* Such analysis should increase self-awareness of management skills. Try to identify possible improvements which could be made. These can be practised and worked on.

It is always valuable to observe other teachers. If possible arrange to visit lessons taught by colleagues in your own and other subjects. Do this with sensitivity. Few teachers are not experiencing problems of one sort or another with at least one class, group or individual but it can be difficult to admit this, especially to a student or newly-qualified teacher. Use the outline suggested above to structure your observation. In considering and analysing your data (perhaps, by agreement, with the teacher concerned) you might like to consider some of the following questions.

- How far does the creation of a good working climate depend on personality or can you identify common skills such as those defined in this chapter?

- Does the demand for different skills vary from subject to subject?

- What are the teachers who are good at this doing which others aren't?

- How did they learn to do it?

- How is the need for a controlled environment balanced with learning objectives?

- What can you learn from this observation?

## 2 | MANAGING CLASSROOM EPISODES

'Flow' is an important summary criterion which can be used to describe classroom management. By 'flow' we mean the degree of continuity and coherence which is achieved in a learning session. It implies a steady, continuous movement in a particular direction. The suggestion is thus that we should work with pupils to develop a coherent sense of purpose within our lessons; should organize our classrooms in ways which are consistent with those purposes; and should manage the pupils, phases and events so that educational objectives are cumulatively reinforced. We would suggest that if this can be done then energy, interest and enthusiasm for learning is likely to be focused productively.

Achieving such a flow of activities requires a high degree of awareness, sensitivity and skill and it is sometimes the case that events seem to conspire to produce jerky, fragmented incoherent sequences of activities which lack momentum.

There are three classroom episodes which pose particular management challenges to the flow of sessions. These are 'beginnings' of lessons; 'transitions' between phases of lessons or between lessons themselves; and 'endings' of lessons. We will discuss each in turn.

## 2.1 Beginnings

The beginning of a lesson is often seen as important because of the way in which it sets a tone. The aim is usually to introduce and interest pupils in the planned activities; to provide them with a clear indication of what they are expected to do; and to structure the activity in practical, organizational terms. It would be useful at this stage to use Checklists 12.1, 12.2 and 12.3 as a basis for observation and discussion with teachers in your subject area.

---

### Checklist 12.1

*Aim:* To consider how we get the attention of the class and keep it.

1. How do we call for attention? Is a recognized signal used (e.g. standing in the front, waiting in silence, clapping hands, a cue word such as 'Right!')?

2. How do we know if we have got their attention?
   Have they stopped what they were doing?
   Are they looking?
   Are they listening?

3. Has the speaker maximized conditions for listening?
   Are the listeners facing the speaker (so those who hear little can see facial expressions)?
   Is it quiet (so those who hear 'too much' have fewer distractions)?

---

## Checklist 12.2

*Aim:* To consider how pupils are motivated at the start of a session. Some possibilities are:

- Finding a point of relevance with pupils' interests or experiences
- Challenging them to investigate, interpret
- Arousing their curiosity – artefacts, models, posters, stories, videos etc.

1. Which of these (if any) is used most in your subject?

2. What other strategies are used?

3. Which is the most commonly used approach?

4. What approach has been most/least successful – why and when?

## Checklist 12.3

*Aim:* To consider how the pupils are orientated to know exactly what is expected of them.

1. Do they know why they are doing this activity?

2. Do they know how this fits in with previous lessons/learning?

3. Do they know what they are going to learn from it?

4. Do they know what outcomes are expected?

5. Do they know about any targets and time limits set?

6. Do they know on what criteria work is to be assessed?

7. Do they know what they are going to do with completed work?

8. Do they know which activity they are to go on to next?

## Practical activity 12.2

*Aim:* To review the beginnings of lessons.

*Method:* Use the suggestions below to carry out an observation (or several observations) of lessons in your subject.

We suggest you use a simple framework like the one below and structure your observations around points made in Checklists 12.1, 12.2 and 12.3.

**Lesson beginnings**

Class:              Date:              Time:              Observer:

| Minutes | Teacher activity | Pupil activity |
|---------|------------------|----------------|
| 1       |                  |                |
| 2       |                  |                |
| 3       |                  |                |
| 4       |                  |                |
| 5       |                  |                |
| 6       |                  |                |
| 7       |                  |                |
| 8       |                  |                |

For each minute (up to eight, by which time most lessons will be moving into the next phase) note the 'story' of the lesson as it unfolds. Wherever possible record verbatim what is said, especially by the teacher. (Audio-taping might provide you with a useful aide-memoire, but do this unobtrusively.)

Consider questions such as:
How do pupils come into the room? What do they do? What is the teacher doing? Is there any interaction between pupils and teacher? How does the teacher get the pupils' attention? Is a register taken? Is there any other administration, e.g. related to homework? Where does the teacher stand/sit? Is there any movement round the room? How does the teacher start the lesson? How does the teacher introduce the topic of the lesson? How do the pupils respond? Is it clear what the overall shape of the lesson will be? Are any targets/outcomes identified?

Now analyse the story you have recorded in some other ways. What is the balance of time between administration, management of the class, teaching/learning? How is the pupil/teacher relationship established and maintained during this period? How would you describe the atmosphere of this opening period e.g. informal, confused, purposeful, casual, repressive? How would you describe the pupils' attitude, e.g. interested, co-operative, bored, challenging, friendly, respectful, wary? How (if at all) did the teacher's actions determine this atmosphere and these attitudes?

*Follow-up:* If possible ask teachers you have observed about how they approach the beginnings of lessons. What could you learn from this observation for your own teaching?

In addition to observing others you could ask a colleague to use this approach to observe the beginnings of one or more of your lessons. Analyse the data together.

## 2.2 'Transitions'

Transitions are a regular cause of control difficulties, particularly for student teachers. This often arises when expectations about behaviour concerning one activity are left behind and those of the new one have yet to be established. In these circumstances, a skilled teacher is likely to take an initiative early and to structure the transition carefully.

For example, there are a number of potential hazards in moving from teacher-centred whole-class exposition to individual or group tasks. We would suggest that it is important to break down a transition such as this into discrete stages. The skill lies in trying to anticipate problems before they arise; in prestructuring the next phase; and in orienting pupils to the next task, trying to ensure that they are motivated and clear about what is to be done. These principles apply to any transition, planned or embarked on as a result of professional judgement about pace and the need to re-structure. Checklist 12.4 provides a basis for thinking about managing transitions.

Practical Activity 12.3 suggests how you might gather data on your own and other teachers' management of transitions.

---

## Checklist 12.4

*Aim:* To monitor a transition.

1. Did I have everything organized for a smooth transition?

2. Did I correctly anticipate and avoid problems?

3. Did I give an early warning of the transition?

4. Did I give clear instructions for leaving existing work?

5. Did I give the pupils clear instructions for the transition and for any movement that was necessary?

6. Did I effectively orientate and motivate pupils to the next phase?

---

## 2.3 Endings

Ending a session is a further management issue and four aspects will be reviewed. The first is a very practical one. At the end of any session equipment or resources must be put away, pupils must prepare to leave the room and the classroom must be left tidy for the next lesson. Timing is important, especially in ensuring that pupils (and teacher) are not late for the next lesson. The second aspect relates to discipline and control. Pupils can sometimes anticipate the end of the lesson or may respond to the bell or buzzer rather than the teacher. In lessons before break, dinner or the end of the day, pupils' anxiety to be away may be particularly apparent as priorities other than your subject assert themselves. A degree of awareness and firmness from the teacher is required.

The management procedures which are called for here are similar to those for transitions. Two other aspects involved in ending sessions are more explicitly related to learning. One of these concerns the excellent opportunities which arise for reviewing learning and achievements, for reinforcing good work, for contextualizing activities which have been completed and pointing the way ahead to the next lesson. The other involves the setting of homework in relation to progressing learning. It is important to leave sufficient time for this. Pupils need time to write things down, especially where homework diaries are kept. They should be clear about what they are to do, why they are doing it, what teacher expectations are. If homework is to be given in for marking or will form part of a subsequent lesson, deadlines should be clear. It is wise to leave time for pupils' questions. A final aspect of endings relates to opportunities that arise for asserting the membership of the class as a social learning group. Positive attitudes of groups or individuals, effective teamwork and examples of co-operation can be acknowledged and celebrated.

Overall, a carefully thought out and well-executed ending to a session can contribute to pupil progress in your subject by reinforcing learning and by building up

## Practical activity 12.3

*Aim:* To gather data on lesson transitions

*Method:* Use the suggestions below to carry out an observation (or several observations) of lessons in your subject.

We suggest you use a simple framework like the one below.

**Lesson transitions**

Class:          Date:          Time:          Observer:

| Time | Teacher activity | Pupil activity |
|------|------------------|----------------|
|      |                  |                |

Note the start time of each transition and record the 'story' of the transition as it unfolds. Wherever possible record verbatim what is said, especially by the teacher. (Audio-taping might provide you with a useful aide-memoire, but do this unobtrusively.) Note the time when in your opinion the transition is complete.

Consider questions such as:
How does the teacher signal a transition? How do the pupils respond? What is the teacher doing? Is there any interaction between pupils and teacher? What do the pupils do? How quickly do they settle to the next activity? Are there any problems?

Overall, how successful was the transition? What factors contributed to its quality?

*Follow-up:* If possible, ask the teachers you have observed about how they approach transitions in their lessons. What could you learn for your own teaching from this observation?

In addition to observing others you could ask a colleague to use this approach to observe the transitions in one or more of your lessons. Analyse the data together.

the sense of 'belonging' within the class as a whole. In addition you will earn the gratitude of colleagues by providing a calm and ordered transition between your lesson and theirs,

Checklist 12.5 provides a basis for thinking about managing endings and Practical Activity 12.4 suggests a way to investigate them.

---

### Checklist 12.5

*Aim:* To monitor the end of a session.

1. Did I give early warning of the end of the session?

2. Did I give clear instructions for finishing off and tidying up?

3. Did I reinforce those instructions and monitor the tidying up?

4. Did I leave enough time for setting homework?

5. Did I take opportunities to summarize and reinforce learning, to be explicit about the educational achievements, efforts and progress made, to contextualize learning and point the way ahead?

6. Did I take opportunities to build up the sense of the class as a community?

7. Did I praise the pupils for what they did well?

---

## 2.4 'Crises'

A classroom 'crisis' is obviously an immediate source of disruption to the flow of a session. Crises can come in many forms, from a pupil arriving late, feeling ill or cutting a finger, to a direct challenge to the teacher's authority and judgement. We particularly focus on behavioural challenges in Chapter 14. Here we offer three fairly simple principles which can be applied as a basis for managing other sorts of crises.

The first principle is to minimize the disturbance. A pupil who is ill, hurt or upset cannot be given the attention which they require by a teacher who has continuing classroom responsibilities. Help from the school nurse, secretary, an ancillary helper, or other teachers should be called on either to deal with the problem or to relieve the class teacher so that he or she can deal with it. In this way, disturbance to the classroom flow can be minimized and those in need of undivided attention can receive it. How this happens will vary from school to school and relate to the procedures and organizational structures that exist. It is a good idea to familiarize yourself with these. It is usually helpful to recruit a responsible member of the class who can be sent with a message. A supportive friend of the pupil involved can also be given a role. Of course, a student teacher usually has a full-time teacher upon whom to call.

The second principle for handling a crisis is to maximize calm and reassurance. Pupils can be upset when something unexpected happens; they may react to the event by over-dramatizing or use it as an excuse for opting out or being disruptive. It may well be appropriate to reassert basic classroom routines and expectations.

## Practical activity 12.4

*Aim:* To gather data on lesson endings.

*Method:* Use the suggestions below to carry out an observation (or several observations) of the endings of lessons.

We suggest you use a simple framework like the one below.

**Lesson endings**

Class:          Date:          Time:          Observer:

| Time | Teacher activity | Pupil activity |
| --- | --- | --- |
|  |  |  |

Note the start time of each ending and record the 'story', minute by minute, of the ending as it unfolds. Wherever possible, record verbatim what is said, especially by the teacher. This may cover only the final minute or two of the lesson but will start earlier where a teacher engages in a review of the lesson, sets homework, looks forward to the next lesson or where there is a significant amount of clearing up to do. (Audio-taping might provide you with a useful aide-memoire, but do this unobtrusively.)

Consider the following questions:
How does the teacher signal the winding-up phase? How do the pupils respond? What is the teacher doing? Is there any interaction between pupils and teacher? Is homework set? How is this done? What do the pupils do? How quickly do the pupils organize themselves to leave for the next lesson? Are there any tidying-up activities? How is this organized? Are there any problems? What happens in the last two/three minutes of the lesson? What happens when the bell or buzzer goes?

*Follow-up:* If possible ask the teachers you have observed about how they approach the endings of their lessons. What could you learn for your own teaching from this observation?

In addition to observing others you could ask a colleague to use this approach to observe the endings in one or more of your lessons. Analyse the data together.

If continuing with work in progress seems unlikely to be effective it might be wise to set a relatively straightforward task.

The third principle which is appropriate when a crisis arises concerns oneself and pausing for sufficient thought before making a judgement on how to act. Obviously, this depends on what has happened and some events require immediate action. However, if it is possible to gain time to think about the issues outside the heat of the moment, then it may produce more authoritative and constructive decisions.

### Practical activity 12.5

*Aim:* To monitor responses to a classroom crisis.

*Method:* After a crisis has arisen, you could write a diary-type account of it and of how it was handled (by you or another teacher). This might describe the event, and also reflect the feelings which you experienced as the events unfolded. If the opportunity arises it might be valuable to talk to pupils after the event, so that you can gain an insight into why they behaved as they did.

Use these questions to structure your reflection on the event:

1. Did I minimize disturbance?

2. Did I maximize calm and reassurance?

3. Did I make appropriate judgements on how to act?

4. How do I account for the various pupil reactions I observed?

*Follow-up:* Having examined your feelings and actions (and perhaps pupils' reactions to the crisis) it would probably be helpful to discuss the event and your account with a friend or colleague.

## 3 | COPING STRATEGIES

The previous sections of this chapter have considered classroom management exclusively from the point of view of the teacher's judgements and actions. However, classroom management is a more complex issue than this implies for the obvious reason that it applies to an interactive situation between the teacher and pupils. The process of managing and coping is thus one of active judgement and decision-making on both sides.

The concept of a coping strategy is useful here (Woods 1977, Hargreaves 1978, Pollard 1982). It refers to the strategies which people adopt in response to their circumstances, as a means of sustaining their sense of self. The issues of classroom management, control and survival are all included in this concept. For a teacher, a major question might be 'How do I cope in the classroom with all the constraints I face and a wide range of expectations bearing on me?' For a pupil, a prominent question might be 'How do I cope in the classroom when I am on my own among so many other pupils, having to do certain things, with the teacher judging my work and when my parents and friends expect certain things of me?'

The answer, to both questions, is that action is likely to be tactical, (i.e. based on judgements which are made about actions which will best serve each person's immediate interests). A great many different examples of teacher and pupil strategies have been identified.

## 3.1 Pupils

Among these are the pupil strategies listed below:

- Open negotiation – collaborative participation
  - discussing, reasoning, initiating
  - sharing a joke.

- Seeking recognition/reassurance
  - fake involvement
  - acting.

- Drifting – relying on routines for cover
  - pleasing the teacher
  - docility/resignation
  - right answerism.

- Evasion – apathy
  - time-stealing
  - re-doing work.

- Withdrawal – avoidance
  - minimizing effort.

- Rebellion – aggression
  - messing around
  - 'winding up' the teacher.

Such strategies can be identified by observation and interviews with pupils in primary and secondary schools. They may well strike a chord with your personal experiences of being a pupil, or indeed, cause reflection concerning pupils you have taught. Such strategies are a means by which many pupils 'manage' their classroom experiences.

### Practical activity 12.6

*Aim:* To reflect on the range of coping strategies which pupils use in the classroom.

*Method:* Observe a small group of pupils in a classroom (either in your own class, or a colleague's). Try and work out the meaning and purpose behind what they are doing. Are they trying to demonstrate their 'best work' to the teacher? Are they evading and playing for time? Are they having a laugh? Afterwards you could discuss some of the events with the pupils to gain insights into their interpretation of events, rather than just to rely on your own.

*Follow-up:* Understanding pupil's coping strategies can help us to be more sensitive to their needs when we make managerial decisions. List the coping strategies you think you have observed. How might you manage the lesson with this in mind?

## 3.2 Teachers

The range of strategies employed by teachers to protect and preserve themselves in the classroom is equally wide. Some which have been identified include the following:

- Open negotiation – mutual collaboration
  - discussion and explaining
  - sharing a joke.

- Distancing – avoiding confrontation
  - enforcing rigid routines
  - ritualizing
  - 'routinization' – keeping them busy
  - repetition
  - moderating demands.

- Manipulation
  - using reward/punishment
  - flattery
  - personal appeals.

- Domination/charisma
  - relying on personal charisma
  - intellectual 'showing off'.

- Coercion
  - sarcasm
  - threatening
  - physical restraint (which could, of course, be deemed illegal in many circumstances).

**Practical activity 12.7**

*Aim:* To reflect on the coping strategies which we use when teaching.

*Method:* It can be difficult to collect data in this area. It requires a degree of honesty when we are reflecting subjectively on our own behaviour and the same degree of honesty allied with sensitivity when we are observing others and engaging, as critical friends, in analysis.

One way to collect data is by a combination of personal diary records together with the comments and observations of a colleague. If it can be arranged without a huge impact on behaviour, a video recording of a session followed by analysis could also be a way of collecting information about our own coping strategies.

*Follow-up:* Use the list above as a basis for your analysis of the range of strategies and the types you most frequently used. How consistent is your behaviour? Do you use different strategies in different situations? What causes the variation? The pupils? The room? The time of day? Your mood and state of health?

## 3.3 Interaction

We now turn to the question of the appropriateness and educational effectiveness of different coping strategies.

It is important to note the interactive context of the classroom. Since the actions of teachers and pupils have an immediate effect on each other, a mesh of teacher and pupil strategies tends to develop. This, of course, is closely related to the form of relationships and to the 'working consensus' which has been negotiated (see Chapter 14).

One way of conceptualizing this mesh of strategies is indicated in Figure 12.1

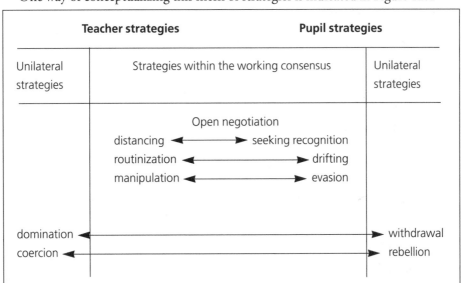

**Figure 12.1** *The inter-relationships between teacher and pupil strategies*

The significant implication of this model of interaction is that the actions of the pupils are clearly related to the actions of the teacher. It suggests that, if difficulties arise in connection with classroom management, it is not sufficient just to review the 'awkward characteristics' of pupils, for this simply passes all responsibility onto them and generates negative ideas about them. It is also necessary to analyse the situation interactively and to consider our responsibilities as teachers.

## CONCLUSION

This chapter has examined aspects of management which help to establish and sustain conditions for successful learning. These questions of management are matters of great concern to teachers, as are the questions of teachers and pupils learning to cope with each other and with learning situations. Most of us soon become more familiar and gradually grow in confidence and competence. Direct experience is irreplaceable in developing competence, but there is also much to be said for sharing ideas, problems and successes through discussion with colleagues.

Many of the issues considered in this chapter relate closely to the content of Chapter 14, 'How are we managing relationships and behaviour?'

### *Notes for further reading*

On classroom management skills, the classic text is:

Kounin, J. S. (1970)
*Discipline and Group Management in Classrooms*,
New York: Holt, Rinehart and Winston.          📖 **Primary Reading 10.6**

There are many good books offering advice on practical issues concerning class management. Among the most useful are:

Waterhouse, P. (1990a)
*Classroom Management*,
Stafford: Network Educational Press.

Marland, M. (1993)
*The Craft of the Classroom: A Survival Guide*,
London: Heinemann.

Laslett, R. and Smith, C. (1992)
*Effective Classroom Management: A Teacher's Guide*,
London: Routledge.          📖 **Primary Reading 10.5**

Kyriacou, C. (1991)
*Essential Teaching Skills*,
London: Simon and Schuster.

Wragg, E. C. (1984)
*Classroom Teaching Skills*,
London: Croom Helm.

Stern, J. (1995)
*Learning to Teach*,
London: David Fulton.

There is now an extensive literature on the coping strategies of both pupils and teachers. For excellent overviews of this work, see:

Woods, P. (1990a)
*Teacher Skills and Strategies,*
London: Falmer Press.

Woods, P. (1990b)
*The Happiest Days? How Pupils Cope with School,*
London: Falmer Press.

Primary Reading 10.8

Clear expositions of the overall theoretical framework are provided in:

Delamont, S. (1990)
*Interaction in the Classroom,*
London: Routledge.

Woods, P. (1983)
*Sociology and the School: an Interactionist Viewpoint,*
London: Routledge.

# CHAPTER 13

# How are we communicating?

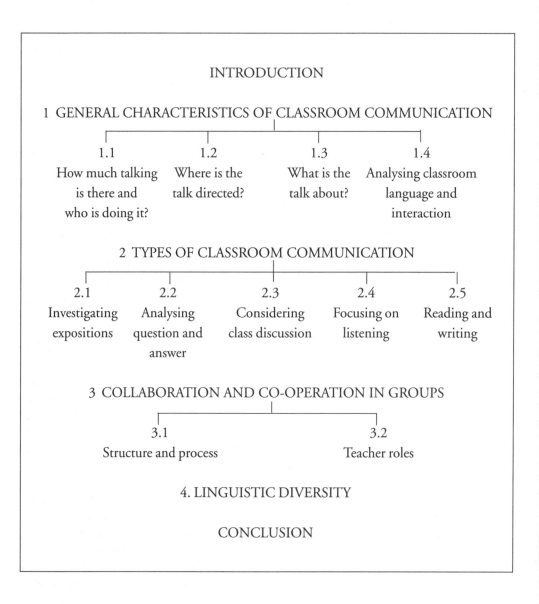

INTRODUCTION

1 GENERAL CHARACTERISTICS OF CLASSROOM COMMUNICATION

| 1.1 | 1.2 | 1.3 | 1.4 |
|---|---|---|---|
| How much talking is there and who is doing it? | Where is the talk directed? | What is the talk about? | Analysing classroom language and interaction |

2 TYPES OF CLASSROOM COMMUNICATION

| 2.1 | 2.2 | 2.3 | 2.4 | 2.5 |
|---|---|---|---|---|
| Investigating expositions | Analysing question and answer | Considering class discussion | Focusing on listening | Reading and writing |

3 COLLABORATION AND CO-OPERATION IN GROUPS

| 3.1 | 3.2 |
|---|---|
| Structure and process | Teacher roles |

4. LINGUISTIC DIVERSITY

CONCLUSION

## INTRODUCTION

So far in Part 2 of this book, we have examined the ways in which knowledge, concepts, skills and attitudes are planned and presented through the curriculum and through classroom organization and management. It is now time to turn directly to teaching and learning processes, and fundamental to these is the language through which teaching and learning is mediated. The Bullock Report (DES 1975) emphasized the crucial role of language in learning and suggested that *all* teachers should be seen as 'language teachers'. This has sometimes been taken to mean the shared responsibility of all teachers for improving their pupils' grammar, spelling and punctuation, and a need for subject teachers to consider developing pupils' reading and research skills in their content area. Such goals are important and, in some schools, are the subject of policies for language and skill development across the curriculum.

More fundamentally however, we need to consider the various forms of communication which contribute to learning. A central task of teaching is to make new knowledge, skills and conceptual frameworks available to pupils and this takes us back to the theories of learning reviewed in Chapter 9. There we suggest that learning involves using language to engage with and order experience so that new patterns of thinking and new ways of understanding and representing reality are developed. We learn through language and we express our understanding in language. Each subject has its own special language which is bound up with its way of thinking, talking and writing. In addition, there is the speech and writing style which Barnes *et al.* (1969) refers to as 'the language of secondary education'.

How best then can we enable pupils to become confident members of these new language communities? This chapter explores that question by focusing on the nature of classroom interactions, how teachers use language, how pupils use language and the implications of both for learning.

A constant dilemma for secondary teachers is how to select teaching strategies which enable both pupils to learn well and teachers to 'cover' the syllabus. Embedded in that dilemma are a number of questions. How effective is teaching by telling? How much can pupils learn from talking to each other? How do we know if it's the right kind of talk? How can we make discussion work better? How good are we at asking questions? Is whole-class discussion valuable? What's the best way to set up small-group discussion? It is no accident that all these questions involve communication. Sharpening our awareness of classroom communication and interaction will help us to resolve the dilemma and make best use of the time available.

Communicating is a complicated business and it is not surprising that it frequently goes wrong. In the rapidity of encoding and decoding processes, there are endless possibilities for misunderstanding. Of course, language skills are fundamental but, since communication involves people, it requires social skills as well. In addition, since communication is usually focused on some meaningful topic, it calls for appropriate cognitive capacities, knowing something about the subject under consideration and being able to think about and process what we want to communicate to others and what they are trying to communicate to us. Nor can we forget the attitudes of the participants, the relationship between them, and the context itself, for these add another layer of meanings to the encounter.

Para-verbal and non-verbal features of oral language contribute to the effectiveness of how we communicate. Apart from what we say, a great deal is conveyed by how we say it. Thus, tone of voice, pace, pitch and how we project our voice are all part of the communication process. Meanings which we convey by these para-verbal features are open to misinterpretation, particularly by those from different cultures and backgrounds. In addition, there are non-verbal aspects such as looks and gestures, and the ways in which we move, which accompany what we say. These can sometimes extend our meanings but they can also sometimes confuse or even contradict what we say.

In classroom situations, teachers and pupils will act as both speakers and listeners. Hence, if classroom communication and learning is to be assured, all the participants need to have knowledge, skills and attitudes which are appropriate to both talking and listening in schools. This cannot be assumed.

This chapter considers such issues in more detail. Section 1 reviews the most significant characteristics of classroom communication: how much, by whom, to whom and about what. This is followed by a focus on particular types of classroom 'talk', a consideration of the demands made in 'listening', and in 'reading and writing'. Section 3 is on group interaction and collaboration in groups. Finally, the chapter concludes by addressing the important subject of linguistic diversity.

## 1 | CHARACTERISTICS OF CLASSROOM COMMUNICATION

If we examine classroom interaction closely a number of characteristics can be identified. These can provide important clues to the quality of the teaching-learning processes being observed.

## 1.1 How much talking is there and who is doing it?

A classic research study carried out in American secondary schools indicated that, in the teaching sessions observed, two thirds of the time was spent in talk and two thirds of that talking was done by the teacher (Flanders 1970). The picture was of a predominantly teacher-dominated situation. Although a wider range of teaching strategies are now used, teacher direction of talk and activities in secondary school classrooms remains at the core of practice. This has been characterized as a 'transmission' model.

The diagram below (Barnes 1975, **Primary Reading 11.2**), was developed as a hypothesis about the relationship in classroom communication between 'transmission' and 'interpretation' and the distinction between 'school knowledge' and 'action knowledge'. If a teacher sees knowledge as content (as existing, prescribed subject-matter which pupils are required to accept), then the communication will be mainly transmission and assessment will also predominate. As a consequence, pupils' talk and writing will be mostly as final draft presentation and the resulting learning will be 'school knowledge'. It is suggested that this is what is 'known' in lessons and is useful for answering teacher's questions, but it is quickly forgotten and has no impact on the learner's personal understanding and life outside school. However, if the teacher sees knowledge as existing in the learner's ability to interpret, then communication will be interactive, and there will be negotiation between the teacher's knowledge and the pupils' knowledge. Talk and writing will be collaborative and exploratory, and will support the struggle to understand as new knowledge is related to the learner's 'action knowledge'. There are clear resonances here with the contrasting views of learning which were reviewed in Chapter 9.

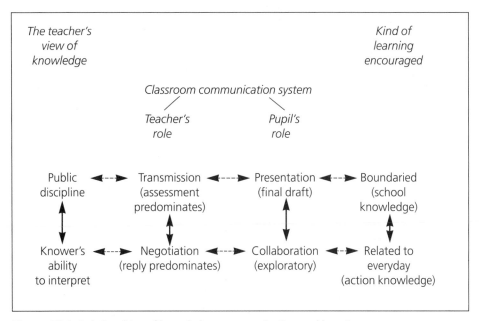

**Figure 13.1** *Relationships of knowledge, communication and learning*

It is important to recognize that to advocate interpretation does not mean that teachers should never tell pupils things or present knowledge directly. Rather, it implies that transmission should be part of patterns of communication which are fundamentally designed to allow pupils to negotiate their own way into new knowledge and understanding. Equally, communication systems that appear pupil-centred sometimes turn out to be simply more subtle forms of transmission. For instance, a study involving analysis of teacher-pupil interaction in group work (Edwards and Mercer 1987) showed teachers maintaining tight control over the activity and the discourse, even while overtly espousing the principle of pupil-centred experiential learning. The result was that pupils' grasp of concepts was what the study defined as 'ritual' (knowing what to do or say) rather than 'principled' (based on conceptual understanding). The interactions between teacher and pupils relied heavily on 'cued elicitation' (where to be 'right' the pupils had to guess what the teacher was thinking) and the teacher's main concern was to get through the set of planned activities. There are echoes here of reasons advanced for the predominance of the transmission mode by Barnes *et al.* (1986). He points to teachers' need to keep pupils on-task and under control, and also to external pressures to cover the syllabus, to emphasize the 'basics' and to assessment procedures which stress performance rather than depth of understanding.

For the authors of both studies, the issue has wider implications.

In making the ethical decision to prepare pupils for choice and responsibility, teachers implicitly choose also an interpretation view of learning. Teaching in which transmission predominates is the negation of 'education for living (Barnes 1975, p. 149)

The asymmetry of teacher and learner is essential to the 'zone of proximal development', and so also is the notion of control. . . . Just as verbal thought originates as social discourse, so self-regulated behaviour begins with the regulation of one's behaviour by other people. The successful process involves a gradual handover of control from teacher to learner, as the learner becomes able to do alone what could previously be done only with help. In formal education, this part of the process is seldom realized. For most pupils, education remains a mystery beyond their control, rather than a resource of knowledge and skill with which they can freely operate. (Edwards and Mercer 1987, p.168)

Here and now, at the turn of the century, such paradoxes and dilemmas are even more evident. A rapidly changing society requires pupils to learn to be flexible, adaptable, multi-skilled problem-solvers who can apply learning in new situations. At the same time there is emphasis on qualifications, examination success, 'standards' and statistical comparison of results – all linked explicitly or by inference to economic and moral revival. In addition, the National Curriculum is expressed in subjects and underpinned by the idea of cultural transmission. In making choices about classroom communication teachers are thus balancing a number of potentially conflicting demands, and the decisions they make about 'who does the talking' will inevitably reflect their values, beliefs and responses to some of these unresolved dilemmas.

To begin to reflect on classroom communication, a reflective teacher is likely to want to collect data rather than rely on impressions. Tape-recording can be a useful technique for collecting certain kinds of data on classroom talk (see Chapter 4, Section 3.6). An alternative way of collecting information about particular aspects of teacher talk is to devise appropriate checklists. These can be helpful both as a guide when preparing a session, or as a framework within which to reflect afterwards. A third approach is to devise an observation schedule which focuses on specific categories of behaviour. For example, four categories could be used, such as when the teacher asks a question, explains a task, manages the situation or disciplines a pupil (questioning, explanation, management, discipline). Each time one of these behaviours is noted it can be 'marked up' using a tally system: see Chapter 4, Section 3.3.

## Practical activity 13.1

*Aim:* To investigate time spent in talking and listening, in a whole-class teaching session.

*Method:* Choose your method of gathering data during a whole-class teaching session.

- Audio recording

- An observation schedule

- A checklist system.

Depending on which method you choose, you may want to gather data on your own teaching or that of another teacher.

Now select the aspect of interaction you want to focus on. For instance:

- How much talking is there?

- Who is doing the talking?

- Are there any differences between boys/girls, high/low attainers?

- What is the teacher talk about?

- What is the pupil talk about?

Information of this kind can highlight the pattern of talk in a classroom. It can often reveal aspects which surprise us, because it is so difficult to be aware of how much we talk, to whom and why, while we are engrossed in the process of teaching itself. Having identified the pattern of talk we need to decide whether what we do is consistent with our aims.

*Follow-up:* You could use a similar approach to investigate different aspects of classroom interaction, e.g. teacher-pupil interaction in group work; pupil-pupil interaction, generally or in small-group work.

You will find suggestions for other observations in subsequent Practical Activities in this chapter.

## 1.2   Where is the talk directed?

Given that much of the interaction in a classroom is teacher-controlled it is useful to consider how the teacher's time is distributed between whole-class, groups and individuals. There is plenty of evidence that, in the context of curriculum pressures, large class sizes and the demands of assessment, parity of attention is difficult to achieve. One feature which often causes problems is that there are variations in both the quantity and quality of teacher attention which is given to different categories of pupils.

There are four fairly obvious categories around which such variations have often been found: ability, gender, ethnicity and social class. The impact of integrating pupils with special needs also has to be considered. In busy classrooms, it is very understandable that teachers tend to deal first with pupils whose needs press most or whose actions necessitate an immediate response. However, the danger is that some other pupils may be consistently passed over as they move from class to class. Whilst the needs of all the pupils in a class cannot be satisfied simultaneously by any teacher, we do have a responsibility to ensure that teacher effort is distributed equitably.

### Practical activity 13.2

*Aim:* To identify if, when interacting with pupils, there are any patterns in the quantity and quality of teacher-child contacts.

*Method:* To assess the *quantity of interaction*, it may be advisable to enlist the help of a colleague as an observer. Alternatively a video-recording of a session could be made for later personal analysis. A simple schedule will be required on which to record contacts. This could distinguish between contacts with girls/boys, ethnic groups, attainment groups, etc. or even with particular individuals. It is then possible to make a tally of the different kinds of contacts. Decisions about whether to try to record all contacts or whether to adopt time sampling techniques will have to be taken (see Chapter 4, Section 3). If the latter is chosen, some practice is essential for the observer. It is also possible to focus on an individual child and to monitor the contacts with just that child. It may be interesting to note pupil-initiated interaction with the teacher.

To assess the *quality of contacts* requires a different approach. By quality we have in mind, following Rogers (1980), the 'genuineness, acceptance and empathy' that is conveyed through the contact, in combination with, following Bennett *et al.* (1984), the cognitive 'match' of task to pupil. Subjective interpretations are more likely to play a dominant part in this analysis, so it is probably helpful to use a video or for an observer to make field notes concerning the nature of contacts made. It would be particularly useful if time could be made for discussion with the teacher and pupils after the session.

*Follow-up:* You might want to share your observations with a friend or colleague. How do you interpret what you have found? How will it affect your planning and your teaching?

## 1.3   What is the talk about?

Teacher talk in the classroom can be divided into three categories: talk related to learning (e.g. exposition, questioning); administrative talk to ensure the management of tasks and activities; and disciplinary talk concerned with managing behaviour and maintaining control. The balance of time given to these different kinds of teacher talk in a lesson indicates the quality of the learning taking place.

As reflective teachers it is particularly important to consider the significance of teacher talk – processes which can be seen in the development work of the National Oracy Project (NCC 1991) and the Language in the National Curriculum Project (Carter 1990, DES 1990–1). For example, what might be the effects on pupils? What impressions might they gain about learning and about their own role in the learning process? What kinds of attitudes towards learning might pupils acquire? What types of learning are likely to take place?

### Practical activity 13.3

*Aim:* To identify patterns in the purpose of teacher contacts with pupils.

*Method:* We suggest the development of a schedule which lists different kinds of contact. This should be in terms of descriptive and visible actions (so that the amount of inference is low) and which do not overlap (so that the categories are exclusive). For example, you could try classifying teacher contacts with pupils using categories such as: 'instructional', 'managerial', 'social' and 'other'. Data might then be collected by time-sampling or a tally. The results could then be analysed to try to identify any different patterns of contact based on gender, ethnicity, attainments, abilities or personalities.

*Follow-up:* You might want to consider looking at pupil-initiated contacts, or at pupil-pupil interaction in a similar way (see below).

Of interest too is the kind of talk involved in pupil-pupil interaction. How much of pupils' talk is learning-related and 'on-task'? How much is social, and might be deemed to be 'off-task'? Of on-task talk, how much is related to managing the task (fetching equipment, sharpening pencils, rubbing out) and how much to carrying out the work and developing understanding? Some sorts of activities – cutting out, colouring in, routine procedures – seem to precipitate social talk. As one Year 9 pupil explained, 'I can colour in and talk at the same time.' What should our reaction be to this?

Looking at what talk is about leads us also to consider the issue of the specialized language of each subject. Most noticeably this concerns technical terms and specialist vocabulary. We need to think about how we introduce and use these in our expositions and their interactions. Equally, observations of pupil talk will help us to consider whether they are taking on the language of the subject as part of their conceptual development (as a significant act of ownership which is the basis for further thinking) or whether they are using terms as 'labels' with no real understanding. We have to remind ourselves that pupils in the secondary years are taking on many new subject 'languages' simultaneously. They are also having to adjust to words carrying different meanings in different contexts. For instance, think about some of the concepts which secondary pupils are likely to meet: matter, force, energy, credit, pressure, stress, mass, balance, texture, tone, rhythm, flow, inequality, status, power, competition, permeability, erosion, population density – and continue the list from your own experience.

Vocabulary is not the only aspect of language involved in subject learning. Successful learners will take on the syntactical structures and style of discourse associated with different disciplines. Talking for thinking makes considerable demands on linguistic competence. For instance, consider the demands in your subject for any of these syntactic structures – 'because' structures, to identify cause and effect; 'conditional' structures (if, if-then, unless); 'although' structures, to identify exclusions and apparent contradictions; 'therefore' structures, to draw conclusions; structures for hypothesizing and speculating (what if . . . , let, assume, suppose) – and for the structures which underpin evaluating, responding, describing, comparing, explaining, defining. Style of discourse can be observed by using the idea of continua – colloquial/formal; personal/impersonal; simple/complex. In textbooks, the discourse tends to the formal, impersonal, complex end of the spectrum. In classrooms, teachers may move up and down the scale in the same lesson but there is evidence (Richards 1978) that teachers of mathematics and the sciences use more textbook-style talk especially in exposition, when defining terms and when information is to be recorded. The influence of 'the language of science' is very strong. There are links here between the speaking and listening and the reading and writing that happens in subject learning. We consider this further in Section 2.5 below.

## 1.4 Analysing classroom language and interaction

We conclude this section with reference to a technique which was designed to look at literacy learning across the curriculum (Webster, Beveridge and Reed 1996) but which can be applied to teaching and learning processes as a whole. The model which is set out in Figure 13.2 can be used to highlight particular characteristics and qualities of interaction between teachers and learners.

The teacher axis runs vertically and represents the degree of teacher involvement in the learning interaction ('high' to 'low'). A learner's axis runs horizontally and represents the degree of learner initiative (from 'high' to 'low'). The model thus plots two key variables in any teaching and learning interaction (the teacher's involvement in the learning process, and the pupils' potential to take the initiative in learning). These combine to give four distinctive 'quadrants of interaction'. In an empirical study using the framework (Webster, Beveridge and Reed 1996), a comparison was drawn between the quadrant from which teachers thought they derived their pedagogy and what they were actually observed to do in the complex realities of their lessons. Of course, teacher and pupil talk is, with observed behaviour, a clear source of evidence on matters of this sort. Practical Activity 13.4 suggests how you might undertake such an investigation. Using this type of representation allows teachers to examine and develop beliefs and practices concerning teaching and learning. Indeed, developing such insights into both belief and practice is at the heart of a reflective pedagogy.

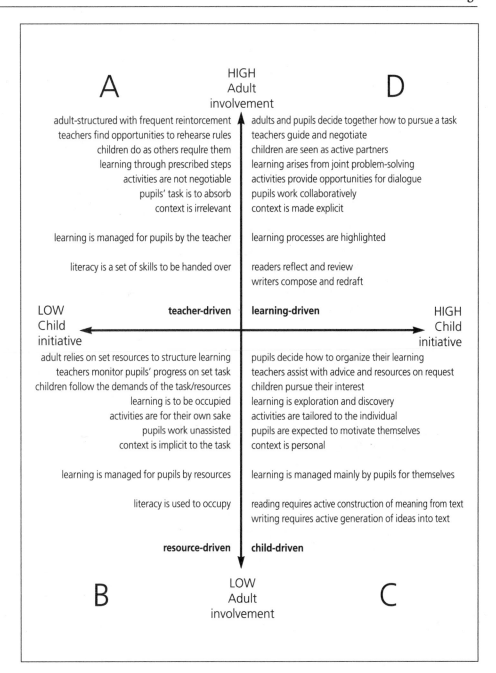

**Figure 13.2** *A model of adult–pupil proximation: literacy learning in classrooms (Webster, Beveridge and Reed 1996)*

### Practical activity 13.4

*Aim:* To consider the qualities of interaction in a lesson, by reflecting on differences between a lesson plan and the lesson as actually taught.

*Method:* First, you will need to produce a full lesson plan, setting out your educational objectives and teaching strategies (see Chapter 7).

Then you need to teach the lesson, and collect some evidence about it. Perhaps you could use some of the methods suggested in Chapter 4, or elsewhere in this book. Having gathered some data, take stock of it and produce a clear description of what happened.

The third stage is more analytical:

* On two sheets of blank paper, draw two copies of the basic four-quadrant framework (the skeleton without the writing) given in Figure 13.2.

* On your first copy: rework the lesson plan, by placing the key events you intended in the appropriate quadrant.

* On your second copy: rework your lesson description (or evaluation), by placing the key events as they actually happened in the appropriate quadrant.

Consider the differences between your two versions. What might these indicate to you about the dilemmas faced by teachers and the struggle for control over learning which takes place in classrooms?

*Follow-up:* How would you evaluate your findings? What strategies might you develop to shift pupils' initiative into a 'higher' quadrant?

## 2 | TYPES OF CLASSROOM COMMUNICATION

There are four particularly common types of oral classroom communication. These are:

* *Expositions:* where the speaker describes, informs, instructs, or explains
* *Question-and-answer exchanges:* frequently for testing and checking purposes, where there is often one right answer, (i.e. a 'closed' situation); also to encourage thinking, speculation, to develop understanding.
* *Discussions:* where the participants (whole class or small group) explore ideas and feelings together, (i.e. an 'open' situation).
* *Listening:* where the receiver hears and responds to the speech of other people.

Each of these situations has features in common as well as features which are unique to itself. For example, since every communicative situation is at least a two-way process, we need to consider the speakers as well as the listeners. In an 'exposition' situation the listeners are not likely to participate verbally very much. Nevertheless, the speaker should be aware of the listeners and watch the listeners for signs of understanding or otherwise, so that adjustments can be made. The listeners must listen, must be able to react and show if understanding has taken place, or, if not, must be able to ask for clarification. In addition, the listeners may also want to respond more actively. Hence 'expositions' can sometimes become 'discussions'. In such situations the roles of speaker and listener may change rapidly. The listeners will have to respond to the speaker and hold on to their own ideas, and wait their turn so that their ideas can be added later. Hence, in an interactive situation of this kind, considerable linguistic, social and cognitive demands are made.

Each situation, in fact, calls for particular types of awareness about the rules of communication. In order to participate productively, the rules must be clear and each participant must understand and accept those rules. Learning to speak and to listen are thus very important skills. Neither skill can be considered 'passive', for they both take place through interaction.

We now turn to examine the first of the four main types of oral communication that we find in the classroom exposition.

## 2.1 Investigating expositions

For an effective teaching session it is necessary both to stimulate your pupils and to provide structure for the subsequent activities. These requirements are just as pertinent for whole-class sessions as for group or individual work. Expositions, therefore, are a very common aspect of any teacher's talk. Although less commonly required of pupils, from time to time they may be asked to make a formal report back on an activity or a prepared presentation. In any such situation the opening 'moves' are particularly important in setting the tone of the session.

A number of different aspects of exposition might be considered:

1. Getting attention
2. Motivating the listeners
3. Orientating, so that expectations about the session are clear
4. Constructing and delivering the exposition itself.

The first three of these aspects have already been discussed in Chapter 12, Section 2.1, as part of our consideration of classroom management. Here therefore, we suggest some checklists to help to focus our attention on the fourth aspect of expositions – constructing and delivering the exposition itself.

## Checklist 13.1

*Aim:* To investigate aspects in the delivery of expositions.

When the speaker delivers the exposition:

- Is eye contact sustained, to hold attention and give interim feedback?
- Is an interesting, lively tone of voice used?
- Is the pace varied for emphasis and interest?
- Is the exposition varied by encouraging orderly participation?
- Are pauses used to structure each part of the exposition?
- Are appropriate examples, objects or pictures used to illustrate the main points?
- Are appropriate judgements made regarding the level of cognitive demand, size of conceptual steps, and length of the concentration span required?
- Is a written or illustrated record of key points provided as a guide, if listeners need memory aids?

## Checklist 13.2

*Aim:* To examine how an exposition is structured.

Are the instructions, directions, descriptions and explanations clear, concise and coherent?

Has the speaker:

- planned what is going to be said?
- stated the outline structure of the exposition? ('advance organizers' e.g. 'We are going to find out . . .').
- selected the key points: identified and made explicit the relevance of each and their relationship to each other? ('There are four things we need to think about . . . because . . .')
- sequenced key points appropriately?
- used short, simple sentences: explained specialist vocabulary if it needs to be used, given concrete examples or asked the listeners to generate their own?
- signalled when a new point is made? ('Now let's look at . . .' 'The third thing to look out for is. . .')
- summarized key points (or got the listeners to summarize)?
- sought feedback to check understanding (at each point if necessary)?

*Practical activity 13.5*

*Aim:* To observe and consider exposition as a teaching strategy.

*Method:* Use Checklists 13.1 and 13.2 to structure your observation and analysis of teaching by exposition. You may be observing another teacher or asking a colleague to observe you. It may be possible to do some self-evaluation by means of an audio (or video) recording (see Chapter 4 and Practical Activity 13.1).

*Follow-up:* What are the implications for your teaching of what you have discovered? It may be helpful to talk with your mentor about this or share your analysis with a friend who has also undertaken a similar observation.

## 2.2 Analysing question-and-answer techniques

Teachers, and pupils, use questions for a wide range of purposes and they can be seen as a vital tool for teaching and learning (Perrot 1982, **Primary Reading 11.8**). Asking questions provides immediate feedback on how participants are thinking and on what they know and it accounts for a high proportion of teacher talk.

Question-and-answer techniques are therefore seen as an essential means of helping us to understand learning processes. Listening to the 'answers', and not prejudging them, is an important way of learning about a learner.

Particular aspects concerning questions which might be reviewed are:

- the purpose, or function, of questions
- the form in which questions are asked
- the ways in which responses are handled.

Each of these aspects are now considered in further detail.

### The purpose, or function, of questions

Questions can be grouped in many different ways. However, two main categories commonly occur. The first is psycho-social questions: those which centre on relationships between pupils or between a teacher and the pupils. The second category is 'pedagogic' questions: those which relate to more specifically educational concerns, and to the teaching and learning of skills, attitudes, concepts and knowledge. Questions are frequently designated 'open' or 'closed'. A closed question has a specific answer; an open question can be answered in a variety of ways. Advice to teachers sometimes appears to suggest that it is better to ask open rather than closed questions. It is more useful to be clear about why questions are being asked, how we think we are using them to develop thinking and support learning. There are situations where closing down the questioning is a very useful strategy, perhaps for instance during recapping work or within an interactive sequence if it becomes necessary to re-establish focus or assert control.

It may be more profitable to think of questions in terms of the level of demand on pupils' thinking. Lower-order questions do not require pupils to go beyond recall of information previously taught or already known. Answers are 'right' or 'wrong'.

Higher-order questions require pupils to apply, re-organize, extend, evaluate, analyse information in some way. In this context it is important to consider the level of thinking indicated by a pupil's answer. A 'lower order' question may produce a 'higher order' answer and vice-versa.

Checklist 13.3 offers a framework for considering different kinds of questions in relation to purposes.

---

## Checklist 13.3

*Aim:* To provide a framework for analysing classroom questions. See how many uses of classroom questions you can spot in your school.

*Purposes of psycho-social questions:*
- *to encourage* shy or reluctant members to integrate by participating (e.g. 'Jan, you keep tropical fish don't you?')
- *to show interest* in and value for group members (e.g. 'You made a good point just now, Norita. Will you say it again for all of us?')
- *to develop respect* for each others' views (e.g. 'What do you think you would have done?')
- *to assert control* (e.g. 'Wayne, what are you up to?')
- *to implement routines and procedures* (e.g. 'Ahmed, what did I tell you to do next?')

*Purposes of pedagogical questions:*
- *to recall information* – for testing, consideration or feedback (e.g. 'Where is Ethiopia?')
- *to develop understanding* – selecting relevant information, describing, interpreting data (reading graphs, tables; comparing, contrasting (e.g. Which area has more rain in the summer? How does what you eat compare with this person's diet from a hundred years ago?)
- *to apply knowledge of rules or processes to new variables* – (e.g. 'What formula would you use for this?' 'Is this writer using metaphors?' 'What are the grid references for this town?')
- *to encourage analysis* – by identifying cause and effect, drawing conclusions, inferring, generalizing, finding evidence (e.g. 'From your observations what are the most significant factors affecting . . . ? 'What does this tell us about how people regarded pupils at that time?')
- *to explore information and ideas* with no set 'answer' (reasoning/interpreting, hypothesizing/speculating, imagining/inventing) (e.g. 'How do you think the hero would feel if . . . ?')
- *to encourage synthesis* of information and ideas by focusing on contradictions, discrepancies, different sources of evidence (e.g. 'What do you think really happened . . . ?')
- *to encourage evaluations, decision-making, and judgements* (e.g. 'Would it be fair if . . . ?' 'What is your opinion on . . . ?')
- *to encourage the transfer of ideas* and application of knowledge, (e.g. 'How is what we've found out useful. . . ?')

## *The form in which questions are asked*

Among the most important issues associated with classroom questioning techniques is the form in which the question is posed in relation to its purpose. The form of a question can have very diverse effects. For example, a teacher wants to encourage an evaluative response to personal reading and asks a 'higher order', 'open' question.

> Q. 'Did you like the book?'
> A. 'Yes/No.'

How could you reformulate this question to avoid this kind of monosyllabic answer?

In a testing situation what kind of information about what a pupil knows are we getting from this question and answer?

> Q. 'Has potato got starch in it?'
> A. 'Yes/No.'

Another form is the 'direct' question, which is short and simple in construction and has a single specified focus. For instance:

> Q. 'How did the Vikings make their boats?'

to which the answer may be lengthy though straightforward and factual, or:

> Q. 'What makes a good book?'

to which the answer may also be lengthy but consisting of opinions and ideas which may be complex to articulate.

Very different effects might result from using a 'direct' question compared to one which invites a monosyllabic response. A reflective teacher would need to consider whether such a form would be appropriate if the aim was to encourage exploration, evaluation, or to focus contributions on a particular suggestion.

A third form of question is the 'indirect' question. This is a long, composite question which may include a number of different leads. Again, such a question can be very useful in some situations but inappropriate in others. For example, 'indirect' questions can offer a number of different suggestions which might help in opening out a discussion and in providing a range of possible leads to explore. It would be less suitable in a testing situation, as the focus of the question would be relatively unclear. It could also be confusing to a pupil who found it hard to take everything in and who therefore got lost.

This latter example raises the question of formulating questions to match pupils' learning needs. This includes thinking about appropriate language and about the sequencing of questions to promote thinking which will lead to the development of understanding or the acquisition of knowledge. Analysis of lessons observed in the Leverhulme Project (Brown and Edmundson 1984) provides a very useful diagrammatic representation of some typical sequences (Figure 13.3).

| Type | | Description |
|---|---|---|
| Extending | 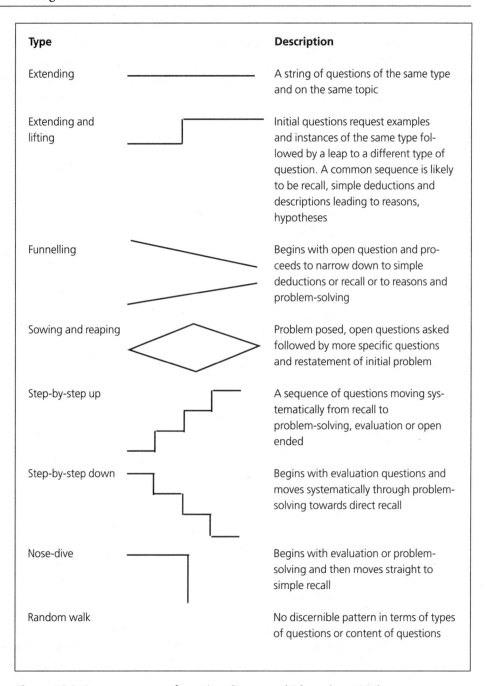 | A string of questions of the same type and on the same topic |
| Extending and lifting | | Initial questions request examples and instances of the same type followed by a leap to a different type of question. A common sequence is likely to be recall, simple deductions and descriptions leading to reasons, hypotheses |
| Funnelling | | Begins with open question and proceeds to narrow down to simple deductions or recall or to reasons and problem-solving |
| Sowing and reaping | | Problem posed, open questions asked followed by more specific questions and restatement of initial problem |
| Step-by-step up | | A sequence of questions moving systematically from recall to problem-solving, evaluation or open ended |
| Step-by-step down | | Begins with evaluation questions and moves systematically through problem-solving towards direct recall |
| Nose-dive | | Begins with evaluation or problem-solving and then moves straight to simple recall |
| Random walk | | No discernible pattern in terms of types of questions or content of questions |

**Figure  13.3** *Some sequences of questions (Brown and Edmondson 1984)*

In effective questioning sequences, teachers hold in mind the key questions for the learning they have planned. Around these they ask related questions which they formulate based on their professional judgement of pupils' needs. It is possible to plan these sequences (four or five questions) but as important is the questioning that arises from careful listening to pupils' responses. Where the teacher is too concerned to lead pupils towards a predetermined answer it is easy to miss hearing important clues to how understanding (or misunderstanding) is developing.

## *The ways in which responses are handled*

The third aspect of questioning, that of the ways in which responses are handled, is important to consider because it is the means by which feedback is offered to the pupils. Often a teacher's immediate and instinctive response is to evaluate, repeat or restate an answer.

Even when a teacher question is well formulated and well judged pupils' responses may be less than expected: silence, 'Don't know', a half-answer, a weak answer, an incorrect answer are all possible. In such circumstances, teachers still have many alternative strategies which can be used. Much will depend on the situation in which the question and answer exchange occurs. In a one-to-one encounter a single pupil can be taken though a specific sequence of questioning. In a small-group context this is also possible and other pupils can be encouraged to listen and be drawn into the interaction by redirected questions. In a large group or whole-class interaction we have to consider more factors. How can we keep everyone involved, listening and thinking? If we reject or pass over a response ('No, I'm afraid that's not right') what will be the effect on the pupil? Should we just give the right answer and move on? Adapted for context, the most useful strategies involve various kinds of pacing, prompting, probing, redirecting, recording and, not least, praising and developing rapport.

## *Pacing*

It has been found that, on average, a classroom teacher waits only two seconds before either repeating the question, rephrasing it, redirecting it to another child, or extending it. Student teachers, understandably nervous, often do not wait so long. The question of pace in relation to questioning takes us back to purpose.

For some purposes, a 'quick-fire' series of questions may be just what is needed. At other times we want pupils to give more thoughtful and considered responses. It is very helpful if such expectations are made explicit. For example, 'Now we are going to spend five minutes on what we covered last lesson and studied for homework. I am going to ask some quick questions and I want very short, factual answers. OK?' There are lots of ways of deciding which pupils answer. For instance, you can take answers on a 'hands up' basis, request particular respondents, or even allow each pupil who answers correctly to nominate the next person to answer. Make clear to the class how it will work. To engage the whole class, always ask the question before the next answerer is nominated. Have a strategy for moving on after wrong answers. For this purpose, keep the interaction fast with minimum evaluation.

On the other hand, if you are looking for more considered answers you might start with, 'I am going to ask a question and I want you to take time to think about your answer so I'm going to give you a few moments before we hear what you have to say. Try to make your answers as full as possible.' Wait four or five seconds after your question (which should, of course, be phrased in an appropriately challenging way). After working with your class for a while, you will be able to signal your approach in a shorthand – 'OK, quick-fire questions' or 'Thinking time for this question.'

### Prompting, probing and redirecting

Prompting may be necessary to elicit an initial answer, or to support a pupil in correcting his or her response. This can be done in many ways, including: simplifying, closer focusing, taking the pupil back to known material, giving hints or clues, asking leading questions, accepting what is right and prompting for a more complete answer. Probing questions are designed to help pupils give fuller answers, to clarify their thinking or to take their thinking further. There are a number of possible formulations, for example: 'Can you say that in another way?', 'Can you say a bit more about that?', 'Could you give us an example?', 'Can you say why you think that?', 'Is that always the case?', 'I'm not sure I understand. Can you make it clearer?', 'Does this remind you of anything we found when we were studying . . . ?'

Redirecting questions to other pupils can be a productive way of probing and keeping the class or group involved in the thinking. For example: 'Can anyone else help?', 'Can we accept that answer?', 'How does that fit with your idea, Susan?', 'You've nearly got it. Can anyone else explain the last step?', 'Does that help us with this . . . ?', 'Can we think of a better way to put that?'

### Recording

Another approach allows you to accumulate a range of responses to a question and to avoid evaluating individual answers. In this case you hold a string of answers (by recording on chalkboard, overhead projector or by repeating aloud) for general consideration and discussion. In the same way you can build up a teaching sequence, such as: solving a mathematical challenge, restructuring or analysing an investigation, considering 'for' and 'against'. Recording answers allows thinking to be held for more careful consideration and evaluation. In the same way recapping or summarizing responses is helpful in keeping thinking focused.

### Praising and developing rapport

As always, remember the value of encouragement and praise: 'That's a new point', 'We could use that idea', ' Simon knows something about this', 'I hadn't thought of that. Well done', 'You've nearly got it . . .'

Additionally, there is much value in encouraging pupils to formulate and ask questions for themselves and each other. Nor do you lose face by acknowledging that you don't always get it right, 'That wasn't a very good question, let's try another one.' Indeed, question-and-answer sessions are an important form of classroom interaction for the development of rapport. They have an evaluative element and, as relatively overt and public, they are potentially threatening to pupils. Respectful interaction, perhaps even with a little humour, is likely to be greatly appreciated.

Practical Activities 13.5 and 13.6 suggest ways of examining question-and-answer sessions with regard to asking questions and handling responses. In addition these activities invite you to consider the management of such sessions in particular in connection with the distribution of questions/responses between boys and girls/pupils of different attainment. Also of interest are the patterns of participation in a session, whether pupils volunteer or are nominated. It is useful to note the context, e.g. one-to-one, group, whole class.

## Practical activity 13.6

*Aim:* To investigate teacher questions within 'question-and-answer' exchanges.

*Method:* Either tape-record a suitable teaching session, or, by agreement, observe a colleague. Choose three five-minute periods in the teaching session, (e.g. beginning/middle/end), and write down the questions the teacher asks during each period.

It may also be possible to code the audience to whom the questions were addressed, (e.g. B = boy, Bb = group of boys, G = girl, Gg = group of girls, Mg = mixed group, C = class).

The questions could be classified using the pedagogic or psycho-social categories from Checklist 11.3.

*Follow-up:* Classifying questions should highlight the variety and level of the cognitive demands that were made. It is then possible to consider whether what we do matches our intentions and, if not, what changes could be made.

If the audience has been noted, it is also possible to analyse the distribution of questions and to consider any implications.

The activity could be repeated to analyse pupils' questions.

## Practical activity 13.7

*Aim:* To investigate teachers' handling of pupils' responses within 'question-and-answer' exchanges:

*Method:* Choose three five-minute periods during a teaching session (beginning/middle/end), and record how the teacher handles pupil responses during each period.

The responses can be related to the use of pausing, prompting and probing discussed above. Remember that the use of these strategies should be matched to teacher's purpose.

*Follow-up:* Analysing the data may help reflection upon the teacher's intentions, and whether they were fulfilled. It may also illuminate the extent to which pupil responses are 'heard' and engaged with by teachers. What effects can be identified resulting from the ways in which pupil responses were handled?

## 2.3   Considering class discussions

Discussion makes an absolutely fundamental contribution to learning. Its importance is well established for the development of very young children, and Wells (1986, **Primary Reading 11.3**) coined the attractive image of 'conversation as the reinvention of knowledge'. This is just as relevant to secondary pupils, indeed for learners of all ages. Barnes (1975) refers to pupils 'talking themselves into understanding', a process which we will probably all recognize if we reflect on our own learning processes and the element of exchange, construction and interpretation which is involved. Of course the psychological theories of Vygotsky and Bruner are central to this (see Chapter 9, Section 1.3, **Primary Readings 6.4, 6.5, 6.8 and 6.9**).

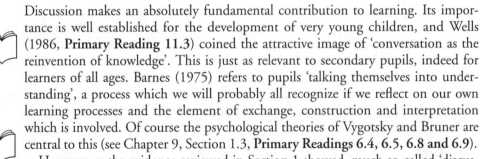

However, as the evidence reviewed in Section 1 showed, much so-called 'discussion' in schools takes the form of teacher-dominated transmission of pre-established knowledge. One common result of such tight teacher control is that pupils' engagement may become relatively routinized and ritualistic. According to Edwards and Mercer (1987, **Primary Reading 11.4**), classroom discussions certainly function to 'establish joint understandings' and 'common knowledge' between teachers and pupils. However, as we saw when their work was discussed in Section 1.1 of this chapter, they conclude that 'The basic process is one of introducing pupils into the conceptual world of the teacher. . . . It is essentially a process of cognitive socialization through language' (1987, p. 157).

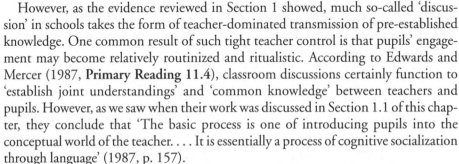

Because of the imbalance of power in classrooms between pupils and teachers – important both for learning and control – pupils normally do what the teacher has decided. Thus the idealized conception of the handover of control from teacher to self-directed learner is seldom realized, even in higher education. Whilst such teacher control is appropriate for some purposes, a genuine class discussion must start with some attempt to elicit opinions and knowledge from the pupils, to treat these views seriously and to explore their consequences. It is also productive to make the purposes of such activity explicit for pupils in terms of learning goals.

To be clear about distinctions between the varied forms and purposes of discussion is particularly important for teachers. At the beginning of a session a teacher may wish to find out what pupils already know about the topic on which he or she wishes to focus. This 'elicitation' may be achieved through open questioning. The elicitation may call for factual knowledge or opinions. If, however, the information that is elicited is also examined, interrogated and re-interpreted, then the episode becomes a more open-ended 'exploration'. It is the latter, exploratory situation which can be identified as a discussion. The content of what is discussed may vary considerably and may include what is believed to be factual knowledge, opinions, hypotheses, etc. It is the manner in which the content is treated rather than the content itself which is the distinguishing factor between elicitation and exploration. The teacher's role is to structure learning activity which involves discussion and to ensure that pupils develop the associated skills which make the process possible and effective (Phillips 1985, **Primary Reading 11.7**). We deal with this in more detail in Section 3 of this chapter, where we consider group work.

## 2.4   Focusing on listening

If communication is a two-way process, we have dwelt long enough on the speaker, or 'initiator'. It is also necessary for teachers and pupils to be competent listeners, or 'receivers'. However, we have already noted how the position of 'initiator' is usually taken by the teacher and that the role of 'receiver' is more often than not assigned to the pupils.

It is possible to identify different types of listening situations within classrooms, which serve specific purposes and impose particular demands. These purposes can be categorized in the following way:

- *Interactive listening* such as during a discussion, where the role of speaker and listener changes rapidly. In such circumstances participants need to exercise 'bidding' skills, for example, by raising a hand; sitting more upright and forwards; or by starting to move their lips. Some individuals will not have acquired any such skills and thus find it very hard to draw attention to the fact that they want to join in. Others may find it hard to notice tentative moves by group members and therefore may not 'let others in'.
- *Reactive listening* where listeners follow an exposition. For example, a set of instructions may be given which pupils are then expected to act upon, or an extended input of information may be provided, which the listeners are expected to be able to 'take in', possibly 'take notes' on, and then respond to. In reactive and interactive listening, the emphasis is on following the meaning of the speakers. Differences are often in the degree of formality and the status of the speaker *vis-à-vis* listeners.
- *Discriminative listening* where listeners have to discriminate between and identify sounds rather than meaning. For example, phonic sounds for spelling or reading purposes, or environmental/musical sounds.
- *Appreciative listening* where listeners listen for aesthetic pleasure, perhaps to musical or environmental sounds. For example, to the rhythm or sounds of words in poems and stories; or to other languages or accents.

It is useful to distinguish between these different types of listening so that we can be aware of the demands we make upon ourselves and the pupils. For example, how often do we allow appreciative listening, requiring perhaps a receptive level of listening? Do we convey how we want the pupil to listen actively in such a situation? How often do we demand extended attention, in a reactive situation, so that we hear someone out, follow a line of argument, consider a large amount of information, before moving into discussions?

As reflective teachers, we may want to be aware of the different demands that each type of listening makes. We also need to consider how many different listening contexts are experienced and how this might affect our listening and that of pupils (Dickson 1981).

### *Practical activity 13.8*

*Aim:* To analyse listening demands in the lesson.

*Method:* During a session or series of lessons try to note down how much time a teacher or pupils spend:

1. on each of the four types of listening mentioned above

2. in each of the four contexts indicated below.

The results could be recorded on a matrix for each session/series.

| Types of listening | Contexts of listening | | | |
|---|---|---|---|---|
| | Where (informal to formal) | To whom (known to unknown) | What (familiar to unfamiliar) | For how long |
| Interactive | | | | |
| Reactive | | | | |
| Discriminative | | | | |
| Appreciative | | | | |

*Follow-up:* Having collected the data, it is then possible to consider the range of listening experience pupils encounter. Is there a particular kind of listening which is important in your subject? How much attention is given specifically to assessing the level of listening skill pupils have and to how these might be developed? Are you making assumptions about pupils' listening skills which are not realistic?

It could be interesting to collect data on listening across the curriculum by undertaking this activity for one class through a day.

### Practical activity 13.9

*Aim:* To appraise the listening skills of individuals

*Method:* Record, or observe, a range of individuals (including the teacher) during a normal teaching-learning session in a classroom.

Note the types of listening called for and the contexts. Also, note any child's behaviour that might indicate that they heard, understood, or responded. For example, did they: look at the speaker, or look around; appear to agree, answer questions, offer suggestions; show awareness of others' needs, take turns?

*Follow-up:* By watching individuals closely, it may be possible to pin-point more precisely any difficulty a child might have, and whether it is specific to certain types of listening or contexts.

## 2.5 Reading and writing

Pupils also interact with written material as they read textbooks, worksheets and other related material. Their reading and their experience of speaking and listening will all feed into their writing.

Teachers of other subjects could usefully look at the content of the National Curriculum in English to identify pupil entitlement through the Key Stages. In helping pupils to talk, think, read, write, research in your subject area it is helpful to know how this meshes with what they are doing in English. Writing approaches which involve pupils talking about and evaluating their own writing in discussion with their teacher or peers at drafting and final 'publishing' stages may be also be appropriate for your subject. The role of speaking and listening is integral to developing literacy, and the experience of written language feeds back into talking and thinking.

If you wish to develop your awareness and understanding of this central aspect of pupil learning you will find more sources in the Notes for Further Reading. Here we will confine ourselves to some basic strategies you could use to develop your pupils as readers and writers in your subject area.

### Considering structure

A simple request: 'For homework, please read pages 10–15 in your textbook.' However, even such apparently straightforward requests can present pupils with considerable challenge. Narrative writing, which constitutes the main reading diet of the primary school years, is basically linear, but most subject reading in secondary school textbooks is non-narrative – a style of writing which can be very daunting because of its complex structures and conventions. Pupils may well need help to see how ideas and information are set down in your subject. Spending time occasionally to look at how paragraphs or even whole passages or chapters are constructed supports reading and offers models for writing, note-making and summarizing.

It may well be worth while helping pupils to identify the logic of some text in your subject, say a paragraph. How does it work? Find the main idea, any supporting or subsidiary ideas and work out how they are related. Using coloured pens or creating a diagram can help to reveal the structure, e.g. main idea and lists of examples; main idea with causes and effects; main idea with comparisons and contrasts; main idea and supporting evidence. Not all informational writing lends itself to neat analysis – try working out for yourself how ideas and information are presented in the books, worksheets etc. that you use.

Pupils faced with longer reading assignments will be helped by some discussion of analysis of the type and overall structure of the material. Help them to identify introductions, explanations, illustrations and examples, definitions, links and transitions, summaries and conclusions. Advising pupils to read conclusions first to get an overall idea is a simple strategy and could be part of a short pre-reading briefing in which you deal with possible barriers (difficult vocabulary), or give advice on how to tackle the reading. For example: 'The first part makes a suggestion for what might be done; the rest gives arguments for and against. Try to make two lists of these and we will talk about them next lesson'; or, 'You'll need to look very carefully at the diagrams – the writing explains them in more detail', 'Use the map to help you follow the information in the text.'

### Using 'signposts'

In English, words like 'and', 'but', 'so' indicate the relationship between ideas in speech and writing (they are 'connectives'). Being alert to the function of such words is very helpful to both readers and writers. The list which follows (based on Robinson 1975, Marland 1977) could be used to enable you to help pupils locate these signals in their reading and writing.

| *Go signals* | *Stop signals* |
|---|---|
| These indicate a continuing idea, another example, more in the same line of thought: | These are stronger than caution signals and indicate that something specially significant will follow: |
| and | without question |
| first, second, third | significantly |
| next | without doubt |
| finally | unquestionably |
| furthermore | absolutely |
| in addition | |
| similarly | |
| moreover | |
| at the same time | |
| also | |

*Caution signals*

These warn the reader to slow down because there is more coming on this point – it is often a conclusion or a summary so is likely to be important or useful for the reader:

thus
therefore
consequently
accordingly
in retrospect
hence
in conclusion
in brief
to summarize
as a result

*Turn signals*

These are particularly important as a warning to the reader that an opposing idea is coming or that there is a change in the direction of the argument:

but
yet
on the contrary
nevertheless
notwithstanding
on the other hand
otherwise
in spite of
although
despite
conversely
however

*Relationship signals*

These are most important in that they are used to create the structure of argument and ideas. The most frequently found are:

| | |
|---|---|
| Cause and effect | because |
| | since |
| | so that |
| | accordingly |
| Condition | if |
| | unless |
| | though |
| Illustration | for instance |
| | for example |
| Apparent contradiction | despite the fact that |
| | although |

**Figure 13.4** *Signposts in reading*

Drawing attention to particular structural features of written text in your subject helps pupils as writers as well as readers. Where pupils are inexperienced in constructing appropriate forms and formats it can be helpful to provide frameworks with headings and/or lead-in phrases or sentences which pupils can fill in or follow. As they become familiar with such conventional formats and regularly encounter models for writing in the reading you ask them to do, they will become more independent in structuring their own writing. Encouraging (and helping) pupils to make personal glossaries or dictionaries for your subject can also help with the use and understanding (and spelling) of specialist vocabulary.

*Finding out*

'Before the next lesson I want you to find out as much as you can about . . .'

It is important to ensure that pupils understand the different conventions that will help them to access information from a variety of sources such as libraries, books, dictionaries, maps, CD Rom, Internet, etc. In the same way as with signposts, it is useful to draw attention to the conventions of information texts and explain how they help to convey sense and meaning through the use of headings, sub-headings, bold text, italic text, captions, etc. Pupils will invariably need help with note-taking (you could provide frameworks, request them to identify key words/main points, teach techniques such as concept mapping) and with collating information from more than one source. Developing the ability to evaluate a source, detect bias, weigh up conflicting evidence, separate relevant from irrelevant information and other such skills are important for all learners and underpin the effectiveness of teaching and learning in many subjects.

There may well be a school policy on the cross-curricular development of these fundamental learning skills. In addition, many faculties, departments or subject groups work collaboratively on the review and development of learning materials with pupils' reading abilities in mind.

## 3 │ COLLABORATION AND CO-OPERATION IN GROUPS

In recent years a great deal of emphasis has been placed on the use of group work in classrooms based on the knowledge that it is a very common means of working in the adult world (Lloyd and Beard 1995, Kutnick and Rogers 1995, Cohen 1994, Galton and Williamson 1992, Bennett and Dunne 1992, **Primary Reading 11.6**). Indeed, the success of the human species itself has been attributed to the capacity to co-operate (Schmuck 1985). Group work also, of course, fits well within the social constructivist model of learning, which we considered in Chapter 6. Vygotskian ideas emphasize the importance and meaningfulness of the social context in which the learner acts and this is exactly what co-operative classroom group work, at its best, can provide.

### 3.1 Structure and process

There are many formulations of structures and processes for this kind of learning. The model we offer here is based on the one used in the Avon Collaborative Learning Project (1993). The structure described was designed to encourage collaborative group work in which discussion would play a major part.

The structure comprises four explicit and sequential stages: preparation, planning, action and review. See Figure 13.5 below.

During the preparation and planning stages, decisions and ideas could be recorded by a designated scribe – a standard *pro forma* is useful in the early stages of working in this way. Groups can also be encouraged to select one member to act as observer of the group process and report back findings at the review stage.

Group work often fails where pupils do not share a clear appreciation of the goal or

During this stage pupils consider questions such as:

*Why are we doing this task?*
*What are we trying to learn?*
*What will we end up with when it is finished?*
*What will it look like? Who is it for?*
*How will we know if we have a successful outcome?*
*How will we know if we have learned what we set out to?*

Clarify the purpose and aims of the task in hand; identify the outcomes required, set standards for the task outcome.

During this stage pupils consider questions such as:

*What do we know already?*
*What ideas do we have?*
*What do we need to know?*
*What resources do we have already?*
*What resources will we need?*
*What could each of us do that might help?*
*How long have we got to complete this task?*
*Who will do what?*
*When should we do it?*

Identify and assemble relevant facts and skills; decide what has to be done; translate this into a detailed action plan.

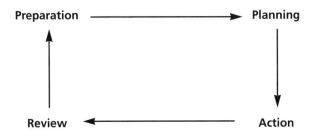

Review learning. The review can be concerned with the achievement of the task, the quality of the outcome, the success of the process.

Task review questions might include:

*Have we achieved what we set out to?*
*Have we met the standards we set ourselves?*
*What have we learned about the content of the task?*

Process review questions might include:

*What has gone well?*
*What problems occurred? How could we avoid these in future?*
*What have individuals done that helped?*
*When did the group make progress and why?*
*How could we co-operate better next time?*

Put the plan into action as a team. Build, stage-by-stage, on previous planning and preparation to meet the collective goals.

During this stage pupils consider questions such as:

*Are we doing what we planned to do?*
*How are we doing for time/targets?*
*Do we need to check/discuss what we have done so far?*
*Are we using our collective skills most effectively?*

**Figure 13.5** *Stages in collaborative group work*

when they lack necessary skills to accomplish the task to their own satisfaction. Learning may be superficial if the talk is not developing thinking. However, research has shown how, with appropriate guidance, even infant and junior pupils can become very skilled discussants in collaborative group-work situations (Ede and Wilkinson 1980, Tann and Armitage 1986). Secondary teachers can certainly develop this further. Many examples of classroom initiatives can also be found in the work of the National Oracy Project (Norman 1990, NCC 1991).

It is also useful to recognize the kinds of group roles which participants might adopt which affect the dynamics of the group: leaders and followers, jokers, inquisitors, non-participants, obstructionists and many other 'characters' might emerge.

An implicit aim of collaborative group work is the development of skills of interaction which foster collaboration, encourage respect for individuals and the contribution they make, support the development and articulation of ideas and minimize conflict. These include: active listening, taking turns, communicating clearly and concisely, being aware of the effect of one's actions on other individuals, encouraging others, nurturing not criticizing ideas, tolerating opposition, creating enthusiasm. Checklist 13.4 may be useful for shaping observation of these interactive skills.

---

### Checklist 13.4

*Aim:* To examine communicative and interpersonal skills in group work.

A reflective teacher may find it useful to consider some of the following questions:

1. Do the participants take turns or do they frequently talk over each other or interrupt?
   Do they invite contributions, re-direct contributions for further comments, give encouragement?
   Do they listen to each other? Are they willing to learn from each other (i.e. respond and react to each other's contributions)?
   Do they indulge in 'parallel' talk (i.e. continue their own line of thinking)?
   Does conflict emerge or is harmony maintained?
   Is conflict positively handled?
   – by modifying statements, rather than just reasserting them?
   – by examining assumptions, rather than leaving them implicit?
   – by explaining/accounting for claims?
2. Do participants elaborate their contributions?
   – by giving details of events, people, feelings?
   – by providing reasons, explanations, examples?
   Do they extend ideas?
   – by asking for specific information?
   – by asking for clarification?
   Do they explore suggestions?
   – by asking for alternatives?
   – by speculating, imagining and hypothesizing?
   Do they evaluate?
   – by pooling ideas and suspending judgement before making choices?

---

*Practical activity 13.10*

*Aim:* To analyse the dynamics of group interaction.

*Method:* Tape-record (or video) a group discussion. General features can be monitored on the following schedule. Additional detailed analysis can be carried out using Checklist 13.4 above.

| Group characteristics | Comments |
| --- | --- |
| 1. Composition of the group (e.g. size, sex, ability) | |
| 2. Seating arrangement (draw diagram) | |
| 3. Was there a leader, or scribe? | |
| 4. Was this challenged? | |
| 5. Did anyone not participate? (How did the others respond?) | |
| 6. In what ways did the group collaborate? | |
| 7. Was help needed/requested? | |
| 8. What intervention was given? | |
| 9. In what ways was the task successful? | |
| 10. Did the group feel satisfied? | |

*Follow-up:* Information gained from such schedules can help in the analysis of group interaction. It can help in understanding the roles of the members and whether these change if the composition of the group changes. Devising our own schedule can make us more aware of what we are aiming at. It also provides a framework for action to develop the potential of the group.

## 3.2 Teacher's role in collaborative group work

The essential elements of the teacher's role in collaborative group work are:

- designing tasks, matching the needs of the curriculum to pupils' development, group composition
- organizing the classroom to ensure appropriate space and resources are available
- explaining and clarifying tasks
- observing group process
- intervening in the process (as planned or as necessary) in order to move the group forward. This may be to re-shape or extend ideas/concepts or to solve a problem in the dynamics of the group.

- monitoring and assessing the outcomes of the process – learning, completed tasks and interpersonal development
- using this assessment in the design of future tasks or activity – both for individuals and groups.

Perhaps the most important contributory factor to successful group work is the nature of the task itself , and this has both social and cognitive aspects (Bennett and Dunne 1992, **Primary Reading 11.6**). It is important to decide whether a task could just as effectively be done by an individual or whether there is a genuine need for a group. This, of course, depends on the purpose of the task and on the way it is presented.

Several sorts of group activity are possible, as the following examples show:

- *Buzz groups:* various sizes of buzz group can be used to stimulate ideas and generate alternative approaches to initiate follow-up action. These are essentially limited to no more than five minutes, often much shorter and sharper. Large groups may cause more reticent pupils to remain silent. As an alternative, a pyramid group process could be used. Individuals think of their views or contribution; they share it with another child; each pair talks to another pair and agrees the ideas which they want to offer to the whole group; all the ideas are then pooled.
- *Problem-solving groups:* these are used where a single outcome is required from member collaboration. It is often successful in small- to medium-sized groups of four or five. This is particularly common in drama, technology, science and maths.
- *Forum work:* when carefully structured, this works well for large groups, such as the whole class, debating ideas or controversial issues (e.g. Troyna and Carrington 1988). Good preparation by the participants is essential.
- *Sharing groups:* where teachers want to encourage a positive interchange of views in a mutually trusting atmosphere, they can often succeed by using smaller, more intimate groups. Expecting the group to provide feedback on the processes of their discussion and/or the outcome is useful in helping to focus the participants' views. The end product, in such instances, could be a list of feelings or a poster depicting group conclusions for action.

As well as matching purpose to task and group size we need to think about the composition of groups. There is much discussion about creating single- or mixed-sex groups, attainment-based or mixed ability groups. Bennett and Dunne (1992) claim clear findings that mixed-ability groups of about four pupils are effective and that high attainers do not suffer. Compatibility of the group members is probably more important than just attainment. Sometimes friendship groupings can be successful, but not if friendship is more highly prized by the members than critical exploration which might reveal friendship differences. Many pupils have well-formed perceptions about who is good to work with – not always close friends. Interest groupings might be useful, but not where personalities might clash destructively. A teacher therefore needs to be very alert to the social groupings within the class, to the placement of shy or less popular pupil and with regard to the possible interaction of different personalities.

The other major management issue for teachers is whether and how much to intervene. A teacher's presence can inhibit learning. Early work in this field demonstrated that the teacher's presence often inhibited pupils and prevented them from putting the issues in their own language and focusing on questions which they wanted to raise. Instead, participants were found to be engaged in a game of 'Guess what's in the teacher's mind': trying to anticipate correct answers rather than raise questions or explore issues (Barnes *et al.* 1969, 1986). Without a teacher present, it is suggested, pupils could learn to take responsibility for their own learning. Some advocate a 'hands-off' approach, even to the extent of allowing groups to make mistakes from which they will learn. However, without a clear perception of the nature of the task and the purpose of the activity, teacher-less small group activity can become a time for 'chat and mucking about', rather than for 'discussion and work' (Tann 1981) It is a matter of professional judgement when to intervene to rescue a situation or move a group on. Others advocate 'planned intervention'. The National Oracy Project (Norman 1992) for instance stresses the importance of teachers as models for 'ways of saying' in groups. By planning to work specifically with each group in turn for an extended period the teacher, it is argued, can extend thinking and understanding, introduce a new aspect, help pupils to make connections and gain valuable information about individuals. The focus of the Oracy project was language and it is perhaps not surprising that their approach echoes that of the seminal Bullock Report, *A Language for Life* (1975) which prompted much discussion of language across the curriculum and still repays reading.

One danger of this way of working is that the desired learning of knowledge, skills and concepts becomes subservient to the production of an acceptable 'outcome', particularly if this outcome is some form of artefact or performance. If talking is learning then the challenge is to devise tasks which incorporate demands for abstract talking and thinking. This is not the kind of talk that pupils generate easily and they will need time, space and support in the form of teacher modelling.

An alternative model for structuring group work (Bennett and Dunne 1992) suggests a more active role for the teacher at the start by including a presentation stage. The cycle as set out below acts as a planning aid and aide memoire for the teacher. Its focus on monitoring and assessment in the final two stages requires the teacher to make decisions about what is to be assessed – individual learning or group process? And how this will happen – observation, discussion, tape-recording, written evidence?

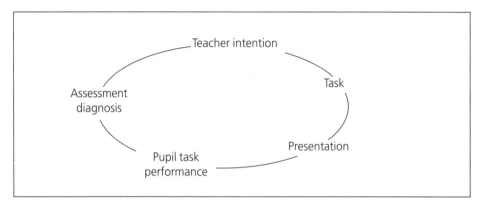

**Figure 13.6** *A teaching cycle*

Considerable interest in learning from British and American experience is being demonstrated by many European countries, from France and Spain to the new, post-communist states of central Europe, in which co-operative forms of learning may be seen as 'democratic'. Despite many of the positive outcomes which can emerge from such collaborative, learner-centred contexts, large classes with a wide range of pupil abilities, personalities, aptitudes and experiences pose severe challenges to any teacher. Indeed, the most consistent finding from the research is that, despite the commitment to this form of classroom practice, teachers have difficulty in implementing it consistently. As a less demanding strategy, co-operative groups with short-term targets can be set up within whole-class activities where each group reports back to the whole class. With an appropriate task, this can be contained within a single lesson and provide useful controlled practice in this way of working. Success creates a positive sense of purpose for teacher and pupils alike.

Whatever strategy you choose will depend on your purposes, on your assessment of pupil need, and on the task you have designed.

## 4 | LINGUISTIC DIVERSITY

Attitudes to oral language have changed dramatically in the last twenty years. For instance, there is much less consensus about the way to talk or write, as is evident from broadcasters and the diversity of written styles in use in modern society. This has occurred partly because of changes in two separate spheres. First, there has been a change in our understanding of the efficiency, as means of communication, of different styles of language. Early work by Labov (1969) identified the grammars of Black teenagers in New York and argued that their language was not 'deficient', 'sloppy' or sub-standard. He suggested that their grammars were 'different' and just as regularly rule-bound as more socially accepted forms of standard English. Second, there has been a change in the social acceptability of a wider range of different styles of language. This has meant that the notion of 'appropriateness' has increasingly come to be used (i.e. that different kinds of language are suitable for different purposes, audiences and situations). This is a contrast to the notion of 'accuracy' as an absolute  standard to be used to judge all language situations (see Stubbs 1983, **Primary Reading 11.9**, for further discussion of this issue).

Within classroom contexts, this led to two further developments. The first of these was support for the importance of accepting a pupil's language because it is part of accepting the child and thereby strengthening a positive self-image. This, in turn, led into the broader issue of the acceptability of language varieties. The use of non-standard English has for long had negative social consequences, of a discriminatory nature. Now, however, there is greater acceptance among educationalists that, whilst speaking in standard English should be part of the linguistic repertoire of each child, variation in language style should not be equated with language deficit, intellectual deficiency or social disadvantage (Edwards 1983, Stubbs and Hillier 1983). The necessity for an understanding of the distinction to be drawn between accent and dialect is also well understood. Using standard English dialect does not require the speaker to acquire Received Pronunciation (RP, at one time referred to as BBC

English). We have plentiful evidence of standard English spoken with a regional or other accent – though some still have higher status than others.

The necessity for a constructive and appreciative approach of this sort is most obvious when considering the extent of linguistic diversity in modern societies. For instance, a 1987 language census in London (ILEA 1987) found that no fewer than 172 different languages were spoken by school pupils. Some of such languages have been mapped in terms of the geolinguistic areas from which they are derived (Alladina and Edwards 1991) and this is shown in Figure 13.6.

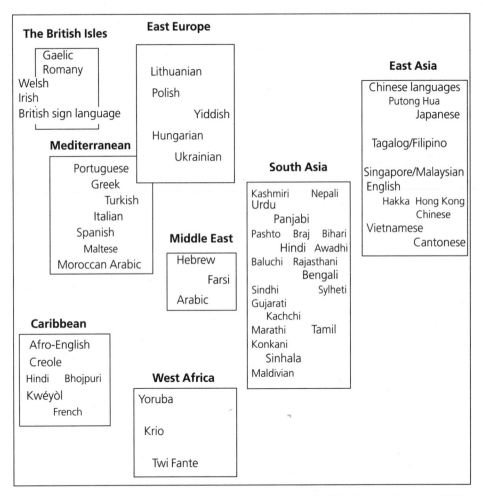

**Figure 13.6** *Geolinguistic areas of language spoken in Britain (Alladina and Edwards 1991)*

Language varieties used within a society with a single dominant language, such as English, reflect far more than simply an alternative means of communication (Pinsent 1992). Language is intimately connected to cultural identity and is thus closely associated with the life-experiences of minority ethnic groups in diverse societies. Often, of course, such groups are both economically and socially disadvantaged. As Pattanayak has so clearly expressed it, countries such as the UK have a poor record of affirming and working with different social groups, and yet the opportunity remains. He writes:

> As the identity of the various oppressed groups is threatened, identity assertion movements ensue. Ethnicity, which in the literature is variously expressed as assertion of cultures, communal upsurges, revival of religions, voices and movements of marginalized peoples, hurts the power elites. . . . Britain is on the crossroads. It can take an isolationist stance in relation to its internal cultural environment. The second road would be working together with cultural harmony for the betterment of the country. The choice is between mediocrity and creativity. (Pattanayak 1991, p. X)

Teachers have a particularly important and sensitive role to play here. The danger is that 'educational' concerns become overly framed by dominant mono-lingual conceptions of traditional English culture and language. Indeed, they may also become structured by socially unaware requirements of national curricula and assessment procedures. Whatever the circumstances, we would suggest that reflective teachers should work to affirm the positive value of minority languages and cultures, wherever they teach.

 This is likely to mean affirming and building on the bilingual capacities of many pupils (Bourne 1989, Levine 1990, Miller 1983, **Primary Reading 11.10**). The official advice in England is slightly different in emphasis. Thus SCAA's 'Framework for Policy' (1996) suggests how schemes of work should be developed so that pupils 'learn English; learn through English; and learn about English'. There is thus a dilemma between affirming and building on the first language of pupils, and teaching them to be competent in English as an 'additional language'.

Further, there is the expectation that pupils will be encouraged to 'be aware' of their own use of language in speaking and listening, reading and writing and be aware of the linguistic, cognitive and social processes involved in using language. This broader conceptualization of what it means 'to be literate' is very much in line with current work in Australia as well as the USA. The Kingman Report (1988) and the subsequent LINC project (Language in the National Curriculum) (Carter 1990) gave teachers rich insights into what was meant by 'awareness' and how such awareness might be developed. However, the English curriculum has been something of a political football in the 1990s and there is still pressure from some groups to narrow it. For secondary pupils, the social and political advantages of good control of standard English in their writing is undeniable. However, we will also want to aim at enabling them to make choices about when, where and for what purposes they will use different varieties of spoken English. Whilst there are advantages in being able to 'speak standard', the variety and integrity of regional or other accents are deeply embedded in cultures and identities. They must therefore be treated with respect.

Practical Activity 13.11 may help you to sort out some of your ideas on this subject.

## Practical activity 13.11

*Aim:* To highlight some of our own responses to language varieties.

*Method:* Use the results of this provocative rating scale for discussion with the results that colleagues obtain.

|  | I tend to agree | I tend to disagree |
|---|---|---|
| 1. Dialects are ungrammatical forms of English | | 1  2  3  4  5 |
| 2. In general middle-class pupils speak better than working-class pupils | | 1  2  3  4  5 |
| 3. Pupils should speak standard English at all times in school, including in the playground | | 1  2  3  4  5 |
| 4. The first task for all pupils in Britain is to learn good English | | 1  2  3  4  5 |
| 5. Dropping your 'H's is sloppy, and creates a bad impression | | 1  2  3  4  5 |
| 6. Poor grammar and spelling should be corrected at all times | | 1  2  3  4  5 |
| 7. All pupils should learn to appreciate Shakespeare | | 1  2  3  4  5 |
| 8. It is confusing for pupils to speak two languages in school | | 1  2  3  4  5 |
| 9. We should not use expressions like 'black mark' as they illustrate racist language | | 1  2  3  4  5 |
| 10.We should always try to use books which show different people as equals | | 1  2  3  4  5 |
| 11.Books with class, gender or race stereotypes can be used with care | | 1  2  3  4  5 |

*Follow-up:* The exercise above should produce some interesting discussion, but actual knowledge and understanding of these issues is another thing. Among speakers of majority languages, the most common state is one of relative ignorance regarding language varieties and the cultures and social circumstances of different social groups. The Notes on Further Reading may provide some ideas.

# CONCLUSION

This chapter has raised a large number of issues relating to communication which takes place within teaching-learning situations. Communication has been viewed as a key component of classroom life and therefore as an important influence on the learning which might take place. Chapter 15 looks at the assessment of that learning and how reflective teachers might analyse and respond to it. Before that we extend the discussion of the role of communication and interaction to take in the important topic of managing of relationships and behaviour. This is the subject of Chapter 14.

## *Notes for further reading*

For two classic studies of the use of language in the secondary classroom see:

Barnes, D., Britton, J. and Rosen, H. (1969)
*Language, the Learner and the School,*
Harmondsworth: Penguin.

*New edition*
Barnes, D., Britton, J. and Torbe, M. (1986)
Harmondsworth: Penguin.

Edwards, A. D. and Furlong, V. J. (1978)
*The Language of Teaching: Meaning in Classroom Interaction,*
London: Heinemann.

Other extremely useful overviews of classroom talk are provided by:

Tsui, A. B. M. (1995)
*Introducing Classroom Interaction,*
London: Penguin.

Graddul, D., Cheshire, J. and Swann, J. (1987)
*Describing Language,*
Buckingham: Open University Press.

Perera, K. (1987)
*Understanding Language,*
London: National Association of Advisers in English.

An excellent guide to methods of investigating classroom language is:

Edwards, A. D. and Westgate, D. P. G. (1987)
*Investigating Classroom Talk,*
London: Falmer.

High quality research-based analyses of teachers' classroom language and interaction are:

Sinclair, J. McH. and Brazil, D. (1982)
*Teacher Talk,*
Oxford: Oxford University Press.

Webster, A., Beveridge, M. and Reed, M. (1996)
*Managing the Literacy Curriculum,*
London: Routledge.

Cazden, C. B (1988)
*Classroom Discourse: The Language of Teaching and Learning,*
Portsmouth, N.H.: Heinemann.

There have been three excellent development projects on language in the UK, with publications which are practical, imaginative and firmly rooted in an understanding of pupils' learning. Some of their publications are in the form of pamphlets, booklets or newsletters but are worth a search.

However, on the National Writing Project see, for instance:

National Writing Project (1989a)
*A Question of Writing,*
Walton-on-Thames: Nelson.

National Writing Project (1989b)
*Becoming a Writer,*
Walton-on-Thames: Nelson.

National Writing Project (1989c)
*Writing and Learning,*
Walton-on-Thames: Nelson.

On the National Oracy Project see:

Norman, K. (1992)
*Thinking Voices: The Work of the National Oracy Project,*
London: Hodder and Stoughton.

National Curriculum Council (1991)
*Teaching Talking and Learning in Key Stage 3,*
York: NCC and National Oracy Project.

On the Language in the National Curriculum Project (LINC Project), see:

Carter, R. (ed.) (1990)
*Knowledge About Language and the National Curriculum,*
London: Hodder and Stoughton.

Department of Education and Science (1990–1)
*Language in the National Curriculum (LINC): Materials for Professional Development,*
London: HMSO.

For practical advice on teaching skills such as explaining and questioning, see:

Brown, G. A. (1978)
*Lecturing and Explaining,*
London: Methuen.

Perrot, E. (1982)
*Effective Teaching,*
London: Longman.      📖 **Primary Reading 11.8**

Harris, J. M. (1995)
*Presentation Skills for Teachers,*
London: Kogan Page.

On developing discussion, see work from the National Oracy Project referred to above. See also the classic, and salutary:

Barnes, D. (1976)
*From Communication to Curriculum,*
London: Penguin.      📖 **Primary Reading 11.2**

Barnes, D and Todd, F. (1977)
*Communication and Learning in Small Groups,*
London: Routledge.

Dillon, J. T. (1994)
*Using Discussion in Classrooms,*
Buckingham: Open University Press.

For more on the Avon model of collaborative group work, see:

Chambers, M., Jackson, A. and Rose, M. (1993)
*Children Developing as Readers: the Avon Collaborative Reading Project.*
Bristol: County of Avon.

On the management of groupwork, see:

Lloyd, C. and Beard, J. (1995)
*Managing Classroom Collaboration,*
London: Cassell.

Kutnick, P. and Rogers, C. (1995)
*Groups in Schools,*
London: Cassell.

Cohen, E. G. (1994)
*Designing Groupwork: Strategies for the Heterogeneous Classroom,*
New York: Teachers College Press.

An interesting analysis of the characteristics of 'Standard English' is provided by:

Wilkinson, J. (1995)
*Introducing Standard English,*
London: Penguin.

The linguistic diversity of our culturally rich modern societies is reflected in:

Alladina, S. and Edwards, V. (eds) (1991)
*Multilingualism in the British Isles,* Two volumes,
London: Longman

Linguistic Minorities Project (1985)
*The Other Languages of England,*
London: Routledge and Kegan Paul.

On providing for bilingual children, see:

Verma, M. K., Corrigan, K. P. and Firth, S. (1995)
*Working with Bilingual Pupils,*
Clevedon: Multilingual Matters.

Levine, J. (ed.) (1990)
*Bilingual Learners and the Mainstream Curriculum,*
London: Falmer.

Miller, J. (1983)
*Many Voices: Bilingualism, Culture and Education,*
London: Routledge.

**Primary Reading 11.10**

# CHAPTER 14

# How are we managing relationships and behaviour?

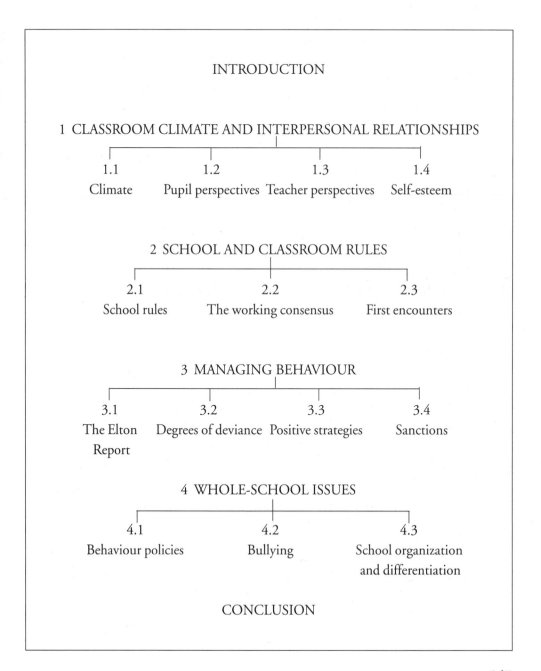

INTRODUCTION

1 CLASSROOM CLIMATE AND INTERPERSONAL RELATIONSHIPS

| 1.1 | 1.2 | 1.3 | 1.4 |
| Climate | Pupil perspectives | Teacher perspectives | Self-esteem |

2 SCHOOL AND CLASSROOM RULES

| 2.1 | 2.2 | 2.3 |
| School rules | The working consensus | First encounters |

3 MANAGING BEHAVIOUR

| 3.1 | 3.2 | 3.3 | 3.4 |
| The Elton Report | Degrees of deviance | Positive strategies | Sanctions |

4 WHOLE-SCHOOL ISSUES

| 4.1 | 4.2 | 4.3 |
| Behaviour policies | Bullying | School organization and differentiation |

CONCLUSION

## INTRODUCTION

Good classroom relationships are considered to be important in facilitating learning, in providing both teachers and pupils with a sense of self-fulfilment, and in underpinning the positive, purposefully disciplined working atmosphere which all teachers aim to create. Nor should we forget that such relationships reflect certain values and help to define a type of moral order for the classroom. In so doing, they model codes and principles of interaction which have wider and longer-term significance and thus contribute to the social, ethical and moral education of pupils.

However, despite its importance, the issue of classroom relationships often seems to defy analysis. Perhaps this is so because relationships are the product of such very particular, complex, and subtle personal interactions between teachers and pupils. Despite such inherent difficulties, the issue is of such significance that reflective teachers are likely to have it almost constantly in mind and this chapter sets out a framework for consideration of the issue. The framework is based on various analytic models of classroom relationships and is largely derived from interpretive studies.

This chapter is structured in four main parts. It is particularly concerned with the importance of the mutual awareness of classroom rules, with pupils' perspectives, with defining deviance and with developing positive strategies for managing behaviour. It also addresses whole-school issues as they impact on discipline. The chapter begins by considering some of the insights on classroom climates and interpersonal relationships which have been developed by social psychologists.

## 1    CLASSROOM CLIMATES AND INTERPERSONAL RELATIONSHIPS

### 1.1    Classroom climate

The influence of classroom environments on teachers and pupils has been a research topic for many years. One obvious question which emerged was how to define the 'environment'. Withall (1949) answered this by highlighting the 'socio-emotional climate' as being particularly significant. Indeed, he attempted to measure it by classifying various types of teacher statement – learner supportive, problem structuring, neutral, directive, reproving and teacher self-supportive. Understanding of the topic moved on when researchers began to define classroom environment in terms of the perception of teachers and children, rather than relying on outside observers (see Moos 1979, Walberg 1979). Further developments in this field have been comprehensively reviewed by Fraser (1986).

The climate of any one classroom is a product of the interaction of the teacher and pupils involved. Organizational factors (discussed in Chapters 5, 7 and 11 and later in this chapter) may have a part to play; but the nature and quality of interpersonal relationships is the most telling feature. In secondary schools where teachers work with many classes the climate of any one lesson is greatly influenced by the relationships built up over time and which are a 'given' whenever those involved meet together in an assigned space for a specific time. It is the quality of those relationships that determines how effectively (or otherwise) a positive climate is maintained in the face of major or minor difficulties and challenges. With this in mind we will not be surprised to find a variety of 'climates' in secondary school classrooms, nor that the same teacher may be involved in different climates with different classes: 'My Year 8s are a pleasure. We get on really well. They work hard and seem to enjoy being pushed. But the Y9s – they think they can get away with anything and they don't want to work. I think they hate me for trying to make them; I can't seem to get through to them; I can barely control them.'

Conventionally teachers and pupils are portrayed as opposing forces, engaged, openly or deviously, in a struggle for domination. The roles in this 'them and us' situation are encapsulated in D. H. Lawrence's description of school in *The Rainbow*: 'children . . . must be compelled by a stronger, wiser will. Against which they must always strive to revolt.' In theory teachers have the superior power; but pupils have the ability to resist and subvert, individually and collectively. How far the contested ground becomes a battlefield depends on how the opposing parties choose to deploy their strengths, the strategies each chooses. In general, research indicates, an 'understanding' emerges based on various forms of negotiation, open or informal, and which accommodates the interests of those concerned (Ball 1987 Hargreaves *et al.* 1975) (we discuss this idea of a 'working consensus' in more detail in the next section of this chapter). As we suggested in Chapter 12, the interpersonal relationships in a class both contribute to and are a product of this negotiation. The process is complex but two contrasting typologies of 'climate' may serve as a starting-point for analysis. A 'coercive' climate stresses power and authority as the basis for control; an 'incorporative' climate encourages participation and emphasizes the interpersonal (Reynolds and Sullivan 1979). Alongside this broad categorization it is interesting to take the 'emotional temperature' of classroom climate from 'warm/supportive' through 'cool/detached' to 'cold/antagonistic' and to consider what teachers do and say to establish the 'temperature' of the relationship. Practical Activity 14.1 will help you to investigate this.

One excellent source of insights on relationships is the work of Rogers (1961, 1969, 1980) on counselling. He suggests that three basic qualities are required if a warm, 'person-centred' relationship is to be established – acceptance, genuineness and empathy. If we apply this to teaching, it might suggest that acceptance involves acknowledging and receiving pupils 'as they are'; genuineness implies that such acceptance is real and heartfelt; whilst empathy suggests that a teacher is able to appreciate what classroom events feel like to learners. Rogers introduced the challenging idea of providing 'unconditional positive regard' for his clients and perhaps this can also provide an ideal for what teachers should offer pupils. Good relationships are, according to Rogers, founded on understanding and on 'giving'.

Rogers' three qualities have much in common with the three key attitudes of the reflective teacher, discussed in Chapter 1. Being able to demonstrate acceptance and genuinely empathize requires 'open-mindedness' and a 'wholehearted' commitment to learners. It also necessitates 'responsibility' when considering the long-term consequences of our feelings and actions.

However, this analysis is not really adequate as a guide to classroom relationships because additional factors are involved. For a number of reasons, the warmth and positive regard which teachers may wish to offer their classes can rarely be 'unconditional'. In the first place, they are constrained by their responsibility for ensuring that their pupils learn adequately and appropriately.

Indeed as Entwistle (1970) argued, 'loving' our pupils, establishing personal rapport (although it may help with disciplinary relationships) is not sufficient. Pupils need teachers to offer not themselves but the knowledge, skills and attitudes of their subject discipline. Second, issues of class management and discipline must always condition teachers' actions. Good relationships in classrooms must, then, be based on each teacher establishing a framework for order and earning the respect of the pupils. Without this, a mutual positive regard between teacher and class is unlikely to be developed. Instead, pupils are likely to regard the teacher as 'soft', 'weak' or 'muddled'. Teachers who successfully combine order with warmth and rapport achieve this in different ways. However, there are some features which they seem to have in common: use of pupil names; eye contact; willingness to help with work (e.g. a firm reprimand followed soon after by a deliberately supportive interaction); acknowledging and getting to know pupils out of class; being prepared to apologize if they get things wrong; use of humour (Woods 1979, Wragg 1984). We look in more detail at these and other teacher strategies in later sections of this chapter. At this point we focus on the pupils' perspectives.

## 1.2 Pupils' perspectives

One way for teachers to investigate the climate in their own classrooms is the Classroom Environment Scale (Fraser 1986). This can give direct and structured feedback on pupils' feelings about classroom life which could be obtained, for example, at the beginning and end of a school year (see Practical Activity 14.2).

## Practical activity 14.2

*Aim:* To 'measure' overall classroom environment for a subject at a particular point of time.

*Method:* Each pupil will need a copy of the questionnaire below. As a class (or in a group) pupils should be asked to circle the answer which 'best describes what their classroom is actually like in this subject'. Pupils could simply record their view, or the statements could be read out in turn for pupils to give simultaneous, but individual responses. They should answer 'True' if 'mostly true' and 'False' for 'mostly false'.

Scoring of answers can be done using the 'Teachers' column. Items not underlined and without the letter 'R' are scored 3 for True and 1 for False. Items with an 'R' are scored in reverse. Omitted or indecipherable answers are scored 2.

There are six scales, made up by adding various items, i.e.

| | |
|---|---|
| Involvement (I) | Items 1, 7, 13, 19 |
| Affiliation (A) | Items 2, 8, 14, 20 |
| Teacher support (TS) | Items 3, 9, 15, 21 |
| Task orientation (TO) | Items 4, 10, 16, 22 |
| Order and organization (OO) | Items 5, 11, 17, 23 |
| Rule Clarity (RC) | Items 6, 12, 18, 24 |

| Name | School | Class |
|---|---|---|

| Remember you are describing your **actual** classroom. | Circle your answer | Teacher use only |
|---|---|---|
| 1. Pupils put a lot of energy into what they do here. | True    False | _____ |
| 2. Pupils in this class get to know each other really well. | True    False | _____ |
| <u>3.</u> This teacher spends very little time just talking with pupils. | True    False | R_____ |
| <u>4.</u> We often spend more time discussing outside pupil activities than class-related material. | True    False | R_____ |
| 5. This is a well-organized class. | True    False | _____ |
| 6. There is a clear set of rules for pupils to follow. | True    False | _____ |
| <u>7.</u> Pupils daydream a lot in this class. | True    False | R_____ |
| <u>8.</u> Pupils in this class aren't very interested in getting to know other pupils. | True    False | R_____ |

9. The teacher takes a personal
   interest in pupils       True    False       _____

10. Getting a certain amount of
    classwork done is very
    important in this class.    True    False       _____

11. Pupils are almost always
    quiet in this class.      True    False       _____

12. Rules in this class seem to
    change a lot.         True    False    R _____

13. Pupils are often
    'clockwatching' in this class.   True    False    R _____

14. A lot of friendships have
    been made in this class.    True    False       _____

15. The teacher is more like a
    friend than an authority.    True    False       _____

16. Pupils don't do much
    work in this class.       True    False    R _____

17. Pupils don't fool around a
    lot in this class.        True    False    R _____

18. The teacher explains what
    will happen if a pupil
    breaks a rule.         True    False       _____

19. Most pupils in this class
    really pay attention to what
    the teacher is saying.     True    False       _____

20. It's easy to get a group
    together for a project.    True    False       _____

21. The teacher goes out of his/
    her way to help pupils.    True    False       _____

22. This class is more a social
    hour than a place to learn
    anything.           True    False    R _____

23. This class is often very noisy. True    False    R _____

24. The teacher explains what
    the rules are.         True    False       _____

I _____    A _____    TS _____    TO _____    OO _____    RC _____

Source: Fraser (1986)

*Follow-up:* Mean scores for each scale will provide some indication of the quality of the overall classroom climate and may raise issues for further consideration. (It should be noted that the inventory reproduced here is a short form of a longer inventory and is not a statistically reliable measure of the feelings of individuals.)

The use of instruments, such as the 'Classroom Environment Scale' can provide a helpful description of pupils' collective feelings and thus go some way towards representing their understanding of the classroom climate. However, such techniques arguably fail to grasp either the subtleties of the interpersonal relationships to which many teachers aspire, or the dynamic complexity of teacher-pupil interaction. Those studies which have involved data collected from pupils indicate strongly that pupils have accurate and perceptive understandings of classroom events and relationships. They also tend to agree in their observations of individual teachers. They understand how teachers define (or fail to define) rules of behaviour, how case law establishes limits. They can also predict how their teachers would respond in given situations (Wragg 1984).

Findings identifying pupils' likes and dislikes about teachers are remarkably consistent. Pupils like teachers who are consistent, efficient at organizing and teaching, stimulating, patient, fair, interested in individuals, and who have a sense of humour. They dislike teachers who are domineering, critical, boring, unkind, unpredictable, and unfair. It is noticeable that the features they select for comment are associated with three central concerns of the classroom: teaching and learning, control, and relationships. Pupils expect to be taught, to be helped (or in many cases 'made') to learn. Above all they don't want to be 'bored' (often a blanket term for anything disliked or difficult) and they want to feel a sense of achievement. They have a desire for order, rules, predictability and in general they expect this to be imposed. However, their attitude to the manner of the imposition is not simple. They will 'test' individual teachers to discover where the lines are drawn, how far rules can be manipulated. Strict/soft are two common constructs which pupils use, where 'softness' is usually regarded as a sign of weakness. 'Firm but fair' is positively valued. 'Fairness' in this context relates to matching punishment to offence in a way that is perceived as appropriate and does not involve the 'innocent' with the 'guilty'. 'Firm but friendly' involves getting a balance between discipline and warmth; teachers who are aloof and distant are not usually liked. In relationships pupils also hope for respect: to be allowed to retain a sense of dignity, not to be publicly humiliated or adversely compared to other individuals or groups, to be known and valued as individuals. Universally they respond positively to teachers who can 'have a laugh' or 'take a joke'.

Ethnographic studies of classrooms since the early 1980s have used the idea of strategies to analyse events (see Woods 1983, 1990 for reviews). To see pupil, as well as teacher, behaviour as 'strategic' with specific aims and intentions allows us greater insight into why situations arise and how they might be constructively managed. Robertson (1981) identified five main areas of pupil goals which are connected with disruptive behaviour:

- *immediate pay-offs* – these are normally acceptable acts which occur at the wrong time or in the wrong place, e.g. a pupil talking to another because there is something to say but when the teacher has required silence.
- *attention-seeking* – behaviour that will keep the pupil at the centre of the teacher's attention and be noticed by other pupils. Can be for peer acceptance or approval.
- *avoiding boredom* – a search for excitement to alleviate frustration or boredom; interfering with the course of the lesson or creating episodes to break the tedium.
- *status-seeking* – more extreme forms of confrontation with the teacher in the form

of challenge to authority or subtle forms of ridicule can create excitement and advance pupil prestige with peers. A degree of brinkmanship is frequently involved.

- *avoiding work* – passive resistance, creating 'incidents', delaying tactics can all serve the purpose of not doing work, avoiding risk or challenge.

Some of these categories may seem to overlap but it is interesting to consider pupil behaviour using this framework. For instance what is the goal of a pupil who persistently balances and rocks on the back legs of a chair? Is this a need to be noticed, a response to boredom, a challenge to authority or a way of avoiding work? How would you react? If you 'misread' the pupil's goal how might your proposed response be received?

### Practical activity 14.3

*Aim:* To consider the idea of pupils' goals and apply this idea to various forms of disruptive behaviour.

*Method:* As an observer you will be able to focus more consistently on a pupil than would be possible for a busy teacher. Make notes on the behaviour of individual pupils that could be considered to be disruptive (or potentially disruptive). Use the categories suggested above to identify possible pupil goals that lie behind the behaviour. Note how the teacher responds to the behaviour. Is the response appropriate for the goals you have assigned to the behaviour? How does the pupil react to the teacher's response?

Use your notes to reflect on the idea of pupil goals, teacher response, and 'misreadings'.

*Follow-up:* You might like to discuss this with your mentor or with colleagues. Try to have the idea of pupil goals in mind when you teach. Ask your mentor or a colleague to include this aspect in an observation of your teaching.

In considering the perspectives of secondary pupils it is important to remember the differences that exist in different age groups. As we saw in Chapter 8, pupils in Years 9 and 10 are experiencing a period of emotional, physical and social change and development. Aspects of relationships with peers, perceptions of the 'outside world' may not be congruent with the school's priorities and preoccupations. These are the years which notoriously are more difficult to handle. Issues of personal dignity and self-esteem (see 1.4) need to be approached with sensitivity.

## 1.3 Teacher's perspectives

So far a number of suggestions have been made about how a teacher can take account of the perspectives, feelings and position of children. Now it is time to change the focus onto ourselves as teachers for, as was discussed in Chapter 8, the self-image of a teacher is just as important to maintain as the self-image of the child. The fact that we have feelings, concerns and interests in the classroom means that we, too, need to feel the benefit of a degree of acceptance, genuineness and empathy if we are to give of our best.

Good teaching has never been easy, for to some extent it has always meant placing the learner's needs before the teacher's. However, classroom relationships are a very special and subtle phenomenon. On the one hand the nature of the working consensus (see Section 2.2) is related to disciplinary issues and problems which are likely to confront the teacher. But on the other hand, the quality of the relationships can, potentially, provide a continuous source of personal pleasure and self-fulfilment for a teacher. Coping with the dilemmas created by the natural tension between these two can be acute and painful. A survey conducted in sixteen comprehensive schools to identify sources of teacher stress puts pupil misbehaviour (noisy, difficult classes, impolite, cheeky pupils, non-acceptance of authority) at the top of the list (Kyriacou 1989). Such anxiety in itself creates problems: those under stress can over-react, misconstrue events, and feel forced into behaviour which runs counter to their values and aspirations.

Traditionally judgements about teaching ability are associated with classroom control; good control = good teaching. We may want to claim that a class may be well controlled without being well taught, but it is indisputable that good discipline makes teaching possible. For this reason problems with control can seriously damage a teacher's self-image and are especially worrying for student teachers and the newly qualified. Associated closely with this is the issue of 'noise level'. The attitude to noise in schools is complex and fascinating (Denscombe 1980, 1985). New teachers soon discover what level of noise is considered acceptable, what exceptions exist which are related to specific subjects, areas, or types of activity. A noisy class can be assumed to be out of control with the result that student teachers become preoccupied with keeping the class quiet and reluctant to attempt teaching which might generate too much noise.

If our feelings as teachers are an important factor in maintaining a positive working consensus, then ways of monitoring our feelings may be useful.

## Practical activity 14.4

*Aim:* To monitor and place in perspective our own feelings on classroom relationships.

*Method:* Probably the best way to do this is by keeping a diary. This does not have to be an elaborate, time-consuming undertaking, but simply a personal statement of how things have gone and how we felt.

You may want to focus on your relationship with the class or, more probably, with specific individuals. Incidents related to control may find a place.

Diary-keeping tends to heighten awareness and, at the same time, it supplies a document which can be of great value in reviewing events.

We would suggest that, once a diary has been kept for a fortnight or so, some time is set aside to read it carefully and to reflect upon it with a view to drawing reasonably balanced conclusions regarding ourselves and our planning of future policies in the classroom.

*Follow-up:* It would be valuable to discuss the issues which are raised with a colleague or friend.

## 1.4   Developing pupils' confidence and self-esteem

A constant theme through this chapter is the powerful interaction between learning and behaviour and the part that classroom climate and interpersonal relationships plays in this. Where learners feel they are failing, behaviour can deteriorate and a downward spiral begins. Pupils, even those who present themselves as hardened adolescents, often feel vulnerable in classrooms, particularly because of their teacher's power to control and evaluate. This affects how they experience school and their openness to new learning. A considerable responsibility is thus placed on teachers to reflect on how they use their power and on how this use affects their pupils .

First there is the positive aspect of how teachers use their power constructively to encourage, to reinforce appropriate actions and to enhance self-esteem (Lawrence 1987). 'Being positive' involves constant attempts to ensure and build on success. The point is to offer suitable challenges and then to make maximum use of pupil achievements to generate still more (see Chapter 10 for more on 'match'). This policy assumes that each learner will have some successes. Sometimes successes may be difficult to identify. Such difficulties often reveal more about the inability of an adult to understand and diagnose what a child is experiencing. As the psychologist Adler argued many years ago (Adler 1927), irrespective of the baseline position, there is always an associated level of challenge – a target for learning achievement which is appropriate and which can be the subject of genuine praise. The appropriateness of the achievement is a matter for a teacher to judge, but the aim should be to encourage all learners to accept challenges and achieve successes (Merrett and Wheldall 1990).

### Practical activity 14.5

*Aim:* To assess the degree and type of positive reinforcement given to pupils.

*Method:* There are many possibilities here:

1. Self-monitoring, that is trying to remain conscious of the need to praise efforts and achievements which pupils make. This involves actively looking for possibilities, but they must be genuine. The essence of this activity is expressed in the phrase 'Catch 'em being good'. Awareness is also likely to be heightened if the learning stages of each pupil and the tasks in which they are engaged are thoroughly appreciated and matched (see Chapter 9). Try keeping a diary-type record for a period noting your success (or otherwise) in being positive.

2. Observing by colleagues. A colleague who is able to sit in on a session to observe will be able to provide invaluable feedback. A suggested observational schedule is:

| Pupil's initial action | Teacher's reinforcing action | Pupil's response |
|---|---|---|
|  |  |  |

A discussion would be very helpful after the session, particularly to identify any patterns in pupil responses and to consider whether any other appropriate opportunities for reinforcement are being missed.

3. Analysis of written feedback to children. Pupils' workbooks provide a permanent record of teacher responses to their efforts. A tally of 'types of comment' is an easy exercise. Some headings might be:

|  | Pupil A | Pupil B | Pupil C | Pupil D |
|---|---|---|---|---|
| Encouragement given: |  |  |  |  |
| a phrase |  |  |  |  |
| a sentence |  |  |  |  |
| Diagnostic advice given: |  |  |  |  |
| Extension proposed: |  |  |  |  |
| No comment given: |  |  |  |  |
| Discouragement given: |  |  |  |  |

*Follow-up:* There is a simple point to be made in considering attempts to be positive as a whole. If, as an outcome of this monitoring, it is found that some pupils do not receive adequate reinforcement, bearing in mind their apparent needs, then the teacher should both check that opportunities for praise are not missed and make provision so that genuine opportunities occur. These can then be monitored. This is another, motivational, aspect of the 'match' (see Chapter 8, Section 2.5 and Chapter 10, Section 2.1) which is very important for the personal development of any learner.

The significance of self-esteem in determining pupils' attitudes to learning and consequently in affecting behaviour is well established. Much effort has been given to ways, such as those outlined above, to help learners develop a positive self-image. However, this must be done with understanding. Of late some of these methods have been questioned for being over-reliant on 'empty praise' and generalized assertions of worth. 'Self-esteem . . . should come as a result of doing something good, not being constantly told you're smart' (Gardner 1995). This echoes earlier findings that pupils who are praised for effort when they feel their achievement is poor may view the teacher's judgements as untrustworthy, putting more strain on an uneasy relationship (Covington and Beery 1976). Praise must be judicious. In building relationships and developing self-esteem it is more useful to remember that most pupils respond to teachers who respect their opinions, empathize with their problems and failures, encourage them to stick at learning, show them how to improve and celebrate their achievements.

We have concentrated here on pupils' learning achievements. It is of course possible to take a similarly 'positive' approach to 'catching them being good' in connection with attitudes and behaviour.

We now turn to the potential for the destructive use of teacher power. This can specifically relate to pupil learning but here we want to focus on the way in which control is used and to 'avoiding destructive action'. In most situations teachers try to be calm, firm and fair – they act within the bounds of the working consensus and use various types of legitimate 'routine censure' to maintain discipline.

Unfortunately, there is a well-documented tendency for teachers to reprimand pupils over-personally when telling them off in the heat of the moment. Or routinely to use destructive sarcasm. The effect of this can be that the pupils may feel attacked and humiliated so that, rather than conforming more, they 'want to get back at' the teacher who has 'picked on' them 'unfairly'. Here, the problem is that the teacher's action is 'unilateral' and lies outside the understandings of the working consensus. The recommended way of enforcing authority whilst at the same time protecting the self-esteem of individuals is to express disapproval of the action rather than of the perpetrator and focus positively on the preferred action (Hargreaves *et al.* 1975). A reprimand can then be firmly given, but the self-image of the pupil is left relatively intact. He or she then has the choice to conform with dignity. This will be discussed further in Section 3.2 where we focus on positive strategies for managing behaviour.

Thus, reflective teachers are likely to attempt to use their power positively and constructively, and they will be particularly aware of the potential damage to relationships which can be done by over-hasty reactions to some classroom crises.

A further reflection on relationships and self-esteem concerns the degree of involvement in the class by pupils. Here we want to return to the notion of the 'incorporative' approach (see Section 1.1). An 'incorporative classroom' is one which is consciously designed to enable each pupil to act as a full participant in class activities and also to feel themselves to be a valued member of the class. Classes vary in the degree to which differences between pupils and their abilities are valued. Such differences between people must inevitably exist, but a contrast can be drawn between classes in which the strengths and weaknesses of each pupil are recognized and in which the particular level of achievement of each individual is accepted as a starting point, and classes in which specific qualities or abilities are regarded as being of more value than others in absolute terms. In the case of the latter, the stress is often on achievements rather than on the effort which may have been made; the ethos is often competitive rather than co-operative; the success of some is made possible only at the cost of the relative failure of others. The overall effect is to marginalize some pupils whilst the work of others is praised and regarded as setting a standard to which others should aspire.

Quality of work and standards of achievement are crucially important considerations, but there are also many other factors to bear in mind. For instance, we would suggest that an incorporative classroom will produce better classroom relationships and more understanding and respect for others than one which emphasizes the particular success of a few. Such issues are particularly significant when specific assessment information is gathered. Pupils come to secondary schools with the results of Teacher Assessment and standardized assessment testing from the end of Key Stage 2. In the context of league tables and discussion of the concept of 'value added', schools may administer additional tests to ascertain 'baseline' positions. This emphasis on attainment must be handled very carefully if it is not to threaten the self-esteem of lower-achieving pupils. Schools have ways of recognizing and celebrating individuals' considerable other strengths and achievements including 'pupil portfolios' or 'records of achievement'.

Thus, there are some central questions about how pupils are valued which should be answered by a reflective teacher. Among them are those which are suggested in Practical Activity 14.6 below. This time it takes the form of a checklist.

## Practical activity 14.6

*Aim:* To consider the degree to which the classroom is structured and run so that each pupil can fully identify with class activities.

*Method:* There are several indicators which might be considered:

1. Which is emphasized most: the absolute achievement of pupils or the efforts which are made?

2. How wide-ranging are the pupil achievements which are valued? Does everyone experience at least some success?

3. In decisions about content, are the interests of each of the pupils recognized and given appropriate attention? Is the previous experience of pupils equally drawn on in selection of content and teaching approaches?

4. How is the work of the class represented in displays, in assemblies, in more public situations? Are there some pupils whose work features more often and others whose work is seen less often?

5. Are pupils helped to learn to respect each other?

6. Does any unnecessary and divisive competition take place?

7. Is assessment activity and its reporting handled sensitively?

*Follow-up:* Having completed your review, consider any insights related to the different experiences of e.g. boys/girls, ethnic groups, pupil attainment, particular individuals. Could you do anything to increase the sense of inclusion for all pupils?

Overall then, teachers wishing to sustain an incorporative classroom will set out to provide opportunities for pupils to feel valued and to 'join in'. At the same time they will attempt to eliminate any routines or practices which would undercut such aims by accentuating the relative weaknesses of some pupils (Prutzman *et al.* 1978, Putnam and Burke 1992, see also Clegg and Billington 1994).

Checklist 14.1 will help in recognizing pupil behaviour that we associate with low self-esteem.

---

## *Checklist 14.1*

*Aim:* To recognize pupil behaviour that is associated with low self-esteem.

Check 'Yes' or 'No' against these statements of pupil behaviour. Do any of your pupils:

- try to get others into trouble/tell tales/complain?
- deliberately stop others from working?
- engage in destructive name-calling?
- criticize others?
- argue constantly?
- destroy their own or others' work?
- develop avoiding tactics with reference to work?
- need reassurance/constantly ask for help?
- find it impossible to say anything good about themselves?
- find it difficult to accept praise?
- never ask questions or volunteer information?
- play the joker or class clown?

A predominance of 'Yes' answers for individuals or the class as a whole indicates that specific attention to raising self-esteem through appropriate strategies might well be beneficial.

---

## 2 | RULES AND RELATIONSHIPS

### 2.1 School rules and ethos

Newcomers, pupils or teachers, will encounter one expression of the school's ethos in the form of the school rules, usually to be found in the school handbook. Schools have very different approaches to rule definition as these contrasting statements from case studies of two schools illustrate (McManus 1989). In each case it is the headteacher speaking:

We have few rules written down and I can't think of any off hand. They tend to lead to silly situations: we have requests, not rules. For example, we have no rules about uniform but we ask the pupils to dress reasonably. If a pupil came to school in wholly unsuitable clothing then we would certainly not send them home or show them up in front of others. The pupil's tutor might compliment them on the outfit but point out it was not suitable for school. They would have shown it off to friends and to us and not got into trouble. They would usually leave it at home the next day. (p. 32)

Some pupils make it impossible for their teachers to teach. For example, we had one pupil who broke our rules from almost the day he came here. In his first year he broke the uniform rules on eight occasions: these included wearing the wrong jumper, having no tie, and coming to school dressed in a jean suit and wearing a hat in school. In the end we had to suspend him when he came to school with a shaved head. It may seem a minor matter in itself, but we feel we have to get compliance in the small things or we find ourselves in battle over things that should never be challenged by pupils. Defeat on the issue of uniform will lead, domino-style, to defeat in total. (p. 33)

While these examples may represent the extremes of the school rules' continuum, in general most schools have abandoned long lists of DON'TS, many about where and when it was not permitted to run, talk, eat etc. These, like rigidly prescriptive uniform rules, provide opportunities for pupils to attack and challenge the system and require disproportionate amounts of staff time to uphold. However, in some cases prohibitions and prescriptions have been replaced by a list of aspirations – concern for others, caring and generous behaviour towards one another – which are too general for specific application or capable of being misunderstood.

The Elton Report (DES/WO 1989) on discipline (See 3.1 below) considered that:

schools which simply have long lists of prohibitions and no consistent behaviour policy are more likely to be troubled by bad behaviour than those which have harmonized all the features of the institution concerned with behaviour. (p. 98)

Elton recommended that:

the number of rules should be kept to an essential minimum, and only include ones which the school will enforce. The reasons for each rule should be obvious. . . . The distinction between rules which are a direct application of fundamental principles, such as an absolute ban on physical violence, and administrative regulations, such as the name tagging of clothes, should be made quite clear. (p. 100)

It may be clear to teachers why particular rules are necessary. It is not always clear to pupils or parents. Rational authority depends on understanding. Any rule for which no rational explanation can be provided is suspect.

It can also be interesting to follow the example of one school (White 1990) where the staff considered school rules where 'everyone' had been substituted for 'all pupils'. They were surprised to discover how often staff behaviour appeared to suggest exemption from the rules, leaving pupils room to doubt the 'rational explanation' for the rule.

*Practical activity 14.7*

*Aim:* To consider school rules as an expression of school ethos.

*Method:* Obtain a copy of the 'official school rules'. What is the status of this document? Is this the form in which the school rules are communicated to pupils and parents as well as staff? Try to identify all the ways in which school rules are expressed and communicated to different groups.

Consider the school rules in the light of the observations in the Elton Report noted above.

What do the rules and the way they are expressed say about the school's ethos and approach?

*Follow-up:* If possible discuss the role of school rules with senior and/or middle managers in the school.

Many schools provide staff with 'official guidelines' which exemplify recommended approaches to situations relating to discipline and control, e.g. movement of pupils around school, unruly behaviour outside the classroom, lateness, litter. In some cases these may extend to school-wide recommended routines and procedures for classrooms, e.g. entering and leaving, seating, moving furniture, visiting the toilet. In effect, these are rules in action. Schools vary in the extent to which they seek to influence or support the individual teacher in managing the class. In reality however, because of the uncertainty of classroom life and the uniqueness of teachers and pupils the negotiation of classroom rules is essentially personal and individual. It is to this process that we turn in the next section.

## 2.2   The working consensus

If, as reflective teachers, we are to take full account of the interpersonal climate in our classrooms, we need a form of analysis which goes beyond description and measurement. It needs to recognize both the speed at which things can happen in classrooms and the inevitable power relationships between teachers and children. One such form of analysis, we suggest, is offered by adopting an interpretive approach and, in particular, by using the concept of a 'working consensus'.

Classroom order and discipline, as the Elton Report (DES/WO 1989) repeatedly emphasized, is most constructively based on good relationships and a sense of community. The concept of 'working consensus' (Hargreaves 1972) helps us to identify the factors involved in the dynamic relationships between teacher and pupils.

A working consensus is based on a recognition of the legitimate interests of other people and on a mutual exchange of dignity between the teacher and the pupils in a class. Embedded in this is a tacit recognition of the coping needs of the other and a shared understanding that the 'self' of the other will not be unduly threatened in the classroom (Pollard 1985).

In a classroom, both teachers and pupils have the capacity to make life very difficult for each other and a pragmatic basis for negotiation thus exists. However, a positive relationship, or working consensus, will not just appear. To a very great extent, the development and nature of this relationship will depend on initiatives made by teachers, as they try to establish rules and understandings of the way they would like things to be in their classes.

Pupils expect such initiatives from teachers and they are unlikely to challenge their teacher's authority to take them, so long as the teacher acts competently and in ways which pupils regard as 'fair'. However, it is also the case that, through negotiating the working consensus, the pupils recognize the greater power of the teacher. As they do so they also expect that the teacher's power will be partially circumscribed by the understandings which they jointly create within the classroom. Hopefully, these teacher initiatives will be based on appropriate principles and values.

Understandings and 'rules' develop in classrooms about a great many things. These might include, for example, rules about noise levels, standards of work, movement, interpersonal relationships. The first few lessons with a class – the period of 'initial encounters' (Ball 1981) – is a particularly important opportunity during which a teacher can take initiatives and introduce routines and expectations (Hamilton 1977, see Section 2.3). This is often a 'honeymoon period' when teachers attempt to establish their requirements and pupils opt to play a waiting game. However, both the 'rules' and the teacher's capacity to enforce them are normally tested before long, for pupils usually want to find out 'how far they can go' and 'what the teacher is like' when pressed.

As a working consensus is negotiated, both overt and tacit rules are produced. These are normally accepted by the majority of the class and become taken-for-granted.

Whilst some classroom rules are overt there are many more which are tacit. Awareness of this is very important for all teachers, but it is especially necessary for a student teacher who is likely to be working with pupils who have already established a set of understandings with their normal teacher. Two things have to be done: the first is to find out what the rules are; the second is to check that when attempting to enforce and act within them, student teachers are doing so in ways which will be regarded as 'fair'. This is essential if teachers are to establish the legitimacy of their actions in the eyes of the pupils. The concept of 'fairness' is vitally important in establishing a working consensus. Because of this, reflective teachers need to develop a variety of ways of monitoring children's perspectives and the criteria by which they make judgements about teachers. For this reason, a number of possible techniques are suggested in Practical Activities 14.8 and 14.9.

To be unaware of classroom rules and understandings is likely to produce a negative response from the pupils, because actions which they regard as incompetent or unfair will almost inevitably be made.

In addition to the content and legitimacy of classroom rules, on which practical activities have been suggested, there are several other aspects of rules which can also be productively considered. In particular, the 'strength' and the 'consistency' of rules can be identified.

### Rule frame

The strength of rules indicates the extent to which situations or events are 'framed' by expectations. This concept is referred to as 'rule frame' (Pollard 1980). It relates to the

## *Practical activity 14.8*

*Aim:* To identify the overt and tacit content of class rules.

*Method:* The overt rules may be available in school or departmental guidelines. They may be displayed in the class, especially if they relate to health and safety. The best way to gather information on tacit rules is to observe, note and study the patterns which exist in what people do. From your observations you should be able to infer the various categories of rules. Another way is to record the events which lead to pupils being reminded of 'the way we do things here' or to being 'told off'.

Asking the pupils is a possible next step. With care, this can be done in informal discussion. Ask them to explain to you what the rules are for this lesson with this teacher. Which ones are most sacred? What would you have to do to be really in trouble? Which ones are not so important? What would the teacher let you get away with?

Finally, try to check your assumptions and inferences with the teacher by asking for his or her account of class rules and how rigidly they are applied.

*Follow-up:* Knowing the overt and tacit content of rules in a classroom makes it easier to evaluate social situations accurately, to act with the competence of a 'member' and to use such rules in achieving goals.

## *Practical activity 14.9*

*Aim:* To check that we are acting in ways which are regarded as being 'fair'.

*Method:* Again, the only really valid source of information on this is the pupils. Whilst it is possible to discuss the issue openly with them, it is probably less contentious and as satisfactory to watch and note their responses to teacher actions. This should be a continuous process for teachers who are sensitive to the way pupils feel about lessons, but it is worthwhile to focus on the issue from time to time. Both verbal and non-verbal behaviour could be noted and interpreted – the groans and the expressions of pleasure, the grimaces and the smiles. From such information, and from the awareness to be gained from such an activity, it should be possible to analyse classroom actions in terms of the classification which is discussed below.

One obvious but important point to note here is that not all pupils will feel the same about teacher actions. This requires careful consideration,

*Follow-up:* The feedback which this activity should produce, could contribute to the smooth running of the class and to the maintenance of the working consensus. If rules which were previously established are being broken by a new teacher, then pupils are likely to become resentful. If classroom rules are not being maintained and enforced by the teacher, then pupils may well consider the teacher to be 'soft' and may try to 'play him or her up' for a 'laugh' at their expense.

way in which action is constrained by understandings of appropriate behaviour which are developed for particular situations. For instance, one might compare the strong rule frame which may exist in a hushed library, with the relatively weak rule frame which often exists in classrooms during wet dinner breaks. For some purposes, such as a transition between phases of a lesson (see Chapter 12) one might want the rule frame to be strong, thus ensuring very tight control. On other occasions, such as during an indoor break time in social areas, a weak rule frame may be perfectly acceptable and may allow pupils considerable choice. Situations of difficulty often arise where a strong rule frame is expected by a teacher but pupils act as if the rule frame is weak. If this happens, a teacher has to act quickly to clarify and define the situation and to re-establish the rules in play.

Teachers can influence the degree of rule frame by their actions, statements and movements. For example, an active, purposeful entry to a classroom is a clear signal that a teacher wants to get attention and one which will normally tighten the frame immediately. Conversely, acting rather casually, or withdrawing into conversation with a visiting adult, will usually cause the rule frame to weaken and may result in pupils relaxing in their approach to activities.

The ability of a teacher to manage the strength of rule frame has a great deal to do with classroom discipline. In particular, skilful management provides a means of pre-empting serious difficulties through giving clear expectations about acceptable behaviour. By its very nature, though, the development of such understandings cannot be rushed and frequently needs to be reviewed explicitly by teachers and pupils.

The degree of consistency with which rules are maintained provides an underlying structure for learning sessions. Conversely, teacher inconsistency tends to reduce the integrity of the working consensus and the sense of fairness on which it is based. This, in turn, can lead to a variety of subsequent control difficulties.

Relationships between teacher and pupils, which derive from a working consensus, have important implications for discipline and control. Figure 14.1 provides a simple model which may help us to reflect on the types of action which teachers and children may make in classrooms when a working consensus exists. The most important distinction is between actions which are bounded by the understandings of the working consensus and those which are not. Five basic 'types of action' can be identified.

- *Non-legitimate censure.* This is the type of teacher action which pupils dislike and cannot understand. It often occurs when a teacher loses his or her temper or feels under great pressure. The effect of such actions is that pupils feel attacked and

| Teacher Acts | | | Pupil Acts | |
|---|---|---|---|---|
| Unilateral | Within working consensus | | | Unilateral |
| Non-legitimate censure | Legitimate routine censure | Conformity | Legitimate routine deviance | Non-legitimate rule-framed disorder |

**Figure 14.1** *A classification of types of teacher and pupil clasroom action*

unable to cope. They perceive teacher power being used without justification. Such actions lie outside the bounds of the working consensus and are likely to lead to a breakdown in relationships.

- *Routine censure.* This is the typical teacher response to pupils' routine deviance – a mild reprimand. It will be regarded by pupils as legitimate, insofar as such a reprimand will not threaten their dignity nor be employed inappropriately. Censures of this type are within the bounds of the working consensus.
- *Conformity.* These actions, by teachers or pupils, are 'as expected'. They are according to the tacit conventions and agreements of the working consensus.
- *Routine deviance.* This is the type of mischief or petty misdemeanour which is accepted as being part of the normal behaviour of pupils for this lesson. Talking too loudly, 'having a laugh' and working slowly are examples. Such activities are partly expected by teachers and are not normally intended by pupils as a threat. They are thus within the bounds of the working consensus.
- *Non-legitimate, rule-framed disorder.* This is a type of pupil action which teachers dislike and find hard to understand. It often occurs when a pupil or a group of pupils feels unable to cope with a classroom situation and thus seek to disrupt it. They are particularly prone to do this if they perceive themselves to have been treated 'unfairly' or feel that their dignity has been attacked. Action of this type usually reflects the cultural rules of peer groups and can be used to build up a type of 'solidarity' or an alternative source of positive self-esteem.

The Practical Activity suggested below is designed to assist in the analysis of classroom relationships, using this basic classification. The central argument is that 'good relationships' are based on the existence of a negotiated sense of acceptability and fairness which teachers and children share.

### *Practical activity 14.10*

*Aim:* To consider the idea of consistency from the pupil's perspective.

*Method:* Arrange to talk to a group of pupils from a class you teach and/or have observed. Ask them to tell you, from their point of view, about the rules that apply in that particular class. Try to find out how they came to know about these rules. Ask whether the rules are always applied in the same way. Try to get examples of when the rules are not consistently applied. How does it vary? With pupil behaviour? From pupil to pupil? With teacher mood? Day of the week? Time of day? How do the pupils feel about this? Do they see what happens as 'fair'?

Consider the pupils' answers in the light of the classifications in Figure 14.1, above.

If possible extend the discussion by trying to find out whether teachers differ in how consistently they apply classroom rules.

*Follow-up:* You might like to repeat this with another group of pupils from another class. Discuss your findings with your mentor or a colleague. How will this reflect how you approach establishing classroom rules?

## 2.3 First encounters

First encounters with new classes are seen as extremely important by teachers. In their first few lessons with a group they make conscious efforts to establish a classroom climate and working consensus for the school year. Student teachers, coming in later and for a limited time, are faced with the challenge of how to manage a class where routines, rules and relationships are already firmly in place. One study (Wragg 1984) looked in some detail at teachers' first encounters with their classes. The teachers, who were interviewed and observed, were both experienced and students in training. We want here to use the findings of this study to characterize generally what experienced teachers do and to identify some of the issues for students.

Teachers appear to have three main objectives for first encounters:

- to establish some degree of dominance
- to establish ethos, rules, routines and procedures
- to begin to build relationships.

We will take each of these in turn.

### *Dominance*

To establish 'dominance' teachers consciously project a confident, business-like image of 'being in charge'. Strategies employed include: controlling entry into the room, choice of seating, movement around the space; taking up a central position in the room; frequently scanning the room, making sure this is obvious to the pupils; making and holding eye contact with individuals; referring to 'my' space/rules/ways. They also deliberately project a larger-than-life version of themselves, possibly building on an established 'reputation' in the school.

### *Ethos, rules, routines and procedures*

The focus of first lessons is usually management. However, this is done within an understanding that effective control is achieved *through* teaching. Establishing the subject and a work ethic quickly is a priority but the lesson content is selected to be interesting and not too demanding. Teachers concentrate on establishing expectations, rules and routines.

Rule-setting is dealt with in different ways:

- directly by stating 'my rules'
- discussion of rules to ensure understanding – rules not negotiable
- indirectly, to be inferred from 'case law', i.e. teacher instructions/reprimands
- by negotiation (not a frequent strategy).

The most frequently observed rules were concerned with: 'No talking when the teacher is talking'; territory (who can go where); respect for property; working procedures (hands up, don't interfere with others, how to present work); safety. A moral dimension was evident in the handing over of responsibility to pupils for books, equipment etc., and in the establishing of a work ethic.

Teachers indicated the importance of rules and their intention that they be kept in different ways. In some cases they exercised their personal authority, issuing a reprimand combined with a sudden change of voice or a rapid movement. Other teachers placed rules in a wider social context, emphasizing responsibility or respect for others. All, quite explicitly and obviously, reprimanded any rule transgressions in the early sessions, leaving fine-tuning till later.

### Relationships

Teachers' long-term aspirations are to substitute dominance with order based on mutual understanding and relationships. They give indications of this in a number of ways in early lessons:

- using a higher than normal level of praise, encouragement, reassurance
- deliberately making contact with individuals
- apologizing for errors
- explaining why things are to be done
- offering help with work
- using pupils' names
- using humour.

Of these, pupils particularly appreciated teachers' willingness to apologise for mistakes etc. and to give explanations and reasons for things. Learning pupils' names gives teachers a powerful edge. Many make considerable efforts to learn names quickly, sometimes making this a public activity/personal challenge shared with the pupils. Being able to name individuals is useful both for control and for building relationships. There are dangers though of stereotyping pupils whose names have been targeted and associated with certain behaviour.

Humour is a slippery attribute. It can be both positive and destructive; it can encompass banter, cheerful insults, self-deprecating references. Its success relies very much on the relationship between those involved and is generally assumed to appear later in teacher-pupil interactions. In this study however it appeared very early in the lesson sequences of some teachers and helped to build relationships. Male teachers made more (and earlier) use of humour.

### Issues for student teachers

It is obvious that in teaching there is no substitute for experience. Confidence grows with experience and it is this characteristic that was, not surprisingly, most obviously lacking in student teachers in the study. Their acknowledged fears about surviving in the classroom often led them to behave in ways they hoped they wouldn't, even though in most cases they got pupils working and experienced little misbehaviour.

Making a good start is clearly important for teachers and pupils. It is generally considered that student teachers can expect a 'honeymoon period' of about six lessons *except* where the first one or two lessons make a negative impression. What might help to ensure a positive start? First of all, we have to consider the problems involved in taking over someone else's working consensus. You have to establish your own control and you want to teach in your way but you don't have a blank sheet to work on. It is useful to find out as much as you can about the existing ethos, rules, routines of the school and the classes you are working with. This will enable you to avoid asking, for example, 'What does Mr X do about . . . ?'; 'What do you usually do . . . ?'. Instead make your understanding of rules and routines explicit by saying, 'I know that you . . .' The explicitness is necessary as it indicates that you are associating yourself with the prevailing consensus; you can't assume that pupils will automatically work with you as they do with their usual teacher. If you want to change something you can explain 'I know that you usually . . . but today I want you to . . .'

The concern of experienced teachers to concentrate on management in first encounters contrasts with a tendency for student teachers to focus on content, starting with something spectacular to impress pupils (and perhaps mentor or tutor). Planning less ambitious activities leaves you freer to concentrate on being business-like and clarifying the working consensus. Take your cue from experienced teachers and work on appearing 'in charge': position yourself where you can dominate; be mobile (come out from behind the desk); be brisk and firm, resist distracting questions; scan class, stare at individuals; work on tone and pitch of voice; stop and wait if necessary. Like a theatre audience with actors, pupils would prefer you to be in charge than to fail.

Gradually understanding and adopting an existing classroom rule-system is comparatively straightforward, but you have to build your own relationships. Often the realization that this is so important makes it more difficult to approach. Student teachers worry about what will happen if they are too informal and this can lead them to be more distant and aloof than they ideally want. Learning names will help you with control and with making relationships. Warmth will come as you feel confident in your management. The strategies used by experienced teachers (see above) can be helpful. Practical Activity 14.11 will help you to think about using praise and encouragement. Chapter 12, 'How are we managing our classes?', is also relevant here.

## 3 | MANAGING BEHAVIOUR

## 3.1 The Elton Report

Good discipline and order in classrooms and schools are the products of a great many factors and influences. When they break down though, there tends to be an almost instinctive, but oversimplified, response to 'sort out the troublemakers'. This can even occur at a national level. In March 1988 a Committee of Enquiry, chaired by Lord Elton, was set up in the United Kingdom following a media outcry over reports of teachers being physically attacked by pupils and about 'indiscipline in schools today'. Wisely however, the Elton Committee took a balanced and wide-ranging view of the issues involved and this is reflected in their report (DES/WO 1989). As the Elton Report stated:

> The behaviour of pupils in a school is influenced by every aspect of the way in which it is run and how it relates to the community it serves. It is the combination of all these factors which give a school its character and identity. Together, they can produce an orderly and successful school in a difficult catchment area; equally, they can produce an unsuccessful school in what should be much easier circumstances. (DES/WO 1989, p. 8)

## Practical activity 14.11

*Aim:* To develop the use of praise and encouragement.

*Method:* It is worth spending time quite deliberately developing your repertoire of words and phrases for praise and encouragement. It is very easy to get stuck with the routine 'Good' which rapidly becomes a meaningless punctuation and loses its effect on the pupils. Think also about the value of being explicit about the reasons for your praise of work or behaviour.

Make a list of words, phrases and statements that could be used. A thesaurus might be useful. Some suggestions to start you off:

Well done!, Good try!, Excellent, Great

That was good because . . .

Good start – can you see where you might go next?

Good idea – can you say a bit more about that?

That's an interesting point . . .

Neil's just said something helpful . . .

I really like that idea . . .

You must have worked hard on that . . .

Well done everyone. I know that was a difficult task but you all tried really hard today.

I know you're trying not to be distracted by people, Sue. You did well today; keep it up.

From your list choose those you think you will feel comfortable using. Practise saying them aloud. (Remember, teaching is part acting.)

*Follow-up:* Consider the research that found secondary teachers tend to reprimand twice as often as they praise (Rutter *et al.* 1979). Try out some of your formulations for praise and encouragement and reflect on the outcome.

The report went on to emphasize the importance of having clearly stated boundaries of acceptable behaviour, of teachers responding promptly and firmly to those who test boundaries, of motivating pupils to learn, of providing a stimulating and appropriately differentiated curriculum, of managing groups skilfully, of creating a positive school atmosphere based on a sense of community and shared values, of achieving the highest possible degree of consensus about standards of behaviour among staff, pupils and parents, of promoting values of mutual respect, self-discipline and social responsibility. Furthermore, it drew attention to the role of governors, local education authorities, training organizations and government in supporting teachers.

The holistic approach of the Elton Committee is well founded and the issues to which they drew attention are considered thoroughly in various chapters of this book. School and classroom discipline problems should be pre-empted where purposeful communities of people exist; with teachers acting sensitively, skilfully and authoritatively to maintain the values, rules, expectations and activities which provide an infra-structure for order and meaning.

Only 1 per cent of the 2,540 secondary teachers who responded to the Elton survey thought that there were 'serious' discipline problems in their schools. However, only 4 per cent felt that there was 'no problem at all'. In classrooms, teachers were more concerned with persistent irritating behaviour rather than serious violent behaviour. Around the school the main problems were identified as unruly rather than aggressive behaviour. Problems were more frequently described as 'serious' in relation to inner city locations, lower-attaining pupils, pupils from ethnic minorities, and boys.

In a smaller study undertaken by the Elton Committee, 100 teachers in ten inner-city comprehensive schools were interviewed. They identified the following areas as important for development in relation to strategies for dealing with misconduct:

- the school's system of incentives and sanctions
- shared understanding and mutual support among school staff
- ways of talking things through with pupils
- teaching styles
- home-school relationships.

The Elton Report includes a statement of eleven 'principles of classroom management' (DES/WO 1989, p. 71). You will find all these points discussed at various points in Part 2 of this book. However, we have drawn them together in Checklist 14.2 below, in the form of questions for use in planning, undertaking and reflecting on classroom practice.

---

## Checklist 14.2

*Aim:* To reflect on classroom management and discipline using the Elton Report's 'principles or classroom management'.

Do I:

1. Know my pupils as individuals – names, personalities, interests, friends?
2. Plan and organize both the classroom and the lesson to keep pupils interested and minimize the opportunities for disruption – furniture layout, pupil grouping, matching of work, pacing lessons, enthusiasm, humour?
3. Involve pupils in establishing the rules for classroom behaviour and routinely reinforce why they are necessary?
4. Act flexibly to take advantage of unexpected events rather than being thrown by them?
5. Continually observe or 'scan' the behaviour of the class?
6. Remain aware of, and control, my own behaviour, including stance and tone of voice?
7. Model the standards of courtesy that I expect from pupils?
8. Emphasize the positive, including praise for good behaviour as well as good work?
9. Make sparing and consistent use of reprimands – being firm not aggressive, targeting the right pupil, using private not public reprimands, being fair and consistent, avoiding sarcasm and idle threats?
10. Make sparing and consistent use of punishments – avoiding whole-group punishment and pupil humiliation which breed resentment?
11. Analyse my own classroom management performance and learn from it?

As the Elton Committee concluded, Item 11 is 'the most important message of all'.

---

## 3.2  Defining disruption

The idea of schools (especially those classified as 'inner-city') as 'blackboard jungles' where pupils threaten teachers and other pupils with physical violence, property is destroyed and teachers are under siege has been a recurring feature of public perception. However, research into behaviour in schools (Lawrence *et al.* 1977, Wragg 1984, DES/WO 1989) consistently indicates that teachers' definitions of 'disruption' encompass much less extreme forms of deviance. Asked to give examples of behaviour that adversely affects teaching and learning in classrooms they cite refusals to co-operate, noisiness, distraction and inattention, 'messing about', cheekiness or insolence, creating disturbances. Inevitably there is variation in teachers' views about the seriousness of different forms of deviant behaviour. Acts may be labelled 'misbehaviour' (implying a degree of acceptance/normality); 'a problem' (implying something that creates difficulty and requires specific attention); 'immoral' (implying some serious breach of a code); 'delinquent' (implying something markedly anti-social or criminal); 'maladjusted' (implying an association with emotional disturbance). The decisions teachers and schools make about how to respond to disruptive behaviour, challenges to authority will depend on their assessment of the seriousness of the act. Practical Activity 14.12 suggests a way of considering how you view various forms of behaviour you might encounter in the classroom.

There are some issues of gender and ethnicity related to judgements about deviance. Girls it is suggested can be no less deviant but because their actions cause less trouble they get away with it or are treated more leniently. This has been associated with the traditional practice that girls did not receive corporal punishment. Other studies (Davies 1979) indicate that girls oppose authority using different weapons. They harbour resentment longer and in many ways are less amenable to discipline than boys.

The more frequent challenges to authority by African-Caribbean pupils, especially boys, has been remarked. However, studies from the 1970s (Rutter *et al.* 1975, Bagley 1975) noted that many Black pupils experiencing behavioural problems in school did not present problems at home. A number of factors were suggested to explain this, including negative stereotyping and unintentional 'racism' on the part of schools. Extensive equal opportunities and anti-racism work in schools since then (most particularly as a result of the Swann Report, 1985) may have brought some improvements. Nevertheless there is still concern about the unequal outcomes of educational experiences, particularly regarding the underachievement of Black (but not Asian) pupils. African-Caribbean boys are also significantly over-represented in the figures for pupil exclusions (see Section 4.2).

For a consideration of those pupils who do present us with extreme and serious behavioural challenge see Sections 4.1 and 4.2 below. It is now time to turn our attention to positive strategies for dealing with disruptive or potentially disruptive behaviour.

## Practical activity 14.12

*Aim:* To consider your view of disruptive behaviour.

*Method:* Consider the list of pupil behaviours given below and decide how you would classify them according to your view of their seriousness. You might like to use the 'misbehaviour' – 'maladjusted' continuum described in the text or devise your own definitions with reference to the degree to which they pose a threat to your teaching or control.

- non-work-related chat
- refusal to do the work set
- wandering around the room
- making cheeky comments to the teacher
- throwing pencil/rubber across the room
- interrupting other pupils' work
- refusal to remove coat
- not having the necessary equipment or materials
- failure to produce homework
- scribbling in a textbook
- sniggering/double entendres
- making a racist remark
- damaging fittings/equipment
- provocative chair-rocking
- talking when silence has been requested
- arriving late
- making a sexist remark
- muttering under breath after a reprimand
- asking a personal question of the teacher
- swearing at another pupil
- swearing at the teacher
- provoking others to laugh by clowning
- pushing past the teacher
- twanging a ruler
- hitting/attacking another pupil
- shouting and running out of the room
- damaging another pupil's property
- talking to another pupil when teacher is waiting for silence
- tearing up work
- not listening to instructions
- doing work for another subject
- looking at non-school material – comics, photos, cards etc.
- threatening the teacher
- making faces behind the teacher's back
- using obscene gestures
- packing up before told to
- hitting the teacher
- talking constantly

*Follow-up:* You might like to compare your responses and discuss differences with other students, mentors, tutors. When you have read Section 3.3 you might like to consider which strategies would be appropriate for responding to some of these.

## 3.3   Positive strategies

Thinking purposefully about planning, organizing and managing to teach (see Chapters 10, 11 and 12), expressing your approval of appropriate behaviour, making sure that your instructions and explanations are clear and unambiguous (see Chapter 13), being supportive of problems encountered should enable you to minimize the possibilities of disruptive behaviour. Tightening the frame during transitions, constant monitoring and being 'withit', will help you to anticipate undesirable behaviour which threatens the working consensus (see Section 2.2) and to 'nip it in the bud'. Nevertheless, difficulties are bound to occur from time to time and a prudent teacher is likely to want to think through possible strategies in advance so that they can act confidently in managing such situations. A range of strategies exist which might be used to meet possible incidents.

### *Strategies to respond to misbehaviour*

1. Ignore it if it only occurs once.

2. If repeated:
    2.1   Make eye contact, stare; use non-verbal gesture.
    2.2   Move towards the pupil.
    2.3   Invite the pupil to participate – ask a question or encourage a comment, direct focus to work.

3. If persistent, in addition to the responses above:
    3.1   Name the pupil firmly and positively.
    3.2   Move to the pupil.
    3.3   Stop the action.
    3.4   Briefly identify the inappropriate behaviour, avoid implying disapproval of the individual, keep voice low, avoid nagging/lecturing, don't confuse respect and fear.
    3.5   Clearly state the desired behaviour.
    3.6   Give pupils a choice, a chance to conform, take back a remark, apologize.
    3.7   If necessary, isolate the pupil – avoid a contagious spread, a public clash and an 'audience' which can provoke 'showing-off'.
    3.8   Focus on the principal individual involved; don't be drawn into discussion with a group; followers will conform if you control the leader.
    3.9   Deal with the situation as quickly and neatly as possible; don't be drawn into long arguments; don't let the situation distract your attention from the rest of the class.
    3.10  Find out the facts if the situation is ambiguous; avoid jumping to conclusions.

4. Closure/after the event:
    4.1   Take anyone involved on one side – preserve their dignity, avoid 'supporters' chipping in.
    4.2   Encourage the pupil to identify what had been wrong, thus sharing responsibility.

4.3 Try to be fair; if necessary apologize.

4.4 Invite the pupil to draw up a 'contract' of what the pupil and the teacher will do and with which tangible rewards.

4.5 Modify behaviour by withdrawal of privileges and by providing opportunities to earn praise.

4.6 Conclude with peace terms clear to all parties.

5. If punishment is in mind:

5.1 Don't threaten disciplinary action too soon.

5.1 Be sure it is appropriate and that you can ensure it is carried through.

5.2 Avoid indiscriminate punishment of class or group.

6. If the situation escalates to confrontation:

6.1 Keep voice low, posture relaxed, avoid exaggerated gestures.

6.2 Stay cool and dispassionate while indicating your disapproval.

6.3 If necessary apply procedures from school/departmental behaviour policy.

6.4 Where a pupil has to be removed from the class lead them out while stating clearly and briefly the procedure you are following and what is about to happen.

The 1997 Education Act enables teachers to restrain pupils with 'such force as is reasonable in the circumstances'. However, corporal punishment remains illegal.

One problem with the working consensus is that the lines of acceptable behaviour are inclined to shift from lesson to lesson depending on what kinds of activity are happening and how people are feeling. Gordon (1974) suggests a metaphor of 'above or below the line' as a way of providing greater clarity about expectations.

> Imagine a line which defines your level of tolerance. Some behaviours are above the line and cause you no concern. Others are below it and it is these which you find unacceptable and which will provoke a reaction. Some pupils are good at sensing where the line is and when it is moving. Others are less sensitive or observant and would benefit from greater explicitness.

This is a strategy which involves giving pupils explanations and reasons for what is happening and the expectations we have of them. For example: 'today we are going to concentrate on improving how we discuss in groups, especially taking turns and listening; so shouting out and interrupting is below the line'; or 'for the next fifteen minutes I want each of you to write a list of all the points you can think of in connection with X; so any talking, asking questions is absolutely below the line'; or even 'I've got a bad headache so a lot of noise is below my line today'.

Other major, ongoing problems can also exist in any classroom. These may be quite general or associated with an individual pupil (or pupils) who have particular difficulties. In such instances, it is important to analyse the behaviour and try to identify the possible causes before any positive action can be taken. One might consider the conditions, characteristics and consequences of the behaviour.

### Conditions

When exactly does the disruption occur?
- Is it random or regular?
- Is it always the same pupil(s)?
- Is it always in connection the same type of task?
- Does it happen with other teachers?

### Characteristics

What exactly happens?
- Is it a verbal reaction?
- Is it a physical reaction?

### Consequences

What are the effects:
- on the child, the teacher?
- on the class, the school?
- do they join in, ignore, retaliate?

Such major, persistent problems are best discussed with other colleagues in the department and from the pastoral system so that a common strategy can be worked out. This might also involve the whole class, and the parents if necessary, so that a consistent approach can be adopted (see Section 4.1 below) .

Whether a problem is associated with an individual child or most of the class, a consistent approach is essential and would, hopefully, provide security for the pupils as well as support for the teacher. Learners respond to situations and experiences. We, as teachers, structure such experiences. Thus, if pupils respond problematically, we must reflect on the experiences which we provide rather than simply trying to apportion blame elsewhere.

### Practical activity 14.14

*Aim:* To analyse and reflect on your management of specific behaviour.

*Method:* As a diary entry record an incident when you were managing the behaviour of a particular pupil. Note as accurately as you can recall what happened step by step. What did the pupil do? What did you do? What was the outcome? How did you feel? How do you think the pupil felt? What do you think caused the incident? Could you have anticipated it? Could you have prevented it? Was your strategy effective? With hindsight would you change what you did?

*Follow-up:* You might want to discuss your analysis with a colleague or a mentor.

## Practical activity 14.15

*Aim:* To consider strategies appropriate to managing different behavioural challenges.

*Method:* If possible do this activity with a colleague or in a group. Use the list in Practical Activity 14.12 as the basis for discussing and deciding which strategies would be appropriate to dealing with different situations.

Or, consider the situations below. How would you respond?

- A pupil destroys or defaces the work and says, 'This is boring. I don't want to do this.'

- A pupil points at another and says 'It's no use asking him; he's a spastic.'

- You have asked a pupil to move to another seat. She sits tight, folds her arms, looks at her friends and says, 'I'm not moving. You can't make me.'

- After a reprimand a pupil bursts out, 'It's not fair, you're always picking on me. I wasn't the only one. Why is it always me that gets it?'

- You have explained a task to the class and reinforced this individually with a pupil. In spite of being asked to get on now with the set task this pupil continues to pester you and other pupils with questions about what to do and how it should be done.

*Follow-up:* Discuss your ideas for managing these situations with colleagues and your mentor. Which presented you with the greatest challenge? Can you say why this is?

## Practical activity 14.16

*Aim:* To reflect on the experience of managing behaviour.

*Method:* Read the following account by a newly qualified science teacher.

*The first term was a 'baptism of fire'. Suddenly I had a form to look after, 200 names to remember, staff to get to know, routines to comprehend and many discipline battles with unruly teenagers to survive. . . . Even a wander over to the staff room found me embroiled in some minor behaviour problem on the way.*

*My Year 9s and to a greater extent my Year 10s thought they could 'have me for dinner' and I was plunged into a discipline battle. I found myself reacting to breaches of discipline with explosions of anger and getting myself into a confrontation. This is not good. Having a 13-year-old boy, in front of the whole class, shouting 'You can't make me do that' or 'I hate you, Sir!' got to me and sapped my confidence. . . . It was just one control command after another, so no flow to the lessons could be maintained. I did learn a great deal about classroom management, using sanctions and discipline, but it also taught me to disassociate myself from the teacher that the pupils see.*

*I discovered that shouting is not always useful and perhaps just looking at the pupil with an air of dissatisfaction and remaining calm can defuse a situation quicker. Another method I picked up was giving the pupils a choice to decide their behaviour. I will say: 'The choice is on your shoulders, either you sit quietly and listen or I will move you.' Then if they still carry on talking I say: 'Look, I gave you the choice and you have decided that you want to move.' This is fair and usually does not lead to any further problems or resentment.*

*Throwing a million and one detentions at a child is fruitless because I have to be there and the said pupil generally has two million detentions anyway!*

*After ten weeks the Year 9 class had settled down. I had learned how to be 'hard'. They now believed my threats. There are still one or two pupils whose disruptive behaviour I am still struggling to curtail – I have tried many different approaches, ignoring them, isolating them, individual tuition, but they have all met with limited success. And no training ever taught me to cope with the boy who came into my laboratory, put his hands in the air and shouted 'I am every teachers' worst nightmare!'*

*The Year 7 and 8 classes have been extremely enjoyable and I've nurtured some very good relationships. . . . This not only aids the smooth running of the lesson but also underpins any discipline as the pupils know where the 'line' is. In these classes I have been confident and creative. . . .*

*If I could say anything to a teacher in their first year it would be ignore the old teacher adage 'Don't smile until Christmas' – as it is a load of rubbish. The job is hard, is tiring, yet I have found it immensely enjoyable and satisfying. (Unitt 1994)*

What is your reaction to this account? How does it relate to your own experiences? What points are you most struck by? Think about the benefits of 'disassociating' your self from yourself as Teacher.

If possible discuss the account and your response to it with some colleagues.

*Follow-up:* Think about this teacher's experiences when you next prepare to go into a difficult class.

## 3.4  Sanctions

However positive and well managed a school or classroom environment, there will be occasions when the behaviour of a pupil requires a member of staff to take some action to prevent its recurrence or reduce its frequency. The use of any of a range of sanctions is an indication of strong disapproval, by an individual teacher or by the institution. Use of sanctions is more likely to be effective if they are clearly defined as part of a whole-school behaviour policy (see 4.1 below).

Punishment systems work best where the punishment is rarely given and when the majority of pupils are not the subject of sanctions. Punishment itself is generally ritualized or symbolic and its chief deterrence lies in the associated shame and loss of approval combined with the inconvenience imposed. In some cases the form of punishment (e.g. detention, lines) may have little deterrent effect, especially where they are a regular feature for some pupils. There may also be pupils who seem not to feel shame and for whom withdrawal of approval is, apparently, not significant. Withdrawal of privileges may be more effective provided the 'privilege' is one that is valued by the pupil and he or she accepts the fairness of the penalty. In general, if we are to avoid alienating pupils or forcing them into face-saving expressions of personal bravado which may undermine the system, the following principles are useful to have in mind:

- punishment should be seen to be fair and rational and applied consistently
- pupils should be clear about the distinction between the punishment given for minor and more serious misbehaviour
- any punishment imposed should be appropriate to the wrongdoing and accepted and understood by the pupil(s) involved
- meaningful acts related to putting right the wrongdoing may be more effective than ritualized punishment
- punishments can be negotiated.

## Practical activity 14.17

*Aim:* To consider the range of sanctions operating in your school.

*Method:* Make a comprehensive list of the sanctions used in your school. Distinguish between those which are 'school-wide' and those which may be used by individual teachers. Can you create a hierarchy of severity for these? From your own observation how are the sanctions applied throughout the school?

Try to talk to pupils. What is their view of various sanctions? How do they feel when they are punished? Which punishments do they think are most effective? Which least effective? How would they go about dealing with people who break the rules or misbehave?

*Follow-up:* Try to get the views of other teachers, students, your mentor. How will thinking about this affect your approach to managing behaviour?

The following reflective note on 'detention' is included because of the wide range of educational issues which it raises. It comes from an experienced teacher, written soon after taking up a post in a boys' secondary school.

I soon realized I was expected after school to corral those pupils who already found normal school hours intolerable. I resented having to punish myself when it was the pupils who had failed to produce homework or who'd already caused me grief in class. On the other hand I accepted the importance of everyone abiding by school policy. I decided to do something useful with the time we were compelled to be together and divided my detainees into two categories: the boys who failed to submit completed homework, and those who behaved badly in class.

It was reasonable to presume that those who had not finished homework might need some help. Sometimes it is easier for adolescents to risk a punitive detention than to admit in front of their peers that they do not understand the work. I encouraged them to tell me what I hadn't explained sufficiently in class. Most had considerable difficulties and I wasn't surprised that they preferred detention to battling in their own time. After the first week, those who had no real difficulty soon preferred to complete homework at home . . .

Pupils in detention for bad behaviour were asked to do the kind of activities which make young people feel better about themselves, e.g. recall their greatest achievement – writing briefly and then talking to the group. . . . Some pupils found it easier to behave than attend these demanding sessions; others found it more difficult to change but the sessions did help to diminish their bad behaviour.

Pupils told me they sometimes misbehaved in order to be put in detention. When I asked why, they said it gave you a chance to talk to teachers. It seemed they craved adult attention even when it was adverse. Boys who lacked confidence in their ability asked if they could come to detention to do homework. Perhaps we should be holding homework clubs instead of retrospective detentions when work is not done. (Lovey 1996)

## 4  WHOLE-SCHOOL ISSUES

### 4.1  Behaviour policies

A recommendation of the Elton Report (DES/WO 1989) was that headteachers and teachers should, in consultation with governors, develop whole-school behaviour policies which are clearly understood by pupils, parents and other school staff. As a result of this, most schools now have a well-developed team approach to discipline, and, following the 1997 Education Act, this must be expressed in a policy document.

A behaviour policy is one expression of a school's ethos in that attitudes and practices in relation to behaviour are inevitably based on shared values and beliefs. Policy documents can be obtained 'off the shelf' from local authorities or freelance consultants. For example, 'assertive discipline' (Canter and Canter 1977) was originally developed in the USA and involves specific techniques for rewarding desired behaviours and implementing sanctions. However, because of the consultations and discussions involved, by the time a school has adopted a policy it has usually made it its own.

There may be some variation in the degree to which consistency is stressed. Some schools place importance on everyone being treated the same, on systems being highly predictable for the pupils. Others tend to greater flexibility and differentiation for age groups, activities and, in some cases, individuals. Nevertheless the behaviour policy of most schools will set out rules and expectations and indicate what sanctions will operate when behaviour is unacceptable. In general these will include detentions, extra work or similar punishments. Where behaviour is persistently a problem the wider pastoral system will be brought in through the form tutor and the Year or House Tutor. A pupil may be put 'on report', a procedure whereby after every lesson the teacher writes a comment about the pupil's behaviour during that session. In this way the pupil is kept under surveillance over an agreed period; parents are informed and progress is reviewed with the pupil. Associated with this is the practice of drawing up contracts with pupils in which targets for improvement are agreed and progress monitored.

In some more extreme cases which may involve aggressive, violent or otherwise unacceptable behaviour a pupil may be taken out of the classroom for 'Time Out'. This may mean sitting in a particular location – outside a deputy's office or in a designated classroom. The aim is to defuse a situation and give the pupil time to reflect on their behaviour. Discussion, as appropriate, with senior staff, form tutor, subject teacher should lead the pupil to some basis for returning to the class. Again, parents may also be informed.

There are, of course, efforts to discover the reasons for disruptive or anti-social behaviour. These may include particularly able pupils who are bored; pupils who find school work difficult and may become frustrated; pupils who have special educational needs; pupils who are new to the school and are having problems fitting in and pupils who have been upset by events in their lives over which they have little control, such as a bereavement, a break-up of their parents' marriage, parental unemployment or even sexual or physical abuse. Such pupils need very sensitive and empathic attention and they may need special help to express their feelings, to put them in perspective, to realize that their teachers and others care about them and to feel that they have tangible and appropriate targets to strive for in their lives. Such care may enable a pupil to take control of their situation, with the support of their teacher, to the extent that this is possible. However, teachers should guard against being amateur therapists. Educational psychologists, education welfare officers, social services, even, though rarely, trained counsellors are available and they will be involved by the school as appropriate.

In some cases a school may feel it necessary to invoke the procedures for exclusion of a pupil. This happens to more than 10,000 pupils each year of which 80 per cent are from secondary schools, a majority in Years 10 and 11. Most of these are boys, with a disproportionate number of these of Afro-Caribbean origin. The main reason for exclusion is aggressive or violent behaviour which cannot be controlled within the school.

Pupils may be excluded permanently or for a maximum of fifteen days. Where exclusion is permanent parents have a right to appeal to the local authority. The LEA and governing bodies have the power to direct headteachers to reinstate pupils. Guidelines from the DFE (10/94) emphasize prompt intervention in cases of disruption and that pupils should be kept in school whenever possible. Variations in the number of exclusions from a school do not necessarily indicate the severity of problems a school faces. Some schools are more reluctant to move to exclusion and will do all they can to help pupils to stay in school. However, larger classes, financial cuts, reduced support from outside agencies and a competitive environment for recruiting pupils have all had an effect. Schools often feel, and are, unsupported. However reluctantly, they have to consider the effects of disruptive pupils on their peers, on league tables, and on parental views and publicity.

Excluded pupils may be sent to another school or to a special Pupil Referral Unit or home tuition may be arranged. Some LEAs consider these pupils as having special educational needs and go through a statementing procedure. The reduction in the availability of special school places as a result of policies of 'mainstreaming' pupils with special needs can make it difficult to place pupils with severe behavioural difficulties.

The official Behaviour Policy is not the only whole-school factor which impacts on behaviour. The PSE programme in conjunction with policies and practices for equal opportunities (especially where these include anti-racist strategies and a broadly-based approach to sexual harassment) can combine productively to influence behaviour. Consultation with parents over a dress code, attendance and homework is also significant, as are any reward systems for recognizing merit and achievement and systems for giving pupils responsibility of different kinds, for example, participation in a school council, jobs to do, prefect roles.

One behavioural issue not mentioned so far is bullying and it is to this we turn in the next section.

## 4.2  Bullying

Recent research evidence on the extent of bullying in schools indicates not only the size of the problem but its widespread prevalence. This is partly the result of a change in definition. Until recently the emphasis has been on physical intimidation; now the serious effects of name-calling and taunting and of undesirable peer pressure have been acknowledged. It is suggested that 1.3 million pupils a year are involved in bullying (McTaggart 1995). A survey by the School Health Education Unit at the University of Exeter (1996) found that, from the 12-year-olds questioned, more than one-third of the girls and one-quarter of the boys reported being afraid to go to school because of bullying. The data were gathered by questionnaire in sixty-five co-ed comprehensive schools in seven varying LEAs. Pupils in all five year-groups were involved and different patterns emerged for boys and girls. The problem is most acute for boys in the first two years of secondary school; for girls, the fear persists until Year 11 when it falls to 17 per cent, with 15 per cent for boys. However, the significant variations in reporting between schools suggests that this is a problem that can be affected by in-school action.

A number of agencies (university departments, independent charities, school governors, the DFE) are involved in the promotion and development of anti-bullying strategies. All agree that no school is free from bullying, even if headteachers claim the opposite. The most universally recommended approaches involve developing the school as a place where bullying is not tolerated. Pupils, teachers, non-teaching staff, parents combine together to create an anti-bullying climate where both bullies and victims can ask for help. The involvement of classes in agreeing rules for social behaviour, raising awareness through the curriculum, the setting up of bully courts with elected pupils involved with teachers in dealing with incidents, are examples of suggested activities which have had positive results. The persistent bully and bullying gangs are more difficult to deal with but the successes that many schools have had as a result of considered and determined action give cause for optimism.

Teachers in general are encouraged to be prepared to listen to children and to be sensitive to even quite small signs that things are not right: a pupil regularly isolated at the end of a queue, reluctance to go out into the playground, complaints that pens/books etc are being taken. The most significant symptoms of bullying are usually identified as:

- deterioration of work
- spurious illness
- isolation
- desire to remain with adults
- erratic attendance.

The lines published in a school magazine recording the despair of a 12-year-old girl at the taunts of 'snob' and 'slut' which she suffered when she was put into a higher maths group than her friends (quoted in *TES*, 5 May 1995) point us to the final section in this part which looks at the possible impact on behaviour of school organization.

> With an empty body, and an empty soul, I stand and pack my books away. I feel a cold stone in the emptiness of my chest. That stone is my heart.

## 4.3  School organization and differentiation

It is a commonplace that control problems are not evenly spread among schools, nor within schools, between years and classes. Factors including location (urban/rural), catchment area (social class composition), selection procedures (ability, single-sex, denominational) all affect the characteristics of schools. More precisely, studies of this phenomenon point to the influence on behaviour of in-school differentiation (the process of separating pupils into groups according to ability). The conclusions of three studies – one in a secondary modern school (Hargreaves 1967), one in a grammar school (Lacey 1970) and one in a comprehensive school (Ball 1981) – are remarkable consistent. In each case processes of streaming, setting, banding and option choice produced polarized groups, including anti-school sub-cultures which presented teachers with behavioural problems.

In Hightown Grammar (Lacey 1970), pupils began Year 1 as a homogeneous, undifferentiated group with an image of themselves as 'best pupils' selected for grammar school. In Year 2 they were streamed by ability and from then until Year 4 the bottom stream exhibited increasingly anti-school attitudes and behaviour, such that by Year 4 strenuous efforts were being made to get rid of some pupils, often at their request. Lacey's analysis points up the place of social class in this.

In Stephen Ball's account of Beachside Comprehensive (1981) pupils were separated into three broad 'bands' from the start on the basis of primary school recommendations. Pupils from middle-class non-manual families were more likely to be allocated to Band One, those from working-class manual homes to Band Two. Very early a 'second band mentality' emerged characterized by misbehaviour, disruption, low participation and rejection of school. Band Three classes were perceived as more manageable. Here pupils were 'remedial', in smaller groups and receiving specialist teaching; behaviour problems were defined as emotional problems or maladjustment.

Band Two classes received a different curriculum and syllabuses. Teaching approaches also differed from Band One, often because the focus was on teaching to effect order and control rather than instruction. Ball concluded that streaming in comprehensive schools produces 'an unstable, polarized social structure among pupils which in turn gives rise to considerable teaching and control problems for teachers' (p. 283). This polarization, he suggests, is reinforced by teachers' expectations and assumptions about pupils, a tendency to stereotype and to identify more closely with Band One pupils ('like me') than Band Two ('not like me'). Here too, values and social class are in play.

The problems raised by banding persuaded Beachside to move to mixed ability grouping for Years 1–3. This prevented the emergence of a strong anti-school sub-culture. 'Key' individuals were spread around so the formation of a group with shared problems of adjustment (a key feature of sub-cultural deviance) was avoided. The improvements in behaviour were welcomed by teachers but there was considerable opposition to mixed ability organization from some subjects, in particular maths, French and science. These were allowed to retain setting. A similar situation is described in case studies of other schools (Denscombe 1985) where a special case for setting was made by teachers of maths, French, English and physics. For these teachers it seems the gains in social control offered by mixed ability groups are outweighed by the problems of teaching 'academic' subjects to pupils of different attainment. In particular the needs of the 'brighter child' are frequently invoked. Practical Activity 14.18 suggests how you might investigate this in your school.

Now at the millennium and after massive educational change, a new National Curriculum (Chapter 6), new forms of assessment (Chapter 15), and a new qualifications framework, it is interesting to reflect on whether schools are now being successful in preventing the kind of polarization that creates an anti-school culture. What are the effects of our current organizational differentiation on relationships and behaviour? There must be a real fear that the introduction of 'vocational', 'applied' and 'academic' pathways (see Chapter 6, Sections 2.5, 3.3, 3.4 and 3.5) will, although designed to meet particular pupil needs and aptitudes, have the unintended consequence of producing polarization within pupil culture. The outcome will rest on the ways in which the qualifications of the applied and vocational pathways are valued within our society as a whole.

## CONCLUSION

Apart from increasing the enjoyment and educational achievement of individual pupils, teachers who are attentive to the particular needs of individuals and develop good relationships with the class as a whole are likely to find that they encounter fewer disruptive incidents. Perhaps too, an expectation of being caring and respectful towards each other may spread among the pupils and be of longer-term benefit for society more generally.

Managing behaviour inevitably involves socialization. Exactly what forms of social behaviour are most desirable in our society is the subject of much discussion and the discourse suggests a variety of priorities: respect for authority, participation, need to conform to moral values, need to question, personal empowerment, character building, responsibility, good citizenship. Finding usable definitions for these phrases is difficult too in a society where pluralism and relativism in moral values is evident and there are changing attitudes to authority. Teachers may find their personal values in conflict with the dominant ethos of the school and the way that ethos is expressed in policies and practices.

### Practical activity 14.18

*Aim:* To highlight the possible influences of school and classroom differentiation and polarization processes.

*Method:* Simple indicators for both differentiation and polarization are required.

1. For differentiation: positions in attainment-based groups, in teaching schemes, e.g. Maths schemes, can be used to rank individuals or group children into attainment quartiles; teacher judgement could also be sought or standardized test scores if available.
2. For polarization: patterns revealed by a sociogram can be used. (See Chapter 4, Section 3.9.)

These indicators then have to be examined together, for example by setting our friendship groups and recording the differentiation indicators beside each child's name.

Examine the data. Is there any evidence of 'band mentality' or 'anti-school groups'? Are gender, class or ethnicity significant factors here?

*Follow-up:* This exercise may suggest ways in which school and teacher practices interact with children's responses to create or reinforce social and individual differences. As a reflective teacher consider what your attitude is to this.

A concern with the idea of 'managing behaviour' may lie in the connotations of fear, imposition, and manipulation that hang about the idea of control. For many of us the aim for our pupils is the development of a moral sense which positively informs behaviour, and the ability to use self-restraint and assertiveness as appropriate. We want them to be 'disciplined' in the best sense of the word. It is in the relationships we develop with them that we hope to express our values and our ideals. Our ability to hold on to these even when pushed into compromise and pragmatic action is a mark of our commitment to the job and our pupils.

### Notes for further reading

For Withall's classic study on 'socio-emotional climate', see:

Withall, J. (1949)
'The development of a technique for the measurement of social-emotional climate in classrooms', *Journal of Experimental Education*, No. 17, pp. 347–61.     See also **Primary Reading 5.1**

One of a number of classic books by Carl Rogers on 'person-centred' theory is:

Rogers, C. (1969)
*Freedom to Learn,*
New York: Merrill.

A thoughtful book linking teacher effectiveness with pupil relationships is:

Kyriacou, C. (1986)
*Effective Teaching in Schools,*
Oxford: Basil Blackwell.

An overviews of research on classroom processes and relationships is:

Wittrock, M. C. (ed.) (1986)
*Handbook of Research on Teaching,*
New York: Macmillan.

Cooper, P. and McIntyre, D. (1996)
*Effective Teaching and Learning: Teachers' and Students' Perspectives,*
Buckingham: Open University Press

Learning pupil names is an important start in developing relationships. Try:

Buzan, T. (1984)
*Using Your Memory,*
London: BBC Books.

On pupils' confidence and self-esteem the books below provide a conceptual overview, a research review and practical ideas respectively:

Lawrence, D. (1987)
*Enhancing Self-Esteem in the Classroom,*
London: Paul Chapman.

**Primary Reading 5.6**

Burns, R. B. (1982)
*Self-concept Development and Education,*
London: Routledge & Kegan Paul.

Cranfield, J. and Wells, H. (1976)
*100 Ways to Enhance Selfconcept in the Classroom,*
Englewood Cliffs, NJ: Prentice-Hall.

On rules in educational contexts see:

Hargreaves, D. H., Hestor, S. K., and Mellor, F. J. (1975)
*Deviance in Classrooms,*
London: Routledge & Kegan Paul.

**Primary Reading 10.7**

For expositions of the interpretive approach to classroom relationships which has informed much of this chapter see:

Delamont, S. (1990)
*Interaction in the Classroom,*
London: Routledge.

Woods, P. (1983)
*Sociology and the School: an Interactionist Viewpoint,*
London: Routledge.

The original use of the concept of working consensus is well worth following up. It can be found in:

Hargreaves, D. H. (1972)
*Interpersonal Relationships and Education,*
London: Routledge & Kegan Paul.

For fascinating studies on collaborative learning and relationships, see:

Salmon, P. and Claire, H. (1984)
*Classroom Collaboration,*
London: Routledge & Kegan Paul.

Biott, C. and Easen, P. (1994)
*Collaborative Learning in Staffrooms and Classrooms,*
London: David Fulton.

Humphreys, T. (1995)
*A Different Kind of Teacher,*
London: Cassell.

Ingram, J. and Worrall, N. (1993)
*Teacher-Child Partnership: The Negotiating Classroom,*
London: David Fulton.

On the management of behaviour, the Elton Report is well worth consulting, together with some of the work which has derived directly from it.

DES/WO (1989)
*Discipline in Schools,*
Report of the Committee of Enquiry chaired by Lord Elton,
London: HMSO.  Primary Reading 10.9

Wheldall, K. (1991)
*Discipline in Schools: Psychological Perspectives on the Elton Report,*
London: Routledge.

To sample the many sources of practical advice on managing classroom behaviour, see:

Laslett, R. and Smith, C. (1992)
*Effective Classroom Management: A Teacher's Guide,* (second edition)
London: Routledge.  Primary Reading 10.5

Fontana, D. (1986)
*Classroom Control: Understanding and Guiding Classroom Behaviour,*
London: Routledge.

McManus, M. (1989)
*Troublesome Behaviour in the Classroom: A Teacher's Survival Guide,*
London: Routledge.

McNamara, S. and Moreton, G. (1995)
*Changing Behaviour: Teaching Children with Emotional and Behavioural Difficulties in Primary and Secondary Classrooms,*
London: David Fulton.

Merrett, F. (1993)
*Encouragement Works Best: Positive Approaches to Classroom Management,*
London: David Fulton.

For books which approach disciplinary issues more explicitly at a whole-school level see:

Farmer, A., Cowin, M., Freeman, L., James, M., Drent, A. and Arthur, R. (1991)
*Positive School Discipline: A Practical Guide to Developing Policy,*
London: Longman.

Cooper, P. (1993)
*Effective Schools for Disaffected Students,*
London: Routledge.

Canter, L. and Canter, M. (1977)
*Assertive Discipline,*
New York: Lee Canter Associates.

Blyth, E. and Milner, J. (eds) (1996)
*Exclusion from School,*
London: Falmer Press.

On bullying, see:

Elliott, M. (ed.) (1992)
*Bullying: A Practical Guide to Coping for Schools,*
London: Longman.

Hazler, R. J. (1996)
*Breaking the Cycle of Violence,*
London: Taylor and Francis.

For two classic studies on school organization and social differentiation emphasizing social class, plus demonstrations of the further influence of race, gender, see:

Hargreaves, D. H. (1967)
*Social Relations in a Secondary School,*
London: Routledge and Kegan Paul.

Ball, S. J. (1981)
*Beachside Comprehensive,*
Cambridge: Cambridge University Press.

Gillborn, D. (1995)
*Racism and Antiracism in Real Schools,*
Buckingham: Open University Press.

Measor, L. and Sikes, P. (1992)
*Gender and Schools,*
London: Cassell.

# CHAPTER 15

# How are we assessing pupils' learning?

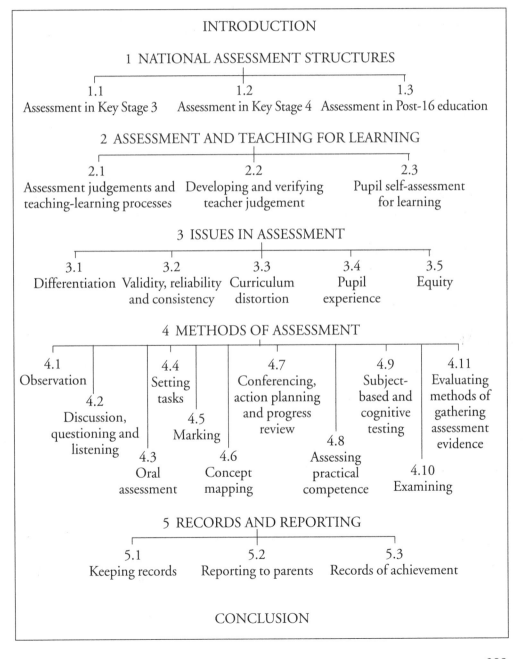

INTRODUCTION

1 NATIONAL ASSESSMENT STRUCTURES

| 1.1 | 1.2 | 1.3 |
|---|---|---|
| Assessment in Key Stage 3 | Assessment in Key Stage 4 | Assessment in Post-16 education |

2 ASSESSMENT AND TEACHING FOR LEARNING

| 2.1 | 2.2 | 2.3 |
|---|---|---|
| Assessment judgements and teaching-learning processes | Developing and verifying teacher judgement | Pupil self-assessment for learning |

3 ISSUES IN ASSESSMENT

| 3.1 | 3.2 | 3.3 | 3.4 | 3.5 |
|---|---|---|---|---|
| Differentiation | Validity, reliability and consistency | Curriculum distortion | Pupil experience | Equity |

4 METHODS OF ASSESSMENT

| 4.1 | 4.4 | 4.7 | 4.9 | 4.11 |
|---|---|---|---|---|
| Observation | Setting tasks | Conferencing, action planning and progress review | Subject-based and cognitive testing | Evaluating methods of gathering assessment evidence |

4.2 Discussion, questioning and listening

4.3 Oral assessment

4.5 Marking

4.6 Concept mapping

4.8 Assessing practical competence

4.10 Examining

5 RECORDS AND REPORTING

| 5.1 | 5.2 | 5.3 |
|---|---|---|
| Keeping records | Reporting to parents | Records of achievement |

CONCLUSION

# INTRODUCTION

In recent years and in most parts of the world, assessment has become more and more important in education. This has occurred for two reasons.

The first, and by far the most significant, has been the concern of governments to introduce ways of 'measuring' educational outputs. In the United Kingdom, this was seen as a way of informing parents about the progress of their children and as a way of comparing school performance to inform an educational market based on choice and diversity (e.g. Major 1991, DES 1992). In this scenario, assessment is expected to raise standards of pupil achievement. *Output* assessment data, of the sort required by these arguments, is known as 'summative'.

The second reason for the growth in interest in assessment derives from teachers, who have increasingly come to realize the value of continuous, on-going assessment in informing the process of their teaching. Thus, as a course of study or a lesson progresses, a teacher gathers evidence of pupil responses and adjusts the learning programme to meet pupil needs. Teachers are thus able to engage more directly and accurately with the development of the learner's thinking and understanding. *Process* assessment data, of the sort required by these arguments, is known as 'formative'.

The basic difference in purpose between these two forms of assessment produces serious tensions – for instance, output versus process, comparison versus support, standardized assessment procedures versus locally produced procedures. Many assessment experts suggest that the effectiveness of one form of assessment is likely to have the unfortunate effect of undermining the effectiveness of the other (see Harlen *et al.*, 1992, **Primary Reading 12.1** for an important discussion of the purposes of assessment). In particular, when summative testing is emphasized, there is a tendency for teaching to be narrowly directed towards whatever the tests measure. A broad and balanced curriculum, as required by the Education Reform Act, 1988, is thus distorted (e.g. Gipps 1990). Other commentators feel that the two major forms of assessment can be mutually supportive – formative assessment supports the process of learning, summative assessment measures the result.

The latter view was strongly endorsed by the Task Group on Assessment and Testing (TGAT) which produced the reports from which assessment in the UK was initially derived (TGAT 1987, 1988). The Task Group suggested that: 'Promoting pupils' learning is the principal aim of schools. Assessment lies at the heart of this process', but: 'The assessment process should not determine what is to be taught and learned. It should be the servant, not the master, of the curriculum' (TGAT 1988, para. 3/4).

With this overall commitment in mind, TGAT set out four criteria for the assessment system. It should be:

- *Criterion-referenced:* relate directly to what pupils can do, rather than to how they compare with others (norm referenced) (see Croll 1990, **Primary Reading 12.2** for further explanation of this distinction).
- *Formative:* provide a basis for teacher decisions about further learning needs.
- *Moderated:* be made consistent and fair across schools.
- *Relate to progression:* reflect expected routes of pupils' development and learning.

Of course, there is a crucially important issue underlying all assessment activity which takes place in secondary education, and this concerns its role in *certifying* attainments when young people begin to seek employment or go on to other forms of education or training. Secondary education is a phase during which the life-chances and career trajectories of young people often begin to become quite overt, and assessment certification certainly contributes to this. Assessment activity is thus 'high stakes' not only because it contributes to learning, but also because it helps to shape the opportunities available in life. As we shall see, such concerns led to a considerable dilution of TGAT's criteria. They were judged to provide an inadequate basis for the public scrutiny of 'standards', with the result that national assessment systems in England and Wales developed during the 1990s with much more emphasis on the measurement of summative attainments. There is plenty in the history of such developments for a reflective teacher to dwell on.

This chapter is organized in five parts. We begin by reviewing basic assessment structures and requirements at Key Stages 3 and 4 and for Post-16 education and training. Part 2 considers the direct and positive support for learning which can, in principle, derive from assessment, whilst in Part 3 we address some of the difficult issues which may also emerge. Part 4 provides an account of various ways of gathering evidence and conducting both teacher-controlled and externally-set assessments and examinations. Finally, Part 5 concerns records, reporting and Records of Achievement.

## 1    NATIONAL ASSESSMENT STRUCTURES

### 1.1   Assessment in Key Stage 3

Assessment at Key Stage 3 is directly related to curricular structures and requirements, so that cross-referencing to Chapter 6, Section 2.5 could be useful.

The following forms of assessment are likely to be found at Key Stage 3:

- *Base-line assessment,* where Key Stage 2 test results are not deemed sufficient. Taken early in Year 7, to help in the assessment of pupil needs and to enable the school to calculate 'added value' at some later point (see Sections 3.6 and 4.9).
- *Teacher assessment,* on a continuous basis as decided by individual teachers or required by the school or subject department assessment policy (see the many methods reviewed in Part 4 of this chapter). It is meant to be used formatively, to support the teaching-learning process.
- *Teacher Assessment (TA),* as a statutory requirement which is formalized during Year 9 and reported to parents (see below and Section 5.2). TA may be used formatively, but must also be used to make judgements about the level of attainment of pupils in National Curriculum subjects.
- *National tests* (formerly known as SATs) as a statutory requirement which is enacted in the summer of Year 9 and reported to parents (see below and Section 5.2). National tests are a summative form of assessment.

The assessment structures and procedures of the National Curriculum identify eight levels of attainment for each subject. Each of these is specified with attainment targets (see Figure 6.3) and 'level descriptions' or 'end of Key Stage descriptions', against which both formative and summative assessments are made at the end of Key Stages 1, 2 and 3. We will address each of these elements in turn.

- *Attainment targets (ATs),* as we saw in Chapter 6, Section 2.4, are defined from within programmes of study to represent the knowledge, skills and understanding which pupils are expected to master as they progress through school. Pupil attainment for each attainment target is described in terms of eight 'levels of attainment', using either 'level descriptions' or 'end of Key Stage descriptions'.
- *Levels of attainment* identify points of knowledge, skill and understanding for each subject, against which pupil attainment can be assessed. In principle, this is a criterion referenced form of assessment. Expectations of the range of attainment for pupils at the end of each Key Stage of the National Curriculum are indicated on Figure 15.1 below.

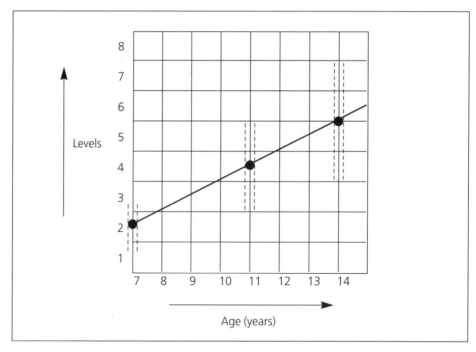

**Figure 15.1** *Sequence of pupil achievement, ages 7 to 14 (adapted from TGAT 1988 to show 1995 revisions)*

- *Level descriptions* indicate the types, quality and range of performance that a pupil working at a particular level 'characteristically should demonstrate' over a period of time. They are used for the subjects of English, Welsh, mathematics, science, technology, information technology, history and geography. Teachers should exercise their professional judgement to weigh up the pupil's strengths and weaknesses and to decide what description 'best fits' the pupil's overall performance in relation to a particular attainment target.

- *End of Key Stage descriptions* set out the standard of performance expected of the majority of pupils at the end of each Key Stage. They apply to art, music and physical education only. In conjunction with available evidence, teachers use their professional judgement to decide the extent to which a pupil's attainment relates to the expected standard of performance at each Key Stage. The statements are broadly equivalent to Level 2 at Key Stage 1, Level 4 at Key Stage 2, and Level 5 or 6 at Key Stage 3.

Aggregated results of national tests and teacher assessments are published, and information about each pupil is given to parents. An important recommendation of the Dearing Review of the National Curriculum (Dearing 1994) was that teacher assessment should have parity with the results of nationally set tests. However, this has been extremely difficult to bring about and, in discussion of 'results', the media tend to focus almost exclusively on test results.

### *Practical activity 15.1*

*Aim:* To investigate national assessment requirements for a particular subject.

*Method:* Collect National Curriculum and assessment documentation for your specialist subject. For instance:

> The National Curriculum programme of study and attainment targets
> Level descriptions or end of Key Stage descriptions
> Official paperwork on national test procedures
> Test papers which have been set in the past.

Taking each document in turn, summarize the assessment requirements for your subject. Where possible, discuss with subject teachers how national requirements are implemented.

*Follow-up:* Consider some of the issues raised by assessment requirements for your subject. For instance, how much do you think assessment influences what is taught? How do you think the learning of higher- and lower-attaining pupils is affected?

## 1.2 Assessment in Key Stage 4

Assessment at Key Stage 4 is directly related to curricular structures and requirements, and this section should therefore be cross-referenced with Chapter 6, Section 2.6.

At Key Stage 4, the following forms of assessment are likely to be found:

- *Teacher assessment,* on a continuous basis as decided by individual teachers or required by the school or subject department assessment policy.
- *Pupil self-assessment,* which can be extremely effective, particularly when focused in the run-up to exams.
- *Coursework assessment,* contributing to up to 25 per cent of GCSE marks and spread throughout Years 10 and 11.

- *Assessment of practical or vocational work,* particularly in association with GNVQ Part 1.
- *Examinations,* taken in the summer of Year 11.

*Teacher assessment* is meant to be used formatively, to support the teaching-learning process. The methods reviewed in Part 4 of this chapter are appropriate for this and many are very commonly used.

*Pupil self-assessment* is extremely important in supporting pupils in becoming independent and constructively self-critical in their work. The form of assessment most directly connected to the learning process (see Section 2.3).

*Coursework assessment* is important in GCSE, GNVQ Part 1, and many vocational courses. Teachers' marking (see Section 4.5) is carried out using criteria and mark schemes provided by the exam boards. There may be forms of standardization or agreement trialling, perhaps using a portfolio of pupil work (see Section 5.1), and the work is normally sent to external examiners for moderation.

*Assessment of practical or vocational work* (see Section 4.8) is often focused on particular skills and frequently takes place in applied contexts, such as workshops or workplaces. Assessment is normally against clear behavioural criteria.

*Examinations* (see Section 4.10) are the most important form of assessment in GCSE. Requirements, scheduling and marking are externally controlled by exam boards, working within national frameworks and subject to various accountability mechanisms. Teachers prepare their pupils for the exams, drawing attention to the published criteria and honing exam techniques, but they then lose control of the marking and moderation process. However, many teachers act as external markers for work coming from other schools. 'Mock exams' are often taken in the late Autumn or early Spring of Year 11, with the real examinations in the early Summer. Results are available in August.

Qualifications are associated with particular curricular pathways and levels (see Figure 6.5).

- Within the 'academic pathway', GCSE A*–C is 'intermediate level', whilst GCSE D–G is 'foundation level'.
- Within the 'applied pathway', Level 2 GNVQ is 'intermediate level', whilst Level 1 GNVQ is 'foundation level'.
- Within the 'vocational pathway', Level 2 NVQ is 'intermediate level', whilst Level 1 NVQ is 'foundation level'.

This structure of qualifications reflects the Dearing framework (as discussed in Chapter 6, Section 3.2 and set out in Table 6.5, p. 140). Sir Ron argued that each of the three pathways should be recognized as suiting young people with different aptitudes, but achieving broadly equivalent levels of attainment. He therefore suggested that there should be an overarching system of 'National Awards' which would certify the equivalence and help to establish parity of esteem between the pathways.

The National Award for the end of Key Stage 4 is at 'intermediate level' and will be integrated within the National Record of Achievement. Demonstration of competence in 'key skills' is a compulsory feature of the award.

## 1.3   Assessment and awards in Post-16 education

Assessment in Post-16 education is directly related to curricular structures and requirements, and this section should therefore be cross-referenced with Chapter 6, Part 3.

In Post-16 education and training, the following forms of assessment are likely to be used:

- *Teacher assessment,* on a continuous basis
- *Student self-assessment,* directly affecting personal capabilities and reflexivity
- *Coursework assessment,* which can directly affect final marks
- *Assessment of practical or vocational work,* particularly in association with NVQs or some GNVQs
- *Examinations,* taken in the summer of Year 13.

*Teacher assessment* will continue to be used formatively, to support the teaching-learning process. Most of the methods reviewed in Part 4 of this chapter remain useful for Post-16 work.

*Student self-assessment* becomes even more significant as young people move towards adulthood. Their powers of 'self-regulation' and 'meta-cognition' are of paramount importance to their future adaptability as learners (see Chapter 9, and this chapter, Section 2.3).

*Coursework assessment* remains important for advanced level courses, though examinations have increasing significance, particularly for A-level. Teacher marking (see Section 4.5) continues to be informed by criteria and mark schemes provided by the exam boards. Standardization or agreement trials may take place, and some coursework is normally sent to external examiners for possible moderation.

*Assessment of practical or vocational work* (see Section 4.8) is likely to be focused on specified behavioural criteria or competences. It may take place in applied settings, such as workshops or workplaces, and may draw on a 'portfolio of evidence' about work which has been done, particularly for NVQs.

*Examinations* (see Section 4.10) are the most important form of assessment for A-level. As at GCSE, requirements, scheduling and marking are externally controlled by exam boards, working within national frameworks and subject to various accountability mechanisms. Teachers again have limited control, once the young people have completed their course and their revision programme. Following the Capey Report (1995) external testing is being introduced to assess GNVQs (from 1998).

Qualifications are associated with particular curricular pathways and, for Post-16, the majority of students are expected to work at 'advanced level' (see Figure 6.5, p. 140).

- Within the 'academic pathway', AS- and A-level
- Within the 'applied pathway', Level 3 GNVQ
- Within the 'vocational pathway', Level 3 NVQ

Other Post-16 students may work at GCSE or other levels of GNVQ or NVQ.

As at Key Stage 4, this structure of Post-16 qualifications reflects the Dearing framework (see Chapter 6, Section 3.2). On his recommendation, attempts have been made to establish parity of esteem for attainments within the three pathways. Hence the creation of an overarching system of 'National Awards' which officially certifies that equivalence.

National Awards at Post-16 are intended to be integrated within the National Record of Achievement, and demonstration of competence in 'key skills' will be a compulsory feature of the awards.

As the new Labout government minister, Baroness Blackstone, explained:

> We want to develop a single over-arching certificate for young people, allowing them to undertake A-levels or vocational qualifications, while also embracing the key skills of communication, application of number and information technology. This would become the basis for progression to higher education and employment at age 18. (Press Release, 11 June 1997)

Sadly however, history suggests that it will be difficult to achieve parity of esteem across the academic, applied and vocational routes which lead to a unified national certificate. This issue is discussed further in Chapter 6, Section 3.7.

## 2 | ASSESSMENT AND TEACHING FOR LEARNING

This section of the chapter is directly concerned with the ways in which assessment can support learning processes. It thus emphasizes formative aspects which can be incorporated into classroom practice, rather than the summative requirements which, as we saw in Section 1, tend to be nationally specified.

## 2.1 Assessment judgement in teaching-learning processes

The social constructivist model reviewed in Chapter 9, Section 1.3, conceives of teachers analysing pupil skill and understanding, in the course of an activity or task, so that appropriate information, questions, explanations or advice can be offered. A teacher acts, we suggested, as a 'reflective agent' who makes accurate judgements, provides an appropriate teaching input and thereby scaffolds the learner's understanding across what Vygotsky called the 'zone of proximal development'. Pupils' knowledge and understanding is thus extended, by appropriate teaching, to levels which could not have been attained without the teacher intervention.

This process is fundamentally dependent on the quality of the teacher's judgement and formative assessment, backed by appropriate subject knowledge and pedogogic skill. Without these, an intervention could easily be inappropriate and confuse the pupil's attempt to construct a meaningful understanding. This then, is the direct link between assessment and learning in modern secondary school practice. Without it, no teacher can hope to support pupils' learning appropriately.

It is worth looking at the various stages of this process in more detail and we represent it, schematically, in Figure 15.2. Five phases of a teaching programme are distinguished in this model. They build, progressively, from the pupil's existing knowledge, understanding and skill and, at each point, the role of teacher assessment is emphasized.

| | Purposes | Assessment Opportunities | Possible Processes |
|---|---|---|---|
| **Orientation** | Arousing pupils' interest and curiosity. Ensures that the pupils are focused on the topic. | Provides an opportunity to assess pupils' motivation regarding the topic. | Introducing Explaining Discussing |
| **Elicitation/ structuring** | Helping pupils to find out and clarify what they think | Enables the teacher to assess pupil understanding in order to plan appropriate next steps. | Questioning Discussing Predicting |
| **Intervention/ restructuring** | Encouraging pupils to test, develop, extend or replace their ideas or skills. Provides opportunities for pupils to engage, actively, in learning tasks. | Enables the teacher to observe pupil behaviour and, by assessing their skill and understanding, to make appropriate teaching interventions. | Practising Observing Measuring Recording Speculating |
| **Review** | Helping pupils to evaluate the significance and value of what they have done. Offers a chance for pupils to take stock of their learning and for the teacher to guide them in consolidating their understanding. | Provides an opportunity for the teacher to assess learning which has taken place and to consider next steps. | Recording Discussing Explaining Hypothesizing Reporting Evaluating |
| **Application** | Helping pupils to relate what they have learned to their everyday lives. Enables the pupils to locate new learning meaningfully in the wider context of their lives. | Provides an opportunity for the teacher to ensure that key points are reinforced and consolidated. | Relating to experience Discussing Interpreting |

**Figure 15.2** *Phases of teaching, learning and assessment*

Such a model is helpful in highlighting the significance of formative assessment. Continuous assessment of this kind is the crucial means through which a teacher 'connects' with the pupils' thinking, and is thus able to extend, challenge and reinforce it as appropriate.

### Practical activity 15.2

*Aim:* To study key phases of a teaching session.

*Method:* Plan to teach a session involving some new learning to a group of pupils. As you plan, think about the five phases which were identified in Figure 15.2 and about the role of assessment. Consider how best to orientate the pupils, how to elicit and then make use of what they already know, etc. Having thought about the possibilities, be prepared to respond to their input.

Prepare for obtaining a record of what happens. For instance, you could ask a colleague to observe you. Try to get your colleague to make detailed notes on what is said by both you and the pupils. Alternatively, you could try setting up a video if you have access to one – but allow time to explain what you are doing to your pupils.

Teach the session.

Analyse what happened. Were the five phases apparent and helpful? What opportunities for assessment occurred? Were they used to maximize the quality and appropriateness of the teacher input?

*Follow-up:* This is primarily an activity to raise awareness. We suggest you try it from time to time, mulling over the results and considering ways in which you could apply the insights about your teaching which you obtain.

## 2.2   Developing and verifying teacher judgement

Of course, the correctness of teacher judgement in constructive interventions in the learning process cannot be assumed. Indeed, high quality judgement is something which has to be worked at and maintained.

A common recommendation for this is through gathering actual evidence of pupils' skill, knowledge and understanding. As we illustrate in Section 4 of this chapter, there are many ways of doing this, with observation, listening, questioning, viewing products and setting tasks, tests and examinations being commonly used in one way or another. Of course, many of these methods are used routinely by all teachers and contribute both to ongoing formative assessment and, where appropriate, to summative judgements of pupil attainment.

The vital step is the collection and analysis of evidence. In itself, this sounds very simple, and in one sense it is. However, if collection is undertaken rigorously and analysis is approached with an open mind, the results are invariably interesting, are often surprising and may be challenging. Investigating pupils' learning in detail has shown, time after time, how little we know as teachers and how fascinating it is to find out, even when we may think that we can sum up a pupil accurately.

> ### *Practical activity 15.3*
>
> *Aim:* To test the value of collecting evidence in informing teacher judgement.
>
> *Method:* Pose yourself a question: 'How do I know what I know?' To follow this up, select a pupil about whose attainment you are confident and focus on an area of your subject. Review any relevant attainment targets, level descriptions or other curricular or training targets. Record your present view of the pupil's knowledge, skill and understanding.
>
> Then select, from Part 3 of this chapter, some appropriate ways of gathering evidence of the pupil's attainment. Phase these into a practical teaching programme and record the evidence in some way.
>
> Assemble and analyse your evidence.
>
> To what extent have your presuppositions been reinforced or amended?
>
> *Follow-up:* If detailed consideration of evidence brings insights which you might not otherwise have had, how could you incorporate such procedures into your routine classroom activity?

Of course, whilst the collection of detailed evidence is vital in refining judgement, we must also note its impracticality on a large scale. Indeed, with large class sizes it is simply not possible for any subject teacher to collect detailed evidence about everyone and everything encountered in their work. The use of evidence gathered from the whole class or of more intuitive teacher judgements is therefore inevitable. However it is gathered, evidence makes three vital contributions.

First, it is a means of developing and verifying the quality of teacher judgement. Wise and reflective teachers will not trust their opinions without some form of regular check. Gathering evidence on pupil attainment for assessment purposes is thus a form of staff development. It attunes teacher thinking and it provides a professional justification for the use of more intuitive judgements.

Second, the gathering of evidence should be undertaken when problem-solving is necessary, such as when the performance of a pupil is causing concern, or perhaps when a very new subject topic is taught. On such occasions, systematic consideration of evidence can take teacher thinking forward considerably, as well as delivering attainment data.

Third, evidence collected in each classroom can contribute to the process of achieving consistency of teacher judgements concerning the official 'levels' of attainment which pupils have reached (see also Section 3.2). One possible procedure is for a department to make up a subject portfolio comprising the work of pupils at different 'levels'. This is then used in standardization or moderation activities when it is necessary for teachers to negotiate and agree the meaning of particular 'levels'. Exemplar material is also supplied by national assessment authorities to help in this process (e.g. SCAA 1995a).

## 2.3 Pupil self-assessment for learning

Self-assessment is a process through which people learn to monitor and evaluate their own learning strategies and achievements. In psychological terms, self-assessment contributes to processes of 'meta-cognition', which we discussed in Chapter 9, Section 2.5. The key capacity is that of being able to stand back from a learning experience and to make an open, personal evaluation so that future actions can be adjusted. For pupils, it supports the gradual development of independence as external support for learning provided by teachers, parents and others becomes less necessary. The development of 'action plans', 'target setting' and 'reviews' are a common manifestation of this process in secondary schools (see also Section 4.6).

When developing pupil self-assessment through target setting, it may be helpful to think of three stages of work

### Stage one: share aims and plan targets

This is the vital first step and foundation for everything else. Learning objectives and criteria must be discussed fully and be clearly understood by the pupils. It is likely that teachers will have to support pupils in drafting their targets so that they are both focused and discrete. Such precision is important, but targets may still range between skills, knowledge and understanding. Some key questions may help:

- When learning a skill, a pupil may clarify her target by asking herself: 'What will I be able to do?'
- When the target concerns learning or finding out new knowledge, a pupil may ask himself: 'What will I know about?'
- When focusing on the development of understanding, a pupil may ask: 'What will I explain?'

Such targets may be recorded on 'planning sheets', placed in a personal record, shared and discussed with a group or the class or treated in any other way which will establish the clear priority for the future efforts of each pupil. One excellent practice, particularly for young people who need structured support, is to develop individual 'action plans' which are designed to help them in meeting agreed targets.

### Stage two: review and record achievements

At an appropriate point after the setting of targets for pupil self-assessment, pupils should be encouraged to review their progress. In the first place this may be fairly general but it is then useful to make it quite specific by selecting and discussing examples of work which illustrate the achievement of the targets. The point of this is to develop understanding by challenging subjective impressions with actual evidence.

The outcome of the review should be recorded and may result in revised targets (perhaps as part of an action plan). Examples of work could be placed in a pupil portfolio of work, and successes may be logged in a Record of Achievement (see Section 5.3).

*Stage three: help report progress*

This is another powerful phase in which it is possible to gain an enormous amount from pupil involvement. The basic idea is that the pupils themselves take a leading role in reporting their progress to their peers, or even to parents. With teacher support as required, pupils could produce an account of their progress as part of a report to the class, discuss it with their parents and then participate in the teacher/parent interview at a parent's evening (see also Section 5.2).

One example of the value of pupil self-assessment has been provided by Bell *et al.* (1993), who investigated the meta-cognitive skills of pupils aged 10–16 studying mathematics. A variety of ways of enhancing these skills was developed and, as part of the study, the pupils themselves acted as assessors. Strategies to raise pupil awareness of their own learning included: constructing tests; devising and using mark schemes; diagnosing errors; assessing themselves against statements of attainment; and predicting their own performance. The study found that asking pupils to construct tests was an effective way of enhancing their awareness of content, particularly when this was accompanied by discussions of the relationships between topics and their relative importance. It led pupils to realize more fully their own level of understanding and sometimes led to a re-evaluation of their own state of knowledge.

For any form of education or training, the learner's engagement with their learning is greatly affected by the degree to which they recognize its purposes and value. Such understanding underpins the processes through which they begin; as Vygotsky said, to become 'self-regulated' (Vygotsky 1978, **Primary Readings 6.4, 6.5**). Unfortunately however, there is a very consistent research finding that school pupils are very often unsure of the educational aims of tasks which are set by their teachers. In reality, we tend to tell them what to do, but rarely explain the reasoning behind tasks or the criteria for assessment. Attainment targets, such as those embedded in the National Curriculum, provide a very general way of sharing information with pupils, but more specific provision can only come from teacher-devised systems for the particular subject content which is being taught. An excellent practice, often found where pupils are beginning GCSE coursework, is the presentation to pupils of the official criteria against which they will be assessed.

We will return to this subject later in the chapter in the context of records of achievement (Section 5.3). At this point it is enough to recognize the power of self-assessment as a learning strategy and as an important contribution to lifelong learning. Through encouraging it, we can both build on primary school work in supporting 'independent learning', and respond to the regular calls from industry for flexible, resilient, self-motivating and reflective learners.

## 3 | ISSUES IN ASSESSMENT

The introduction of national assessment procedures tends to cause anxiety. However, we should not forget that assessment happens informally, and quite naturally, all the time in relationships with people. Whenever people meet, judgements are made and expectations developed. When people part, knowledge of each other may be reinforced, refined or changed. These new understandings are then brought to the next encounter. Such processes enable people to build reciprocal expectations, to develop close relationships and to become aware of needs. Sensitivity to others, empathy and understanding are thus founded, one way or another, on naturally occurring forms of assessment.

However, there is a world of difference between this naturally occurring interpersonal awareness and assessment procedures which are required by the State and are intended to be formally institutionalized in schools, detailed in league tables and made available to the press. The potential destructive power of such a system is immense, and in this section we consider some of the main issues which are raised.

## 3.1 Differentiation

Differentiation in assessment is the process of enabling pupils of all abilities to show what they know, understand and can do (DES 1985b). Within any teaching group there will always be a range of abilities and experiences, with the result that pupils will respond to assessments in different ways. In practical terms then, the basis of differentiation is that pupils learn in different ways, to different levels of attainment and at different rates. In assessment terms this means ensuring that assessments meet the criteria of fitness for purpose, and use language, resources or tasks that are appropriate to the pupils and the situation.

The most common forms of differentiation of teaching activities are 'by task' and 'by outcome'.

*Differentiation by task:* describes tasks and activities which are set for particular pupils according to a teacher judgement of their learning needs. For instance, pupils might be carrying out a science topic on electricity. To provide a challenge for all the pupils in the class, the teacher ensures that some tasks are complex and challenging, there are plenty of choices for the majority of the pupils, whilst some tasks are relatively simple. Teacher or pupils decide the appropriate task for them based upon previous performance. In history, a teacher may want to test pupils' skill in analysing sources. Some pupils may be asked to work on copies of original sources. However, others with relatively weak reading skills may be offered different materials in which the language is more accessible.

A major national example of differentiation by task is provided by GCSE examination procedures which offer 'tiered' examination papers. The purpose of tiering is to set tasks at an appropriate level for measuring pupil attainments. Indeed, SCAA (1996f) explains that 'tiering provides pupils with the opportuntity to show what they know, understand and can do by presenting them with question papers that are targeted at a band of attainment' (p. 3). From 1998, in order to regularize some complexity, English, English literature, science, information technology, design and techology, modern foreign languages, geography and home economics are to be examined through a 'foundation tier' covering grades G to C, and a 'higher tier' covering grades D to A*. Maths will retain three tiers.

Differentiation by task always carries the risk that pupils may not perform as anticipated. For instance, early studies of GCSE mathematics papers (Good and Cresswell 1988) indicated large numbers of pupils being ungraded when entered for a higher tier paper which proved to be too difficult, whilst some pupils were entered for too low a tier.

*Differentiation by outcome:* describes open-ended tasks and activities which offer appropriate levels of challenge for a wide range of learners. For instance, pupils might be given the task of producing a poster about the effects of acid rain on the environment. The shared stimulus produces a range of responses from the pupils, and thus reveals their abilities and attainments. In another form, differentiation by outcome may be explicitly planned into a form of assessment. For instance, pupils may be given a series of stepped questions that become increasingly complex. Some are only able to answer the first few questions in any depth while others reach much higher levels.

Regarding national use of differentiation by outcome, (SCAA 1996f) explain that, 'for some subjects, the evidence shows that it is possible to set questions in examination papers that are accessible and challenging to pupils across the whole ability range' (p 3). Thus GCSE examinations for history, music, art, performing arts, physical education, humanities and religious studies do not use tiering.

## 3.2 Validity, reliability and consistency

Validity and reliability are technical terms of immense importance. Do assessments actually represent what they purport to measure (validity)? Can the procedures be implemented in ways which ensure consistency in assessments across the country and from year to year (reliability)? In addressing the latter question regarding teacher assessment, SCAA (1995a) prefer to use the term 'consistency'.

Opinions and evidence about the validity and reliability of any assessment system are crucial to its long-term credibility. If high standards on both criteria are not met, then criticism is likely to follow. Where validity is low, assessments will be regarded as partial, limited and crude because of the factors which they ignore or cannot measure (arguments which, in 1993, caused many English teachers to withdraw co-operation for Key Stage 3 tests). Where reliability is low, assessments will be regarded as inconsistent, unfair and unreliable because of the variation in the procedures by which the assessment results were produced (arguments which, in 1995, caused a public outcry over Key Stage 2 test administration).

The technical problems in constructing and implementing a national system of assessment are considerable and, unfortunately, there is an element of tension between validity and reliability . The quest for validity tends to lead in the direction of assessment procedures which are designed for normal classroom circumstances, covering a wide curriculum and using a range of assessment techniques which are likely to be administered by teachers. In the specialist literature, this is known as 'authentic assessment'. However, the drive for reliability tends to suggest simplification in both assessment procedures and in the range of the curriculum to be assessed, so that there is more chance of comparability being attained. The result of this is likely to be greater use of methods which can be tightly controlled, such as pencil and paper testing and examinations.

In the 1990s, this tension was played out for GCSEs in England and Wales. Since the inception of the GCSE in 1986, teachers had developed a wide range of assessment techniques to obtain a broad overview of pupils' abilities. The aim was to increase the validity of the judgements made and to feed back into the learning process. However, government concern to raise 'standards' through publication of assessment results led to a drive to increase reliability. Restrictions on the proportions of teacher-assessed work were therefore introduced and an increased emphasis was placed on externally set, terminal examinations. Procedures for the administration and accreditation of examination boards became more rigorously controlled and a mandatory code of conduct was accompanied by rationalization of the number of syllabuses available (a process which the Qualifications and Curriculum Authority is likely to continue).

There is a similar story regarding teacher assessment. In the early 1990s, the role of teacher assessment in informing the teaching-learning process was emphasized. As TGAT put it, such assessment evidence was to 'feed forward' and enable teachers to meet pupil needs more precisely. The profession endorsed this view wholeheartedly, and a great deal of work was done in schools and LEAs to develop the approach (see  also **Primary Readings 12.5, 12.8 and 12.9**). By 1995 however, the School Curriculum and Assessment Authority were presenting a new form of teacher assessment (now known as 'TA') almost exclusively as a means of assessing and reporting pupil attainment against National Curriculum levels. Rather than draw out the potential contribution to teaching and learning, SCAA emphasized the need to 'define the standard' of National Curriculum levels and put stress on 'the benefits of consistency' for reporting purposes (SCAA 1995a). For instance:

> Consistency in assessment helps to ensure that, when judgements are made against the standards in the revised National Curriculum, there is fairness for pupils across classes, schools and key stages.

> Effective approaches to consistency can enhance teachers' knowledge and increase confidence in their own assessments. It can establish a basis for trust in the judgement of other teachers. This, in turn, results in a greater willingness to value and build on prior assessments of pupils.

> Properly planned and co-ordinated assessment activity . . . helps to develop a collective view of assessment, a shared expertise in the planning of teaching and assessment, and an agreed understanding of standards, expectations and pupils' achievements throughout the school. These can provide helpful support to teachers when they make the judgements at the end of a key stage. (SCAA 1995a, p.5)

To increase consistency, SCAA recommended the development of school portfolios containing samples of work which are agreed to represent each level (see also Sections 2.1 and 5.1).

The trend during the 1990s has thus been in the same direction for both standard and teacher assessment, with the formative role of assessment regarding teaching and learning being gradually subordinated to the production of summative assessment information. In the drive to improve reliability so that the performance of pupils and schools can be monitored (see Section 3.6), it is quite possible that assessment arrangements may be tightened still further. However, this is likely to continue to reduce validity. The results may become more precise and comparable, but they may also become more narrow, less meaningful and less helpful to teachers in contributing to future teaching.

> ### *Practical activity 15.4*
>
> *Aim:* To highlight the dilemma between validity and reliability.
>
> *Method:* Thinking of your main teaching subject, identify a specific target for pupil attainment.
>
> First, drawing on an appropriate form of assessment, consider how the competence and understanding of pupils *across the country* could be assessed with regard to this selected attainment target.
>
> Now change your focus, by thinking about *particular individual pupils* whom you know. How do you think each of these would cope with your form of assessment? Would it reveal all of what they really know?
>
> Pose yourself this question: Can an assessment method reflect what is really involved in understanding and competence (validity), and yet be administered in standard and consistent ways by teachers wherever or whoever they are (reliability)?
>
> *Follow-up:* Consider any test materials with which you are familiar. How do you feel that test designers have tried to resolve the validity/reliability dilemma? What compromises have they made? Do you think it is possible to devise assessment with high validity and high reliability for all subjects?

Achieving reliability, validity and consistency of assessments is thus a constant struggle, as anyone who has marked pupils' work and tried to agree a mark with colleagues will know. National Curriculum and assessment authorities tend to exercise their responsibilities by seeking technical solutions to such problems, but others argue that there are endemic difficulties. For instance, Broadfoot (1994) suggests that 'educational assessment can never be scientific' and points out that scientists have long recognized both the relativity of scientific observation and the ways in which scientific measurement depends on the relationship between the observed and the observer. Broadfoot argues that, because all kinds of educational measurement are ultimately interpersonal in character, there are inevitably inaccuracies. These can include examinee effects such as the exam stress, lack of coverage of content for the exam, type of test, questions asked and boredom; and also marker effects such as different interpretations of mark schemes, tiredness and inconsistencies over time.

Similarly Wiliam (1996) argues that 'standards' are socially constructed, rather than representing something precisely measurable:

> Examination results are 'social facts'. Like bank notes they depend for their value on the status that is accorded to them within a social system. As foreign currency markets have found out to their cost, it is not possible to create comparability by

fiat. Similarly, all attempts to define 'standards' or 'equivalence' independently of the social setting in which they are created have failed, and indeed are bound to fail. Two qualifications are comparable only to the extent that there are people who are prepared to believe they are comparable. (p. 304)

## 3.3 Curriculum distortion

The tension between validity and reliability is so endemic that it is unlikely that a completely satisfactory resolution will ever be found. Where assessment is used formatively, to inform the teaching/learning process, this is of less significance because the information can still be used constructively within each school. However, where assessment is used summatively, and published with the claim that it reflects pupil and school performance, then the stakes become high both for pupils and schools. In these circumstances there is a well-documented tendency for teachers and pupils to  'work to the test' (Harlen *et al.* 1992, **Primary Reading 12.1**). The result is likely to be a narrow curriculum and, whilst standards may rise in those areas of the curriculum which are tested, a reduction in overall standards across the broader curriculum may occur.

Concern is justified by the experience of the United States of America, where a great deal of testing has been used for many years (Shepard 1987, Corbett and Wilson 1991, Rottenberg and Smith 1990, Romberg and Zavinnia 1989). As Rottenberg and Smith comment: 'As the stakes become higher, in that more hangs on the results, teaching becomes more 'test-like', such that testing tends to result in the substitution of means for ends.'

It is interesting to note the determined moves in the United States to move away from 'high-stakes testing' (such as tests with league tables) towards formative, authentic testing (Resnick and Resnick 1991).

### Practical activity 15.5

*Aim:* To investigate ways in which high-stakes assessment distorts curriculum provision.

*Method:* Talk to several teachers about the assessments which they carry out and, in particular, about those which have to be reported publicly. Ask them about any concerns which they may have. Enquire about ways in which they feel they have had to shape curriculum provision to ensure that the pupils can perform on publicly reported tests and examinations. Ask if public reporting of assessment results has broadened, narrowed or made no difference to the curriculum which they provide.

*Follow-up:* You could reflect on a potentially very significant dilemma here. The National Curriculum sets broad curriculum targets, whilst national assessment procedures test only a narrow range. Does one undermine the other?

## 3.4 Pupil experience

We have already discussed the potential threat which increased assessment activity could pose through narrowing the curriculum as teachers 'teach to the test'. Some teachers also fear that assessment pressure can worsen the quality of pupils' education experiences and undermine the self-confidence of less successful pupils. Of course, these effects are likely to vary between subjects according to the differing requirements of the National Curriculum and according to the steps taken by teachers to mitigate any adverse consequences of overt assessment. Assessment pressure can also 'gee up' some pupils, and cause them to increase their efforts and performance.

Evaluation of early Key Stage 3 tests showed that they were too long and that pupils found it difficult to concentrate for long enough to show their true levels of attainment (CATS 1992). The changes to the structures of the tests since these findings appear to have alleviated the problem (SCAA 1995b). As the core subjects (science, English and mathematics) have gone through changes both to their curricula and to their testing arrangements in recent years, the focus of the national tests has changed towards short, timed, written tests which can be taken under controlled conditions. In some ways this has allowed teachers to be more flexible in their approach to assessment and to see the Key Stage 3 tests as simply one part of the information which they are collecting. In other foundation subjects the emphasis is also on Teacher Assessment for reporting purposes.

As we approach the millennium and see the full implementation of Dearing's concept of 'vocational' and 'academic' pathways, assessment processes are likely to produce distinctly different experiences and forms of public certification. The ways in which assessment results influence the expectations which teachers have of pupils, pupils have of each other, and pupils have of themselves is not yet documented for this new era, but there is considerable evidence of how the experiences of pupils have diverged in secondary schools in the past. In a series of studies, sociologists such as Hargreaves (1967), Lacey (1990), Ball (1981) and Turner (1985) have demonstrated that when a school 'differentiates' its pupils for organizational purposes or as a result of assessment, this has consequences for social relations within the pupil culture. Termed 'polarization', the basic process is that some pupils come to favour the school more, and to try harder at their studies, whilst others become dispirited and are likely to become more deviant (see also Chapter 14, Section 4.3). Such divisive processes are particularly likely to emerge as assessment processes become more overt and 'high stakes'. However, setting, option choices and allocation for different parts of tiered GCSE papers are all examples of differentiation which it is almost impossible to avoid, but may well lead to pupils adopting progressively different attitudes to school. In what is essentially a multiplier effect, we then find schools publicly promoting the achievements of its high attainers (with half an eye on boosting enrolments), whilst also developing increasingly sophisticated systems for behavioural control and reluctantly contributing to a steady rise in pupil exclusions. In part, these are the unintended consequences of the competitive and assessment-led climate in which schools of the late 1990s must survive, develop and provide, as best they can, for their pupils.

There is little doubt that national assessment procedures will have long-term effects on pupils. For many pupils, these effects will be positive, in that the quality of teaching and learning will be enhanced. Reflective teachers though, will prudently monitor effects which could both damage the self-image and self-confidence of pupils and have other divisive effects for our society as a whole.

### Practical activity 15.6

*Aim:* To investigate the impact of assessment activity on pupils.

*Method:* One simple method would be to ask the pupils what they think about being assessed in your subject through coursework, testing or examination. An interesting way of doing this might be to set up a debate, with groups putting the case for, and against, particular forms of assessment. Observation could provide another source of data. Watch the pupils carefully next time they are being assessed. How do they respond? Are some relaxed? Are others tense or anxious? Make some notes on your observations and let these accumulate over a week or so. Then review what you have found. Alternatively, if you want to obtain a large amount of material which can be analysed more systematically, you could ask pupils to express their views in writing.

As you gather data, look out for patterns. For instance, are there any differences between high achievers and lower achievers, between boys and girls?

*Follow-up:* Assessment is, necessarily, a means of differentiating between pupils (see Pollard 1987, **Primary Reading 13.8**). Thus, despite the fact that one major purpose of assessment is that pupil needs can be identified, it remains somewhat threatening. Consider then, how you can both maintain constructive assessment activity and sustain the self-confidence of all the pupils in your class (see Thorne, 1993, **Primary Reading 13. 9** for some suggestions).

### Practical activity 15.7

*Aim:* To consider people's feelings when experiencing assessment.

*Method:* We suggest that you join with a colleague and talk in pairs, each person taking it in turns to talk. First, each shares a personal experience from their childhood about which they felt positively. Second, each shares a personal childhood experience of being assessed about which they felt negatively. We suggest that each person talks, without interruption, for about five minutes.

When each person has shared their experiences, you should work together to identify the issues which were involved. Did any of the following come up: dignity, self-esteem, anxiety, humiliation, unfairness, pleasure, pride, recognition, affirmation?

*Follow-up:* Do you think the young people with whom you work in school have feelings now which are similar to those which you once had yourself?

## 3.5 Equity

This is an extremely important, but complex, topic which we will approach by addressing three questions.

### What do we mean by 'equity'?

There is a broad consensus that our society should be 'open' and 'fair', but what exactly do we want? 'Equality of opportunity' for people from all social groups is often contrasted with 'equality of outcome'. Equality of opportunity articulates with present conceptions of individual advancement and of market competition. However, it remains somewhat simplistic as a commitment, for inequalities are created by a multiplicity of factors which even a supposedly 'equal' starting point can do little to offset. On the other hand, if we believe that all social groups have the same inherent potential, then perhaps, in the long term, we should be aiming for the equality of outcome. Yet the unique qualities of people are also to be celebrated and it is unlikely that we want to produce a bland, equal homogeneity. Gipps and Murphy (1994) offer the term 'equity' to by-pass these dilemmas and they endorse a 'spirit of justice' in which 'assessment practice and interpretation of results are fair and just for all groups' (p. 18). Although still somewhat vague, perhaps such commitment is the only realistic position to take?

### Is there equality in educational outcomes?

There is not. For instance, regarding gender, a recent study by the Equal Opportunities Commission and OFSTED (1996) has shown how girls outperform boys at ages 7, 11 and 14 in English and are more successful at every level and in almost every subject at GCSE (the exception is physics). However, these differences disappear at A-level. Inspection evidence suggests that about one-fifth of secondary schools are 'weak' in meeting the needs of one sex or the other, though very few schools explicitly discriminate against either sex. Regarding social class there has been a very consistent and strong finding of its direct relationship with academic achievement: the higher the social class, the higher the achievement. There are also distinct differences regarding ethnic origin with African Caribbeans tending to perform less well than Whites, whilst Asians tend to do as well, or better (Gillborn and Gipps 1996). The Youth Cohort Study provides an unusual data set of all these factors, and shows that the strongest influence remains social class (Drew and Gray 1990) (see Figure 15.3).

### Are our forms of assessment equitable?

Ultimately, this seems most unlikely. The issue can be approached in many ways. For instance, Apple (1988) suggests distinguishing between 'curricular' and 'assessment' questions which might be asked with regard to different social groups. Thus:

- Whose knowledge is taught? Whose knowledge is assessed?
- Why is this knowledge taught in this particular way to this particular group? Are the form, content and mode of assessment appropriate for different groups and individuals?
- How do we enable the histories and cultures of different social groups to be taught in responsible and responsive ways? Is this range of cultural knowledge reflected in definitions of achievement?

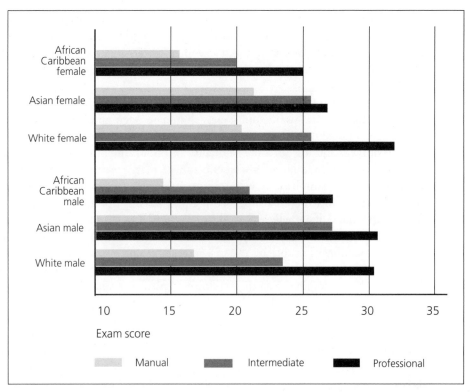

**Figure 15.3** *Average exam scores by ethnic origin, gender and social class (England and Wales, 1985) (adapted from Drew and Gray, 1990, p. 114 and cited by Gillborn and Gipps, 1996)*

These are very difficult questions, but the point to be clear about is that it is the case that different forms of assessment do produce differences in measured attainment and can be manipulated to adjust these outcomes. Assessment practices are therefore not 'objective' in any absolute sense: they measure what they are designed to measure. They are socially constructed, and to some extent so is the performance or capability of the pupil (see Chapter 9, Section 2).

There are many ways in which unintended differences in assessed performance may occur, an issue which is closely linked to that of validity (Gipps and Murphy, 1994). The *form* of an assessment instrument may affect some pupils; for instance, multiple choice response questions have been found to favour boys and coursework tasks girls (Murphy 1982). In terms of the *content* to be assessed, ethnic, social and cultural background, as well as gender of pupils, will affect how meaningful a task or question is to pupils and therefore on whether their performance in the assessment reflects their real understanding. The *social contexts* in which assessment activities are carried out have also been shown to impact on performance (James 1996, Filer 1995), with administrative procedures being a more specific example of this factor. A further issue of great significance concerns the *expectations* of significant others, such as teachers, peers or parents. These affect performance indirectly, through their influence on the self-confidence of the pupil. However, the influence of expectations may also be felt very directly thorough the access, or lack of it, to assessment at particular levels, for instance, when tiered examination entry is required (see Section 3.1). Indeed, higher level results may be inaccessible to some pupils simply by their not being entered for relevant assessments in the first place. Low expectations by teachers is regarded as a much bigger problem than high expectations (Woodhead 1995, Blair 1996), and may perhaps be echoed by pupils themselves. *Marking practices* are also vulnerable to teacher expectations for, as Hargreaves, Hestor and Mellor (1975) demonstrated, teachers tend to classify pupils in relatively stable and holistic ways, which may well become self-perpetuating.

This review of possible sources of distortion in assessment is clearly linked to many other issues of equity in education and is part of the argument that 'there is no such thing as an objective assessment' (Broadfoot 1994). There are also links with the issue of academic differentiation, addressed in Section 2.1 of this chapter, and social differentiation, considered in Chapter 14, Section 4.3 and in Section 3.7 of the present chapter. The most important thing for teachers is to recognize that some forms of assessment can be misleading. As reflective practitioners we cannot take the 'objectivity' of assessment practices for granted and we must be prepared to maintain an alert commitment to equity and the 'spirit of justice' when we assess pupils.

## 4 METHODS OF GATHERING ASSESSMENT EVIDENCE

There are many ways of gathering evidence for assessment. Some of the methods reviewed in Chapter 4 will be helpful, others more specific to assessment practices are introduced in this section.

The pattern of methods used in schools is likely to vary by subject and Key Stage, and will reflect both school policies and different departmental policies for both formative assessment and for discharging statutory obligations. However, some common patterns at Key Stage 3 are as follows.

### English
- For AT1 (Speaking and Listening) using classroom discussions, debates, readings or drama.
- For AT 2 and 3 (Reading; Writing) using classroom reading and written work, homework tasks, writing under test conditions, assessment of effort and achievement, pupil self-assessment and keeping samples of 'good work' in a portfolio.
- Portfolios of work may be used in departmental standardization meetings to discuss the meaning of particular 'levels' of attainment.

### Mathematics
- For AT1 (Using and Applying Mathematics) using set investigations or problem-solving tasks carried out in class or as part of homework, perhaps with agreed performance criteria.
- For AT2, 3, 4 and 5 (Number; Algebra; Space, Shape and Measures; Handling Data) marking of classwork and homework, observation of pupils at work in the class and occasional class testing.
- Finally, marks from the various elements of assessment may be aggregated.

### Science
- For AT1 (Experimental and Investigative Science) using assessments of practical work, with agreed criteria.
- For AT2, 3 and 4 (Life Processes and Living Things; Materials and their Properties; Physical Processes) using regular tests, perhaps based on AT-related modules and multiple choice. Also end-of-year examinations.
- Annual aggregation of practical, class test and exam scores.

We reproduce Figure 15.4 opposite, to summarize the techniques which are specifically introduced in this book. All italicized methods are particularly appropriate for the assessment of pupil learning. Those in bold italic are discussed in detail in Chapter 13; those in plain italic are discussed in this chapter. All other methods are considered in Chapter 4. Comprehensive Notes for Further Reading on data gathering are also provided at the end of Chapter 4.

## 4.1  Observation

This is probably the method which we use most frequently in the classroom and yet is possibly least recognized as a form of assessment. As the introduction to part 2 of this chapter points out, we are constantly making judgements about people in our everyday relationships with them. This is just as true in the classroom as anywhere else. The difference in a teaching situation is that we need to be more conscious of the judgements we make and need to develop ways of ensuring that decisions based on these judgements are the most appropriate for our pupils. We also need to remember the 'invisible' pupils in our classes, with whom we may have few direct interactions and about whom we feel we have less personal knowledge. We need to target them more directly in our observations.

## 4.2  Discussion, questioning and listening

These are three of the most important and natural ways by which teachers form assessment judgements, particularly of individual pupils. The great advantages of discussion, questioning and listening are that they are immediate, interactive and can be used for both formative and summative purposes. Potentially then, they are amongst the most sensitive, subtle and useful skills in any teacher's teaching and assessment repertoire. Please see Chapter 13 for further discussion on 'communication' and for many suggestions of Practical Activities.

## 4.3  Oral activities

The most common use of *formal* oral assessment is in English, Welsh and Modern Foreign Languages where 'speaking' is a target for pupil attainment. It also has a very important role in Drama in which oracy is a key skill.

The development of oral assessment in recent years recognizes the vital role of the use of language. However, as a form of assessment, it poses some challenges. These

| | Looking | Listening | Asking |
|---|---|---|---|
| ROUTINELY OCCURRING | Participant observation (C4, 3.1, C15, 4.1) Document analysis (C4, 3.2) *Marking pupils' work* (C15, 4.5) | ***Active listening*** (C13, 2.4) | ***Questioning*** (C13, 2.2) *Setting tasks* (C15, 4.4) *Subject based tests* (C15, 4.9) |
| | | ***Discussing*** (C13, 2.3) *Oral assessment* (C15, 4.3) *Conferencing* (C15, 4.7) | |
| | *Assessing practical competence* (C15, 4.8) | | |
| SPECIALLY UNDERTAKEN | Systematic observation (C4, 3.3) Photography (C4, 3.4) | Audio recording (C4, 3.6) | Interviewing (C4, 3.7 and C15, 4.7) *Concept mapping* (C15, 4.6) Questionnaires (C4, 3.8) Sociometry (C4, 3.9) Personal constructs (C4, 3.10) Curriculum matrices (C4, 3.11) Checklists (C4, 3.12) *Examining* (C15, 4.10) *Cognitive testing* (C15, 4.9) |
| | Video recording (C4, 3.5) | | |

**Figure 15.4** *A typology of data-gathering methods and their location in the book*

include: manageability where numbers of pupils are high; the difficulty of providing evidence where this is needed (tape recordings or pupil accounts of speaking assignments are often used alongside teacher notes); and the risk of teacher judgements being influenced by speech style, dialect or accent (Satterly, 1989). Overall, oral assessment provides a good example of a form of assessment which has high validity and is targeted at a very important skill, but which, for a variety reasons, has relatively low reliability (see Section 3.2 for further discussion of these concepts).

Oral assessment is also used *informally* in many other subjects where pupils' understanding and contribution to classroom activities are considered. Presentations may be made, or debates held, and these may provide useful insights for teachers. Similarly, questioning allows the teacher to explore knowledge, understanding and the development of thinking in a detailed and comprehensive manner.

Oral assessment may be particularly useful with pupils, such as those suffering from dyslexia, whose written skills are poor. In these circumstances, it allows the teacher to check knowledge and understanding in an extremely flexible manner. However, although oral assessment can be very useful for pupils who for various reasons underperform in written tests, it should be recognized that it can also cause anxiety for some pupils.

## 4.4   Setting tasks

Perhaps the most routinely available source of evidence of pupil learning is that which arises, lesson by lesson, as pupils engage in the activities and tasks which the teacher has prepared for them.

Teachers who are aware of the importance of formative assessment and of the potential for gathering evidence from routine classroom activities should be able to focus tasks so that pupil actions and performance reveal what they know, can do and understand. The teacher's skill thus lies in providing tasks which are appropriate and accessible for all the pupils but which also highlight what particular pupils have learned. This is a form of 'differentiation by outcome' – the development of understanding about the needs and capacities of the pupil by evaluating 'how they got on'.

Bennett (1992b) has developed a model (see Figure 15.5) of the teaching phases which are involved in setting and using tasks . It is clear from the research evidence that the role of the teacher is particularly significant. Over time, it should be the aim of every teacher to develop a repertoire of tasks, suitable for assessment, which can be drawn on as appropriate.

The strengths of using tasks for assessment purposes derive both from the frequency and routine nature of the opportunities which are available and from the high validity which this form of assessment is likely to have. After all, it is embedded in everyday classroom processes. It should provide a rich source of insights about pupil learning strategies and attainments, which can be used formatively.

*Practical activity 15.8*

*Aim:* To evaluate and develop the use of tasks as a means of pupil assessment.

*Method:* A review and comparison of tasks which are already routinely set should provide initial insights. Three criteria could be used: appropriateness and accessibility for all pupils; potential for yielding differentiated outcomes; manageability. In other words, can the tasks involve and motivate everyone and produce some clear insights into the pupils' capacities in a way which is practical to use?

| Tasks for comparison | Accessibility for all pupils | Potential for differentiation of outcomes | Manageability |
|---|---|---|---|
| 1. | | | |
| 2. | | | |
| 3. etc. | | | |

If some tasks are more useful than others for assessment purposes, can you identify what it is about the best ones that makes them so useful?

*Follow-up:* Think about some specific learning targets which you have for the pupils. What tasks could you devise to help you assess their progress and attainment?

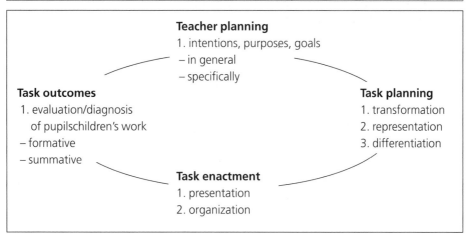

**Teacher planning**
1. intentions, purposes, goals
   – in general
   – specifically

**Task planning**
1. transformation
2. representation
3. differentiation

**Task enactment**
1. presentation
2. organization

**Task outcomes**
1. evaluation/diagnosis of pupilschildren's work
– formative
– summative

**Figure 15.5** *A cycle for classroom tasks (from Bennett 1992b)*

## 4.5  Marking

The most common way for teachers to monitor pupils' learning is to 'mark' work which has been completed, either in class or through homework. This can be anything from a verbal or written comment (e.g. 'What an exciting story!' or 'See me'), to setting spelling corrections at the end of an excercise, or allocating a grade or mark. For practical reasons, marking is often done by the teacher in the absence of the pupil concerned, so that there is no opportunity to talk with them and find out how they set about the task. In such cases, marking is more evaluative than diagnostic.

However, marking can be used in conjunction with other forms of monitoring. For instance, teacher judgement when marking is often informed by observations as when the teacher circulates around the room during classwork and also by discussions which may have taken place during lessons.

When marking, there are two ways of deriving additional information which takes available insights beyond the limits of any particular piece of work.

First, each piece of work by a single pupil can be considered in sequence. By comparing each example with previous work, it is possible to assess what learning has taken place and what significance to attach to any mistakes. If such mistakes, or 'miscues', are analysed carefully they can provide valuable clues to possible learning difficulties. For instance, it is revealing to note whether errors are consistent or one-off. If a pattern emerges then a future teaching-learning point has been identified. Such diagnostic marking can provide useful information upon which to base subsequent discussion, or be used when making judgements about matching future tasks.

Second, pupils' work can be considered in the context of the class as a whole. In this way, it may be possible to identify any difficulties which our teaching may be creating. Spotting patterns of errors across a selection of pupils will allow us to see these.

Most schools or subject departments have a marking policy, which teachers will be required to follow. These policies attempt to ensure consistency so that a pupil will develop an increasingly mature sense of how to interpret comments made on his or her work. Sometimes references to National Curriculum levels may be expected. Comments should encourage pupils to value their work in a positive but self-critical way.

Teachers will also need to think about the strategy of asking pupils to mark their own work. This is a valuable activity (not just to save teachers' time!), since it helps pupils interpret their responses against some 'model answers' provided by their teacher. This will, in itself, help develop pupils' understanding of the work they are doing and of its underlying purposes. The skill of marking their own work is one which will need to be developed. Pupils are often very 'hard' on themselves and do not find it easy to interpret their work flexibly if it does not precisely match the answer they are given.

## Practical activity 15.9

*Aim:* To mark a pupil's work to identify their achievements and weaknesses.

*Method:* Collect examples of a pupil's work which form a sequence. Contrast the early and later work and note the major developments. Then list and prioritize continuing weaknesses. Talk with the pupil and affirm their progress. Negotiate with the pupil to agree targets for future development.

*Follow-up:* This is a way to use marking formatively for an individual. Marking the work of the whole class on a particular piece of work is also helpful in identifying teaching which several pupils may need or for gauging understanding and competence in the class as a whole. Look back through your marking though. How often is it encouraging? How often do your comments engage with what the pupil was trying to do?

## Practical activity 15.10

*Aim:* To investigate pupils' feelings about routine marking of their work.

*Method:* We suggest that you begin work with one of your classes and hold a discussion on the two questions below.

'What is marking for?'
'How would you like your work to be marked?'

Then you could consider some examples of marking relating to your subject. Perhaps you could use some written work that has been produced and look at any comments and corrections which you made. How do the pupils feel about your responses?

*Follow-up:* What ways of protecting pupils' dignity can you develop, whilst still providing appropriate assessment feedback to them? Could you negotiate with the pupils to establish criteria by which their work will be evaluated?

The term 'mapping' denotes a procedure which requires pupils to 'map' out what they have learnt and how it appears to 'fit' together (see, for instance. Figure 15.6). Such a map would represent the ideas, concepts and knowledge that the pupils have been working with during a particular unit of work, as perceived by the pupil. The procedure might begin by listing aspects of the topic which were covered (e.g. glaciation, moraine, ice age, U-shaped valleys, cirques, etc.). The pupils then map the relationships between the different elements explaining how they see any links. This provides a way of seeing what they have understood. It can then provide a basis for teacher and pupil to talk over understandings and misunderstandings. In a sense then, this is a technique for gaining some access to the 'curriculum-as-experienced' (see the Introduction to Chapter 6).

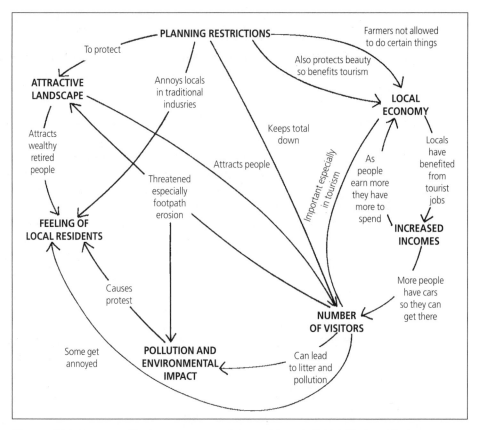

**Figure 15.6** *A geographical concept map of the problems in British National Parks, produced by an able Year 10 pupil (Leat and Chandler 1996)*

## Practical activity 15.11

*Aim:* To practise and evaluate concept mapping as a means of investigating pupils' understanding.

*Method:* If you can, we suggest you work first with a group, then try concept mapping with a whole class.

There are lots of ways of approaching concept mapping and you may have to adapt our suggestion to reflect your subject. Each pupil can be asked to think what the topic you have just taught them 'was about' and to write each element or idea on small pieces of paper. These can be arranged on a larger sheet and moved around experimentally to eventually reflect, by their proximity to each other, the relationships between the various aspects of the topic as seen by the pupil. The small pieces of paper can then be glued on and lines drawn between them to represent the relationships which have been identified. Finally, a few words expressing these relationships should be written on each line.

*Follow-up:* You could relate the concept maps which you create both to your plans and to relevant learning targets. This is likely to underline the fact that, whatever we teach, pupils make sense of it in their own ways.

## 4.7  Conferencing, action planning and progress review

These are terms used to describe forms of extended discussion, usually with a specific goal and outcome, which takes place between a teacher and pupil. Such a session offers an opportunity for a teacher and pupil to come to a mutual understanding concerning an issue which has arisen (conferencing), to agree future learning or behavioural targets (action planning) or to discuss the outcomes of previous efforts (progress review). Such discussions should allow a teacher and pupil to talk about their feelings concerning events and activities, thus also building their relationship. Such processes are also closely related to our previous discussion of pupil self-assessment for learning (Section 2.3) and they are important skills for lifelong learning and career management (see SCAA 1996a).

Of course, the in-depth discussions which are involved in conferencing, action planning and progress review could pose management problems for any teacher. How to fit in neccessary discussions? What preparation is necessary? What will other pupils be doing whilst the teacher is thus engaged? The length of the discussions will vary with the needs of the pupil. However, it may be wise to plan to set aside a certain amount of time, perhaps during a set lesson period, when the class knows that you must not be disturbed, if at all possible.

For some topics, discussions with a group might be appropriate, and collective action plans or targets could result. However, it is important that a group context does not inhibit some of the more reticent individuals.

> ### Practical activity 15.12
>
> *Aim:* To experiment with conferencing, action planning or target setting.
>
> *Method:* We suggest that conferencing, action planning or target setting is initially tried on a relatively small scale, with a few identified pupils, so that it does not take too much time.
>
> **Who:** Begin by thinking with which pupils you wish to engage. Perhaps you will identify pupils with whom you wish to negotiate some learning targets for your subject, or changes in behaviour?
>
> **When:** The question of timing is crucial for the practicality of this one-to-one activity. Decide how you will make time for it, with particular attention to what the other pupils will be doing.
>
> **What:** Be clear and specific concerning what you wish to discuss, and, if possible, agree this with the pupil. If at all possible, define your focus so that you can reach a target and an agreement together. Aim for small successes and build on them.
>
> **How:** Consider how you are going to discuss the issue with the pupil. What will be the most appropriate strategy? Can you suggest ways of monitoring the achievement of the target?
>
> *Follow-up:* Review the practicality and value of your experience. Was it valuable? Do conferencing, action planning and target setting have a role in your repertoire of assessment and teaching methods?

## 4.8 Assessing practical competence

This is a crucial form of assessment and is central to the vocational pathway and NVQs. However, it is also an important and necessary requirement for some GNVQs in the applied pathway. We will focus on NVQ assessment, which will illustrate some of the more developed forms of assessment of practical competence.

It might be helpful to refer back to Chapter 6, Figure 6.6, in which the national framework for NVQs and the criteria for the five 'levels' are set out.

How, then, can competences be assessed in workplaces?

The first challenge is to be clear about what is meant by 'competence'. NCVQ (1995b) have a highly developed scheme for structuring this. First, they suggest an *analysis of functions* which will support broadly based and transferable capabilities. The various *elements* of competence are then stated in the form of: 'a verb specifying an activity', 'the object of the activity' and 'the conditions of the activity'. For instance, 'to adapt methods of communication to different customers'. *Performance criteria* are each required to specify 'a critical outcome' and 'an evaluative statement'. For instance, 'candidate records are complete, legible and accurate'. *Range statements* set out the breadth or scope of each element by defining the various circumstances in which they may be applied. *Knowledge specifications* specify the extent to which the candidate should be able to transfer performance, produce new solutions and deal with the unexpected. Finally, there are various *evidence requirements* for the assessment of each competence.

In terms of the practical organization of assessment processers, the NCVQ has worked closely with industry (e.g. CBI 1994) to create a structure of assessors, internal verifyers, managers, external verifiers and awarding bodies. This structure is illustrated by Figure 15.7, below

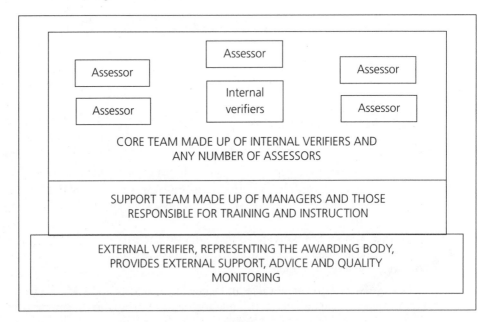

**Figure 15.7** *The structure of an NVQ Assessment Team*

Each assessment team has the role of assessing and verifying the capabilities of each NVQ candidate, officially defined as a 'competence'. This is done through the collection of evidence. 'Performance evidence' shows what a candidate can do. 'Knowledge evidence' shows what a candidate knows and understands. Such evidence is related to standards of performance criteria and range statements (see Chapter 6, Section 3.5). Common sources of evidence (Cook 1994) are:

- *Observation of performance*
  Used in work situations in relation to set tasks, simulations, training exercises or assessment. Mainly offers performance evidence.

- *Questioning*
  Verbal, while performing activities or at a review meeting; or written, such as multiple-choice tests, essays or projects. Primarily offers knowledge evidence.

- *Reports*
  Reflective reports by candidates on their experience, activities and role; work diaries, procedural notes, assignments and projects. Give both performance and knowledge evidence.

- *Testimonies*
  Managers, colleagues and clients give verbal or written evidence about the candidate's performance and/or knowledge. Provides both performance and knowledge evidence.

- *Products*
  Items that are produced as a result of performance such as letters/memos, computer printouts, documents, finished products (such as food, hairstyle, painting or brickwork).

## Practical activity 15.13

*Aim:* To explore the specification of a workplace competence and its assessment.

*Method:* Consider a workplace setting (a shop, a cafe, a pub, a school). Focus on one person who works there and on a key aspect of his or her role. With reference to the text in Section 4.8, try to express this in NCVQ terms as a competence and in terms of elements. Attempt to construct performance criteria and a range statement. Now consider what evidence you might collect to assess the extent to which this competence has been developed.

*Follow-up:* To what extent did the NCVQ framework assist you in thinking more rigorously about the workplace competence of the person on whom you focused? Can you see a role for such analysis in school settings?

## 4.9 Subject-based and cognitive testing

Testing takes many forms and is used for a wide range of purposes. In the list below, we distinguish the main differences between major types of test and testing practice.

### Teacher tests/published tests

Test which teachers devise themselves and are directly related to what has been taught, may be contrasted with published tests which are intended to be generally applicable to a wide range of situations. Teacher tests are widely used for diagnostic purposes to assess the extent to which pupils have learned a particular, locally developed unit of work. Such tests can also be used reflectively to assess a teacher's effectiveness in implementing specified learning objectives. On the other hand, published tests offer convenient assessment resources. They are often associated with established courses in subjects, such as French and Mathematics, where incremental learning is necessary.

### Criterion referenced/norm referenced tests

Criterion referenced tests are concerned with assessing whether each pupil's performance satisfies specified criteria. For instance, this is the basis of national testing at Key Stages 1, 2 and 3 and of many 'mastery' tests such as those of graded sports awards, cycling proficiency and vehicle driving tests. They may be compared to tests which provide 'standardized' comparisons of individuals in terms of 'normal' expectations of achievement. These are well established through 'IQ tests' and other forms of cognitive measure of verbal or mathematical reasoning. At present, the latter are often regarded as being more reliable than criterion referenced tests such as national Key Stage 3 tests. For instance, where there are reservations about national testing at the end of Key Stage 2, it remains common for secondary schools to ask each new intake of Year 7 pupils to take cognitive and/or subject based forms of norm referenced tests on entry. These are used as a 'base-line' from which value added later in the school can be measured.

### Open response/closed response

Many classroom tests pose questions to which there is room for imagination and creativity, such as an essay, review, synopsis, investigation or problem-solving task. Such open response tests are particularly common in English and the humanities, but even these may also use closed tests in relation to issues such as spelling, dates, capital cities or other forms of factual information. Closed response tests presume that there is one right answer, and multiple choice questions, with selection between pre-specified answers, are the most extreme example of this. Such tests are often used in the sciences, but science teachers may also use open response tests in association with experiments and problem-solving.

Criterion referenced testing is supposed to underly all statutory assessment activity in the UK (TGAT 1987, 1988, see the Introduction of this chapter) and is the specific rationale for the creation of the structure of levels, attainment targets and statements of attainment. However, research has shown that normative assumptions tend to creep back into the judgements which teachers and others make when carrying out both teacher and standardized assessment procedures (Broadfoot 1996, Croll 1990, **Primary Reading 12.2**).

There is no doubt that appropriate comparative scores for pupils can be helpful in any review of the attainments of pupils, teachers or schools. However, whatever type of test is used, it is most important for a reflective teacher to try to identify its strengths, weaknesses and its underlying assumptions about learning. Taking an example of a reading test (the classics like Schonell, Daniels and Diack, Neale, or more up-to-date tests from NFER, SCAA or the QCA), on what evidence does the test actually rely as an indication of 'reading'? Is the test founded on an appropriate conceptualization of learning to read? Does the test generate valid data so that it really measures what it is supposed to measure? Can the test be reliably used so that results are consistent?

### Practical activity 15.14

*Aim:* To practise and evaluate the use of tests as a means of assessment.

*Method:* Decide on a worthwhile topic for testing, consider the type of test you require (see above) and devise a short test. Plan how you are going to manage the test in the classroom.

Carry out your testing plan with some pupils.

Make notes on what happened.

Evaluate the results.

*Follow-up:* Consider questions such as:

Did your test provide useful information?
Can you use the information in future teaching?
How did the less successful pupils respond to the test?
Was the test a valid indicator of what you wanted to find out about?
Was the test completed reliably? (Any pupils distracted, interrupted, tired, disturbed?)
How did your test compare with national tests?

## 4.10 Examining

In most secondary schools the public examination system has always had an enormous influence on curriculum and teaching, particularly in Key Stage 4 and Post-16 education as young people begin to approach the 'world of work'. This is where the role of the education system in producing 'certification' of the capabilities of potential employees or students in further study becomes particularly important.

From the 1950s to the mid-1980s GCE O-levels and A-level examinations dominated secondary education, though largely relying on examinations taken at the end of each course and providing awards to a relatively small proportion of school-leavers. For example, the 1966 O-level exams were passed by only 22 per cent of school-leavers. The introduction of GCSE in 1988 with its emphasis on assessing what pupils know, understand and can do was accompanied by the use of more varied assessment techniques, and significant proportions of coursework. It was welcomed by many teachers as a motivator for many pupils and began to achieve results, so that by 1996 46 per cent of 16-year-olds achieved five GCSEs graded A–C (the O-level equivalent). However, worries about coursework plagiarism and 'falling standards' resulted in the introduction of a mandatory code of practice (1995) and a 25 per cent ceiling on the permitted levels of coursework. A similar debate on A-level took place in 1996 concerning the effect on standards of the increasingly popular 'modular' courses, in which examinations are spread thoughout the course, thus allowing 'retakes'.

Whilst Wales, Scotland and Northern Ireland have had single unified examinations boards for many years, a particular feature of this period in England has been the multiplicity of boards and thus of syllabuses for each subject. For instance, in 1996 GCSE and A-level courses in England were available from eight different exam boards, co-ordinated within four examination groups:

- Northern Examining and Assessment Board (NEAB)
- Midland Examining Group (MEG)
- University of London Examinations and Assessment Council (ULEAC)
- Southern Examining Group (SEG).

Given the pressure on schools to 'raise' standards, the selection of appropriate boards and syllabuses for particular subjects and pupil groups became a specialized strategic game. If anything, the situation regarding vocational qualifications was even more varied, with the most significant providers being:

- National Council for Vocational Qualifications (NCVQ)
- Business Training and Enterprise Council (BTEC)
- Royal Society of Arts Examinations Board (RSA)
- City and Guilds of London Institute (CGLI).

Following the Dearing Review, the DfEE has begun to rationalize some of this diversity and now publishes an approved list of qualifications for use in schools. A new framework for qualifications has been established (see Chapter 6, Parts 2 and 3). With the Qualifications and Curriculum Authority taking an overview, there is likely to be further rationalization of awarding bodies and integration of vocational and academic qualifications.

Of course, public examinations are very different from most of the other forms of assessment which have been discussed in this chapter because teachers essentially begin to lose control of the process. Pupil work passes into the special examination books and then out of the school to external examiners. There is nothing more that a teacher can do. For this reason, there is particular skill in preparing pupils in both revision and exam technique.

### Revision

Encourage pupils to think strategically. What percentage of marks are associated with each exam? What are the pupil's aims? What is their present mark level, and what are their realistic targets? How then, should they allocate revision time?

Given a sound strategy, Wragg (1996) suggests helping pupils to reflect on their own learning strategies, so that they can organize a successful revision programme for themselves. For instance:

- Encourage pupils to think about and use revision techniques which suit them. For instance, highlighting, underlining or writing out notes for those with a strong visual memory, making audio tapes of vital information for those with a strong auditory memory, explaining to parents or friends for those who prefer some inter-personal support. Perhaps varying such approaches to maintain concentration.
- Encourage pupils to reflect on their favoured organizational approach. Is a revision plan to be produced? Are they going to work in concentrated blocks on each subject or spread the revision out? Are all subjects to be treated the same, or will there be variation? Will this change as the exams approach? Given the amount of material to be revised, how will boredom be avoided? Should there be some targets, and some rewards for meeting them?
- Encourage pupils to review their approach to revision, and change it if necessary. Above all, help them to build confidence.
- At an appropriate point, study previous exam papers. Again, encourage pupils to think strategically. How many questions are there usually? What are these questions normally like? What criteria are being applied? What would constitute 'good' answers? Then try some 'mock exams'.

### Exam technique

Wragg suggests offering the following guidelines to pupils who are about to take exams:

- Share out the time properly
- Read the instructions carefully
- Read the whole paper and decide a strategy
- Read the question carefully, and analyse what has to be done
- Answer the question
- Do whatever you can in each part of the exam
- Watch spelling, grammar and punctuation
- Leave time to check.

Reflective teachers will use all the available good practice to inform their teaching and it is clear that some are able to instil in their pupils good exam technique.

> ### *Practical activity 15.15*
>
> *Aim:* To develop a strategic plan to prepare a class for a subject examination.
>
> *Method:* First, it may be helpful to address the following questions:
>
> How much time is there to prepare?
> How much of the subject do the pupils know and understand?
> What have they still to be taught?
> How much time will be needed for revision?
> How confident are the pupils in exam technique?
>
> It should then be possible to draw up a schedule for preparation, and it will be important to share this with the pupils so that they can take some ownership of the process, working *with* you.
>
> *Follow-up:* We suggest that you work though the programme, carefully evaluating it as it develops, and being flexible as necessary. Above all, seek to maximize pupil confidence (without creating false expectations).

## 4.11 Evaluating methods of gathering assessment evidence

Within this book, as Figure 15.4 summarized, we have reviewed a very large array of different ways of gathering evidence of pupil learning for assessment purposes. Nor is this coverage exclusive. Indeed, we know that creative teachers will develop other methods which meet their needs and circumstances.

However, all methods of gathering data, whatever their origin, can be evaluated against criteria such as worthwhileness, validity, reliability and practicality (see Chapter 3). Those that seem effective should pass into the repertoire of teachers so that they can be drawn on when needed. Practical Activity 15.16 suggests taking stock through an overall evaluative review.

## 5 | RECORDS AND REPORTING

## 5.1 Keeping records

Records are important for many reasons, including the following.

### To inform future teaching

As teachers of our subject, we need accurate and relevant information about the pupils in our classes on which we can base our curriculum planning and our ongoing teaching judgements. Such records should make it easier to achieve an appropriate match between pupils, curriculum and tasks.

## Practical activity 15.16

*Aim:* To evaluate different techniques for gathering assessment evidence.

*Method:* Draw up a three-column table, with some chosen techniques for gathering assessment evidence listed on the left, and two adjacent columns for the advantages and disadvantages of each.

Fill in the table bearing in mind:

Why gather evidence in this way?
For whom is this assessment being done?
What can be most appropriately monitored in this way?
How often might this technique be used?
In what situations can this technique be used?
How can the results be interpreted?
Are there any unforeseen effects of such assessment?
Are the techniques valid and free from cultural bias?

*Follow-up:* Having made your own decisions about the 'pros' and 'cons' of different techniques for gathering assessment evidence, you should now be in a position to choose which techniques you will use for various purposes, and in which contexts. This should help you to devise a flexible and powerful set of techniques to assess processes and products within your classroom.

### To support personal reflection

A review of records of pupil achievements, particularly in conjunction with a portfolio of work, can provide a partial mirror on our own teaching which, for the self-aware teacher, can provide a constructive spur to further pedagogic or curricular development.

### To underpin continuity and progression

Records exchanged between teachers provide a crucial means of ensuring that there is continuity and progression in the pupils' learning experiences from year to year or across subject teams. Continuity in the Programmes of Study of the National Curriculum between Key Stages 3 and 4, and the development of whole-school planning, is increasingly being reflected in school-wide assessment policies. Many departments now keep portfolios of pupils' work for the purpose of agreeing 'levels' for teacher assessment, and engage in progressive target setting and action planning with each pupil.

### To contribute to assessment and accountability processes

Records and evidence of pupil attainments are increasingly needed for assessment purposes – particularly when teacher judgement is drawn on in conjunction with more standardized summative assessments. Such records are directly helpful when reporting to parents. Where 'league tables' are constructed such data may also be used to compile indicators of teacher, subject department, school or local education authority performance.

Keeping accurate and consistent records is thus of major significance for schools and is likely to be structured by whole-school policies. Individual classroom teachers and pupil teachers can certainly keep whatever personal records they wish, but are likely to be required to contribute to an official faculty, subject department or whole-school system. Obviously it is vital that information is collected in manageable ways and that it is possible to organize, analyse and use it effectively. Inappropriately elaborate and time-consuming systems are likely to be discarded. For Key Stages 3 and 4 in England and Wales, the basic legal requirement is that individualized records of attainment in each National Curriculum subject must be kept for each pupil. Of course, this is time consuming but there may be significant elements of record systems – perhaps to do with curriculum activities – that pupils could maintain for themselves.

Among the most valuable form of record is a portfolio of each pupil's work and assessment information, which provides evidence for understanding the development and achievements of the young person. There is a slowly developing trend towards the use of such portfolios, gradually built up over Key Stages 3 and 4 (though, unfortunately, not often linked to pre-existant primary school portfolios). Such portfolios can incorporate material from activities such as classwork, homework, class tests, cognitive tests and end-of-year examinations, and they provide an excellent resource for reviewing progress.

In most countries there are moves towards increasing access to records. For instance, in England and Wales teachers can keep personal records of their own, but any official record which may be transferred to other teachers or other professionals must also be made available to parents on request. The issue reflects more general ethical concerns about the central accumulation and recording of information about individuals, whether it is medical information, financial, criminal or anything else. Indeed, most of us would probably want to know what was being kept on us and many people take the view that this should be a right. Continuous awareness of the possible audiences for teacher-created records is thus necessary.

It is useful to think of the range of alternative forms in which records could be kept. For example, personal teacher records may simply be jotted in an exercise book. More formal records for faculty, department or whole-school systems are likely to be recorded with a standardized *pro forma* employed by all staff. LEAs, publishers, exam boards and accreditation agencies sometimes provide schools with standardized sheets to use. However, these are not always successful as schools often prefer to devise their own formats to reflect their particular circumstances. A more elaborate method is to put pupil information onto a computer database, where it can be easily updated and quickly accessible. In addition to providing normal access to parents, such databases must be registered appropriately – in England, under the terms of the Data Protection Act 1985.

> ## Practical activity 15.17
>
> *Aim:* To identify information about the pupils which it is important for you, as their present teacher in your subject, to know and record.
>
> *Method:* Thinking of one of your classes, take notes, under the following headings, of:
>
> 1. What information do you think is important for you to know about pupils in your class?
> 2. Why is it important?
> 3. How would you use it?
> 4. How would you record it?
> 5. How would you check on the objectivity and fairness of your records?
> 6. Who has a right of access to your records?
>
> *Follow-up:* Asking such basic questions could provide a check on the keeping of records. Procedures should be reviewed unless they are demonstrably useful to teaching, manageable, consistent with school policies, contribute to accountability requirements and are ethically sound.

## 5.2 Reporting to parents

Written reports to parents are important documents which contain a range of types of information and have complex purposes.

For parents, they are the principal means of obtaining 'official' information about the progress of their children and they also implicitly provide information about the school, its teachers and their values and emphases. If appropriately written, reports can encourage parents to work with teachers and will go a long way towards making an effective relationship to support pupils' learning.

For the young people being reported on, written reports can be somewhat threatening, since they provide an explicit occasion when connections between the 'world of home' and the 'world of school' are made. For those who prefer to manage their identities in quite different ways in such settings, this can be somewhat unnerving. Pupil feelings thus have to be taken into account in the ways in which reporting is managed. If handled correctly, both 'good' and 'bad' reports can stimulate pupils' commitment to work harder and it is important for schools to find ways to capitalize on this.

Within the school, written reports provide a record of pupils' performance across the curriculum and an opportunity, particularly for class tutors, year group leaders or headteachers, to take stock of a pupil's achievements as a whole. They provide an explicit opportunity, in other words, for the pastoral system to consider the pupil's overall academic profile and trajectory.

Annual written reports to parents are also a legal requirement and the minimum information they must contain is prescribed for England and Wales by the DFEE (see Circular 3/96).

- *For all pupils,* reports must include:
  – 'brief particulars' of progress in all subjects and activities studied as part of the curriculum, the results of any public examinations and any vocational qualifications (or credits towards them)
  – details of general progress (academic, behaviour, special achievements)
  – details of the arrangements for parents to discuss the report with the school.
- *Where pupils are of compulsory school age,* reports must also include: 'brief particulars' of pupil attainment for each National Curriculum foundation subject studied (including religious education) and a summary of the pupil's attendance record.
- *For pupils at the end of Key Stage 3,* reports must also include: the pupil's test results in English, mathematics and science, in the form of an overall level for each; the pupil's teacher assessed levels in these subjects; a brief commentary on what these levels show about the pupil's progress; comparative information about levels achieved by pupils at the school, compared with national data.
- *For pupils at the end of Key Stage 4,* the report must include information about the subjects in which the pupil has been assessed at GCSE or for other certificates, with grades if available. It is suggested that the format of the National Record of Achievement could be used for this report, and this is the practice in many secondary schools.
- *For pupils aged 16 or over,* information must be given about any A-level, AS level or GNVQ entries, and both academic and vocational qualifications achieved or credits which have been given towards them. Record of Achievement formats are again often used for this.
- For pupils aged 18 or over, the annual report should be sent directly to each pupil, though a copy can also be sent to parents.

These specifications, by including items such as attendance records and comparative data, have increased the amount of information provided to parents. However, they have not necessarily made it more understandable or accessible, as a report from OFSTED (1995c) described. OFSTED commented that many reports give too much detail, often in National Curriculum 'jargon' which is difficult for parents to understand.

In relation to a 'partnership' model of parent-teacher relationships, OFSTED (1995c) suggested that teacher comments in reports are unduly positive. Indeed, they judged that more than half of reports they saw failed to diagnose pupils' weaknesses in understanding and skills and failed to provide guidance for improvement. This last point is important for parents and pupils alike. For parents, a teacher's comments can be very helpful in suggesting how they could contribute to their child's education. For the pupil also, the stimulus to action which a report can provide will be more effective if it contains positive suggestions for steps to be taken.

Reciprocal reporting, in which parents make comments on aspects of their children's progress when they know more than the school does, can be a way of enriching the school's picture of the pupil as well as giving the parent a real stake in the content of the report. This complements the involvement which a pupil can have if Records of Achievement, to which pupils have contributed, form the basis for the report. Of course, such strategies need to be treated with appropriate sensitivity and within a clear procedural framework to recognize the issues of privacy and confidentiality which are involved in gaining this more holistic picture of a young person.

In the requirement for comparative information to be provided, national reporting requirements were also intended to feed the 'consumer' model of education. This is most starkly represented by 'league tables' of schools, which politicians and the media have expected to produce a flurry of parental and community debate following the annual publication of results, closely followed by enrolment decisions (see Section 3.7). Because of the financial significance of such decisions, the 'market' for education would determine which schools flourished and grew, and which declined. In fact, research shows how constrained and patterned choices actually are, so that at best, education is a 'quasi-market' only (Glatter *et al.* 1997, Gewirtz, Ball and Bowe 1995). For most parents, there is very little choice, and for many communities, allowing their school to wither is not an acceptable option (see Chapter 16, Introduction).

It is by no means certain how this tension between partnership and consumerist models of parent-school relationships will develop. Whilst the consumer model is projected centrally, teachers, parents and employers seem to be increasingly aware of the need to focus constructively on *supporting* the learning process. Perhaps a commitment to the partnership model remains? If this is so, one of the most explicit ways of manifesting it will be through the processes which a school adopts in reporting pupil achievements to parents.

## Practical activity 15.18

*Aim:* To develop a constructive procedure for reporting to parents and receiving information from them.

*Method:* This activity must be tailored to circumstances. Discuss with appropriate subject colleagues the aims and scope of a reporting exercise which you could pilot. If you are a pupil-teacher, you might want to limit this to reflect a block of teaching which you have completed, build it into an end-of-term open day or focus it on just one class, or even on a few specific pupils.

Then consider the following questions in relation to your subject:

How could you provide appropriate information to parents?
How could you elicit information and support from parents?
How could you involve the pupils in the reporting process?

*Follow-up:* Evaluate your reporting procedure. What did you learn, and can now act upon? What do you think the parents learned, and can now act upon? How did the pupils benefit? Did you find consumerist or partnership expectations from parents – or both? What reporting procedure will you try when your next opportunity arises?

## 5.3 Records of achievement

The introduction of Records of Achievement in many schools during the 1980s produced considerable development in the involvement of pupils in the assessment of their own learning (DES 1984, Broadfoot 1986, Hitchcock 1986, Broadfoot, James, McMeeking, Nuttall and Stierer 1988). Records of Achievement provided a structure within which pupils were encouraged to take part in a (usually) written dialogue with their teachers about their learning. This often took the form of a sheet to be completed at fixed intervals, sometimes accompanied by a discussion of the pupils' comments with their teachers. Teachers added their comments to those of the pupils and the sheets often formed part of a report to parents on their child's progress. This was a powerful development which took place in most LEAs and secondary schools, often with very creative systems being developed. According the DES (1984), such approaches were intended to:

- recognize, acknowledge and give credit for what pupils have achieved
- contribute to pupil's personal development and progress by improving their motivation, providing encouragement and increase awareness of strengths, weaknesses and opportunities
- help schools identify the all-round potential of their pupils and to consider how well their curriculum, teaching and organization enable pupils to develop
- provide a record and summary document for reporting to others.

However, the use of Records of Achievement began to decline in the early 1990s in the face of the multiple policy-led and national innovations of that period, despite continuing professional commitment. In September 1997, realizing that something of considerable value was declining in use, the DFEE relaunched the scheme as a National Record of Achievement which would cover not only Key Stages 3 and 4, but also Post-16 education and training. This development followed Sir Ron Dearing's recommendations for Post-16 education and has much integrative potential as a way of representing a holistic profile of young people, whether they draw on the academic, applied or vocational pathways.

Records of Achievement are very important documents, providing evidence of the achievements, qualities and experiences of each young person. Many will draw on their Record of Achievement documents as they negotiate one of the most important transitions in life – from school to employment.

## CONCLUSION

Assessment has been, and remains, a controversial issue in education. It is a very important element of public education policy and is often seen as a means of raising standards of pupil attainment.

Professional practice has tended to be shaped by the assessment purposes which have been given priority, and in recent years, summative performance measures for pupils and schools have been emphasized extremely strongly. However, the direct contribution of formative assessment, at the heart of the teaching-learning process, should never be forgotten. Similarly, Records of Achievement, providing an overall representation of young people's education and training, have a uniquely holistic character. Each of these forms of assessment contribute to the achievement of educational quality.

## *Notes for further reading*

Assessment in schools is a crucial issue of social policy and various responses have historically been adopted in different parts of the world. In most cases though, assessment processes are becoming more prominent. A contradiction between assessment as a means of enabling learning and assessment as a means of certificating and measuring learning continues. Such issues are explored in three wide-ranging books:

Gipps, C. (1994)
*Beyond Testing: Towards a Theory of Educational Assessment,*
London: Falmer Press.

Hargreaves, A. (1989)
*Curriculum and Assessment Reform,*
Buckingham: Open University Press.

Broadfoot, P. (1996)
*Education, Assessment and Society: A Sociological Analysis,*
Buckingham, Open University Press.

Butterfield, S. (1995)
*Educational Objectives and National Assessment,*
Buckingham: Open University Press.

For an excellent overview of issues to do with **equity and assessment,** drawing on research from across the world, see:

Gipps, C. and Murphy, P. (1994)
*A Fair Test? Assessment, Achievement and Equity,*
Buckingham: Open University Press.

For **reviews of school practices** in England prior to the Education Reform Act, and of policy developments after it (including the 1993 Dearing Report), see:

Gipps, C., Steadman, S. Blackstone, T. and Stierer, B. (1983)
*Testing Children: Standardized Testing in LEAs and Schools,*
London: Heinemann.

Daugherty, R. (1995)
*National Curriculum Assessment: A Review of Policy, 1987–1994,*
London: Falmer Press.

During the 1990s assessment policy for England and Wales was reviewed and changed for each age phase and curriculum pathway:

Dearing, R. (1993)
*The National Curriculum and its Assessment: Final Report,*
London, SCAA.                                                    **Primary Reading 7.12**

Dearing, R. (1996)
*Review of Qualifications for 16–19 Year Olds: Full Report,*
London, SCAA.

Capey, J. (1995)
*GNVQ Assessment Review,*
London: NCVQ.

OFSTED (1996)
*Assessment of National Vocational Qualifications in Schools, 1995/96,*
London: HMSO.

For concise **introductions to the technical aspects of assessment** and much more besides, see:

Desforges, C. (1989)
*Testing and Assessment,*
London: Cassell.

Gipps, C. (1990)
*Assessment: A Teachers' Guide to the Issues,*
London: Hodder and Stoughton.

On monitoring school performance, see:

Fitz-Gibbon, C. T. (1995)
*Monitoring Education: Indicators, Quality and Effectiveness,*
London: Cassell.

Gray, J. and Wilcox, B. (1995)
*'Good School, Bad School': Evaluating Performance and Encouraging Improvement,*
Buckingham: Open University Press.

For an interesting general book on **techniques of assessing pupil learning and a compendium of techniques** see :

White, R. T. and Gunstone, R. F. (1992)
*Probing Understanding,*
London: Falmer.

Brown, S., Race, P. and Smith, B. (1996)
*500 Tips on Assessment,*
London: Kogan Page.

An important US book provides case-studies of schools in which innovative forms of 'authentic assessment' have been implemented – a challenge to many aspects of summative, national assessment systems.

Darling-Hammond, L., Ancess, J. and Falk, B. (1995)
*Authentic Assessment in Acton: Studies of Schools and Students at Work,*
New York: Teachers College Press.

For consideration of authentic assessment in the UK, see:

Torrance, H. (ed.) (1994)
*Evaluating Authentic Assessment,*
Buckingham: Open University Press.

For a useful resource on the assessment of speaking and listening skills, seek out the video and guidance material produced by SCAA and NCVQ. This is suitable for GCSE or Part 1 GNVQ.

*DFEE News* 311/96 24 September 1996.

To develop the marking of pupils' work, see:

Dunsbee, T. and Ford, T. (1980)
*Mark My Words*,
London: NATE and Ward Lock.

National Writing Project (1989)
*Responding to Writing*,
Walton-on-Thames: Nelson.

On working on action plans with pupils, try:

Squirrell, G. (1994)
*Individual Action Planning: A Practical Guide*,
London: David Fulton.

For an excellent overview of issues and practices in assessing practical competences, see:

Wolf, A. (1995)
*Competence-based Assessment*,
Buckingham: Open University Press.

A specific book on record-keeping, but with many generalizable ideas is:

Lawson, H. (1992)
*Practical Record Keeping for Special Schools*,
London: David Fulton

National recording and reporting requirements vary in different countries. In England, see:

Department of Education and Science (1990)
London, DES.

On the implementation of Records of Achievement in a school, see:

Pole, C. (1993)
*Assessment and Recording Achievement*,
Buckingham: Open University Press.

On **profiling** and constructive **attempts to involve parents** through reporting assessments of their pupil's learning, see:

Wolfendale, S. (1992)
*Involving Parents in Schools*,
London: Cassell.

Jowett, S. and Baginsky, M. (1991)
*Building Bridges: Parental Involvement in Schools*,
London: Routledge.

# PART 3

# BEYOND CLASSROOM REFLECTION

# CHAPTER 16

# School improvement

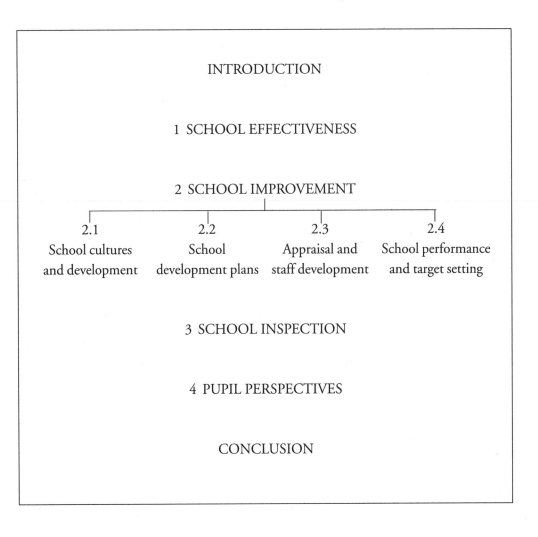

INTRODUCTION

1 SCHOOL EFFECTIVENESS

2 SCHOOL IMPROVEMENT

| 2.1 | 2.2 | 2.3 | 2.4 |
|---|---|---|---|
| School cultures and development | School development plans | Appraisal and staff development | School performance and target setting |

3 SCHOOL INSPECTION

4 PUPIL PERSPECTIVES

CONCLUSION

## INTRODUCTION

In this chapter we focus on the development of the whole school. However, this must itself be set in the wider policy context.

There are many perspectives on how to develop high quality in schools and we will identify three here. First, there are those who believe in various forms of school self-evaluation, quality management and review as internally driven processes. An alternative view is that of external inspection, in which the work of a school is assessed against standardized national criteria. Finally, there are those who emphasize the power of competition in a quasi-market for education.

Despite their distinct origins, in recent years these approaches have begun to be combined. Thus, for example, a 1996 White Paper, *Competitiveness: Creating the Enterprise Centre of Europe* (DFEE 1996a), identified the three elements as forms of 'quality assurance':

- self-assessment
- external inspection
- published information on performance.

Each of these approaches assumes that schools are essentially responsible, themselves, for the quality of their provision. Before the late 1980s, schools had been only semi-autonomous and were managed within the multilayered structure of each local education authority. However, during the 1990s there was an enormous increase in the significance of schools as free-standing and self-managed organizations. Legislation gradually moved state schools from the shelter of local education authority support structures and their associated lines of accountability. By the late 1990s almost all schools had control of their budgets, policies and practices and, whilst now constrained by national structures, were formally accountable to their own governors and parents.

In respect of internally driven, professional perspectives, the importance of organization cultures has been asserted consistently. For example, Rosenholz (1989) identified 'high consensus' schools in which principals and teachers appear to 'agree on the definitions of teaching', and in which 'their instructional goals occupy a place of high significance' (pp. 206–8). She expressed this in ways which echo the concept of a 'learning organization':

> A spirit of continuous improvement seemed to hover school-wide, because no one ever stopped learning to teach. It was assumed that improvement in teaching is a collective rather than an individual enterprise, and that analysis, evaluation and experimentation in concert with colleagues was a collective rather than individual enterprise. (Rosenholz 1989, p. 73)

However, Rosenholz's model may seem somewhat idealistic and she herself drew attention to schools at the other end of the continuum. In such 'low consensus' schools there was no support for change or improvement; teachers were able to learn little from their colleagues and no one seemed to feel responsible for helping struggling teachers to improve; teachers experienced frustration, failure, tedium; they complained about the pupils and were self-defensive. Rosenholz described such schools as 'stuck', in contrast to the schools which are 'moving' forward. Of course, in some cases the schools in which reflective teachers find themselves may well also be static, 'routinized' and locked into 'taken-for-granted' conventions. As will be apparent throughout this chapter, the process of building a collaborative culture is neither easy nor quick.

Perhaps it was the difficulty of achieving consistent quality through self-assessment which led to the introduction of a very significant infrastructure for external inspection of schools through the 1990s. This is the main subject of Section 3 of this chapter, but it is worth emphasizing the ways in which inspection reports are made available to parents and others. This, together with the public reporting of examination results and national assessment scores in 'league tables', is a way of providing 'information on performance' for parents and others.

As we have seen in Chapter 2, Section 1.4, and in Chapter 5, Section 1, the emphasis on self-management, school development, inspection and public reporting is closely associated with the expectation that competition between schools for pupil enrolments will lead overall standards of pupil attainment to rise.

Of course, there was a sustained attempt during the 1990s to increase the amount of 'choice and diversity' within the education system by creating new types of school outside LEA structures. Thus legislation of 1992 encouraged schools to 'opt out' of LEA control altogether and to become 'grant maintained' (GMS) with annual funding direct from the central Funding Agency for Schools. By 1996, one in five of state educated secondary pupils were in such schools (DFEE 1996a). A small number of specialist schools were also created. By 1996 there were fifteen City Technology Colleges and seventy-six schools designated as Technology or Language Colleges. These initiatives were often resisted by teachers and LEAs, and the majority of the 5,000 secondary schools remained within LEA control. The Conservative government also supported an 'assisted places scheme', which offered parents means-tested payment of fees at almost 300 independent schools, and proposed to encourage schools to put themselves forward to become grammar schools. In contrast, the Labour Party emphasized 'excellence for everyone' (1995) and argued for increasing the quality of education provided *within* all schools (see Blair 1996, in **Practical Activity 8.5**). However, the Labour Party withdrew a previous commitment to abolish grant-maintained status.

There is no doubt therefore, that pressure to compete between schools will remain very important and this will certainly impact on educational standards in schools. However, it is by no means proven that all these effects will be positive. Indeed, as Dale (1996, **Primary Reading 15.5**) and Gewirtz *et al.* (1995) have argued, the danger is that schools which are perceived to be 'good' draw pupils away from other local schools, thus causing financial difficulties and threatening a spiral of decline. This is already a problem in some major centres of population where middle-class pupils travel out of city schools into rural or suburban schools.

Of course, these are essentially political issues, and this chapter is primarily focused on internal factors in school development. However, to consider these without an awareness of the wider context would be extremely misleading.

We now move to consider work on school effectiveness.

## 1 | SCHOOL EFFECTIVENESS

School effectiveness is concerned with finding answers to questions about how and in what way pupils are affected by their experiences at school. Does it matter which school a child attends? What are the features of a school that make a difference? Defining the measures by which effectiveness are judged is obviously significant. These are frequently related to pupil attainment, more latterly to the 'value added' between attainment when the pupil enters the school, and subsequent results.

Governments throughout the world have an active interest in school effectiveness. Indeed, there is a widespread desire to raise the achievement of pupils to strengthen international competitiveness, but this also usually constrained by the costs of education. So an interest in effectiveness is also an interest in efficiency, or value for money.

Work on school effectiveness began thirty years ago in the United States. In the UK, detailed research on twelve London secondary schools, *Fifteen Thousand Hours* (Rutter *et al.* 1979), indicated very clearly that schools do make a difference to pupils' behaviour and attainments and that variations in outcome were 'systematically and strongly associated with the characteristics of schools as social institutions' (p. 205). In addition, the research identified which school variables were associated with good behaviour and attainment, and which were not. These more specific findings have been confirmed by subsequent studies so there is now a generally agreed set of factors associated with school effectiveness. For instance, the following eleven 'key factors' derive from a recent review of school effectiveness research (Sammons, Hillman and Mortimore, 1995).

1. Effective headteachers are firm and purposeful, appoint effective teachers, create consensus and unity of purpose; they share and delegate responsibilities and involve all teachers in decision-making; they are 'leading professionals' with an understanding of classrooms and how teaching and learning can be improved.
2. In the school there must be 'shared vision and goals': necessary for lifting aspirations and creating consistency of practice through whole-school policies and contracts.
3. The 'learning environment' is attractive, orderly and encourages self-control among pupils; this is a prerequisite for a positive classroom ethos.
4. There is a clear priority focus on teaching and learning as the school's primary purpose. Four factors: time spent on learning, amount of homework, effective learning time, learning time for different subjects are measures indicating the practical implementation of this focus.
5. Teaching is purposeful, well-organized and clear about objectives, well-prepared, appropriately paced and structured, questioning focuses pupil attention.
6. There is a general culture which has high expectations of everyone: teachers, pupils and parents.
7. Better pupil outcomes follow from positive reinforcement, clear feedback, rewards and clear rules for behaviour. These are more successful than punishment or criticism.
8. Monitoring progress keeps track of whether the school is meeting its targets and goals, maintains awareness of targets and goals among staff, pupils and parents,

informs planning and teaching, sends clear messages to pupils that teachers are interested in their progress.

9. Giving pupils rights and responsibilities and enabling them to play an active role in the life of the school is important for raising self-esteem and encouraging taking responsibility for their own learning.

10. Partnerships that encourage and foster parent support for learning have positive effects on achievement; successful schools made demands on parents as well as encouraging involvement.

11. Effective schools are 'learning organizations' where teachers and senior managers, as well as pupils, continue to be learners, improve their practice and keep up with change.

Of these factors, those that are concerned with the quality of teaching (4 and 5) and expectations (6) are most significant for fostering pupils' learning and progress. However, the other factors are important in that they provide the overall framework within which teachers and classrooms operate, enable the development of consistent goals and ensure that pupils' educational experiences are linked as they progress through the school.

The National Commission on Education (1995) identified a similar set of positive features in their detailed study of eleven schools which were effective despite being located in disadvantaged areas. They reported a 'can do better culture' and 'shared vision', together with leadership which was confident, positive, proactive and able to set strategic priorities. The most effective leadership enabled participation in the process of change by everyone in the school, including parents; encouraged shared leadership and teamwork: and developed unity of purpose and consistency of practice. An orderly and industrious climate for learning, clear policies on behaviour and discipline, high expectations of pupils expressed through curriculum planning, assessment and reporting, high levels of care for the physical environment (even where it was inadequate) were all identified as important.

The importance of internal school management and culture is confirmed by studies of the variations of school exam performance. For instance, Sammons *et al.* (1995) studied the GCSE results of 11,000 pupils from schools in Lancashire and inner London. Adjusting for pupils' home background and for attainment levels on entry to secondary school, they found that the schools can make a difference of as much as 10 per cent of GCSE marks – the equivalent of several grades. Interestingly, the study showed that some schools are more effective with low attainers than high attainers (and vice versa); some with girls than boys, and others with different ethnic groups. Similarly, school effectiveness often varies from year to year, and consistent improvement is hard to achieve. Where there was clear leadership and a shared whole-school emphasis on pupil learning, there was less variation in achievement between departments. In other schools it was harder for departments to be effective due to lack of overall leadership, shared goals and vision, poor expectations and inconsistent policies.

## Practical activity 16.1

*Aim:* To evaluate the significance of 'key factors' of school effectiveness.

*Method:* Review the list of key factors produced by Sammons, Hillman and Mortimore (1995) in the light of your knowledge of a school which you know well. Go through, point by point, and consider the position which the school takes in relation to the identified factors. How is the school's effectiveness affected?

*Follow-up:* Reconsider the factors in relation to other schools which you know. Comparing with caution, and recognizing contextual variations, what do you think are the most significant factors producing differences in the effectiveness of the schools?

Ideas about school effectiveness are playing an increasingly important role in the formulation of education policy. The DFEE has now established a school effectiveness division, schools are being encouraged to set 'targets' and league tables documenting the 'value added' by schools are being developed (see Section 2.4 below). However, identifying factors that indicate levels of school effectiveness does not, in itself, bring about school improvement. Research into processes of school improvement has thus developed alongside and in conjunction with the measurement of effectiveness. It is to this work that we now turn.

## 2 | SCHOOL IMPROVEMENT

How can a school improve itself? Finding answers to this question involves seeking out the connections between how pupils learn, how teachers teach, school organization, management and decision-making, and many other factors.

Characteristically, a move to improvement includes:

- identifying the school's strengths and weaknesses, including its leadership and culture
- seeking the views of pupils, parents, employers and other interested groups,
- seeking necessary help and support from outside sources
- agreeing targets which are ambitious but accepted as achievable
- planning and implementing changes in management
- planning and implementing changes in classroom teaching
- systematically monitoring and evaluating the process and the outcomes of the changes.

The process is certainly complex and calls for very high quality leadership. Arguably, the *sine qua non* of this is an understanding of how to manage change within the particular culture of the school.

## 2.1 School cultures and development

Research into the implementation of development in schools has provided many useful insights and understandings. Fullan (1992) identifies four elements that have been found to be important in the process of achieving change:

- active initiation and participation
- pressure and support
- changes in behaviour and belief
- the overriding problem of ownership.

Getting started requires a clear impetus, though this may at first involve only a small group. Change may seem more manageable by starting small and putting the emphasis on action and learning by doing. Maintaining a balance between pressure and support is important, for, as Fullan puts it: 'pressure without support leads to resistance and alienation; support without pressure leads to drift or waste of resources' (p. 25). The relationship between behavioural and belief change, Fullan suggests, is reciprocal and ongoing. Changing behaviour and trying something new most frequently precedes the development of ideas and understanding. It is also necessary to remember that with much innovation and change things often get worse before they get better. Ownership of the new is not easily or rapidly achieved. Indeed, even when there is 'acceptance', there may not be complete understanding or adequate levels of skill. The development of clarity, skill and commitment is progressive: growing in the middle of a project and stronger still at the end. In particular, ownership has to be achieved by each of the individuals who together make up the social system that is the school.

An understanding of the subtlety and complexity of this process, the ways in which the factors can interact, combine, undercut each other, is necessary in order to select and devise appropriate strategies for achieving positive reforms that deliver improvement and offering leadership. The distinction between leadership and management identified by Louis and Miles (1990) may be helpful here. Leadership involves articulating a vision, inspiring and motivating those involved, planning the overall strategy. Management is concerned with administration and interacting with people: planning, resourcing, negotiating, co-ordinating, problem-solving. However, the successful management of change requires the skills and abilities associated with both leadership and management. They have to be present in one person or appropriately dispersed among the members of a team. A characteristic of effective leadership is the skill of delegating roles or assigning tasks so that the necessary skills are in the right place. Head teachers who are particularly effective are those who develop teachers' commitment to implementation and create a strong culture for improvement and change (Leithwood and Jantzi 1989, 1990).

As we suggested in Chapter 5, Section 1.6 a great deal is written about 'school culture' without problematizing the concept itself. From the sociological point of view, all sorts of normative assumptions are embedded within the idea. At its most developed, for instance by Nias *et al.* (1989), the proposition is that individuals working in a school may identify personally and collectively with official goals and values – a 'culture of collaboration'. Fulfilment is thus achieved through institutional policies, practices and achievements. But to what degree can aims, understandings, conventions, habits and routines really be held collectively by a school staff and fulfilled corporately though the organization? Arguably, the concept implies more consensus and commitment than is realistic in most situations, particularly in complex organizations such as secondary schools.

Nevertheless, the idea of schools having a 'learning culture' is important as an ideal. To the extent that it is achieved, teachers will have the confidence to respond constructively to change; disagreement and debate will be possible because relationships are secure; individuals and groups will feel able to take risks; values and their relationship to school practices can be continuously considered; and both individuals and groups will feel collectively affirmed.

However attractive the ideal, a culture of collaboration may turn out to be more apparent than real. Hargreaves (1992, **Primary Reading 14.1**) has suggested the idea of 'contrived collegiality' in which the management attempts to build collegiality but the hearts and minds of staff do not follow. A common factor which can impede the development of a collaborative culture is the existence of strong pre-existing group identities – sometimes referred to as 'balkanization'. As we noted in Chapter 5, Section 2.2, balkanized cultures are particularly evident in secondary schools where there is a strong subject-department structure and identity, and may produce concerns and struggles about territory in terms of time, space, resources, practices and procedures. Another common problem is the situation which may be characterized as 'comfortable collaboration' where teachers work together in well-established, warm and casual ways. There are many shared understandings, but not much questioning, enquiry or investigation of the *status quo*. Processes associated with systematic reflective practice are not in evidence (Levine and Eubanks 1989).

Phenomena such as Balkanized cultures or 'comfortable collaboration' may be better understood in terms of micro-political analysis (Ball 1987, Hoyle 1986). In this form of analysis, school policies and practices are seen as temporary and negotiated products which reflect the existing balance of power and influence within a school. In a sense, they reflect an apparent consensus, which hides continuing conflicts concerning issues which are constantly being contested within ever-changing circumstances. The influence of any one individual at any given time, will depend on their degree of status, power, charisma and authority. The role of both internal alliances and of other external factors, such as parental views and governor, LEA or government policies must also be recognized.

The most important player is likely to be the headteacher, who has both formal authority and a great deal of power. As Ball concludes, in one way or another this position is likely to be used to 'dominate' so that apparent agreement is achieved:

> I have tried to indicate the conflictual basis of the school as an organization. Concomitantly, I have attempted to indicate that the control of school organizations, focused on the position and role of the headteacher, is significantly concerned with domination (the elimination or pre-emption of conflict). Thus domination is intended to achieve and maintain particular definitions of the school over and against alternative definitions. (Ball 1987, p. 278)

Ball offers an interestingly provocative analysis of forms of participation in school decision-making (see Figure 16.1).

|  | Forms of participation | Responses to opposition | Strategies of control |
| --- | --- | --- | --- |
| **Authoritarian** | Prevents public access to voice | Stifle | Insulation, concealment and secrecy |
| **Managerial** | Formal committees, meetings and working parties | Channel and delay | Structuring, planning, control of agendas, time and context |
| **Interpersonal** | Informal chats and personal consultation and lobbying | Fragment and compromise | Private performances of persuasion |
| **Adversarial** | Public meetings and open debate | Confront | Public performances of persuasion |

**Figure 16.1** *Forms of participation in school decision-making*

We are thus left with an image of school organizations as settings in which values, priorities and practices are contested by headteachers, management teams, departments, faculties and individuals. Sometimes such micro-political activity may be considerable, such as when a new headteacher arrives. There may also be periods of relative stability when 'comfortable collaboration' may exist for a while.

*Practical activity 16.2*

*Aim:* To consider micro-politics in schools.

*Method:* Thinking of a school in which you have worked, reflect on the various groups of staff and their perspectives and actions within the school. What relationships exist between these groups? Thinking of a significant incident or event, what variations were there in the responses of different individuals and groups? What strategies does the leadership team use in managing the different positions? To what extent do you feel that the culture of the school is affected by the influence which particular groups or individuals exert?

*Follow-up:* Consider the strategies of the headteacher in terms of Ball's forms of participation. To what extent is the head authoritarian, managerial, interpersonal or adversarial?

During the 1990s, the growing emphasis on external accountability, school effectiveness, school development, target setting and inspection has meant that schools can no longer be considered as relatively closed and semi-autonomous institutions. Whether a school is best characterized in terms of its collaborative culture or its micro-politics makes little difference to the accountability and performance requirements which have to be met. The consequence of this structuring of external requirements, pressures and constraints is that schools are now managed in much more purposive and explicit ways than many were in the past. The major means of doing this are through school development planning and target setting, and it is to these issues which we now turn.

## 2.1 School development plans

School development plans are produced annually and, as part of the policy of encouraging individual school autonomy, have been seen as enabling schools to become 'empowered' (Hargreaves and Hopkins 1991, **Primary Reading 14.3**). They are the prime means by which staff and governors can exercise coherent and forward-looking control over curriculum and school development. In most schools, development plans include consideration of:

1. aims and philosophy
2. the present situation
   - catchment and enrolment
   - organization
   - staffing
   - curriculum provision
   - resources
   - achievements
3. assessed needs for future development
   - organizational development
   - staff development
   - curriculum development
   - resource development
4. how the assessed needs are to be met.

The last point is a significant one, for it brings the planning process up against practicalities – for instance of budgets. School budgeting should be 'curriculum led' rather than be driven by financial considerations but this is not always possible. Nevertheless, in the words of HMI (1992) development planning provides: 'a more rational and coherent framework in which to identify priorities, plan for change and allocate resources. In the best practice, development plans paid attention to teaching and learning, specified manageable timescales, and outlined arrangements for monitoring and evaluation' (HM Senior Chief Inspector of Schools 1992, p. 20).

The whole-school development process is designed to lead to change and Miles (1986) identifies three overlapping stages in such innovation:

- *Initiation* – deciding to start, developing commitment, defining purposes and processes, appointing key people, make links with key issues for whole-school explicit, guarantee support for involvement.
- *Implementation* – the first cycle, a learning process; focus on co-ordination, adequate and sustained support in the form of INSET, supply cover; positive reinforcement. Skills and understanding are being acquired; groups of teachers may become self-governing as they move forward.
- *Institutionalization* – development planning becomes part of the normal pattern of how the school does things; management arrangements have evolved to support further development and maintenance – they also are part of the pattern. The impact of development planning is seen in classroom practice and the innovation is no longer new.

Where there are a number of priorities and initiatives, developments are likely to overlap and interconnect, and each will have its own timescale. A coherent planning and development process will permeate the normal work of the school and, as Miles suggests, will eventually become encompassed in routine activity. Figure 16.2 illustrates this multi-level integration as a 'development cone'.

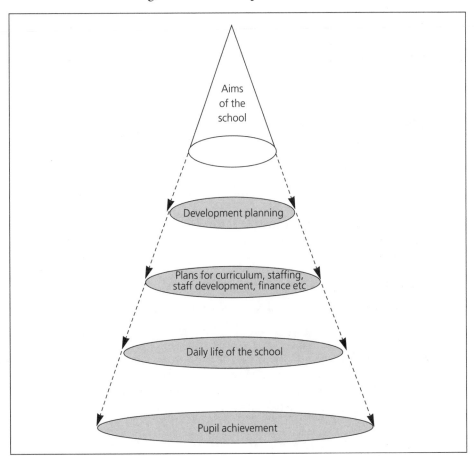

**Figure 16.2** *The development planning cone (Hargreaves and Hopkins 1991)*

However, there are a number of reasons why some schools do not succeed with development planning. As with 'contrived collegiality', development can become a 'bolt-on' activity which happens rather procedurally but has no fundamental impact on the way the school works. Equally, it is possible to underestimate the need for the process to be managed, especially where this itself requires significant changes in established management practice. Associated with this is a failure to create the conditions under which change and innovation can happen; to be unaware, for example, of the distinctive nature of the three stages identified by Miles and of the different management and support required by each phase. Finally, it is possible to produce a development plan as a management document but give little or no thought to the processes by which it will be implemented.

Anning (1983) suggested that new headteachers attempting curriculum innovation face a course rather like that of the Grand National. The first jump, the improvement of the environment, and the second, that of producing new policy statements and curriculum guidelines, are accomplished smoothly. Becher's Brook looms when it is realized that actual practice in the classroom may not be changing as fast and cannot be influenced by aesthetics and documents alone. This is a problem which faces everyone for it is never easy to bring practice into line with ideals, let alone in the difficult circumstances which schools have faced in recent years. Indeed, many headteachers have found that the apparent ordered rationality of school development planning is disrupted by the turbulence of external events (Wallace 1994, **Primary Reading 14.4**), so that the whole process becomes something of a diversion from managing the 'real world'.

In an insightful research study, MacGilchrist and her colleagues (1995) identified four types of school development plan: the 'rhetorical plan' (no sense of ownership by head or staff), the 'singular plan' (produced by the headteacher alone), the 'co-operative plan' (with partial involvement of teaching staff), and the 'corporate plan'. The latter was 'characterized by a united effort to improve . . . and a focus on teaching and learning' (p. 195). Of the four types, the rhetorical plan had a negative impact, while the corporate plan had 'a very significant positive impact on both the efficiency and the effectiveness of the school'.

Clearly, implementing a school development plan is far from easy, and is intimately connected with school culture, and management of the school's micro-politics.

### Practical activity 16.3

*Aim:* To consider a school development plan.

*Method:* Ask a headteacher if you may study the school development plan for their school. Consider it and the process of its implementation in the light of the points made in this section. If possible, discuss with the head, a member of the senior management team and/or your mentor the circumstances of the plan's production and the reasons for the priorities given. Talk with other staff in your subject and if possible other subjects. From your discussion, consider to what extent they are able to identify purposefully with the plan.

*Follow-up:* Could you classify the plan using MacGilchrist's typology?

## 2.3 Appraisal and staff development

In management terms, staff appraisal and development processes flow directly from school development planning.

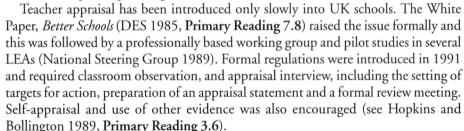

Teacher appraisal has been introduced only slowly into UK schools. The White Paper, *Better Schools* (DES 1985, **Primary Reading 7.8**) raised the issue formally and this was followed by a professionally based working group and pilot studies in several LEAs (National Steering Group 1989). Formal regulations were introduced in 1991 and required classroom observation, and appraisal interview, including the setting of targets for action, preparation of an appraisal statement and a formal review meeting. Self-appraisal and use of other evidence was also encouraged (see Hopkins and Bollington 1989, **Primary Reading 3.6**).

However, in a research survey Wragg *et al.* (1996) found considerable variation between schools in how appraisal was managed. Almost 70 per cent of teacher respondents felt that appraisal had benefited them personally and mentioned improved confidence, self-awareness, clarification of priorities and other forms of professional development. However, only half said that appraisal had actually affected their classroom practice. There was widespread concern about finding time to do the appraisal properly and also about finding time and resources to follow up the targets identified and agreed for development. Teachers were also concerned about the possible use of appraisal information in determining redundancies or promotions.

A collation of evidence by HMI concluded that appraisal processes were making very little impact, with only 20 per cent of schools visited by HMI in which appraisal had led to observable improvements in teaching. In the majority of schools, appraisal was seen as about self-development of teachers, rather than concerned with the relationship between the work of the individual and the policies and needs of the school as a whole. As HMI conclude: 'There is a need to set sharper targets, better linked to classroom practice and school management' (OFSTED 1996b, p. 11).

Although there are clear managerial advantages in making connections between appraisal and school improvement processes, the considerable suspicion amongst many teachers is a reality. Perhaps this is not surprising, for if a micro-political perspective is adopted, appraisal may be seen as an attempt to impose conformity, rather than as an invitation to join in with a collaborative goal. This brings us back to the recognition that any form of change, review or evaluation is interpersonally sensitive, in that personal interests are likely to be affected.

If such issues are clearly recognized then it is easier to understand the responses of an individual teacher who is involved in processes of change. Doyle and Ponder (1976) identified three typical responses.

- The 'rational adapter' who, by recognizing problems or issues and enacting logical procedures to tackle them, accepts innovation and help to bring it about.
- The 'pragmatic sceptic' who assesses the consequences of change in a calculative way by considering the gains and losses from change in time, energy and personal development before deciding how to act.
- The 'stone-age obstructionist' who, by rejecting the value position and judgements upon which a need for change is based and by refusing to become fully involved, attempts to retain the *status quo*.

Clearly these are caricatures which simplify the complexity of people's motivations and involvements but they do begin to describe the essence of three basic sorts of compliance (Etzioni 1966).

- *Moral:* in which commitment is based on intrinsic acceptance of purposes and value concerns.
- *Calculative:* in which compliance is based on extrinsic judgements of personal interests.
- *Alienative:* in which compliance is reluctant and is based on a powerlessness to resist.

The existence of such different types of perspectives and commitment clearly has serious implications for those who may wish to bring about changes in schools.

### Practical activity 16.4

*Aim:* To review our own attitudes on appraisal.

*Method:* Consider your feelings about being appraised (if you are a student teacher, try to imagine yourself on the staff of a school which you know well). Do you see it as a wonderful opportunity to tell a senior manager how you feel about your job, and to get some affirmation or help? Do you see it as an intrusion on your privacy and as an insult to your professionalism? Do you see it as an occasion to consider how you could make a greater contribution to the school?

Imagining your appraiser as your next line-manager, how frank would you feel able to be? Would you feel comfortable with his or her observation, interpretation and judgement on your teaching?

Reflecting on your feelings, where would you place yourself: rational adapter, pragmatic sceptic or stone-age obstructionist? Or where?

*Follow-up:* Think about the situation in reverse, now taking the appraiser role. How could you set your appraisees at ease? Consult Hopkins and Bollington (**Primary Reading 3.6**) for further discussion of the issues, particularly in appraisal interviews.

## 2.4   School performance and target setting

National assessment results have increasingly been used as indicators of school performance. This began in the Summer of 1992 when a number of newspapers published unofficial 'league tables' of secondary schools, based on GCSE results. Official data on secondary schools was issued from 1993, but such 'league tables' showed measured attainment levels only. They did not show the progress of pupils, or the circumstances of the families, schools and communities which influence attainment. However, if 'baseline' data on pupil attainment on entry and adequate data on social circumstances is available, it is possible, by statistical methods, to measure the 'value added' by schools (the progress of pupils from entry to exit) (Sammons and Nuttall 1992). Many schools and LEAs now subscribe to a variety of services (usually research-inspired) that provide baseline assessments, predict performance at 16 or 18, and analyse results. The analysis usually involves comparison with national figures and may well also incorporate other contextual factors such as gender, parental occupation, ethnicity, eligibility for free school meals. The information provided by such statistical analyses is confidential to the school and used to help identify and target subjects, groups of pupils or individual pupils for attention. At present, these value-added projects are not designed or used to construct alternative league tables.

The policies of the major political parties in the UK illustrate a gradual alignment in approaches to the use of raw data and value-added calculations. For most of the early 1990s, the Conservative government advocated the simple use of raw data. This practice was criticized for failing to take account of pupil and school circumstances, and for fuelling the 'market' in education in misleading ways as parents interpreted only raw results when choosing schools. In 1995 the Department for Education announced that value-added measures would now be developed to compare raw score gains of pupils from school entry. The Labour Party then accepted that performance tables should 'allow sensible comparisons to be made' but particularly advocated the development of value-added measures which could take account of social circumstances. They stated that:

> This process should not be used to develop a competitive market in education. The information should be used to lift and support schools, rather than to embarrass or denigrate them. The key way to raise standards is to set targets for pupils and schools and then set out the steps to achieve them. (Labour Party 1995, pp. 26–7)

Given the existence of performance data, the obvious next step is to plan improvements. In 1996, the concept of 'target setting' was endorsed by DFEE who published a *Survey of Good Practice*. For instance, Figure 16.3 shows changes from 1989–95 in the aggregated performance in all GCSE subjects of a hypothetical secondary school, compared with aggregated LEA and national scores. What, then, should the school's future targets be? 'D', to maintain present standards; 'C', some improvement; 'B', the LEA average; or even 'A', the national average?

At a more detailed level, such evidence can also be provided for particular subjects, departments or faculties, thus making it possible to set particular targets for individuals, teachers or teams of staff. Comparisons of, for example, Year 11 GCSE results across different subjects may be particularly provocative. How, for example, can extreme variation be explained if the basic cohort of pupils is the same? Of course, the issues are complicated, but the spur to reflection is considerable.

Analysis of performance and consequent target-setting involves schools in looking at many aspects of teaching and learning, management and organization. Figure 16.4 is a model developed by Spours and Hodgson (1996) and indicates the multiplicity of factors to be considered when issues associated with value added are followed through institutionally.

Of course, analysis of results is not the only source of evidence that will inform review and analysis in order to identify new targets for school improvement. A more penetrating source is that of school inspection.

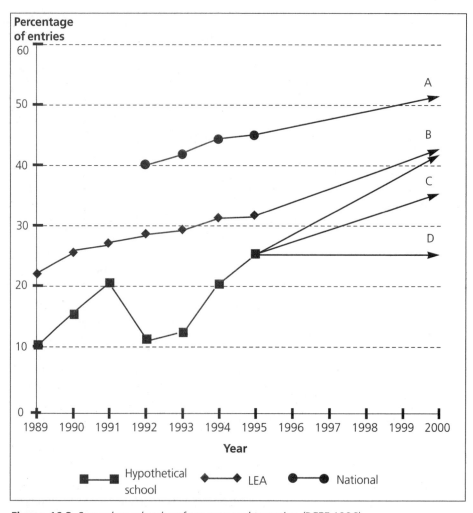

**Figure 16.3** *Secondary school performance and targeting (DFEE 1996)*

## Practical activity 16.5

*Aim:* To consider school performance and target setting for your subject.

*Method:* Gather some performance data for your subject from a school which you know well. This could be in the form of simple tables of exam results for different years. However, if possible, study an added-value analysis based on Year 7 entry and GCSE scores for successive cohorts. Consider variations in these datasets – for instance, over time and between departments.

Talk with other subject teachers, and ask for their interpretations of any patterns. How are trends and annual variations explained?

Consider what future targets might be appropriate for your subject.

*Follow-up:* Take your data set and compare it with similar schools and with national figures for your subject.

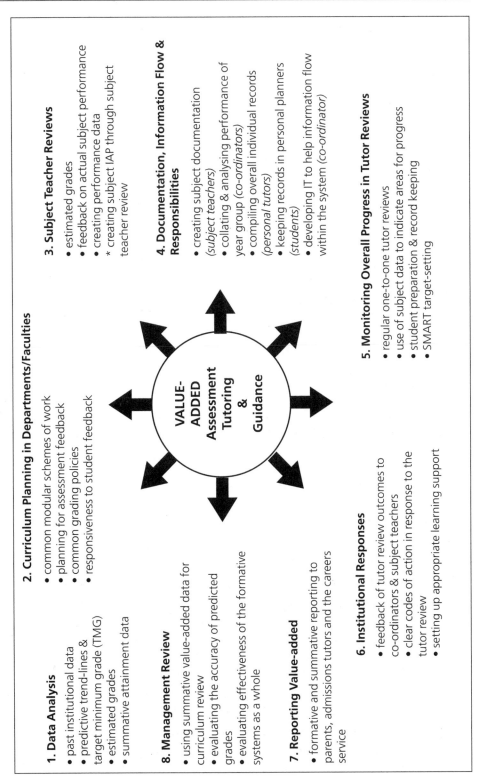

**2. Curriculum Planning in Departments/Faculties**
- common modular schemes of work
- planning for assessment feedback
- common grading policies
- responsiveness to student feedback

**3. Subject Teacher Reviews**
- estimated grades
- feedback on actual subject performance
- creating performance data
* creating subject IAP through subject teacher review

**4. Documentation, Information Flow & Responsibilities**
- creating subject documentation *(subject teachers)*
- collating & analysing performance of year group *(co-ordinators)*
- compiling overall individual records *(personal tutors)*
- keeping records in personal planners *(students)*
- developing IT to help information flow within the system *(co-ordinator)*

**5. Monitoring Overall Progress in Tutor Reviews**
- regular one-to-one tutor reviews
- use of subject data to indicate areas for progress
- student preparation & record keeping
- SMART target-setting

**1. Data Analysis**
- past institutional data
- predictive trend-lines & target minimum grade (TMG)
- estimated grades
- summative attainment data

**8. Management Review**
- using summative value-added data for curriculum review
- evaluating the accuracy of predicted grades
- evaluating effectiveness of the formative systems as a whole

**7. Reporting Value-added**
- formative and summative reporting to parents, admissions tutors and the careers service

**6. Institutional Responses**
- feedback of tutor review outcomes to co-ordinators & subject teachers
- clear codes of action in response to the tutor review
- setting up appropriate learning support

**VALUE-ADDED Assessment Tutoring & Guidance**

**Figure 16.4** *Components of institutional value-added, assessment and guidance systems (Spours and Hodgson 1996)*

## 3   SCHOOL INSPECTION

A national school inspection system has existed from Victorian times (see **Primary Reading** 7.4) and there is a long tradition of Her Majesty's Inspectors providing professional advice to government. Until 1993 this was achieved by HMI sampling schools for particular purposes and reviewing developments and quality in the system overall. For more specific information on standards of attainment, evidence had been provided by the Assessment of Performance Unit (APU), which regularly tested a representative sample of pupils at different ages. Local education authority Advisers provided more immediate support and advice to schools.

In 1992, with a new emphasis on the provision of more specific information to parents about particular schools, the Education (Schools) Act established new procedures for the regular inspection of all schools, to be co-ordinated by a new body, the Office for Standards in Education (OFSTED). The numbers of HMI were reduced and large numbers of new inspectors were trained. Teams of inspectors, led by a 'Registered Inspector', were then invited to bid for contracts to inspect particular schools, each of which was to be inspected every four years (see Rose 1995, **Primary Reading** 14.8 for a rationale for the approach).

Inspectors are required to report on:

- the quality of the education provided by the school
- the education standards achieved in the school
- whether the financial resources made available to the school are managed efficiently
- the spiritual, moral, social and cultural development of pupils at the school.

Inspection visits to secondary schools of average size usually last for a whole week. The team must include inspectors with expertise to cover the full range of subjects and vocational courses offered by the school. One of the team must be a 'lay inspector', that is someone without personal experience of managing or providing education in a school.

The diagram below (Figure 16.5) from the 1995 OFSTED *Handbook for the Inspection of Secondary Schools*, shows the structure of both the inspection schedule and the framework for the eventual report. It sets out the context of the school and 'highlights the distinction between *outcomes,* with an emphasis on attainment and progress, and the *factors which contribute to these outcomes,* particularly teaching' (p. 42).

In compiling their report, inspectors must assemble evidence for their judgements. Approximately 60 per cent of inspection time is devoted to observing lessons, sampling pupils' work and talking to pupils. Amongst the many sources of evidence used are the following.

### The pre-inspection context and school indicator (PICSI)

This is compiled by OFSTED and contains: key performance data from earlier years to enable trends to be identified; information about the social and economic characteristics of the area in which the school is sited; comparative data to enable school data to be set in a national context.

| CONTEXT | | | | | |
|---|---|---|---|---|---|
| | 3.1 Characteristics of the School | | | | |

| OUTCOMES | | | | |
|---|---|---|---|---|
| | 4.2 | 4.1 | 4.3 | |
| Educational standards achieved | Attitudes, behaviour and personal development | Attainment & progress | Attendance | |

| CONTRIBUTORY FACTORS | | | | | |
|---|---|---|---|---|---|
| | 5.2 | 5.3 | 5.1 | 5.4 | 5.5 |
| Provision | The curriculum & assessment | Pupils' spiritual, moral, social & cultural development | Teaching | Support, guidance & pupils' welfare | Partnership with parents & the community |
| | 6.2 | | 6.1 | 6.3 | |
| Management | Staffing, accommodation & learning resources | | Leadership & management | The efficiency of the school | |

**Figure 16.5** *The structure of the inspection schedule (OFSTED 1995)*

## The headteacher's form and statement

This includes quantitative data required by OFSTED and commentary on the characteristics of the school, the pupils, the features of the area it serves which influence its work.

## Data on attainment and progress

This is considered in relation to national standards and expectations including National Targets for Education and Training. The data should cover attainment in all subjects and that of pupils with statements of special educational need. It is used to reveal trends and to consider whether targets for improvement set by the school are appropriate, achievable and well met. It will also be used to highlight any significant variations in attainment among pupils of different gender, ethnicity or background. Data includes: National Curriculum assessments (tests and teacher assessment); examination results; any data from testing on entry; teacher records and assessment; marking of pupils' work; observation and discussion with pupils.

## Documents

The school prospectus, statement of aims, staff handbook, policy statements (e.g. assessment, behaviour and discipline, equal opportunities, pupil support and guidance), governing body minutes, staff job descriptions. Schemes of work, syllabuses, teachers' planning, curriculum audits/reviews/analyses. Samples of pupils' work – three pupils from each Year Group to represent above-average, average and below-average attainment; work from pupils with statements of special need. School self-review and development plan.

### Records
Pupil attendance, exclusions.

### Parents' views
As a minimum there must be a meeting with inspectors open to all parents.

### Observation and discussion
Of teachers and pupils in lessons; discussion with teachers and pupils; sampling of pupils' work; observation of behaviour, attitudes and relationships; collective worship; extra-curricular activities; resource provision including accommodation, facilities, central and departmental resource collections.

Following an inspection visit, the inspection report is made publicly available and a summary is sent to parents. Governors must consider the report and, within forty days, must produce an 'action plan' which sets out what it is going to do about the 'key issues for action' identified in the report.

The first phases of the new inspection system were not a complete success, and it is not expected that it will continue in its present form once the first cycle of inspections of all schools has been completed. There were practical problems, with recruiting sufficient inspectors, and the cost in 1995 was almost £100 million. More fundamentally, there were doubts about the conception, with some influential commentators suggesting that the system highlights problems but fails to provide adequate support for school improvement (e.g. OECD 1995, **Primary Reading 14.8**). There have been problems of stress and diversion, with many teachers suffering anxiety, and schools feeling that the inspection process interrupts their long-term development plans. There have been problems of trust and legitimacy, with professionals questioning the basis of inspectors' judgements on grounds of validity, reliability, consistency, subjectivity and rigour (Maw 1995, Fitzgibbon 1995, Wilcox and Gray 1996). There has also been a feeling that the system has been used to undermine public confidence in schools. For instance, a 1996 CfBT report stated:

> Very many still believe that OFSTED's inspections are punitive Government exercises against the teaching profession, and the reports are little more than vehicles for reinforcing Government dogma. (cited in *TES*, 2. January 1996, p. 3)

This feeling has not been helped by the promotion, from both major political parties, of the concept of 'failing schools'. This concept derives from the Education Act 1993 and was developed in Labour's policy statement, *Excellence for Everyone* (1995). OFSTED has established some indicators that would place a secondary school on the 'at risk' register:

- unsatisfactory standards in four or more subjects – across the school or in particular Key Stages
- unsatisfactory or poor teaching in more than 25 per cent of lessons
- bad behaviour of pupils and poor relationships between pupils and staff
- ineffectual management
- poor value for money
- attendance rates below 90 per cent
- more than twenty-five exclusions
- fewer than 20 per cent of pupils achieving five or more GCSE grades at A–C.

### Practical activity 16.6

*Aim:* To consider teacher perceptions of inspection.

*Method:* Talk with a subject teacher and/or a member of middle or senior management about the three 'problems' with inspection which were discussed above:

- conception and practicality
- stress and diversion
- trust and legitimacy.

What concerns do they raise? Make sure that you also ask about the positive aspects of inspection. Then consider if the benefits outweigh the difficulties.

*Follow-up:* Study an inspection report of your school, or of another school known to you. Consider what you can learn from it which would help you in improving your practice.

A recent revision of inspection arrangements reduces the frequency of formal school inspection from every four years to every six years. OFSTED's efforts will be concentrated on identifying schools with 'serious weaknesses' which will be scrutinized much more frequently. For instance, it is possible that weak measures of value added could lead to inspection.

The 1997 Education Act extended inspection procedures to cover local education authorities.

## 4 | PUPIL VIEWS ON SCHOOL IMPROVEMENT

One group rarely heard or consulted in investigations of effectiveness are the pupils. We conclude this section with reference to a study which was based on a belief that 'young people are observant and often capable of analytical and constructive comment and usually respond well to the responsibility, when given it, of helping to identify what it is about their schooling that gets in the way of learning'. Interviews conducted with ninety pupils in three secondary schools (Rudduck *et al.* 1996) suggested that most pupils want to succeed. From the pupil responses, the researchers identified six principles that make a significant difference to pupils' learning and would lead to them responding constructively in school.

1. *Respect* for pupils as individuals and as a body occupying a significant position in the institution of the school. Teachers recognizing pupils' readiness to take more responsibility as they grow older and engaging with them in as adult a way as possible.
2. *Fairness* to all students irrespective of their class, gender, ethnicity or academic status. In particular, teachers not prejudging pupils on the basis of past incidents.
3. *Autonomy* as both right and a responsibility in relation to physical and social maturity.
4. *Intellectual challenge* that helps pupils to experience learning as a dynamic, engaging and empowering activity. Teachers ensuring that they make all pupils feel confident they can do well and achieve something worthwhile.
5. *Social support* in relation to both academic and emotional concerns. Teachers are able to talk to pupils about learning and school work (and not just about behaviour).
6. *Security* in relation to the physical setting of the school and in interpersonal encounters (including anxiety about threats to self-esteem). Teachers are sensitive to the tone and manner of their discourse with pupils, as individuals and in groups, so that they do not humiliate them, criticize them in ways that make them 'feel small' (especially in front of their peers) or shout at them.

Patterns of commitment and confidence of pupils are also affected by the organizational structures and systems of the school that make it more or less possible for these principles to be enacted. Overall, the research suggests that we should be concerned about the messages that teacher-pupil interaction communicates to pupils about themselves, both as learners and as people. Figure 16.6 presents diagramatically the set of relationships that for Rudduck *et al.* constitute 'the conditions of learning'.

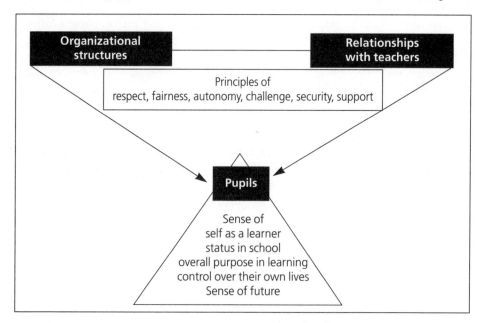

**Figure 16.6** *A framework for understanding the 'conditions of learning' (Rudduck et al. 1996)*

## Practical activity 16.7

*Aim:* To investigate pupil views on school improvement.

*Method:* Select a small group of responsible pupils and hold a discussion with them about the school. Structure this first by a focus on the school's strengths and weaknesses; then by a focus on 'how the school could be improved'. If possible tape or take notes on what is said. Later, review the discussion. How many of the issues raised relate to the six principles identified by Rudduck *et al.*: respect, fairness, autonomy, intellectual challenge, social support and security?

*Follow-up:* The slightly more challenging activity is to repeat the discussion, but this time with a group of pupils who may feel less positive about the school. What variations do you find? Can you relate this to processes of differentiation and polarization (see Chapter 14, Section 4.3)?

## CONCLUSION

In this chapter, we began by looking at the policy context within which schools work and at various approaches to school improvement, including the pressure of market competition. We reviewed the main findings of school effectiveness research and then focused on various factors which are important to school improvement: school culture and micro-politics; development planning; staff appraisal; and the measurement of performance and setting of targets. We then focused on the school inspection system before concluding with some insights into the perceptions of pupils – after all, they are what it is all about, aren't they?

### Notes for further reading

The outstanding introduction to the importance of school contexts for the quality of educational provision is:

Fullan, M. (1991)
*The New Meaning of Educational Change,*
London: Cassell.

'Local Management of Schools' (LMS) has brought particular challenges for headteachers. Much has been written on the subject, but for an excellent research study and sources of practical advice, see:

Levacic, R. (1995)
*Local Management of Schools: Analysis and Practice,*
Buckingham: Open University Press.

Caldwell, B. J. and Spinks, J. M. (1988)
*The Self-managing School,*
London: Falmer Press.

Cave, E. and Wilkinson, C. (1990)
*Local Management of Schools: Some Practical Issues,*
London: Routledge.

Two excellent sources on the impact of 'market competition' between schools are:

Gewirtz, S., Ball, S. J. and Bowe, R. (1995)
*Markets, Choice and Equity in Education,*
Buckingham: Open University Press.

Glatter, R., Woods, P. A. and Bagley, C. (eds) (1997)
*Choice and Diversity in Education,*
London: Routledge.

Work on school effectiveness has been very considerable in recent years. We list the UK classic first, together with three other illustrative collections:

Rutter, M., Maugan, B., Mortimore, P. and Ouston, J. (1979)
*Fifteen Thousand Hours: Secondary Schools and their Effects on Children,*
London: Open Books.

Reynolds, D. and Cuttance, P. (eds) (1992)
*School Effectiveness: Research, Policy and Practice,*
London: Cassell.

Ainscow, M. (ed.) (1991)
*Effective Schools for All,*
London: David Fulton.

Riddell, S. and Brown, S. (eds) (1991)
*School Effectiveness Research: Its Messages for School Improvement,*
Edinburgh: HMSO.

There has been considerable emphasis on making schools function more like businesses. In one manifestation, the ideas of 'total quality management' are being applied. For instance, see:

West-Burnham, J. (1992)
*Managing Quality in Schools,*
London: Longman.

Murgatroyd, S. and Morgan, C. (1992)
*Total Quality Management and the School,*
Buckingham: Open University Press.

On approaches to school improvement and implementation, and on the uncertainties of change, see:

Fullan, M. G. (1992)
*Successful School Improvement,*
Buckingham: Open University Press.

Fullan, M. G. (1993)
*Change Forces,*
London: Falmer Press.

For interpretive approaches using the concepts of school culture:

Hargreaves, A. (1991) 'Cultures of teaching', in Hargreaves, A and Fullan, M. G. (eds) (1992)
*Understanding Teacher Development,*
London, Cassell.                                                        📖 **Primary Reading 14.1**

Nias, J., Southworth, G. and Yeomans, R. (1989)
*Staff Relationships in the Primary School: A Study of Organizational Cultures,*
London: Cassell.                                                        📖 **Primary Reading 14.2**

For the influential micro-political perspective on school organizations see:

Ball, S. (1987)
*Micropolitics of the School: Towards a Theory of School Organisation,*
London: Routledge.

Hoyle, E. (1986)
*The Politics of School Management,*
London: Hodder and Stoughton.

The issues raised by headship and management of schools are very evident in the case-study accounts provided by Mortimore and Mortimore below. Hall offers excellent accounts and analysis of the particular struggles of women in school management.

Mortimore, P. and Mortimore, J. (ed.) (1991)
*The Secondary Head,*
London: Paul Chapman.

Hall, V. (1996)
*Dancing on the Ceiling: A Study of Women Managers in Education,*
London: Paul Chapman.

An important publication from the National Commission on Education sets out how schools in disadvantaged areas can maintain effectiveness.

National Commission on Education (1995)
*Success Against the Odds,*
London: Routledge.

Constructive books on the topic of school-based planning and development are indicated below. The first by Hargreaves and Hopkins sets out the rationale very clearly. Their second qualifies it somewhat in the light of experience. MacGilchrist *et al.* provide an excellent study of implementation, of great relevance to all schools.

Hargreaves, D. H. and Hopkins, D. (1991)
*The Empowered School: The Management and Practice of Development Planning,*
London: Cassell.                                    📖 **Primary Reading 14.3**

Hargreaves, D. H. and Hopkins, D. (eds) (1994)
*Development Planning for School Improvement,*
London: Cassell.

MacGilchrist, B., Mortimore, P., Savage, J. and Beresford, C. (1995)
*Planning Matters: The Impact of Development Planning in Primary Schools,*
London: Paul Chapman.

The most useful sources on school appraisal are:

OFSTED (1996b)
*The Appraisal of Teachers: 1991–1996,*
London: OFSTED.

Wragg, E. C., Wikeley, F. J., Wragg, C. M. and Haynes, C. S. (1996)
*Teacher Appraisal Observed,*
London: Routledge.

School performance and target setting is well illustrated in:

DFEE (1996c)
*Setting Targets to Raise Standards: A Survey of Good Practice,*
London: DFEE.

See also the DFEE School Improvement Database on the internet for cases of 'good practice':

http://www.open.gov.uk/dfee/dfeehome/

For a more analytic approach to the issues, see:

Gray, J. and Wilcox, J. (1995)
'*Good School, Bad School*': *Evaluating Performance and Encouraging Improvement,*
Buckingham: Open University Press.

Fitz-Gibbon, C.T. (1995)
*Monitoring Education: Indicators, Quality and Effectiveness,*
London: Cassell.

The official framework for inspection is:

OFSTED (1995a)
*Guidance on the Inspection of Secondary Schools,*
London: OFSTED.

On evaluation of the provision of inspection and advice, see:

Ouston, J., Earley, P. and Fidler, B. (1996)
*OFSTED Inspections: the Early Experience,*
London: David Fulton.

Centre for Educational Research and Innovation (1995)
*Schools Under Scrutiny,*
Paris: OECD.                                        📖 **Primary Reading 14.9**

Wilcox, B. and Gray, J. (1996)
*Inspecting Schools: Holding Schools to Account and Helping Schools to improve,*
Buckingham: Open University Press.

An excellent book on pupil perspectives in secondary education is:

Rudduck, J., Chaplain, R and Wallace, G. (eds) (1996)
*School Improvement: What Can Pupils Tell Us?*
London: David Fulton.

For international perspectives on school change, effectiveness and quality see:

Husen, T., Tuijnman, A. and Halls, W. D. (eds) (1992)
*Schooling in Modern European Society,*
London: Pergamon.

Finally, a principled polemic on how teachers and headteachers should pull together, is:

Fullan, M. and Hargreaves, A. (1992)
*What's Worth Fighting for in Your School? Working Together for School Improvement,*
Buckingham, Open University Press.

# CHAPTER 17

# Reflective teaching and society

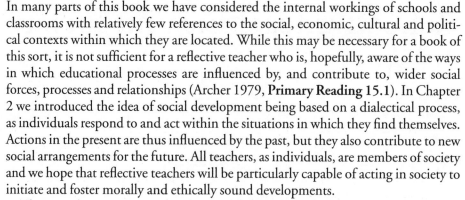

## INTRODUCTION

In many parts of this book we have considered the internal workings of schools and classrooms with relatively few references to the social, economic, cultural and political contexts within which they are located. While this may be necessary for a book of this sort, it is not sufficient for a reflective teacher who is, hopefully, aware of the ways in which educational processes are influenced by, and contribute to, wider social forces, processes and relationships (Archer 1979, **Primary Reading 15.1**). In Chapter 2 we introduced the idea of social development being based on a dialectical process, as individuals respond to and act within the situations in which they find themselves. Actions in the present are thus influenced by the past, but they also contribute to new social arrangements for the future. All teachers, as individuals, are members of society and we hope that reflective teachers will be particularly capable of acting in society to initiate and foster morally and ethically sound developments.

There are three sections in this chapter. The first discusses the relationship between education and society and reviews the theoretical framework which was first introduced in Chapter 2. The second considers the classroom responsibilities of a socially aware and reflective teacher and discusses the formation of classroom policies. The final section focuses on the actions which a reflective teacher could take as a citizen in trying to influence democratic processes of decision-making by local, regional and national governments.

## 1 | EDUCATION AND SOCIETY

Two major questions have to be faced with regard to the relationship between education and society. The first is, 'What should an education system be designed to do?' The second is, 'What can actually be achieved through education? We will address these in turn and draw out the implications for reflective teachers.

Education has very often been seen as a means of influencing the development of societies, and we will identify three central areas of purpose. These are:

- wealth creation through preparation for economic production
- cultural production and reproduction
- developing social justice and individual rights.

### Wealth creation

One educational priority is certainly likely to be wealth creation. For instance, in the latter part of the industrial revolution in Great Britain, an important part of the argument for the establishment of an elementary school system was that it should provide a workforce which was more skilled and thus more economically productive. The idea became the linchpin of 'human capital' theory in the 1960s (Schultz 1961) and many new nations, influenced by analyses such as Rostow's *The Stages of Economic Growth* (1962), put scarce resources into their education systems. The economics of education is still a flourishing area of policy and research (Aldcroft 1990). In Britain, the links between education and economic productivity are constantly being drawn by the government, with particular attention to the standard of basic skills achieved in schools and to the proportion of young people acquiring advanced knowledge and skills in higher education. See **Primary Reading 15.2** for a liberal manifestation of this concern from the National Commission on Education (1993). There are parallel developments in the USA, Europe, SE Asia, Australasia and elsewhere.

### Cultural reproduction

Alternatively, there are those who would highlight the 'function' of education in the production and reproduction of a national culture. Again there were elements of the nineteenth-century British experience which illustrate this. For instance, the arguments and influence of Arnold (1986) helped to define the traditional classical curriculum which remains influential today. Indeed, the necessity for pupils to study Shakespeare and key episodes in English history were insisted upon in the construction of the National Curriculum. Even so, some remain concerned about the erosion of national identity in modern society (see Tate 1995, **Primary Reading 15.3**).

A particularly clear example of cultural production is that of the USA in the twentieth century where the education system was required to 'assimilate' and 'integrate' successive groups of new immigrants into an 'American culture'. The education system was seen as a vital part of the 'melting pot'. Of course, a highly questionable assumption here was that there was a single American culture, but the notion of the existence of a set of 'central values' was important in this formative period of the development of the USA. There are thus costs in the use of education to develop or assert a national culture, and these costs are usually borne by minority or less powerful groups. The historical case of the education provided in the colonies of the British Empire provides a particularly graphic example of this last point (Mangan 1993).

However, use of an education system for the production of a sense of shared national identity is common in many parts of the world, particularly where independent or democratic states have been established relatively recently. Of course, other forms of political structure can also be supported by education. Thus, at the turn of the century, we have many emergent forms of regional identity within the nations which make up the European Union. Education plays a part in producing and reproducing culture at each of these levels. Thus, for example, the people of Wales preserve an important part of their culture through the teaching of Welsh in their schools, but, at the same time, their education system inducts Welsh children into the culture of the United Kingdom and Europe. Another educational priority can thus be an integrative one, relating to the production or reproduction of 'culture' within political structures.

### Social justice

Contributing to social justice is a third central purpose which is often identified for education systems. This concern was very much at the forefront of thinking in the production of the 1944 Education Act in the UK and also in the subsequent introduction of comprehensive schools. It has been an important element of policy in the USA and features prominently in the educational goals which are set by many countries in Europe and across the world (for a European example, see the 1985 *Memorandum of the Council of Europe*, **Primary Readings 15.4**). One critical point to make is that 'equality of opportunity' and the meritocratic ideal, which often lie behind policies on this issue, are concepts which are vulnerable to rhetoric. They can be used in ways which ignore the structural inequalities of wealth, status and power which exist. If such issues are glossed, then the promotion of social justice through education policy is very unlikely to be successful.

The concern for social justice through education can partly be seen as a desire to ensure that there is an acceptable and legitimated system for allocating jobs in democratic societies and for facilitating social mobility. However, there are more individualized and fundamental concerns which are perhaps more relevant to reflective teaching. A very clear exposition of such issues is contained in the Universal Declaration of Human Rights (United Nations 1948).

Article 1 of the Declaration states that:

> All human beings are born free and equal in dignity and rights. They are endowed with reason and conscience.

These rights are to be enjoyed, according to Article 2:

> Without distinction of any kind, such as race, colour, sex, language, religion, political or other opinion, national or social origin, property, birth or other status.

There then follow many articles dealing with rights and fundamental freedoms of movement, thought, religion, assembly, political participation, work, leisure, and an adequate standard of living. Article 26 deals with education and asserts that:

> Education shall be directed to the full development of the human personality and the strengthening of respect for human rights and fundamental freedoms. It shall promote understanding, tolerance and friendship among all nations, racial and religious groups.

Education was expected to have a crucial role in the dissemination of the UN Declaration across the world, for it was to be 'displayed, read and expanded principally in schools and other educational institutions' in all member states. Needless to say, the achievement of social justice and individual rights for all citizens remains a noble and appropriate goal, but one which will probably always be with us, for it is optimistic to think that educational provision alone can overcome structural inequalities in any society. Indeed, the necessity of adopting a United Nations Convention on the Rights of the Child in 1989, underlines that fact.

Education policies and systems can thus be designed to emphasize economic production, cultural production or reproduction, social justice or individual rights. Whilst such goals are not necessarily conflicting, various tensions and dilemmas are often posed. One obvious issue concerns the rights of minority groups to maintain an independent culture and sense of identity within a majority culture. Another is the dilemma between the demands of individual development and those of economic production. We have raised these issues in Chapter 8 and argued that a reflective teacher should make informed and responsible judgements about them. The ways in which action might follow will be discussed further, below.

We now move on to the second question: 'What can actually be achieved through education?'

There has been a long-running debate on this topic. Some people, such as Coleman *et al.* (1966), Jencks *et al.* (1972), and Bowles and Gintis (1976, **Primary Reading 13.1**), have argued that education can make little difference to social development. Although coming to the issue from different theoretical perspectives, they argue that educational processes reflect and reproduce major features of existing societies, particularly with regard to distinctions related to social class. The suggestion is that relationships of power, wealth, status and ideology are such that education should be seen as a part of the dominant social system, rather than as an autonomous force within it.

Others, such as Berger and Luckman (1966), may be seen as taking a more idealistic theoretical position. They argue that, since our sense of reality is 'socially constructed' by people as they interact together, there is, therefore, scope for individuals to make an independent impact on the course of future social development. Thus there is potential for education to influence change. What we have here are the competing positions of those who believe in social determinism ranged against those who believe in individual voluntarism. As we have already seen, education is very often expected to bring about social and economic developments and it is an area which tends to attract idealists. However, we also have to recognize that the major structural features of societies are extremely resistant to change. What is needed then is a theoretical position which recognizes the importance of action and of constraint. Such a position would accept that education has a degree of relative autonomy and would thus legitimate action by individuals to contribute to future social development.

Such a theoretical framework is provided by what we call the dialectic of the individual and society (see Chapter 2 and, in particular, **Primary Readings 2.1 and 2.2**). As Berlak and Berlak (1981, **Primary Reading 1.3**) put it: 'Conscious creative activity is limited by prevailing social arrangements, but human actions and institutional forms are not mere reflections of them' (p. 121).

The clear implication is that people can make their own impact and history but must do so in whatever circumstances they find themselves. If this theoretical framework is adopted, social developments can be seen as the product of processes of struggle and contest between different individuals and groups in society (**Primary Readings 15.1, 15.7**). Such processes are ones in which education must, inevitably, play a part.

Our answer to the question of what education can actually achieve must thus be based on a guarded and realistic optimism. The dialectical model of the influence of individuals and social structures recognizes constraints but asserts that action remains possible. This places a considerable responsibility on a reflective teacher.

## 2 | CLASSROOM TEACHING AND SOCIETY

One implication of the adoption of a dialectical model of the relationship between individuals and society is that it highlights the possible consequences, for the 'macro' world of society, of actions, experiences and processes which take place in the 'micro' world of the classroom. In Chapter 1, we raised this issue with the assertion that 'reflective teaching implies an active concern with aims and consequences as well as with technical efficiency' and we must pick up the themes again here. One of the most important issues concerns the influence of a reflective teacher's own value commitments.

In Chapter 1, we argued that reflective teachers should accept democratically determined decisions but should act both as responsible professionals and as autonomous citizens to contribute to such decision-making processes. We also suggested that attitudes of 'open-mindedness' and 'responsibility' are essential attributes. Open-mindedness involves a willingness to consider evidence and argument from whatever source it comes. It is thus the antithesis of closure and of habituated or ideological thinking. There are parallels here with the guidelines issued by the UK Politics Association regarding teaching politics in school (Jones 1986). Jones suggests that the objective should be to achieve a 'comprehensive awareness' and an 'overall understanding of political processes and issues'. On the basis of such awareness, children should be encouraged to form their own views and participate in the democratic process. An open-minded tolerance to the exposition of a variety of views and opinions is obviously an initial necessity here and we would say the same for reflective teaching.

However, the Politics Association also asserts the importance of a teacher's social responsibility with its guideline that 'the teacher cannot be neutral towards those values which underpin liberal democracy'. But what are such values? Clear guidance on this has been provided by the Council of Europe (1985, **Primary Reading 15.4**). In a recommendation to all member states of the European Union, the Council of Ministers reaffirmed the understandings embodied in the United Nations' Universal Declaration of Human Rights and the European Convention of Human Rights. The Council suggested that study in schools should 'lead to an understanding of, and sympathy for, the concepts of justice, equality, freedom, peace, dignity, rights and democracy' (Council of Europe 1985, Appendix). These are seen as being fundamental to democratic societies, and all schools, including those for young children, are encouraged to introduce them to their pupils and to develop their understanding. Hugh Starkey (1987) claims that the United Nations' Declaration is accepted as a worldwide moral standard and that fundamental freedoms are what make effective political democracies possible.

This brings us directly back to the issues of individual dignity, equality and freedom. It again raises issues such as sexism, racism and other forms of discrimination on the basis of social class, age, disability or sexual orientation and it focuses attention once more on the quality of relationships and the use of power in classrooms. These are issues upon which, we would argue, children have rights about which socially responsible teachers should not compromise. We take this to constitute a 'bottom line', a value commitment to the fundamental rights of citizens in a democratic society and a necessary underpinning for professionality.

Such a value commitment by reflective teachers might be manifested in two ways. First, classroom processes might be monitored with such specific issues in mind; indeed we have made various suggestions of this sort with regard to race, disability and gender. The second way of manifesting this value commitment follows logically from such monitoring. It is to develop classroom social policies for the long term, so that actions which are taken in the immediacy of classroom decision-making, support concerns with individual dignity, equality and freedom rather than undercut them. Classroom social policies may be seen as attempts to anticipate, plan and prestructure activities and procedures so that teacher actions reflect a consistent and socially responsible value-position.

We will illustrate these steps through the suggestion of practical activities. We begin with Practical Activity 17.1, designed to monitor the care of a pupil with a special educational need.

### Practical activity 17.1

*Aim:* To monitor the experience of a pupil with a physical disability in a class.

*Method:* We would suggest a form of focused child study here. Data collection methods might include observation and field notes, collecting examples of work, sociometry, and discussions with the pupil. Other colleagues might also observe and provide comments on teacher-pupil interaction.

*Follow-up:* The criteria for analysis might ultimately be in terms of maximizing the pupil's dignity, equality and freedom but more specific questions which could be used to interrogate the data might be:

1. To what extent is the pupil able to participate in class activities?
2. To what extent is tolerance and understanding of the pupil's disability shown by other pupils?
3. What is the quality of the relationship between the pupil and yourself?
4. What is the quality of the pupil's learning and achievement?

Having monitored an existing situation it is then necessary to take action and to establish policy. The establishment of classroom policy is by no means easy. It requires a sound analysis of the issues both in terms of the specific situation and in the light of alternative approaches, experiences and research findings from elsewhere. Above all it requires knowledge of oneself and personal commitment to implementation. In our view, it is very hard to develop such understanding without the insights of others and opportunities to discuss the issues with colleagues and 'critical friends'. The establishment of a classroom policy might then take the form as suggested in Practical Activity 17.2. Again we use the example of provision for pupils with special educational needs.

Activities such as these should help in the development of socially aware teaching and can be applied to issues such as race, social class, beliefs, moral values and gender. Classroom practice can never, following a dialectical model, fail to have some influence on the development of society at large in particular through the ways in which it influences the identity, values and life-chances of individuals. The development of classroom social policies thus enables the reflective teacher to take conscious control and to contribute productively to micro-macro linkages and to the future of both individual biographies and social history (Mills 1959, **Primary Reading 2.1**).

## Practical activity 17.2

*Aim:* To develop a classroom policy to maximize the participation of pupils with special educational needs.

*Method:* We would suggest the following stages:

1. Read some of the literature about provision for pupils with special educational needs in classrooms (e.g. Ashdown, Carpenter and Borair 1991, Lowe 1989).

2. Discuss with colleagues how they make provision. Gather examples of practice elsewhere.

3. Consider your present provision. Are the physical resources, the learning activities and the quality of interactions in the classroom such that all children can participate, feel valued and maintain their dignity?

4. Discuss these issues with colleagues. Brainstorm on ways of providing support for children with particular needs. Sort out the ideas which seem to be both productive and practical.

5. Draw out the implications for practice so that explicit policy decisions for one's actions are identified.

*Follow-up:* Attempt to develop classroom action which is guided by policy. Monitor your degree of success.

---

### 3  REFLECTIVE TEACHING AND THE DEMOCRATIC PROCESS

In Chapter 1 we suggested that, in addition to professional responsibilities to implement democratically determined decisions, teachers as citizens also have responsibilities to act to influence the nature of such decisions. Teachers have rights and it is perfectly reasonable that they should be active in contributing to the formation of public policy. This role, as White (1978) suggested, is close to that of the activist and the methods to be utilized are those which have been well developed in recent years by a variety of pressure groups.

There are six basic elements of successful pressure group activity:

1. Identifying decision-makers
2. Preparing the case
3. Forming alliances
4. Managing the media
5. Lobbying decision-makers
6. Following up.

## Practical activity 17.3

*Aim:* To investigate processes of political activity and decision-making with regard to an educational issue.

*Method:* A necessary basic strategy here is to focus on one issue and to trace the debates in the media and elsewhere. This is best done with colleagues so that the workload is shared. The issue could be local or national.

Newspapers provide useful sources of easily retrievable information. Some, such as *The Times* and *Times Educational Supplement* publish an index and are available on CD Rom and the Internet.

Having gathered a variety of statements about the issue in question, an attempt should be made to classify them so that the competing positions are identified. From this point, it may be possible to gather policy statements directly from the participants, by letter, discussion, interview or library search.

Finally, the decision point can be studied. Were the public arguments influential? What interests seem to have prevailed when decisions were taken?

*Follow-up:* Having studied an example of political influence on decision-making it is worth taking stock of what has been learned. Did you feel that the debate reflected appropriate educational concerns? Could educationalists have made more constructive contributions?

Such techniques have been evident in UK debates about the curriculum in secondary schools where lobbying of Members of Parliament has taken place. For instance, when standardized assessment tests were imposed at the end of Key Stage 3 many teachers of English were particularly concerned about its effects. Members of the National Association for the Teaching of English were encouraged to write to MP's and the views of the association were made clear to Education Ministers, journalists and the public through letters to the press and media interviews. The techniques have also been deployed on more general educational issues such as cutbacks in educational expenditure, the issue of grant-maintained schools, the abolition of corporal punishment in schools and the question of the sort of 'moral education' which schools are expected to provide. Some national educational pressure groups are now well established. These include CASE (The Campaign for the Advancement of State Education) and NAME (The National Anti-racist Movement in Education). Professional associations such the NUT, NAS/UWT, AMMA and PAT are also active, though the most influential in recent years have been the headteacher associations of NAHT and SHA.

At the more local level, pressure group activity and lobbying by individuals of councillors and education officials also takes place regularly. For instance, in the mid-1990s an independent religious foundation applied to the Secretary of State for a grant to open and maintain a new secondary school to serve a large area of new housing near Bristol. Through lobbying and discussion, considerable support was initially obtained within the community, which at that time had no secondary school. However, the local education authority opposed the scheme and initiated a process of much wider consultation involving other schools, local industry, other community groups, parents in the area, etc. The issue featured regularly in the local press and media and various groups pressing for non-denominational provision emerged. Lobbying of local MPs and of the Secretary of State grew, and the application was eventually turned down.

Pressure group activity and collective action by individuals can thus both bring about new policy priorities and lead to a reappraisal of existing policies. This is an essential feature of democratic decision-making and we would suggest that reflective teachers have both the right and responsibility to contribute to such processes.

We are conscious, though, that this is a book which is primarily designed to support student teachers during periods of school-based work and that activities to influence wider policies may seem inappropriate. We include them because such activity is a logical consequence of taking reflective teaching seriously and because some preparation for such activity is perfectly possible before taking up a full-time teaching post. One of the most important aspects of this is to demystify the democratic process itself and we will make various suggestions on this and with regard to the six elements of pressure group activity which we have identified. These might be followed up by small groups of students or teachers, perhaps by taking an educational issue as a case study, or indeed, by facing a real current issue.

### Demystifying the democratic process

There is a tendency to regard decision-making as something which is done by 'them'– an ill-defined, distant and amorphous body. In fact, decisions in democracies are taken by people who are elected representatives and the connection between the ordinary citizen and decision-makers can be much more close, direct and specific. Some possible ways forward here are:

- Visit a relevant meeting of your local or regional council or the House of Commons. Council committee meetings are normally open to the public and attendance at an education committee meeting is likely to be very interesting to reflective teachers.
- Visit a local elected representative, MP, councillor or a candidate. Alternatively, set up a meeting which they can attend. Discuss their views on educational issues and get them to explain the constraints and pressures within which they serve.
- Attend a meeting of the governing body of your school. Note who the governors are and their powers over the affairs of the school. Consider the potential for partnership between teachers and governors.

### Identifying decision-makers

Lists of MPs and councillors are normally available in local libraries and from council offices. It is then necessary to identify those who have a particular interest in education and those who have a particular degree of influence over decisions. A list of members of the education committee on a council or of members of the House of Commons with an interest in education will be helpful. The names of school governors will be available in your school.

It is also often appropriate to identify the leaders of political groups and those who speak on education issues. In addition, the chair of the finance committee on a local council or Treasury Ministers in the House of Commons are likely to be worth identifying depending, of course, on the issue under consideration.

A further group to identify are the education officers and civil servants who advise decision-makers and implement many decisions. Chief education officers, for instance, can be extremely influential.

### Preparing the case

It is essential to prepare a case well. This requires at least three things:

- Appropriate factual information about the issue.
- Good educational arguments in support of whatever is being advocated.
- Some understanding and responses to the interests and concerns of those whom it is hoped to influence.

Statistical information can be gathered from various sources at a local or national level. For instance, in England the Statistics Branch of the Department for Education publishes a *Statistical Bulletin* every month and other important statistics on more general issues are available from *Social Trends and Regional Trends*, both of which are annual government publications from the Central Statistical Office and should be available in good libraries. Similar statistics are available from the Scottish Office, Welsh Office and Northern Ireland Office.

Other sorts of information can be collected through discussion with those people who may be involved locally with the issue under consideration. Sources within your school should be one starting point. Newspapers also offer a regular source of reports and comment on educational developments and can be monitored for relevant material. Bearing in mind the nature of some journalism, it is worth checking stories if possible.

For good educational arguments, one might want to consult the literature and certainly would wish to discuss the issues under consideration with colleagues.

Regarding the interests of those whom one wishes to influence, a good place to start is with any published policy statements or manifestos. This could be followed up by discussion and by making judgements regarding the pressures and constraints which they face.

### Forming alliances

Representative democracy is designed as a system which links decision-making with the views of a majority. It follows that the most successful type of campaigning is likely to be one which is broadly based – one which is produced by an alliance of interested parties bringing concerted pressure to bear on policy-makers.

Reflective teachers may thus wish to act with others if and when they wish to influence public policy. Obvious places to look for allies are:

- Other colleagues, perhaps through professional associations, trade union links or the General Teaching Council to which the new Labour government is committed. The fragmentation of the profession into different unions has been a considerable source of weakness on some issues in the past.

- Parents, and the importance of parental support cannot be underestimated. It can help to establish the legitimacy of educational arguments and is a source of much energy and commitment to educational quality.
- Other workers in the public services.
- Existing national pressure groups such as those listed earlier in this section.
- Local community and interest groups who may be directly or indirectly affected by the issues under consideration.

### Managing the media

Possibilities here include:

- Carrying out a review of the types of media which might be interested in educational issues – press, radio, television etc.
- Holding discussions with people who have had experience of managing publicity to learn from them.
- Carrying out an analysis of the types of stories or news that each media outlet is likely to be interested in and, crucially, of the ways in which they are likely to handle educational issues.
- Considering the timing constraints which appropriate media outlets face.
- Holding discussions with selected journalists to get first-hand knowledge of their concerns.
- Preparing some press releases and considering suitable images for photographic or filming purposes.
- Identifying and supporting a spokesperson for press follow-up.

### Lobbying decision-makers

There are any number of possibilities here and we provide a few examples:

- Discrete lobbying through discussion
- Letter-writing by individuals
- Letter-writing campaigns
- Delegations to put arguments
- Petitions
- Leafleting
- Demonstrating with supporters
- Attending council or House of Commons debates to observe.

One important strategy is to try to ensure, for as long as possible, that any policy changes can be introduced by politicians with dignity. Not many politicians enjoy being forced to change course, but most are open to persuasion if they have not previously taken up a hard, public position.

### Following up

There is no mystery here. If agreement for changes in policy or practice is reached, it is simply necessary to check that the agreement is enacted.

# CONCLUSION

Education is inevitably concerned not just with 'what is' but also with what 'ought to be' (Kogan 1978). We hope that this book will help teachers and student teachers to develop not only the necessary skills of teaching but also the awareness and commitment which will ensure the positive nature of their contribution to the education service in the future.

## *Notes for further reading*

The inexorable links between education and society have tended to be glossed in recent years, as concern to maximize the 'technical efficiency' of schooling has predominated. A very valuable reminder of the wider social, political and philosophical issues is Carr and Hartnett's historical account:

Carr, W. and Hartnett, A. (1996)
*Education and the Struggle for Democracy,*
Buckingham: Open University Press.

Many of the resources suggested as further reading for Chapters 1 and 2 will also be relevant here. Two of those books which we have found particularly challenging are:

Apple, M. (1982)
*Education and Power,*
London: Routledge and Kegan Paul.

Stenhouse, L. (1982)
*Authority, Education and Emancipation,*
London: Heinemann.

One more general way of following up many of these issues, particularly to gather information, would be through the use of textbooks in the sociology of education. For two of the most recent see:

Burgess, R. G. (1986)
*Sociology, Education and Schools,*
London: Batsford.

Reid, I. (1986)
*The Sociology of School and Education,*
London: Fontana.

For an important analysis of the impact of market competition between schools, see:

Dale, R. (1996)
'Mechanisms of differentiation between schools: the four 'M's'.
Mimeo, Auckland: University of Auckland.                     📖 **Primary Reading 15.5**

Human rights is an extremely important topic. The most important documents to consider are:

*The Universal Declaration of Human Rights,*
New York: United Nations.

This Declaration was initially agreed in 1948 and is available through United Nations Associations.

The European Convention on Human Rights,
Strasbourg: Council of Europe.

This Convention represents a collective guarantee of a number of the principles contained in the Universal Declaration. It came into force in 1953 and all of the twenty-one member states of the Council of Europe have ratified it. It is backed by the European Court of Human Rights. Copies of the Convention and further information is available from: Directorate of Human Rights, Council of Europe, F-67006 Strasbourg, France.

The United Nations Convention on children's rights is another important international statement. For an excellent account of both it and its implications for the UK, see:

Newell, P. (1991)
*The UN Convention and Children's Rights in the UK,*
London: National Children's Bureau.

For specific guidance and ideas on classroom practice see also:

Council of Europe, (1985)
*Teaching and Learning about Human Rights in Schools,*
Recommendation No. R (85) 7 of the Committee of Ministers to Member States,
Strasbourg: Council of Europe. **Primary Reading 15.4**

Starkey, H. (1987)
*Practical Activities for Teaching and Learning about Human Rights in Schools,*
Strasbourg: Council of Europe.

There is also a considerable literature which is more specifically about children's rights. For an important handbook, see:

Franklin, B. and Hammarberg, T. (1995)
*The Handbook of Children's Rights: Comparative Legislation and Practice,*
London: Routledge.

For consideration of some of the issues to do with political balance which may be raised, see:

Jones, B. (1986)
'Politics and the pupil',
*Times Educational Supplement,* 30 May 1986.

Wellington, J. J. (ed.) (1986)
*Controversial Issues in the Curriculum,*
Oxford: Blackwell.

An element of political struggle between central government and the teaching profession has been clear through the 1990s. On this see Carr and Hartnett (as cited above) and:

Ball, S. J. (1994)
*Education Reform: A Critical and Post-structural Approach,*
Buckingham: Open University Press. **Primary Reading 15.6**

Action by reflective teachers within the democratic process calls for some knowledge of political structures and processes. For excellent introductions, see:

Coxall, B. and Robins, L. (1991)
*Contemporary British Politics,*
London: Macmillan.

Kingdom, J. (1991)
*Government and Politics in Britain,*
Oxford: Polity Press.

Byrne, T. (1992)
*Local Government in Britain,*
London: Penguin.

For analyses of recent conditions among local authority policy-makers, advisers and school governors respectively, see:

Hewton, E. (1986)
*Education in Recession: Crisis in County Hall and Classroom,*
London: Allen and Unwin.

Heller, H. and Edwards, P. (1992)
*Policy and Power in Education: The Rise and Fall of the LEA,*
London: Routledge.

Ranson, S. (1992)
*The Role of Local Government in Education,*
London: Longman.

Winkley, D. (1985)
*Diplomats and Detectives: LEA Advisers at Work,*
London: Robert Royce.

Kogan, M., Johnson, D., Packwood, T. and Whitaker, T. (1984)
*School Governing Bodies,*
London: Heinemann.

Deem, R., Brehony, K. and Heath, S. (1995)
*Active Citizenship and the Governing of Schools,*
Buckingham: Open University Press.                    📖 **Primary Reading 14.7**

Beckett, C., Bell, L. and Rhodes, C. (1991)
*Working with Governors in Schools: Developing a Professional Partnership,*
Buckingham: Open University Press.

# BIBLIOGRAPHY

Abbs, P. (ed.) (1987) *Living Powers: The Arts in Education*, Lewes: Falmer Press.

Abraham, J. (1995) *Divide and School: Gender and Class Dynamics in Comprehensive Education*, London: Falmer Press.

ACAS (1986) *Report of the Appraisal/Training Working Group*, London: ACAS.

Acker, S. (ed.) (1989) *Teachers, Gender and Careers*, London: Falmer Press.

Adam Smith Institute (1984) *Omega Report – Education Policy*, London: Adam Smith Institute.

Adelman, C. and Walker, R. J. (1975) *A Guide to Classroom Observation*, London: Methuen.

Adler, A. (1927) *The Practice and Theory of Individual Psychology*, New York: Harcourt.

Aggleton, P. (1987) *Rebels Without a Cause?*, London: Falmer Press.

Ainscow, M. (ed.) (1991) *Effective Schools for All*, London: David Fulton.

Aldcroft, D. H. (1992) *Education, Training and Economic Performance 1994–1990*, Manchester: Manchester University Press.

Alladina, S. and Edwards, V. (eds) (1991) *Multilingualism in the British Isles*, two volumes, London: Longman.

Altbach, P. G. and Kelly, G. P. (eds) (1986) *New Approaches to Comparative Education*, Chicago: University of Chicago.

Althusser, L. (1971) 'Ideology and the ideological state apparatuses', in Cosin, B. R. (ed.) *Education, Structure and Society*, Harmondsworth: Penguin.

Altrichter, H., Posch, P. and Somekh, B. (1993) *Teachers Investigate Their Work: An Introduction to the Methods of Action Research*, London: Routledge.

Anderson, A. J. B. (1989) *A First Course in Statistics*, London: Routledge.

Anderson, B. (1983) *Imagined Communities*, London: Verso.

Anderson, R. J., Hughes, J. A. and Sharrock, W. (1986) *Philosophy and the Human Sciences*, London: Routledge.

Anning A. (1983) 'The three year itch', *Times Educational Supplement*, 24 June.

Apple, M. (1982) *Education and Power*, London: Routledge & Kegan Paul.

Apple, M. (1988) *Teachers and Texts: A Political Economy of Class and Gender Relations in Education*, London: Routledge.

Archer, M. (1979) *The Social Origins of Educational Systems*, London: Sage Publications.

Arnold, M. (1986) *Selected Works*, Oxford: Oxford University Press.

Arnot, M. and Barton, L. (eds) (1992) *Voicing Concerns: Sociological Perspectives on Contemporary Education*, Wallington: Triangle Press.

Arnot, M. and Weiler, K. (1993) *Feminism and Social Justice in Education*, London: Falmer Press.

Ashdown, R., Carpenter, B. and Borair, K. (1991) *The Curriculum Challenge: Access to the National Curriculum for Pupils with Learning Difficulties*, London: Falmer Press.

Badderley, A. (1990) *Human Memory: Theory and Practice*, London: Allyn and Bacon.

Bagley, C. (1975) 'The background of deviance in black children in London', in Bagley, C. and Verma, G. (eds) *Race and Education Across Cultures*, London: Heinemann.

Baird, J. R. and Mitchell, I. J. (eds) (1986) *Improving the Quality of Teaching and Learning: an Australian Case Study – 'The Peel Project'*, Melbourne: Monash University.

Ball, S. J. (1981) *Beachside Comprehensive*, Cambridge: Cambridge University Press.

Ball, S. (ed.) (1984) *Comprehensive Schooling: a Reader*, Lewes: Falmer Press.

Ball, S. and Goodson, I. (eds) (1985) *Teachers' Lives and Careers*, London: Falmer Press.

Ball, S. J. (1987) *Micropolitics of the School: Towards a Theory of School Organisation*, London: Routledge.

Ball, S. J. (1990) *Politics and Policy Making in Education*, London: Routledge.

Ball, S. J. (1994) *Education Reform: A Critical and Post-structural Approach*, Milton Keynes: Open University Press.

Balshaw, M. H. (1991) *Help in the Classroom*, London: David Fulton.

Barber, M. (1991) *Education and the Teacher Unions*, London: Cassell.

Barber, M. (1996) *The Learning Game: Arguments for an Educational Revolution*, London: Gollancz.

Barker, R. G. (1978) *Habitats, Environments and Human Behaviour*, San Francisco: Jossey Bass.

Barnes, B. *et al.* (1987) *Learning Styles in TVEI: Evaluation Report No. 3*, Leeds: Leeds University MSC.

Barnes, D. (1975) *From Communication to Curriculum*, London: Penguin Books.

Barnes, D., Britton, J. and Rosen, H. (1969) *Language, the Learner and the School*, Harmondsworth: Penguin.

Barnes, D., Britton, J., Torbe, M. (1986) *Language, the Learner and the School*, third edition, revised, Harmondsworth: Penguin.

Barrow, R. and Woods, R. (1988) *An Introduction to Philosophy of Education*, London: Routledge.

Barrow, R. (1984) *Giving Teaching back to Teachers*, Brighton: Wheatsheaf.

Barth, R. S. (1990) *Improving Schools from Within*, San Francisco: Jossey Bass.

Bartholome, L. (1994) 'Beyond the methods fetish: towards a humanising pedagogy', *Harvard Education Review*, Vol. 64, No. 2, 173–93.

Barton, L., Barrett, E., Whitty, G., Miles, S. and Furlong, J. (1994) 'Teacher education and teacher professionalism in England: some emerging issues', *British Journal of Sociology of Education*, 15 (4).

Barton, L. and Lawn, M. (1980/81) 'Back inside the whale: a curriculum case study', *Interchange*, 11 (4).

Bassey, M. (1990) 'Creating education through research', *Research Intelligence Autumn*, 40–44.

Bates, I. and Riseborough, G. (eds) (1993) *Youth and Inequality*, Buckingham: Open University Press.

Bauman, Z. (1990) *Thinking Sociologically*, Oxford: Blackwell.

Beardon, T., Booth, M., Hargreaves, D. and Reiss, M. (1992) 'School-led Teacher Training: The Way Forward', *Cambridge Education Papers No. 2*, Cambridge: University of Cambridge Department of Education.

Beckett, C., Bell, L. and Rhodes, C. (1991) *Working with Governors in Schools: Developing a Professional Partnership*, Buckingham: Open University Press.

Bell, A., Crust, R., Shannon, A. and Swan, M. (1993) *Awareness of Learning, Reflection and Transfer in School Mathematics*, Shell Centre for Mathematical Education, University of Nottingham.

Bell, J. (ed.) (1995) *Teachers Talk about Teaching*, Buckingham: Open University Press.

Benn, C. and Chitty, C. (1995) *Thirty Years On: Is Comprehensive Education Alive and Well, or Struggling to Survive?*, London: David Fulton.

Benn, C. and Simon, B. (1970) *Half Way There*, Maidenhead: McGraw Hill; second edition (1972) Harmondsworth: Penguin Education.

Bennett, N. (1979) 'Recent research on teaching: a dream, a belief and a model', in Bennett, S. N. and McNamara, D. (eds) *Focus on Teaching*, London: Longman.

Bennett, N., Desforges, C., Cockburn, A. and Wilkinson, B. (1984) *The Quality of Pupil Learning Experiences*, London: Lawrence Erlbaum Associates.

Bennett, N. and Dunne, E. (1992) *Managing Classroom Groups*, Hemel Hempstead: Simon and Schuster.

Bentley, D. and Watts, M. (1992) *Communicating in School Science*, London: Falmer Press.

Benton, P. (1990) *The Oxford Internship Scheme: Integration and Partnership in Initial Teacher Education*, London: Calouste Gulbenkian Foundation.

Berger, P. L. and Luckman, T. (1967) *The Social Construction of Reality*, London: Allen Lane.

Berger, P. L. (1963) *Invitation to Sociology: a Humanistic Perspective*, New York: Doubleday.

Berlak, H. and Berlak, A. (1981) *Dilemmas of Schooling*, London: Methuen.

Bernstein, B. (1971) 'On the Classification and Framing of Educational Knowledge', in M. F. D. Young (ed.), *Knowledge and Control: New Directions for the Sociology of Education*, London: Collier Macmillan.

Best, R. (ed.) (1995) *Pastoral Care and Personal Social Education: Entitlement and Provision*, London: Cassell in association with NAPCE.

Beveridge, S. (1993) *Special Education Needs in School*, London: Routledge.

Beynon, J. (1986) *Initial Encounters in the Secondary School*, London: Falmer Press.

Biklen, S. K. (1995) *School Work: Gender and the Cultural Construction of Teaching*, New York: Teachers College Press.

Biott, C. and Easen, P. (1994) *Collaborative Learning in Staffrooms and Classrooms*, London: David Fulton.

Blair, M., Holland, J. with Sheldon, S. (eds) (1995) *Identity and Diversity: Gender and the Experience of Education*, Clevedon: Multilingual Matters in association with the Open University.

Blair, T. (1996) *New Britain: My Vision of a Young Country*, London: Fourth Estate.

Blase, J. and Anderson, G. (1995) *The Micropolitics of Educational Leadership*, London: Cassell.

Blishen, E. (1969) *The School That I'd Like*, Harmondsworth: Penguin.

Bliss, T. and Tetley, J. (1993) *Circle Time for Infant Junior and Secondary Schools*, Portishead: Lame Duck Publishing.

Bloom, B. S. (ed.) (1956) *Taxonomy of Educational Objectives: Handbook 1, Cognitive Domain*, London: Longman.

Bloom, B. S., Krathwohl, D. and Masica, B. (eds) (1964) *Taxonomy of Educational Objectives: Handbook 1, Affective Domain*, London: Longman.

Blyth, E. and Milner, J. (eds) (1996) *Exclusion from School*, London: Falmer Press.

Board of Education (1926) *The Education of the Adolescent*, Report of the Consultative Committee (The Hadow Report), London: Board of Education.

Board of Education (1931) *Report of the Consultative Committee on the Primary School*, (The Hadow Report), London: HMSO.

Boas, G. (1966) *The Cult of Childhood, Studies of the Warburg Institute: 29*, Warburg Institute, University of London.

Bolster, A. (1983) 'Towards a more effective model of research on teaching', *Harvard Educational Review*, 53 (3), 294–308.

Book Trust (1996) *School Spending on Books*, London: Book Trust.

Booth, M., Furlong, J. and Wilkin, M. (1990) *Partnership in Initial Teacher Training*, London: Cassell.

Borg, W. R. (1981) *Applying Educational Research: A Practical Guide for Teachers*, New York: Longman.

Bottery, M. (1990) *The Morality of the School*, London: Cassell.

Bourdieu, P. and Passeron, J. C. (1977) *Reproduction in Education, Society and Culture*, London: Sage.

Bourne, J. (1989) *Moving into the Mainstream, LEA Provision for Bilingual Pupils*, London: Routledge.

Bowe, R. and Ball, S. J. with Gold, A. (1992) *Reforming Education and Changing Schools*, London, Routledge.

Bowles, S. and Gintis, H. (1976) *Schooling in Capitalist America*, London: Routledge & Kegan Paul.

Boyson, R. (1975) 'Maps, chaps and your hundred best books', *Times Educational Supplement*, 17 October.

Brantlinger, E. A. (1993) *The Politics of Social Class in Secondary School: Views of Affluent and Impoverished Youth*, New York: Teachers College Press.

Breakwell, G. (1986) *Coping with Threatened Identities*, London: Methuen.

Bridges, D. and McLaughlin, T. (eds) (1994) *Education and the Market-Place*, London: Falmer Books.

Brighouse, T. (1990) *What Makes a Good School?*, Stafford: Network Educational Press.

Broadfoot, P. (ed.) (1986) *Profiles and Records of Achievement*, London: Cassell.

Broadfoot, P. (1994) 'The myth of measurement', inaugural lecture, University of Bristol.

Broadfoot, P. (1996) *Education, Assessment and Society: A Sociological Analysis*, Buckingham: Open University Press.

Broadfoot, P., Abbott, D., Croll, P., Osborn, M., Pollard, A. and Towler, L. (1991) 'Implementing national assessment: issues for primary teachers', *Cambridge Journal of Education*, Vol. 21, No. 2, 153–168.

Broadfoot, P., James, M., McMeeking, S., Nuttall, D. and Stierer, B. (1988) *Records of Achievement*, Report of the National Evaluation of Pilot Schemes, London: HMSO.

Bronfenbrenner, U. (1979) *The Ecology of Human Development; Experiments in Nature and Design*, Cambridge, Mass: Harvard University Press.

Brophy, J. E. and Good, T. L. (1974) *Teacher-Student Relationships*, New York: Cassell.

Brown, G. A. (1978) *Lecturing and Explaining*, London: Methuen.

Brown, G. A. and Edmundson, R. (1984) 'Asking Questions' in Wragg, E. C. (ed.) *Classroom Skills*, London: Croom Helm.

Brown, S. and McIntyre, D. (1993) *Making Sense of Teaching*, Buckingham: Open University Press.

Brown, S., Race, P. and Smith, B. (1996) *500 Tips on Assessment*, London: Kogan Page.

Bruner, J. S. (1966) *Towards a Theory of Instruction*, Cambridge, Massachusetts: Harvard University Press.

Bruner, J. S. (1986) *Actual Minds, Possible Worlds*, Cambridge, Massachusetts: Harvard University Press.

Bruner, J. S. (1990) *Acts of Meaning*, Cambridge, Massachusetts: Harvard University Press.

Bruner, J. S. and Haste, H. (1987) *Making Sense: The Child's Construction of the World*, London: Methuen.

Burgess, R. G. (ed.) (1982) *Field Research: A Sourcebook and Field Manual*, London: Allen & Unwin.

Burgess, R. G. (1983) *Experiencing Comprehensive Education: A Study of Bishop McGregor School*, London: Methuen.

Burgess, R. G. (1984) *In the Field: An Introduction to Field Research*, London: Allen and Unwin.

Burgess, R. G. (1986) *Sociology, Education and Schools*, London: Batsford.

Burns, R. B. (1982) *Self-concept Development and Education*, London: Routledge & Kegan Paul.

Burstall (1995) 'Leaked report Fuels A-level Fears' in *Times Educational Supplement*, 20 January.

Butterfield, S. (1995) *Educational Objectives and National Assessment*, Buckingham: Open University Press.

Button, L. (1981) *Group Tutoring for the Form Teacher: a Developmental Model, 1 Lower Secondary School*. Programmes and Working Papers, London: Hodder and Stoughton.

Button, L. (1982) *Group Tutoring for the Form Teacher: a Developmental Model, 2 Upper Secondary School*. Programmes and Working Papers, London: Hodder and Stoughton.

Buzan, T. (1984) *Using Your Memory*, London: BBC Books.

Byrne, C. J. (1983) 'Teacher Knowledge and Teacher Effectiveness', paper presented at NERA, New York State.

Byrne, E. (1978) *Women and Education*, London: Tavistock.

Byrne, T. (1992) *Local Government in Britain*, London: Penguin.

Calderhead, J. (1984) *Teachers' Classroom Decision Making*, London: Holt, Rinehart, Winston.

Calderhead, J. (ed.) (1987) *Exploring Teachers' Thinking*, London: Cassell.

Calderhead, J. (1988a) 'Learning from Introductory School Experience', *Journal of Education for Teaching*, 4 (1), 75–83.

Calderhead, J. (1988b) *Teachers' Professional Learning*, London: Falmer Press.

Caldwell, B. J. and Spinks, J. M. (1988) *The Self-managing School*, London: Falmer Press.

Callaghan, J. (1976) 'Towards a national debate', *Education*, Vol. 148, No. 1, 332–3.

Campbell, J. and Neill, S. R. St. J. (1992) *Teacher Time and Curriculum Manageability at Key Stage 1*, London: AMMA.

Campbell, R. J. and Neill, S. R. St.J. (1994) *Secondary Teachers at Work*, London: Routledge.

Canter, L. and Canter, M. (1977) *Assertive Discipline*, New York: Lee Canter Associates.

Capey, J. (1995) *GNVQ Assessment Review*, London: NCVQ.

Capra, F. (1982) 'Buddhist physics', in Kumar, S. (ed.) *The Schumacher Lectures*, London: Abacus.

Carnoy, M. and Levin, H. M. (1985) *Schooling and Work in the Democratic State*, Stanford, California: Stanford University Press.

Carr, W. and Hartnett, A. (1996) *Education and the Struggle for Democracy*, Buckingham: Open University Press.

Carr, W. and Kemmis, S. (1986) *Becoming Critical*, London: Falmer Press.

Carter, R. (ed.) (1990) *Knowledge About Language and the National Curriculum*, London: Hodder and Stoughton.

Cattell, R. B. and Kline, P. (1977) *The Scientific Analysis of Personality and Motivation*, London: Academic Press.

Cave, E. and Wilkinson, C. (1990) *Local Management of Schools: Some Practical Issues*, London: Routledge.

Cazden, C. B (1988) *Classroom Discourse: The Language of Teaching and Learning*, Portsmouth, NH: Heinemann.

Central Advisory Council for Education (England) (1967) *Children and their Primary Schools*, London: HMSO.

Centre for Educational Research and Innovation (1995) *Schools Under Scrutiny*, Paris: OECD.

Chambers, M., Jackson, A., Rose, M. (1993) *The Avon Collaborative Learning Project*, Bristol: County of Avon Advice, Monitoring and Development Service.

Child, D. (1986) *Psychology and the Teacher*, London: Cassell.

Chubb, J. and Moe, T. (1990) *Politics, Markets and America's Schools*, Washington, DC: Brookings.

Clandinin, D. J. (1986) *Classroom Practice: Teacher Images In Action*, London: Falmer Press.

Clarke, P. B. (1993) *Finding Out in Education: A Guide to Sources of Information*, London: Longman.

Claxton, G. (1989) *Being a Teacher: A Positive Approach to Change and Stress*, Buckingham: Open University Press.

Clegg, D. and Billington, S. (1994) *The Effective Primary Classroom: Management and Organisation of Teaching and Learning*, London: David Fulton.

Clough, P. and Barton, L. (1995) *Making Difficulties: Research and the Construction of SENs*, London: Paul Chapman.

Cohen, E. G. (1994) *Designing Group Work: Strategies in the Heterogeneous Classroom*, New York: Teachers College Press.

Cohen, L. (1976) *Educational Research in Classrooms and Schools: A Manual of Materials and Methods*, London: Harper & Row.

Cohen, L. and Holliday, M. (1979) *Statistics for Education*, London: Harper & Row.

Cohen, L. and Manion, L. (1990) *Research Methods in Education* (third edition), London: Croom Helm.

Cohen, S. (1972) *Folk Devils and Moral Panics*, Oxford: Martin Robinson.

Cole, M. and Walker, S. (eds) (1989) *Teaching and Stress*, Buckingham: Open University Press.

Coleman, A. M. (1994) *Companion Encyclopedia of Psychology*, London: Routledge.

Coleman, J. (ed.) (1992) *School Years: Current Issues in the Socialization of Young People*, London: Routledge.

Coleman, J. S., Coser, L. A. and Powell, W. W. (1966) *Equality of Educational Opportunity*, Washington: US Government Printing Office.

Collins, R. (1977) 'Some comparative principles of educational stratification', *Harvard Educational Review*, Vol. 47, No. 1, 1–27.

Combs, P. H. (1985) *The World Crisis in Education: The View from the Eighties*, Oxford: Oxford University Press.

Commission for Racial Equality (1987) *Learning in Terror: A Survey of Racial Harassment in Schools*, London: CRE.

Confederation of British Industry (1994) *Quality Assessed: The CBI Review of NVQs and SVQs*, London: CBI.

Connell, R. W. (1985) *Teachers' Work*, London: Allen & Unwin.

Connell, R. W., Ashden, D. J., Kessler, S. and Dowsett, G. W. (1982) *Making the Difference: Schools, Families and Social Divisions*, Sydney: Allen & Unwin.

Connelly, F. M. and Clandinin, D. J. (1988) *Teachers as Curriculum Planners*, New York: Teachers College Press.

Connor, M. (1990) *Secondary Education*, London: Cassell.

Consortium on Assessment and Testing in Schools (1992) *Evaluation of Key Stage 3 Tests*, London: CATS.

Cook, C. (1994) *Assessor Workbook*, London: Macmillan.

Cooper, P. (1993) *Effective Schools for Disaffected Students*, London: Routledge.

Cooper, P. and McIntyre, D. (1996) *Effective Teaching and Learning: Teachers' and Students' Perspectives*, Buckingham: Open University Press.

Corbett, H. D. and Wilson, B. L. (1991) 'Unintended and unwelcome: the local impact of state testing', in Niblett, G. W. and Fink, W. T. A. (eds) *Testing, Reform and Rebellion*, New York: Ablex Publishing Corporation.

Corrigan, P. (1979) *Schooling the Smash Street Kids*, London: Routledge.

Council of Europe (1953) *The European Convention on Human Rights*, Strasbourg: Council of Europe.

Council of Europe (1985) *Teaching and Learning about Human Rights in Schools*, Recommendation No. R (85) 7 of the Committee of Ministers to Member States, Strasbourg: Council of Europe.

Covington, M. and Beery, R. (1978) *Self Worth and School Learning*, New York: Holt, Rinehart and Winston.

Cox, C. B. and Dyson, A. E. (eds) (1969) *Fight for Education: A Black Paper*, London: Critical Quarterly Society.

Cox, C. B. and Marks, J. (eds) (1982) *The Right to Learn*, London: Centre for Policy Studies.

Coxall, B. and Robins, L. (1991) *Contemporary British Politics*, London: Macmillan.

Cranfield, J. and Wells, H. (1976) *100 Ways to Enhance Self-concept in the Classroom*, Englewood Cliffs, NJ: Prentice-Hall.

Croll, P. (1986) *Systematic Classroom Observation*, London: Falmer Press.

Croll, P. (1990) *Norm and Criterion Referenced Assessment*, Redland papers, 1, Summer, 8–11, Bristol: Bristol Polytechnic.

Crombie White, R., Pring, R. and Brockington, D. (1995) *14–19 Education and Training: Implementing a Unified System of Learning*, Royal Society of Arts.

Cruickshank, D. R., Bainer, D. and Metcalf, K. (1995) *The Act of Teaching*, New York: McGraw-Hill.

Cullingford, C. (1991) *The Inner World of the School*, London: Cassell.

Dahllof, U. and Lundgren, U. P. (1970) *Macro- and Micro Approaches Combined for Curriculum Process Analysis*, Goteborg, Sweden: University of Goteborg, Institute of Education.

Dale, R. (1996) *Mechanisms of Differentiation Between Schools: the Four 'Ms'*, Mimeo, Auckland: University of Auckland.

Daniels, H. (1996) *An Introduction to Vygotsky*, London: Routledge.

Darling-Hammond, L., Ancess, J. and Falk, B. (1995) *Authentic Assessment in Action: Studies of Schools and Students at Work*, New York: Teachers College Press.

Daugherty, R. (1995) *National Curriculum Assessment: A Review of Policy, 1987–1994,* London: Falmer Press.

Davies, L. (1979) 'Deadlier than the Male? Girls' conformity and deviance in school', in Barton, L. and Meighan, R. (eds) *Schools, Pupils and Deviance,* Driffield: Nafferton.

Davies, L. (1984) *Pupil Power: Deviance and Gender in School,* London: Falmer Press.

De Bono, E. (1972) *Children Solve Problems,* London: Penguin Education.

Dean, J. (1996) *Beginning Teaching in the Secondary School,* Buckingham: Open University Press.

Dearden, R. F. (1968) *The Philosophy of Primary Education,* London: Routledge & Kegan Paul.

Dearing, R. (1993) *The National Curriculum and its Assessment: Final Report,* London: SCAA.

Dearing, R. (1996) *Review of Qualifications for 16–19 Year Olds: Full Report,* London: SCAA.

Deem, R. (1994) 'School governing bodies: public concerns and private interests', in Scott, D. (ed.) *Accountability and Control in Educational Settings,* London: Cassell.

Deem, R., Brehony, K. and Heath, S. (1995) *Active Citizenship and the Governing of Schools,* Buckingham: Open University Press.

Delamont, S. (1983) *Interaction in the Classroom* (second edition), London: Methuen. Reprinted 1990, London: Routledge.

Delamont, S. (ed.) (1984) *Readings on Interaction in the Classroom,* London: Methuen.

Delamont, S. and Galton, M. (1986) *Inside the Secondary Classroom,* London: Routledge.

Denscombe, M. (1980) 'Keeping 'em quiet: the significance of noise for the practical activity of teaching', in Woods, P. (ed.) *Teacher Strategies,* London: Croom Helm.

Denscombe, M. (1985) *Classroom Control: a Sociological Perspective,* London: George, Allen and Unwin.

Department for Education (1994) *Code of Practice for Special Educational Needs,* London: HMSO.

Department of Education and Science/Welsh Office (1989) *Discipline in Schools,* Report of the Committee of Enquiry chaired by Lord Elton, London: HMSO.

Department for Education/Welsh Office (1992) *Initial Teacher Training (Secondary Phase),* DFE Circular 9/92, WO Circular 35/92, London: DFE.

Department for Education and Employment (1996a) *Competitiveness: Creating the Enterprise Centre of Europe,* London: HMSO.

Department for Education and Employment (1996b) *Learning to Compete: Education and Training for 14–19 Year Olds,* London: HMSO.

Department for Education and Employment (1996c) *Setting Targets to Raise Standards: A Survey of Good Practice,* London: DFEE.

Department of Education and Science (1975) *A Language for Life (The Bullock Report),* London, HMSO.

Department of Education and Science (1977) *Curriculum 11–16,* London: HMSO.

Department of Education and Science (1984) *Records of Achievement: A Statement of Policy,* London: DES.

Department of Education and Science (1985a) *Better Schools: A Summary,* London: HMSO.

Department of Education and Science (1985b) *The Curriculum from 5 to 16,* HMI, Curriculum Matters Series, London: HMSO.

Department of Education and Science (1987) *The National Curriculum 5–16: A Discussion Document,* London: HMSO.

Department of Education and Science (1988a) *Advancing A-levels,* London: HMSO.

Department of Education and Science (1988b) *The Kingman Report: Report of the Committee of Enquiry into the Teaching of the English Language,* London: HMSO.

Department of Education and Science (1990–1) *Language in the National Curriculum (LINC): Materials for Professional Development,* London: HMSO.

Department of Education and Science (1991a) *Education Statistics for the United Kingdom,* London: HMSO.

Department of Education and Science (1991b) *The Parent's Charter,* London, Department of Education and Science.

Department of Education and Science (1992) *Choice and Diversity: A New Framework for Schools*, London, HMSO.

Desforges, C. (1989) *Testing and Assessment*, London: Cassell.

Dewey, J. (1902) 'The Child and the Curriculum' in Boydston, J. (ed.) *John Dewey: The Middle Works*, Vol. 2, Carbondale: Southern Illinois University Press.

Dewey, J. (1916) *Democracy and Education*, New York: Free Press.

Dewey, J. (1933) *How We Think: A Restatement of the Relation of Reflective Thinking to the Educative Process*, Chicago: Henry Regnery.

Dickinson, C. and Wright, J. (1993) *Differentiation: A Practical Handbook of Classroom Strategies*, Coventry: National Council for Educational Technology.

Dickson, W. P. (ed.) (1981) *Children's Oral Communication Skills*, New York: Academic Press.

Dillon, J. (1983) 'Problem solving and findings', *Journal of Creative Behaviour*, Vol. 16, No. 2, 97–111.

Dillon, J. T. (1994) *Using Discussion in Classrooms*, Buckingham: Open University Press.

Docking, J. (1996) *National School Policy: Major Issues in Education Policy for Schools in the UK*, London: David Fulton.

Donald, J. and Rattansi, A. (eds) (1992) *'Race', Culture and Difference*, London: Sage.

Donaldson, M. (1978) *Children's Minds*, Glasgow: Collins/Fontana.

Doyle, W. and Ponder, C. A. (1976) 'The Practicality Ethic in Teacher Decision-Making', *Interchange* 8.

Doyle, W. (1977) 'Learning the classroom environment: an ecological analysis', *Journal of Teacher Education*, Vol. XXVIII, No. 6, 51–54.

Doyle, W. (1986) 'Classroom organisation and management', in Wittrock, M. C. (ed.) *Handbook of Research on Teaching* (third edition), New York: Macmillan.

Doyle, W. and Carter, K. (1984) 'Academic Tasks in Classrooms', in *Curriculum Inquiry* 14, 129–49.

Doyle, W., Sanford, J. P., Schmidt French, B. S., Emmer, E. T. and Clements, B. S. (1985) *Patterns of Academic Work in Junior High School Science, English and Mathematics Classes: a Final Report*, Austin, Texas: University of Texas, Research and Development Centre for Teacher Education.

Drew, D. and Gray, J. (1990) 'The fifth year examination achievements of Black young people in England and Wales', *Educational Research*, 32 (3), 107–17.

Dreyfus, S. E. (1981) *Four Models v. Human Situational Understanding*, US Air Force, Office of Scientific Research.

Duncan, C. (1989) *Pastoral Care: An Antiracist/Multicultural Perspective*, Oxford: Blackwell.

Dunford, J. (1995) '14–19 Education: a coherent approach', in *Forum*, Vol. 37, No. 2.

Dunham, J. (1992) *Stress in Teaching*, London: Routledge.

Dunkin, M. J. and Biddle, B. J. (1974) *The Study of Teaching*, Holt, Rinehart and Winston.

Dunn, J. (1988) *The Beginnings of Social Understanding*, Oxford: Blackwell.

Dunsbee, T. and Ford, T. (1980) *Mark My Words*, London: NATE and Ward Lock.

Dweck, C. and Bempechat, J. (1983) 'Children's theories of intelligence: consequences for learning', in Paris, S. G., Olson, G. M. and Stevenson, H. W. (eds), *Learning and Motivation in the Classroom*, Hillsdale, NJ: Lawrence Erlbaum Associates.

Dweck, C. S., (1986) 'Motivational processes affecting learning', *American Psychologist*, October, 1040–46.

Easen, P. (1985) *Making School-Centred INSET Work*, London: Croom Helm.

Eckert, P. (1989) *Jocks and Burnouts: Social Categories and Identity in the High School*, New York: Teachers College Press.

Ede, J. and Wilkinson, J. (1980) *Talking, Listening and Learning*, London: Longman.

Edwards, A. D. and Furlong, V. J. (1978) *The Language of Teaching: Meaning in Classroom Interaction*, London: Heinemann.

Edwards, A. D. and Westgate, D. P. G. (1987) *Investigating Classroom Talk*, London: Falmer Press.

Edwards, D. and Mercer, N. (1987) *Common Knowledge: The Development of Understanding in Classrooms*, London: Methuen.

Edwards, V. (1983) *Language in the Multicultural Classroom*, London: Batsford.

Egan, M. and Bunting, B. (1991) 'The effects of coaching on 11+ scores', *British Journal of Educational Psychology*, Vol. 61, No. 1, 85–91.

Eisenhart, M., Behm, L. and Riomagnano, L. (1991) 'Learning to Teach: Developing Expertise of Rite of Passage?', *Journal of Education for Teaching*, 7 (1).

Eisner, E. (1994) *Cognition and Curriculum Reconsidered*, New York: Teachers College Press.

Eisner, E.W. (1967) 'Educational Objectives: Help or Hindrance?', *School Review*, 75, 200–60.

Eisner, E. W. (1979) *The Educational Imagination*, New York: Macmillan.

Eisner, E. W. and Vallance, E. (eds) (1974) *Competing Conceptions of the Curriculum*, Berkeley: McCutchan.

Elbaz, F. (1983) *Teacher Thinking: a Study of Practical Knowledge*, London: Croom Helm.

Elliott, J. (1990) 'Competency Based Training and the Education of the Professions: Is a Happy Marriage Possible?' Unpublished paper, Norwich: University of East Anglia, Centre for Applied Research in Education.

Elliott, J. (1991) *Action Research for Educational Change*, Buckingham: Open University Press.

Elliott, J. (1996) *Changing Curriculum*, Buckingham: Open University Press.

Elliott, J. and Adelman, C. (1973) 'Reflecting where the action is; the design of the Ford Teaching Project', *Education for Teaching*, 9 (2), 8–20.

Elliott, M. (ed.) (1992) *Bullying: A Practical Guide to Coping for Schools*, London: Longman.

Ely, M. (1990) *Doing Qualitative Research: Circles within Circles*, London: Falmer Press.

Entwistle, H. (1970) *Child-centred Education*, London: Methuen.

Entwistle, N. (ed.) (1985) *New Directions in Educational Psychology: Learning and Teaching*, London: Falmer Press.

Entwistle, N. (1987) *Understanding Classroom Learning*, London: Hodder and Stoughton.

Epstein, D. (1993) *Changing Classroom Cultures: Anti-racism, Politics and Schools*, Stoke-on-Trent: Trentham Books.

Ernest, P. (1991) 'Does the National Curriculum in mathematics need revising?', *Research Intelligence*, Autumn, British Educational Research Association, 49–50.

Etzioni A. (1996) *A Comparative Analysis of Complex Organisations*, New York: Free Press of Glencoe.

Evans, J. (1985) *Teaching in Transition: The Challenge of Mixed-ability Grouping*, Buckingham, Open University Press.

Evans, K. M. (1962) *Sociometry and Education*, London: Routledge & Kegan Paul.

Everard, B. and Morris, G. (1996) *Effective School Management*, London: Paul Chapman.

Evetts, J. (1990) *Women in Primary Teaching: Career, Contexts and Strategy*, London: Routledge.

Evetts, J. (1995) *Becoming a Secondary Headteacher*, London: Cassell.

Eysenck, H. J. and Cookson, D. (1969) 'Personality in primary school children, I: Ability and achievement', *British Journal of Educational Psychology*, No. 39, 109–22.

Farmer, A., Cowin, M., Freeman, L., James, M., Drent, A. and Arthur, R. (1991) *Positive School Discipline: A Practical Guide to Developing Policy*, London: Longman.

Filer, A. (1993) 'Contexts of assessment in a primary classroom', *British Educational Research Journal*, Vol. 19, No. 1, 95–108.

Filer, A. (1995) 'Teacher assessment: social process and social product', *Assessment in Education*, Vol. 2, No. 1, 23–38.

Finegold, D., Keep, E., Milibrand, D., Spours, K. and Young, M. (1990) *A British Baccalaureate: Ending the Divisions Between Education and Training*, Institute for Public Policy Research.

Fink, A. and Kosecoff, J. (1986) *How to Conduct Surveys: A Step by Step Guide*, London: Sage.

Fitz, J., Halpin, D. and Power, S. (1993) *Grant-Maintained Schools: Education in the Marketplace*, London: Kogan Page.

Fitz-Gibbon, C. T. (1995) *Monitoring Education: Indicators, Quality and Effectiveness*, London: Cassell.

Flanders, N. (1970) *Analysing Teaching Behaviour*, Reading, Massachusetts: Addison-Wesley.

Flavell, J. H. (1979) 'Metacognition and Cognitive Monitoring', *American Psychologist*, 34 (10), 906–11.

Flude, M. and Hammer, M. (1990) *The Education Reform Act 1988*, London: Falmer Press.

Fontana, D. (1986) *Classroom Control: Understanding and Guiding Classroom Behaviour*, London: Routledge.

Fontana, D. (1988) *Psychology for Teachers*, London: Macmillan.

Franklin, B. and Hammarberg, T. (1995) *The Handbook of Children's Rights: Comparative Legislation and Practice*, London: Routledge.

Fraser, B. J. (1986) *Classroom Environment*, London: Croom Helm.

Fraser, B. J. and Walberg, H. J. (eds) (1991) *Educational Environments: Evaluation, Antecedents and Consequences*, London: Pergamon Press.

Freeman, J. (1991) *Gifted Children Growing Up*, London: Cassell.

Freeman, P. L. (1986) 'Don't talk to me about lexical meta-analysis of criterion-referenced clustering and lap-dissolve spatial transformations: a consideration of the role of practising teachers in educational research', *British Education Research Journal*, Vol. 12, No. 2, 197–206.

Fullan, M. (1991) *The New Meaning of Educational Change*, London: Cassell.

Fullan, M. and Hargreaves, A. (1992) *What's Worth Fighting for in Your School?*, Buckingham: Open University Press.

Fullan, M. G. (1992) *Successful School Improvement*, Buckingham: Open University Press.

Fullan, M. G. (1993) *Change Forces*, London: Falmer Press.

Fuller, M. (1980) 'Black girls in a London comprehensive school', in Deem, R. (ed.) *Schooling for Women's Work*, London: Routledge.

Furlong, J. (1996) 'Do Student Teachers Need Higher Education?', in Furlong, J. and Smith, R. (eds) (1996) *The Role of Higher Education in Initial Teacher Education*, London: Kogan Page.

Furlong, J., Hirst, P. H., Pocklington, K. and Miles, S. (1988) *Initial Teacher Training and the Role of the School*, Buckingham: Open University Press.

Furlong, J. and Maynard, T. (1995) *Mentoring Student Teachers: The Growth of Professional Knowledge*, London: Routledge.

Furlong, J. and Smith, R. (eds) (1996) *The Role of Higher Education in Initial Teacher Training*, London: Kogan Page.

Furlong, J., Whitty, G., Barrett, E., Barton, L. and Miles, S. (1994a) 'Integration and Partnership in Initial Teacher Education – Dilemmas and Possibilities', *Research Papers in Education*, Vol. 9 (3), 281–301.

Furlong, J., Wilkin, M., Maynard, T. and Miles, S. (1994b) *The Active Mentoring Programme*, Cambridge: George Pearson Publishing.

Furlong, V. J. (1985) *The Deviant Pupil*, Buckingham: Open University Press.

Gage, N. L. and Berliner, D. C. (1975) *Educational Psychology*, Chicago: Rand McNally.

Gagné, R. M. (1965) *The Conditions of Learning*, New York: Holt Rinehart and Winston.

Galloway, D. (1990) *Pupil Welfare and Counselling: an Approach to PSE across the Curriculum*, London: Longman.

Galloway, D. and Edwards, A. (1992), *Secondary School Teaching and Educational Psychology*, London: Longman.

Galton, M. and Williamson, J. (1992) *Groupwork in the Primary Classroom*, London: Routledge.

Galton, M., Simon, B. and Croll, P. (1980) *Inside the Primary Classroom*, London: Routledge & Kegan Paul.

Gamble, A. (1986) 'The political economy of freedom', in Levitas, R. (ed.) *The Ideology of the New Right*, Oxford: Polity Press.

Gardner, H. (1985) *Frames of Mind: The Theory of Multiple Intelligences*, London: Paladin Books.

Gardner, H. (1993) *The Unschooled Mind*, London: Fontana.

Gardner, H. (1995) 'Machines of the Brain', *Times Educational Supplement*, 17 March.

Gardner, P. (1993) 'The Early History of School Based Teacher Training' in McIntyre, D., Hagger, H. and Wilkin, M. (eds) *Mentoring: Perspectives on School Based Teacher Education*, London: Kogan Page.

Gardner, P. (1996) 'Higher Education and Teacher Training: A Century of Progress and Promise' in Furlong, J. and Smith, R. (eds) *The Role of Higher Education in Initial Teacher Training*, London: Kogan Page.

Gewirtz, S., Ball, S. J. and Bowe, R. (1995) *Markets, Choice and Equity in Education*, Buckingham: Open University Press.

Gibbs, G. and Habeshaw, T. (1989) *253 Ideas for Your Teaching*, Bristol: Technical and Educational Services Ltd.

Gibson, J. (1996) *All You Need to Know About GNVQs*, London: Kogan Page.

Giddens, A. (1989) *Sociology*, Oxford: Polity Press.

Gillborn, D. (1995) *Racism and Antiracism in Real Schools*, Buckingham: Open University Press.

Gillborn, D. and Gipps, C. (1996) *Recent Research on the Achievement of Ethnic Minority Pupils*, an OFSTED Research Review, London: HMSO.

Ginsberg, H. and Opper, S. (1969) *Piaget's Theory of Intellectual Development*, New York: Prentice Hall.

Gipps, C. (1990) *Assessment: A Teacher's Guide to the Issues*, London: Hodder and Stoughton.

Gipps, C. (1994) *Beyond Testing: Towards a Theory of Educational Assessment*, London: Falmer Press.

Gipps, C. and Murphy, P. (1994) *A Fair Test? Assessment, Achievement and Equity*, Buckingham: Open University Press.

Gipps, C., Steadman, S., Blackstone, T. and Stierer, B. (1983) *Testing Children: Standardised Testing in LEAs and Schools*, London: Heinemann.

Glaser, B. and Strauss, A. (1967) *The Discovery of Grounded Theory*, Chicago: Aldine.

Glass, G. V., Cahan, L. S., Smith, M. and Filby, N. (1979) *School Class Size, Research and Policy*, Beverley Hills: Sage.

Glatter, R., Woods, P. and Bagley, C. (eds) (1996) *Choice and Diversity in Schooling: Perspectives and Prospects*, London: Routledge.

Glover, L. (1995) *GNVQ into Practice*, London: Cassell.

Gold, A. (1996) *Managing a Department*, London: Heinemann.

Gold, Y. and Roth, R. (1994) *Teachers Managing Stress and Preventing Burnout*, London: Falmer Press.

Goldthorpe, J. H. (1987) *Social Mobility and Class Structure in Modern Britain*, Oxford: Oxford University Press.

Good, F. and Cresswell, M. (1988) *Grading the GCSE*, London: Secondary Examinations Council.

Goodson, I. F. (1984) *Social Histories of Secondary Curriculum: Subjects for Study*, Lewes: Falmer Press.

Goodson, I. F. (1992) *Studying Teachers' Lives*, London: Routledge.

Goodson, I. F. (1994) *Studying Curriculum: Cases and Methods*, Buckingham: Open University Press.

Goodson, I. F. and Walker, R. (eds) (1991) *Biography, Identity and Schooling*, London: Falmer Press.

Goodson, I. and Marsh, C. J. (1996) *Studying School Subjects: A Guide*, London: Falmer Press.

Gordon, T. (1974) *Teacher Effectiveness Training*, NewYork: Peter H. Wyden.

Grace, G. (1978) *Teachers, Ideology and Control*, London: Routledge and Kegan Paul.

Grace, G. (1985) 'Judging teachers; the social and political contexts of teacher evaluation', *British Journal of Sociology of Education*, Vol. 6, No. 1, 3–16.

Graddul, D., Cheshire, J. and Swann, J. (1987) *Describing Language*, Buckingham: Open University Press.

Gramsci, A. (1978) *Selections from Political Writings*, Vols 1 and 2, London: Lawrence and Wishart.

Gray, J. and Wilcox, B. (1995) *'Good School, Bad School': Evaluating Performance and Encouraging Improvement*, Buckingham: Open University Press.

Gray, J., McPherson, A. F. and Raffe, D. (1982) *The Reconstructions of Secondary Education: Theory, Myth and Practice Since the War*, London: Routledge.

Green, A. (1990) *Education and State Formation*, London: Macmillan.

Grieve, R. and Hughes, M. (1990) *Understanding Children*, Oxford: Blackwell.

Griffin, C. (1985) *Typical Girls? Young Women from School to the Job Market*, London: Routledge.

Griffiths, M. (1995) *Feminism and the Self: The Web of Identity*, London: David Fulton.

Griffiths, M. and Davies, C. (1995) *In Fairness to Children*, London: David Fulton.

Gross, M. (1992) *Exceptionally Gifted Children*, London: Routledge.

Hagger, H., Burn, K. and McIntyre, D. (1993) *The School Mentor Handbook*, London: Kogan Page.

Hall, E. and Hall, C. (1988) *Human Relations in Education*, London: Routledge.

Hall, S. and Jefferson, T. (eds) (1976) *Resistance Through Rituals: Youth Sub-Cultures in Post-War Britain*, London: Unwin Hyman. Originally published (1975) as a Working Paper, Centre for Contemporary Cultural Studies, University of Birmingham.

Hall, V. (1996) *Dancing on the Ceiling: A Study of Women Managers in Education*, London: Paul Chapman.

Halpin, D., Fitz, J. and Power, S. (1993) *The Early Impact and Long-term Implications of the Grant-Maintained Schools Policy*, Stoke-on-Trent: Trentham Books.

Halsey, A. H. (1986) *Change in British Society*, Oxford: Oxford University Press.

Halsey, A. H., Heath, A. F. and Ridge, J. M. (1980) *Origins and Destinations*, Oxford: Oxford University Press.

Hamilton, D. (1977) *In Search of Structure*, Edinburgh: Scottish Council for Research in Education.

Hammersley, M. (1986) *Controversies in Classroom Research*, Buckingham: Open University Press.

Hammersley, M. and Atkinson, P. (1984) *Ethnography: Principles in Practice*, London: Tavistock.

Hampson, S. E. (1988) *The Construction of Personality: An Introduction*, London: Routledge.

Hansen, D. T. (1995) *The Call to Teach*, New York: Teachers College Press.

Hargreaves, A. and Fullan, M. G. (eds) (1992) *Understanding Teacher Development*, London: Cassell.

Hargreaves, A. (1978) 'Towards a theory of classroom coping strategies', in Barton, L. and Meighan, R. (eds), *Sociological Interpretations of Schooling*, Driffield: Nafferton Books.

Hargreaves, A. (1989) *Curriculum and Assessment Reform*, Buckingham: Open University Press.

Hargreaves, A. (1991) 'Cultures of teaching', in Hargreaves, A. and Fullan, M. G. (eds) (1992) *Understanding Teacher Development*, London: Cassell.

Hargreaves, A. (1994) *Changing Teachers, Changing Times: Teachers' Work and Culture in the Postmoderm Age*, New York: Teachers College Press.

Hargreaves, D. H. (1967) *Social Relations in a Secondary School*, London: Routledge & Kegan Paul.

Hargreaves, D. H. (1972) *Interpersonal Relationships and Education*, London: Routledge & Kegan Paul.

Hargreaves, D. H. (1982) *The Challenge for the Comprehensive School: Culture, Curriculum and Community*, London: Routledge & Kegan Paul.

Hargreaves, D. H. (1996) 'Teaching as a research-based profession: possibilities and prospects', Teacher Training Agency Annual Lecture, London: TTA.

Hargreaves, D. H. and Hopkins, D. (1991) *The Empowered School: The Management and Practice of Development Planning*, London: Cassell.

Hargreaves, D. H. and Hopkins, D. (eds) (1994) *Development Planning for School Improvement*, London: Cassell.

Hargreaves, D. H., Hestor, S. K., and Mellor, F. J. (1975) *Deviance in Classrooms*, London: Routledge & Kegan Paul.

Harlen, W., Broadfoot, P., Gipps, C. and Nuttall, D. (1992) 'Assessment and the improvement of education', *The Curriculum Journal*, Vol. 3, No. 3, 215–30.

Harré, R. (1972) *The Philosophies of Science*, Oxford: Oxford University Press.

Harris, A., Jamieson, I. and Russ, J. (1995) 'Characteristics of successful departments in secondary schools', *School Organisation*, Vol. 15, No. 3.

Harris, J. M. (1995) *Presentation Skills for Teachers*, London: Kogan Page.

Hart, S. (1996) (ed.) *Differentiation and the Secondary Curriculum*, London: Routledge.

Hartley, D. (1985) *Understanding the Primary School*, London: Croom Helm.

Hashweh, M. Z. (1985) 'An exploratory study of teacher knowledge and teaching', cited in Wilson, S., Shulman, L. and Richert, A. '150 different ways of knowing: representations of knowledge in teaching', in Calderhead, J. (ed.) *Exploring Teachers' Thinking*, London: Cassell.

Haviland, J. (1988) *Take Care, Mr Baker!*, London: Fourth Estate.

Hawthorne, R. K. (1992) *Curriculum in the Making: Teacher Choice and the Classroom Experience*, New York: Teachers College Press.

Haydon, G. (1996) *Teaching About Values: a Practical Approach*, London: Cassell.

Hazler, R. J. (1996) *Breaking the Cycle of Violence*, London: Taylor and Francis.

Heilbronn, R. and Jones, C. (1996) *The Quality of Our Learning: Beginning Teachers and Staff Development in an Urban Comprehensive*, Stoke-on-Trent: Trentham Books.

Heller, H. and Edwards, P. (1992) *Policy and Power in Education: The Rise and Fall of the LEA*, London: Routledge.

Hendry, L. (1993) *Young People's Leisure and Lifestyles*, London: Routledge.

Hendry, L., Sanders, D. and Glendinning, A. (1996) *New Perspectives on Disaffection*, London: Cassell.

Henry, M., Taylor, S., Knight, J. and Lingard, R. (1990) *Understanding Schooling*, London: Routledge.

Her Majesty's Inspectors (1978) *Mixed Ability Work in Comprehensive Schools*, London: HMSO.

Her Majesty's Inspectors/DES (1992) *Education of Very Able Children in Maintained Schools; A Review*, London, HMSO.

Her Majesty's Inspectors/Scottish Education Department (1990) *Management of Education Resources 4. Curriculum, Staffing and Timetabling: A Commentary on Aspects of Secondary School Management*, Edinburgh: HMSO.

Her Majesty's Inspectors/Scottish Office Education and Industry Department (1995) *Achievement for All: A Report on Selection Within Schools*, Edinburgh: HMSO.

Hewett, P. (1993) *About Time: The Revolution in Work and Family Life*, London: River Oram Press.

Hewton, E. (1986) *Education in Recession: Crisis in County Hall and Classroom*, London: Allen and Unwin.

Hextall, I., Lawn, M., Menter, I., Sidgwick, S. and Walker, S. (1991), 'Imaginative projects: arguments for a new teacher education', *Evaluation and Research in Education*, Vol. 5, Nos. 1 and 2, 79–95.

Hey, V. (1996) *The Company She Keeps: an Ethnography of Girls' Friendships*, Buckingham: Open University Press.

Higham, J., Sharp, P. and Yeomans, D. (1996) *The Emerging 16–19 Curriculum: Policy and Provision*, London: David Fulton.

Hillgate Group (1986) *Whose Schools? A Radical Manifesto,* London: Hillgate Group.

Hillgate Group (1987) *The Reform of British Education*, London: Hillgate Group.

Hilsum, S. and Strong, C. (1978) *The Secondary Teacher's Day*, Windsor: NFER.

Hirst, P. (1967) 'The logical and physiological aspects of teaching a subject', in Peters, R. (ed.) *The Concept of Education*, London: Routledge & Kegan Paul.

Hitchcock, G. (1986) *Profiles and Profiling*, London: Longman.

Hitchcock, G. and Hughes, D. (1995) *Research and the Teacher: A Qualitative Introduction to School-Based Research*, London: Routledge.

Hodgson, A. and Spours, K. (eds) (1997) *Dearing and Beyond: 14–19 Qualifications, Frameworks and Systems*, London: Kogan Page.

Hodgson, N. (1988) *Classroom Display: Improving the Visual Environment in Schools*, Diss: Tarquin.

Holt, J. (1982) *How Children Fail*, London: Penguin.

Hopkins, D. (1986) *A Teacher's Guide to Classroom Research*, Buckingham: Open University Press.

Hopkins, D. and Bollington, R. (1989) 'Teacher appraisal for professional development: a review of research', *Cambridge Journal of Education*, Vol. 19, No. 2, 165–79.

Hopkins, D., Ainscow, M. and West, M. (1994) *School Improvement in an Era of Change*, London: Cassell.

Howe, M. J. A. (1990) *The Origins of Exceptional Abilities*, London: Basil Blackwell.

Howe, M. J. A. (1991) Review of Richardson, K. 1991, 'Understanding Intelligence', *British Journal of Educational Psychology*, Vol. 61, Part 3, 382–3.

Hoyle, E. (1986) *The Politics of School Management*, London: Hodder and Stoughton.

Hoyle, E. and John, P. (1995) *Professional Knowledge and Professional Practice*, London: Cassell.

Huberman, M. (1993) *The Lives of Teachers*, New York: Teachers College Press.

Hughes, M. (ed.) (1994) *Perceptions of Teaching and Learning*, Clevedon: Multilingual Matters.

Humphreys, T. (1995) *A Different Kind of Teacher*, London: Cassell.

Humphries, S. (1982) *Hooligans or Rebels?*, Oxford: Blackwell.

Husen, T., Tuijnman, A. and Halls, W. D. (eds) (1992) *Schooling in Modern European Society*, London: Pergamon.

Hustler, D. and McIntyre, D. (1996) *Developing Competent Teachers: Approaches to Professional Competence in Teacher Education*, London: David Fulton.

Hustler, D., Cassidy, T. and Cuff, T. (eds) (1986) *Action Research in Schools and Classrooms*, London: Allen & Unwin.

Hutton, W. (1995) *The State We're In*, London: Cape.

Hyland, T. (1994) *Competence, Education and NVQs*, London: Cassell.

Ingram, J. and Worrall, N. (1993) *Teacher-Child Partnership: The Negotiating Classroom*, London: David Fulton.

Inhelder, B. and Piaget, J. (1958) *The Growth of Logical Thinking from Childhood to Adolescence*, London: Routledge.

Inner London Education Authority (1987) *Language Courses*, London: ILEA Research and Statistics.

Irving, A. (1996) *Study and Information Skills Across the Curriculum*, London: Heinemann.

Jackson, B. and Marsden, D. (1962) *Education and the Working Class*, London: Ark.

Jackson, P. W. (1968) *Life in Classrooms,* New York: Holt, Rinehart and Winston.

James, A. and Prout, A. (eds) (1990) *Constructing and Reconstructing Childhood: Contemporary Issues in the Sociological Study of Childhood*, London: Falmer Press.

James, D. (1996) 'Mature studentship in HE: beyond a "species" approach', in *British Journal of Sociology of Education*, Vol. 16, No. 4, 451–66.

Jencks C. *et al.* (1972) *Inequality: a Reassessment of the Effect of Family and Schooling in America*, New York: Basic Books.

Jenkins, D. (1973) 'Integrated Studies Project', in *Evaluation in Curriculum Development: Twelve Case Studies*, Schools Council Research Studies, London: Macmillan Education for the Schools Council.

John, P. D. (1993) *Lesson Planning for Teachers*, London: Cassell.

Johnson, D. W. and Johnson, R. (1982) *Joining Together Group Theory and Groups Skills*, Englewood Cliffs, NJ: Prentice Hall.

Johnson, L. (1993) *The Modern Girl: Girlhood and Growing Up*, Buckingham: Open University Press.

Jones, B. (1986) 'Politics and the pupil', *Times Educational Supplement*, 30 May.

Jones, K. (1989) *Right Turn: the Conservative Revolution in Education*, London: Hutchinson Radius.

Jones, K. and Charlton, T. (1992) *Learning Difficulties in the Primary Classroom*, London: Routledge.

Jowett, S. and Baginsky, M. (1991) *Building Bridges: Parental Involvement in Schools*, London: Routledge.

Kagan, J. *et al.* (1964) 'Information processing in the child: significance and reflective attitudes', *Psychological Monographs*, No. 78.

Kay-Shuttleworth J. (1868) *Memorandum on Popular Education* (1969 edition), London: Woburn Books.

Keddie, N. (1971) 'Classroom Knowledge' in Young, M. F. D.(ed.) *Knowledge and Control: New Directions for the Sociology of Education*, London: Collier Macmillan.

Kegan, R. (1982) *The Evolving Self: Problem and Process in Human Development*, London: Harvard University Press.

Kelly, A. V. (1978) *Mixed-ability Grouping: Theory and Practice*, London: Harper and Row.

Kemmis, S. and McTaggert, R. (1981) *The Action Research Planner*, Victoria: Deakin University.

Kerckhoff, A. *et al.* (1996) *Going Comprehensive in England and Wales*, Woburn Press.

Kerry, T. (1984) 'Analyzing the Cognitive Demand made by Classroom Tasks in Mixed Ability Classes', in Wragg, E. C. (ed.) *Classroom Teaching Skills*, London: Croom Helm.

Kerry, T. and Sands, M. K. (1984) 'Classroom Organization and Learning', in Wragg, E. C. (ed.) *Classroom Teaching Skills*, London: Croom Helm.

Kerry, T. and Shelton Mayes, A. (eds) (1995) *Issues in Mentoring*, London: Routledge.

Keys, W and Fernandes, C. (1993) *What Do Students Think About School? Research into the Factors Associated with Positive and Negative Attitudes to School and Education*, Slough: NFER.

Kingdom, J. (1991) *Government and Politics in Britain*, Oxford: Polity Press.

Klein, G. (1993) *Education Towards Race Equality*, London: Cassell.

Kleinig, J. (1982) *Philosophical Issues in Education*, London: Croom Helm.

Klemp, G. O. (1977) *Three Factors of Success in the World of Work*, Boston: McBer & Co.

Kline, P. (1991) *Intelligence: the Psychometric View*, London: Routledge.

Kogan, M. (1978) *The Politics of Educational Change,* London: Fontana.

Kogan, M., Johnson, D., Packwood, T. and Whitaker, T. (1984) *School Governing Bodies*, London: Heinemann.

Kohl, H. (1986) *On Becoming a Teacher,* London: Methuen.

Kohlberg, L. and Lickona, T. (1986) *The Stages of Ethical Development from Childhood Through Old Age*, New York: Harper and Row.

Kohler, W. and Winter, E. (trans) (1957) *The Mentality of Apes*, Harmondsworth: Penguin.

Kohler, W. (1969) *The Task of Gestalt Psychology*, Princeton: Princeton University Press.

Kounin, J. S. (1970) *Discipline and Group Management in Classrooms*, New York: Holt, Rinehart and Winston.

Kroger, J. (1996) *Identity in Adolescence*, London: Routledge.

Kutnick, P. and Rogers, C. (1995) *Groups in Schools*, London: Cassell.

Kyriacou, C. (1986) *Effective Teaching in Schools*, Oxford: Basil Blackwell.

Kyriacou, C. (1991) *Essential Teaching Skills*, London: Simon and Schuster.

Labour Party (1993) *Opening the Doors to a Learning Society*, London: Labour Party.

Labour Party (1995) *Excellence for Everyone: Labour's Crusade to Raise Standards*, London: Labour Party.

Labov, W. (1973) 'The logic of non-standard English', in Keddie, N. (ed.) *Tinker, Tailor . . . the Myth of Cultural Deprivation*, Harmondsworth: Penguin.

Lacey, C. (1970) *Hightown Grammar*, Manchester: Manchester University Press.

Lacey, C. (1977) *The Socialisation of Teachers*, London: Methuen.

Laslett, R. and Smith, C. (1992) *Effective Classroom Management: A Teacher's Guide*, London: Routledge.

Lawlor, S. (1988) *Correct Core: Simple Curricula for English, Maths and Science*, Policy Study No. 93, London: Centre for Policy Studies.

Lawn, M. and Grace, G. (1987) *Teachers: The Culture and Politics of Work*, London: Falmer Press.

Lawn, M. and Ozga, J. (1981) 'The educational worker: a reassessment of teachers', in Ozga, J. (ed.) *School Work: Approaches to the Labour Process of Teaching*, Buckingham: Open University Press.

Lawn, M. and Ozga, J. (1986) 'Unequal partners: teachers under indirect rule', *British Journal of Sociology of Education*, 7 (2).

Lawrence, D. (1987) *Enhancing Self-Esteem in the Classroom*, London: Paul Chapman.

Lawrence, J., Steed, D. and Young, P. (1977) *Disruptive Behaviour in a Secondary School*, London: University of London.

Lawson, H. (1992) *Practical Record Keeping for Special Schools*, London: David Fulton.

Lawton, D. (1983) *Curriculum Studies and Educational Planning*, London: Hodder and Stoughton.

Lawton, D. (1995) *The Tory Mind on Education: 1979–1994*, London: Falmer Press.

Learner, R., Nagai, A. K. and Rothman, S. (1995) *Molding the Good Citizen: the Politics of High School History Texts,* Westport, CT: Greeenwood.

Leat, D. and Chandler, S. (1996) 'Using concept mapping in geography teaching', *Teaching Geography*, July, 109–12.

Lees, S. (1987) 'The structure of sexual relations in school', in Arnot, M. and Weiner, G. (eds) *Gender and the Politics of Schooling*, Buckingham: Open University Press.

Leithwood, K. and Jantzi, D. (1990) 'Transformational leadership: how principals can help reform school culture.' Paper presented at AERA annual conference.

Levacic, R. (1995) *Local Management of Schools: Analysis and Practice*, Buckingham: Open University Press.

Levine, D. and Eubanks, E (1989) 'Site-based nanagement: engine for reform or pipe-dream?' Unpublished MS cited in Fullan, M. and Hargreaves, A. (1992) *What's Worth Fighting For in Your School?*, Buckingham: Open University Press.

Levine, J. (ed.) (1990) *Bilingual Learners and the Mainstream Curriculum*, London: Falmer Press.

Lewin, K. (1946) 'Action research and minority problems', *Journal of Social Issues*, Vol. 2, 34–6.

Lieberman, A. (1990) *Schools as Collaborative Cultures: Creating the Future Now*, London: Falmer Press.

Linguistic Minorities Project (1985) *The Other Languages of England*, London: Routledge & Kegan Paul.

Little, J. W. and McLaughlin, M. W. (1993) *Teachers' Work: Individuals, Colleagues and Contexts*, New York: Teachers College Press.

Lloyd, C. and Beard, J. (1995) *Managing Classroom Collaboration*, London: Cassell.

Lloyd-Smith, M. and Davies, J. (eds) (1995) *On the Margins: The Education Experience of 'Problem' Pupils*, Stoke-on-Trent: Trentham Books.

Lortie, D. (1975) *Schoolteacher: A Sociological Study*, Chicago: University of Chicago Press.

Louis, K. S. and Miles, M. B. (1992) *Improving the Urban High School: What Works and Why*, New York: Teachers College Press.

Lovey, J. (1996) 'How to use Detention Time Constructively', *Times Educational Supplement*, 28 June.

Lowe, P. (1988) *Responding to Adolescent Needs: A Pastoral Care Approach*, London: Cassell.

Lowe, R. (1989) *Changing English Secondary Schools*, London: Falmer Press.

Mac an Ghaill, M. (1988) *Young, Gifted and Black*, Buckingham: Open University Press.

Mac an Ghaill, M. (1995) *The Making of Men: Masculinities, Sexualities and Schooling*, Buckingham: Open University Press.

MacDonald, B. (1973) 'Humanities Curriculum Project', *Evaluation in Curriculum Development: Twelve Case Studies*, Schools Council Research Studies, London: Macmillan Education for the Schools Council.

MacGilchrist, B., Mortimore, P., Savage, J. and Beresford, C. (1995) *Planning Matters: The Impact of Development Planning in Primary Schools*, London: Paul Chapman.

Maden, M. (1996) 'A Tale of Two Tribes', *Times Educational Supplement*, 10 May.

Maines, B. and Robinson, G. (1994) *If it Makes My Life Easier . . . to Write a Policy on Bullying*, Bristol: Lame Duck Publishing.

Major, J. (1991) 'Education – all our futures', speech to the Centre for Policy Studies, Cafe Royal, London, 3 July.

Makins, V. (1969) 'Child's eye view of teachers', *Times Educational Supplement*, 19 and 26 September.

Mangan, J. A. (1993) *The Imperial Curriculum: Racial Images and Education in the British Colonial Experience*, London: Routledge.

Marks, J. (1992) *Value for Money in Education*, York: Campaign for Real Education.

Marks, J. and Pomian-Srzednicki, M. (1985) *Standards in English Schools: Second Report*, London: National Council for Educational Standards.

Marland, M. (1977) *Language Across the Curriculum*, London: Heinemann.

Marland, M. (1989) *The Tutor and the Tutor Group: Developing Your Role as a Tutor*, London: Longman.

Marland, M. (1993) *The Craft of the Classroom: A Survival Guide*, London: Heinemann.

Marsh, C. J. (1991) *Key Concepts for Understanding Curriculum*, London: Falmer Press.

Marsh, C., Day, C., Hannay, L. and McCutcheon, G. (1990) *Reconceptualising School-based Curriculum Development*, London: Falmer Press.

Marshall, B. (1994) *Engendering Modernity: Feminism, Social Theory and Social Change*, Cambridge, Polity Press.

Maslow, A. H. (1970) *Motivation and Personality*, second edition, New York: Harper and Row.

Maw, J. (1995) 'The Handbook for the Inspection of Schools: a Critique', *Cambridge Journal of Education*, Vol. 25, No. 1, 75–87.

Maynard, T. and Furlong, J. (1993) 'Learning to Teach and Models of Mentoring', in McIntyre D., Hagger H. and Wilkin M. (eds) *Mentoring: Perspectives on School-Based Teacher Education*, London: Kogan Page.

McClelland, R., Thomas, G., Vass, P. and Webb, J. (1995) *Parent Choice: A Survey of 659 Parents*, Oxford: Education Services, School of Education, Oxford Brookes University.

McCoy, K. and Wibbelsman, C. (1989) *The Teenage Body Book*, London: Piatkus Books.

McCulloch, G. (1989) *The Secondary Technical School: A Usable Past?*, Lewes: Falmer Press.

McIntyre, D. (1991) 'The Oxford Internship Scheme and the Cambridge Analytical Framework: Models of Partnership in Initial Teacher Education', in Booth M., Furlong J. and Wilkin M. (eds) *Partnership in Initial Teacher Training*, London: Cassell.

McIntyre, D. and Hagger, H. (eds) (1996) *Mentors in Schools: Developing the Profession of Teaching*, London: David Fulton.

McIntyre, D., Hagger, H. and Wilkin, M. (1993) (eds) *Mentoring: Perspectives on School-Based Teacher Education*, London: Kogan Page.

McLaughlin, C., Lodge, C. and Watkins, C. (eds) (1991) *Gender and Pastoral Care: Personal-Social Aspects of the Whole School*, Oxford: Blackwell.

McManus, M. (1989) *Troublesome Behaviour in the Classroom: A Teacher's Survival Guide*, London: Routledge.

McNamara, D. and Desforges, C. (1978) 'The social sciences, teacher education and the objectification of craft knowledge', *British Journal of Teacher Education*, Vol. 4, No. 1, 17–36.

McNamara, S. and Moreton, G. (1995) *Changing Behaviour: Teaching Children with Emotional and Behavioural Difficulties in Primary and Secondary Classrooms*, London: David Fulton.

McNiff, J. (1988) *Action Research: Principles and Practice*, London: Routledge.

McPeck, J. E. (1981) *Critical Thinking and Education*, Oxford: Martin Robertson.

McPherson, A. and Raab, C. D. (1988) *Governing Education: A Sociology of Policy Since 1945*, Edinburgh: Edinburgh University Press.

McRobbie, A. (1991) *Feminism and Youth Culture: From 'Jackie' to 'Just 17'*, London: Macmillan.

McTaggart, M. (1995) 'Signposts on the road to hell', *Times Educational Supplement*, 5 May.

Mead, G. H. (1934) *Mind, Self and Society*, Chicago: University of Chicago.

Measor, L. and Sikes, P. J. (1992) *Gender and Schools*, London: Cassell.

Mecca, A. M., Smelser, N. J. and Vasconcellos, J. (1989) *The Social Importance of Self-esteem*, Berkeley: University of California Press.

Meighan, R. (1981)(second edition 1986) *A Sociology of Educating*, London: Holt, Rinehart & Winston.

Menter, I. (1989) 'Teaching practice stasis: racism, sexism and school experience in initial teacher education', *British Journal of Sociology of Education*, Vol. 10, No. 4, 459–473.

Merrett, F. (1993) *Encouragement Works Best: Positive Approaches to Classroom Management*, London: David Fulton.

Merrett, F. and Wheldall, K. (1990) *Identifying Troublesome Classroom Behaviour*, London: Paul Chapman.

Meyenn, R. J. (1980) 'School girls' peer groups', in Woods, P. (ed.) *Pupil Strategies*, London: Croom Helm.

Miles, M. (1986) 'Research findings on the stages of school improvement', New York: Centre for Policy Research (mimeo).

Miles, T. and Miles, E. (1990) *Dyslexia: A Hundred Years On*, Buckingham: Open University Press.

Miliband, R. (1991) *Divided Societies*, Oxford: Oxford University Press.

Miller, J. (1983) *Many Voices: Bilingualism, Culture and Education*, London: Routledge.

Mills, C. W. (1959) *The Sociological Imagination*, New York: Oxford University Press.

Millett, A. (1996) 'A new agenda for teacher training', speech to the NAS/UWT annual conference, Birmingham.

Mirza, H. S. (1992) *Young, Female and Black*, London: Routledge.

Mitchell, S. and Stocks, A. (1993) *PSE at Key Stages 3 and 4: Student Activities and Staff Support*, Framework Press.

Moore, R. and Ozga, J. (eds) (1991) *Curriculum Policy: A Reader*, Oxford: Pergamon Press in association with the Open University.

Moos, R. H. (1979) *Evaluating Educational Environments: Procedures, Measures, Findings and Policy Implications*, San Francisco: Jossey Bass.

Morley, D. (1986) *Family Television, Cultural Power and Domestic Leisure*, London: Comedia.

Morley, D. (1992) *Television, Audiences and Cultural Studies*, London: Routledge.

Mortimore, P. and Mortimore, J. (eds) (1991) *The Secondary Head: Roles, Responsibilities and Reflections*, London: Paul Chapman.

Mortimore, P. and Mortimore, J. with Thomas, H. (1994) *Managing Associate Staff: Innovation in Primary and Secondary Schools*, London: Paul Chapman.

Mortimore, P., Sammons, P., Stoll, L., Lewis, D. and Ecob, R. (1988) *School Matters: The Junior Years*, Wells: Open Books.

Mungham, G. and Pearson, G. (eds) (1975) *Working-Class Youth Culture*, London: Routledge.

Murgatroyd, S. and Morgan, C. (1992) *Total Quality Management and the School*, Buckingham: Open University Press.

Murphy, R. (1982) 'Sex differences in objective test performance', *British Journal of Educational Psychology*, 52, 213–19.

Murray, R. with Paechter, C. and Black, P. (1994) *Managing Learning and Assessment Across the Curriculum*, London: HMSO.

Myers, K. (ed.) (1992) *Genderwatch! After the Education Reform Act*, Cambridge: Cambridge University Press.

Myers, K. (ed.) (1995) *School Improvement in Practice: Schools Make a Difference Project*, London: Falmer Press.

Nash, R. (1976) *Teacher Expectations and Pupil Learning*, London: Routledge & Kegan Paul.

National Commission on Education (1995) *Success Against the Odds,* London: Routledge.

National Council for Vocational Qualifications (1995a) *Corporate Plan*, London: National Council for Vocational Qualifications.

National Council for Vocational Qualifications (1995b) *NVQ Criteria and Guidance*, London: NCVQ.

National Curriculum Council (1990a) *The Whole Curriculum*, Curriculum Guidance 3, York: NCC.

National Curriculum Council (1990b) *Cross Curricular Issues. Dimension/skills/themes*, York: NCC.

National Curriculum Council (1990c) *Education for Citizenship: Curriculum Guidance 8*, York: NCC.

National Curriculum Council (1991) *Teaching Talking and Learning in Key Stage 3*, York: NCC and National Oracy Project.

National Steering Group (1989) *School Teacher Appraisal: A National Framework*, London: HMSO.

National Writing Project (1989a) *A Question of Writing*, Walton-on-Thames: Nelson.

National Writing Project (1989b) *Becoming a Writer*, Walton-on-Thames: Nelson.

National Writing Project (1989c) *Writing and Learning*, Walton-on-Thames: Nelson.

National Writing Project (1989d) *Responding to Writing*, Walton-on-Thames: Nelson.

Neave, G. (1992) *The Teaching Nation: Prospects for Teachers in the European Community*, Oxford: Pergamon.

Nelson, I. (1994) *Time-management for Teachers*, London: Kogan Page.

Newell, P. (1991) *The UN Convention and Children's Rights in the UK*, London: National Children's Bureau.

Newman, D., Griffin, P. and Cole, M. (1989) *The Construction Zone: Working for Cognitive Change in Schools*, Cambridge: Cambridge University Press.

Newman, J. W. (1990) *America's Teachers*, New York: Longman.

Newsam, P. (1996) 'Capital Idea', *Times Educational Supplement*, 7 June.

Nias, J., Southworth, G. and Yeomans, R. (1989) *Staff Relationships in the Primary School: A Study of Organizational Cultures*, London, Cassell.

Nicholls, J. G. (1983) 'Conceptions of ability and achievement motivation: a theory and its implications for education', in Paris, S. G., Olson, G. M. and Stevenson, H. W., *Learning and Motivation in the Classroom*, Hillsdale, NJ: Lawrence Erlbaum Associates.

Nisbet, J. and Shucksmith, J. (1986) *Learning Strategies*, London: Routledge.

Nixon, J. (ed.) (1981) *A Teacher's Guide to Action Research*, London: Grant McIntyre.

Nixon, J., Martin, J., McKeown, P. and Ranson, S. (1996) *Encouraging Learning: Towards a Theory of the Learning School*, Buckingham: Open University Press.

No Turning Back Group of MPs (1986) *Save Our Schools*, London: Conservative Party Centre.

Norman, K. (1990) *Teaching, Talking and Learning in Key Stage One*, York: National Curriculum Council.

Norman, K. (1992) *Thinking Voices: The Work of the National Oracy Project*, London: Hodder and Stoughton.

NUT (1991) *Lesbians and Gays in School: An Issue for Every Teacher*, London: NUT.

O'Hear, A. (1981) *An Introduction to the Philosophy of Education*, London: Routledge.

O'Hear, A. (1991) *Education and Democracy: Against the Educational Establishment*, London: Claridge.

O'Keeffe, D. (1988) 'A critical look at the national curriculum and testing: a libertarian view', paper presented to the American Educational Research Association, New Orleans, April.

OFSTED (1995a) *Guidance on the Inspection of Secondary Schools*, London: HMSO.

OFSTED (1995b) *Partnership: Schools and Higher Education in Partnership in Initial Teacher Training*, London: HMSO.

OFSTED (1996a) *Assessment of National Vocational Qualifications in Schools, 1995/96*, London: HMSO.

OFSTED (1996b) *The Appraisal of Teachers, 1991–1996*, London: OFSTED.

OFSTED (1996c) *School Inspection: A Guide to the Law*, London: OFSTED.

OFSTED/DFEE (1996) *Setting Targets to Raise Standards: A Survey of Good Practice*, London: DFEE.

OFSTED/EOC (1996) *The Gender Divide: Performance Differences Between Boys and Girls in School*, London: HMSO.

OFSTED/TTA (1996) *Framework for the Assessment of Quality and Standards in Initial Teacher Training, 1996/97*, London: HMSO.

Olson, J. (1991) *Understanding Teaching: Beyond Expertise*, Buckingham: Open University Press.

Ouston, J., Earley, P. and Fidler, B. (1996) *OFSTED Inspections: the Early Experience*, London: David Fulton.

Ozga, J. (1988) *Schoolwork: Approaches to the Labour Process of Teaching*, Buckingham, Open University Press.

Paechter, C. (1995) *Crossing Subject Boundaries: the Micropolitics of Curriculum Innovation*, London: HMSO.

Parsons, T. (1951) *The Social System*, London: Routledge & Kegan Paul.

Parsons, T. (1959) 'The school class as a social system', *Harvard Educational Review*, Vol. 29, 297–318.

Pasch, M., Sparks-Langer, G., Gardner, T. G., Starko, A. J. and Moody, C. D. (1991) *Teaching as Decision Making: Instructional Practices for the Successful Teacher*, New York: Longman.

Pate-Bain, H., Achilles, C., Boyd-Zacharias, J. and McKenna, B. (1992) 'Class size does make a difference', *Phi Delta Kappan*, November, 253–5.

Pattanayak, D. P. (1991) 'Foreword' in Alladina, S. and Edwards, V. (eds) 1991 *Multilingualism in the British Isles*, Vol. 1, London: Longman.

Perera, K. (1987) *Understanding Language*, London: National Association of Advisers in English.

Perrot, E. (1982) *Effective Teaching: A Teaching Guide to Improving Your Teaching*, London: Longman.

Peter, M. (ed.) (1992) *Differentiation: Ways Forward*, Stafford: National Association for Special Educational Needs.

Peters, R. S. (1966) *Ethics and Education*, London: Allen & Unwin.

Phillips, T. (1985) 'Beyond lip-service: discourse development after the age of nine', in Wells, G. and Nicholls, J. (eds) *Language and Learning: An Interactional Perspective*, London: Falmer Press.

Phoenix, A. and Tizard, B. (1993) *Black, White, or Mixed Race?*, London: Routledge.

Piaget, J. (1926) *The Language and Thought of the Child*, New York: Basic Books.

Piaget, J. (1950) *The Psychology of Intelligence*, London: Routledge & Kegan Paul.

Piaget, J. (1951) *Play, Dreams and Imitation*, New York: Norton.

Piaget, J. (1961) 'A genetic approach to the psychology of thought', *Journal of Educational Psychology*, Vol. 52, 151–61.

Pilkington, P. (1991) *End Egalitarian Delusion: Different Education for Different Talents*, Centre for Policy Studies.

Pinsent, P. (1992) *Language, Culture and Young Children*, London: David Fulton.

Polanyi, M. (1958) *Personal Knowledge*, London: Routledge & Kegan Paul.

Pole, C. (1993) *Assessment and Recording Achievement*, Buckingham: Open University Press.

Pole, C. J. and Chawla-Duggan, R. (1996) *Reshaping Education in the 1990s: Perspectives on Secondary Education*, London: Falmer Press.

Pollard, A. (1980) 'Teacher interests and changing situations of survival threat in primary school classrooms', in Woods, P. (ed.) *Teacher Strategies*, London: Croom Helm.

Pollard, A. (1982) 'A model of coping strategies', *British Journal of Sociology of Education*, Vol. 3, No. 1, 19–37.

Pollard, A. (1985) *The Social World of the Primary School*, London: Cassell.

Pollard, A. (1987) 'Social differentiation in primary schools', *Cambridge Journal of Education*, Vol. 17, No. 3, 158–61.

Pollard, A. with Filer, A. (1996) *The Social World of Children's Learning*, London: Cassell.

Pollard, A. and Filer, A. (forthcoming) *The Social World of Pupil Careers*, London: Cassell.

Popkewitz, T. (ed.) (1993) *Changing Patterns of Power: Social Regulation and Teacher Education Reform in Eight Countries*, New York: State University of New York Press.

Popper, K. R. (1968) *The Logic of Scientific Discovery*, London: Hutchinson.

Powell, R. (1990) *Resources for Flexible Learning*, Stafford: Network Educational Press.

Power, S. (1996) *The Pastoral and the Academic: Conflict and Contradiction in the Curriculum*, London: Cassell.

Preedy, M. (ed.) (1993) *Managing the Effective School*, London: Paul Chapman in association with the Open University.

Preedy, M., Glatter, R. and Levacic, R. (eds) (1997) *Educational Management: Strategy, Quality and Resources*, Buckingham: Open University Press.

Price, M. (ed.) (1986) *Development of the Secondary Curriculum: Subjects for Study*, Lewes: Falmer Press.

Pring, R. (1996) *The New Curriculum*, London: Cassell.

Prutzman, P., Burger, M. L., Bodenhamer, G., and Stern, L. (1978) *The Friendly Classroom for a Small Planet*, New Jersey: Avery Publishing.

Putnam, J. and Burke, J. B. (1992) *Organising and Managing Classroom Learning Communities*, New York: McGraw Hill.

Quicke, J. (1988) 'The "New Right" and education', *British Journal of Educational Studies*, Vol. 36, No. 1, 5–20.

Quicke, J. (1994) 'Metacognition, pupil empowerment and the school context', *School Psychology International*, 15(3), 247–60.

Quicke, J. and Winter, C. (1994) 'Teaching the language of learning: towards a metacognitive approach to pupil empowerment', *British Education Research Journal*, 20 (4) 429–46.

Ranson, S. (1992) *The Role of Local Government in Education*, London: Longman.

Raphael-Reed, L. (1994) *If it Makes my Life Easier . . . to Write a Policy on 'Equal Opportunities'*, Bristol: Lame Duck Publishing.

Raphael-Reed, L. (1995a) 'Reconceptualising equal opportunities: a study of radical teacher culture' in Griffiths, M. and Troyna, B. (eds) *Anti-racism, Culture and Social Justice*, Stoke-on-Trent: Trentham Books.

Raphael-Reed, L. (1995b) 'Working with boys: a new research agenda', *Redland Papers 3*, Bristol: University of the West of England.

Reeder, D. (1979) 'A recurring debate: education and industry', in G, Bernbaum (ed.) *Schooling in Decline*, London: Macmillan.

Reid, I. (1986) *The Sociology of School and Education*, London: Fontana.

Reid, I. (1989) *Social Class Differences in Britain: Life Chances and Life-Styles*, London: Fontana.

Resnick, L. and Resnick, D. (1991) 'Assessing the thinking curriculum: new tools for educational reform', in Gifford, B. and O'Connor, M. (eds) *Future Assessments: Changing Views of Aptitude, Achievement and Instruction*, New York: Kluwer Academic Publishers.

Reynolds, D. and Cuttance, P. (eds) (1992) *School Effectiveness: Research, Policy and Practice*, London: Cassell.

Reynolds, D. and Sullivan, M. (1979) 'Bringing Schools Back In', in Barton, L. and Meighan, R. (eds) *Schools, Pupils and Deviance*, London: Nafferton.

Richards, J. (1978) *Classroom Language: What Sort?*, London: George Allen and Unwin.

Richards, M. and Light, P. (1986) *Children of Social Worlds*, Cambridge: Polity Press.

Richardson, K. (1991) *Understanding Intelligence*, Buckingham: Open University Press.

Richardson, R. (1996) *Fortunes and Fables: Education for Hope in Troubled Times*, Stoke-on-Trent: Trentham Books.

Riddell, S. and Brown, S. (eds) (1991) *School Effectiveness Research: Its Messages for School Improvement*, Edinburgh: HMSO.

Rieser, R. and Mason, M. (eds) (1990) *Disability Equality in the Classroom: A Human Rights Issue*, London: ILEA Publications.

Robertson, J. (1981) *Effective Classroom Control*, Oxford: Blackwell.

Robinson, E. (1983) 'Meta-cognitive development', in Meadows, S. (ed.) *Developing Thinking*, London: Methuen.

Robinson, G. and Maines, B. (1988) *You Can . . . You Know You Can!*, Portishead: Lame Duck Publishing.

Robinson, G., Sleigh, J. and Maines, B. (1995) *No Bullying Starts Today*, Portishead: Lame Duck.

Robinson, H. A. (1975) *Teaching, Reading and Study Strategies*, Allyn and Bacon.

Roger, I. A. and Richardson, J. A. S. (1985) *Self-Evaluation for Primary Schools*, London: Hodder & Stoughton.

Rogers, C. (1969) *Freedom to Learn*, New York: Merrill.

Rogers, C. (1980) *A Way of Being*, Boston: Houghton Mifflin.

Rogoff, B. and Lave, J. (ed.) (1984) *Everyday Cognition: Its Development in Social Context*, London: Harvard University Press.

Romberg, T. A. and Zavinnia, E. A. (1989) *The Influence of Mandated Testing on Mathematical Instruction*, Madison, WI: National Centre for Mathematical Science Foundation, University of Wisconsin.

Rose, J. (1995) 'OFSTED Inspection – Who is it for?', *Education Review* 9 (1), 63–66.

Rosenberg, M. (1965) *Society and the Adolescent Self-image*, Princeton, NJ: Princeton University Press.

Rosenholz, S. (1989) *Teachers' Workplace: the Social Organisation of Schools*, New York: Longman.

Rostow, W. W. (1962) *The Stages of Economic Growth*, Cambridge: Cambridge University Press.

Rottenberg, C. and Smith, M. L. (1990) 'Unintended effects of external testing in elementary schools', paper presented to the annual conference of the American Educational Research Association, Boston, April.

Rowland, S. (1987) 'An interpretive model of teaching and learning', in Pollard, A. (ed.) *Children and their Primary Schools*, London: Falmer Press.

Rowland, S. (1993) *The Enquiring Tutor: Explorations in Professional Learning*, London: Falmer Press.

Rudduck, J., Chaplain, R. and Wallace, G. (eds) (1996) *School Improvement: What Can Pupils Tell Us?*, London: David Fulton.

Rutter, M. and Madge, N. (1976) *Cycles of Disadvantage*, London: Heinemann.

Rutter, M., Maugham, B., Mortimore, P. and Ouston, J. (1979) *Fifteen Thousand Hours: Secondary Schools and their Effects on Children*, London: Open Books.

Salisbury, J. and Jackson, D. (1996) *Challenging Macho Values: Practical Ways of Working With Adolescent Boys*, London: Falmer Press.

Salmon, P. (1995) *Psychology in the Classroom: Reconstructing Teachers and Learners*, London: Cassell.

Salmon, P. and Claire, H. (1984) *Classroom Collaboration*, London: Routledge & Kegan Paul.

Salter, G. and Tapper, T. (1985) *Power and Policy in Education: The Case of Independent Schooling*, London: Falmer Press.

Sammons, P., Hillman, J. and Mortimore, P. (1995) *Key Characteristics of Effective Schools*, London: London University Institute of Education, ISEIC for OFSTED.

Sammons, P. and Nuttall, D. (1992) 'Differential school effectiveness: results from a reanalysis of the ILEA's Junior School Project data', paper presented at the annual conference of the British Educational Research Association, Stirling, August.

Sarason, S. B. (1996) *Revisiting 'The Culture of the School and the Problem of Change'*, New York: Teachers College Press.

Satterly, D. (1989) *Assessment in Schools*, (second edition), Oxford: Blackwell.

Sayer, J. (1992) *The Future Governance of Education*, London: Cassell.

SCAA (1994) *Code of Practice for GCE A and AS Examinations*, London: SCAA.

SCAA (1995a) *Consistency in Teacher Assessment Guidance for Schools*, London: SCAA.

SCAA (1995b) *Review of Assessment and Testing*, London: SCAA.

SCAA (1995c) *Planning the Curriculum at Key Stages 1 and 2*, London: SCAA.

SCAA (1995d) *Discussion Paper 3, Spiritual and Moral Development*, London: SCAA.

SCAA (1996a) *Skills for Choice: Developing Pupils' Career Management Skills*, London: SCAA.

SCAA (1996b) *Education for Adult Life: the Spiritual and Moral Development of Young People*, Discussion Paper No. 6, London: SCAA.

SCAA (1996c) *A Guide to the National Curriculum*, London: SCAA.

SCAA (1996d) *Teaching English as an Additional Language: A Framework for Policy*, London: SCAA.

SCAA (1996e) *Teaching Environmental Matters Through the National Curriculum*, London: SCAA.

SCAA (1996f) *Tiering in GCSE Examinations: A Guide for Teachers*, London: SCAA.

Scardamalia, M. and Bereiter, C. (1983) 'Child as Co-investigator: Helping Children Gain Insight into Their Own Mental Processes', in Paris, S. G., Olson, G. M. and Stevenson, H. W. (1983) *Learning and Motivation in the Classroom*, Hillsdale, NJ: Lawrence Erlbaum.

Schmuck, R. A. (1985) 'Groupwork', in Slavin, E. R. (ed.) *Learning to Co-operate, Co-operating to Learn*, New York: Plenum.

Schon, D. (1983) *The Reflective Teacher*, London: Temple Smith.

School Health Education Unit (1996) *Bully Off*, University of Exeter.

Schultz T. (1960) 'Investment in Human Capital', *American Economic Review*, 51, 1–17.

Scottish Office Education Department (1992) *Revised Guidelines for Teacher Training Courses*, Edinburgh: Scottish Office Education Department.

Scruton, R. (1986) 'The myth of cultural relativism', in Palmer, F., *Anti-racism: An Assault on Education and Value*, London: Sherwood.

SEAC (1990) *Consultation on the Draft Principles for GCE AS and A Examinations*, London: SEAC.

Secord, P. F. and Backman, C. W. (1964) *Social Psychology*, New York: McGraw-Hill.

Sewell, T. (1996) *Black Masculinities and Schooling*, Stoke-on-Trent: Trentham Books.

Sexton, S. (1987) *Our Schools: A Radical Policy*, Warlington: Institute of Economic Affairs.

Sexton, S. (1988) 'No nationalised curriculum', *The Times*, 9 May.

Sharp, R. and Green, A. (1975) *Education and Social Control*, London: Routledge & Kegan Paul.

Shaw, R. (1995) *Teacher Training in Secondary Schools*, London: Kogan Page.

Sheeran, Y. and Barnes, D. (1991) *School Writing*, Buckingham: Open University Press.

Shepard, L. A. (1987) 'The harm of measurement driven instruction', paper presented to the annual conference of the American Educational Research Association, Boston, April.

Shipman, M. (ed.) (1985) *Educational Research: Principles, Policies and Practice*, London: Falmer Press.

Shulman, L. S. (1986) 'Those who understand: knowledge growth in teaching', *Educational Researcher*, Vol. 15, No. 2, 1–16.

Siegel, H. (1990) *Educating Reason: Rationality, Critical Thinking and Education*, London: Routledge.

Sikes, P. J., Measor, L. and Woods, P. (1985) *Teachers' Careers*, London: Falmer Press.

Silver, H. (1980) *Education and the Social Condition*, London: Methuen.

Simon, B. (1953) *Intelligence Testing and the Comprehensive School*, London: Lawrence and Wishart.

Simon, B. (1985) *Does Education Matter?*, London: Lawrence and Wishart.

Simon, B. (1992) *What Future for Education?*, London: Lawrence and Wishart.

Simons, H. and Elliott, K. (1989) *Re-thinking Appraisal and Assessment*, Buckingham: Open University Press.

Sinclair, J. McH. and Brazil, D. (1982) *Teacher Talk*, Oxford: Oxford University Press.

Siskin, L. S. and Little, J. W. (1995) *The Subjects in Question: Departmental Organisation and the High School*, New York: Teachers College Press.

Skilbeck, M. (1994) 'The Core Curriculum in OECD', in OECD, *The Curriculum Redefined: Schooling for the 21st Century*, Paris: OECD.

Skinner, B. F. (1953) *Science and Human Behaviour*, New York: Macmillan.

Skinner, B.F. (1968) *The Technology of Teaching*, New York: Appleton.

Slavin, R. E. (1990) 'Achievement effects of ability grouping in secondary schools: a best evidence synthesis', *Review of Educational Research*, Vol. 60, No. 3, 471–500.

Smith, F. (1990) *To Think*, New York: Teachers College Press.

Smith, R. (1995) *Successful School Management*, London: Cassell.

Smyth, J. (1991) *Teachers as Collaborative Learners*, Buckingham: Open University Press.

Smyth, J. (ed.) (1995) *Critical Discourses on Teacher Development*, London: Cassell.

Sotto, E. (1994) *When Teaching Becomes Learning*, London: Cassell.

Spaulding, C. L. (1992) *Motivation in the Classroom*, New York: McGraw-Hill.

Spours, K. and Hodgson, A. (1996) *Value Added and Raising Attainment: A Formative Approach*, Poole, Dorset: BP Educational Services.

Spring, J. (1991) *American Education: an Introduction to Social and Political Aspects*, New York: Longman.

Squibb, P. (1973) 'The concept of intelligence: a sociological perspective', *Sociological Review*, Vol. 21, No. 1, 147–66.

Squirrell, G. (1994) *Individual Action Planning: A Practical Guide*, London: David Fulton.

Stables, A. (1995) *Subjects of Choice: The Process and Management of Pupil and Student Choice*, London: Cassell.

Starkey, H. (1987) *Practical Activities for Teaching and Learning about Human Rights in Schools*, Strasbourg: Council of Europe.

Steedman, C., Urwin, C. and Walkerdine, V. (1985) *Language, Gender and Childhood*, London: Routledge.

Steedman, J. and MacKinnon, D. (1991) *The Education Factfile*, London: Hodder and Stoughton.

Stenhouse, L. (1982) *Authority, Education and Emancipation*, London: Heinemann.

Stephens, P. (1996) *Essential Mentoring Skills: A Practical Handbook for School-based Teacher Educators*, Cheltenham: Stanley Thorn Publishers.

Stern, J. (1995) *Learning to Teach*, London: David Fulton.

Stott, D. H. (1976) *Bristol Social Adjustment Guides Manual*, London: Hodder and Stoughton.

Stradling, R., Saunders, L. and Weston, P. (1991) *Differentiation in Action: A Whole School Approach for Raising Standards*, London: HMSO.

Strauss, A. and Corbin, J. (1990) *Basics of Qualitative Research*, New York: Sage.

Stubbs, M. (1983) *Language, Schools and Classrooms*, London: Routledge.

Stubbs, M. and Hillier, H. (eds) (1983) *Readings on Language and Classrooms*, London: Methuen.

Tann, S. (1981) 'Grouping and group-work', in Simon, B. and Willcocks, J. (eds) *Research and Practice in the Primary School*, London: Routledge & Kegan Paul.

Tann, S. and Armitage, M. (1986) 'Time for talk', *Reading*, Vol. 20, No. 3, 184–89.

Task Group on Assessment and Testing (1987) *National Curriculum, Report*, London: DES.

Task Group on Assessment and Testing (1988) *Three Supplementary Reports,* London: DES.

Tate, N. (1994) 'Target Vision', *Times Educational Supplement*, 2 December.

Tate, N. (1995) 'National Cultures', Mimeo: speech to the Shropshire Secondary Headteachers' Annual Conference, July.

Tattum, D. P. and Lane, D. A. (1989) *Bullying in Schools*, Stoke on Trent: Trentham Books.

Taylor, P. H. (1970) *How Teachers Plan Their Courses*, Slough: NFER.

Teacher Training Agency (1996) *Corporate Plan 1996: Promoting Excellence in Teaching*, London: TTA.

Tharp, R. and Gallimore, R. (1988) *Rousing Minds to Life: Teaching, Learning and Schooling in Social Context*, New York: Cambridge University Press.

Thomas, D. (ed.) (1995) *Teachers' Stories*, Buckingham: Open University Press.

Thomas, G. (1989) 'The teacher and others in the classroom, in Cullingord, C. (ed.) *The Primary Teacher: The Role of the Educator and the Purpose of Primary Education*, London: Cassell.

Thomas, G. (1992) *Effective Classroom Teamwork: Support or Intrusion?*, London: Routledge.

Thomas, H. and Martin, J. (1996) *Managing Resources for School Improvement*, London: Routledge.

Thorndike, E. L. (1911) *Human Learning*, New York: Prentice Hall.

Thorne, B. (1993) *Gender Play: Girls and Boys in School*, Buckingham: Open University Press.

Tickle, L. (1994) *The Induction of New Teachers: Reflective Professional Practices*, London: Cassell.

Tizard, B. and Hughes, M. (1984) *Young Children Learning*, London: Fontana.

Tolley, H., Biddulph, M., Fisher, T. (1996) *Beginning Teaching Workbooks 1–6,* Cambridge: Chris Kington Publishing.

Tom, A. (1984) *Teaching as a Moral Craft*, New York: Longman.

Tomlinson, J. (1992) *Small, Rural and Effective: A Study of Secondary Schools*, Stoke-on-Trent: Trentham Books.

Tomlinson, P. (1995) *Understanding Mentoring: Reflective Strategies for School-based Teacher Preparation*, Buckingham: Open University Press.

Torrance, H. (ed.) (1994) *Evaluating Authentic Assessment*, Buckingham: Open University Press.

Trethowan, D. (1991) *Managing with Appraisal: Achieving Quality Schools Through Performance Management*, David M. Trethowan.

Tripp, D. (1993) *Critical Incidents in Teaching: Developing Professional Judgement*, London: Routledge.

Troyna, B. and Carrington, B. (1988) *Children and Controversial Issues: Strategies for the Early and Middle Years of Schooling*, London: Falmer Press.

Troyna, B. and Hatcher, R. (1992) *Racism in Children's Lives*, London: Routledge.

Tsui, A. B. M. (1995) *Introducing Classroom Interaction*, London: Penguin.

TTA (1996a) *Effective Training Through Partnership*, London: TTA.

TTA (1996b) *Teaching as a Research-based Profession: Promoting Excellence in Teaching*, London: TTA.

Turner, G. (1985) *The Social World of the Comprehensive School*, London: Croom Helm.

United Nations (1948) *The Universal Declaration of Human Rights,* New York: United Nations.

Unitt, P. (1994) 'Do Smile Before Christmas', *Times Educational Supplement*, 28 October.

Van Manen, M. (1990) *The Tact of Teaching: The Meaning of Pedagogical Thoughtfulness,* London, Ontario: Althouse Press.

Verma, G. K. and Pumfrey, P. (eds) (1993) *Cross-curricular Themes in Secondary Schools*, London: Falmer Press.

Verma, M. K., Corrigan, K. P. and Firth, S. (1995) *Working with Bilingual Pupils*, Clevedon: Multilingual Matters.

Vulliamy, G. and Webb. R. (1992) *Teacher Research and Special Educational Needs*, London: David Fulton.

Vygotsky, L. S. (1962) *Thought and Language*, Cambridge, MA: Massachusetts Institute of Technology.

Vygotsky, L. S. (1978) *Mind in Society: The Development of Higher Psychological Processes*, Cambridge, Massachusetts: Harvard University Press.

Wade, B. and Moore, M. (1992) *Experiencing Special Education: What Young People with Special Educational Needs Can Tell Us*, Buckingham: Open University Press.

Walberg, H. J. (ed.) (1979) *Educational Environments and Effects: Evaluation, Policy and Productivity*, Berkeley: McCutchan.

Walford, G. (ed.) (1984) *British Public Schools: Policy and Practice*, London: Falmer Press.

Walford, G. (1991) *Doing Educational Research*, London: Routledge.

Walker, R. (1986) *Doing Research: A Handbook for Teachers*, London: Routledge.

Walkerdine, V. (1983) 'It's only natural: rethinking child-centred pedagogy', in Wolpe, A. M. and Donald, J. (eds) *Is There Anyone There from Education?*, London: Pluto Press.

Walkerdine, V. (1988) *The Mastery of Reason: Cognitive Development and the Production of Rationality*, London: Routledge.

Wallace, M. (1994) 'Towards a Contingency Approach to Development Planning in Schools' in Hargreaves, D. H. and Hopkins, D., *Development Planning for School Improvement*, London: Cassell.

Wallace, M. and Hall, V. (1994) *Inside the Senior Management Team: Teamwork in Secondary School Management*, London: Paul Chapman.

Waterhouse, P. (1990a) *Classroom Management*, Stafford: Network Educational Press.

Waterhouse, P. (1990b) *Tutoring*, Stafford: Network Educational Press.

Webb, R. (ed.) (1991) *Practitioner Research in the Primary School*, London: Falmer Press.

Webster, A., Beveridge, M. and Reed, M. (1996) *Managing the Literacy Curriculum*, London: Routledge.

Wellington, J. J. (ed.) (1986) *Controversial Issues in the Curriculum*, Oxford: Blackwell.

Wells, G. (1986) *The Meaning Makers: Children Learning Language and Using Language to Learn*, London: Hodder and Stoughton.

Wertsch, J. V. (1985) *Vygotsky and the Social Formation of Mind*, Cambridge, Massachusetts: Harvard University Press.

West-Burnham, J. (1992) *Managing Quality in Schools*, London: Longman.

Wexler, P., Crichlow, W., Kern, J. and Matusewicz, R. (1992) *Becoming Somebody: Toward a Social Psychology of School*, London: Falmer Press.

Wheelock, A. (1992) *Crossing the Tracks: How Untracking Can Save America's Schools*, New York: The New Press.

Wheldall, K. (1991) *Discipline in Schools: Psychological Perspectives on the Elton Report*, London: Routledge.

White, J. (1978) 'The primary teacher as servant of the state', *Education*, 3–13, Vol. 7, No. 2, 18–23.

White, M. (1990) *Rewards and Sanctions: Towards a New Behaviour Policy*, Calne: John Bently School.

White, R. T. and Gunstone, R. F. (1992) *Probing Understanding*, London: Falmer Press.

Whiting, C., Whitty, G., Furlong, J., Miles, S. and Barton, L. (1996) *Partnership in Initial Teacher Education: A Topography*, London: Health and Education Research Unit, Institute of Education, University of London.

Whitty, G. (1992) 'Education, economy and national culture', in Bocock, R. and Thompson, K. (eds) *Social and Cultural Forms of Modernity*, Oxford: Polity Press.

Whitty, G. (1985) *Sociology and School Knowledge*, London: Methuen.

Whitty, G. (1989) 'The New Right and the National Curriculum: state control on market forces?', *Journal of Education Policy*, Vol. 4, No. 4, 329–42.

Whitty, G. and Willmott, E. (1991) 'Competence-based teacher education: approaches and issues', *Cambridge Journal of Education*, Vol. 21, No. 3, 309–18.

Whitty, G., Rowe, R. and Aggleton, P. (1994) 'Subjects and themes in the secondary-school curriculum', *Research Papers in Education*, Vol. 9, No. 2, 159–83.

Wilcox, B. and Gray, J. (1996) *Inspecting Schools: Holding Schools to Account and Helping Schools to Improve*, Buckingham: Open University Press.

Wiliam, D. (1996) 'Standards in examinations: a matter of trust?', *The Curriculum Journal*, 7 (3) 293–306.

Wilkin, M. (1996) *Initial Teacher Training: The Dialogue of Ideology and Culture*, London: Falmer Press.

Wilkin, M., Furlong, J., Miles, S. and Maynard, T. (1996) *The Secondary Subject Mentor Handbook*, London: Kogan Page.

Wilkinson, J. (1995) *Introducing Standard English*, London: Penguin.

Williams, A. (ed.) (1994) *Perspectives on Partnership: Secondary Initial Teacher Training*, London: Falmer Press.

Willis, P. (1977) *Learning to Labour: Why Working Class Kids Get Working Class Jobs*, London: Saxon House.

Willis, P. (1990) *Common Culture*, Buckingham: Open University Press.

Winkley, D. (1985) *Diplomats and Detectives: LEA Advisers at Work*, London: Robert Royce.

Winter, R. (1982) 'Dilemma analysis', *Cambridge Journal of Education*, Vol. 12, No. 3.

Winter, R. (1989) *Learning From Experience: Principles and Practice in Action-Research*, London: Falmer Press.

Withall, J. (1949) 'The development of a technique for the measurement of social-emotional climate in classrooms', *Journal of Experimental Education*, No. 17, 347– 61.

Withall, J., and Lewis, W. (1963) 'Social/emotional Climate in the Classroom', in Gage, N. L. (ed.) *Handbook of Research on Teaching*, American Educational Research Association.

Wittrock, M. C. (ed.) (1986) *Handbook of Research on Teaching*, New York: Macmillan.

Wolf, A. (1995) *Competence-based Assessment*, Buckingham: Open University Press.

Wolf, A. (1997) *GNVQs 1993–97: A National Survey Report*, London: FEDA.

Wolfendale, S. (1992) *Involving Parents in Schools*, London: Cassell.

Wolpe, A-M. (1988) *Within School Walls: The Role of Discipline, Sexuality and the Curriculum*, London: Routledge.

Wood, D. (1988) *How Children Think and Learn*, Oxford: Blackwell.

Woodhead, C. (1995) *Annual Report of Her Majesty's Chief Inspector of Schools*, London: HMSO.

Woods, P. (1977) 'Teaching for survival', in Woods, P. and Hammersley, M. (eds), *School Experience,* London: Croom Helm.

Woods, P. (1979) *The Divided School*, London: Routledge.

Woods, P. (1983) *Sociology and the School: an Interactionist Viewpoint*, London: Routledge.

Woods, P. (1986) *Inside Schools*, London: Routledge & Kegan Paul.

Woods, P. (1987) 'Managing the Primary School Teachers' Role', in Delamont, S. (ed.), *The Primary School Teacher*, London: Falmer Press.

Woods, P. (1990a) *Teacher Skills and Strategies,* London: Falmer Press.

Woods, P. (1990b) *The Happiest Days? How Pupils Cope with School*, London: Falmer Press.

Woods, P. and Pollard, A. (eds) (1988) *Sociology and Teaching: A New Challenge for the Sociology of Education*, London: Croom Helm.

Wragg, E. C. (1984) *Classroom Teaching Skills*, London: Croom Helm.

Wragg, E. C. (1996) *GCSE and Key Stage 4 of the National Curriculum*, London: Longman.

Wragg, E. C., Wikeley, F. J., Wragg, C. M. and Haynes, C. S. (1996) *Teacher Appraisal Observed*, London: Routledge.

Young, M. (1993) 'A curriculum for the 21st century? Towards a new basis for overcoming academic/vocational divisions', *British Journal of Educational Studies,* Vol. XXXXI, No. 3.

Young, M. D. (ed.) (1971) *Knowledge and Control,* London: Collier-Macmillan.

Zahorik, J. A. (1975) 'Teachers' Planning Models', *Educational Leadership,* 33, 134–9.

Zeichner, K. (1981–2) 'Reflective teaching and field-based experience in pre-service teacher education', *Interchange,* Vol. 12, 1–22.

Zeichner, K. and Liston, D. P. (1996) *Reflective Teaching: An Introduction,* Mahwah, NJ: Lawrence Erlbaum Associates.

Zeichner, K., Melnick, S. and Gomez, M. L. (1996) *Currents of Reform in Pre-service Teacher Education,* New York: Teachers College Press.

# PRACTICAL ACTIVITIES INDEX

# NAME INDEX